June 11–13, 2014
Cambridge, UK

I0047552

**Association for
Computing Machinery**

Advancing Computing as a Science & Profession

e-Energy'14

Proceedings of the Fifth ACM International Conference on
Future Energy Systems

Sponsored by:
ACM SIGCOMM

Supported by:
**University of Cambridge, IEEE UK&RI Communications Chapter,
and IBM**

Association for Computing Machinery

Advancing Computing as a Science & Profession

The Association for Computing Machinery
2 Penn Plaza, Suite 701
New York, New York 10121-0701

Notice to Past Authors of ACM-Published Articles
ACM intends to create a complete electronic archive of all articles and/or other material previously published by ACM. If you have written a work that has been previously published by ACM in any journal or conference proceedings prior to 1978, or any SIG Newsletter at any time, and you do NOT want this work to appear in the ACM Digital Library, please inform permissions@acm.org, stating the title of the work, the author(s), and where and when published.

ISBN: 978-1-4503-2819-7 (Digital)

ISBN: 978-1-4503-3084-8 (Print)

Additional copies may be ordered prepaid from:

ACM Order Department
PO Box 30777
New York, NY 10087-0777, USA

Phone: 1-800-342-6626 (USA and Canada)
+1-212-626-0500 (Global)
Fax: +1-212-944-1318
E-mail: acmhelp@acm.org
Hours of Operation: 8:30 am – 4:30 pm ET

Printed in the USA

ACM e-Energy 2014 General Chairs' Welcome

These are the proceedings of the F ifth ACM International Conference on Future Energy Systems (e-En ergy 2014). T he conference i tself is host ed i n C ambridge Uni versity at the Computer Laboratory June 11–13, 2014, with tw o co-located workshops the preceding day, on Energy-Efficient Data Centres, and on Demand Response.

The breadth and depth of work continues to grow, and we are very grateful to the PC Chairs and the PC and Organization Committee for all of their assistance in preparing the event and the publications, which we sincerely hope you enjoy and learn from.

Jon Crowcroft
e-Energy 2014 General Chair
University of Cambridge, UK

Richard Penty
e-Energy 2014 co-chair
University of Cambridge, UK

ACM e-Energy 2014 Program Chairs' Welcome

Welcome to the ACM e-Energy 2014 Conference being held in Cambridge, UK. As Co-Chairs of the Technical Program Committee (TPC), we are delighted to introduce this year's technical program. The program committee accepted 23 full papers selected from 112 submissions in addition to 20 posters / short papers posters and 2 demos. The substantial increase in submissions illustrates the rapid growth of our field. This year's program includes papers covering topics from building energy management to picogrids, from energy optimization in computer systems to electric vehicle charging, from wind energy management to demand response systems and analysis. ACM e-Energy is truly a global conference — both submitted and accepted papers, posters and demos have authors hailing from over 20 countries. We were fortunate to work with an outstanding technical program committee of 35 members from around the world that brought a diverse range of expertise to the table. Members of the PC were drawn from 4 continents. The hallmark of a high quality conference is a thoughtful and demanding review process that provides valuable feedback to all authors, and ACM e-Energy definitely met that high bar. We are extremely grateful for the hard work, and the very selective and insightful paper reviews, provided by TPC members. In a few cases, we also asked the expertise of external reviewers, who are gratefully acknowledged here.

ACM e-Energy used a two-round review process, with a first round of three reviews for each paper. Papers that did not receive a high-confidence review in the first round or received reviews with high variance were assigned additional reviews in a second round of reviewing. After the second round, we initiated online discussions on all submitted papers. The thoughtful asynchronous discussion of papers in advance of the TPC meeting allowed us to discuss 38 papers in depth during an online, day-long TPC meeting that crafted the final program.

We believe that the collective efforts of the TPC has created an extremely strong and technically vibrant program that will greatly interest and inspire all attendees while setting a high standard for subsequent editions of the conference.

JY Le Boudec
2014 ACM e-Energy TPC Co-Chair
EPFL, Lausanne, Switzerland

Prashant Shenoy
2014 ACM e-Energy TPC Co-Chair
U. of Massachusetts at Amherst, USA

Table of Contents

Session 4: Building Energy Management

Session 5: Smart Grid

Demo and Poster Session

ACM e-Energy 2014 Organization

General Chairs: Jon Crowcroft, *University of Cambridge, UK*
Richard Penty, *University of Cambridge, UK*

Program Chairs: Jean-Yves Le Boudex, *EPFL, Switzerland*
Prashant Shenoy, *University of Massachusetts, Amherst, USA*

Publication/Web Assistants: Stephen Lee, *University of Massachusetts, Amherst, USA*
Andrius Aucinas, *University of Cambridge, UK*

Publicity Chair: Jean-Marc Pierson, *IRIT, France*

Steering Committee: Hermann de Meer, *University of Passau, Germany*
David Hutchison, *Lancaster University, United Kingdom*
S. Keshav, *University of Waterloo, Canada*
Jim Kurose, *University of Massachusetts, Amherst, USA*
Marco Ajmone Marsan, *Politecnico di Torino, Italy*
Antonio Fernandez Anta, *IMDEA Networks, Spain*

Program Committee: Anil Aswani, *UC Berkeley, USA*
Suman Banerjee, *University of Wisconsin, USA*
Zainul Charbiwala, *IBM Research, India*
Sid Chau, *Masdar Institute, UAE*
Minghua Chen, *The Chinese University of Hong Kong, China*
Florin Ciucu, *University of Warwick, UK*
Hermann De Meer, *University of Passau, Germany*
Shiv Kalyanaraman, *IBM Australia*
David Irwin, *UMass Amherst, USA*
S. Keshav, *University of Waterloo, Canada*
Steve Low, *Caltech, USA*
Anirban Mahanti, *NICTA, Australia*
Marco Marsan, *Politecnico Torino, Italy*
Friedemann Mattern, *ETHZ, Switzerland*
Daniel Menasche, *Federal University of Rio de Janeiro, Brazil*
Sean Meyn, *University of Florida, USA*
Klara Nahrstedt, *UIUC, USA*
Pierre Pinson, *UT Denmark, Denmark*
Krithi Ramamritham, *IIT Bombay, India*
Sarvapalli Ramchurn, *University of Southampton, UK*
Catherine Rosenberg, *University of Waterloo, Canada*
Amarjeet Singh, *IIIT Delhi, India*
Ole Sundstrom, *IBM Research, Switzerland*

ACM e-Energy 2014 Sponsor & Supporters

We gratefully acknowledge ACM SIGCOMM, the University of Cambridge and the generous support of IBM and the IEEE UK&RI Communications Chapter.

Sponsor:

Supporters:

Computational Carbon Capture

Berend Smit

UC Berkeley, California, USA

Abstract

The separation of mixtures of volatile molecules presents a critical issue in the clean use of existing fuels and in the generation of alternative fuels. In particular separation of CO_2 is at present one of the mayor barriers for large scale CO_2 sequestration. For example, the conventional technology for capturing CO_2 from the effluent stream of a power plant may require as much as 25% of the electricity being produced. In this presentation an overview will be given on the activities on carbon capture the Energy Frontier Research Center (EFRC) in Berkeley.

In this presentation we describe how computational techniques can be used to screen novel materials for carbon capture. Our starting point is the question how to define the optimal material. We introduce the concept of parasitic energy as a metric to compare different materials; the best material is the material that minimizes the loss of efficiency of a power plant. To compute this parasitic energy one need information on the mixture isotherms of the various components of flue gasses. We show how quantum chemical calculations can be used to predict the adsorption energies. In addition, we show how these calculations can be used to develop a force field that allows us to predict the adsorption properties. We will apply these methods for materials for which experimental data is lacking, or for materials that have not yet been synthesized.

Categories and Subject Descriptors
J.2 Computer Applications, PHYSICAL SCIENCES AND ENGINEERING: Chemistry -- Nouns: SCR

Keywords
Carbon Capture; Materials Genome; Molecular Simulations; nano porous materials

Short Bio

Berend Smit received an MSc in Chemical Engineering in 1987 and an MSc in Physics both from the Technical University in Delft (the Netherlands). He received in 1990 cum laude PhD in Chemistry from Utrecht University (the Netherlands). He was a (senior) Research Physicists at Shell Research from 1988-1997, Professor of Computational Chemistry at the University of Amsterdam (the Netherlands) 1997-2007. In 2004 Berend Smit was elected Director of the European Center of Atomic and Molecular Computations (CECAM) Lyon France. Since 2007 he is Professor of Chemical Engineering and Chemistry at U.C. Berkeley and Faculty Chemist at Materials Sciences Division, Lawrence Berkeley National Laboratory. Since 2009 he is the director of the Energy Frontier Research Center for gas separations relevant for clear air technologies.

Berend Smit's research focuses on the application and development of novel molecular simulation techniques, with emphasis on energy related applications. Together with Daan Frenkel he wrote the textbook Understanding Molecular Simulations and together with Jeff Reimer, Curt Oldenburg, and Ian Bourg the textbook Introduction to Carbon Capture and Sequestration.

e-Energy'14, June 11–13, 2014, Cambridge, UK.
ACM 978-1-4503-2819-7/14/06.
http://dx.doi.org/10.1145/2602044.2604000

An EROI-Based Analysis of Renewable Energy Farms with Storage

Yashar
Ghiassi-Farrokhfal
University of Waterloo
yghiassi@uwaterloo.ca

Srinivasan Keshav
University of Waterloo
keshav@uwaterloo.ca

Catherine Rosenberg
University of Waterloo
cath@uwaterloo.ca

ABSTRACT

Large renewable energy (RE) farms, such as wind or solar farms are usually sited in remote areas, far from the transmission grid which typically interconnects population centers. Thus, they need to be connected on expensive access lines (distribution feeders) with limited capacity. The excess of RE generation over line capacity is wasted; this is called *curtailment*. We study curtailment using the metric of *energy return on investment (EROI)*, defined as the ratio of useful energy extracted from each unit of energy invested in creating the renewable energy generation system. Curtailment reduces EROI. It may appear that we can extract more energy from an RE farm and increase EROI by adding storage to the system, where this storage is charged during generation peaks and discharged during off-peak times. However, manufacturing the storage requires an energy investment, and, after a certain number of cycles of usage, the storage becomes non-functional. Thus, adding storage may actually decrease the EROI. In this work, we study the EROI for RE farms when used with several types of storage technologies. Unlike prior work that makes numerous simplifying assumptions, our work accounts for storage size and storage imperfections and uses actual traces of renewable power generation. We find that lithium-ion batteries increase the EROI of both wind and solar farms, unlike lead-acid batteries which generally decrease their EROI. We also show that increasing access line capacity to achieve a target EROI is much more expensive for solar farms than for wind farms.

Categories and Subject Descriptors

C.4 [**Performance of systems**]: EROI analysis; I.6 [**Simulation and modelling**]: Model validation and analysis

1. INTRODUCTION

Large renewable energy (RE) farms, such as wind farms and solar farms, are usually sited in remote areas [21]. Being far from the transmission network that typically interconnects population centres, they require the provisioning of *access lines* (distribution feeders). Extracting the entire energy from RE farms requires access lines to support generation peaks, because generation in excess of

the line capacity must be *curtailed*[1]. However, increasing access line capacity is costly; hence, line capacity is typically inadequate to support peak generation, which limits the amount of energy and potential revenue that can be extracted from these farms [21]. This waste of power is undesirable for RE farm owners, who must wait longer to recoup their initial capital investment as a result.

We study curtailment using the metric of *energy return on investment (EROI)*, defined as the ratio of useful energy extracted from each unit of energy invested in creating an RE generation system, such as the energy required to manufacture wind turbines and photovoltaic (PV) panels. Curtailment reduces the EROI of the system because it reduces the amount of energy extracted from the energy system.

One way to increase EROI is to use devices that store surplus power that cannot be carried by an access line and discharge it when there is enough spare capacity. It may appear that all storage technologies invariably increase the EROI of RE farms. However, this does not take into account the energy required to manufacture storage systems, which have limited lifetimes. Recent work has shown that adding an energy-intensive and short-lived storage system to prevent curtailment may actually *reduce* the overall EROI: it would be better to simply curtail generation than to use such storage devices [6]. While the conclusions in [6] are drawn based on a simple model, our work formulates an accurate EROI analysis for this problem and makes the following contributions:

1. We provide a generic formulation for computing the EROI for a variable-rate RE generation system coupled with storage, and transmitting power over an access line with limited capacity. Our formulation accounts for the storage state of charge and the physical constraints of the storage technologies.

2. We use actual solar and wind measurement datasets to evaluate system performance. We contradict some of the earlier claims in [6]. We find that for both wind and solar power, some storage technologies increase EROI compared to curtailment and some do not.

3. Our formulation enables us to size storage in order to obtain an EROI arbitrarily close to the EROI of the same storage technology with infinite size. Moreover, it also demonstrates that the required access line capacity for a target EROI is much larger for solar power than for wind power, requiring a more expensive integration system for solar power.

The rest of the paper is organized as follows. We motivate the importance of EROI analysis in Section 2. We discuss the chal-

---

[1]Curtailment may also occur due to lack of sufficient demand. We discuss this in more detail in Section 3.

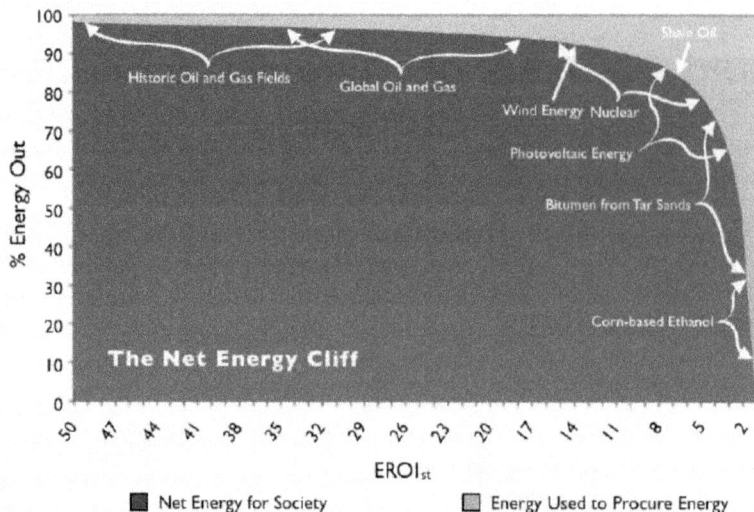

Figure 1: **The net energy cliff [18]:** The light grey area represents the percent of the total energy return that is invested. The dark grey area is the percentage of the energy returned to the total energy invested and returned (i.e., $100 \times \frac{EROI}{EROI+1}$). Note that the net energy is very sensitive to EROI values below 8.

	EROI
Coal	80
Gas	10
Nuclear	9
Wind turbine	18
Solar PV panel	9
Biomass	1.3

Table 1: EROI of some of the power sources [15]

lenges of integrating renewables to the grid in Section 3. We introduce our system model and formulate the EROI for that system in Section 4. Numerical examples and engineering insights are presented in Section 5 and we review the related work in Section 6. We conclude the paper and discuss future work in Section 7.

2. EROI

Designing and evaluating an energy system is carried out largely by focusing on its cost efficiency. As an example, an RE farm is typically sized to maximize its revenues while taking investment costs and some requirement constraints into account. Another important factor, though often ignored, is energy efficiency. The energy efficiency of an energy system mimics its cost efficiency. One of the most widely-used metrics to measure the energy efficiency is the *energy return* of that system during its lifetime per unit *energy invested* to create that system (EROI) [15]:

$$EROI = \frac{\text{Energy returned in } [0, T_{sys}]}{\text{Energy invested in } [0, T_{sys}]}, \qquad (1)$$

where T_{sys} is the lifetime of the system. When T_{sys} is not known, or the system consists of many components with different lifetimes, the following equation is alternatively used to compute EROI

$$EROI = \lim_{T \to \infty} \frac{\text{Energy returned in } [0, T]}{\text{Energy invested in } [0, T]}. \qquad (2)$$

One of the main criticisms of EROI is that it does not take time into account. Specifically, for a given investment, EROI shows the total return, but it does not indicate how soon this return will occur.

EROI is widely used in the literature as a metric for the quality of fuels and energy systems (see Table 1); higher quality fuels are those with higher EROIs. Fossil fuels have a large EROI, which ensures reasonable energy return for any energy system, making cost efficiency the main concern. Thus, EROI analysis has been mostly ignored to date; however, it has recently become an important metric for two reasons.

First, an unfavourable decreasing trend has been observed on the EROI of fossil fuels (except coal). For instance, the global EROI for the production of oil and gas has declined from 30 in 1995, to about 18 in 2006. The second reason motivating EROI analysis is the increasing trend towards RE to reduce carbon use. However, most RE sources have considerably lower EROI values than fossil fuels. Thus, renewables might not be as energy profitable as originally suggested. We believe that the fact that high quality (high EROI) fossil fuels are employed in the creation, transport, and implementation of wind turbine and PV panels needs to be taken into account when performing a viability study of an RE system (along with other aspects such as cost).

When evaluating the EROI of a system, it is important to note that a small change in EROI is far more critical for small values of the EROI than it is for large values. This becomes apparent from Fig. 1. Here, for a given EROI, the dark grey portion represents the percentage of the energy returned as a fraction of the total energy invested and returned (i.e., $100 \times \frac{EROI}{(EROI+1)}$). This is commonly viewed as the *energy efficiency* of the system [18]. It is clear that the impact of changing EROI on energy efficiency is much less pronounced for large values of EROI. As EROI decreases, we reach an energy *cliff*, where slightly decreasing EROI considerably reduces the energy efficiency. This observation highlights the fact that when the EROI of a system is small, even a small change in EROI can significantly affect energy efficiency. Also, note that an EROI lower than 8 yields an energy efficiency lower than 90% and this percentage decreases very steeply with decreasing EROI. We therefore conservatively view an EROI of 8 as the minimum desirable from an RE farm. Although this is a somewhat arbitrary choice, in another work, it has been shown that a minimum EROI value of 3 is needed to support continued economic activity [13].

The EROI of renewables is significantly lower than those of fossil fuels and conventional power sources. Moreover, curtailment

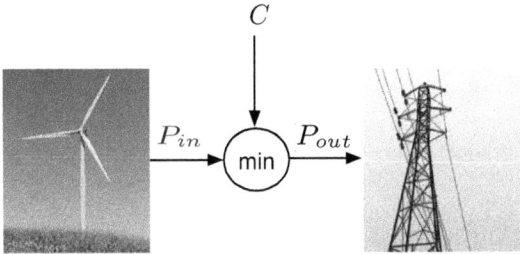

(a) Model of our system

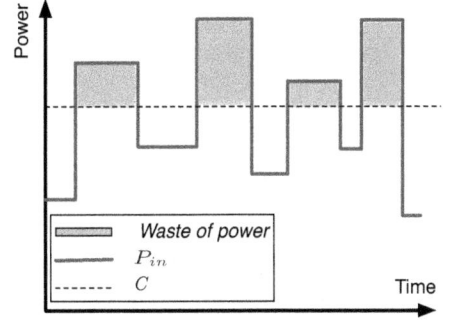

(b) Waste of power due to curtailment

Figure 2: A simple model for curtailment: when a renewable energy source produces more power than can be carried on a transmission line of capacity C, the excess is wasted.

further reduces their EROI. Thus, there is an urgent need to improve the EROI of RE technologies. This can be accomplished using three complementary approaches: (1) reducing the energy needed to create RE systems, (2) increasing the lifetime of RE technologies, and (3) reducing RE curtailment using storage. In the rest of this paper, we focus on the third approach.

3. INTEGRATING RE FARMS

To recap, a major challenge facing RE farms is their reduced energy efficiency due to curtailment. Curtailment is necessary for two reasons: insufficient line capacity for generation peaks and insufficient demand. It has been shown that limited line capacity is the most important reason for reduction in EROI today [10] and is therefore the primary focus of our work.

We also do not consider curtailment due to lack of demand because this is an extremely complex problem. The generation mix needed to meet a given load includes *must run* generators, such as nuclear generators, which are insensitive to demand, and fast spinning generators, such as natural gas turbines or combined hydro generators, which can respond quickly to reduced demand. In the future, moreover, loads may also be met from energy stored in storage devices, that have their own constraints on capacity and ramping rates. Thus, it is difficult to determine the degree to which RE farms must be curtailed due to insufficient load, and we defer consideration of this difficult issue to future work.

In the remainder of this section, we will consider the integration of RE farms in the absence and presence of storage, respectively.

3.1 Systems without storage

In a system without storage, the surplus power exceeding the access line capacity is curtailed (Fig. 2a). Curtailment is a good strategy in that it does not require any new investment. Interestingly, it also has the effect of making RE farms more attractive. This is because curtailment allows an RE farm to be deployed while ignoring, to first order, access line constraints, by simply shedding generation when it peaks exceed capacity. However, increasing RE farm capacity beyond a certain threshold wastes too much power and leads to poor energy and cost efficiencies [9], [16], [19].

3.2 Systems with storage

An alternative to curtailment is to use storage. By adding a storage device adjacent to a transmission line, we can store the non-absorbable power and withdraw it later. The stored energy can be

Name	Description
* $P_{in}(t)$	Available renewable power at time t (W)
* P_{max}	Peak generation capacity of the renewable farm (W)
$P_{out}(t)$	Absorbable power by the access line at time t (W)
$P_{add}(t)$	Part of the $P_{out}(t)$ coming from storage (W)
$P_{direct}(t)$	Part of the $P_{out}(t)$ not coming from storage (W)
* $E_{in}(T)$	Total renewable energy in $[0, T]$ (Wh)
$E_s(T)$	Total energy output from storage in $[0, T]$ (Wh)
$E_{out}(T)$	Energy transmitted over the access line in $[0, T]$ (Wh)
$E_{add}(T)$	Part of the $E_{out}(T)$ coming from storage (Wh)
$E_{direct}(T)$	Part of the $E_{out}(T)$ not coming from storage (Wh)
* C	Access line capacity (W)
$b(t)$	State of charge at time t (Wh)
$EROI_0$	EROI of the curtailment scenario
$EROI_B$	EROI of the storage scenario
* $EROI_e$	EROI of the energy harvesting technology
* $EROI_s$	EROI of the storage device
* ε_s	Energy invested to create a unit of energy storage (Wh)
* $E_{lifetime}$	Total deliverable energy during storage lifetime (Wh)
R_0	Waste of power ratio in a curtailment system
R_B	Waste of power ratio in a system with storage
* B	Storage size (Wh)
* $\alpha_c(\alpha_d)$	Storage charging (discharging) power limit (W)
* η	Storage efficiency
* γ	Storage leakage power rate (W)
* DoD	Storage depth of discharge
* λ	Storage cycle life
λ_{cr}	Critical cycle life

Table 2: Notation. Starred variables are input to the analysis.

used later to fill the gap between the available power and the access line capacity.

There are multiple advantages to using storage for renewable energy integration: reducing power waste, price arbitrage, peak shaving, and power regulation, among others [7]. Adding storage to facilitate renewable energy integration, however, comes at an investment cost, financially (the price of storage) and from energy perspective (the energy invested to create the storage device). In this paper, we are concerned about the latter investment as we study the energy efficiency of adding storage devices to access lines.

In the next section, we formulate and compare the EROI of the two systems above (with and without storage) to understand whether or not adding storage can improve the EROI of the system.

4. EROI FORMULATION AND COMPARISON

We assume a discrete-time model, where time is slotted $t = 0, T_u, 2T_u, \ldots$, with T_u being the time unit. To simplify notation, we drop T_u from our formulation by assuming $T_u = 1$. Generalizing the formulas for any T_u is a matter of additional notations.

We formulate the EROI of the systems without storage and of those using storage, separately, in the following. Please refer to Table 2 for the notation used in the rest of the paper.

4.1 The EROI of a system without storage

Let $P_{in}(t)$ be the available power from an energy harvesting technology, such as a wind or solar farm, at time t. Suppose we want to transport P_{in} over an access line of capacity C (see Fig. 2). Without access to storage in this system, the available power exceeding the access capacity must be curtailed. Hence, the absorbable power, P_{out} (i.e., the power effectively carried by the access line), in this system at any time t, is given by:

$$P_{out}(t) = \min(P_{in}(t), C). \tag{3}$$

Let $E_{in}(T)$ and $E_{out}(T)$ be, respectively, the total available energy from the energy harvesting technology and the total absorbable energy by the access line in the time interval $[0, T]$ for some $T > 0$. This is:

$$E_{in}(T) = \sum_{\tau=0}^{T} P_{in}(\tau) \tag{4}$$

and

$$E_{out}(T) = \sum_{\tau=0}^{T} P_{out}(\tau). \tag{5}$$

A key metric in designing a wind or solar farm is the *waste ratio*, R, defined as:

$$R = \lim_{T \to \infty} \frac{\text{Total wasted renewable energy in } [0, T]}{\text{Total available renewable energy in } [0, T]}. \tag{6}$$

The larger is R, the smaller the dispatchable fraction of the total available renewable power. This, subsequently, impacts the time to return the initial capital cost of the system [4]. With current technologies, prices, and energy market schemes, the average waste ratio for wind power ranges from as large as 16% and as low as 1% [20].

We denote R_0, the waste ratio in a no-storage scenario, which is:

$$R_0 = \lim_{T \to \infty} \frac{\sum_{\tau=0}^{T} [P_{in}(\tau) - C]_+}{\sum_{\tau=0}^{T} P_{in}(\tau)}, \tag{7}$$

where $[x]_+ = \max(0, x)$ for any x.

With the above notation and definitions, we can now formulate the EROI of a system without storage, as illustrated in Fig. 2. In a system without storage, the only energy invested to create the system is the energy used to produce the energy harvesting technology (wind turbine or solar PV panel). Denote $EROI_e$ as the EROI of the energy harvesting technology for each form of renewable energy (e.g., the EROI of wind turbines or solar PV panels). Then, the EROI of a system without storage depicted in Fig. 2, denoted $EROI_0$, is:

$$EROI_0 = (1 - R_0)EROI_e, \tag{8}$$

because only a fraction $(1 - R_0)$ of the total available energy from the energy harvesting tool is eventually absorbed into the system, due to the access line constraint. Formulating EROI for a system

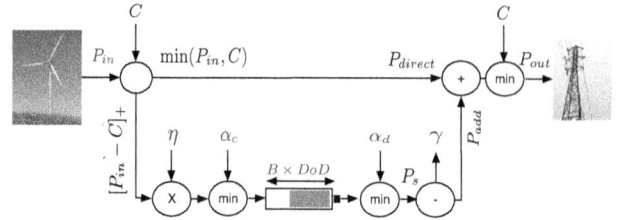

Figure 3: **Integrating renewables using storage devices:** Using a non-ideal storage device with parameters (α_c, α_d, η, DoD, B, γ, λ) to transfer renewable power P_{in} over an access line, with maximum allowable power transmission of C.

using storage is more complicated and is the focus of the next section.

4.2 The EROI of a system with storage

Transmitting renewable energy over an access line using a storage device is depicted in Fig. 3. The available power from the output of the energy harvesting technology at time slot t is $P_{in}(t)$. The maximum allowable power on the access line is C. Thus, $\min(P_{in}, C)$ is transmitted directly over the line (without going through the storage device) and the remaining available power (i.e, $[P_{in}(t) - C]_+$) is sent to be stored in the storage device (if possible). The absorbable power at any time comes either directly from the energy harvesting tool, P_{direct}, or from the energy stored in the storage device P_{add}. Before proceeding with the EROI formulation, we will discuss the non-ideal physical constraints of the storage devices, which influence the analysis.

- **Storage size (B (Wh)):** This is the maximum amount of energy that can be stored in a storage device.

- **Storage charging and discharging rate limit (α_c and α_d (W)):** This is the limit on the charge or discharge power. Typical discharge rates are many times greater ($10\times$ for PbA and $5\times$ for lithium-ion batteries) than charging rates.

- **Self-discharge (γ (W)):** Stored energy leaks over time at rate γ. Large self-discharge rates become problematic when storage devices need to store large amounts of energy for a long time.

- **Efficiency ($0 \leq \eta \leq 1$):** Due to inherent inefficiencies, each unit of energy stored is reduced to η units that can be used later. Storage devices converting electrical energy to other forms typically have lower efficiencies.

- **Depth-of-discharge ($0 \leq DoD \leq 1$):** While the entire capacity of some storage devices can be used for energy storage, in others, the storage life is extended if only a fraction (DoD) of available capacity is used.

- **Cycle life (λ):** Let B be the storage size in Watt-hours (Wh) for a storage device, the total energy delivered by that device throughout its lifetime is [17]:

$$E_{\text{lifetime}} = \lambda \times B \times DoD, \tag{9}$$

where λ is the cycle life of the storage.

A precise state of charge (SoC) analysis must account for the above physical constraints of storage. Although we account for the above physical constraints, there are still some constraints that we do not take into account:

- **Temperature:** The ambient temperature significantly impacts the storage lifetime; the higher the ambient temperature, the lower the battery lifetime.

  We assume that the ambient temperature is not highly variable. This assumption, however, can be simply relaxed and incorporated in our derivations, if the impact of temperature on the storage operation is quantified. This has yet to be modelled in the literature.

- **The impact of partial charging/discharging on cycle life:** For simplicity, we assume that λ in Eq. (9) is a constant for each storage technology. It has, however, been observed that λ of some battery technologies is highly affected by the discharge rate, especially during the first few moments of each discharge cycle [12]. This is known as the *rate capacity effect*. Moreover, it is also a function of the shape of the discharging process. For instance, an intermittent discharging process, which has an on-off duty cycle, leads to a longer lifetime than a steady discharging process. This is known as the *recovery effect*; during periods with no or very low discharge, the battery can recover the capacity lost during periods of high discharge to a certain extent [8]. Thus, the battery lifetime can be improved by using a pulsed current discharge instead of a constant current discharge, due to the recovery effect.

The discharging process of storage systems, when used to back up renewable energy sources, is characterized by highly variable charging power, deep cycling, partial cycling, and infrequent full charging. It has been shown in [14], that although the variability in renewable energy (wind) dramatically decreases the lifetime of PbA batteries, it does not considerably impact the lifetime of lithium-ion batteries. Thus, in our numerical examples, the EROI values of lithium-ion are close to practical values for renewables, while those corresponding to PbA might overestimate the practical values. This is not problematic, however, as the EROI values of PbA in our examples are already below the values of a system without storage.

In the next section, we formulate the EROI, assuming all of the storage imperfections depicted in Fig. 3.

4.3 SoC analysis

Due to the limited access line capacity in the scenario depicted in Fig. 3, the instantaneous surplus power at any time t, $[P_{in}(t) - C]_+$, is sent to be stored in the storage device. However, because of the non-ideal behaviour of the storage devices mentioned earlier, part of this power will be wasted and cannot be withdrawn later. The maximum charging power of the storage cannot exceed a certain threshold α_c and any charging power beyond that, is curtailed. Moreover, the storage device loses a fraction $1 - \eta$ of the total energy being stored in the storage device, due to storage inefficiency. Energy stored in the storage device is discarded with rate γ, due to storage self-discharge. The storage cannot be discharged faster than α_d. The storage lifetime constraint is met if only a DoD fraction≤ 1 of the entire storage is used. Thus, at any moment, the storage state of the charge cannot exceed $DoD \times B$. Finally, at any time t due to the constraint of the line capacity, only up to a maximum of $[C - P_{in}(t)]_+$ can be sent to the line from the storage.

Accounting for all of the above parameters, we can formulate the state of charge $b(t)$ of the storage at any time instant t. The storage device in such a system can be viewed as a buffer. Similar to a buffer content formulation, a *state of charge* formulation can

be expressed by a recursive equation as follows:

$$b(t) = \min\Big(B \times DoD, \Big[\min\left([P_{in}(t) - C]_+, \alpha_c \right) \eta$$
$$- \min([C - P_{in}(t)]_+, \alpha_d) - \gamma + b(t-1) \Big]_+ \Big). \tag{10}$$

To simplify notation, we define $b'(t)$ to be the state of charge at time t before deducting the storage output processes (P_s in the system model in Fig. 3) , i.e.,:

$$b'(t) = \min\Big(B \times DoD, \Big[\min\left([P_{in}(t) - C]_+, \alpha_c \right) \eta$$
$$+ b(t-1) \Big]_+ \Big). \tag{11}$$

Then, the output process from the storage device is:

$$P_s(t) = \min(\min([C - P_{in}(t)]_+, \alpha_d) + \gamma, b'(t)) \tag{12}$$

and the additional power being transmitted over the line with respect to the no-storage scenario is:

$$P_{add}(t) = [P_s(t) - \gamma]_+. \tag{13}$$

Let $E_{in}(T)$ be the total available energy from the energy harvesting device in the interval $[0, T]$ for some $T > 0$, computed from Eq. (4). We also define $E_{direct}(T)$, $E_{add}(T)$, and $E_s(T)$, respectively, as the total energy directly transported from the renewable energy source, the total energy coming from the storage device, and the total energy withdrawn from the storage device in the time interval $[0, T]$. These quantities are, respectively, given by

$$E_{direct}(T) = \sum_{\tau=0}^{T} \min(P_{in}(\tau), C), \tag{14}$$

$$E_{add}(T) = \sum_{\tau=0}^{T} P_{add}(\tau), \tag{15}$$

and

$$E_s(T) = \sum_{\tau=0}^{T} P_s(\tau). \tag{16}$$

Using Eqs. (4)-(14) together with these new definitions and notation, the waste ratio in a system without storage can be rewritten as:

$$R_0 = 1 - \lim_{T \to \infty} \frac{E_{direct}(T)}{E_{in}(T)}. \tag{17}$$

Moreover, the waste ratio (defined in Eq. (6)) in a system with storage is:

$$R_B = R_0 - \lim_{T \to \infty} \frac{E_{add}(T)}{E_{in}(T)}. \tag{18}$$

There are two devices used in the scenario depicted in Fig. 3: the energy harvesting technology and the energy storage with their respective EROI denoted as $EROI_e$ and $EROI_s$. The energy invested to produce a storage system is usually expressed in terms of energy invested to create one unit of that storage system ε_s. The $EROI_s$ of a storage system can be subsequently computed as

$$EROI_s = \frac{\eta E_{\text{lifetime}}}{B \times \varepsilon_s}$$
$$= \frac{DoD \times \lambda \eta}{\varepsilon_s}, \tag{19}$$

	PbA	Lithium-ion	CAES
Efficiency	0.75	0.85	0.68
Charge time (=storage size/charge rate)	8-16h	2-4h	15 min
Discharge rate to charge rate ratio	10	5	4
Self-discharge/day (=self-discharge rate × day/storage size) (%)	0.3	0.1	0
DoD	0.80	0.80	1
ε_s	96	136	22
λ	700	6000	25000

Table 3: Characteristics of storage technologies [1], [6], [22]

where Eq. (9) is used to obtain the second line.

The energy return in the time interval $[0, T]$ in this model is:

$$\text{Energy return in } [0, T] = E_{direct}(T) + E_{add}(T), \qquad (20)$$

and the energy invested in the time interval $[0, T]$ is:

$$\text{Energy invested in } [0, T] = \frac{E_{in}(T)}{EROI_e} + \frac{E_s(T)}{EROI_s}. \qquad (21)$$

Note that Eqs. (20) and (21) compute the *exact* energy return and energy investment in $[0, T]$ based on the actual energy flux in that period. This models the fact that the lower the amount of energy generated by the source, the longer its lifetime. Similarly, if there is zero energy flux through the storage element in that period, there is no degradation in its expected lifetime. Although this is a simplifying assumption, it does reflect the fact that the lifetime of a generator or storage element is coupled to the energy flux it generates, stores, or releases.

Combining Eq. (20)-(21), we have:

$$EROI_B = \lim_{T \to \infty} \frac{E_{direct}(T) + E_{add}(T)}{\frac{E_{in}(T)}{EROI_e} + \frac{E_s(T)}{EROI_s}} \qquad (22)$$

$$= \lim_{T \to \infty} \frac{(1 - R_0) + E_{add}(T)/E_{in}(T)}{\frac{1}{EROI_e} + \frac{E_s(T)}{EROI_s \times E_{in}(T)}}, \qquad (23)$$

where we have used Eq. (17) in the second line.

We learn from Eqs. (8)-(23) that the cycle life of a storage technology must be larger than a critical life cycle λ_{cr}, to be beneficial (with respect to curtailment) to be used for the access line, where:

$$\lambda_{cr} = \lim_{T \to \infty} \frac{(1 - R_0)\varepsilon_s \times EROI_e \times E_s(T)}{\eta \times DoD \times E_{add}(T)}. \qquad (24)$$

Otherwise, curtailment has a larger EROI than a system with storage, and hence, is more energy efficient. Comparing the current life cycle of the storage technologies with λ_{cr} determines if those existing storage technologies outperform curtailment for integrating renewables.

5. NUMERICAL EXAMPLES

In this section, we numerically evaluate the energy efficiency of adding storage to an access line that is used to carry renewable power by comparing the EROI of systems with and without storage. For wind power, we use the measurement traces collected from wind turbines located on the west coast of the United States, with 10-minute time resolution ($T_u = 10$min), freely available in [2]. For solar power, we use the solar irradiance dataset from the atmospheric radiation measurement (ARM) website [3] from the $C1$ station in southern great plains (SGP) permanent site with a 1-minute time resolution. We multiply the solar irradiance by a PV efficiency factor of 0.2 to translate from solar irradiance to the power output of a solar PV panel of unit size ($1m^2$). To obtain the output power of a solar PV farm, the output power of a unit size

PV panel is multiplied by the total surface area of all of the existing solar PV panels in that farm.

We consider three storage technologies in our examples:

1. *Lead-acid battery* (PbA): This storage technology is widely-used, due to its low price, simple manufacturing, and lowest self-discharging rate among all batteries. It has, however, a small charging rate, and a limited life cycle.

2. *Lithium-ion battery* (Li-ion): This type of battery has a low discharge rate and a larger-than-average cycle life, compared to other batteries. A disadvantage is its price, which can be three times that of a PbA battery.

3. *Compressed air energy storage* (CAES): This device stores energy in the form of compressed air and releases it to rotate a turbine for electricity generation. CAES has a low efficiency, but has no restriction on DoD, and a large cycle life.

The characteristics of these technologies are given in Table 3. In our examples, we define P_{max} to be the peak generation capacity of the renewable energy farm, i.e.,:

$$P_{max} = \max_{t \geq 0} (P_{in}(t)). \qquad (25)$$

Our example solar and wind power farms both have $P_{max} = 3\text{MW}^2$. We treat the *normalized access capacity*, defined as C/P_{max}, as the independent variable. This indicates how large the line capacity is with respect to the maximum renewable power.

First, we study the EROI of different storage technologies as a function of normalized access capacity (Section 5.1). We then study how to size access lines to achieve maximum EROI (Section 5.2). Finally, we study the improvements that need to be made in storage cycle life to allow the EROI to at least match that of curtailment (Section 5.3).

5.1 The EROI of storage technologies

In this section, we study whether adding storage increases the EROI of the system compared to curtailment (Fig. 2). We use Eq. (23) to compute the EROI of a system with storage ($EROI_B$) with $B = 10$MWh, accounting for all physical constraints of storage systems. We also include the $EROI$ of an *ideal* storage technology (using Eq. (23) with $B = \infty$, $\alpha_c, \alpha_d = \infty$, $\gamma = 0$, but with the same λ) and the EROI of a system without storage from Eq. (8) ($EROI_0$). Adding storage to the system is beneficial if it improves the EROI of the system with respect to curtailment, i.e., $EROI_B > EROI_0$.

Fig. 4 shows that the EROI impact of adding storage depends on the storage technology, the type of renewable energy (e.g., solar or wind power), and the normalized access capacity C/P_{max}.

---

[2]We choose the surface area of the total PV panels in the solar PV farm such that $P_{max} = 3$ with the given solar irradiance dataset.

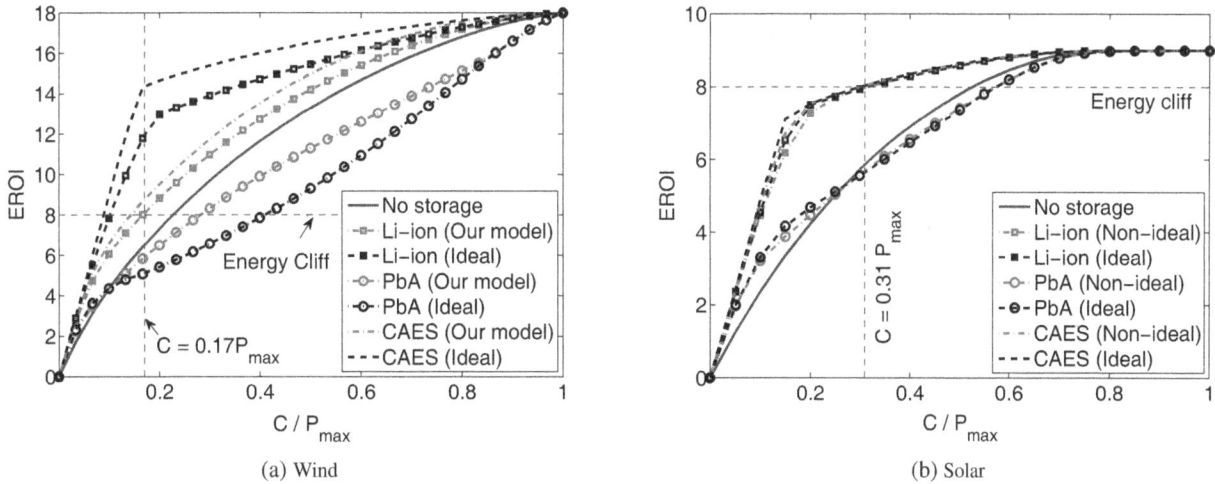

Figure 4: **Energy evaluation of storage systems and comparison with no-storage and ideal storage models:** EROI as a function of the normalized access capacity. The storage sizes of non-ideal models are B = 10MWh.

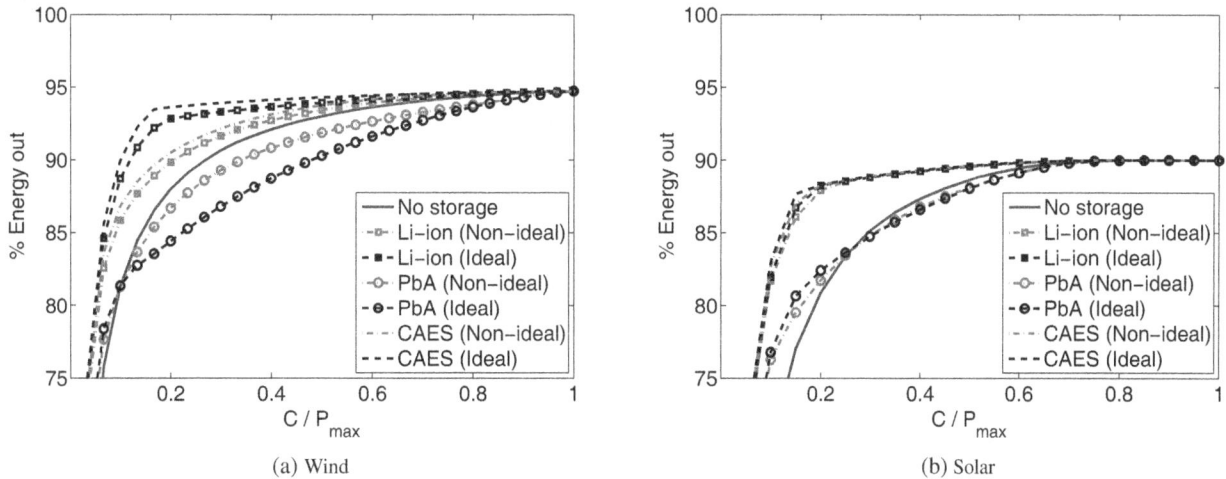

Figure 5: **Illustrating the energy cliff using our analysis and the comparison with no-storage and ideal storage models:** Output energy percentage as a function of the normalized access capacity. The storage sizes of non-ideal models are B = 10MWh. Note that the Y axis does not start at the origin.

In particular, we find that the choice of storage technology determines the EROI gain over curtailment ('No storage'); using some storage technologies is beneficial (such as lithium-ion and CAES), while for some other storage technologies (such as PbA), it is more energy efficient to curtail the surplus power.

Comparing the non-ideal and ideal curves in Fig. 4a for wind power shows that considering non-ideal behaviour of the storage technologies substantially affects the EROI. In other words, an idealized analysis might significantly overestimate or underestimate the EROI, possibly yielding misleading conclusions. In contrast, for the storage size chosen here, the ideal analysis for solar power closely matches that for non-ideal storage. This is because this storage size ($B = 10$MWh) is sufficiently large so that it behaves as an infinite size storage. We study the effect of smaller storage size in Fig. 6. Surprisingly, we find that the EROI of an ideal storage device can be smaller than that of a non-ideal one (e.g., for PbA batteries). This counter intuitive observation occurs because an ideal

storage device carries more energy flux compared to a non-ideal one in the same finite time interval; hence, it increases the energy investment in that interval.

We have drawn a horizontal line at EROI = 8 in Fig. 4, which corresponds to the critical net energy cliff (see Section 2). As discussed in Section 2, we prefer to design energy systems that have an EROI $\geq$ 8. The intersection of the line EROI = 8 and the EROI curves determine the access capacity needed to guarantee that the system operates above the net energy cliff. The access line capacity required to satisfy this constraint depends on the storage technology, storage size, and the type of renewable source. Access lines are expensive and the cost increases with both the length of the line and with its capacity [21]. Thus, the minimum access line capacity that can guarantee a quality constraint (such as $EROI > 8$) is desirable. A comparison of the intersecting points for a non-ideal and ideal storage model suggests that an ideal storage model can be misleading, if it is used to estimate the EROI of a system with

9

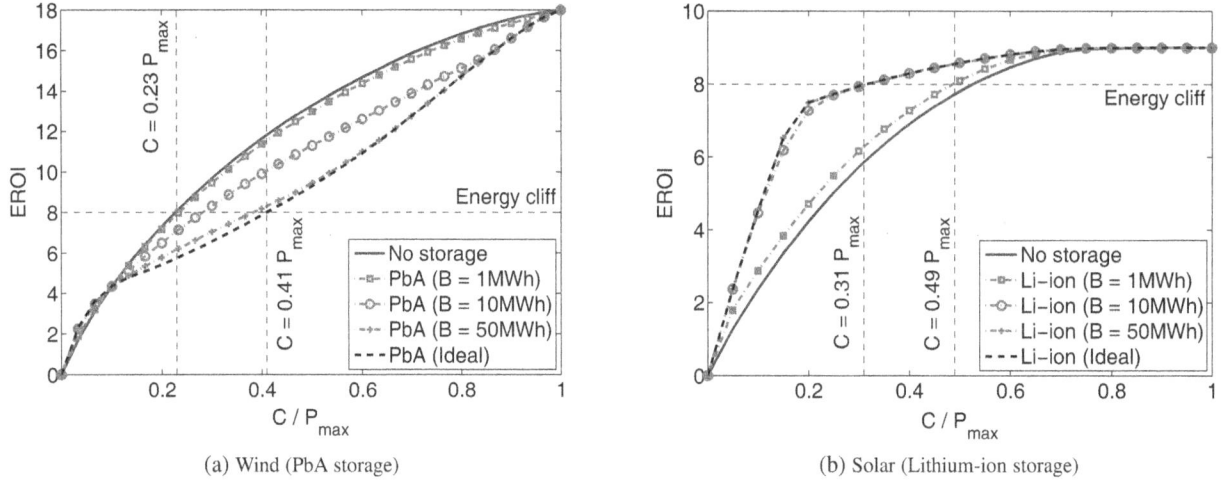

(a) Wind (PbA storage)

(b) Solar (Lithium-ion storage)

Figure 6: **EROI as a function of storage size and normalized access capacity for both ideal and non-ideal storage for specific storage technologies.**

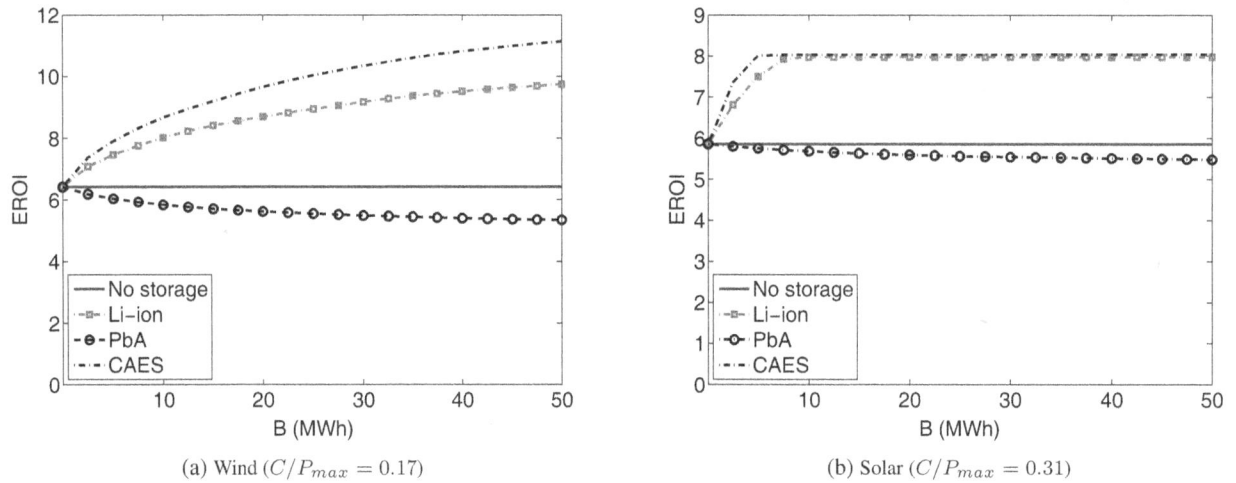

(a) Wind ($C/P_{max} = 0.17$)

(b) Solar ($C/P_{max} = 0.31$)

Figure 7: **The impact of storage size on EROI**: EROI as a function of storage size.

storage. Moreover, a comparison of these intersecting points for wind and solar power reveals that integrating *solar* power is much more expensive than integrating *wind* power. For instance, the required access line capacity for solar power with lithium-ion storage is $C = 0.31P_{max}$ which is almost twice as much as that for wind power $C = 0.17P_{max}$ (recall that P_{max} is equal for both solar and wind power in our examples). This is due to the larger variance of solar power compared to wind power. Specifically, there is an underlying diurnal pattern for solar power which dominates its short-term variations. However, wind power lacks such a deterministic pattern and its variations are nearly unbiased. Thus, for the same P_{max} and C, solar power has a larger curtailment ratio than wind power.

Although the storage size is assumed to be 10MWh in this example, all scenarios with storage coincide with that of a system with no storage when $C/P_{max} = 1$. This is due to the fact that when $C/P_{max} = 1$, the net energy flux through the storage element is zero, thus it has no effect on EROI.

The impact of increasing the access line capacity to avoid the net energy cliff is illustrated in another way in Fig. 5. This graph repeats the example in Fig. 4, however, it shows the percentage of energy return to the total energy (i.e., $\frac{EROI}{EROI+1}$). This graph shows that the energy cliff occurs at different line access capacities, depending on the storage technologies and types of renewable energy sources. Moreover, this figure confirms the need to account for the non-ideal behaviour of storage devices.

5.2 The effect of storage size on the EROI

Fig. 6 shows EROI analysis with both ideal and non-ideal storage for specific storage technologies associated with wind and solar power. It is evident that EROI analysis using idealized storage assumptions can be misleading. Indeed, the difference is more pronounced for smaller storage sizes (note that with idealized storage assumptions we have $B = \infty$). For example, from Fig. 6a, the points corresponding to the net energy cliff (i.e., EROI = 8) are $C/P_{max} = 0.23$ and $C/P_{max} = 0.41$, respectively, for a PbA battery with size $B = 1$MWh and for an ideal storage model. The cor-

(a) Wind

(b) Solar

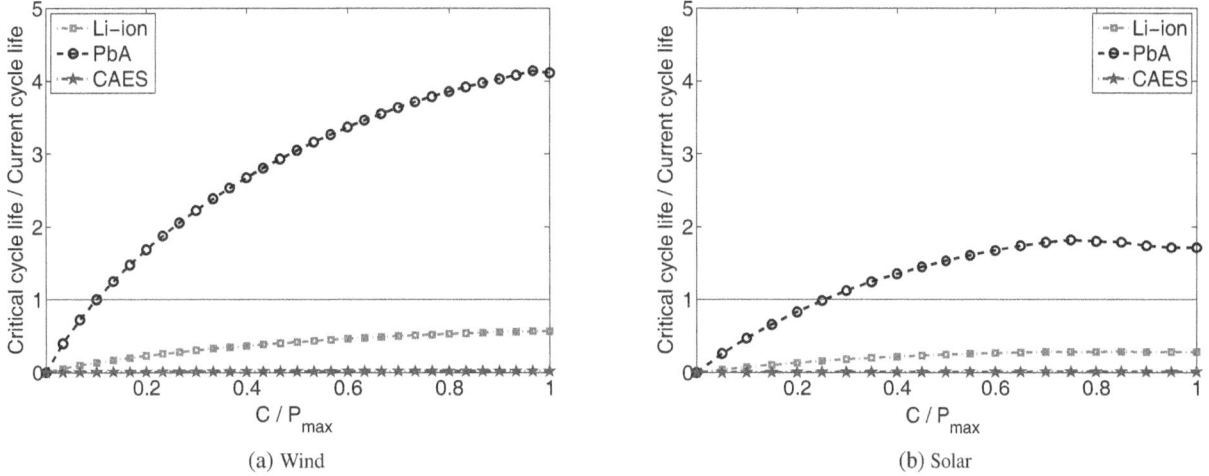

Figure 8: **The ratio of critical cycle life to current cycle life for different storage technologies with B = 10MWh:** The cycle life must be scaled by these values for the storage devices so that they are sufficiently energy efficient to replace curtailment.

responding points in Fig. 6b also differ considerably, with C/P_{max} = 0.49 for a non-ideal storage model and C/P_{max} = 0.31 for that with idealized storage assumptions.

To demonstrate that increasing the storage size can have either a positive or negative impact on EROI, in Fig. 6 we show the $EROI_B$ for three different storage sizes ($B = 1, 10, 50$MWh) of PbA for wind power and lithium-ion for solar power. Indeed, if $EROI_B < EROI_0$ for $B > 0$, then $EROI_B$ is increasing in B. However, if $EROI_B > EROI_0$ for $B > 0$, then $EROI_0$ is decreasing in B.

Unlike the simple model analysis in [6], which is oblivious to the choice of storage size, our analysis takes the storage size into account. Hence, this allows storage sizing for a target performance. Specifically, Fig. 7 illustrates the impact of increasing the storage size from another perspective. In this graph, for a fixed operation point of $C/P_{max} = 0.31$ for solar power and $C/P_{max} = 0.17$ for wind power, we compute $EROI$[3]. At $B = 0$, the curtailment and storage systems are equivalent. As B increases, the EROI monotonically converges to a system with the same storage technology with infinite size. The speed of convergence depends on the storage technology, type of renewable energy, and point of operation. If $EROI_B < EROI_0$ for $B > 0$, then the optimal storage size is zero. If $EROI_B > EROI_0$ for $B > 0$, then the optimum storage size is the minimum storage size which achieves an EROI satisfactorily close to the EROI of an infinite storage size with the same storage technology. The monotonic trend observed in Fig. 7 is attributed to the fact that the storage size only limits the amount of power that can be absorbed or discharged, but it does not directly impact EROI analysis. Indeed, the EROI of an ideal storage device is independent of B.

5.3 Critical cycle life for a storage technology

Following [6], we now study the *critical* cycle life, which is defined as the cycle life for which the EROI of a system with storage is equal to that of a system with no storage. This is denoted as λ_{cr} in Eq. (24). The critical cycle life is helpful in assessing the improvements necessary to make a storage technology viable.

Fig. 8 illustrates the ratio of the critical cycle life to the current cycle life for existing technologies (i.e., $\lambda_{cr}/\lambda_{now}$) as a function of normalized access capacity. If this ratio is less than unity for a storage technology, then using this storage increases EROI compared to the curtailment scenario. Otherwise, that storage technology is not preferred to curtailment, and future improvements need to scale its cycle life by $\lambda_{cr}/\lambda_{now}$. As Fig. 8 shows, with the existing technologies, it is efficient to use lithium-ion batteries and CAES for both wind and solar power. However, PbA batteries are not yet efficient enough to compete with pure curtailment.

As shown in Fig. 8, the critical cycle life mostly increases as the access line capacity increases. This is because the critical cycle life from Eq. (24) is proportional to $(1 - R_0)$, and this term usually increases as the access capacity increases. The physical interpretation is that as the access capacity increases, the waste ratio decreases, thus, there is less power to be saved by storage. Thus, a storage technology must have a larger cycle life to increase EROI beyond curtailment for large values of C/P_{max}. Note that this ratio does not always increase with access line capacity; there is also a small decrease in λ_{cr} when C/P_{max} increases for the case of PbA. It can be shown that this is due to the high self-discharge rate of this technology.

6. RELATED WORK

Cost efficiency is a significant–if not the only–factor that has been studied in the literature to decide whether to add storage to an energy system. The fundamental problem studied in these cases is whether the additional revenue obtained from an energy system by adding storage is larger than the investment cost to buy that storage. The results of such a study are highly dependent on the use to which the energy system is put to, as well as the storage technology. For example, it is shown in [11] that adding Sodium-Sulphur batteries at current costs increases the revenue for RE farms. In another work [5], a cost/benefit analysis was conducted by comparing the annual cost of different storage technologies with the total profit for both the utility and an RE farm owner. The results show that integrating storage with the distribution system is economically feasible only when the least expensive storage (Zn-Br) is used.

---

[3]These are the corresponding operating points at which the systems with lithium-ion batteries in Fig. 4 reach the energy cliff (EROI = 8).

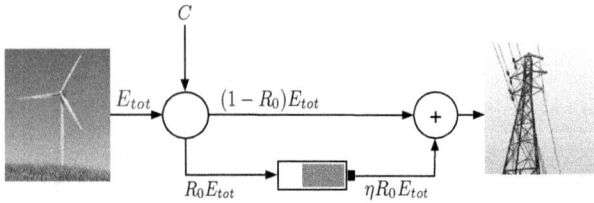

Figure 9: **Simple model used in [6]:** Idealized storage assumption ($B = \infty$, α_c, $\alpha_d = \infty$, and $\gamma = 0$) and no access capacity constraint on the power transmitted from the storage.

Evaluating the *energy efficiency* of an energy system using EROI analysis has drawn much attention over the last few years. Prior studies are mostly focused on the following five topics [18]: (1) energy efficiency of corn ethanol; (2) comparing the EROI of major fuel types; (3) energy return on water invested (EROWI); (4) the relation between EROI and the economy; and (5) an attempt to calculate the minimum EROI for a sustainable society. None of these are directly related to our work.

Evaluating the energy efficiency of adding storage to RE farms was recently proposed by Barnhart *et al* [6]. This work introduced the fresh, new perspective of EROI analysis to study this important problem. Using a simple model of an RE farm (see Fig. 9) and approximate analysis, their work showed that, in contrast to conventional wisdom, the EROI of an RE farm sometimes decreases by adding storage.

In their model, if E_{tot} represents the total available energy from an RE harvesting technology (such as wind turbine or photovoltaic) over a long time interval, then only a fraction $(1 - R_0)$ of that total energy can be transmitted over an access line. The rest of the energy is stored in the storage device and $R_0\eta$ portion of that is withdrawn later, where η is the efficiency of that storage system. This model has several shortcomings:

First, it makes strong assumptions on storage: infinite storage capacity, infinite charge and discharge rates, and zero self-discharge. Second, it permits infinite discharge rate from the storage device into the access line. Third, it treats, R_0, the waste of power ratio with no storage, as an independent variable, rather than an outcome of the underlying storage charge/discharge process. Not only does this disregard the dynamics of the system but also, given that the waste ratio in a system with storage is smaller than R_0 (compare Eq. (7) and Eq. (18)), it is technically incorrect to compare $EROI_0$ and $EROI_B$ for the same R_0 in the first place.

How important are these shortcomings? Figs. 4, 5, and 6 show that even when we consider only one of the inaccuracies in the simple model–assuming an ideal store– the resulting EROI considerably differs from that computed from a more complete analysis. This suggests that the conclusions in [6] may have substantial shortcomings. For instance, this work claims that using any type of storage device for solar power always increases EROI and that using batteries for wind power always decreases EROI. Our results contradict these conclusions, as discussed next.

7. CONCLUSIONS AND FUTURE WORK

Integrating RE farms into the power grid is challenging due to inherent unpredictable fluctuations. One of the problems arising in energy integration is that the peak power bursts cannot be absorbed to the grid due to the limited access line capacity. A common solution to this problem is to simply curtail excess power. Curtailment is simple and does not need any additional hardware; however, it leads to significant power waste. A promising solution to reduce

the waste ratio is to use storage devices to store some of the curtailed power. Recent work suggests that to fairly evaluate the energy benefits of adding storage to a system, the energy invested to create the storage device must also be taken into account [6]. This can be achieved by using a well-known metric called *energy return on investment* (EROI); adding a storage device to an energy system is *energy efficient* only if it improves the EROI of that system.

In this work, we present an accurate EROI analysis for RE farms. This analysis accounts for several storage imperfections and tracks the dynamics of the state of charge process. Other than illustrating why imperfections of a storage system must be accounted for, our analysis when applied to actual solar and wind power measurement traces leads to several new insights:

- The required access line capacity to achieve a certain EROI is much larger for solar power than for wind power. This implies that solar power integration is more expensive than wind power.

- EROI always monotonically varies as a function of storage size; it could, however, be either increasing or decreasing.

- Some existing technologies, such as lithium-ion batteries and CAES increase the EROI in comparison with curtailment whereas some others such as PbA have a lower EROI than curtailment.

- We contradict earlier claims in [6] that *no* battery technology is energy efficient for wind and *all* battery technologies are energy efficient for solar power.

We caution that these insights might be sensitive to the numerical values in our analysis.

In future work, we plan to use the insights gained here to tackle the complex problem of EROI analysis of RE farms whose output is curtailed due to limited demand.

8. REFERENCES

[1] http://batteryuniversity.com.

[2] http://wind.nrel.gov/Webnrel/.

[3] http://www.archive.arm.gov.

[4] E. W. E. Association. *Wind energy–the facts: a guide to the technology, economics and future of wind power*. Earthscan, 2009.

[5] Y. M. Atwa and E. F. El-Saadany. Optimal allocation of ESS in distribution systems with a high penetration of wind energy. *IEEE Transactions on Power Systems*, 25(4):1815 – 1822, 2010.

[6] C. J. Barnhart, M. Dale, A. R. Brandt, and S. M. Benson. The energetic implications of curtailing versus storing solar- and wind-generated electricity. *Energy Environment Science*, 6:2804 – 2810, 2013.

[7] A. Carvallo and J. Cooper. *The Advanced Smart Grid: Edge Power Driving Sustainability*. Artech House, 2011.

[8] C. Chiasserini and R. R. Rao. A model for battery pulsed discharge with recovery effect. In *Proc. of IEEE WCNC*, pages 636 – 639, 1999.

[9] R. A. F. Currie, G. W. Ault, and J. R. McDonald. Methodology for determination of economic connection capacity for renewable generator connections to distribution networks optimised by active power flow management. *IEE Proceedings- Generation, Transmission and Distribution*, 153(4):456 – 462, 2006.

[10] P. Denholm. Energy storage to reduce renewable energy curtailment. In *IEEE Power and Energy Society General Meeting*, pages 1 – 4, 2012.

[11] S. Gill, G. W. Ault, and I. Kockar. The optimal operation of energy storage in a wind power curtailment scheme. In *Proc. of IEEE Power and Energy Society General Meeting*, pages 1– 8, 2012.

[12] J. Groot. *State-of-Health Estimation of Li-ion Batteries: Cycle Life Test Methods*. PhD thesis, Chalmers University of technology, 2012.

[13] C. A. S. Hall, S. Balogh, and D. J. R. M. What is the minimum EROI that a sustainable society must have? *Energies*, 2(1):25 – 47, 2009.

[14] E. M. Krieger. *Effects of variability and rate on battery charge storage and lifespan*. PhD thesis, Princeton University, 2013.

[15] J. Lambert, J. Hall, S. Balogh, A. Poisson, and A. Gupta. EROI of global energy resources preliminary status and trends. Technical report, State University of New York, College of Environmental Science and Forestry, November 2012.

[16] S. N. Liew and G. Strbac. Maximising penetration of wind generation in existing distribution networks. *IEE Proceedings-Generation, Transmission and Distribution*, 149(3):256 – 262, 2002.

[17] N. Michelusi, L. Badia, R. Carli, L. Corradini, and M. Zorzi. Impact of battery degradation on optimal management policies of harvesting-based wireless sensor devices. In *Proc. of IEEE INFOCOM*, pages 590 – 594, 2013.

[18] D. J. Murphy and C. A. S. Hall. Year in review: EROI or energy return on (energy) invested. *Annals of the New York Academy of Sciences*, 1185(1):102 – 118, 2010.

[19] L. F. Ochoa, C. J. Dent, and G. P. Harrison. Distribution network capacity assessment: Variable DG and active networks. *IEEE Transactions on Power Systems*, 25(1):87 – 95, 2010.

[20] J. Rogers, S. Fink, and K. Porter. Examples of wind energy curtailment practices. Technical Report SR-550-48737, National Renewable Energy Library, July 2010.

[21] S. Stoft, C. Webber, and R. H. Wiser. Transmission pricing and renewables: Issues, options, and recommendations. Technical Report LBNL-39845, LBNL, May 1997.

[22] D. Wang, C. Ren, A. Sivasubramaniam, B. Urgaonkar, and H. Fathy. Energy storage in datacenters: what, where, and how much? In *Proc. of ACM SIGMETRICS/PERFORMANCE*, pages 187–198, June 2012.

Control of Systems that Store Renewable Energy

Neda Edalat, Mehul Motani
Department of Electrical and
Computer Engineering,
National University of
Singapore
neda@nus.edu.sg,
motani@nus.edu.sg

Jean Walrand
Department of Electrical
Engineering and Computer
Sciences,
University of California
Berkeley
wlr@eecs.berkeley.edu

Longbo Huang
Institute for Interdisciplinary
Information Sciences,
Tsinghua University, Beijing
longbohuang@tsinghua.edu.cn

ABSTRACT

This paper studies the control of systems that store renewable energy. The problem is to maximize the long-term utility of the energy by controlling how it is used. The methodology for designing the control policy depends on the size of the battery. If the battery is small, the control policy is determined by solving a Markov decision problem. If the battery is large, this problem is complex but one can replace it by a simpler problem where the constraint is on the average power usage. When the battery is large, the average power usage should not exceed the average power harvested by the source. When the battery size is moderate, the control is based on the large deviations of the battery charge. This paper illustrates these methods with a number of examples.

Keywords

Renewable energy; storage; control; large deviations; Markov chain; occupation measure.

1. INTRODUCTION

By increasing the use of renewable energy sources, the energy usage control of the systems that operates with such sources are the great of interest. Unlike conventional power sources, the output power of renewable sources cannot be controlled as there are daily and seasonal fluctuations and inaccurate energy prediction. This makes the control of the systems that operates with such sources challenging [1].

The paper is concerned with systems that utilize renewable energy and are equipped with a battery to adjust for the variability in available power and energy usage. Examples include wireless sensor nodes and buildings.

The problem under study is how to best use the stored energy to maximize the long-term utility. For instance, in the case of a wireless sensor node, the average power used must be less than the average power of the source. How-

ever, unless the battery is very large, the variability may cause the battery to go empty even when that condition is met. In such a situation, one suspects that the energy use should take into account the instantaneous amount of energy stored in the battery. One approach is to formulate this problem as a Markov decision in which the state of the system is the amount of stored energy, together with the state of the environment. Unless the battery is small, the size of the state space of this Markov decision problem is very large, which makes the problem difficult to solve. Moreover, this formulation results in a complex control strategy that depends on the stored energy. However, intuition suggests that if the battery is moderate in size, then using energy at an average rate slightly less than the average rate of the source should guarantee that the battery rarely goes empty. This paper explains how to make that intuition precise using the theory of large deviations. The large deviation analysis leads to the constraint for energy usage. The novelty of the analysis is that the source and usage are both variable, in contrast with the theory of effective bandwidth [6] and [7]. Indeed, the usage affects the large deviations of the battery discharge, so that the large deviations appear as constraints for the optimization problem. One contribution of the paper is a formulation that enables the analysis of the large deviations of the battery in a numerically tractable way that can be included in the optimization problem. We compare this approach to the large deviations analysis based on the occupation measure of a Markov chain. We also examine the case when the variability of the energy source and that of the load are independent.

It would be tempting to use a Gaussian approximation [11] to study the large deviations. However, simple examples show that this approximation is very poor.

The paper is structured as follows. We introduce the system model and problem formulation in Section 2. This is followed by Section 3 which is approximating the control policy by replacing the constraint based on large deviation techniques. In Section 4, the large deviation techniques are applied in three ways: direct method which is based on the Chernoff's inequality, a method based on occupation measure and a Gaussian approximation method. Sections 5 and 6 explain the evaluation of the approach for random walk and 2-state Markov chain, respectively. In Section 6, we present the same problem for the case when the variability of the energy source and that of the load are independent. In order to clarify the proposed approach, Section 7 provides several examples. Section 8 concludes and summarizes the paper.

1.1 Background and related work

Resource management techniques for energy harvesting systems with uncertain resource availability pose a new set of challenges. These techniques lead to utility maximization considering the energy constraint. For energy harvesting wireless sensor networks EH-WSNs where the resources of interest are energy and data, the transmission rate and data sampling rate maximization satisfying the energy constraint are two important problems. These problems have been addressed in [12]- [17]. The authors in [12] proposed the solution for rate maximization for multiple fading channels of a transmitter. They develop the directional water filling heuristic. The authors in [14] designed a solution for fair and high throughput data extraction from all nodes guaranteeing fairness while maximizing the sampling rate and throughput. Mao et al. in [16] proposed a joint data queue and battery buffer control algorithm, thus the long-term average sensing rate maximization subject to stability of data queue and desired data loss ratio could be achieved. They considered the static channel model and offline knowledge about the energy input. A policy with decoupled admission control and power allocation decisions is developed in [15] that achieves asymptotic optimality for sufficiently large battery capacity to maximum transmission power ratio (explicit bounds are provided). The authors in [17] obtained the energy management policies that are throughput optimal and minimize the mean delay in the queue. They mainly assume that the capacity of the rechargeable battery is large enough; however, they did not consider the consequence of large state space on designing the methodology and algorithms. In this paper, we show that by considering the storage capacity of the system, one can design efficient and simple algorithms. The main advantage of our approach is that the control policy for the energy usage rate does not involve the instantaneous amount of energy stored in the nodes, when the size of the battery is moderate or large.

In this paper, the core idea is to convert the complex Markov decision problem to a simple optimization problem where its constraint is based on large deviation theory. Large deviations theory refers to the collection of techniques to estimate the properties of rare events, such as their frequency and most likely manner of occurrence. Some references on large deviations include Bahadur (1971) [2], Varadhan (1984) [3], Deuschel and Stroock (1989) [5], and Dembo and Zeitouni (1998) [4]. Large deviations are often caused by a large number of unlikely events occurring together, rather than a single event of small probability. The theory of large deviations has been applied to the analysis of Asynchronous Transfer Mode (ATM) networks [6] and [7]. ATM is a packet switching standard that aimed to limit the rate of cell losses due to buffer overflow to negligible values, comparable to losses caused by transmission errors.

In this paper, the state of the system is modeled as a finite Markov chain. There are a few possible approaches to study the large deviations of a Markov chain. One method is based on the occupation measure of Markov chains [9]. The basic idea of this approach is that the most likely way for a Markov chain to have an empirical distribution that differs from the invariant distribution is for it to behave as if it had different transition probabilities consistent with the observed empirical distribution. This is the essence of the contraction mapping theorem [3].

Another approach, that we call the direct method, is to start with Chernoff's inequality and calculate the relevant moment generating functions using the first step equations of a Markov chain.

Yet another approach is to consider a Gaussian approximation for the changes of the Markov chain over a number of steps [10], [11]. However, we explain that this method yields poor estimates of the likelihood that the battery becomes empty for realistic system parameters, which should not be surprising since large deviations typically depend strongly on the higher moments of the distributions.

2. MODEL

A discrete time model of the system is as follows. At time $n \geq 0$, the battery, with capacity B, has accumulated an amount $X_n \in \{0, 1, \ldots, B\}$ of energy, the environment state such as weather condition is Y_n, a Markov chain on some finite state space $\mathcal{Y}$ with a transition probability matrix P, and one uses a control action $U_n \in \mathcal{U}$ where $\mathcal{U}$ is a finite set. The net amount of battery discharge at time n is a function of Y_n and U_n denoted as $g(Y_n, U_n)$. Hence, $E[g(Y_n, U_n)]$ can take positive as well as negative values. A negative value means that the battery tends to recharge more than drain. Also, $r(Y_n, U_n)$ represents the reward of taking action U_n in state Y_n. The action u is possible at time n only if $g(Y_n, u) \leq X_n$. The objective is to choose the control actions to maximize the long term average value of $r(Y_n, U_n)$. That is, the problem is as follows:

$$
\begin{aligned}
\text{Maximize} \quad & E(r(Y_n, U_n)) \\
\text{over} \quad & U_n \\
\text{s.t.} \quad & g(Y_n, U_n) \leq X_n \\
\text{and} \quad & X_{n+1} = [X_n - g(Y_n, U_n)]_0^B.
\end{aligned}
$$

Note that in the above problem formulation U_n is the function of state of the system and energy level of the battery. In the last expression, we use the notation

$$
[x]_0^B = \max\{0, \min\{x, B\}\}.
$$

Since (X_n, Y_n) is a Markov chain controlled by U_n, this is a Markov decision problem. It can be solved by Dynamic Programming. The size of the state space of this problem is $(B + 1) \times |\mathcal{Y}|$ and it can be very large unless the battery capacity B is not relatively small. More importantly, the resulting control strategy is complex as it depends on the instantaneous amount of stored energy.

For the purpose of simplifying the solution of the problem and also for deriving some insight into the solution, we examine approximation methods that we explore in the next section.

3. APPROXIMATIONS

If the battery is not too small, the fact that it goes empty is a large deviation under a suitable operating regime. This suggests that one can replace the constraint $g(Y_n, U_n) \leq X_n$ by a constraint on the probability that the battery goes empty. Moreover, this constraint can be guaranteed by using a control strategy that depends only on Y_n and is designed so that the statistics of U_n make it very unlikely to deplete the battery faster than it charges for a duration long enough to empty it. This approach has the benefit of resulting in a much simpler control scheme that does not have to depend on the state of charge of the battery. Moreover, the calculation of the control strategy is also much simpler.

Specifically, we consider the problem

$$\text{Maximize} \quad E(r(Y_n, U_n))$$
$$\text{over} \quad q$$
$$\text{s.t.} \quad P[U_n = u | Y_n = y] = q(y, u)$$
$$\text{and} \quad P(X_n = 0) \leq \beta$$
$$\text{and} \quad X_{n+1} = [X_n - g(Y_n, U_n)]_0^B.$$

In this formulation, β is a small probability. Also, q defines a stationary control strategy that depends only on Y_n, not on X_n. Thus, we have relaxed the tight constraint $g(Y_n, U_n) \leq X_n$ by replacing it by the constraint $P(X_n = 0) \leq \beta$. We will enforce this constraint by considering the large deviations of the process X_n. Specifically, if $E(g(Y_m, U_m)) < 0$, which is a necessary requirement for the battery to have a small probability of being empty, one can expect the probability, under the stationary distribution, to be on the order of

$$K \exp\{-B\psi(q)\}$$

where K is a constant and $\psi(q)$ depends on the control policy q. That is, the constraint $P(X_n = 0) \leq \beta$ can be replaced by

$$\psi(q) \geq \frac{\delta}{B} \tag{1}$$

where δ is chosen so that $K \exp\{-\delta\} = \beta$.

To determine $\psi(q)$, one argues as follows. The battery becomes empty after $n = B/c$ steps if it discharges at an average rate c for these n steps for some $c > 0$. Thus, one is led to study the probability of such a discharge rate, i.e., the probability

$$P(Z_1 + \cdots + Z_n \geq nc)$$

where

$$Z_m = g(Y_m, U_m).$$

We will show that, when $E(Z_n) < 0$, this probability is approximately equal to

$$\exp\{-n\phi(c, q)\}.$$

Accordingly, with $n = B/c$, we see that this probability is of the order of

$$\exp -B\frac{\phi(c, q)}{c}.$$

Since every $c > 0$ is a possible discharge rate that would empty the battery in B/c steps, the probability that the battery empties is the sum over all $c > 0$ of these probabilities. If B is not too small, this sum is well approximated by the term that corresponds to the smallest exponential rate of decay as a function of B. That is, the probability is well approximated by

$$\exp\{-B\psi(q)\}$$

where

$$\psi(q) := \inf_{c>0} \frac{\phi(c, q)}{c}.$$

To analyze the probabilities, we note that for a given q the random variables (Y_n, U_n) form a Markov chain. Thus, Z_n is a function of a Markov chain. Now, the main concern is how to calculate the value of $\phi(., .)$ and $\psi(.)$. This is explained in next section.

Before proceeding, we review some results about Markov chains.

4. LARGE DEVIATIONS

To develop our estimates, we need to study the large deviations of the process $Z_1 + \cdots + Z_n$ driven by the Markov chain Y_n. To do this, we consider three methods: a direct method, an analysis of the occupation measure of a Markov chain, and a Gaussian approximation. We explain that the direct method is numerically simple and yields good estimates. We use the occupation measure to derive properties of the large deviations. We show that the Gaussian approximation is not satisfactory for our problems.

Direct Method

The direct method is based on Chernoff's inequality and on the first step analysis of a Markov chain.

For $y \in \mathcal{Y}$, $\theta > 0$ and $n \geq 1$, let

$$s_n(y) := E[\exp\{\theta(Z_1 + \cdots + Z_n)\}|Y_1 = y], \forall y \in \mathcal{Y}.$$

Note that (see Appendix A)

$$s_{n+1}(y) = E[\exp\{\theta Z_1\}|Y_1 = y] \sum_{y'} P(y, y') s_n(y'), \forall y \in \mathcal{Y}.$$

Let $\mathbf{s}_n$ be the column vector with components $\{s_n(y), y \in \mathcal{Y}\}$. Then

$$\mathbf{s}_{n+1} = G_\theta \mathbf{s}_n, n \geq 1$$

where

$$G_\theta(y, y') = h_\theta(y) P(y, y')$$

with

$$h_\theta(y) = E[\exp\{\theta Z_1\}|Y_1 = y] = \sum_u q(y, u) \exp\{\theta g(y, u)\}.$$

Consequently,

$$\mathbf{s}_n = G_\theta^n \mathbf{s}_0$$

where $\mathbf{s}_0 = [1, 1, \ldots, 1]'$. Also, from conditional expectation we have,

$$E[\exp\{\theta(Z_1 + \cdots + Z_n)\}] = \pi \mathbf{s}_n = \pi G_\theta^n \mathbf{s}_0 \tag{2}$$

where π is the distribution of Y_1.

Let $\lambda(\theta)$ be the largest eigenvalue of G_θ. We can approximate the mean value above by

$$E[\exp\{\theta(Z_1 + \cdots + Z_n)\}] \approx K\lambda(\theta)^n, n \gg 1$$

where K is a constant. To see this approximation, note that if the eigenvalues of G_θ are distinct, then one can use the eigendecomposition of matrix G_θ

$$G_\theta = VDV^{-1}$$

where D is the diagonal matrix of eigenvalues. Then,

$$G_\theta^n = VD^nV^{-1}$$

and the approximation follows. If the eigenvalues are not distinct, one replaces D by the block Jordan matrix and the same approximation results.

We use that approximation to study the large deviations of Z_n. One has Chernoff's inequality for $\theta > 0$:

$$P(Z_1 + \cdots + Z_n \geq nc) \leq E(\exp\{\theta(Z_1 + \cdots + Z_n - nc)\})$$
$$\approx K\lambda(\theta)^n \exp\{-n\theta c\} = K\exp\{-n(\theta c - \log(\lambda(\theta)))\}.$$

Since this inequality holds for all $\theta > 0$, one can minimize the right-hand side over $\theta > 0$ and find

$$P(Z_1 + \cdots + Z_n \geq nc) \leq K\exp\{-n\phi(c,q)\}$$

where

$$\phi(c,q) = \sup_{\theta > 0}\{\theta c - \log(\lambda(\theta))\}.$$

As we explained earlier, $\psi(q) = \inf_{c>0} \phi(c,q)/c$, so that

$$\psi(q) = \inf_{c>0}\frac{\phi(c,q)}{c} = \inf_{c>0}\frac{1}{c}\sup_{\theta>0}\{\theta c - \log(\lambda(\theta))\}. \quad (3)$$

The value of c that minimizes $\frac{\phi(c,q)}{c}$ is the average draining rate which results in the battery to go empty rarely. Moreover, $\psi(q)$ is a strictly decreasing function in terms of our control policy q. Hence, the value of q such that $\psi(q)$ is equal to $\frac{\delta}{B}$ from constraint (1) is the optimum control policy.

Occupation Measure

For the purpose of deriving properties of the large deviations, we consider an estimate based on the occupation measure of the Markov chain $V_n = (Y_n, U_n)$. We use the occupation measure to obtain an expression for the probability that a Markov chain with a given transition matrix behaves as if it had another transition rate matrix over a long period of time.

Consider a Markov chain V_n with transition matrix P_0. For another transition matrix P_1 and a sequence $\mathbf{v} = (v_0, \ldots, v_n)$, let

$$L(\mathbf{v}) = \frac{\pi_0(v_0)P_0(v_0,v_1)\ldots P_0(v_{n-1},v_n)}{\pi_1(v_0)P_1(v_0,v_1)\ldots P_1(v_{n-1},v_n)}$$

where π_1 is invariant under P_1 and π_0 is invariant under P_0. Note that

$$\log(L(\mathbf{v})) = \log\left(\frac{\pi_0(v_0)}{\pi_1(v_0)}\right) + \sum_{v,v'} N_n(v,v')\log\left(\frac{P_0(v,v')}{P_1(v,v')}\right) \quad (4)$$

where $N_n(v,v')$ is the number of transitions from v to v' in $\mathbf{v}$. Thus, $L(\mathbf{v})$ is the ratio of the likelihood of $\mathbf{v}$ under P_0 divided by its likelihood under P_1. Note that under P_1, one has

$$N_n(v,v') \approx n\pi_1(v)P_1(v,v').$$

Consequently, for the random sequence $V^n = \{V_1 \ldots, V_n\}$, if we get an exponential from both sides of (4), under P_1 we have,

$$L(V^n) \approx \exp\{-nH(P_1)\} \quad (5)$$

where

$$H(P_1) = -\sum_{v,v'}\pi_1(v)P_1(v,v')\log\left(\frac{P_0(v,v')}{P_1(v,v')}\right).$$

Consider a set A of sequences $\mathbf{v}$ that are typical under P_1. These sequences satisfy the law of large numbers for the Markov chain so that (5) holds and, moreover,

$$P_1(A) \approx 1. \quad (6)$$

We claim that

$$P_0(A) = E_1(1_A(V^n)L(V^n)) \approx \exp\{-nH(P_1)\}. \quad (7)$$

To see the first equality, note that for any function $f(V^n)$ one has

$$E_0(f(V^n)) = \sum_{\mathbf{v}} P_0(\mathbf{v})f(\mathbf{v}) = \sum_{\mathbf{v}} P_1(\mathbf{v})\frac{P_0(\mathbf{v})}{P_1(\mathbf{v})}f(\mathbf{v})$$
$$= \sum_{\mathbf{v}} P_1(\mathbf{v})L(\mathbf{v})f(\mathbf{v}) = E_1(f(V^n)L(V^n)).$$

To get the approximation in (7), we use (5) and (6).

This calculation shows that the likelihood that the Markov chain V_n with transition matrix P_0 behaves as if its transition matrix were P_1 for n steps is exponentially small in n and given by the expression (7).

The next step is to estimate the likelihood $\kappa(\pi_1, n)$ that the empirical distribution of $\{V_1, \ldots, V_n\}$ is π_1. One can use the contraction principle (see e.g., [4] and [3]) to argue that this likelihood is the maximum over P_1 of the probability that the Markov chain behaves as if its transition matrix were P_1, where the maximum is over all P_1 with empirical distribution π_1. Hence, one finds that

$$\kappa(\pi_1, n) = \max_{P_1 : \pi_1 P_1 = \pi_1}\exp\{-nH(P_1)\} \approx \exp\{-nR(\pi_1)\}$$

where

$$R(\pi_1) := \inf_{P_1 : \pi_1 P_1 = \pi_1} H(P_1)$$

with $H(P_1)$ as given above.

Now, consider the likelihood that the empirical average value of $\{Z_1, \ldots, Z_n\}$ is $c > 0$, where

$$Z_m = g(V_m), m = 0, 1, \ldots, n.$$

One argues that this likelihood is the maximum of the probabilities that V_n has an empirical distribution π_1, where the maximum is over all π_1 such that

$$\sum_v \pi_1(v)g(v) = c.$$

Thus, this probability is estimated as $\exp\{-n\phi(c,q)\}$ where

$$\phi(c,q) = \min_{\pi_1 : \sum_v \pi_1(v)g(v) = c} R(\pi_1). \quad (8)$$

Finally, one argues that the likelihood that the battery discharges is of the order of

$$\exp\{-B\psi(q)\}$$

where

$$\psi(q) = \min_{c>0}\frac{\psi(c,q)}{c}. \quad (9)$$

Gaussian Approximation

The Gaussian approximation considers that

$$Z_1 + \cdots + Z_n \approx \mathcal{N}(n\alpha, n\sigma^2),$$

where $\alpha = E(Z_n)$ is as before and $n\sigma^2 \approx \text{var}(Z_1 + \cdots + Z_n)$.

As we will see below, this approximation is not satisfactory.

5. EVALUATION

We have explained three methods for estimating the likelihood that the battery gets discharged: a direct method, a method based on the occupation measure of the Markov chain, and a Gaussian approximation. In the following subsections, we evaluate these methods for a random walk and two-state Markov chain.

5.1 Evaluation for Random Walk

Let Z_n be i.i.d. with $P(Z_n = 1) = a$ and $P(Z_n = -1) = 1 - a =: b$. We assume that $E(Z_n) = a - b = 2a - 1 < 0$, so that the battery tends to charge more than it discharges. We consider the Markov chain W_n defined by

$$W_{n+1} = (W_n + Z_n)^+, n \geq 0.$$

This is a random walk reflected at 0 that models the discharge process of the battery. The state X_n of charge of the battery can be seen to be essentially $B - W_n$, so that if W_n reaches the value B, the battery gets discharged.

Direct Method

The reflected random walk W_n is a simple Markov chain on $\{0, 1, \dots\}$ with

$$P(k, k+1) = a \text{ and } P(k+1, k) = b, \forall k \geq 0.$$

Also, $P(0, 0) = b$. We can analyze explicitly this Markov chain without having to resort to Chernoff's bound. If $a < b$, the invariant distribution of X_n is π where

$$\pi(k) = (1 - \rho)\rho^k, k \geq 0 \text{ with } \rho := \frac{a}{b}.$$

In particular,

$$P(W_n \geq B) = \sum_{k=B}^{\infty} \pi(k) = \rho^B =: p_Q(B). \tag{10}$$

Occupation Measure

Using (7), we find that the likelihood that the increments Z_n behave as if $P(Z_n = 1) = a'$ instead of a over n steps is approximately

$$\phi(a') := \exp\{-nH(a')\}$$

where

$$H(a') = -a' \log(\frac{a}{a'}) - (1 - a') \log(\frac{1-a}{1-a'}).$$

Thus, according to (8),

$$\phi(c) := \min\{H(a')|E_{a'}(Z_n) = a' - (1-a') \geq c\} = H(\frac{1+c}{2}).$$

Hence, by (9),

$$\psi_O := \inf_{c>0} \frac{\phi(c)}{c} = \log(\frac{1-a}{a}).$$

Finally, we get the estimate for the probability that the battery gets empty as

$$\exp\{-B\psi_O\} = (\frac{a}{1-a})^B,$$

which agrees with (10).

Gaussian Approximation

A Gaussian approximation for this process would work as follows. We argue that for $n \gg 1$,

$$\frac{Z_1 + \cdots + Z_n - n\alpha}{\sqrt{n}} \approx \mathcal{N}(0, \sigma^2)$$

where

$$\sigma^2 = \text{var}(Z_n) = E(Z_n^2) - (E(Z_n))^2 = 1 - \alpha^2.$$

Recall that if W is $\mathcal{N}(0, 1)$, then

$$P(W > x) \leq \frac{1}{x\sqrt{2\pi}} \exp\{-\frac{x^2}{2}\}, \forall x > 0.$$

Moreover, this upper bound on the error function is asymptotically tight. Thus, if $V = Z_1 + \cdots + Z_n - n\alpha$, one uses the (poor) approximation $V =_D \sqrt{n\sigma^2}W$, so that

$$P(V > na) = P(W > \frac{na}{\sqrt{n\sigma^2}}) = P(W > \sqrt{n}\frac{a}{\sigma})$$

$$\leq \frac{\sigma}{a\sqrt{n}} \exp\{-n\frac{a^2}{2\sigma^2}\}.$$

Note that this approximation is a bad application of the Central Limit Theorem. Using this approximation, we get

$$P(Z_1 + \cdots + Z_n > n(\alpha + a)) \approx \frac{\sigma}{a\sqrt{n}} \exp\{-n\frac{a^2}{2\sigma^2}\}.$$

This leads to the probability of the battery going empty being of the order of

$$\exp\{-B\psi\}$$

where

$$\psi = \inf_{a:a+\alpha>0} \frac{1}{a+\alpha} \frac{a^2}{2\sigma^2} = -\frac{2\alpha}{\sigma^2},$$

which gives the following estimate for the probability that the battery goes empty:

$$\exp\{B\frac{2\alpha}{\sigma^2}\} = \exp\{B\frac{2\alpha}{1-\alpha^2}\} =: p_G(B). \tag{11}$$

Thus, the correct expression is given by (10) and the Gaussian approximation is given (11). Note that

$$\frac{1}{B} \log(p_Q(B)) = \log(\frac{a}{1-a})$$

and

$$\frac{1}{B} \log(p_G(B)) = \frac{2\alpha}{\sigma^2} = \frac{2a-1}{2a(1-a)}.$$

Figure 1 compares these expressions as functions of a. We note that the Gaussian approximation is not very good. This is to be expected since one knows that the Central Limit Theorem provides good estimates of the probability

$$P(Z_1 + \cdots + Z_n > \alpha n + \delta\sqrt{n}),$$

but not of

$$P(Z_1 + \cdots + Z_n > \alpha n + (c - \alpha)n).$$

5.2 Evaluation for 2-state Markov Chain

Next, we compare and validate the estimates obtained by the direct method and from the occupation measure in the case of a $\{-1, 1\}$-Markov chain Z_n with $P(-1, 1) = a$ and

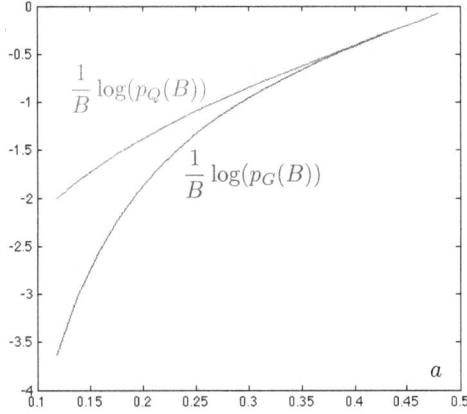

Figure 1: Comparison of (10) and (11). The Gaussian approximation underestimates the probability of large deviations.

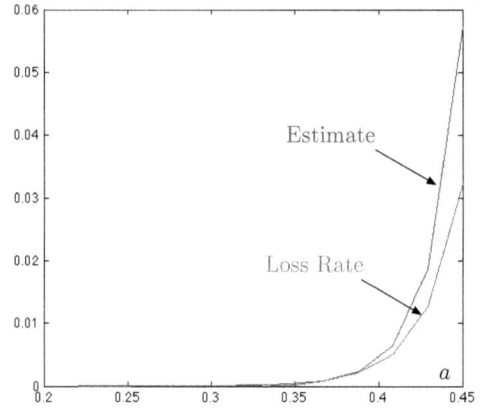

Figure 2: Comparison of actual loss rate and estimate. Here, $b = 0.5$ and $B = 30$.

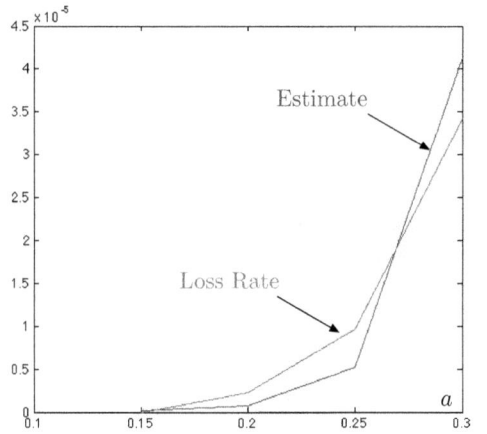

Figure 3: Comparison of actual loss rate and estimate for smaller values of a. Here, $b = 0.5$ and $B = 30$.

$P(1, -1) = b$. The goal is to estimate the probability that the process

$$Z_1 + \cdots + Z_n$$

reaches some large value B. This probability, say $p(B)$ is of the order of $\exp\{-B\psi\}$. We will derive three estimates for ψ: ψ_D, ψ_O and ψ_G using the three methods.

Direct Method for two-state Markov Chain

We find

$$G_\theta = \left[\begin{array}{cc} e^{-\theta}(1 - a) & e^{-\theta}a \\ e^{\theta}b & e^{\theta}(1 - b) \end{array} \right].$$

We can then evaluate the largest eigenvalue $\lambda(\theta)$ of G_θ and calculate ψ_D using (3).

Occupation Measure

We use (7), (8) and (9) for the two-state Markov chain and we find that the probability of the battery going empty is

$$\exp\{-B\psi_O\}$$

where

$$\psi_O = \inf_{c>0} \left(\min_{\{P_1 : E_1(Z_n) = c\}} H(a', b') \right)$$

with

$$H(a', b') = -\frac{a'}{a' + b'}[(1 - a')\log(\frac{1 - a}{1 - a'}) + a'\log(\frac{a}{a'})]$$
$$- \frac{b'}{a' + b'}[(1 - b')\log(\frac{1 - b}{1 - b'}) + b'\log(\frac{b}{b'})].$$

Occupation Measure vs. Simulations

We compare $p(B)$ measured from simulations to the estimates given by the occupation measure approach.

Figure 2 shows representative results measured by simulating X_n for 10^6 steps for every value of a. The loss rate calculates as the number of times that the battery goes empty over the number of steps (for example here is 10^6). The estimate is based on the large deviation of the occupation measure as explained above.

Figure 3 shows more results for smaller values of a. Here, the loss rate is measured by simulating X_n for 10^8 for every value of a.

Gaussian Approximation

For this Markov chain, one finds that (see Appendix)

$$\sigma^2 := cd\frac{2 - a - b}{a + b} \text{ with } c = \frac{a}{a + b}, d = 1 - c.$$

This gives the estimate

$$\exp\{B\frac{2\alpha}{\sigma^2}\} = \exp\{-B\frac{2(b - a)(a + b)^2}{ab(2 - a - b)}\}.$$

Comparison

Figure 4 compares the values of ψ for the probability

$$\exp\{-B\psi\}$$

that the battery becomes empty derived using the three methods. The values are shown for $b = 0.5$ and as a function of $a < b$. As in the case of the random walk, we find that the

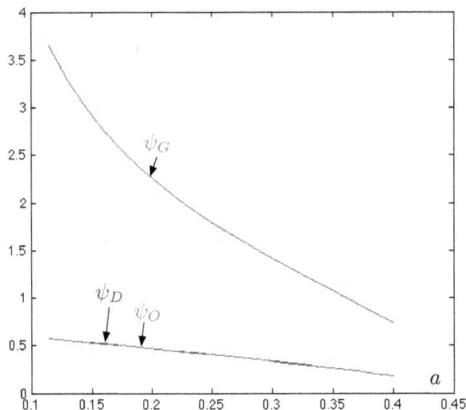

Figure 4: Comparison of estimates with occupation measure, direct method and Gaussian approximation. As before, $b = 0.5$ and $B = 30$.

Gaussian approximation yields poor estimates, which should not be surprising.

6. INDEPENDENT SOURCE AND LOAD

In this section we consider the case where $Y_n = (Y_n^1, Y_n^2)$ and

$$g(Y_n, U_n) = -a(Y_n^1) + b(Y_n^2, U_n).$$

Here, the Markov chains Y_n^1 and Y_n^2 are independent.

For instance, Y_n^1 models the weather that affects the charging rate $a(Y_n^1)$ of the battery and Y_n^2 models the quality of a transmission channel, which affects the reward of transmitting with a given power. We assume that the control policy is defined by q_0 where

$$P[U_n = u | Y_n^1 = y_1, Y_n^2 = y_2] = q_0(y_2, u).$$

The empirical average value of $g(Y_n, U_n)$ differs from its expected value if Y_n^1, Y_n^2 and U_n given Y_n^2 make large deviations. The likelihood of a large deviation where Y_n^1 behaves as if its transition matrix were P^1 instead of P_0^1, Y_n^2 as if its transition matrix were P^2 instead of P_0^2 and U_n given Y_n^2 behaves as it its condition distribution were q instead of q_0 is exponentially small with exponent

$$H(P^1) + H(P^2) + K[q|\pi_2]$$

where

$$H(P^1) = -\sum_{y_1, y_1'} \pi_1(y_1) P^1(y_1, y_1') \log\left(\frac{P_0^1(y_1, y_1')}{P^1(y_1, y_1')}\right)$$

$$H(P^2) = -\sum_{y_2, y_2'} \pi_2(y_2) P^2(y_2, y_2') \log\left(\frac{P_0^2(y_2, y_2')}{P^2(y_2, y_2')}\right)$$

$$K[q|\pi_2] = -\sum_{y_2, u} \pi_2(y_2) q(y_2, u) \log\left(\frac{q_0(y_2, u)}{q(y_2, u)}\right).$$

In these expressions, π_1 is invariant for P^1 and π_2 is invariant for P^2. Thus, the empirical rate of $a(Y_n^1)$ is some value a and the empirical rate of $g(Y_n^2, U_n)$ is some value b with an exponentially small probability with an exponent

$$\phi_1(a) + \phi_2(b).$$

The empirical drain rate of the battery is then $b - a$.

CLAIM 1. *The likelihood that a battery of size B drains is exponentially small in B with an exponent*

$$\inf_{b > a} \frac{\phi_1(a) + \phi_2(b)}{b - a}.$$

PROOF. Assume that there is some value of c such that, for all $a > c$ and $b < c$,

$$\frac{\phi_1(a)}{a - c} \geq \gamma \text{ and } \frac{\phi_2(b)}{c - b} \geq \gamma.$$

Then

$$\phi_1(a) \geq \gamma(a - c) \text{ and } \phi_2(b) \geq \gamma(c - b),$$

so that

$$\frac{\phi_1(a) + \phi_2(b)}{a - b} \geq \gamma.$$

The interpretation of this result is as follows. Assume that there is some constant rate c such that if the battery drains at rate c, its likelihood of getting empty has an exponent γ and also that if the battery recharges at rate c, then the likelihood that the load makes it go empty also has an exponent γ. Then, the combined system with variable charging and discharging rate has rate at least γ. □

A converse of that result is as follows.

CLAIM 2. *Assume that the combined system has an exponent γ. Then there is some rate c such that each of the two decoupled systems has an exponent γ.*

PROOF. To see this, let a^* and b^* be the minimizers of

$$\frac{\phi_1(a) + \phi_2(b)}{b - a}$$

and let γ be the minimum value. The first order conditions are

$$\phi_1'(a^*) = -\phi_2'(b^*) = \gamma.$$

Now, choose c so that

$$\frac{\phi_1(a^*)}{c - a^*} = \gamma.$$

Then we see that

$$\phi_1'(a^*)(c - a^*) = \phi_1(a^*),$$

so that a^* minimizes

$$\frac{\phi_1(a)}{a - c}$$

and the minimum is γ. Similarly, b^* minimizes

$$\frac{\psi_2(b)}{c - b}$$

and the minimum is also γ, which proves the claim. □

7. EXAMPLES

To clarify the analysis, we consider a few simple examples.

No Control

In our first example, $Y_n \in \{0,1\}$ with $P(0,1) = a_0, P(1,0) = b_0, g(0) = -1, g(1) = 1$. We also assume that $U_n = Y_n$, so that there is no randomization of the control. Finally, assume that $a_0 < b_0$, so that

$$E(g(U_n)) = E(g(Y_n)) = \frac{a_0 - b_0}{a_0 + b_0} < 0.$$

Using the occupation method approach, we note that a transition matrix $P(0,1) = a$ and $P'(1,0) = b$ is such that $E(Y_n) = c$ if

$$b = a\frac{1-c}{1+c}.$$

Substituting this value of b in $H(P)$ and minimizing over a, we find

$$\phi(c) = \min_a H(P).$$

We then minimize $\phi(c)/c$ over c. The results is ψ and the likelihood that the battery goes empty is

$$\exp\{-\psi B\}.$$

Numerical examples give the values of ψ, in terms of a and b, shown in Table 1.

a_0	b_0	ψ_O	ψ_D
0.1	0.15	0.057	0.067
0.2	0.3	0.134	0.155
0.3	0.45	0.241	0.282
0.4	0.6	0.406	0.472
0.2	0.4	0.288	0.288
0.3	0.6	0.560	0.561
0.4	0.8	1.099	1.101

Table 1: Values of ψ when $U_n = Y_n$ obtained using the occupation measure (ψ_O) and the direct method (ψ_D)

This table shows that the battery is less likely to get empty (ψ is larger) when b_0 increases or a_0 decreases. Moreover, that is also the case if a_0 and b_0 increase, for a given value of a_0/b_0. Thus, for a given value of $E(g(Y_n))$, the battery is less likely to get empty if Y_n changes faster instead of staying equal to 1 for longer periods of time. This results confirm our intuition.

Using the direct method, we consider the matrix

$$G_\theta(y,y') = e^{\theta y} P(y,y')$$

and define $\lambda(\theta)$ to be its largest eigenvalue. Then

$$\psi_D = \min_{c>0} \frac{1}{c} \sup_{\theta>0}[\theta c - \log(\lambda(\theta))].$$

Control

We now consider the same situation as in the previous example, except that

$$P[U_n = 1|Y_n = 1] = \gamma_0 \text{ and } P[U_n = 1|Y_n = 0] = 0.$$

As a concrete example, say that $a_0 = 0.2$ and $b_0 = 0.3$. We saw that $\psi = 0.134$ if $U_n = Y_n$. This corresponds to a probability of a battery of size 20 going empty that is of the order of

$$\exp\{-20 \times 0.134\} = \exp\{-2.5\} = 0.07,$$

which is not acceptable. Thus, it makes sense to choose the value $U_n = 1$ only a fraction γ_0 of the time that $Y_n = 1$.

A large deviation of $g(U_n)$ occurs when its empirical mean value c is different from its expected value

$$E(g(U_n)) = \gamma_0 P(Y_n = 1) - (1 - \gamma_0)P(Y_n = 1) - P(Y_n = 0)$$
$$= \frac{2a_0\gamma_0}{a_0 + b_0} - 1.$$

This can occur as a combination of two events: Y_n can be equal to 1 a fraction of time $\pi(1)$ that differs from $a_0/(a_0 + b_0)$) and the fraction of time that $U_n = 1$ when $Y_n = 1$ can be γ instead of γ_0.

Using the occupation method approach, the resulting empirical mean value of $g(U_n)$ is then

$$\frac{2a\gamma}{a+b} - 1$$

with a probability that is of the order of

$$\exp\{-nH(P) - nK[\gamma|P]\}$$

where $H(P)$ is as before and

$$K[\gamma|P] = -\pi(1)\gamma \log\left(\frac{\gamma_0}{\gamma}\right) - \pi(1)(1-\gamma)\log\left(\frac{1-\gamma_0}{1-\gamma}\right)$$

Using the direct method, one calculates ψ_D from (3). Table 2 shows some numerical results that again confirm the intuition.

a_0	b_0	γ_0	ψ_O	ψ_D
0.1	0.15	0.9	0.096	0.101
0.1	0.15	0.8	0.152	0.155
0.1	0.15	0.6	0.360	0.361
0.2	0.3	0.9	0.215	0.225
0.2	0.3	0.6	0.608	0.607

Table 2: Values of ψ when $P[U_n = 1|Y_n = 1] = \gamma_0$

Optimization

The setup is the same as in the previous example. However, in this example we want to choose γ_0 to maximize

$$E(r(Y_n, U_n))$$

subject to

$$P(W_n = 0) \approx \beta.$$

Assume that $r(0,u) = r(y,0) = 0$ and $r(1,1) = 1$. Thus, we want to maximize γ_0 such that $\psi \geq \beta/B$. The goal is to have a probability of the battery going empty of the order of $\exp\{-\beta\}$.

Say that $\beta = 4.6$, so that $\exp\{-\beta\} = 1\%$. Then, we find the results shown in Table 3 for $a = 0.1$ and $b = 0.15$. (We used the direct method.)

Not surprisingly, if the battery is smaller, one has to be more cautious in using it.

Wireless Sensor Node

Figure 5 illustrates the power flow in a wireless sensor node. The node is equipped with a solar cell that generates a variable amount of power, depending on the state of the weather. Here, for the purpose of illustration, we think of the time

B	γ_0
50	0.92
40	0.87
30	0.80
20	0.70
10	0.54

Table 3: Values of γ_0 for optimization problem

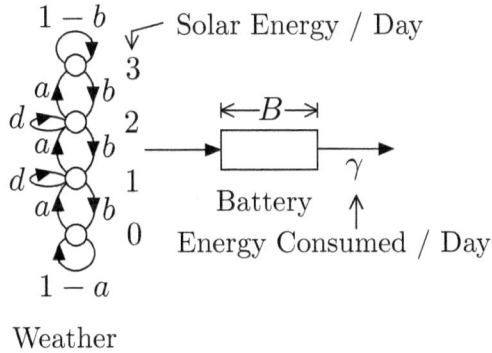

Figure 5: A wireless sensor node equipped with a solar cell.

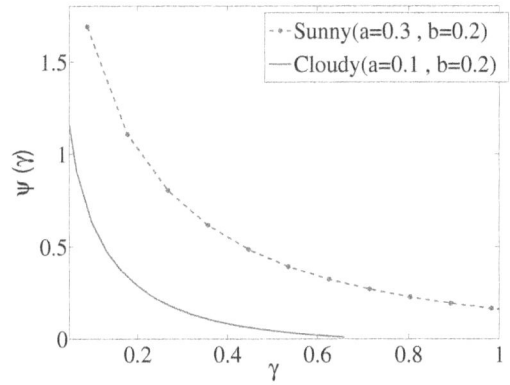

Figure 6: Exponential rate of decay as a function of γ in cloudy and sunny environments.

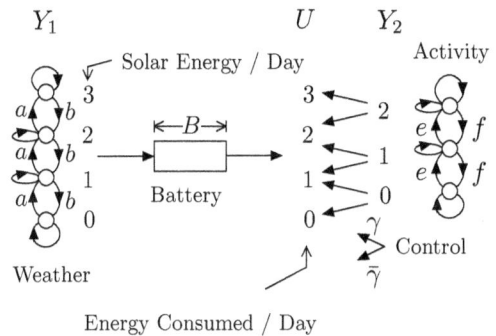

Figure 7: A self-sufficient building with a control parameter γ.

unit being one day. The system is designed to transmit an amount of energy equal to γ per day. The problem is to determine the maximum value of γ such that the probability that the battery goes empty is about 1%.

We use the direct method, with the model that

$$P[U_n = 1 | Y_n = y] = \gamma \text{ and } P[U_n = 0 | Y_n = y] = 1 - \gamma.$$

Let $Y_n \in \{0, 1, 2, 3\}$ be the Markov chain that represents the weather. In the figure, $d := 1 - a - b$. The increment in the battery discharge is then

$$Z_n = V_n - Y_n,$$

where the V_n are i.i.d. Bernoulli with mean γ and are independent of the weather.

Using the direct method, we let

$$s_n(y) = E[\exp\{\theta(Z_1 + \cdots + Z_n)\} | Y_1 = y]$$

and we find that

$$\mathbf{s}_{n+1} = G_\theta \mathbf{s}_n$$

where

$$G_\theta(y, y') = h(y)P(y, y')$$

with

$$h(y) = E(\exp\{\theta(V_1 - y)\}) = [\gamma e^\theta + (1 - \gamma)]e^{-y\theta}.$$

We calculate the largest eigenvalue of G_θ then proceed as before, by using (3). Figure 6 shows the exponential rate of decay $\psi(\gamma)$ as a function of γ for relatively sunny and cloudy weathers.

From these curves, one can determine the maximum value of the usage of the sensor node described by γ as a function of the target error probability and of the battery size.

Building with Solar Panels and Variable Load

Figure 7 sketches the power flow of a building with a solar cell, a battery, and a variable load. The control parameter

γ is the probability of using a higher rate instead of a lower one, given the level of activity in the building and $\bar{\gamma} = 1 - \gamma$. The problem is to determine the largest possible value of γ so that the probability that the battery gets depleted is acceptably small. As before, we compute $\psi(\gamma)$. The one-day depletion of the battery is

$$Z(n) = U(n) - Y_1(n).$$

As before, we find

$$\mathbf{s}_{n+1} = G_\theta \mathbf{s}_n$$

where

$$G_\theta(y, y') = h(y)P(y, y'),$$

where

$$h(y) = E[\exp\{\theta(U(1) - y_1)\} | Y_2(1) = y_2]$$
$$= e^{\theta(y_2 - y_1)}[\gamma e^\theta + 1 - \gamma].$$

Figure 8 shows the numerical results.

8. CONCLUSIONS

This paper explored a methodology for addressing the variability of renewable energy and the electric load in the control of systems with energy storage. The main idea is to replace a Markov decision problem formulation by an opti-

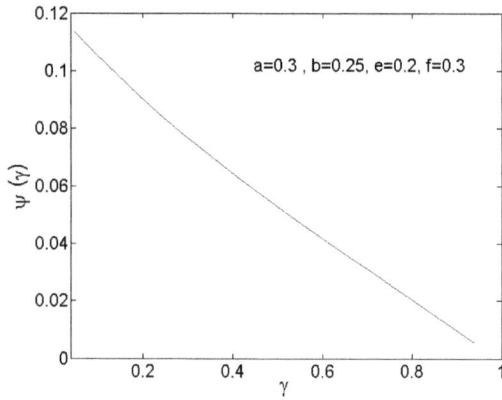

Figure 8: The numerical result for the building model.

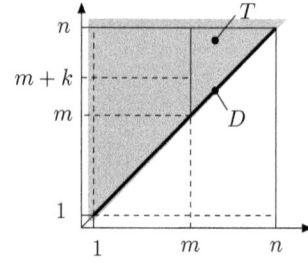

Figure 9: The sum over $(m, n) \in \{1, \ldots, n\}^2$ is decomposed into twice the sum over T minus the sum over D because the terms are symmetric in (m, n).

mization problem with constraints based on the theory of large deviations.

We compared three methods for evaluating the small probability that the battery goes empty for a given control policy. These methods use the fact that the battery discharge increments are functions of a Markov chain. The three methods are: 1) a direct method based on Chernoff's inequality and the first step equations of a Markov chain; 2) a method based on the analysis of the occupation measure and the contraction principle; 3) a Gaussian approximation method.

Our examples indicate that the direct method and the occupation measure yields essentially the same estimates, but that the first approach is numerically simpler. The examples confirm that the Gaussian approximation usually yields poor estimates that are not satisfactory to address the optimization problems.

Using the occupation measure approach, we could derive properties of the large deviations. We showed a decomposition result when the source and the load are functions of independent Markov chains.

We demonstrated the use of the approach for two simple problems: a wireless sensor node equipped with a solar panel and a self-sufficient building. The methodology applies to much more complex situations. The benefit is that the resulting control law is simple, as it does not depend on the instantaneous charge of the battery.

9. ACKNOWLEDGEMENTS

The research of the third author is supported in part by NSF-NetSE grants 1024318 and 0910702.

10. APPENDIX A: STATEMENT IN DIRECT METHOD

This is to show:

$$s_{n+1}(y) = E[\exp\{\theta Z_1\}|Y_1 = y] \sum_{y'} P(y, y') s_n y', \forall y \in \mathcal{Y}.$$

Starting from LHS, we have,

$$
\begin{aligned}
s_{n+1}(y) &= E[\exp\{\theta(Z_1 + \cdots + Z_{n+1})\}|Y_1 = y], \\
&= E[\exp\{\theta Z_1\} \cdot \exp\{\theta(Z_2 + \cdots + Z_{n+1})\}|Y_1 = y], \\
E[\exp\{\theta(Z_2 + \cdots + Z_{n+1})\}|Y_1 = y] \\
&= \sum_{y' \in \mathcal{Y}} E[\exp\{\theta(Z_2 + \cdots + Z_{n+1})\} \mathbf{1}\{Y_2 = y'\}|Y_1 = y], \\
&= \sum_{y' \in \mathcal{Y}} E[\exp\{\theta(Z_2 + \cdots + Z_{n+1})\}|Y_2 = y'] \\
&\quad \times P[Y_2 = y'|Y_1 = y], \forall y \in \mathcal{Y}.
\end{aligned}
$$

11. APPENDIX B: GAUSSIAN APPROXIMATION FOR MARKOV CHAIN

Let $\{X_n\}$ be a $\{0, 1\}$-Markov chain with $P(0, 1) = a$ and $P(1, 0) = b$. We want to show that

$$\text{var}(X_1 + \cdots + X_n) \approx n\sigma^2$$

where

$$\sigma^2 := cd(\frac{2}{a + b} - 1)$$

where $c := a/(a + b)$ and $d := 1 - c$.

We have (see Figure 9)

$$E((\sum_{m=1}^{n} X_m)^2) = 2T - D$$

where

$$T := \sum_{m=1}^{n} \sum_{k=0}^{n-m} E(X_m X_{m+k})$$

and

$$D := \sum_{m=1}^{n} E(X_m^2) = \sum_{m=1}^{n} E(X_m) = nc.$$

One can verify that

$$P^k(1, 1) = c + d\lambda^k, \text{ with } \lambda = 1 - a - b.$$

Now,

$$T = \sum_{m=1}^{n} \sum_{k=0}^{n-m} P(X_m = 1)P[X_{m+k} = 1|X_m = 1]$$

$$= \sum_{m=1}^{n} \sum_{k=0}^{n-m} cP^k(1,1)$$

$$= \sum_{m=1}^{n} \sum_{k=0}^{n-m} c(c + d\lambda^k)$$

$$= \sum_{m=1}^{n} \sum_{k=0}^{n-m} c^2 + cd \sum_{m=1}^{n} \sum_{k=0}^{n-m} \lambda^k$$

$$= c^2 \frac{n^2 + n}{2} + cd \sum_{m=1}^{n} (1 + \lambda + \cdot + \lambda^{n-m}).$$

Also,

$$\sum_{m=1}^{n} (1 + \lambda + \cdots + \lambda^{n-m}) = \sum_{m=1}^{n} \frac{1 - \lambda^{n-m+1}}{1 - \lambda}$$

$$= \frac{n}{1 - \lambda} - \frac{1}{1 - \lambda} \sum_{m=1}^{n} \lambda^{n-m+1}$$

$$= \frac{n}{1 - \lambda} - \frac{\lambda(1 - \lambda^n)}{(1 - \lambda)^2}.$$

Hence,

$$T = c^2 \frac{n^2 + n}{2} + \frac{ncd}{1 - \lambda} - \frac{cd\lambda(1 - \lambda^n)}{(1 - \lambda)^2}$$

$$\approx c^2 \frac{n^2 + n}{2} + \frac{ncd}{1 - \lambda}.$$

Finally, we get

$$E((\sum_{m=1}^{n} X_m)^2) \approx c^2(n^2 + n) + \frac{2cdn}{1 - \lambda} - nc.$$

Thus,

$$\text{var}(X_1 + \cdots + X_n) \approx c^2(n^2 + n) + \frac{2cdn}{1 - \lambda} - nc - n^2 c^2$$

$$= n[c^2 + \frac{2cd}{1 - \lambda} - c] = ncd\frac{1 + \lambda}{1 - \lambda}$$

$$= ncd\frac{2 - a - b}{a + b},$$

as we wanted to show.

12. REFERENCES

[1] H Bevrani, A Ghosh, G Ledwich "Renewable energy sources and frequency regulation: survey and new perspectives," *Renewable Power Generation,* IET 4, no. 5, pp. 438-457, 2010.

[2] R. R. Bahadur. " Some Limit Theorems in Statistics," *SIAM,* Philadelphia, 1971.

[3] S.R.S. Varadhan. " Large Deviations and Applications," *CBMS86,* SIAM, 1986.

[4] A. Dembo, O. Zeitouni. " Large Deviations Techniques and Applications," *Springer,* 1998.

[5] J. D. Deuschel, and D. W. Stroock . " Large Deviations," *Academic Press,* Inc., Boston, MA 1989.

[6] G. Kesidis, J. Walrand, C. S. Chang, " Effective bandwidths for multiclass Markov fluids and other ATM sources," *IEEE/ACM Transactions on Networking,* vol. 1, no. 4, pp. 424-428, 1993.

[7] G. D. Veciana, J. Walrand, "Effective bandwidths: Call admission, traffic policing and filtering for ATM networks." *Queueing Systems* 20, no. 1, pp. 37-59, 1995.

[8] R. S. Ellis. " Large Deviations for the Empirical Measure of a Markov Chain with an Application to the Multivariate Empirical Measure," *The Annals of Probability,* vol. 16, no. 4, Oct., 1988.

[9] I. H. Dinwoodie, P. Ney. " Occupation measures for Markov chains," *Journal of Theoretical Probability,* vol. 8, no. 3, pp 679-691, July 1995.

[10] S. Halfin, W. Whitt. " Heavy-Traffic Limits for Queues with Many Exponential Servers," *Operations Research,* 1981.

[11] R. Guerin, H. Ahmadi, M. Naghshineh, "Equivalent capacity and its application to bandwidth allocation in high-speed networks," *IEEE Journal on Selected Areas in Communications,* vol. 9, no. 7, pp 968-981, 1991.

[12] O. Ozel, K. Tutuncuoglu, J. Yang, S. Ulukus, and A. Yener, "Transmission with energy harvesting nodes in fading wireless channels: Optimal policies," *IEEE Journal on Selected Areas in Communications,* vol. 29, no. 8, 2011.

[13] K. Tutuncuoglu and A. Yener, "Optimum transmission policies for battery limited energy harvesting nodes," *IEEE Transactions on Wireless Communications,* vol. 11, no. 3, 2012.

[14] R.-S. Liu, K.-W. Fan, Z. Zheng, and P. Sinha, "Perpetual and fair data collection for environmental energy harvesting sensor networks," *IEEE/ACM Transactions on Networking,* vol. 19, no. 4, 2011.

[15] M. Gatzianas, L. Georgiadis, and L. Tassiulas, "Control of wireless networks with rechargeable batteries," *IEEE Transactions on Wireless Communications,* vol. 9, no. 2, 2010.

[16] Z. Mao, C. E. Koksal, and N. B. Shroff, "Near optimal power and rate control of multi-hop sensor networks with energy replenishment: Basic limitations with finite energy and data storage," *IEEE Transactions on Automatic Control,* vol. 57, no. 4, 2012.

[17] V. Sharma, U. Mukherji, V. Joseph, and S. Gupta, "Optimal energy management policies for energy harvesting sensor nodes," *IEEE Transactions on Wireless Communications,* vol. 9, no. 4, 2010.

Modeling and Online Control of Generalized Energy Storage Networks

Junjie Qin, Yinlam Chow, Jiyan Yang
Computational and Mathematical Engineering
Stanford University
Stanford, CA, 94305
{jqin, ychow, jiyan}@stanford.edu

Ram Rajagopal
Civil and Environmental Engineering
Stanford University
Stanford, CA, 94305
ramr@stanford.edu

ABSTRACT

The integration of intermittent and volatile renewable energy resources requires increased flexibility in the operation of the electric grid. Storage, broadly speaking, provides the flexibility of shifting energy over time; network, on the other hand, provides the flexibility of shifting energy over geographical locations. The optimal control of general storage networks in uncertain environments is an important open problem. The key challenge is that, even in small networks, the corresponding constrained stochastic control problems with continuous spaces suffer from curses of dimensionality, and are intractable in general settings. For large networks, no efficient algorithm is known to give optimal or near-optimal performance.

This paper provides an efficient and provably near-optimal algorithm to solve this problem in a very general setting. We study the optimal control of generalized storage networks, *i.e.*, electric networks connected to distributed generalized storages. Here generalized storage is a unifying dynamic model for many components of the grid that provide the functionality of shifting energy over time, ranging from standard energy storage devices to deferrable or thermostatically controlled loads. An online algorithm is devised for the corresponding constrained stochastic control problem based on the theory of Lyapunov optimization. We prove that the algorithm is near-optimal, and construct a semidefinite program to minimize the sub-optimality bound. The resulting bound is a constant that depends only on the parameters of the storage network and cost functions, and is independent of uncertainty realizations. Numerical examples are given to demonstrate the effectiveness of the algorithm.

Categories and Subject Descriptors

C.4 [**Performance of Systems**]: Modeling techniques, Performance attributes; G.4 [**Mathematical Software**]: Algorithm design and analysis

General Terms

Algorithms, Design, Theory

Keywords

Energy systems, energy storage, stochastic control, online optimization

1. INTRODUCTION

To ensure a sustainable energy future, deep penetration of renewable energy generation is essential. Renewable energy resources, such as wind and solar, are intrinsically variable. Uncertainties associated with these intermittent and volatile resources pose a significant challenge to their integration into the existing grid infrastructure [1]. More flexibility, especially in shifting energy supply and/or demand across time and network, are desired to cope with the increased uncertainties.

Energy storage provides the functionality of shifting energy across time. A vast array of technologies, such as batteries, flywheels, pumped-hydro, and compressed air energy storages, are available for such a purpose [2, 3]. Furthermore, flexible or controllable demand provides another ubiquitous source of storage. Deferrable loads – including many thermal loads, loads of internet data-centers and loads corresponding to charging electric vehicles (EVs) over certain time interval [4] – can be interpreted as *storage of demand* [5]. Other controllable loads which can possibly be shifted to an earlier or later time, such as thermostatically controlled loads (TCLs), may be modeled and controlled as a storage with negative lower bound and positive upper bound on the storage level [6]. These forms of storage enable intertemporal shifting of excess energy supply and/or demand, and significantly reduce the reserve requirement and thus system costs.

On the other hand, shifting energy across a network, *i.e.*, moving excess energy supply to meet unfulfilled demand among different geographical locations with transmission or distribution lines, can achieve similar effects in reducing the reserve requirement for the system. Thus in practice, it is natural to consider these two effects together. Yet, it remains mathematically challenging to formulate a sound and tractable problem that accounts for these effects in electric grid operations. Specifically, due to the power flow and network constraints, control variables in connected buses are coupled. Due to the storage constraints, control variables in different time periods are coupled as well. On top of that, uncertainties associated with stochastic generation and demand dramatically complicate the problem, because of the large number of recourse stages and the need to account for all probable realizations.

Two categories of approaches have been proposed in the literature. The first category is based on exploiting structures of specific problem instances, usually using dynamic programming. These structural results are valuable in providing insights about the system, and often lead to analytical solution of these problem instances. However, such approaches rely heavily on specific assumptions of the type of storage, the form of the cost function, and the distribution of uncertain parameters. Generalizing results to other specifications and more complex settings is usually difficult, and consequently this approach is mostly used to analyze single storage systems. For instance, analytical solutions to optimal storage arbitrage with stochastic price have been derived in [7] without storage ramping constraints, and in [8] with ramping constraints. Problems of using energy storage to minimize energy imbalance are studied in various contexts; see [9, 10] for reducing reserve energy requirements in power system dispatch, [11, 12] for operating storage co-located with a wind farm, [13, 14] for operating storage co-located with end-user demands, and [15] for storage with demand response.

The other category is to use heuristic algorithms, such as Model Predictive Control (MPC)[16] and look-ahead policies [17], to identify sub-optimal storage control rules. Usually based on deterministic (convex) optimization, these approaches can be easily applied to general networks. The major drawback is that these approaches usually do not have any performance guarantee. Consequently, it lacks theoretical justification for implementing them in real systems. Examples of this category can be found in [16] and references therein.

This work aims to bring together the best of both worlds, *i.e.*, to design online deterministic optimizations that solve the stochastic control problem with provable guarantees. It contributes to the existing literature in the following ways. First, we formalize the notion of *generalized storage* as a dynamic model that captures a variety of power system components which provide the functionality of storage. Second, we formulate the problem of storage network operation as a stochastic control problem with general cost functions, and provide examples of applications that can be encapsulated by such a formulation. Third, we devise an online algorithm for the problem based on the theory of Lyapunov optimization [1], and prove guarantees for its performance in terms of a bound of its sub-optimality. We also show that the bound is independent of the realizations of the uncertain parameters. The bound is useful not only in assessing the worst-case performance of our algorithm, but also in evaluating the performance of other sub-optimal algorithms when the optimal costs are hard to obtain. It can also be used to estimate the maximum cost reduction that can be achieved by *any* storage operation, thus provides understanding for the limit of a certain storage system. To the best of our knowledge, this is the first algorithm with provable guarantees for the storage operation problem with general electric networks.

Our methodology is closely related to that of [14], where the focus is on solving the problem of operating an idealized

[1] Although closely related to the classical Lyapunov theory for stability, the theory and techniques of Lyapunov optimization are relatively recent. See [18] for more details.

energy storage (with no energy dissipation over time, and no charging/discharging conversion loss) at data-centers. Our objective is to provide an algorithm to operate generalized storage network in a wide range of different settings. This requires an extended or a new analysis in the following aspects. From the modeling perspective, in order to capture applications such as deferrable loads and TCLs, we do not assume storage level is non-negative, instead, we only assume each storage is feasible (see Assumption 2.1 for more details). Furthermore, modeling the dissipation of energy over time leads to a new sub-optimality bound; the bound in [14] becomes a special case of our bound when the dissipation factor (or storage efficiency) is one. A semidefinite program is constructed to decide parameters of the algorithm in order to minimize the sub-optimality bound. Finally, the aspect of power network appears to be completely new.

The rest of the paper is organized as follows. Section 2 formulates the problem of operating a generalized storage network under uncertainty. Section 3 gives the online algorithm and states the performance guarantee. Section 4 analyzes the single bus case in detail with a generalized storage, and Section 5 provides a summary of results for general storage networks. Numerical examples are then given in Section 6. Section 7 concludes the paper.

2. PROBLEM FORMULATION

2.1 Generalized Storage Models

We start by defining a generalized storage model for each fixed bus of the electric network. A diagram is shown in Figure 1. Such a model may be used for a single bus system by setting the network inflow to be zero, or as a component of an electric network as discussed in Section 2.3. We work with a slotted time model, where t is used as the index for an arbitrary time period. Given that the actual length of each time interval is constant, this allows for simple conversion from power units (*e.g.*, MW) to energy units (*e.g.*, MWh) and vice versa. Thus we assume all quantities under consideration in this paper are in energy units, albeit many power system quantities are conventionally specified in power units.

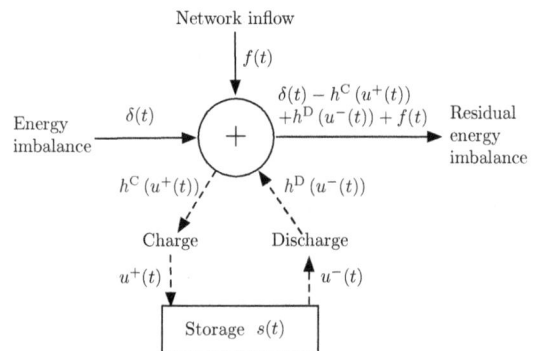

Figure 1: Diagram of a single-bus storage system.

For the bus under consideration and time period t, the local *energy imbalance* $\delta(t)$ is defined to be the difference between the local generation and demand. Both the local generation and demand can be stochastic, and therefore $\delta(t)$ is stochastic in general. The bus may be connected to other

28

parts of the network, whose net energy inflow is denoted by $f(t)$. The bus is also connected to a *generalized storage*, which is specified by the following elements:

- The *storage level* or State of Charge (SoC) $s(t)$ summarizes the status of the storage at time period t. If $s(t) \geq 0$, it represents the amount of energy in storage; if $s(t) \leq 0$, $-s(t)$ can represent the amount of currently deferred (and not fulfilled) demand. It satisfies $s(t) \in [S^{\min}, S^{\max}]$, where $S^{\max}$ is the storage capacity, and $S^{\min}$ is the minimum allowed storage level.

- The *storage operation* $u(t)$ summarizes the charging (when $u(t) \geq 0$) and discharging (when $u(t) \leq 0$) operations of the storage. It satisfies charging and discharging ramping constraints, *i.e.*, $u(t) \in [U^{\min}, U^{\max}]$, where $U^{\min} \leq 0$ whose magnitude is the maximum discharge within each time period, and $U^{\max} \geq 0$ is the maximum charge within each time period. We also use $u^{+}(t) = \max(u(t), 0)$ and $u^{-}(t) = \max(-u(t), 0)$ to denote the charging and discharging operations respectively.

- The *storage conversion function* h maps the storage operation $u(t)$ into its effect on the bus. In particular, it is composed of two linear functions, namely the *charging conversion function* h^{C}, and the *discharging conversion function* h^{D}, such that the quantity $h^{C}(u^{+}(t))$ is the amount of energy that is withdrawn from the bus due to $u^{+}(t)$ amount of charge, and $h^{D}(u^{-}(t))$ is the amount of energy that is injected into the bus due to $u^{-}(t)$ amount of discharge, whence

$$h(u(t)) = h^{D}(u^{-}(t)) - h^{C}(u^{+}(t))$$

is the net energy injection into the bus.

- The *storage dynamics* is then

$$s(t+1) = \lambda s(t) + u(t), \tag{1}$$

where $\lambda \in (0, 1]$ is the *storage efficiency* which models the loss over time even if there is no storage operation.

The storage parameters satisfy the following consistency conditions.

Assumption 2.1 (Feasibility). *Starting from any feasible storage level, there exists a feasible storage operation such that the storage level in the next time period is feasible, that is*

1. $\lambda S^{\min} + U^{\max} \geq S^{\min}$,

2. $\lambda S^{\max} + U^{\min} \leq S^{\max}$.

The *residual energy imbalance*, after accounting for the network inflow and storage operation, is then given by:

$$\delta(t) + h(u(t)) + f(t) = \delta(t) - h^{C}(u^{+}(t)) + h^{D}(u^{-}(t)) + f(t). \tag{2}$$

We give a few examples of generalized storage models as follows.

Example 2.2 (Storage of energy). *Storage of energy can be modeled as a generalized storage with $S^{\max} \geq S^{\min} \geq 0$. Here $U^{\min}$ and $U^{\max}$ correspond to the power rating of the storage, up to a multiple of the length of each time period. By setting $h^{C}(u^{+}(t)) = (1/\mu^{C})u^{+}(t)$, and $h^{D}(u^{-}(t)) =*

$\mu^{D}u^{-}(t)$, *one models the energy loss during charging and discharging operations. Here $\mu^{C} \in (0, 1]$ is the charging efficiency; $\mu^{D} \in (0, 1]$ is the discharging efficiency; and the round-trip efficiency of the energy storage is $\mu^{C}\mu^{D}$. For instance, based on the information from [19], a NaS (sodium sulfur) battery can be modeled with parameters:*

$$(S^{\min}, S^{\max}, U^{\min}, U^{\max}, \mu^{C}, \mu^{D}, \lambda) = (0\,MWh, 100\,MWh,$$
$$- 10\,MW \times 1h, 10\,MW \times 1h, 0.85, 0.85, 0.97),$$

and a CAES (compressed air energy storage) can be modeled with parameters:

$$(S^{\min}, S^{\max}, U^{\min}, U^{\max}, \mu^{C}, \mu^{D}, \lambda) = (0\,MWh, 3000\,MWh,$$
$$- 300\,MW \times 1h, 300\,MW \times 1h, 0.85, 0.85, 1.00).$$

Example 2.3 (Storage of demand). *Pre-emptive deferrable loads may be modeled as storage of demand, with $-s(t)$ corresponding to the accumulated deferred (but not yet fulfilled) load up to time t, and with $u(t)$ corresponding to the amount of load to defer/fulfill in time period t. We have $S^{\min} \leq S^{\max} \leq 0$ in this case. Storage of demand differs from storage of energy in the sense that it has to be discharged before charging is allowed. The conversion function can usually be set to $h(u(t)) = u(t)$, and generally $\lambda = 1$ in deferrable load related applications.*

Example 2.4 (Generalized battery models). *It is shown recently that an aggregation of TCLs may be modeled as a generalized battery [6]. A discrete time version of such a model can be cast into our framework by setting $S^{\min} = -S^{\max}$ and $S^{\max} \geq 0$. Other storage parameters can be set properly according to Definition 1 of [6], and we have $\lambda \leq 1$ to model energy dissipation.*

We consider the following *stochastic piecewise linear cost function* for each fixed bus

$$g(t) = \sum_{\ell=1}^{L} p(t, \ell) \Big(\alpha^{\delta}(\ell)\delta(t) - \alpha^{C}(\ell)h^{C}(u^{+}(t)) \tag{3}$$
$$+ \alpha^{D}(\ell)h^{D}(u^{-}(t)) + \alpha^{F}(\ell)f(t) + \alpha^{Const}(t, \ell) \Big)^{+},$$

where the parameter $p(t, \ell)$ is in general stochastic, and follows a prescribed probability law, and $\alpha^{\delta}(\ell)$, $\alpha^{C}(\ell)$, $\alpha^{D}(\ell)$, $\alpha^{F}(\ell)$ and $\alpha^{Const}(t, \ell)$ are constants, for each $\ell = 1, \ldots, L$ and t. This cost function serves as a generalization of positive (and/or negative) part cost function of the residual energy imbalance, and it encapsulates many applications of storage as shown in Section 2.2. Our analysis applies to a more general class of cost functions; see Appendix A for more details.

2.2 Applications in Single Bus Systems

The storage operation problem on a single bus system ($f(t) = 0$) can be posed as an infinite horizon average cost stochastic control problem as follows:

$$\text{minimize} \quad \lim_{T \to \infty} \frac{1}{T} \mathbb{E} \left[\sum_{t=1}^{T} g(t) \right] \tag{4a}$$

$$\text{subject to} \quad s(t+1) = \lambda s(t) + u(t), \tag{4b}$$

$$S^{\min} \leq s(t) \leq S^{\max}, \tag{4c}$$

$$U^{\min} \leq u(t) \leq U^{\max}, \tag{4d}$$

where we aim to find a control policy that maps the state $s(t)$ to storage operation $u(t)$, minimizes the expected average cost and satisfies all constraints for each time period t. Here, the initial state $s(1) \in [S^{\min}, S^{\max}]$ is given.

Combining some specific cases of the generalized storage model given in Examples 2.2-2.4 with properly defined cost functions leads to possible problem instances of optimal control of storage under uncertainty. Here we provide examples that are considered in the literature.

Example 2.5 (Balancing). *Storage may be used to minimize residual energy imbalance given some stochastic $\{\delta(t) : t \geq 1\}$ process. Typical cost functions penalize the positive and negative residual energy imbalance differently, and may have different penalties at different time periods . (For example, to model the different consequences of load shedding at different times of the day.) The problem of optimal storage control for such a purpose can be modeled by problem (4) with the cost function*

$$g(t) = q^+(t)\Big(\delta(t) - h^{\mathrm{C}}(u^+(t)) + h^{\mathrm{D}}(u^-(t))\Big)^+$$
$$+ q^-(t)\Big(\delta(t) - h^{\mathrm{C}}(u^+(t)) + h^{\mathrm{D}}(u^-(t))\Big)^-$$
$$= q^+(t)\Big(\delta(t) - h^{\mathrm{C}}(u^+(t)) + h^{\mathrm{D}}(u^-(t))\Big)^+$$
$$+ q^-(t)\Big(-\delta(t) + h^{\mathrm{C}}(u^+(t)) - h^{\mathrm{D}}(u^-(t))\Big)^+,$$

where $q^+(t)$ and $q^-(t)$ are the penalties[2] for each unit of positive and negative residual energy imbalance at time period t, respectively.

Example 2.6 (Arbitrage). *Given that the locational marginal prices $\{p^{\mathrm{LMP}}(t) : t \geq 1\}$ are stochastic, a storage may be used to exploit arbitrage opportunities in electricity markets. The problem of maximizing the expected arbitrage profit using storage operations can be cast as an instance of (4), with the cost function (i.e., negative profit) given by:*

$$g(t) = p^{\mathrm{LMP}}(t)(h^{\mathrm{C}}(u^+(t)) - h^{\mathrm{D}}(u^-(t)))$$
$$= p^{\mathrm{LMP}}(t)\Big(h^{\mathrm{C}}(u^+(t)) - h^{\mathrm{D}}(u^-(t))\Big)^+$$
$$- p^{\mathrm{LMP}}(t)\Big(-h^{\mathrm{C}}(u^+(t)) + h^{\mathrm{D}}(u^-(t))\Big)^+.$$

Example 2.7 (Storage co-located with a stochastic generation or demand). *Applications of this type may be cast into our framework using $\{\delta(t) : t \geq 1\}$ to model the stochastic generation or demand process, and $\{p(t,\ell) : t \geq 1\}$ to model the stochastic prices. A possible cost function is*

$$g(t) = p^{\mathrm{LMP}}(t)\Big(-\delta(t) + h^{\mathrm{C}}(u^+(t)) - h^{\mathrm{D}}(u^-(t))\Big)^+,$$

where the residual energy is curtailed with no cost/benefit, and the residual demand is supplied via buying energy from the market at stochastic price $p^{\mathrm{LMP}}(t)$.

2.3 Network Models

The electric network can be modeled as a directed graph $G(V,E)$. Let $n = |V|$, $m = |E|$, and E^{R} be the edge set with all edges reversed. We use the notation $e \sim v$ to indicate that $e \in \{(v',v) \in E \cup E^{\mathrm{R}} : v' \in V\}$. Each edge models

a transmission (or distribution) line, and is associated with some power flow. Assuming the power system is operated in steady state, and the power flow is approximately a constant over each time period t, the energy flow through the line can be obtained by multiplying the power flow by the length of each time period and is denoted by $f_e(t)$ for $e \in E$, with the direction of the edge indicating the positive direction of the flow.[3] The flow vector $\mathbf{f}(t) \in \mathbb{R}^m$ satisfies power flow constraints, which can be compactly summarized by the following set of linear constraints using the classical DC power flow approximations to AC power flow equations [20]:

$$\mathbf{f}(t) \in \mathcal{F}, \quad \mathcal{F} = \{\mathbf{f} \in \mathbb{R}^m : -\mathbf{F}^{\max} \leq \mathbf{f} \leq \mathbf{F}^{\max}, K\mathbf{f} = 0\}, \tag{5}$$

where $\mathbf{F}^{\max} \in \mathbb{R}^m$ is the vector of the line capacities of the network, and $K \in \mathbb{R}^{(m-n+1) \times m}$ is a matrix summarizing the Kirchhoff's voltage law. The construction of this K matrix from network topology and line parameters can be found in [21]. Note that additional network constraints may be included in the definition of the set $\mathcal{F}$.

Each node models a bus in the electric network. On bus $v \in V$, a set of variables as described in Section 2.1 is defined, with a subscript v attached to each of the bus variables, and the network inflow is replaced by network flows to the bus from incident lines. The cost for bus v and time period t is then given by

$$g_v(t) = \sum_{\ell=1}^{L_v} p_v(t,\ell)\Big(\alpha_v^\delta(\ell)\delta_v(t) - \alpha_v^{\mathrm{C}}(\ell)h_v^{\mathrm{C}}(u_v^+(t)) \tag{6}$$
$$+ \alpha_v^{\mathrm{D}}(\ell)h_v^{\mathrm{D}}(u^-(t)) + \alpha_v^{\mathrm{F}}(\ell)\sum_{e \sim v} f_e(t) + \alpha_v^{\mathrm{Const}}(t,\ell)\Big)^+,$$

and the networked storage stochastic control problem is defined as follows:

$$\text{minimize} \quad \lim_{T \to \infty} \frac{1}{T}\mathbb{E}\left[\sum_{t=1}^{T}\sum_{v \in V} g_v(t)\right] \tag{7a}$$

$$\text{subject to} \quad s_v(t+1) = \lambda_v s_v(t) + u_v(t), \tag{7b}$$
$$S_v^{\min} \leq s_v(t) \leq S_v^{\max}, \tag{7c}$$
$$U_v^{\min} \leq u_v(t) \leq U_v^{\max}, \tag{7d}$$
$$\mathbf{f}(t) \in \mathcal{F}. \tag{7e}$$

In this problem, we aim to find a control policy that maps the state $\mathbf{s}(t)$ to storage operation $\mathbf{u}(t)$ and network flow $\mathbf{f}(t)$, and minimizes the expected average cost objective function(7a), such that constraints (7b)-(7d) hold for each t and v, and (7e) holds for each t.

3. ONLINE ALGORITHM AND PERFORMANCE GUARANTEES

This paper provides an online algorithm for solving (7) with provable performance guarantees. Here we give a preview of the algorithm (Algorithm 1) and its sub-optimality bound (Theorem 3.3). The performance theorem will hold under the following additional technical assumptions.

---

[2]These penalties are usually prescribed deterministic sequences [9].

[3]To lighten the notation, for each $e = (v_1, v_2) \in E$, we also define $f_{e'}(t) = -f_e(t)$ for $e' = (v_2, v_1)$, and therefore for all $v \in V$, the net inflow $\sum_{e \sim v} f_e(t) = \sum_{e=(v',v) \in E} f_e(t) + \sum_{e=(v',v) \in E^{\mathrm{R}}} f_e(t) = \sum_{e=(v',v) \in E} f_e(t) - \sum_{e=(v,v') \in E} f_e(t)$.

Algorithm 1 Online Lyapunov Optimization for Storage Network Control

Input: (i) Storage specifications $(S_v^{\min}, S_v^{\max}, U_v^{\min}, U_v^{\max}, h_v^{\mathrm{C}}, h_v^{\mathrm{D}}, \lambda_v)$, (ii) cost parameters in $g_v(t)$ (including an upper bound and a lower bound on the sub-derivative of $g_v(t)$ with respect to $u_v(t)$, denoted by $\overline{D}g_v(t)$ and $\underline{D}g_v(t)$, and excluding any information about stochastic parameters $\delta_v(t)$ and $p_v(t,\ell)$, $\ell = 1, \ldots, L_v$) for each bus $v \in V$, and (iii) network parameters K and $\mathbf{F}^{\max}$.

Offline-Phase: Determine algorithmic parameters Γ_v, for each bus $v \in V$, and W by solving semidefinite program (24).

Online-Phase:
for each time period t **do**

Each bus $v \in V$ observes realizations of stochastic parameters $\delta_v(t)$ and $p_v(t,\ell)$, $\ell = 1, \ldots, L_v$.

Solve the following deterministic optimization for storage operation $\mathbf{u}(t)$ and network flow $\mathbf{f}(t)$:

$$\text{minimize} \sum_{v \in V} \lambda_v (s_v(t) + \Gamma_v) u_v(t) + W g_v(t) \quad (8a)$$

$$\text{subject to } \mathbf{U}^{\min} \leq \mathbf{u}(t) \leq \mathbf{U}^{\max}, \quad (8b)$$

$$\mathbf{f}(t) \in \mathcal{F}. \quad (8c)$$

end for

Assumption 3.1. *For each bus $v \in V$, the range of storage control is smaller than the effective capacity of the storage, i.e., $U_v^{\max} - U_v^{\min} < S_v^{\max} - S_v^{\min}$.*

Since the bounds for storage control $U_v^{\max}$ and $U_v^{\min}$ are the product of the power rating of storage (in unit MW for example) and the length of each time period, this assumption holds for most systems as long as the length of each time period is made small enough. For instance, this assumption is satisfied for both energy storage examples in Example 2.2.

We make the following assumption on the stochastic parameters of the system.

Assumption 3.2. *Let the collection of stochastic parameters be $\boldsymbol{\theta}(t) = \{\delta_v(t), p_v(t,\ell), \ell = 1, \ldots, L_v, v \in V\}$. Then one of the following two assumptions is in force:*

1. *$\boldsymbol{\theta}(t)$ is independent and identically distributed (i.i.d.) across time t, and is supported on a compact set.*

2. *$\boldsymbol{\theta}(t)$ is some deterministic function of the system stochastic state $\omega(t)$, which is supported on an (arbitrarily large) finite set Ω, and follows an ergodic Markov Chain.*

The first assumption is used to give a simple proof of the performance theorem and provide insights on the construction of our algorithm. The second alternative assumption intends to generalize the performance bounds to non-i.i.d. cases. The additional assumptions such as that $\omega(t)$ lies in a finite set are introduced to reduce the required technicality in view of the page limit. The same result can be obtained in a more general setting where $\{\boldsymbol{\theta}(t) : t \geq 1\}$ follows a renewal process. The performance bounds in these setting are the same, up to a multiple of the mean recurrence time of the stochastic process under consideration.

Under Assumptions 3.1 and 3.2, the following performance guarantee holds.

Theorem 3.3. *The control actions $(\mathbf{u}(t), \mathbf{f}(t))$ generated by Algorithm 1 are feasible for (7) and sub-optimal, whose sub-optimality[4] is bounded by a constant that depends only on the parameters of the storages and cost functions, and is independent of realizations of the stochastic parameters.*

The precise expressions of the sub-optimality bounds for the single bus case and general network case are given in Section 4 and Section 5, respectively, both under the i.i.d. assumption (Assumption 3.2.1). The bounds for settings with the Markov assumption (Assumption 3.2.2) are given in [21].

Remark 3.4 (Convexity). *Our result holds without assuming that $g_v(t)$ is convex in $u_v(t)$, $v \in V$. However, we do assume the online optimization (8) can be solved efficiently, and in all numerical examples we work with convex cost functions.*

4. ANALYSIS FOR SINGLE BUS SYSTEMS

To demonstrate the proof ideas without unfolding all technicalities, we prove Theorem 3.3 for a single bus system under the following simplifying assumptions.

Assumption 4.1. *We assume in this section:*

- *the imbalance process $\{\delta(t) : t \geq 1\}$ is independent and identically distributed (i.i.d.) across t and is supported on a compact interval $[\delta^{\min}, \delta^{\max}]$;*

- *for each $\ell = 1, \ldots, L$, the process $\{p(t,\ell) : t \geq 1\}$ is i.i.d. across t and is supported on a compact interval $[p^{\min}(\ell), p^{\max}(\ell)]$.*

Define

$$\bar{u} \triangleq \lim_{T \to \infty} \frac{1}{T} \mathbb{E}\left[\sum_{t=1}^{T} u(t)\right], \quad \bar{s} \triangleq \lim_{T \to \infty} \frac{1}{T} \mathbb{E}\left[\sum_{t=1}^{T} s(t)\right].$$

Note that for $s(1) \in [S^{\min}, S^{\max}]$,

$$\bar{u} = \lim_{T \to \infty} \frac{1}{T} \mathbb{E}\left[\sum_{t=1}^{T} s(t+1) - \lambda s(t)\right] = (1-\lambda)\bar{s}.$$

As $s(t) \in [S^{\min}, S^{\max}]$ for all $t \geq 0$, the above expression implies

$$(1-\lambda)S^{\min} \leq \bar{u} \leq (1-\lambda)S^{\max}.$$

Problem (4) can be equivalently written as follows

P1:
$$\text{minimize} \lim_{T \to \infty} \frac{1}{T} \mathbb{E}\left[\sum_{t=1}^{T} g(t)\right] \quad (9a)$$

$$\text{subject to } s(t+1) = \lambda s(t) + u(t), \quad (9b)$$

$$S^{\min} - \lambda s(t) \leq u(t) \leq S^{\max} - \lambda s(t), \quad (9c)$$

$$U^{\min} \leq u(t) \leq U^{\max}, \quad (9d)$$

$$(1-\lambda)S^{\min} \leq \bar{u} \leq (1-\lambda)S^{\max}, \quad (9e)$$

where bounds on $s(t)$ are replaced by (9c), and (9e) is added without loss of optimality.

The proof procedure is depicted in the diagram shown in Figure 2, where we use $J_{\mathrm{P1}}(u)$ to denote the objective value

---

[4]Here the sub-optimality is defined as the difference between the objective value of (7) with $(\mathbf{u}(t), \mathbf{f}(t))$ generated by Algorithm 1 and the optimal cost of (7).

of **P1** with storage operation sequence u (as an abbreviation of $\{u(t) : t \geq 1\}$), $u^\star(\mathbf{P1})$ to denote an optimal sequence of storage operation for **P1**, $J^\star_{\mathrm{P1}} \triangleq J_{\mathrm{P1}}(u^\star(\mathbf{P1}))$, and we define similar quantities for **P2** and **P3**. Here **P2** is an auxilliary problem we construct to bridge the infinite horizon storage control problem **P1** to online Lyapunov optimization problems **P3** (8) (or (15) for single storage case). It has the following form

$$\mathbf{P2:} \quad \underset{T \to \infty}{\text{minimize}} \lim \frac{1}{T} \mathbb{E}\left[\sum_{t=1}^{T} g(t)\right] \tag{10a}$$

$$\text{subject to } U^{\min} \leq u(t) \leq U^{\max}, \tag{10b}$$

$$(1-\lambda)S^{\min} \leq \bar{u} \leq (1-\lambda)S^{\max}. \tag{10c}$$

Notice that it has the same objective as **P1**, and evidently it is a relaxation of **P1**. This implies that $u^\star(\mathbf{P2})$ may not be feasible for **P1**, and

$$J^\star_{\mathrm{P2}} = J_{\mathrm{P1}}(u^\star(\mathbf{P2})) \leq J^\star_{\mathrm{P1}}. \tag{11}$$

The reason for the removal of state-dependent constraints (9c) (and hence (9b) as the sequence $\{s(t) : t \geq 1\}$ becomes irrelevant to the optimization of $\{u(t) : t \geq 1\}$) in **P2** is that the state-independent problem **P2** has easy-to-characterize optimal stationary control policies. In particular, from the theory of stochastic network optimization [18], the following result holds.

Lemma 4.2 (Optimality of Stationary Disturbance-Only Policies). *Under Assumption 4.1 there exists a stationary disturbance-only[5] policy $u^{\mathrm{stat}}(t)$, satisfying (10b) and (10c), and providing the following guarantees for all t:*

$$(1-\lambda)S^{\min} \leq \mathbb{E}[u^{\mathrm{stat}}(t)] \leq (1-\lambda)S^{\max}, \tag{12}$$

$$\mathbb{E}[g(t)|u(t) = u^{\mathrm{stat}}(t)] = J^\star_{\mathrm{P2}}, \tag{13}$$

where the expectation is taken over the randomization of $\delta(t)$, $p(t,\ell)$, $\ell = 1, \ldots, L$, and (possibly) $u^{\mathrm{stat}}(t)$.

Equation (13) not only assures the storage operation induced by the stationary disturbance-only policy achieves the optimal cost, but also guarantees that the expected stage-wise cost is a constant across time t and equal to the optimal time average cost. This fact will later be exploited in order to establish the performance guarantee of our online algorithm. By the merits of this Lemma, in the sequel, we overload $u^\star(\mathbf{P2})$ to denote the storage operation sequence obtained from an optimal stationary disturbance-only policy.

An issue with $u^\star(\mathbf{P2})$ for the original problem is that it may not be feasible for **P1**. To have the $\{s(t) : t \geq 1\}$ sequence induced by the storage operation sequence lie in the interval $[S^{\min}, S^{\max}]$, we construct a virtual queue related to $s(t)$ and use techniques from Lyapunov optimization to "stabilize" such a queue. Let the queueing state be a shifted version of the storage level:

$$\tilde{s}(t) = s(t) + \Gamma, \tag{14}$$

where the shift constant Γ will be specified later. We wish to minimize the stage-wise cost $g(t)$ and at the same time to maintain the queueing state close to zero. This motivates us to consider solving the following optimization online (*i.e.*,

---

[5]The policy is a pure function (possibly randomized) of the current disturbances $\delta(t)$ and $p(t,\ell)$, $\ell = 1, \ldots, L$.

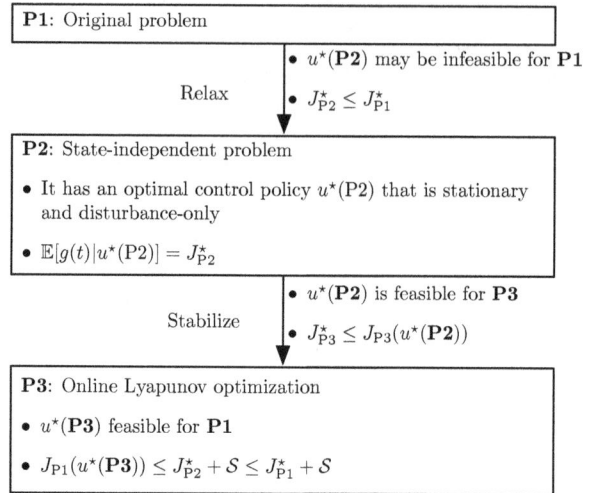

P1: Original problem

↓ Relax
- $u^\star(\mathrm{P2})$ may be infeasible for **P1**
- $J^\star_{\mathrm{P2}} \leq J^\star_{\mathrm{P1}}$

P2: State-independent problem
- It has an optimal control policy $u^\star(\mathrm{P2})$ that is stationary and disturbance-only
- $\mathbb{E}[g(t)|u^\star(\mathrm{P2})] = J^\star_{\mathrm{P2}}$

↓ Stabilize
- $u^\star(\mathrm{P2})$ is feasible for **P3**
- $J^\star_{\mathrm{P3}} \leq J_{\mathrm{P3}}(u^\star(\mathbf{P2}))$

P3: Online Lyapunov optimization
- $u^\star(\mathbf{P3})$ feasible for **P1**
- $J_{\mathrm{P1}}(u^\star(\mathbf{P3})) \leq J^\star_{\mathrm{P2}} + \mathcal{S} \leq J^\star_{\mathrm{P1}} + \mathcal{S}$

Figure 2: An illustration of the proof procedure as relations between problems considered in Section 4. Here $\mathcal{S}$ denotes the sub-optimality bound.

at the beginning of each time period t after the realizations of stochastic parameters $p(t,\ell)$, $\ell = 1, \ldots, L$, and $\delta(t)$ have been observed)

$$\mathbf{P3:} \quad \text{minimize } \lambda\tilde{s}(t)u(t) + Wg(t) \tag{15a}$$

$$\text{subject to } U^{\min} \leq u(t) \leq U^{\max}, \tag{15b}$$

where the optimization variable is $u(t)$, the stochastic parameters in $g(t)$ are replaced with their observed realizations, and $W > 0$ is a weight parameter. Note that the objective here is a weighted combination of the stage-wise cost and a linear term of $u(t)$, whose coefficient is positive when $s(t)$ is large, and negative when $s(t)$ is small. We use the notation $u^{\mathrm{ol}}(t)$ for the solution to **P3** at time period t, $u^\star(\mathbf{P3})$ for the sequence $\{u^{\mathrm{ol}}(t) : t \geq 1\}$, $J_{\mathrm{P3},t}(u(t))$ for the objective function of **P3** at time period t, and $J^\star_{\mathrm{P3},t}$ for the corresponding optimal cost. In the rest of this section, we give conditions for parameters Γ and W such that solving **P3** online will result in a feasible $\{s(t) : t \geq 1\}$ sequence (Section 4.1), characterize the sub-optimality of $u^\star(\mathbf{P3})$ as a function of Γ and W and state the semidefinite program for identifying the optimal Γ and W pair (Section 4.2).

4.1 Feasibility

We start with a structural result for the online optimization problem **P3**. It follows from Lemma A.1 which is proved for general cost functions in Appendix A.

Lemma 4.3. *At each time period t, the solution to **P3**, $u^{\mathrm{ol}}(t)$, satisfies*

1. $u^{\mathrm{ol}}(t) = U^{\min}$ whenever $\lambda\tilde{s}(t) \geq -W\underline{D}g$,

2. $u^{\mathrm{ol}}(t) = U^{\max}$ whenever $\lambda\tilde{s}(t) \leq -W\overline{D}g$,

where

$$\underline{D}g \triangleq \inf\left\{\xi \in \partial_{u(t)}g(t) \,\middle|\, \begin{matrix} u(t) \in [U^{\min}, U^{\max}], \\ p(t,\ell) \in [p^{\min}(\ell), p^{\max}(\ell)], \,\forall \ell, \\ \delta(t) \in [\delta^{\min}, \delta^{\max}], \\ \mathbf{f}(t) \in \mathcal{F}, \, t \geq 1 \end{matrix}\right\},$$

and

$$\overline{D}g \triangleq \sup \left\{ \xi \in \partial_{u(t)} g(t) \; \middle| \; \begin{array}{l} u(t) \in [U^{\min}, U^{\max}], \\ p(t, \ell) \in [p^{\min}(\ell), p^{\max}(\ell)], \; \forall \ell, \\ \delta(t) \in [\delta^{\min}, \delta^{\max}], \\ \mathbf{f}(t) \in \mathcal{F}, \; t \geq 1 \end{array} \right\}$$

are the greatest lower bound and the least upper bound of the sub-derivatives of $g(t)$, respectively.

Remark 4.4 (Evaluation of $\overline{D}g$, $\underline{D}g$). *Any finite lower bound and upper bound for the sub-derivative of the cost $g(t)$ can be used as $\underline{D}g$ and $\overline{D}g$, respectively. Here we use the greatest lower bound and least upper bound to provide the tightest performance bounds. For cases with simple cost functions, e.g., for idealized storage with $L = 1$, $\underline{D}g$ and $\overline{D}g$ can be easily obtained from $p^{\min}(\ell)$, $p^{\max}(\ell)$, and constants in the cost function $g(t)$ (such as $\alpha^C(\ell)$ and $\alpha^D(\ell)$). In cases where $g(t)$ is differentiable with respect to $u(t)$, $\overline{D}g$ and $\underline{D}g$ may be obtained by solving a simple optimization problem.*

This allows us to construct the following sufficient condition that will assure the feasibility of the $\{s(t) : t \geq 1\}$ sequence induced by $u^\star(\mathbf{P3})$.

Theorem 4.5 (Feasibility). *Suppose the initial storage level satisfies $s(1) \in [S^{\min}, S^{\max}]$, then the storage level sequence $\{s(t) : t \geq 1\}$ induced by the sequence of storage operation $u^\star(\mathbf{P3})$ is feasible with respect to storage level constraints, i.e., $s(t) \in [S^{\min}, S^{\max}]$ for all t, provided that*

$$\Gamma^{\min} \leq \Gamma \leq \Gamma^{\max}, \tag{16}$$

$$0 < W \leq W^{\max}, \tag{17}$$

where

$$\Gamma^{\min} = \frac{1}{\lambda} \left[-W \underline{D}g + (U^{\max} - (1 - \lambda) S^{\max})^+ \right] - S^{\max}, \tag{18}$$

$$\Gamma^{\max} = \frac{1}{\lambda} \left[-W \overline{D}g - \left((1 - \lambda) S^{\min} - U^{\min} \right)^+ \right] - S^{\min}, \tag{19}$$

and

$$W^{\max} = \frac{1}{\overline{D}g - \underline{D}g} \left[\lambda(S^{\max} - S^{\min}) - \left((1 - \lambda) S^{\min} - U^{\min} \right)^+ \right.$$
$$\left. - (U^{\max} - (1 - \lambda) S^{\max})^+ \right]. \tag{20}$$

Proof. The result is proved by induction, where Lemma 4.3 is used to partially characterize the $u^{\text{ol}}(t)$ sequence. See Appendix B for more details. □

4.2 Performance

In the previous result, we have established that $u^\star(\mathbf{P3})$ is feasible for $\mathbf{P1}$ as long as parameters Γ and W satisfy (16) and (17). In the next theorem, we characterize the sub-optimality of $u^\star(\mathbf{P3})$ for fixed Γ and W.

Theorem 4.6 (Performance). *The sub-optimality of storage operation $u^\star(\mathbf{P3})$ is bounded by $M(\Gamma)/W$, that is*

$$J_{\mathrm{P1}}^\star \leq J_{\mathrm{P1}}(u^\star(\mathbf{P3})) \leq J_{\mathrm{P1}}^\star + M(\Gamma)/W, \tag{21}$$

where

$$M(\Gamma) = M^u(\Gamma) + \lambda(1 - \lambda) M^s(\Gamma),$$

$$M^u(\Gamma) = \frac{1}{2} \max \left(\left(U^{\min} + (1 - \lambda)\Gamma \right)^2, (U^{\max} + (1 - \lambda)\Gamma)^2 \right),$$

$$M^s(\Gamma) = \max \left(\left(S^{\min} + \Gamma \right)^2, (S^{\max} + \Gamma)^2 \right).$$

Proof. A quadratic Lyapunov function is constructed. The relation between the Lyapunov drift and the objective of $\mathbf{P3}$ is exploited, which in turn relates to the objective of $\mathbf{P2}$ and so $\mathbf{P1}$. Appendix B contains the whole proof. □

The theorem above guarantees that the worst-case cost (among different uncertainty realizations) of our online algorithm is bounded above by $J_{\mathrm{P1}}^\star + M(\Gamma)/W$. The sub-optimality bound $M(\Gamma)/W$ reduces to a much simpler form if $\lambda = 1$.

Remark 4.7 (Sub-Optimality Bound, $\lambda = 1$). *For a storage with $\lambda = 1$, we have*

$$M \triangleq M(\Gamma) = (1/2) \max((U^{\min})^2, (U^{\max})^2),$$

and the online algorithm is no worse than M/W sub-optimal. In this case, one would optimize the performance by setting

$$W = W^{\max} = \frac{(S^{\max} - S^{\min}) - (U^{\max} - U^{\min})}{\overline{D}g - \underline{D}g},$$

and the corresponding interval $[\Gamma^{\min}, \Gamma^{\max}]$ turns out to be a singleton, where

$$\Gamma^{\min} = \Gamma^{\max} = -\frac{\overline{D}g(S^{\max} - U^{\max}) + \underline{D}g(U^{\min} - S^{\min})}{\overline{D}g - \underline{D}g}.$$

Let $S^{\max} - S^{\min} = \rho(U^{\max} - U^{\min})$. Suppose $|U^{\max}| = |U^{\min}|$. For efficient storage ($\lambda = 1$), the sub-optimality bound is

$$\frac{M}{W} = \frac{(1/2)(\overline{D}g - \underline{D}g)(U^{\max})^2}{(S^{\max} - S^{\min}) - (U^{\max} - U^{\min})} = \frac{\overline{D}g - \underline{D}g}{4(\rho - 1)} U^{\max}.$$

For fixed $U^{\max}$, as storage capacity increases , i.e., $\rho \to \infty$, the sub-optimality $(M/W) \to 0$. If $U^{\max}$ and $S^{\max}$ increases with their ratio ρ fixed, the bound increases linearly with $U^{\max}$.

The remaining case $\lambda \in (0, 1)$ requires solving an optimization program to identify the bound-minimizing parameter pair (Γ, W). In the next result, we state a semidefinite program to find $(\Gamma^\star, W^\star)$ that solves the following parameter optimization program

P3-PO: minimize $\quad M(\Gamma)/W$

subject to $\Gamma^{\min} \leq \Gamma \leq \Gamma^{\max}$, $0 < W \leq W^{\max}$.

In the current form, this program appears to be non-convex. The next result reformulates **P3-PO** into a semidefinite program. Note that $\Gamma^{\min}$ and $\Gamma^{\max}$ are linear functions of W as defined in (18) and (19).

Lemma 4.8 (Semidefinite Reformulation of **P3-PO**). *Let symmetric positive definite matrices $X^{\min,u}$, $X^{\max,u}$, $X^{\min,s}$, and $X^{\max,s}$ be defined as follows*

$$X^{(\cdot),u} = \begin{bmatrix} \eta^u & U^{(\cdot)} + (1 - \lambda)\Gamma \\ * & 2W \end{bmatrix}, \quad X^{(\cdot),s} = \begin{bmatrix} \eta^s & S^{(\cdot)} + \Gamma \\ * & W \end{bmatrix},$$

*where $(\cdot)$ can be either $\max$ or $\min$, and η^u and η^s are auxilliary variables. Then **P3-PO** can be solved via the following semidefinite program*

minimize $\quad \eta^u + \lambda(1 - \lambda)\eta^s$ (23a)

subject to $\Gamma^{\min} \leq \Gamma \leq \Gamma^{\max}$, $0 < W \leq W^{\max}$, (23b)

$\quad X^{\min,u}, X^{\max,u}, X^{\min,s}, X^{\max,s} \succeq 0.$ (23c)

Proof. The result follows from Schur complement. See Appendix B for details. □

We close this section by discussing several implications of the performance theorem.

Remark 4.9 (Optimality at the Fast-Acting Limit). *Let the length of each time period be Δt. At the limit $\Delta t \to 0$, the online algorithm is optimal. Indeed, as discussed in Section 2, both $|U^{\min}|$ and $|U^{\max}|$ are linear in Δt, such that $|U^{\max}| \to 0$ and $|U^{\min}| \to 0$ as $\Delta t \to 0$. Meanwhile, $\lambda \to 1$ as $\Delta t \to 0$. So by Remark 4.7, it is easy to verify that the sub-optimality M/W converges to zero as $\Delta t \to 0$.*

Remark 4.10 (Operational Value of Storage and Percentage Cost Savings). *Operational Value of Storage (VoS) is broadly defined as the savings in the long term system cost due to storage operation. Such an index is usually calculated by assuming storage is operated optimally. In stochastic environments, the optimal system cost with storage operation is hard to obtain in general settings. In our notations, let u^{NS} denote the sequence $\{u(t) : u(t) = 0, t \geq 1\}$ which corresponds to no storage operation. Then*

$$\mathrm{VoS} = J_{\mathrm{P1}}(u^{\mathrm{NS}}) - J_{\mathrm{P1}}^\star,$$

and it can be estimated by the interval

$$\left[J_{\mathrm{P1}}(u^{\mathrm{NS}}) - J_{\mathrm{P1}}(u^\star(\mathbf{P3})), \ J_{\mathrm{P1}}(u^{\mathrm{NS}}) - J_{\mathrm{P1}}(u^\star(\mathbf{P3})) + \frac{M}{W}\right].$$

Additionally, for a storage operation sequence u, the percentage cost savings due to storage can then be defined by $(J_{\mathrm{P1}}(u^{\mathrm{NS}}) - J_{\mathrm{P1}}(u))/J_{\mathrm{P1}}(u^{\mathrm{NS}})$. An upper bound of this for any storage control policy can be obtained via $(J_{\mathrm{P1}}(u^{\mathrm{NS}}) - J_{\mathrm{P1}}(u^\star(\mathbf{P3})) + M/W)/J_{\mathrm{P1}}(u^{\mathrm{NS}})$, which to an extent summarizes the limit of a storage system in providing cost reduction.

5. RESULTS FOR NETWORKED SYSTEMS

For completeness, we provide a summary of results for networks with more than one buses and storages; detailed discussions and proofs can be found in [21]. For each bus $v \in V$, we use X_v to denote the corresponding variable X defined for single bus systems in Section 4, and $\mathbf{X}$ to denote the vector $\{X_v\}_{v \in V}$. The online optimization, which corresponds to **P3** in the single bus systems, is as stated in (8). Suppose that Assumption 4.1 is in force for each bus $v \in V$. The following results hold for the control sequence $(\mathbf{u}^\star(\mathbf{P3}), \mathbf{f}^\star(\mathbf{P3}))$ obtained from Algorithm 1.

Theorem 5.1 (Feasibility). *Suppose the initial storage level satisfies $s_v(1) \in [S_v^{\min}, S_v^{\max}]$, for all $v \in V$, then the storage level sequence $\{\mathbf{s}(t) : t \geq 1\}$ induced by the sequence of storage operation $(\mathbf{u}^\star(\mathbf{P3}))$ is feasible with respect to storage level constraints, i.e., $s_v(t) \in [S_v^{\min}, S_v^{\max}]$ for all t and $v \in V$, provided that*

$$\Gamma_v^{\min} \leq \Gamma_v \leq \Gamma_v^{\max}, \ 0 < W \leq W_v^{\max},$$

for all $v \in V$.

Theorem 5.2 (Performance). *The sub-optimality of control sequence $(\mathbf{u}^\star(\mathbf{P3}), \mathbf{f}^\star(\mathbf{P3}))$ is bounded by $M(\mathbf{\Gamma})/W$, that is*

$$J_{\mathrm{P1}}^\star \leq J_{\mathrm{P1}}(\mathbf{u}^\star(\mathbf{P3}), \mathbf{f}^\star(\mathbf{P3})) \leq J_{\mathrm{P1}}^\star + \frac{M(\mathbf{\Gamma})}{W},$$

where

$$M(\mathbf{\Gamma}) = M^u(\mathbf{\Gamma}) + M^s(\mathbf{\Gamma}),$$

$$M^u(\mathbf{\Gamma}) = \sum_{v \in V} M_v^u(\Gamma_v),$$

and

$$M^s(\mathbf{\Gamma}) = \sum_{v \in V} \lambda_v(1 - \lambda_v) M_v^s(\Gamma_v).$$

The semidefinite program for minimizing the bound is as follows.

Lemma 5.3 (Semidefinite Optimization of $M(\mathbf{\Gamma})/W$). *Let symmetric positive definite matrices $X_v^{\min,u}$, $X_v^{\max,u}$, $X_v^{\min,s}$, and $X_v^{\max,s}$, $v \in V$, be defined as follows*

$$X_v^{(\cdot),u} = \begin{bmatrix} \eta_v^u & U^{(\cdot)} + (1 - \lambda_v)\Gamma_v \\ * & 2W \end{bmatrix}, \ X_v^{(\cdot),s} = \begin{bmatrix} \eta_v^s & S^{(\cdot)} + \Gamma_v \\ * & W \end{bmatrix},$$

where $(\cdot)$ can be either $\max$ or $\min$, and η_v^u and η_v^s are auxiliary variables, for any $v \in V$. Then the sub-optimality bound $M(\mathbf{\Gamma})/W$ can be optimized by solving the following semidefinite program

$$\text{minimize} \quad \sum_{v \in V} \eta_v^u + \lambda_v(1 - \lambda_v)\eta_v^s \tag{24a}$$

$$\text{subject to} \ \Gamma_v^{\min} \leq \Gamma_v \leq \Gamma_v^{\max}, \tag{24b}$$

$$0 < W \leq W_v^{\max}, \tag{24c}$$

$$X_v^{\min,u}, X_v^{\max,u}, X_v^{\min,s}, X_v^{\max,s} \succeq 0, \tag{24d}$$

where constraints (24b)-(24d) hold for all $v \in V$.

6. NUMERICAL EXPERIMENTS

6.1 Single Storage Example

We first test our algorithm in a simple setting where the analytical solution for the optimal control policy is available, so that the algorithm performance can be compared against the true optimal costs. We consider the problem of using a single energy storage to minimize the energy imbalance as studied in [9], where it is shown that greedy storage operation is optimal if $\lambda = 1$ and if the following cost is considered

$$g(t) = |\delta(t) - (1/\mu^{\mathrm{C}})u^+(t) + \mu^{\mathrm{D}}u^-(t)|.$$

As in [9], we specify storage parameters in per unit, and $S^{\min} = 0$. Let $\mu^{\mathrm{C}} = \mu^{\mathrm{D}} = 1$ so that the parameterization of storage operation here is equivalent to that of [9]. We assume each time period represents an hour, and $-U^{\min} = U^{\max} = (1/10)S^{\max}$. In order to evaluate the performance, we simulate the $\delta(t)$ process by drawing i.i.d. samples from zero-mean Laplace distribution, with standard deviation $\sigma_\delta = 0.149$ per unit obtained from NREL data [9]. The time horizon for the simulation is chosen to be $T = 1000$. Figure 3(a) depicts the performance of the our algorithm and the optimal cost $J_{\mathrm{P1}}^\star$ obtained from the greedy policy, where it is shown that the algorithm performance is near-optimal, and better than what the (worst-case) sub-optimality bound predicts. [6]

---

[6] By an abuse of notation, in this section, we use $J_{\mathrm{P1}}^\star$ and J_{P1} to denote the results from simulation, which are estimates of the true expectations.

A slight modification of the cost function would render a problem which does not have an analytical solution. Consider the setting where only unsatisfied demand is penalized with a higher penalty during the day (7 am to 7 pm):

$$g(t) = \begin{cases} 3\left(\delta(t) - (u^+(t)/\mu^C) + \mu^D u^-(t)\right)^-, & t \in \mathcal{T}^{\text{Day}}, \\ \left(\delta(t) - (u^+(t)/\mu^C) + \mu^D u^-(t)\right)^-, & \text{otherwise}, \end{cases} \quad (25)$$

where $\mathcal{T}^{\text{Day}} = \{t \geq 1 : 7 \leq t \bmod 24 < 19\}$. We run the same set of tests above, with the modification that now $\mu^C = \mu^D = 0.95$. Note that the greedy policy is only a sub-optimal heuristic for this case. Figure 3(b) shows our online algorithm performs significantly better than the greedy algorithm. The costs of our algorithm together with the lower bounds give a narrow envelope for the optimal average cost J^*_{P1} in this setting, which can be used to evaluate the performance of other sub-optimal algorithms numerically. In both experiments, we also plot the costs of predictive/nominal storage control, whose solution can be shown to be $u(t) = 0$ for all t. Consequently, the costs of such operation rule are the same as the system costs when there is no storage.

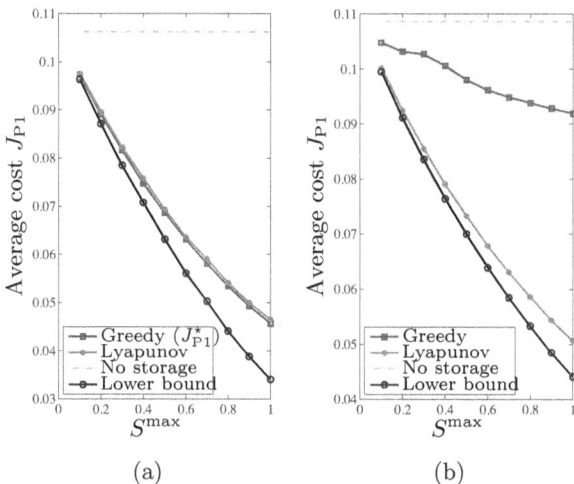

(a)　　　　　　(b)

Figure 3: Performance of algorithms in a single bus network. Note that, different from the setup in Remark 4.7, we scale $U^{\min}$, $U^{\max}$ together with $S^{\max}$ in this and the following numerical examples.

Figure 4 translates the results in Figure 3 into percentage cost savings due to storage operation, which are computed following the discussion in Remark 4.10. Using the cost of our online algorithm and the theoretical sub-optimality bound, we obtain an upper bound of percentage cost reduction of energy storage for *any control policy* (see black curve in each panel of Figure 4). It indicates the systemic limit of using storage to provide cost reduction, and is useful for system design considerations especially when the optimal cost cannot be calculated efficiently.

6.2　Storage Network Example

We consider a setting similar to that in the single storage numerical example, in which now distributed storages are coordinated to minimize the power imbalance over a tree network with N buses. We assume the storage network is homogeneous, *i.e.*, the storage installed on each bus of the

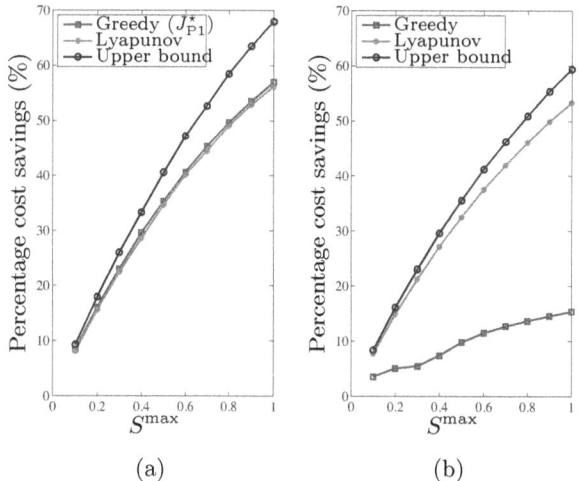

(a)　　　　　　(b)

Figure 4: Percentage cost savings of a single storage operated for balancing.

network has the same specifications and the same cost functions. Two cases with different cost functions are considered. In the first case, time homogeneous costs of the form

$$g^{\text{H}}_v(t) = \left(\delta_v(t) - (1/\mu^C_v)u^+_v(t) + \mu^D_v u^-_v(t) + \sum_{e \sim v} f_e(t)\right)^-, \quad (26)$$

are considered, where $\mu^C_v = \mu^D_v = 0.95$, and $\delta_v(t)$ is i.i.d. following the same distribution as in the single storage example. In the second case, each bus has a cost function similar to (25):

$$g_v(t) = \begin{cases} 3g^{\text{H}}_v(t), & t \in \mathcal{T}^{\text{Day}}, \\ g^{\text{H}}_v(t), & \text{otherwise}, \end{cases}$$

with $g^{\text{H}}_v(t)$ as defined in (26). We consider non-idealized storages which are operated frequently such that $\lambda_v = 0.999$ for all $v \in V$. As in the single storage example, we fix $-U^{\min}_v = U^{\max}_v = (1/10)S^{\max}_v$. The storages are connected in a star network, with $N = 5$ and $F^{\max}_e = \sigma_\delta$ for each line $e \in E$. The time horizon for the simulation is chosen to be $T = 1000$. Figure 5 shows the percentage cost savings, where it is demonstrated that the online algorithm performs consistently superior to the greedy heuristic, and leads to percentage cost savings values that are close to the derived upper bound. Therefore near-optimal performance is achieved by our algorithm in both cases.

7.　CONCLUSIONS AND FUTURE WORK

This work is motivated by the fundamental question of how to *optimally* shift energy over space and time to achieve uncertainty reduction and to facilitate renewable integration. To this end, we consider the problem of optimal control of generalized storage networks under uncertainty. The notion of generalized storage is proposed as a dynamic model to capture many forms of storage conveniently. An online control strategy is then proposed to solve the corresponding constrained stochastic control problem, whose performance is analyzed in detail. We prove that the algorithm is near optimal, and its sub-optimality can be bounded by a constant that only depends on the parameters of the storage network

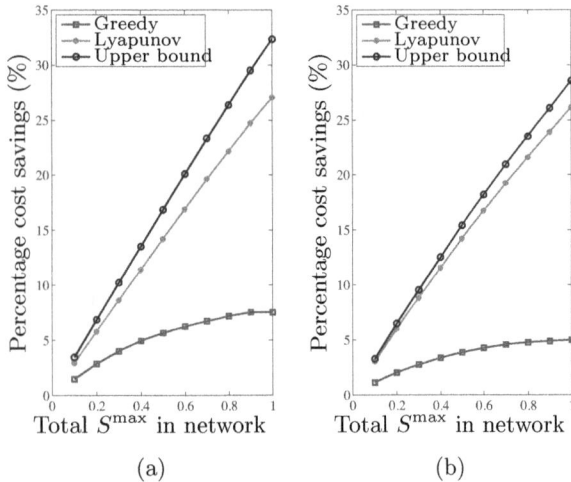

Figure 5: Percentage cost savings of a storage network operated for balancing.

and cost functions, and is independent of the realizations of uncertainties.

Although we have provided analysis for a relatively general setting (see [21] for more details), potential improvements can be achieved in many directions. (i) Our formulation starts by minimizing the long run *expected average* cost, and lands on an online algorithm that has *robust* performance guarantees in the form of a sub-optimality bound that holds for all uncertainty realizations. Relaxing such requirements may result in approaches that trade *risk* with *performance*. Better performance guarantees (in terms of smaller sub-optimality) may hold with large probability (instead of with probability one), which leads to, in a sense, probably approximately correct (PAC) algorithms[22]. (ii) While our online control solves deterministic optimization respecting network constraints, the sub-optimality bound is derived independent of network topology and network parameters such as line capacities. Utilizing such information may lead to a tighter performance bound or a more informed choice of algorithmic parameters. (iii) It can be an advantage or a disadvantage that our online algorithm does not use any statistical information about the uncertain parameters, depending on whether such information is readily available. Observe that our approach in fact can be generalized immediately to settings with additional *same-stage variables* which do not affect the (temporal) states of the system. Incorporating statistical information and forecast updates may improve the performance of the algorithm, and make the algorithm applicable to other settings where *lookahead variables* (such as wind farm contract level for the next stage) are considered together with storage operation. (iv) While the focus of this paper is on energy networks, the algorithm may be applied to other networks since our analysis does not rely on properties of the given constraints on network flow. This also implies that a more accurate AC power model can be used in this study as long as the online optimization can be solved efficiently. Recent advances in tight convex relaxation of AC optimal power flow [23] can be utilized for such purposes. (v) This paper provides a procedure to convert the hard stochastic problem to a sequence of easy deterministic problems which fit into

today's grid operational paradigms (especially for transmission grids operated by centralized system operators). For the future, the integration of distributed energy resources would require a decentralized solution to these problems. We note that many methods have been developed for distributed/decentralized *deterministic* optimization (*cf.* [24]); incorporating these methods for solving the online problems is an important future direction.

Acknowledgments

This work was supported in part by TomKat Center for Sustainable Energy, in part by a Satre Family Fellowship, and in part by a Powell Foundation Fellowship. The authors wish to thank Walter Murray for useful comments.

8. REFERENCES

[1] National Renewable Energy Laboratory. Western Wind and Solar Integration Study, 2010.

[2] National Renewable Energy Laboratory. The Role of Energy Storage with Renewable Electricity Generation, 2010.

[3] D. Lindley. Smart Grids: The Energy Storage Problem. *Nature*, 463(7277):18, 2010.

[4] B. Daryanian and R. E. Bohn. Sizing of Electric Thermal Storage under Real Time Pricing. *IEEE Transactions on Power Systems*, 8(1):35–43, 1993.

[5] G. O'Brien and R. Rajagopal. A Method for Automatically Scheduling Notified Deferrable Loads. In *Proc. of American Control Conference*, pages 5080–5085, 2013.

[6] H. Hao, B. M. Sanandaji, K. Poolla, and T. L. Vincent. Aggregate Flexibility of Thermostatically Controlled Loads. *IEEE Transactions on Power Systems*, submitted.

[7] J. Qin, R. Sevlian, D. Varodayan, and R. Rajagopal. Optimal Electric Energy Storage Operation. In *Proc. of IEEE Power and Energy Society General Meeting*, pages 1–6, 2012.

[8] A. Faghih, M. Roozbehani, and M. A. Dahleh. On the Economic Value and Price-Responsiveness of Ramp-Constrained Storage. *ArXiv e-prints*, 2012.

[9] H. I. Su and A. El Gamal. Modeling and Analysis of the Role of Energy Storage for Renewable Integration: Power Balancing. *IEEE Transactions on Power Systems*, 28(4):4109–4117, 2013.

[10] J. Qin, H. I. Su, and R. Rajagopal. Storage in Risk Limiting Dispatch: Control and Approximation. In *Proc. of American Control Conference (ACC)*, pages 4202–4208, 2013.

[11] E. Bitar, R. Rajagopal, P. Khargonekar, and K. Poolla. The Role of Co-Located Storage for Wind Power Producers in Conventional Electricity Markets. In *Proc. of American Control Conference (ACC)*, pages 3886–3891, 2011.

[12] J. H. Kim and W. B. Powell. Optimal Energy Commitments with Storage and Intermittent Supply. *Operations Research*, 59(6):1347–1360, 2011.

[13] P. M. van de Ven, N. Hegde, L. Massoulie, and T. Salonidis. Optimal Control of End-User Energy Storage. *ArXiv e-prints*, 2012.

[14] R. Urgaonkar, B. Urgaonkar, M. J. Neely, and A. Sivasubramaniam. Optimal Power Cost Management Using Stored Energy in Data Centers. In *Proc. of the ACM SIGMETRICS Joint International Conference on Measurement and Modeling of Computer Systems*, SIGMETRICS '11, pages 221–232, 2011.

[15] L. Huang, J. Walrand, and K. Ramchandran. Optimal Demand Response with Energy Storage Management. In *Proc. of IEEE Third International Conference on Smart Grid Communications*, pages 61–66, 2012.

[16] L. Xie, Y. Gu, A. Eskandari, and M. Ehsani. Fast MPC-Based Coordination of Wind Power and Battery Energy Storage Systems. *Journal of Energy Engineering*, 138(2):43–53, 2012.

[17] National Renewable Energy Laboratory. The Value of Energy Storage for Grid Applications, 2013.

[18] M. J. Neely. Stochastic Network Optimization with Application to Communication and Queueing Systems. *Synthesis Lectures on Communication Networks*, 3(1):1–211, 2010.

[19] P. Mokrian and M. Stephen. A Stochastic Programming Framework for the Valuation of Electricity Storage. In *Proc. of 26th USAEE/IAEE North American Conference*, pages 24–27, 2006.

[20] B. Stott, J. Jardim, and O. Alsac. DC Power Flow Revisited. *IEEE Transactions on Power Systems*, 2009.

[21] J. Qin, Y. Chow, J. Yang, and R. Rajagopal. Modeling and Online Control of Generalized Energy Storage Networks. Technical report, 2014. Available at http://www.stanford.edu/~jqin/pdf/QCYR2014report.pdf.

[22] A. Strehl, L. Li, E. Wiewiora, J. Langford, and M. Littman. PAC Model-Free Reinforcement Learning. In *Proc. of the 23rd International Conference on Machine Learning*, pages 881–888. ACM, 2006.

[23] B. Zhang and D. Tse. Geometry of Feasible Injection Region of Power Networks. *IEEE Transactions on Power Systems*, 28(2):788–797, 2013.

[24] S. Boyd, N. Parikh, E. Chu, B. Peleato, and J. Eckstein. Distributed Optimization and Statistical Learning Via the Alternating Direction Method of Multipliers. *Foundations and Trends® in Machine Learning*, 3(1):1–122, 2011.

APPENDIX

A. STRUCTURAL PROPERTIES OF THE ON-LINE OPTIMIZATION

We consider replacing the $g(t)$ defined in (3) with an extended real-valued function

$$g(t) = \phi_t(u(t), \kappa(t)), \qquad (27)$$

where $\kappa(t)$ is a vector of auxiliary parameters that captures both stochastic parameters and deterministic parameters, and it is supported on a compact set C_K. Observe that this would make our analysis applicable to general cost functions. Similar to discussions in Section 4, we are interested in solving the following optimization in each time period t for $u(t)$

$$\text{minimize } \lambda \tilde{s}(t)u(t) + W\phi_t(u(t), \kappa(t)) \qquad (28a)$$

$$\text{subject to } U^{\min} \leq u(t) \leq U^{\max}, \qquad (28b)$$

after observing the realization of $\kappa(t)$.

Lemma A.1 (Structural Properties of Single Bus Online Optimization). *For an extended real valued function $\phi_t(u(t), \kappa(t))$, let $\hat{\phi}^\kappa(u) \triangleq \phi_t(u, \kappa)$, where κ is equal to the observed value of $\kappa(t)$. The following statements hold, regardless of the realizations of $\kappa(t)$.*

1. *if $\lambda \tilde{s}(t) + W\underline{D}\hat{\phi}^\kappa(u) \geq 0$, then $u^{ol}(t) = U^{\min}$;*

2. *if $\lambda \tilde{s}(t) + W\overline{D}\hat{\phi}^\kappa(u) \leq 0$, then $u^{ol}(t) = U^{\max}$.*

Here,

$$\underline{D}\hat{\phi}^\kappa(u) \triangleq \inf\left\{\xi \in \partial\hat{\phi}^\kappa(u) \,\middle|\, \begin{array}{l} u \in [U^{\min}, U^{\max}], \\ \kappa \in C_K \end{array}\right\},$$

$$\overline{D}\hat{\phi}^\kappa(u) \triangleq \sup\left\{\xi \in \partial\hat{\phi}^\kappa(u) \,\middle|\, \begin{array}{l} u \in [U^{\min}, U^{\max}], \\ \kappa \in C_K \end{array}\right\}.$$

and $\partial\hat{\phi}^\kappa(u)$ is the sub-differential of $\phi^\kappa(u)$[7].

Proof. To show the set of sufficient conditions for $u^{ol}(t)$ takes $U^{\max}$ (or $U^{\min}$), notice that the condition

$$\lambda \tilde{s}(t) \leq -W\overline{D}\hat{\phi}^\kappa(u)$$

implies $\partial J_t^{\kappa, \tilde{s}}(u) \subseteq (-\infty, 0]$ for any $u(t)$, $\kappa(t)$, $\tilde{s}(t)$. Thus, for every given $u \in [U^{\min}, U^{\max}]$, if β is a constant such that

$$J_t^{\kappa, \tilde{s}}(v) - J_t^{\kappa, \tilde{s}}(u) \geq \beta \cdot (v - u), \ \forall v \in [U^{\min}, U^{\max}],$$

then the sub-differential condition implies that $\beta \leq 0$. Now, by substituting $u = U^{\max}$ in the above expression, one obtains $\beta \cdot (v - u) \geq 0$ and $J_t^{\kappa, \tilde{s}}(v) \geq J_t^{\kappa, \tilde{s}}(U^{\max})$, for all $v \in [U^{\min}, U^{\max}]$. Therefore, one concludes that $u(t) = U^{\max}$ attains an optimal solution in problem (28). Similarly, the condition

$$\lambda \tilde{s}(t) \geq -W\underline{D}\hat{\phi}^\kappa(u)$$

implies $\partial J_t^{\kappa, \tilde{s}}(u(t)) \subseteq [0, \infty)$. Based on analogous arguments, one concludes that $u(t) = U^{\min}$ attains an optimal solution in problem (28). $\square$

B. PROOF OF SINGLE BUS RESULTS

Proof of Theorem 4.5 We first validate that the intervals of Γ and W are non-empty. Note that from Assumption 3.1, $W^{\max} > 0$, thus it remains to show $\Gamma^{\max} \geq \Gamma^{\min}$. Based on (20), $W \geq 0$, and $\overline{D}g \geq \underline{D}g$, one obtains

$$W(\overline{D}g - \underline{D}g) \leq \lambda(S^{\max} - S^{\min}) - (U^{\max} - (1-\lambda)S^{\max})^+ - ((1-\lambda)S^{\min} - U^{\min})^+.$$

Re-arranging terms results in

$$\left[-W\underline{D}g + (U^{\max} - (1-\lambda)S^{\max})^+\right] - \lambda S^{\max}$$
$$\leq \left[-W\overline{D}g - \left((1-\lambda)S^{\min} - U^{\min}\right)^+\right] - \lambda S^{\min}$$

---

[7]We say β is a sub-derivative of an extended real-valued function ϕ at $u_0 \in \mathbb{R}$ if $\beta \cdot (u - u_0) \leq \phi(u) - \phi(u_0)$, for any $u \in \mathbb{R}$, and denote the set of all such β, namely the sub-differential of ϕ at u_0, by $\partial\phi(u_0)$.

which further implies $\Gamma^{\max} \geq \Gamma^{\min}$.

We proceed to show that

$$S^{\min} \leq s(t) \leq S^{\max}, \qquad (29)$$

for $t = 1, 2, \ldots$, when $u^\star(\mathbf{P3})$ is implemented. The base case holds by assumption. Let the inductive hypothesis be that (29) holds at time t. The storage level at $t + 1$ is then $s(t + 1) = \lambda s(t) + u^{\mathrm{ol}}(t)$. We show (29) holds at $t + 1$ by considering the following three cases.

Case 1. $-W\underline{D}g \leq \lambda \tilde{s}(t) \leq \lambda(S^{\max} + \Gamma)$.

First, it is easy to verify that the above interval for $\lambda \tilde{s}(t)$ is non-empty using (18) and $\Gamma \geq \Gamma^{\min}$. Next, based on Lemma 4.3, one obtains $u^{\mathrm{ol}}(t) = U^{\min} \leq 0$ in this case. Therefore

$$s(t+1) = \lambda s(t) + U^{\min} \leq \lambda S^{\max} + U^{\min} \leq S^{\max},$$

where the last inequality follows from Assumption 2.1. On the other hand,

$$\begin{aligned}
s(t+1) &= \lambda s(t) + U^{\min} \geq -W\underline{D}g - \lambda\Gamma + U^{\min} \\
&\geq -W\underline{D}g - \lambda\Gamma^{\max} + U^{\min} \\
&\geq \left((1-\lambda)S^{\min} - U^{\min}\right)^+ + \lambda S^{\min} + U^{\min} \geq S^{\min},
\end{aligned}$$

where the third line used $\overline{D}g \geq \underline{D}g$.

Case 2. $\lambda(S^{\min} + \Gamma) \leq \lambda \tilde{s}(t) \leq -W\overline{D}g$.

The above interval for $\lambda \tilde{s}(t)$ is non-empty by (19) and $\Gamma \leq \Gamma^{\max}$. Lemma 4.3 implies $u^{\mathrm{ol}}(t) = U^{\max} \geq 0$ in this case. Therefore, using Assumption 2.1,

$$s(t+1) = \lambda s(t) + U^{\max} \geq \lambda S^{\min} + U^{\max} \geq S^{\min}.$$

On the other hand,

$$\begin{aligned}
s(t+1) &= \lambda s(t) + U^{\max} \leq -W\overline{D}g - \lambda\Gamma + U^{\max} \\
&\leq -W\overline{D}g - \lambda\Gamma^{\min} + U^{\max} \\
&\leq -(U^{\max} - (1-\lambda)S^{\max})^+ + \lambda S^{\max} + U^{\max} \leq S^{\max},
\end{aligned}$$

where the third line again is by $\overline{D}g \geq \underline{D}g$.

Case 3. $-W\overline{D}g < \lambda \tilde{s}(t) < -W\underline{D}g$.

By $U^{\min} \leq u^{\mathrm{ol}}(t) \leq U^{\max}$, one obtains

$$\begin{aligned}
s(t+1) &= \lambda s(t) + u^{\mathrm{ol}}(t) \leq \lambda s(t) + U^{\max} \\
&< -W\underline{D}g - \lambda\Gamma + U^{\max} \\
&\leq -W\underline{D}g - \lambda\Gamma^{\min} + U^{\max} \\
&\leq -(U^{\max} - (1-\lambda)S^{\max})^+ + \lambda S^{\max} + U^{\max} \leq S^{\max}.
\end{aligned}$$

On the other hand,

$$\begin{aligned}
s(t+1) &= \lambda s(t) + u^{\mathrm{ol}}(t) \geq \lambda s(t) + U^{\min} \\
&> -W\overline{D}g - \lambda\Gamma + U^{\min} \\
&\geq -W\overline{D}g - \lambda\Gamma^{\max} + U^{\max} \\
&\geq \left((1-\lambda)S^{\min} - U^{\min}\right)^+ + \lambda S^{\min} + U^{\min} \geq S^{\min}.
\end{aligned}$$

Combining these three cases, and by mathematical induction, we conclude (29) holds for all $t = 1, 2, \ldots$.

Proof of Theorem 4.6 Consider a quadratic Lyapunov function $L(s) = s^2/2$. Let the corresponding Lyapunov drift be

$$\Delta(\tilde{s}(t)) = \mathbb{E}\left[L(\tilde{s}(t+1)) - L(\tilde{s}(t))|\tilde{s}(t)\right].$$

Recall that $\tilde{s}(t+1) = s(t+1) + \Gamma = \lambda \tilde{s}(t) + u(t) + (1-\lambda)\Gamma$, and so

$$\begin{aligned}
\Delta(\tilde{s}(t)) &= \mathbb{E}\big[(1/2)(u(t) + (1-\lambda)\Gamma)^2 - (1/2)(1-\lambda^2)\tilde{s}(t)^2 \\
&\quad + \lambda\tilde{s}(t)u(t) + \lambda(1-\lambda)\tilde{s}(t)\Gamma|\tilde{s}(t)\big] \\
&\leq M^u(\Gamma) - (1/2)(1-\lambda^2)\tilde{s}(t)^2 \\
&\quad + \mathbb{E}\big[\lambda\tilde{s}(t)u(t) + \lambda(1-\lambda)\tilde{s}(t)\Gamma|\tilde{s}(t)\big] \\
&\leq M^u(\Gamma) + \mathbb{E}\left[\lambda\tilde{s}(t)(u(t) + (1-\lambda)\Gamma)|\tilde{s}(t)\right]. \quad (30)
\end{aligned}$$

It follows that, with arbitrary storage operation $u(t)$,

$$\begin{aligned}
&\Delta(\tilde{s}(t)) + W\mathbb{E}[g(t)|\tilde{s}(t)] \qquad (31) \\
&\leq M^u(\Gamma) + \lambda(1-\lambda)\tilde{s}(t)\Gamma + \mathbb{E}\left[J_{\mathrm{P3},t}^\star(u(t))|\tilde{s}(t)\right],
\end{aligned}$$

where it is clear that minimizing the right hand side of the above inequality over $u(t)$ is equivalent to minimizing the objective of **P3**. Given that $u^{\mathrm{stat}}(t)$, the disturbance-only stationary policy of **P2** described in Lemma 4.2, is feasible for **P3**, the above inequality implies

$$\begin{aligned}
&\Delta(\tilde{s}(t)) + W\mathbb{E}[g(t)|\tilde{s}(t), u(t) = u^{\mathrm{ol}}(t)] \qquad (32) \\
&\leq M^u(\Gamma) + \lambda(1-\lambda)\tilde{s}(t)\Gamma + \mathbb{E}\left[J_{\mathrm{P3},t}^\star|\tilde{s}(t)\right] \\
&\leq M^u(\Gamma) + \lambda(1-\lambda)\tilde{s}(t)\Gamma + \mathbb{E}\left[J_{\mathrm{P3},t}(u^{\mathrm{stat}}(t))|\tilde{s}(t)\right] \\
&\overset{(a)}{=} M^u(\Gamma) + \lambda\tilde{s}(t)\mathbb{E}\left[u^{\mathrm{stat}}(t) + (1-\lambda)\Gamma\right] + W\mathbb{E}[g(t)|u^{\mathrm{stat}}(t)] \\
&\overset{(b)}{\leq} M(\Gamma) + W\mathbb{E}[g(t)|u^{\mathrm{stat}}(t)] \overset{(c)}{\leq} M(\Gamma) + WJ_{\mathrm{P1}}^\star.
\end{aligned}$$

Here (a) uses the fact that $u^{\mathrm{stat}}(t)$ is induced by a disturbance-only stationary policy; (b) follows from inequalities $|\tilde{s}(t)| \leq \left(\max\left((S^{\max} + \Gamma)^2, (S^{\min} + \Gamma)^2\right)\right)^{1/2}$ and $|\mathbb{E}\left[u^{\mathrm{stat}}(t)\right] + (1-\lambda)\Gamma| \leq (1-\lambda)(\max((S^{\max} + \Gamma)^2, (S^{\min} + \Gamma)^2))^{1/2}$; and (c) used $\mathbb{E}[g(t)|u^{\mathrm{stat}}(t)] = J_{\mathrm{P2}}^\star$ in Lemma 4.2 and $J_{\mathrm{P2}}^\star \leq J_{\mathrm{P1}}^\star$. Taking expectation over $\tilde{s}(t)$ on both sides gives

$$\begin{aligned}
&\mathbb{E}\left[L(\tilde{s}(t+1)) - L(\tilde{s}(t))\right] + W\mathbb{E}\left[g(t)|u(t) = u^{\mathrm{ol}}(t)\right] \\
&\leq M(\Gamma) + WJ_{\mathrm{P1}}^\star. \qquad (33)
\end{aligned}$$

Summing expression (33) over t from 1 to T, dividing both sides by WT, and taking the limit $T \to \infty$, we obtain the performance bound in expression (21).

Proof of Lemma 4.8 Based on the following re-parametrizations:

$$\eta^u = M^u(\Gamma)/W, \quad \eta^s = M^s(\Gamma)/W,$$

(since $W > 0$) one can easily show that problem **P3-PO** has a same solution as the following optimization problem:

$$\begin{aligned}
\text{minimize} \quad & \eta^u + \lambda(1-\lambda)\eta^s \\
\text{subject to} \quad & \Gamma^{\min} \leq \Gamma \leq \Gamma^{\max}, 0 < W \leq W^{\max}, \\
& 2\eta^u W \geq \left(U^{\min} + (1-\lambda)\Gamma\right)^2, \\
& 2\eta^u W \geq (U^{\max} + (1-\lambda)\Gamma)^2, \\
& \eta^s W \geq \left(S^{\min} + \Gamma\right)^2, \eta^s W \geq (S^{\max} + \Gamma)^2.
\end{aligned}$$

The proof is completed by applying Schur complement on the last four constraints of the above optimization.

Windy with a Chance of Profit - Bid Strategy and Analysis for Wind Integration

Sagar Kurandwad, Chandrasekar Subramanian,
Venkata Ramakrishna P, Arunchandar Vasan,
Venkatesh Sarangan, Vijaysekhar Chellaboina
Innovation Labs,
TATA Consultancy Services
IIT Madras Research Park, Chennai 600113, India
venkataramakrishna.p@tcs.com

Anand Sivasubramaniam
Dept. of Comp. Sci. & Eng.
Pennsylvania State University
University Park, PA 16802, USA
anand@cse.psu.edu

ABSTRACT

Integration of wind power with the grid has become an important problem. For integration, a producer needs to bid in a time-ahead market to deliver an amount of energy at a future point in time. Because wind speed and price are both uncertain, a producer needs to place bids on the basis of expected wind power yield and price. To this end, improving the accuracy of the prediction of wind speed has received much attention. However, the trade-off between expected profit and the prediction errors over a multi-period setting has been less studied.

We fill this gap by quantifying trade-offs between profits and prediction errors. First, we obtain, under idealized conditions on the price and the yield processes, an optimal bid strategy as a closed-form expression. Next, we evaluate the profit-vs-prediction trade-off using this idealized bidding strategy on synthetic datasets which satisfy all the idealistic assumptions. We also consider two baselines - a naive strategy and an oracle strategy that has perfect knowledge over a limited horizon. Finally, we relax our assumptions and evaluate all strategies under real-world datasets. We identify and work around limitations of the idealized bidding strategy when the underlying assumptions are violated.

On synthetic datasets, with no buffering and a (relative) prediction error of 25% , we find that our bidding approach performs significantly better than a naive approach and compares favourably (86%) to an oracle with a look-ahead of two time-slots and infinite buffer. On real-world datasets, with buffer equivalent to 20% of the maximum yield, our approach exceeds the naive approach by 25%, while remaining within 62% of a two-step look-ahead oracle that uses infinite buffering.

Categories and Subject Descriptors

G.3 [**Probability and Statistics**]: Stochastic processes; J.7 [**Computers in Other Systems**]

Keywords

Renewable integration; Wind prediction; Bidding strategy

1. INTRODUCTION

The global demand for energy is expected to grow by 56% from 2010 to 2040 [20]. With increasing awareness of the carbon emissions of fossil-fuel based power generation such as coal, gas, etc., it has become important for utilities to diversify their energy basket across cleaner sources of energy. Renewable and nuclear energy are the fastest growing cleaner sources of energy [20]. While hydroelectricity has traditionally been considered a clean source of energy, there are significant ecological and financial issues in commissioning new hydroelectric power projects. At this juncture, wind energy installations are expected to grow by 20% per annum [23].

Integration of wind power with the grid involves a producer making a bid to supply an agreed quantity of electricity at a future time. This involves placing a bid in a time-ahead market. For instance, a day-ahead bidding process would mean that the producer makes a bid for supplying wind power one day ahead of the actual generation. When a producer makes a bid for supplying energy, they do so under the following sources of uncertainty: 1) the actual amount of energy produced; 2) the price of energy some time ahead. The uncertainty in energy production can result in a producer producing more or less energy than what they bid for. In the former case, the excess energy produced may or may not be buffered. In the latter case, the producer has to pay a (Unscheduled Interchange - UI) penalty to the utility for failing to meet the contract obligation.

In developing economies (e.g., India, South Africa), where the energy market is still evolving evolving, wind integration primarily involves avoidance of penalties of under-delivery. For instance, in India, a shortage in delivered power beyond 30% of the bid placed, will incur a penalty for the shortage at the UI rate. In developed economies (e.g., UK, EU), the wind producer can seek to maximize profits by participating in spot and future energy markets. In either case, it is important to have a bidding strategy that maximizes the operating profits of the producer [9].

For a small producer of electricity, the pricing of the spot market is largely unaffected by its bid. In other words, the bidding process is the only control knob available to them in the face of the uncertainty. The bid of the producer is determined by the trade-offs between the expected price in the electricity market and the wind power yield. This requires a model for wind power prediction whose expected values can drive the bidding process. In this context, two natural questions arise:

1. How should a producer bid under uncertainty?

2. What is the economic impact of prediction errors?

Wind power prediction has been very well studied in the literature (e.g., [18]). Question 1 has also been addressed very extensively under a variety of assumptions about the price market and the wind yields (e.g., [5,17,21], detailed related work is in Section 2). Question 2, on the other hand, has received little attention and has been typically addressed for one-period problems [4]. The economic impact of the prediction accuracy depends on the how the bidding process uses information about the prediction. While several approaches have been proposed to answer question 1, the trade-off between prediction errors and profits has not been widely studied over a multi-period horizon. We fill this gap and complement existing work by focusing on the economic impact of wind power (mis)prediction.

Exact analysis under simplifying assumptions: First, we develop, *under idealized assumptions*, a closed form analytical expression for idealized bidding (IB). Specifically, we assume an 1) arbitrary price process that is independent of our bidding strategy; 2) a Markovian wind power yield process that is conditionally uniform and independent of the price process; and 3) an infinite buffer. Under these stochastic driving processes, we optimize the expected value of wind power over a finite horizon of one year as opposed to several existing works that focus on optimizing the wind power over the next bidding slot alone. We derive the optimal bidding process by solving the Bellman recursion exactly. The expression for the optimal bid in each timestep involves a) the buffer at the beginning of the timestep; b) the expected wind power yield over that timestep; and c) the expected prices over that timestep and the next (details are in Section 3).

Cross-validation with synthetic datasets: We then cross-validate our analytical derivation of the optimal bidding strategy under idealized conditions. To do this, we derive the price and yield from stochastic models that satisfy the requirements of our analysis. Under this synthetic dataset, we evaluate the profit-prediction trade-off. Specifically, we quantify the impact of prediction errors on the profits over the optimization horizon for varying caps on the buffers to store the excess energy produced. We find that a buffer can help mitigate any mispredictions to a certain extent, beyond which the expected profits almost linearly degrade with increasing prediction error. As two extreme baselines, we use a **naive** approach and an **oracle** based approach. The former makes no use of the buffer information to place a bid, while the latter has perfect knowledge of the price and the yield up to a look-ahead window into the future. With no buffering and a (relative) prediction error of 25% , we find that our bidding approach performs significantly better than a naive approach and compares favourably (86%) to an oracle with a look-ahead of *two time-slots and infinite buffer.*

Empirical evaluation with real-world datasets: Next, we relax each of our simplifying assumptions and evaluate our approach with real-world data and a finite buffer. We identify the limitations of our approach when the data (specifically, the price process) does not match our assumptions. Then we modify our approach to work around this limitation (details in Section 5). We compare our approach by comparing with the two baselines mentioned above. With buffer equivalent to 20% of the maximum yield, our approach exceeds the naive approach by 25%, while remaining within 62% of a two-step look-ahead oracle that uses infinite buffering.

Economic impact of prediction errors: We want to explore the profit vs. prediction error trade-off in a manner that is agnostic to the predictor. Specifically, we do this by constructing sample paths of the predicted yields with a parametrized prediction error from the actual wind yield obtained from real-world data. Then we evaluate the expected profits under our idealized bidding algorithm, and the naive and oracle-based baselines. This quantifies the trade-off between the profits from wind power and the errors in misprediction. For a given tolerance of the profit from the maximum possible, we also quantify the trade-off between the buffer sizing required as a function of the prediction error.

Contributions: Our specific findings and contributions include the following:

- We analyze a one-period ahead bidding strategy to obtain a closed-form expression for the optimal bid under idealized conditions. The closed-form expression provides intuition behind the choice of the bid as a trade-off point between the higher and lower limits of the yield distribution and the expected prices.

- We cross-validate the analytical expression on synthetic datasets for the price and yield processes. The price and yield processes match real-world data in mean and deviation. We quantify the profit vs. prediction error trade-off with varying absolute and relative prediction errors. We find that prediction errors do not matter significantly beyond a buffer capacity of 30% of the maximum generation. For a buffer capacity of 20%, we find that the impact of prediction errors on profits to be less than 1.2%.

- We evaluate our approach on real-world datasets by relaxing the assumptions on the price and the yield processes. Specifically, we modify our approach to account for the fact that price and yield processes in reality violate our idealized assumptions. Under our modified bidding strategy, we quantify the profits vs. prediction error trade-off. We find that modified IB remains stable on the real-world data.

- We present two baselines as comparison with IB for both synthetic and real datasets. At the lower extreme, we consider a naive bid strategy; and at the higher extreme, we consider an oracle that gives perfect prediction of yield and price processes over the next few time-slots.

- We quantify the impact of the increasing penalties on the expected net profits. We find that modified idealized bidding is almost agnostic to variations in the penalty.

The rest of the paper is organized as follows. Related work is surveyed in Section 2. Section 3 presents our analysis of optimal bidding using a Bellman recursion and identifies the formula for the optimal bid. Section 4 evaluates our algorithm on synthetic datasets that satisfy all the assumptions of our analysis. Section 5 evaluates our algorithm on real-world datasets for price and yield and explains how to improve our algorithm when the conditions assumed in the analysis are not met. Section 6 studies the impact of penalty on net profits. Section 7 concludes.

2. RELATED WORK

A number of wind yield prediction techniques have been tried. These techniques are based on statistical methods, numeric weather prediction methods, machine learning models and hybrid forecasting approaches [11]. Reference [18] uses alternative models based on the variables involved and combine these models to obtain the final prediction. Numerical Weather Prediction (NWP) models outperform statistical and machine learning techniques over long term prediction horizons. However, the statistical techniques perform better over shorter horizons [19], [2], [12].

A large section of the related literature focuses on optimal bidding as a one period problem, optimizing for just the next period, under various settings. Usaola et al [22] look at the problem of bidding one period ahead in an intraday market, given a position in a forward market. Botterud et al [5] consider the question of how to make the next bid in a day ahead market for different types of objective functions (Conditional Value at Risk (CVAR), expected profit, etc.). Puglia et al [17] also look at minimization of a risk measure, under the presence of both a day ahead and an ancillary market. Liang et al [13] address the problem of bidding optimally for the next period, provided the wind producer has access to both an energy market and a reserve market. Bitar et al [3] solve the problem of optimally bidding for the next time slot, allowing wind output to vary continuously within the slot. They then generalize the problem somewhat by allowing storage to be used within the slot, but it is still with a constant bid over the entire period. Other papers that look at one-period bidding problems include [16], [24], [6], [7], [8], [25] and [21]

There have been a few papers that have looked at N-period horizon bidding problems. Lohndorf et al [14] consider such an N-period problem, with finite buffers. They model the problem as a Markov decision process, and use an approximate dynamic programming approach to provide approximate solutions to it. Apart from the fact that our paper provides detailed empirical analysis of the value of prediction accuracy to bidding (which is not considered in [14]), a few other differences can also be noted between this work and ours. We allow for an arbitrary price process, while this work models price by an AR(1) process and the solution critically depends on this assumption. Further, our work provides an analytical solution that is optimal. Our optimal solution also turns out to be simple and can be implemented at each state of the system in constant time; on the other hand, the ADP methods used in [14] take significant computational resources. Morales et al [15] solve an N-period problem by reducing continuous variables into discrete scenarios and using linear programming. However, they do not allow buffers (any excess is sold off immediately), and therefore it is fundamentally not different from just a one-period problem. Further, the running time can quickly go up with increasing number of scenarios chosen. Giannitrapani et al [10] employ a similar LP technique as [15]; [10] differs from [15] by allowing buffers, but assuming a constant price and penalty throughout.

One of the main objectives of this paper is to analyze how better prediction accuracy can translate to better bidding, and therefore better profits. There has been some recent initial effort in this area, but only for a one-period case. Bitar et al, in [4], consider a problem of choosing an optimal constant bid for the next time slot, allowing wind output to vary continuously within the slot. They also analyze value of information about next period's wind power to the quality of bidding. Specifically, they quantify information using the conditional value-at-risk (CVaR) measure, and show how better information can increase profits. However, in this paper, we seek to evaluate (empirically) the value of prediction accuracy in a more general situation with multiple periods and with storage.

3. IDEALIZED BIDDING (IB)

Consider a wind power producer who needs to bid at time-slot $t-1$ for supplying energy in the slot t. The bid placed k_t needs to be decided by the producer in response to the predictions of the yield Y_t and the price P_t processes. Suppose buffering is allowed and the buffer at the end of a slot t is b_t, then the energy delivered d_t in slot t is given by $\min(Y_t + b_{t-1}, k_t)$.

If buffering is allowed, the buffer b_t stores any energy that is produced in excess of the bid, and can be used to meet any shortfall in the yield below the bid. We ignore buffer related energy losses in this work. Any unit of energy that is actually delivered from the yield or the buffer earns a revenue of P_t and any energy delivered by procuring from the spot market incurs a penalty of L_t. The net profit is difference between the revenue and the penalty paid. In sum, our problem statement is as follows:

Problem statement: Over an optimization horizon of T (say, a year) divided into equal number of (say, six hour) slots, given (probabilistic) knowledge about the yield and the price, we want to identify a bid strategy that maximizes the expected value of the net profit over the entire duration T at time $t = 0$ with future profits discounted by a factor δ.

Symbol	Meaning
T	Optimization horizon
t	Timeslot id; ranges in $[1..T]$
CF_t	Net profit in slot t
Y_t	Yield in t
y_l	Lower bound on $Y_t | Y_{t-1}$
y_h	Upper bound on $Y_t | Y_{t-1}$
P_t	Unit price in t
b_{t-1}	Buffer at end of $t-1$
k_t	Bid placed at $t-1$ for delivery in t
d_t	Amount actually delivered in t given by $d_t = \min(Y_t + b_{t-1}, k_t)$
L_t	Penalty for each unit of under-delivery
δ	Discount factor to translate cash-flows between slots
p_0	Terminal sale price at last slot T
$\mathbb{E}_t[]$	Expectation given all information up to and inclusive of t
$\mathbf{P}()$	Probability distribution

Table 1: Notation

Notation used is summarized in Table 1. Our goal is to find the optimal strategy $\{k_1^*, ..., k_T^*\}$ to maximize

$$\sum_{t=1}^{T} \delta^t \mathbb{E}_0(CF_t)$$

In other words, we want to identify a strategy that maximises the value function where the expected cash flows of future timeslots are discounted by the factor δ. The cash flow at the terminal time slot T is:

$$CF_T = d_T P_T - [k_T - d_T]L_T + [b_{T-1} + Y_T - d_T]p_0$$

where $d_T = \min(Y_T + b_{T-1}, k_T)$ Specifically, at T, there is no further buffering. Anything in excess of the delivered amount is dumped at the dumping price p_D. The cash flow at slots $t < T$ is:

$$CF_t = d_t P_t - [k_t - d_t]L_t$$

We obtain the optimal strategy using Bellman dynamic programming. The value function is:

$$V_t = CF_t + \delta \cdot \mathbb{E}_t(V_{t+1}^*), t < T$$

with $V_T = CF_T$. We update the buffer at every t as follows:

$$b_t = b_{t-1} + Y_t - d_t$$

The problem at each $t \in \{0, 1, ..., T-1\}$ is:

$$V_t^* = \max_{k_{t+1}} V_t$$

The value under the optimal strategy $\{k_1^*, ..., k_T^*\}$ is V_0^*.

3.1 Assumptions

For the sake of analytical tractability, we make the following simplifying assumptions (that will be relaxed in the experimental evaluation):

- At $t-1$, we bid k_t for delivery during t.
- Y_t is conditionally uniform: $Y_t|Y_{t-1}$ is $\sim U(y_l, y_h)$, where the range is determined by Y_{t-1}.
- Y_t and P_t are independent.
- Buffers are infinite and costless.
- The per-unit price of dumping is low:

$$p_0 < \mathbb{E}_t(P_{t+1}), \forall t \qquad (1)$$

- Penalty is sufficiently large to avoid simple hoarding:

$$\mathbb{E}_{t-1}[L_t] > \mathbb{E}_{t-1}[-P_t + \delta P_{t+1}], \forall t \qquad (2)$$

Essentially, this precludes someone from buying in the spot market at time t and hoarding it to sell it at time $t+1$.

3.2 Preliminaries

Our strategy is to calculate the expected delivery $\mathbb{E}_{t-1}[d_t]$ and see how it changes with the bid value k_t. Since the delivered amount is the minimum of the bid placed and the available energy (the sum of the buffer and the current yield), we proceed as follows:

$$\mathbb{E}_{t-1}[d_t] = \mathbb{E}_{t-1}[b_{t-1} + \min\{Y_t, k_t - b_{t-1}\}] \qquad (3)$$

If Y is a uniform random variable in $[y_l, y_h]$, then for $a \in [y_l, y_h]$

$$\mathbb{E}[\min(Y, a)] = \int_{-\infty}^{a} x f(x) dx + \int_{a}^{\infty} a f(x) dx$$
$$= a\alpha_t - \frac{a^2}{2(y_h - y_l)} + g(y_h, y_l)$$

where $\alpha_t = \frac{y_h}{y_h - y_l}$ and $g(.)$ is a function of only y_h and y_l and independent of a. Using this result in Equation 3, we have

$$E_{t-1}[d_t] = b_{t-1}(1 - \alpha_t) + k_t\alpha_t - \frac{(k_t - b_{t-1})^2}{2(y_h - y_l)} + g(.) \qquad (4)$$

Differentiating $E_{t-1}[d_t]$ with respect to k_t yields,

$$\frac{\partial \mathbb{E}_{t-1}(d_t)}{\partial k_t} = \alpha_t - \frac{(k_t - b_{t-1})}{(y_h - y_l)} \qquad (5)$$

3.3 Solving the Bellman recursion for $t = T$

We solve for the optimal bid in every timestep using Bellman's recursion working from backwards. Recall that the value function is recursively defined with

$$V_t = d_t P_t - [k_t - d_t]L_t + \delta\mathbb{E}_t(V_{t+1}^*)$$

with a terminal condition at:

$$V_T = d_T P_T - [k_T - d_T]L_T + (b_{T-1} + Y_T - d_T)p_0$$

Now $\frac{\partial V_{T-1}}{\partial k_T} = \delta \frac{\partial}{\partial k_T}\mathbb{E}_{T-1}[V_T]$

$$\frac{\partial \mathbb{E}_{T-1}[V_T]}{\partial k_T} = \left(\frac{\partial \mathbb{E}_{T-1}[d_T]}{\partial k_T}\right)\left(\mathbb{E}_{T-1}[P_T + L_T] - p_0\right)$$
$$- \left(\mathbb{E}_{T-1}[L_T]\right) \qquad (6)$$

We use Equation 5 to evaluate $\frac{\partial \mathbb{E}_{T-1}[d_T]}{\partial k_T}$. To solve for the optimal k_T we equate Equation 6 to 0. Under the assumption given in Equation 1, the second derivative w.r.t. k_T (that we omit for the sake of brevity) is negative and hence the local optimum is a maximum. Thus, the optimal bid for T works out to:

$$\boxed{k_T^* = y_h + b_{T-1} - \frac{\mathbb{E}_{T-1}[L_T](y_h - y_l)}{\mathbb{E}_{T-1}[P_T + L_T] - p_0}} \qquad (7)$$

3.4 Solving the Bellman recursion for $t < T$

Solving the recursion for $t < T$ is slightly more involved, and we give only the highlights of the analysis. Recall that

$$V_{t-1} = d_{t-1}P_{t-1} - [k_{t-1} - d_{t-1}]L_{t-1} + \delta\mathbb{E}_{t-1}(V_t^*)$$

$$\frac{\partial V_{t-1}}{\partial k_t} = \delta\frac{\partial}{\partial k_t}\mathbb{E}_{t-1}(V_t^*)$$
$$= \delta\left(\left(\frac{\partial \mathbb{E}_{t-1}[d_t]}{\partial k_t}\cdot\mathbb{E}_{t-1}[P_t + L_t]\right) - \mathbb{E}_{t-1}[L_t]\right)$$
$$+ \delta^2\frac{\partial}{\partial k_t}\mathbb{E}_{t-1}[V_{t+1}^*] \qquad (8)$$

The first term of Equation 8 is similar to the expression for the case of $k = T$ that we saw earlier in Equation 6 (only with p_0 set to zero). Because $t < T$ does not have a terminal condition, we need to evaluate the second term of Equation 8 separately. Using the law of iterated expecations and some algebraic transformations, we have

$$\delta^2\frac{\partial}{\partial k_t}\mathbb{E}_{t-1}[V_{t+1}^*] = -\delta^2\frac{\partial}{\partial k_t}\left(\mathbb{E}_{t-1}[d_t]\cdot\mathbb{E}_{t-1}[P_{t+1}]\right) \qquad (9)$$

Now, substituting Equation 9 back into Equation 8 and equating it to zero, we have

$$k_t^* = \alpha_t(y_h - y_l) + b_{t-1} - \frac{\mathbb{E}_{t-1}[L_t](y_h - y_l)}{\mathbb{E}_{t-1}[P_t - \delta P_{t+1} + L_t]}$$

which is

$$\boxed{k_t^* = y_h + b_{t-1} - \frac{\mathbb{E}_{t-1}[L_t](y_h - y_l)}{\mathbb{E}_{t-1}[P_t - \delta P_{t+1} + L_t]}} \qquad (10)$$

This choice of k_t^* is a maxima because the assumption in Equation 2 ensures that the second derivative is negative.

3.5 Discussion

We make the following observations about the expression for the optimal bid. As $\mathbb{E}_{t-1}[L_t]$ increases, k_t^* decreases, indicating that as the penalty increases, the bidding strategy should be more conservative. Similarly, if $\mathbb{E}_{t-1}[P_t]$ increases, k_t^* increases, but if $\mathbb{E}_{t-1}[P_{t+1}]$ increases, k_t^* decreases. If the expected price in the next slot t is higher, we bid more, if the expected price in the slot $t+1$ is higher, we defer. As y_h increases, k_t^* increases if next period's expected price is relatively more attractive (i.e. if $\mathbb{E}_{t-1}[P_t] > \delta \cdot \mathbb{E}_{t-1}[P_{t+1}]$)

Data	Value	Units
Min Wind Yield	0	KwH
Max Wind Yield	21000	KwH
Average Wind Yield	5358	KwH
Min Unit Price	8.48	£/KwH
Max Unit Price	257.21	£/KwH
Average Unit Price	25.41	£/KwH

Table 2: Digest of real-world data for slots of 6 hours. All yields are normalized to a single turbine. The data is from the UK geography and the prices are in GBP (£)

Parameter	Symbol	Value	Units
Price	μ_P	16.92	£/KwH
	α_P	0.47	
	σ_P	9.41	£/KwH
Yield	μ_Y	1533	KwH
	α_Y	0.73	
	σ_Y	4061	KwH
Risk-free interest rate	r_f	3.5% p.a.	
Discount factor	δ	0.99	
Absolute prediction error σ	Varied		KwH
Relative prediction error ρ	Varied		% of prediction

Table 3: Values of parameters used to generate price and yield processes. The data is from the UK geography and the prices are in GBP (£)

4. EVALUATION ON SYNTHETIC DATASETS

We now evaluate our IB strategy with data that is generated synthetically but matching real-world data in mean and deviation. We use a synthetic dataset to ensure that all the assumptions made for the analysis are satisfied by the dataset. On this, we explore the profit vs. prediction tradeoff for IB.

Time model: We consider a bidding horizon of 1 year. Each bidding slot is 6 hrs, i.e., we consider wind prediction and bid over (non-overlapping) 6 hour blocks. Thus we have $T = \frac{1yr}{6hrs} = 1460$ slots. Under this horizon, we want to maximize the expected profits over all timeslots with the profit at each slot t discounted by δ^t. To get the discount factor δ, we use the annual risk-free rate of interest $r_f = 3.5\%$ and divide it across 6 hour blocks. That is, $\delta = \frac{1}{(1+r_f/T)} = \frac{1}{(1+0.025/1460)} = 0.99$

Price model: For the price process, following [14], we use an AR(1) process. We use real-world datasets obtained from [1] to obtain the mean, variance, and the first-order correlation of the price process. Specifically, the price process is modeled as $P_{t+1} = \alpha_P P_t + \mu_P + \xi_t$, where P_{real} denotes the price from a real-world dataset, $\mu_P = \mathbb{E}[P_{real}](1 - \alpha_P)$ and ξ_t is $\mathcal{N}(0, \sigma)$ with $\sigma^2 = Var[P_{real}](1 - \alpha^2)$.

Under this model the assumption that the bidding knows $\mathbf{P}(P_{t+1}|P_t)$ at time t and hence $\mathbb{E}_t[P_{t+1}]$ is satisfied.

Yield and prediction errors: For the yield process, we similarly use real-world data [1] to identify parameters for an AR(1) process. We first generate a sample path $\hat{Y}(t)$ from an AR(1) process. We introduce a **prediction error** to the actual yield $\hat{Y}_t$ to get a predicted yield Y_t as follows. Specifically, once a sample path $\hat{Y}(t)$ is

---

footnote:

[1] We do not mention the source of real-world data for the wind power yields due confidentiality requirements.

---

generated, we assume that the predicted yield is given by

$$\mathbf{P}(Y_{t+1}|\hat{Y}_t) = \hat{Y}_{t+1} + Uniform[-\sigma, \sigma] \quad (11)$$

to model absolute errors in prediction that are same over the entire region of wind values or

$$\mathbf{P}(Y_{t+1}|\hat{Y}_t) = \hat{Y}_{t+1} + Uniform[-\rho, +\rho] \times \hat{Y}_{t+1} \quad (12)$$

to model relative errors in prediction whose ranges depend on the actual value being predicted. This satisfies the assumption in the analysis that the conditional yield is uniformly distributed and that the lower and upper limits of the uniform distribution are determined by $\hat{Y}_t$. The parameters used for generating the yield and the price processes are shown in Table 3.

Bidding strategies evaluated: We evaluate the following bid strategies:

1. Our approach (IB) described in Section 3. Here y_h would be $\hat{Y}_t + \sigma$ and y_l would be $\hat{Y}_t - \sigma$ in the case of absolute prediction errors and the corresponding ρ term for relative prediction errors.

2. The first baseline strategy (termed **Naive**) bids exactly the expected value of the yield according to the wind prediction model, i.e., $k_t = \hat{Y}_t + $ prediction noise, while the actual yield is $\hat{Y}_t$ and the noise is given in Equations 11 and 12 respectively.

3. The second baseline strategy (termed **Oracle(l)**) is as follows:

   - The bidder knows perfect information about the price for the next l steps.
   - With an infinite buffer, the yield Y_t is always sold at the maximum price in the slots $[t, t + l - 1]$
   - With $l = 1$, slot t's yield is sold off at that slot's price P_t with no penalty at all.

4.1 The profit-prediction tradeoff

Under these generating processes for the price and the yield, we generate an ensemble of 1000 sample paths for each set of parameters. We compute (ensemble average) expected net profit over the entire bidding horizon. Then we plot the prediction error on the X-axis and the expected net profit on the Y-axis for the various bidding strategies. This quantifies the tradeoff between prediction error and the expected net profit.

The results are shown in Figures 1a, 1b, and 1c for IB, naive, and oracle bid strategies when the prediction errors are absolute (i.e., the error magnitude is the same irrespective of the predicted value). The X-axis shows the absolute prediction error, and the Y-axis shows the expected net profits for each of the bidding strategies. Each plot shows a family of curves parametrized by various buffer values (B_{cap}). We make the following high-level observations:

- The expected profits fall with increasing errors in both IB and naive strategies. In the Oracle strategy, with increasing look-ahead knowledge, we have improved profits.

- The rate of fall is higher for the naive strategy than IB despite both using buffers of the same capacities.

- In general, for increasing buffer capacities, the tolerance of the net profit to error increases for both IB and Naive. For IB, beyond a buffer cap of about 6000 KwH (which is 30% of

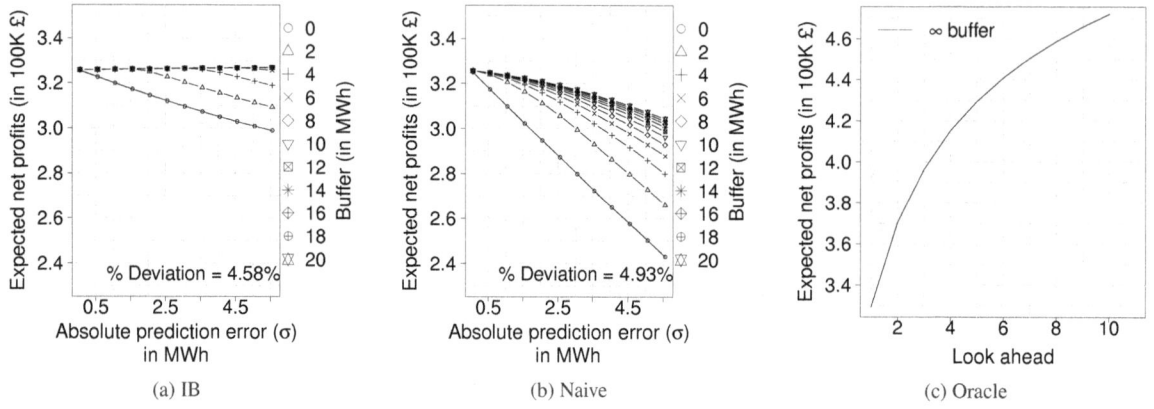

Figure 1: Profit-vs-prediction tradeoff with varying buffer capacities and absolute prediction errors

the peak yield), prediction errors do not matter significantly. With a buffer capacity of 20% of peak yield, the impact of prediction errors on profits is less than 1.2%.

- The Oracle strategy with a perfect look-ahead of length $l = 1$ matches closely with IB, indicating that IB is nearly optimal when the look-ahead knowledge is perfect only over short-intervals.

Figures 2a and 2b show the profit-vs-prediction tradeoff for relative errors in prediction. We note that the trends are similar to the absolute prediction errors. We now analyze each of these bidding strategies in detail.

4.2 Analysis of IB

Figure 1a shows IB's performance for varying values of prediction noise. Specifically, the X-axis shows the absolute error in prediction of the yield. The Y-axis shows the expected value of the cashflow over the entire bidding period. The curves are parametrized by increasing values of the buffer cap (B_{cap}). We see that as the prediction error increases, the expected cash flow falls as one would expect. For very high values of B_{cap}, there is no significant fall as the buffer can handle the excess and deficit over multiple timeslots. For lower values of B_{cap} the expected net cash flow stays flat for lower values of σ, but show a sharp dip when σ exceeds some threshold. All deviations are within 5% of the ensemble means. Figure 2a shows similar results when the errors are no longer absolute but are a constant fraction (ρ) of the predicted value. As before, the X-axis shows increasing values of ρ and the Y-axis shows the expected cash flow. For the sake of brevity, we restrict our analysis of the IB to the case where the prediction errors are absolute (i.e., for the errors parametrized by σ). Specifically, we explain the behaviour of the expected cash flows with increasing σ. We have assumed that the prediction error is uniform in $[-\sigma, +\sigma]$. For sake of brevity, we omit $(t-1)$ in $E_{t-1}[.]$ and use $\mathbb{E}[.]$. Because $P_{t+1} = \alpha_P P_t + \mu + \xi_t$ is a weak-sense stationary process, we have as $\alpha_P < 1$

$$\lim_{t \to \infty} \mathbb{E}[P_t] = \lim_{t \to \infty} \mathbb{E}[P_{t+1}] = \frac{\mu}{(1 - \alpha_P)} \quad (13)$$

Therefore, under the assumption that $\mathbb{E}[L_t] = \lambda \mathbb{E}[P_t]$, the optimal bid k_t^* simplifies to

$$k_t^* = y_h + b_{t-1} - \frac{\lambda}{(1 - \delta) + \lambda} \times (y_h - y_l) \quad (14)$$

Further, because $\delta \approx 1$ (explained earlier in Section 4) we have $k_t^* = b_{t-1} + y_l$. Recall that y_l is the lower limit of the uniform

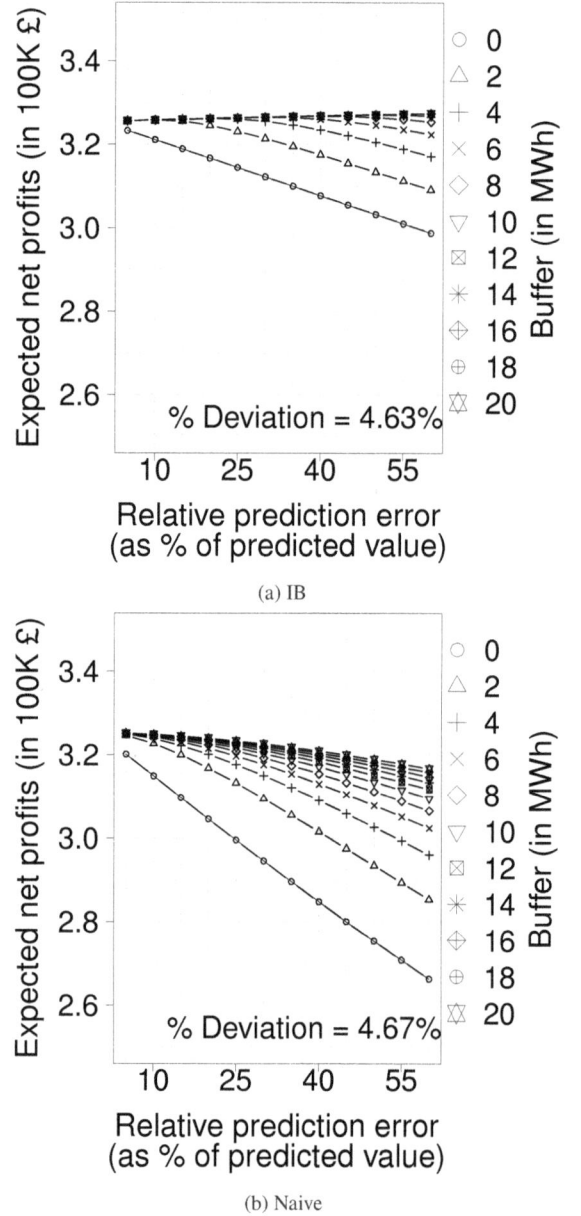

(a) IB

(b) Naive

Figure 2: Profit-vs-prediction tradeoff for varying buffer capacities and relative prediction errors

44

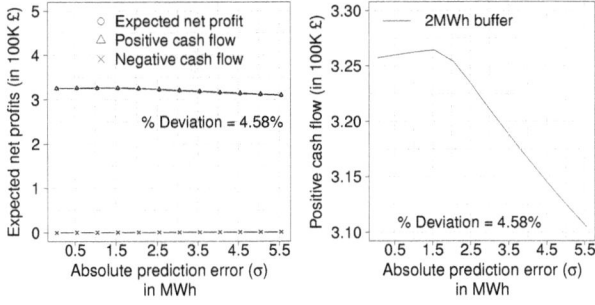

Figure 3: Break-up of the expected net cash flow into the positive and negative cash flows confirming the analytical predictions. The buffer cap used is 2000 KwH.

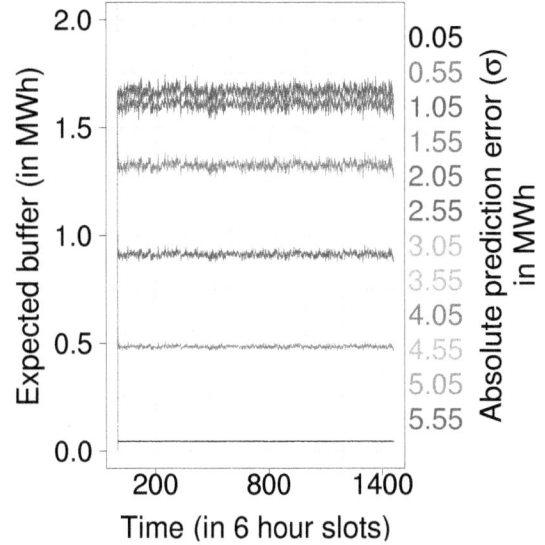

Figure 4: Time evolution of the ensemble average buffer $\mathbb{E}[B_t]$ for $t \in [0, 1460]$ for the bid strategies with prediction errors. IB

marginal $P(Y_{t+1}|Y_t)$. On an average, the expected bid at t is given by $\mathbb{E}[b_{t-1}] + \mathbb{E}[y_l]$ Because we bid at the lower limit, the penalty is never paid. And we store $\mathbb{E}[Y_t - y_l]$ in the buffer. For a constant error of prediction parametrized by σ, we have $\mathbb{E}[Y_t - y_l] = \sigma$. Therefore, we expect to discharge σ from the buffer and store σ on an average over every t.

If the buffer cap $\mathbf{B_{cap}} > \sigma$, all of the yield excess over the bid value can be stored over all timesteps. The expected per-step cash flow over all timesteps would be $\lim_{t \to \infty} \mathbb{E}[Y_t]\mathbb{E}[P_t]$. By our assumptions of independence, this would simplify to $\frac{\mu_Y \mu_P}{(1-\alpha_P)(1-\alpha_Y)}$ which is independent of B_{cap} and σ. Therefore, we get a flat line behaviour. The expected steady-state buffer size is given by σ.

If the buffer cap $B_{cap} < \sigma$, we will expect to lose some energy in every timestep when the yield is in excess of the bid value because the buffer cannot store it. Specifically, the expected per-step cash flow is given by $\mathbb{E}[P_t(b_{t-1} + Y_L) + P_D(Y_t - Y_L)]$. The expected buffer size is given by B_{cap} and $\mathbb{E}[Y_L] = \mathbb{E}[Y_t] - \sigma$. Thus the per-step cash flow becomes

$$\frac{\mu_P}{1-\alpha_P} \times \left(B_{cap} + \frac{\mu_Y}{1-\alpha_Y} - \sigma \right) + (\sigma - B_{cap}) P_{dump}$$

Because $P_{dump} < \frac{\mu_P}{1-\alpha_P}$, the expected cash flow is a linearly decreasing function of σ.

Figure 3 shows the expected net cash flow and the expected negative and positive cash flows of the IB algorithm for varying values of σ for $B_{cap} = 2000$. As we can see, the expected negative cash flow stays almost constant at zero, while the expected positive cash flow decreases after $\sigma > B_{cap}$ as predicted by the analysis thus confirming our analysis of the IB algorithm.

Figure 4 shows the time evolution of the expected buffer size for the IB algorithm. As expected, for $\sigma < B_{cap}$, the steady-state buffer value is approximately σ, while for $\sigma > B_{cap}$, the buffer saturates close to the maximum cap available B_{cap}. Thus our experiments confirm our analytical predictions.

4.3 Analysis of naïve bidding

Figure 1b shows the performance of naïve bidding for various values of the prediction noise.

For the naïve bidding strategy, where $k_t = \mathbb{E}[Y_t]$, we see a smooth behaviour in the curve (as opposed to a threshold-based knee like behaviour seen for IB.) When we bid $E[Y_t]$, any excess of the yield over the bid is buffered and any deficit in the yield can be met from the buffer. However, the buffer value itself is not used to make a bidding decision. Therefore, if $\epsilon_t = E[Y_t] - Y_t$ the

buffer evolves according to the following equations:

$$B_{t+1} = \begin{cases} \min(B_t - \epsilon_t, B_{cap}) & \text{if } \epsilon_t < 0 \\ \max(B_t - \epsilon_t, 0) & \text{if } \epsilon_t > 0 \\ B_t & \text{if } \epsilon_t = 0 \end{cases}$$

Because ϵ_t is uniform in range $[-\sigma, +\sigma]$, we can solve the stochastic difference equation for the steady state behaviour of B_t as $t \to \infty$ similar to diffusion processes with barriers. We omit the analysis for sake of brevity and state the following results:

$$\lim_{t \to \infty} \mathbb{E}[B_t] = B_{cap}/2$$
$$\lim_{t \to \infty} \mathbf{P}(B_t) \xrightarrow{D} Unif[0, B_{cap}]$$
$$\text{with point masses } p_m \text{ at } \{0, B_{cap}\}$$

An illustration of the buffer distribution is shown in Figure 5.

At timeslot t, if there is no penalty, then the expected profit is precisely $E[P_t]E[Y_t]$. However, if the yield happened to be less than the bid **and** the buffer cannot meet the deficit, we end up paying a penalty. To estimate the probability of paying a penalty in the steady-state we proceed as follows. Because Y_t is exogenous, it and, therefore, ϵ_t are independent of B_{t-1}. Recall that ϵ_t and B_{t-1} are continuous and mixed (i.e., continuous with point masses) random variables respectively. So we have

$$\mathbf{P}(\text{penalty}) = \int_x \mathbf{P}(\epsilon_t \in [x, x + dx]) \times \mathbf{P}(B_{t-1} < x)$$

For $B_{cap} > \sigma$, we have

$$\begin{aligned} \mathbf{P}(\text{penalty}) &= \int_0^\sigma \frac{dx}{2\sigma} \times \int_0^x \mathbf{P}(B) dy \\ &= \int_0^\sigma \frac{dx}{2\sigma} \times \left(p_m + \frac{x(1-2p_m)}{B_{cap}} \right) \\ &= \frac{p_m}{2} + \frac{\sigma(1-2p_m)}{4B_{cap}} \end{aligned}$$

Because $\sigma < B_{cap}$ this is an increasing function of p_m, and consequently the penalty would increase with increasing p_m. For

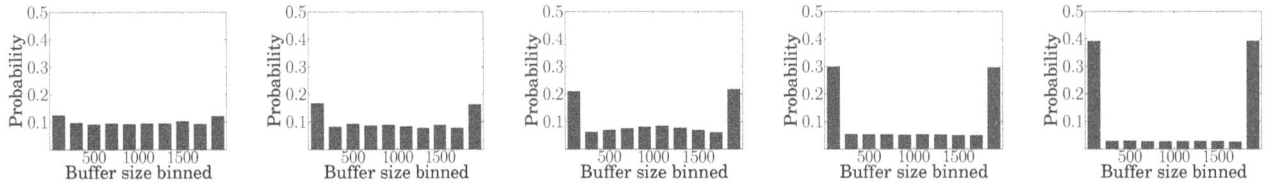

Figure 5: PDF of the steady-state buffer distribution for $B_{cap} = 2000$ units for σ in the list [200, 600, 1000, 2000, 3800] units.

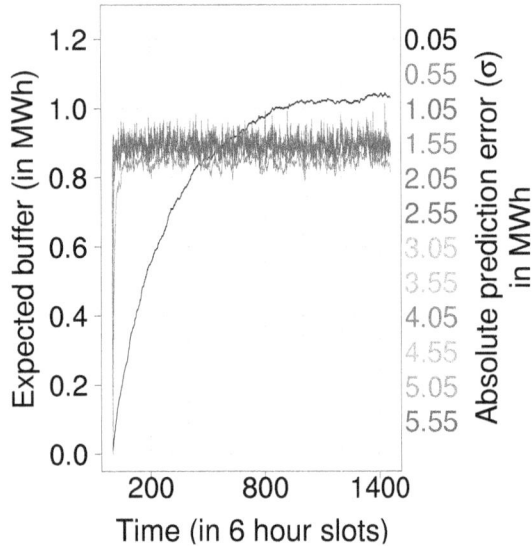

Figure 6: Time evolution of the ensemble average buffer $\mathbb{E}[B_t]$ for $t \in [0, 1460]$ for the bid strategies with prediction errors. Naive approach

$\sigma > B_{cap}$, we have

$$\mathbf{P}(\text{penalty}) = \frac{(\sigma - B_{cap})}{\sigma} + \int_0^{B_{cap}} \frac{dx}{2\sigma} \times \int_0^x \mathbf{P}(B) dy$$
$$= \frac{(\sigma - B_{cap})}{\sigma} + \frac{B_{cap}}{4\sigma}$$

independent of p_m and increases smoothly with σ. For $\sigma = B_{cap}$, the expressions for the latter two cases both simplify to $\frac{1}{4}$ as can be expected.

Summary: Therefore, the expected penalty also increases super-linearly and smoothly with σ for $\sigma < B_{cap}$ as well as $\sigma > B_{cap}$. So the net cash flow falls smoothly. The inflection point occurs at $\sigma = B_{cap}$. Figure 6 shows the time evolution of the expected buffer size averaged across 1000 runs for the range of timeslots for $B_{cap} = 2000$ and various values of σ. As the analysis predicts, it converges to approximately $B_{cap}/2$. The slight deviation from $B_{cap}/2$ is because the empirical evaluation does not allow the yield values to become negative, while the analysis does not explicitly account for the case (instead focusing on the buffer values alone being non-negative).

5. EVALUATION ON REAL-WORLD DATA SETS

As mentioned before, we had access to historical data for wind yield over 2003 and 2005. The price data for the same period was obtained from [1]. Figure 7 shows the price and the yield data for 2003; Figure 8 shows the same for 2005. We evaluated the performance of the IB algorithm and the two benchmarks as follows. The expected value of the wind was uniformly chosen within an interval of the actual wind speed. This makes the prediction error to be uniformly distributed in a pre-determined interval.

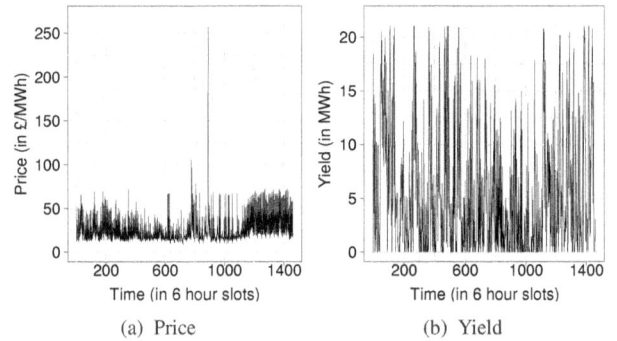

(a) Price

(b) Yield

Figure 7: Price and yield for wind in 2003

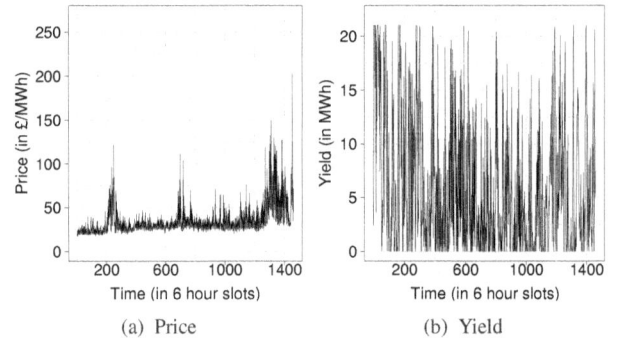

(a) Price

(b) Yield

Figure 8: Price and yield for wind in 2005

Under this assumption on the prediction error, we evaluated the IB algorithm with real-world price and yield data (2003). Figures 9a and 9b show the results for absolute and relative errors respectively. IB performs significantly worse than the other naive bidding algorithms that do not even use the buffer or the buffer state.

Explanation of poor performance of IB: To understand this behaviour, we evaluated if the conditions (specified in Equations 1 and 2) for the IB algorithm to be optimal are valid. The assumption that the price process satisfies the condition that $E[L_t] > E[P_t] - \delta E[P_{t+1}]$ is violated in the real-world price data that we used. Intuitively, the IB algorithm assumes that the price process varies smoothly. Indeed, if $L_t = \lambda P_t$, then $\mathbb{E}[P_{t+1}] < \frac{(1+\lambda)\mathbb{E}[P_t]}{\delta}$. The violation of this assumption has two consequences:

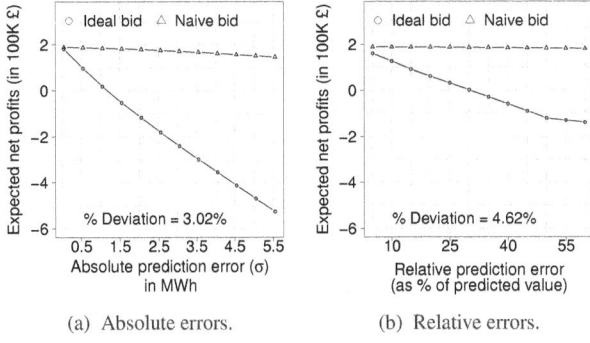

(a) Absolute errors.   (b) Relative errors.

Figure 9: Poor performance of the IB algorithm on the real-world data for 2003.

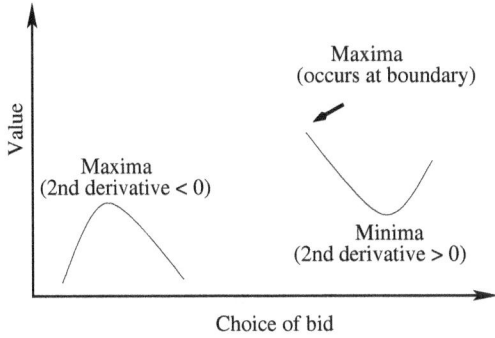

Figure 11: Intuition behind choice of optimal bid when the condition for local maxima is flipped.

- The second derivative used for checking the optimality in the expected per-slot payoff flips signs to become positive and therefore indicative of a minima.

- In the optimal bid formula

$$k_t^* = y_h + b_{t-1} - \frac{\mathbb{E}_{t-1}[L_t](y_h - y_l)}{\mathbb{E}_{t-1}[P_t - \delta P_{t+1} + L_t]}$$

the denominator $\mathbb{E}_{t-1}[P_t - \delta P_{t+1} + L_t]$ becomes negative, and so the bid placed becomes

$$k_t^* = y_h + b_{t-1} + \text{a positive quantity}$$

In other words, IB systematically overbids above the range of possible yields in every timestep leading to a very high negative cashflow and, consequently, a poor performance.

Modifying IB for real-world data: We observe that even under the violation of the price assumption, the expression for the optimal k_t^* still identifies a local extrema. Without going into the details of the mathematics, we give the intuition in Figure 11.

When the second derivative changes sign, we expect the bid to be a local minima rather than a maximum. Because there are no other local extrema, the boundary value of the function at the lowest choice of the bid is the local maxima in that interval. This corresponds to a bid value of precisely 0. Therefore, we modify the **IB algorithm to bid zero** when the condition on the expected price is violated.

Performance of modified IB: We now evaluate the modified IB algorithm with the price and yield data (2005) obtained from real-world sources. We also restrict the buffer capacity to 20% of the maximum yield (i.e., a value of 4 MwH) to avoid unrealistic buffer

sizes. Figure 10a shows the results of IB when the error involved in the prediction is absolute. In both cases, the IB algorithm is relatively stable in the face of increasing errors, while the naive strategy quickly degrades in performance.

6. IMPACT OF PENALTY

So far, we studied the impact of prediction inaccuracy assuming that the penalty is a constant multiple of the bid price. In other words, $L_t = \lambda P_t$ with λ being held constant. We now study the impact of prediction errors on the profits when the L_t varies significantly. Specifically, for a given constant prediction error σ, we vary L_t as follows:

- Relative to P_t, i.e., increasing the value of λ

- Independent of P_t, with L varying from $\frac{P_{max}}{10}$ to $2P_{max}$ in steps of $\frac{P_{max}}{10}$.

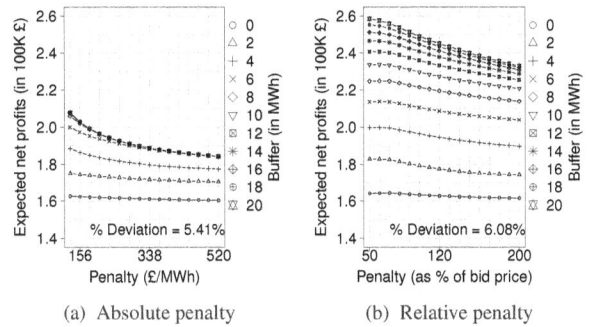

(a) Absolute penalty   (b) Relative penalty

Figure 12: Effect of penalty on the expected profit for IB. Somewhat constant, but falls with increasing values of penalty.

Figures 12a and 12b show the effect of increasing penalty values on the expected profits on the real-world data for IB. These can be understood as follows. Because IB in the real-world data incurs penalties, we expect the expected profit to decline with increasing penalties. This trend is seen across the same value of B_{cap}. With increasing B_{cap}, we expect the effect of penalty to be less as the buffer helps smooth out the bid-yield mismatch. This trend is also observed in both figures. A similar behaviour is seen in Figures 13a and 13b for the naive bidding strategy, except that the penalty increases rapidly with increasing penalty.

For the synthetically generated datasets, as indicated in the analysis in Section 4, the bid formula does not depend on the penalty

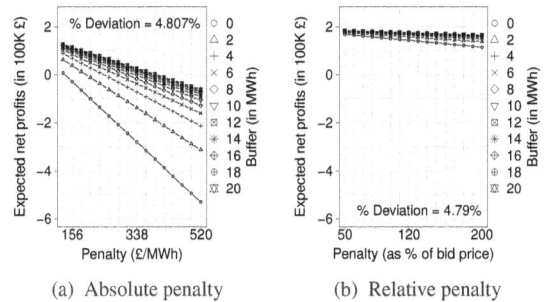

(a) Absolute penalty   (b) Relative penalty

Figure 13: Effect of penalty on the expected profit for naive bidding for 2003 real dataset. The expected profits fall off more rapidly than IB.

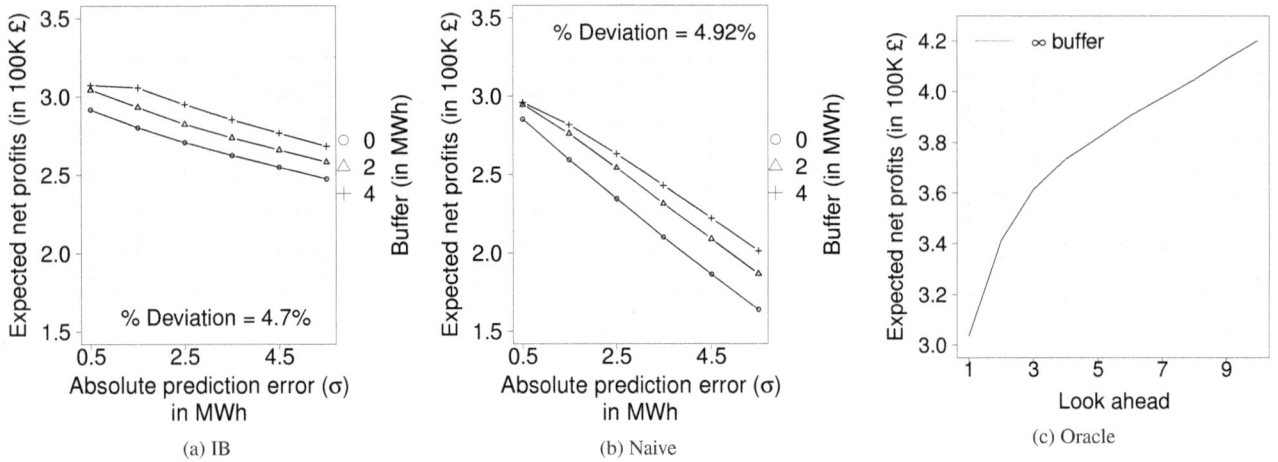

(a) IB   (b) Naive   (c) Oracle

Figure 10: Profit vs. prediction for realistic buffer capacities and absolute prediction errors for IB, Naive, and Oracle approaches. Data is from year 2005.

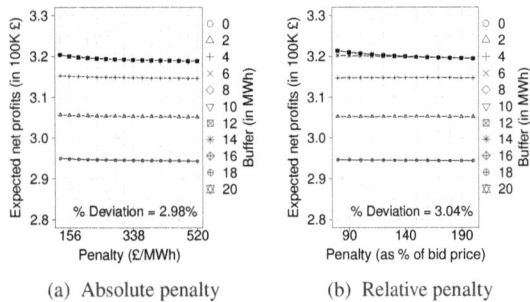

(a) Absolute penalty   (b) Relative penalty

Figure 14: Effect of penalty on the expected profit for synthetic datasets and IB. The net profit is almost independent of the penalty as IB hardly pays any penalties.

value, and the penalty paid is close to zero, and thus the actual value of the per-unit penalty price does not affect the net profit. Figures 14a and 14b confirm the expected trend.

7. CONCLUSIONS

Integration of wind energy with the grid is an important problem. Placing a bid in a time-ahead market is a key mechanism for wind power generators to integrate with the grid. A bidding strategy uses predictions about the wind power yield and the price. To do this, we need a bidding strategy and understand the trade-off between profits and the prediction accuracy. We presented a bidding strategy that computes the optimal bid under idealized situations. We cross-validated this approach under synthetic datasets that match the idealized requirements. Next, we identified the modifications required for our idealized bidding strategy to work on real-world datasets. For both synthetic and real-world datasets, we explored the trade-off between the net profits and the prediction errors. On real-world data, we find that buffers can help reduce the impact of prediction errors significantly, but are not required if the errors are within 10% to achieve 83% of baseline profits. Future directions of work include generalizing the strategy for costs associated with buffering and evaluating the profit-prediction trade-off when buffers incur capital expenditure and operational expenses.

8. REFERENCES

[1] APX Power Exchange, UK. UKPX Historical Reference Price Data.

http://www.apxgroup.com/market-results/apx-power-uk/ukpx-rpd-historical-data/, 2003.

[2] Melam Bhaskar, Amit Jain, and N Venkata Srinath. Wind speed forecasting: Present status. In *Power System Technology (POWERCON), 2010 International Conference on*, pages 1–6. IEEE, 2010.

[3] E. Bitar, A. Giani, R. Rajagopal, D. Varagnolo, P. Khargonekar, K. Poolla, and P. Varaiya. Optimal contracts for wind power producers in electricity markets. In *Decision and Control (CDC), 2010 49th IEEE Conference on*, pages 1919–1926, 2010.

[4] E.Y. Bitar, R. Rajagopal, P.P. Khargonekar, K. Poolla, and P. Varaiya. Bringing wind energy to market. *Power Systems, IEEE Transactions on*, 27(3):1225–1235, 2012.

[5] A. Botterud, Zhi Zhou, Jianhui Wang, R.J. Bessa, H. Keko, J. Sumaili, and V. Miranda. Wind power trading under uncertainty in LMP markets. *Power Systems, IEEE Transactions on*, 27(2):894–903, 2012.

[6] F. Bourry, J. Juban, L. M. Costa, and Kariniotakis G. Advanced strategies for wind power trading in short-term electricity markets. In *European Wind Energy Conference*, Brussels, Belgium, 2008.

[7] Franck Bourry and George Kariniotakis. Strategies for wind power trading in sequential short-term electricity markets. In *European Wind Energy Conference*, 2009.

[8] D.W.H. Cai, S. Adlakha, and K.M. Chandy. Optimal contract for wind power in day-ahead electricity markets. In *Decision and Control and European Control Conference (CDC-ECC), 2011 50th IEEE Conference on*, pages 1521–1527, 2011.

[9] USA Department of Energy. Strategies and Decision Support Systems for Integrating Variable Energy Resources in Control Centers for Reliable Grid Operations. 2011.

[10] Antonio Giannitrapani, Simone Paoletti, Antonio Vicino, and Donato Zarrilli. Optimal bidding strategies for wind power producers with meteorological forecasts. Available at: http://knowledgecenter.siam.org/CP2-0022/2, 2013.

[11] Gregor Giebel, Richard Brownsword, George Kariniotakis, Michael Denhard, and Caroline Draxl. The state-of-the-art in short-term prediction of wind power: A literature overview. Technical report, ANEMOS. plus, 2011.

[12] Matthias Lange and Ulrich Focken. State-of-the-art in wind power prediction in germany and international developments. In *Second Workshop of International Feed-In Cooperation*, volume 94, 2005.

[13] Jiaqi Liang, S. Grijalva, and R.G. Harley. Increased wind revenue and system security by trading wind power in energy and regulation reserve markets. *Sustainable Energy, IEEE Transactions on*, 2(3):340–347, 2011.

[14] Nils Lohndorf and Stefan Minner. Optimal day-ahead trading and storage of renewable energies - an approximate dynamic programming approach. *Energy Systems*, 1(1):61–77, 2010.

[15] J.M. Morales, A.J. Conejo, and J. Perez-Ruiz. Short-term trading for a wind power producer. *Power Systems, IEEE Transactions on*, 25(1):554–564, 2010.

[16] P. Pinson, C. Chevallier, and G.N. Kariniotakis. Trading wind generation from short-term probabilistic forecasts of wind power. *Power Systems, IEEE Transactions on*, 22(3):1148–1156, 2007.

[17] L. Puglia, D. Bernardini, and A. Bemporad. A multi-stage stochastic optimization approach to optimal bidding on energy markets. In *Decision and Control and European Control Conference (CDC-ECC), 2011 50th IEEE Conference on*, pages 1509–1514, 2011.

[18] Ismael Sanchez. Short-term prediction of wind energy production. *International Journal of Forecasting*, 22(1):43–56, 2006.

[19] Saurabh S Soman, Hamidreza Zareipour, Om Malik, and Paras Mandal. A review of wind power and wind speed forecasting methods with different time horizons. In *North American Power Symposium (NAPS), 2010*, pages 1–8. IEEE, 2010.

[20] US Energy Information Administration. International enegry outlook. http://www.eia.gov/forecasts/ieo/pdf/048428201329.pdf, 2013.

[21] J. Usaola and J. Angarita. Bidding wind energy under uncertainty. In *Clean Electrical Power, 2007. ICCEP '07. International Conference on*, pages 754–759, 2007.

[22] J. Usaola and M.A. Moreno. Optimal bidding of wind energy in intraday markets. In *Energy Market, 2009. EEM 2009. 6th International Conference on the European*, pages 1–7, 2009.

[23] World Wind Energy Association. World wind energy report. http://wwindea.org/home/index.php, 2011.

[24] Haifeng Zhang, Feng Gao, Jiang Wu, Kun Liu, and Xiaolin Liu. Optimal bidding strategies for wind power producers in the day-ahead electricity market. *Energies*, 5(11):4804–4823, 2012.

[25] Xiaoxuan Zhang. Optimal wind bidding strategy considering imbalance cost and allowed imbalance band. In *Energytech, 2012 IEEE*, pages 1–5, 2012.

Reducing Electricity Demand Charge for Data Centers with Partial Execution

Hong Xu
Department of Computer Science
City University of Hong Kong
Kowloon, Hong Kong
henry.xu@cityu.edu.hk

Baochun Li
Department of Electrical and Computer
Engineering
University of Toronto
Toronto, ON, Canada
bli@ece.toronto.edu

ABSTRACT

Data centers consume a large amount of energy and incur substantial electricity cost. In this paper, we study the familiar problem of reducing data center energy cost with two new perspectives. First, we find, through an empirical study of contracts from electric utilities powering Google data centers, that demand charge per kW for the maximum power used is a major component of the total cost. Second, many services such as web search tolerate partial execution of the requests because the response quality is a concave function of processing time. Data from Microsoft Bing search engine confirms this observation.

We propose a simple idea of using partial execution to reduce the peak power demand and energy cost of data centers. We systematically study the problem of scheduling partial execution with stringent SLAs on response quality. For a single data center, we derive an optimal algorithm to solve the workload scheduling problem. In the case of multiple geo-distributed data centers, the demand of each data center is controlled by the request routing algorithm, which makes the problem much more involved. We decouple the two aspects, and develop a distributed optimization algorithm to solve the large-scale request routing problem. Trace-driven simulations show that partial execution reduces cost by 3%–10.5% for one data center, and by 15.5% for geo-distributed data centers together with request routing.

Categories and Subject Descriptors

C.4 [**Performance of Systems**]: Modeling techniques; G.1.6 [**Optimization**]: Convex programming

General Terms

Performance, Algorithms

e-Energy'14, June 11–13, 2014, Cambridge, UK.
Copyright is held by the owner/author(s). Publication rights licensed to ACM.
ACM 978-1-4503-2819-7/14/067 ...$15.00.
http://dx.doi.org/10.1145/2602044.2602048 .

Keywords

Energy; Data centers; Demand charge; Partial execution; Distributed optimization; ADMM

1. INTRODUCTION

Data centers are the powerhouse behind many Internet services today. A modern data center, deployed by companies such as Google, Microsoft, and Facebook, often hosts tens or even hundreds of thousands of servers to provide services for millions of users at the global scale [15, 44]. Energy consumption of data centers is enormous: Google's data centers draw 260 MW of power in 2011 [14], and incur millions of dollars of electricity bills.

How to reduce data centers energy cost has thus received much attention over the recent years. Since servers and cooling systems constitute the majority of a data center's power budget [54], reducing energy cost is commonly addressed on these two fronts. Workloads may be shifted across time and location to exploit the diversity of electricity prices [27, 35, 37, 44, 45]. The cooling energy overhead can also be optimized with more efficient cooling systems and integrated thermal management [19, 23, 26, 36, 52, 54].

Despite extensive efforts, the question of how the electricity bill for data centers is actually calculated by utilities is not well understood. Almost all of the previous works simply assume that the cost is solely determined by the total energy consumption in kilowatt hours (kWh). We revisit this question by conducting empirical investigations. Data centers, like other large industrial power users, typically enter long-term contracts with local utilities instead of purchasing power off the market to avoid price volatility [40]. Thus, we collect real-world electricity contracts from utilities that power Google data centers, and study the pricing structures.

Though details vary, we find that the electricity bill for data centers has two major components: energy charge, and demand charge. Energy charge is the commonly studied cost of total kWh used. Demand charge, on the other hand, calculates the cost of *peak* power used in kW during the billing period, and can be much more significant than energy charge. For example for a data center consuming 10 MW on peak and 6 MW on average, the monthly energy charge and demand charge amount to around $24,000 and $165,500, respectively, according to Georgia Power's PLH-8 contract [28]. How to reduce the demand charge, however, has not been fully discussed in the literature.

Motivated by this observation, in this paper, we advocate to reduce the peak power and demand charge of data

51

centers by using a simple idea of *partial execution*. Partial execution has been exploited to improve request completion times for interactive services [32]. Many interactive services execute tasks in a distributed and iterative fashion. Results of a user request will improve in quality given additional processing time and energy. The marginal improvement of response quality however is diminishing. A typical application that exhibits these properties is web search. Fig. 1 plots the empirical search quality profile from 200K queries in a production trace of Microsoft Bing [32]. The quality profile is clearly concave as a result of the diminishing marginal return in quality. Therefore, a request does not necessarily need to be fully executed: at peak hours, partial execution can be used to trade response quality for demand charge savings, in addition to improving the processing time.

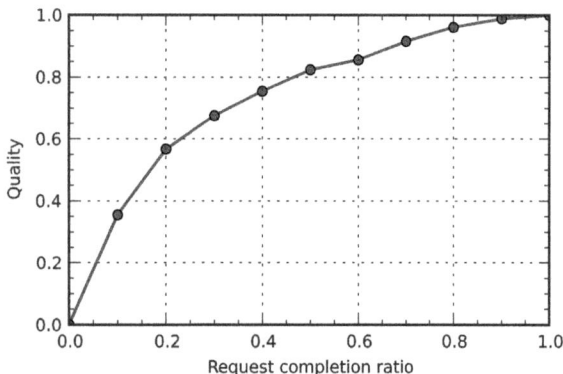

Figure 1: Search quality profile of Microsoft Bing. Data is from 200K queries of a production trace [32].

The technical challenge of using partial execution is to develop efficient workload scheduling algorithms to decide when and how partial execution should be used, so that the demand charge and energy cost are minimized and the Service Level Agreement (SLA) on response quality is satisfied. Towards this end, we make the following contributions.

First we propose a general optimization model to realistically capture both demand charge and energy charge according to our empirical study, and the typical percentile-based SLA constraints. We find that the SLA constraints imply that the optimal solution at each time slot is *binary*, i.e. we only need to decide whether to use a high power mode with high quality, or low power mode with low quality. This greatly simplifies the problem formulation.

Our second contribution is a systematic study of the workload scheduling problem with partial execution. We consider the case of a single data center, where the problem is an integer program, and derive a simple optimal algorithm. We also study the case of multiple geo-distributed data centers, where each data center's request demand as well as power use can be adjusted by the request routing algorithm. This new dimension adds considerable complexity to solving the joint optimization in a practical manner (e.g., every 15 minute). We decouple the problem, by first optimizing request routing without partial execution to reduce the demand fluctuation seen by each data center, and then optimally solving workload scheduling with partial execution. The request routing problem itself is difficult due to its large scale and tight constraint coupling. We rely on the alternat-

ing direction method of multipliers (ADMM) that offers fast convergence [20, 22]. ADMM decomposes the problem into per-user and per-data center sub-problems that are easy to solve, leading to an efficient distributed algorithm.

Finally, we perform trace-driven simulations to evelute the cost reductions of partial execution with our algorithms in Sec. 5. Results demonstrate that our algorithms outperform existing schemes that only focus on energy charge. A saving of 3%–10.5% can be realized for one data center depending on the relative importance of demand charge, and a saving of 15.5% can be achieved for geo-distributed data centers.

2. MOTIVATIONS

Let us start by motivating our key idea in this paper: using partial execution to reduce the energy cost, especially the demand charge of data centers. To make our case concrete, we first present an empirical analysis of the electricity billing method to demonstrate the importance of demand charge. We then introduce some background on the feasibility of partial execution for typical data center workloads, such as Web search.

2.1 Electricity Billing: An Empirical Analysis of Contracts

It is generally assumed that a simple volume-based charging scheme calculates the total energy cost for all kWh a data center consumes. Prices of the day-ahead or hour-ahead future markets operated by ISOs (Independent System Operator) or RTOs (Regional Transmission Operator) are often used as the prices data centers pay per kWh. However, ISOs and RTOs operate their markets mainly for electricity suppliers to balance the supply and demand of the grid in real time [16]. Data centers, as an electricity consumer, do not participate in and purchase power off the ISO or RTO market. They generally enter long-term contracts with their local utilities to obtain fixed electricity prices and avoid volatility [40].

To see how a data center's electricity bill is calculated in practice, we perform an empirical analysis of real-world electricity long-term contracts, which to our knowledge has not been done before. We briefly explain our methodology here. Our study is based on the locations of all six Google data centers in the U.S. [1]. We first determine the local utilities that power each of these data centers according to anecdotal evidence, as shown in Table 1. In many cases there is only one electric utility operating in the region of a Google data center, which makes us believe that our inference is accurate.[1] We then collect the long-term contracts these utilities provide for large industrial users—such as data centers—that has an annual contract demand of more than 10 MW. For simplicity we choose contracts with fixed rates instead of time-of-use pricing. All utilities in our study publish contracts and rate schedules on their websites, and all the contracts we study can be downloaded from [2]. We believe that these contracts faithfully represent the billing method used in the actual contracts data centers enter.

Our empirical study reveals that the monthly electricity bill is, among other things, determined mainly by two meth-

---

[1]We provide references to anecdotal evidence for determining the local utilities that power each Google data center in Table 1. For those without references, they are the only utility in the region.

Table 1: Electric utilities for Google data centers. Monthly cost breakdown based on a 10 MW peak demand and a 6 MW average demand. Data collected in June, 2013.

Location	Utility	Contract Type	Demand Charge	Energy Charge
The Dalles, OR	Northern Wasco County PUD [3]	Primary Service [4]	$38,400	$147,312
Council Bluffs, IA	MidAmerican Energy	Large General Service, South System [5]	$62,600	$114,236
Mayes County, OK	The Grand River Dam Authority [6]	Wholesale Power Service [7]	$103,900	$93,312
Lenoir, NC	Duke Energy [8]	Large General Service LGS-24 [9]	$111,000	$240,580
Berkeley County, SC	South Carolina Electric & Gas Company	Rate 23 – Industrial Power Service [10]	$147,600	$217,598
Douglas County, GA	Georgia Power	Power and Light – High Load Factor PLH-8 [11]	$165,500	$24,002

Table 2: The Industrial Power Service contract, SCEG [10].

Item	Price (USD)
Basic Facilities Charge	$1925.00
Demand Charge	$14.76/kW
Energy Charge	$0.05037/kWh
Miscellaneous	Tax, minimum charge, etc.

ods: a volume-based charging method that charges the total kWh of energy used, and a peak-based charging scheme that charges the maximum demand measured in kW in the billing period. More specifically, utilities install demand meters at customers' facilities to record the average demand in kW for every 15 minutes in general. The customer is billed for the highest 15-minute average demand during the billing cycle. In the utilities' taxonomy, volume-based charging results in *energy charge*, and peak-based charging results in *demand charge*. Table 2 shows the typical structure of a contract that we collected.

Demand charge and energy charge constitute the majority of total energy cost. Intuitively, demand charge helps utilities recover the cost of providing capacity to meet the peak demand, which is more expensive than meeting the average demand especially for large industrial users. Thus, demand charge is in general on par with energy charge, and often significantly higher. We estimate the monthly cost breakdown of all utilities in Table 1, for a typical data center that consumes 10 MW on peak and 6 MW on average. Observe that in the case of Georgia, demand charge is almost 8x energy charge. The importance of demand charge is more salient when the peak-to-average ratio of the demand increases.

Therefore, one needs to take into account demand charge in order to reduce energy cost, which unfortunately has not yet been fully explored. Previous works focus only on reducing the energy charge, that is the total energy consumption. They do not necessarily reduce the peak energy consumption and demand charge.

2.2 Partial Execution: A Feasibility Check

We propose to exploit partial execution of requests to reduce both the peak and total energy consumption. Partial execution is orthogonal to, and can work with existing energy management approaches that focus on energy charge. We now provide a feasibility check for partial execution in the context of Web search, which is one of the most important data center workloads.

An Internet search engine consists of crawling, indexing, and query serving systems. We focus on the query serving system, which is a distributed system with many aggregators and index servers. When a query arrives and hits the cache, the results are immediately returned. Otherwise, it is assigned to an aggregator. The aggregator sends the request to index servers, each of which holds a partition of the entire index for billions of documents. An index server then searches its index for documents matching the keywords in the query. It ranks the matching documents sequentially using a PageRank-like algorithm. This is the most time- and energy-consuming part and it uses over 90% of hardware resources [32], because the ranking algorithm needs to extract and compare many features of the documents.

Web search is best-effort: The query response quality improves as more time and resources are used to run the ranking algorithm with more matching documents. Partial execution can be implemented in a rather straightforward way for a search engine, by setting a threshold for the ranking algorithm's running time. If the elapsed processing time reaches the threshold, the algorithm is terminated, and index servers return the top ranked results they compute. The quality profile as in Fig. 1 is concave, meaning that a small degree of partial execution will not severely impact quality. These observations thus confirm that partial execution is feasible in practice for data centers.

In fact, besides Web search, many other systems also tolerate inexact or tainted results. For example it is acceptable to skip spelling correction when composing a complex web page with many sub-components [25]. Partial execution has already been adopted to rein in the tail request completion times in Google and Microsoft's Internet services [25, 32].

3. SYSTEM MODELS

Before developing algorithms that control when and how partial execution should be used to save cost, we first state our models and assumptions in this section.

We consider a discrete time model, where in each slot t the average power draw is measured at the data center. There is an interval of interest $t \in \{1, \ldots, T\}$. The length of a time slot equals 15 minutes, and the planning horizon T is one day ($T = 96$) in which the demand series can be accurately predicted. This is a valid assumption in practice. Time series analysis and other learning algorithms have been shown to fairly accurately predict the aggregate demand from a large number of users, which exhibits regular patterns [29, 42]. We cannot consider a longer planning horizon, say one month, for which prediction becomes unreliable. However we show through simulations in Sec. 5 that our algorithms perform close to the ideal case when we have limited future information. The partial execution decision is adjusted every 15 minutes for all requests.

3.1 Server Power and Energy Cost

We adopt the empirical model from [26] that calculates the individual server power consumption as an affine function of CPU utilization at t, $E_I + (E_P - E_I) u(t)$. E_I is the server power when idle, E_P is the server power when fully utilized, and $u(t)$ is the average CPU load at t. This model is especially accurate for calculating the aggregate power of a large number of servers [26]. $u(t)$ is determined by the 15-minute request demand $D(t)$, and the request completion ratio $\alpha(t) \in [0,1]$ which we control. Assuming the data center deploys N index servers to process search queries, the cache miss rate is 10%, and each request takes 50 ms to complete with 200 servers running at 100% CPU utilization, we have:

$$u(t) = D(t) \cdot 0.1 \cdot 200 \cdot 0.05 \cdot \alpha(t)/N \cdot 15 \cdot 60 = \alpha(t)D(t)/900N$$

We assume that servers are adequately provisioned and demand can always be handled so that $u(t) \leq 1$ holds, i.e.,

$$N \geq D(t)/900, \forall t. \tag{1}$$

Since servers are always on once commissioned [31, 40], server idle power is an immaterial constant that we do not consider subsequently. The total server usage power in kW at t is then a linear function of both $\alpha(t)$ and $D(t)$:

$$E\big(\alpha(t), D(t)\big) = (E_P - E_I)\frac{D(t)\alpha(t)}{900}. \tag{2}$$

As discussed in Sec. 2.1, the electricity bill has both demand charge and energy charge. Denote the demand price as P^D per kW, and the energy price as P^E per 0.25 kWh (recall a time slot is 0.25 hour). The total energy cost is then:

$$\max_{t \in [1,T]} E(\alpha(t), D(t))P^D + \sum_{t=1}^{T} E\big(\alpha(t), D(t)\big)P^E \tag{3}$$

Since we use partial execution for Web search, we are only concerned with the energy consumption of index servers. Other components of the infrastructure, such as the cooling system, also consume a lot of power [54]. They can be accounted for by a multiplying PUE factor to the server power, which captures the energy overhead as a function of the ambient temperature, humidity, etc. [27, 52], without fundamentally changing the nature of our problem. Thus we do not model them in this paper.

3.2 SLA on Response Quality

For a search engine, response quality is arguably one of the most important performance metrics. Response quality here compares the tainted results of partial execution against those from full execution. Thus many commercial services specify strict Service Level Agreements (SLAs), using both high-percentile and worst-case response quality. High-percentile guarantees ensure consistent high-quality results, at the extremes of the service distribution. For example, a web search may have an SLA that targets a 0.99 quality for at least 95% of requests, referred to as the 95th-percentile quality [32]. Worst-case guarantees, e.g. at least a 0.8 quality needs to be met for all requests, ensure that performance is at an acceptable level as the bottom line.

We model SLAs using the empirical response quality profile of Bing as shown in Fig. 1. Specifically, response quality is a function of the request completion ratio $Q(\alpha) \in [0,1]$. $Q(\alpha)$ can be obtained by applying regression techniques to the empirical data points in Fig. 1:

$$Q(\alpha) = -0.82129975\alpha^2 + 1.67356677\alpha + 0.14773298. \tag{4}$$

Clearly $Q(\alpha)$ is concave in $[0,1]$. To save cost, the operator will use just enough resources to satisfy the SLA. In other words, the operator makes sure that the quality of 95% of the requests is exactly 0.99, and the quality of the rest 5% requests is exactly 0.8 according to our examples above. Thus, in the problem of minimizing energy cost with demand charge, the partial execution decision is *binary*, even though the entire range from 0 to 1 is possible to implement. At each time slot, the operator needs to make a decision of whether to operate in the high power mode where the response quality is 0.99, or in the low power mode where quality is 0.8.

This observation greatly simplifies our model. We let $X(t)$ be a binary indicator of the partial execution decision at each time slot t. $X(t) = 1$ if $Q\big(\alpha(t)\big) = 0.99$, i.e. $\alpha(t) = Q^{-1}(0.99)$, and $X(t) = 0$ if $Q\big(\alpha(t)\big) = 0.8$, i.e. $\alpha(t) = Q^{-1}(0.8)$. It is then only necessary to make sure that the 95th-percentile quality guarantee is satisfied, which amounts to the following:

$$\sum_{t=1}^{T} X(t)D(t) \geq 0.95 \sum_{t=1}^{T} D(t). \tag{5}$$

At this point, some may wonder to what extent could partial execution reduce cost. After all, only 5% of the requests can be served using the low power mode, and they still need to have a 0.8 quality. Notice that since $Q(\alpha)$ is concave, a 0.8 quality can cut the processing time by half from (4), which implies a good amount of power reduction. Also demand charge can be reduced substantially by only using partial execution at a few time slots. Our claims will be verified in Sec. 5.

4. ALGORITHMS

We now systematically study the data center workload scheduling problem with partial execution. We formally introduce the problem formulations and solution algorithms in the cases of both a single data center and multiple geo-distributed data centers.

4.1 The Case of One Data Center

As a starting point, we consider one data center. At $t = 1$, the demand information $\{D(t)\}$ is known for the interval T. Given $\{D(t)\}$, we can formulate the problem as:

$$\min \; \max_{t \in [1,T]} E\big(\alpha(t), D(t)\big)P^D + \sum_{t=1}^{T} E\big(\alpha(t), D(t)\big)P^E$$

$$\text{s.t.} \; \sum_{t=1}^{T} X(t)D(t) \geq 0.95 \sum_{t=1}^{T} D(t),$$

$$\alpha(t) = \left\{ \begin{array}{ll} Q^{-1}(0.99), & \text{if } X(t) = 1, \\ Q^{-1}(0.8), & \text{if } X(t) = 0. \end{array} \right.$$

$$\text{variables: } X(t), \forall t. \tag{6}$$

The workload schedule $\{X(t)\}$ are our optimizing variables. They entail whether the high or the low power mode should be used at each time slot. In words, our problem is to determine the optimal workload schedule that minimizes the total cost for the period while conforming to the SLA.

The optimization (6) is an integer program, which is hard to solve in general. A moment's reflection tells us that it is not the case for our problem. Since we know the demand series, and setting $X(t) = 0$ reduces both terms of the objective function, we can derive the optimal solution with a trial-and-error approach summarized in Algorithm 1. We initialize all $X(t)$ to 1. In the decreasing order of demand, the algorithm goes through all time slots. For each t, it sets each $X(t) = 0$ if this does not violate the SLA, and reverts $X(t)$ to 1 if otherwise.

Algorithm 1 *Optimal Solution for* (6)

---
1. Initialize $X(t)$ to 1 for all t.
2. **while** $\{D(t)\}$ is not empty **do**
3.   Pick the highest $D(t)$, and set $X(t) = 0$.
4.   **if** (5) holds with $X(t) = 0$ **then**
5.   Output $X(t) = 0$.
6.   **else**
7.   Output $X(t) = 1$.
8.   **end if**
9.   Set $D(t) = 0$.
10. **end while**

The optimality of the workload schedule is intuitive. The solution is feasible to problem (6) for at each step we ensure the SLA is satisfied. It is also optimal since we always set the most demanding time slots in low power mode whenever possible, thereby providing the largest cost reduction in both demand and energy charge.

4.2 The Case of Geo-distributed Data Centers

We have assumed a single data center, in which case the problem can be solved relatively easily. In practice we may have multiple data centers geographically distributed over the wide area to improve the service latency and reliability. In this case, the provider deploys some mapping nodes, such as authoritative DNS servers or HTTP ingress proxies [43,51], to route user requests to an appropriate data center based on certain criteria. Thus an individual data center's demand is determined by the request routing algorithm. Request routing has been studied in many recent works to exploit price diversity and save energy charge [27,37,44,52,53]. Yet it has not been studied with demand charge, where the routing decision needs to smooth out the demand series for each data center.

We consider a provider with J data centers, each running N_j index servers. In the subsequent analysis the same subscript j is appended to all the notations introduced in Sec. 3 to denote the location specific quantities when necessary. We allow a mapping node to arbitrarily split a user's request traffic among all data centers. DNS servers and HTTP proxies can achieve such flexibility in commercial products [34,51]. Let I denote the number of users. In this work a user i is simply a unique IP prefix similar to [43]. Now at each time slot, the operator computes the request routing decisions together with workload schedules to better cope with dynamic request demand and reduce cost. The joint problem can be formulated as in (11).

We use $d_{ij}(t)$ to denote the amount of requests routed to data center j from user i at t. $\{d_{ij}(t)\}$ and $\{X_j(t)\}$ are our decision variables. Compared to (6), the objective function is now the sum of costs from all data centers, which can be optimized by both the workload schedule and the request routing decision. There are three additional constraints: (8) is a user workload conservation constraint that requires a user's demand to be fully satisfied at all times; (9) is a user

latency constraint that states a user's average latency should not be worse than L; and (10) is the simple data center capacity constraint as discussed in Sec. 3.1. L_{ij} denotes the end-to-end network latency between user i and j, which can be obtained through active measurements.

The optimization is a mixed-integer program (MIP) with a convex objective function. Adding to the complexity of the problem is its large scale. The number of users I, i.e. unique IP prefixes, can be $O(10^5)$ for a production cloud. The number of data centers J is $O(10)$, and the number of time slots $T = 240$. Thus (11) has $O(10^8)$ variables, and $O(10^6)$ constraints. This prohibits a direct approach of using an optimization package to solve the problem, as it takes more than 15 minutes for a modern solver to solve MIPs with millions of variables and constraints [41].

$$\min \sum_{j=1}^{J} \max_{t \in [1,T]} E_j\left(\alpha_j(t), \sum_{i=1}^{I} d_{ij}(t)\right) P_j^D \qquad (7)$$

$$+ \sum_{j=1}^{J} \sum_{t=1}^{T} E_j\left(\alpha_j(t), \sum_{i=1}^{I} d_{ij}(t)\right) P_j^E$$

$$\text{s.t.} \quad \sum_{t=1}^{T} X_j(t) \sum_{i=1}^{I} d_{ij}(t) \geq 0.95 \sum_{t=1}^{T} \sum_{i=1}^{I} d_{ij}(t), \forall j,$$

$$\sum_{j=1}^{J} d_{ij}(t) = D_i(t), \forall i, t, \qquad (8)$$

$$\sum_{j=1}^{J} d_{ij}(t) L_{ij}/D_i(t) \leq L, \forall i, t, \qquad (9)$$

$$\sum_{i=1}^{I} d_{ij}(t) \leq 900 N_j, \forall j, t, \qquad (10)$$

$$\alpha_j(t) = \begin{cases} Q^{-1}(0.99), & \text{if } X_j(t) = 1, \\ Q^{-1}(0.8), & \text{if } X_j(t) = 0. \end{cases} \forall j.$$

variables: $X_j(t), d_{ij}(t), \forall i, j, t.$ (11)

Since directly solving the joint optimization is infeasible, we decouple the request routing and workload scheduling problem to reduce the complexity. Specifically, we first solve the request routing problem and obtain the solution $d_{ij}^*(t)$ without partial execution, by setting all $X_j(t)$ to 1. We then solve the workload scheduling problem using Algorithm 1 for each data center j given the demand $\sum_i d_{ij}^*(t)$. Though sub-optimal, this approach still allows request routing to effectively smooth out the demand peaks seen by data centers in the worst case.

Thus from now on we focus on solving the decoupled request routing problem with all $X_j(t) = 1$. Since the server power function $E_j(\cdot)$ as in (2) is linear in both $\alpha_j(t)$ and $d_{ij}(t)$, the decoupled request routing problem can be written as:

$$\min \quad \sum_{j=1}^{J} \max_{t \in [1,T]} E_j\left(\sum_{i=1}^{I} d_{ij}(t)\right) P_j^D$$

$$+ \sum_{j=1}^{J} \sum_{t=1}^{T} \sum_{i=1}^{I} E_j(d_{ij}(t)) P_j^E$$

$$\text{s.t.} \quad (8), (9), (10). \qquad (12)$$

Note $\alpha_j(t)$ can now be omitted in $E_j(\cdot)$ without loss of generality. This is a large-scale convex optimization which still has $O(10^8)$ variables and $O(10^6)$ constraints. More importantly, the constraints (8), (9) and (10) couple all variables together, which makes it difficult to solve. The coupling here in this case is especially difficult, because it happens on two orthogonal dimensions simultaneously: The per-user constraints (8) and (9) couple $d_{ij}(t)$ across data centers, and the per data center capacity constraint (10) couples $d_{ij}(t)$ across users.

In these cases we rely on a distributed algorithm that enables parallel computations in data centers. A common approach is to relax the constraints and employ dual decomposition to decompose the problem into many independent sub-problems [24]. Subgradient methods can then be used to update dual variables towards the optimum of the dual problem [21]. Yet, dual decomposition does not apply here, because it requires the objective function to be strictly convex, for otherwise the Lagrangian is unbounded below. Our objective function, including a max and a linear function, is not strictly convex.

Summarizing the discussions, we need to design a practical distributed algorithm that does not require strict convexity of the objective function, and preferably converges fast for large-scale problems. Next, we present such an algorithm based on the alternating direction method of multipliers (ADMM) [22] .

4.3 A Distributed Request Routing Algorithm

We first provide a brief primer on ADMM. Developed in the 1970s [20], ADMM has recently received renewed interest in solving large-scale distributed convex optimization in statistics, machine learning, and related areas [22]. The algorithm solves problems in the form

$$\min \quad f(x) + g(z) \tag{13}$$
$$\text{s.t.} \quad Ax + Bz = c,$$
$$x \in C_1, z \in C_2,$$

with variables $x \in \mathbf{R}^n$ and $z \in \mathbf{R}^m$, where $A \in \mathbf{R}^{p \times n}$, $B \in \mathbf{R}^{p \times m}$, and $c \in \mathbf{R}^p$. f and g are convex functions, and C_1, C_2 are non-empty polyhedral sets. Thus, the objective function is *separable* over two sets of variables, which are coupled through an equality constraint.

We can form the augmented Lagrangian [33] by introducing an extra $\mathcal{L}$-2 norm term $\|Ax + Bz - c\|_2^2$ to the objective:

$$L_\rho(x, z, \lambda) = f(x) + g(z) + \lambda^T(Ax + Bz - c)$$
$$+ (\rho/2)\|Ax + Bz - c\|_2^2. \tag{14}$$

$\rho \, > 0$ is the penalty parameter (L_0 is the standard Lagrangian for the problem). The augmented Lagrangian can be viewed as the unaugmented Lagrangian associated with the problem

$$\min \quad f(x) + g(z) + (\rho/2)\|Ax + Bz - c\|_2^2$$
$$\text{s.t.} \quad Ax + Bz = c,$$
$$x \in C_1, z \in C_2.$$

Clearly this problem is equivalent to the original problem (13), since for any feasible x and z the penalty term is zero. The benefit of the quadratic penalty term is that it makes the objective function strictly convex for all f and g. The

penalty term is also called a regularization term and it helps substantially improve the convergence of the algorithm.

ADMM solves the dual problem with the iterations:

$$x^{t+1} := \operatorname*{argmin}_{x \in C_1} L_\rho(x, z^t, \lambda^t), \tag{15}$$
$$z^{t+1} := \operatorname*{argmin}_{z \in C_2} L_\rho(x^{t+1}, z, \lambda^t), \tag{16}$$
$$\lambda^{t+1} := \lambda^t + \rho(Ax^{t+1} + Bz^{t+1} - c). \tag{17}$$

It consists of an x-minimization step (15), a z-minimization step (16), and a dual variable update (17). Note the step size is simply the penalty parameter ρ. Thus, x and z are updated in an alternating or sequential fashion, which accounts for the term *alternating direction*. Separating the minimization over x and z is precisely what allows for decomposition when f or g are separable, which will be useful in our algorithm design.

The optimality and convergence of ADMM can be guaranteed under very mild assumptions. For more details see [20]. In practice, it is often the case that ADMM converges to modest accuracy within a few tens of iterations [22], which makes it attractive for practical use.

Our request routing problem (12) cannot be readily solved using ADMM. The constraints (8) and (10) couple all variables together as mentioned before, whereas in ADMM problems the constraints are separable for each set of variables.

To address this, we introduce a set of auxiliary variables $b_{ij}(t) = d_{ij}(t)$, and re-formulate the problem:

$$\min_{d,b} \quad \sum_{j=1}^{J} \max_{t \in [1,T]} E_j\left(\sum_{i=1}^{I} d_{ij}(t)\right) P_j^D$$
$$+ \sum_{j=1}^{J} \sum_{t=1}^{T} \sum_{i=1}^{I} E_j(b_{ij}(t)) P_j^E$$
$$\text{s.t.} \quad b_{ij}(t) = d_{ij}(t), \forall i, j, t,$$
$$\sum_{i=1}^{I} d_{ij}(t) \leq 900 N_j, \forall j, t,$$
$$\sum_{j=1}^{J} b_{ij}(t) = D_i(t), \sum_{j=1}^{J} b_{ij}(t) L_{ij}/D_i(t) \leq L, \forall i, t. \tag{18}$$

This technique is reminiscent to [53]. This problem (18) is clearly equivalent to the original problem (12). Observe that the new formulation is in the ADMM form (13). The objective function is now separable over two sets of variables $d_{ij}(t)$ and $b_{ij}(t)$. $d_{ij}(t)$ controls the demand charge, while $b_{ij}(t)$ determines the energy charge. $d_{ij}(t)$ and $b_{ij}(t)$ are connected through an equality constraint. Overall, they control the provider's total energy cost of running the index servers.

The use of auxiliary variables also enables the separation of per-user and per-data center constraints, and is the key step towards reducing the complexity as we demonstrate now. The augmented Lagrangian of (18) is

$$L_\rho(d, b, \lambda) = \sum_j \max_{t \in [1,T]} E_j\left(\sum_{i=1}^{I} d_{ij}(t)\right) P_j^D + \sum_{i,j,t} E_j(b_{ij}(t)) P_j^E$$
$$+ \sum_{i,j,t} \left(\lambda_{ij}(t)(d_{ij}(t) - b_{ij}(t)) + \frac{\rho}{2}(d_{ij}(t) - b_{ij}(t))^2\right), \tag{19}$$

where d, b, λ are shorthands for $\{d_{ij}(t)\}, \{b_{ij}(t)\}, \{\lambda_{ij}(t)\}$.

The dual problem is solved by updating d and b sequentially. At the k-th iteration, the d-minimization step tries to minimize $L_\rho(d, b^{k-1}, \lambda^{k-1})$ over d with the capacity constraints (10) according to (15). By inspecting (19), we can readily see that this is *decomposable* over data centers since all terms related to d are separable over j. Effectively, each data center needs to independently solve the following sub-problem:

$$\min_d \max_{t \in [1,T]} E_j \left(\sum_{i=1}^{I} d_{ij}(t) \right) P_j^D$$
$$+ \sum_{i,t} d_{ij}(t) \left(\lambda_{ij}^{k-1}(t) + \frac{\rho}{2} \left(d_{ij}(t) - b_{ij}^{k-1}(t) \right) \right)$$
$$\text{s.t.} \sum_{i=1}^{I} d_{ij}(t) \leq 900 N_j, \forall t. \tag{20}$$

The physical meaning of the per-data center problem is simple. Each data center computes the optimal request routing solution d that minimizes the sum of its demand charge and the penalty of violating the constraint $d = b^{k-1}$. In other words, the data center also takes into account the users' perspective of the problem represented by b^{k-1}, eventually making sure that both parties converge to the same global optimal solution.

The per-data center sub-problem is a much simpler convex problem with $O(10^7)$ variables and only $T = O(10^2)$ constraints. Since the constraints are not coupled across multiple dimensions as in (12), it can now be efficiently solved using a standard optimization solver.

We have solved the d-minimization step distributively across all data centers by decomposing into J per-data center sub-problem in the form (20). After obtaining the solution d^k, the b-minimization step can also be similarly attacked.

According to (16), the b-minimization step tries to minimize $L_\rho(d^k, b, \lambda^{k-1})$ over b with the workload conservation constraints $\sum_j b_{ij}(t) = D_i(t), \forall i, t$. Readily it can be seen that this can also be decomposed across users, where each user independently solves the following per-user sub-problem:

$$\min_b \sum_j \left(E_j \left(b_{ij}(t) \right) P_j^E + \frac{\rho}{2} b_{ij}^2(t) + \left(\rho d_{ij}^k(t) - \lambda_{ij}^{k-1}(t) \right) b_{ij}(t) \right)$$
$$\text{s.t.} \sum_j b_{ij}(t) = D_i(t), \sum_j b_{ij}(t) L_{ij}/D_i(t) \leq L, \tag{21}$$

which a simple quadratic program for $E_j()$ is linear. Again, the formulation embodies an intuitive interpretation. Here user i, at each t, optimizes its request routing strategy $\{b_{ij}(t)\}$ according to the prices $\{P_j^E\}$ to minimize the energy charge. Meanwhile, it also considers the data center's optimal solution that mainly concerns the demand charge, by staying close to $d_{ij}^k(t)$ and minimizing the quadratic penalty term as much as it can.

Having obtained the optimal d^k and b^k, the final step is to perform the dual variable update:

$$\lambda_{ij}^k = \lambda_{ij}^{k-1} + \rho(d_{ij}^k - b_{ij}^k). \tag{22}$$

The entire procedure is summarized in Algorithm 2. Since the constraint set for d is clearly bounded in our problem, according to [20] the algorithm converges to the optimal solution.

Lemma 1. *Our algorithm based on ADMM converges to the optimal solution d^* and b^* of (18) and equivalently (12).*

Algorithm 2 *Optimal Distributed Solution for (12)*

---

1. Initialize $d^0 = 0$, $b^0 = 0$, $\lambda^0 = 0$, $\rho = 1$.
2. At k-th iteration, solve J per-data center sub-problems (20) in parallel. Obtain d^k.
3. Given d^k, solve $I \cdot T$ per-user sub-problems (21) in parallel. Obtain b^k.
4. Update dual variables λ^k as in (22).
5. Return to step 2 until convergence.

Now to summarize, our algorithm follows a divide-and-conquer paradigm. Recall that d controls the demand charge of processing the requests, while b determines the energy charge. Our algorithm separately optimizes d and b for either aspect of the problem. Additionally, the penalty terms (i.e. the Augmented Lagrangian) force d and b to stay close to each other, eventually ensuring that they converge to the same request routing solution which is also optimal.

4.4 Implementation Issues of Algorithm 2

The distributed nature of Algorithm 2 allows for an efficient parallel implementation in a data center that has abundant server resources. Here we discuss several issues pertaining to such an implementation in reality.

First, at each iteration, step 2 can be implemented on J servers, each solving one instance of the large-scale per-data center sub-problem (20). Step 3 can be implemented even on a single server since it only involves solving quadratic programs (21). A multi-threaded implementation can further speed up the algorithm on multi-core hardware. Thus only J servers are required to run the distributed algorithm.

Second, our algorithm can be terminated before convergence is reached. This is because ADMM is not sensitive to step size ρ, and usually finds a solution with modest accuracy within tens of iterations [22]. A solution with modest accuracy is sufficient in situations of flash crowds of requests and failure recovery. The operator can apply an early-braking mechanism in these cases to terminate the algorithm pre-maturely without much performance loss.

Finally, the message passing overhead of our algorithm is also low. The request routing decisions d need to be disseminated to the mapping nodes and data centers. All the other message passing, for exchanging d, b, and λ amongst servers, happens in the internal network of the designated data center, which in many cases is specifically designed to handle the broadcast and shuffle transmission patterns of HPC applications such as MapReduce [17]. The amount of intermediate data our algorithm produces is much smaller than the bulky data of HPC applications [49]. Thus the message passing overhead incurred to the data center network is low.

5. EVALUATION

To realistically evaluate the cost reduction of partial execution with our algorithms, we conduct trace-driven simulations in this section.

5.1 Setup

We use the Wikipedia request traces [47] to represent the Web search request traffic of a data center. The dataset we use contains, among other things, 10% of all user requests issued to Wikipedia from a 30-day period of September 2007. The prediction of workload can be done accurately as demonstrated by previous work, and in the simulation we simply adopt the measured request traffic as the total demand. The scheduling period is 15 minutes, and the planning horizon T is one day as mentioned in Sec. 3. Fig. 2 plots the request traffic of the traces for 24 hours of the measurement period. The scale of the traces closely matches Google's search traffic, which is roughly 1.2 trillion annual searches in 2012 [12], or equivalently 2.7 million searches per 15 minutes per data center with its 13 data centers [1].

We consider six Google data centers in the U.S. We scale the Wikipedia traffic trace by a factor of six, and time shift it according to the time differences of these locations to synthesize the total demand of the six data centers. In the case of a single data center, the original trace is used. We rely on iPlane [39], a system that collects wide-area network statistics from Planetlab vantage points, to obtain the latency information. We set the number of clients $|\mathcal{I}| = 10^5$, and choose 10^5 IP prefixes from a RouteViews [13] dump. We then extract the corresponding round trip latency information from the iPlane logs, which contain traceroutes made to a large number of IP addresses from Planetlab nodes. We only use latency measurements from Planetlab nodes that are close to our data center locations. Since the Wikipedia traces do not contain any client information, to emulate the geographical distribution of requests, we split the total request traffic among the clients following a normal distribution.

Each data center has $N = N_j = 5,000$ index servers[2], so it can process 4.5 million requests every 15 minutes according to (1), while the peak demand of our trace is about 3.4 million requests. We use the contract prices of the local electric utilities that power these Google data centers as detailed in Sec. 2.1. We assume a server's idle and peak power are $E_I = 400$ W and $E_P = 750$ W, respectively, which are typical for a data center server [48].

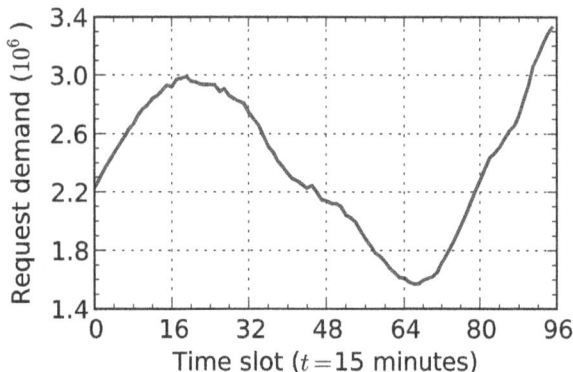

Figure 2: Total request traffic of the Wikipedia traces [47].

5.2 The Case of One Data Center

We start with one data center, and evaluate the benefit of partial execution with Algorithm 1. We solve the workload scheduling problem (6) on a daily basis for the 30-day

---

[2]A data center has more than just index servers. Here we focus on index servers with partial execution.

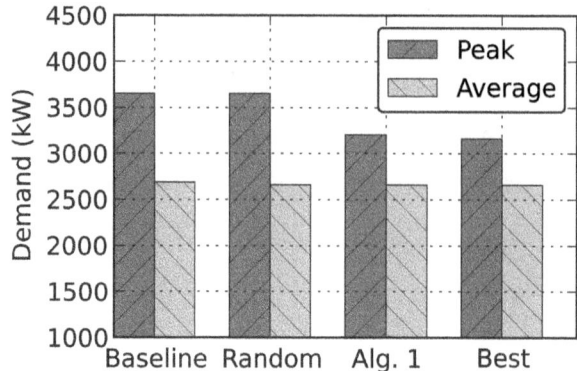

Figure 3: Monthly power consumption comparison for one data center.

period, to obtain the monthly bill. We compare the performance of Algorithm 1, called Alg. 1, with three benchmarks. The first one, called Baseline, is a naive approach that does not use partial execution, and the data center is always operating in the high power mode. The second one, called Random, uses partial execution randomly without our workload scheduling algorithm. This represents state-of-the-art that exploits partial execution for improving latency while satisfying SLA [32], instead of using it to reduce the demand charge. The third one, called Best, assumes that complete demand information for the entire 30-day period is known, and uses Algorithm 1 to obtain the optimal schedule with minimum cost. This benchmark helps us understand the impact of limited future knowledge about the workload demand on reducing energy cost.

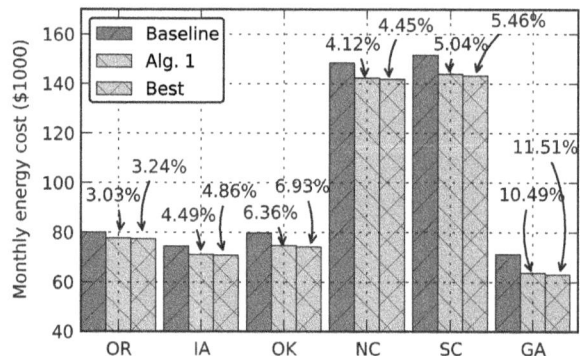

Figure 4: Monthly energy cost comparison for one data center.

Fig. 3 plots the monthly power consumption breakdowns, including both the peak and average demand, for the three benchmarks. Note that this calculation includes server idle power. All schemes reduce the average demand by 5% compared to Baseline, which is the maximum that the SLA allows. First notice that Random only marginally reduces the peak power demand by 0.02%, since it does not utilize partial execution strategically at times when demand is high. Our Algorithm 1 utilizes limited (1-day) information that is practically available, and optimizes the partial execution schedule. Thus it is able to reduce the peak demand more substantially than Random by 12.17%. Also observe that when we have perfect future knowledge, Best reduces the peak demand by 13.36%, only slightly higher than Alg. 1.

This demonstrates that limited future knowledge provides close-to-optimal peak reduction with partial execution.

Fig. 4 shows the monthly energy cost comparison by using the contract prices of all six utilities in order to understand how much cost saving our idea can offer. Clearly we see that given the same demand series and partial execution schedules the total cost varies wildly depending on the prices. NC and SC are the most expensive locations while others are much cheaper. In all cases, Alg. 1 offers 3.04% to 10.49% total cost reductions compared to Baseline without partial execution, and is again very close to Best. The improvement becomes more salient for locations where demand charge is more significant than energy charge, such as OK and GA. In dollar terms, cost savings range from about $2,400 to $7,600 per month. Though the amount seems small for a data center, with the rapid increase of user demand and energy cost even a single digit of cost saving is crucial for operators. Moreover, an operator usually deploys multiple data centers, in which case the cost savings multiply and become more substantial even without optimizing request routing.

5.3 The Case of Geo-distributed Data Centers

We now look at the case of multiple geo-distributed data centers, and examine more closely the cost savings from optimizing request routing, and the performance of Algorithm 2. To do this we turn off partial execution in this set of simulation. We have three benchmarks here. The first, called Baseline, directs user requests to the closest data center as long as capacity allows, and does not attempt to reduce energy cost. The second, called Energy, optimizes request routing only for energy charge, i.e. it only considers the per kWh price and directs user requests to locations where the per kWh price is cheap while conforming to the average latency requirements. This represents a large class of existing works that shift workloads according to geographical diversity of the energy prices [27, 35, 37, 44, 45, 52]. On the other hand, the third, called Demand, optimizes request routing only for demand charge, and tries to smooth out the demand patterns at locations where the per kW price is high. Finally, Alg. 2 refers to our Algorithm 2 that optimizes for both demand and energy charge, subject to the latency constraint.

Fig. 5 shows the breakdowns of the total cost for all six data centers. Observe that the total cost stands around $600K, with $230K demand charge and $380K energy charge as Baseline shows. Energy improves the situation by lowering the energy charge. However, it actually incurs a higher demand charge than Baseline, as it shifts demands to locations with cheaper per kWh price where the per kW prices are not necessarily cheaper. Also the demand series are more fluctuating at those locations. Both factors contribute to the higher demand charge. Demand, on the other hand, effectively reduces the demand charge, with only marginally reduced energy cost. By taking into account both factors, Alg. 2 offers the most cost savings as expected. In all cases, the latency constraint (9) is always satisfied. This confirms the benefits of request routing optimization for geo-distributed data centers.

Fig. 6 further plots the percentage of cost savings provided by different schemes compared to Baseline. Energy and Demand provide 10.8% and 9.8% cost savings, while Alg. 2 is able to offer 14% cost savings. We also calculate the cost savings of joint request routing and partial execution

by using Algorithm 2 together with Algorithm 1, shown as Alg.2 + Alg.1 in the figure. It provides 15.5% cost reduction, amounting to around a monthly saving of $85K for six data centers. Our results establish that our workload scheduling and request routing algorithms are effective in reducing the total energy cost for practical-scale data centers.

5.4 Convergence

We now investigate the convergence and running time of our ADMM based Algorithm 2. For comparison, we use the subgradient method [21] to solve the dual problem of the transformed optimization (18) with the augmented Lagrangian (19). Specifically, the primal variables α and β are jointly optimized instead of sequentially updated as in our ADMM algorithm, and the dual variables λ are updated by the subgradient method. The step size is carefully chosen according to the diminishing step size rule [21].

Fig. 7 plots the CDF of the number of iterations the two algorithms take to achieve convergence for the 30 runs on the traces. Our ADMM algorithm converges much faster than the subgradient methods. Our algorithm takes at most 46 iterations to converge in the worse case, and for 80% of the time converges within 33 iterations. The subgradient method takes at least 72 iterations to converge, and for 80% of the time takes more than 110 iterations. This shows the fast convergence of our ADMM algorithm compared to conventional methods.

6. RELATED WORK

Many related works on thermal management and workload shifting to reduce data center energy cost have been discussed in Sec. 1. Only energy charge is considered in these works. Some other efforts include dynamically shutting down and waking up idle servers [35], using battery and/or on-site generators to absorb workload spikes [30, 46], etc. These proposals are orthogonal to our approach using partial execution. A recent work [38] focuses on the coincidental peak charge which is a form of demand response programs voluntary for data centers to participate to help better balance the grid. Wang et al. [50] consider workload dropping and delaying with penalties to reduce data cente renergy cost, including a peak-based component. We conduct an empirical analysis with real-world contracts from electric utilities which are not present in [38,50], and explicitly focus on reducing the demand charge through the novel use of partial execution.

For partial execution, besides those discussed in Sec. 2.2, [18] develops a flexible system that allows many programs to take advantage of approximation opportunities in a systematic manner to reduce energy. This enables the general implementation of partial execution while we focus more on the algorithmic challenges brought by partial execution and demand charge. We also present a model from empirical data to quantify the trade-off between response quality and energy usage, which has not been studied.

7. CONCLUSION

We proposed to use partial execution to reduce the peak power demand and total energy cost of data centers, given the importance of demand charge as established by our empirical study of real-world electricity contracts. We studied the resulting workload scheduling problem with SLA con-

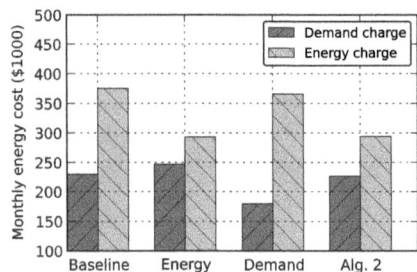

Figure 5: Cost breakdown comparison for geo-distributed data centers.

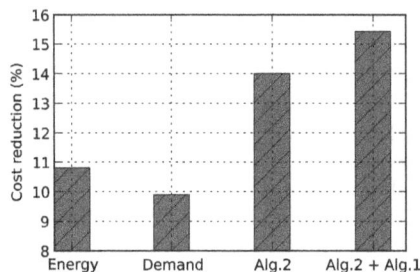

Figure 6: Cost reduction compared to Baseline.

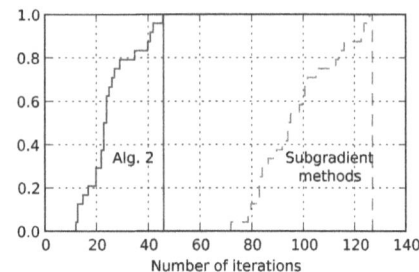

Figure 7: CDF of number of iterations.

straints in detail. The case with a single data center can be optimally solved. For geo-distributed data centers, we tackled the large-scale joint optimization of request routing and workload scheduling following a decoupling approach. Request routing is solved using an efficient distributed algorithm based on ADMM that decomposes the global problem into many sub-problems, each of which can be quickly solved. Trace-driven simulations are conducted to evaluate the algorithm's performance. As future work, we plan to more thoroughly study the impact of partial execution on demand response mechanisms of data centers.

Acknowledgment

The work was supported in part by the Start-up Grant NO. 7200366 from City University of Hong Kong,

We would like to thank Yuxiong He from Microsoft Research Redmond for providing the response quality data from Bing, as well as insightful suggestions on the ideas of this paper. We also thank Minghua Chen from The Chinese University of Hong Kong, and Shaolei Ren from Florida International University for their encouragement and helpful discussions.

8. REFERENCES

[1] https://www.google.com/about/datacenters/inside/locations/.
[2] http://www.cs.cityu.edu.hk/~hxu/share/Contracts.zip.
[3] http://www.oregonlive.com/business/index.ssf/2011/11/do_centers_get_more_than_they.html.
[4] http://www.nwasco.com/commercial-rates.cfm.
[5] http://www.midamericanenergy.com/rates1.aspx.
[6] http://googleblog.blogspot.ca/2012/09/more-renewable-energy-for-our-data.html.
[7] http://www.grda.com/electric/customer-service/wholesale-sales/.
[8] http://googleblog.blogspot.ca/2013/04/expanding-options-for-companies-to-buy.html.
[9] http://www.duke-energy.com/rates/progress-north-carolina.asp.
[10] http://www.sceg.com/en/commercial-and-industrial/rates/electric-rates/default.htm.
[11] http://www.georgiapower.com/pricing/business/large-business.cshtml.
[12] http://www.google.com/zeitgeist/2012/#the-world.
[13] http://www.routeviews.org.
[14] Google details, and defends, its use of electricity. http://www.nytimes.com/2011/09/09/technology/google-details-and-defends-its-use-of-electricity.html, September 2011.
[15] Google throws open doors to its top-secret data center. http://www.wired.com/wiredenterprise/2012/10/ff-inside-google-data-center/all/, October 2012.
[16] http://en.wikipedia.org/wiki/ISO_RTO, 2013.
[17] M. Al-Fares, A. Loukissas, and A. Vahdat. A scalable, commodity data center network architecture. In Proc. ACM SIGCOMM, 2008.
[18] W. Baek and T. M. Chilimbi. Green: A framework for supporting energy-conscious programming using controlled approximation. In Proc. ACM PLDI, 2010.
[19] C. Bash and G. Forman. Cool job allocation: Measuring the power savings of placing jobs at cooling-efficient locations in the data center. In Proc. USENIX ATC, 2007.
[20] D. P. Bertsekas and J. N. Tsitsiklis. Parallel and Distributed Computation: Numerical Methods. Athena Scientific, 1997.
[21] S. Boyd and A. Mutapcic. Subgradient methods. Lecture notes of EE364b, Stanford University, Winter Quarter 2006-2007. http://www.stanford.edu/class/ee364b/notes/subgrad_method_notes.pdf.
[22] S. Boyd, N. Parikh, E. Chu, B. Peleato, and J. Eckstein. Distributed optimization and statistical learning via the alternating direction method of multipliers. Foundations and Trends in Machine Learning, 3(1):1–122, 2010.
[23] Y. Chen, D. Gmach, C. Hyser, Z. Wang, C. Bash, C. Hoover, and S. Singhal. Integrated management of application performance, power and cooling in datacenters. In Proc. NOMS, 2010.
[24] M. Chiang, S. H. Low, A. R. Calderbank, and J. C. Doyle. Layering as optimization decomposition: A mathematical theory of network architectures. Proc. IEEE, 95(1):255–312, January 2007.
[25] J. Dean. Achieving rapid response times in large online services. Berkeley AMPLab Cloud Seminar, http://research.google.com/people/jeff/latency.html, March 2012.
[26] X. Fan, W.-D. Weber, and L. A. Barroso. Power provisioning for a warehouse-sized computer. In Proc. ACM/IEEE Intl. Symp. Computer Architecture (ISCA), 2007.
[27] P. X. Gao, A. R. Curtis, B. Wong, and S. Keshav. It's not easy being green. In Proc. ACM SIGCOMM, 2012.
[28] Georgia Power. Power and light high load factor schedule: "PLH-8".

`http://www.georgiapower.com/pricing/files/`
`rates-and-schedules/5.10_plh-8.pdf`.

[29] Z. Gong, X. Gu, and J. Wilkes. PRESS: PRedictive Elastic ReSource Scaling for cloud systems. In *Proc. IEEE CNSM*, 2010.

[30] S. Govindan, D. Wang, A. Sivasubramaniam, and B. Urgaonkar. Aggressive datacenter power provisioning with batteries. *ACM Trans. Comput. Syst.*, 31(1):1–31, February 2013.

[31] A. Greenberg, J. Hamilton, D. A. Maltz, and P. Patel. The Cost of a Cloud: Research Problems in Data Center Networks. *SIGCOMM Comput. Commun. Rev.*, 39(1):68–73, 2009.

[32] Y. He, S. Elnikety, J. Larus, and C. Yan. Zeta: Scheduling interactive services with partial execution. In *Proc. ACM SoCC*, 2012.

[33] M. R. Hestenes. Multiplier and gradient methods. *Journal of Optimization Theory and Applications*, 4(5):303–320, 1969.

[34] R. Krishnan, H. V. Madhyastha, S. Srinivasan, S. Jain, A. Krishnamurthy, T. Anderson, and J. Gao. Moving beyond end-to-end path information to optimize CDN performance. In *Proc. ACM IMC*, 2009.

[35] M. Lin, A. Wierman, L. L. H. Andrew, and E. Thereska. Dynamic right-sizing for power-proportional data centers. In *Proc. IEEE INFOCOM*, 2011.

[36] Z. Liu, Y. Chen, C. Bash, A. Wierman, D. Gmach, Z. Wang, M. Marwah, and C. Hyser. Renewable and cooling aware workload management for sustainable data centers. In *Proc. ACM Sigmetrics*, 2012.

[37] Z. Liu, M. Lin, A. Wierman, S. H. Low, and L. L. Andrew. Greening geographical load balancing. In *Proc. ACM Sigmetrics*, 2011.

[38] Z. Liu, A. Wierman, Y. Chen, and B. Razon. Data center demand response: Avoiding the coincident peak via workload shifting and local generation. In *Proc. ACM Sigmetrics*, 2013.

[39] H. V. Madhyastha, T. Isdal, M. Piatek, C. Dixon, T. Anderson, A. Krishnamurthy, and A. Venkataramani. iPlane: An information plane for distributed services. In *Proc. USENIX OSDI*, 2006.

[40] D. A. Maltz. Challenges in cloud scale data centers. In *Keynote, ACM Sigmetrics*, 2013.

[41] H. Mittelmann. Mixed integer linear programming benchmark (serial codes). `http://plato.asu.edu/ftp/milpf.html`, 2011.

[42] D. Niu, H. Xu, B. Li, and S. Zhao. Quality-assured cloud bandwidth auto-scaling for video-on-demand applications. In *Proc. IEEE INFOCOM*, 2012.

[43] E. Nygren, R. K. Sitaraman, and J. Sun. The Akamai network: A platform for high-performance Internet applications. *SIGOPS Oper. Syst. Rev.*, 44(3):2–19, August 2010.

[44] A. Qureshi, R. Weber, H. Balakrishnan, J. Guttag, and B. Maggs. Cutting the electricity bill for Internet-scale systems. In *Proc. ACM SIGCOMM*, 2009.

[45] L. Rao, X. Liu, L. Xie, and W. Liu. Minimizing electricity cost: Optimization of distributed Internet data centers in a multi-electricity-market environment. In *Proc. IEEE INFOCOM*, 2010.

[46] J. Tu, L. Lu, M. Chen, and R. K. Sitaraman. Dynamic provisioning in next-generation data centers with on-site power production. In *Proc. ACM e-Energy*, 2013.

[47] G. Urdaneta, G. Pierre, and M. van Steen. Wikipedia workload analysis for decentralized hosting. *Elsevier Computer Networks*, 53(11):1830–1845, July 2009.

[48] A. Vasan, A. Sivasubramaniam, V. Shimpi, T. Sivabalan, and R. Subbiah. Worth their watts? — An empirical study of datacenter servers. In *Proc. IEEE HPCA*, 2010.

[49] V. Vasudevan, A. Phanishayee, H. Shah, E. Krevat, D. G. Andersen, G. R. Ganger, G. A. Gibson, and B. Mueller. Safe and effective fine-grained TCP retransmissions for datacenter communication. In *Proc. ACM SIGCOMM*, 2009.

[50] C. Wang, B. Urgaonkar, Q. Wang, G. Kesidis, and A. Sivasubramaniam. Data center power cost optimization via workload modulation. In *Proc. IEEE/ACM International Conference on Utility and Cloud Computing (UCC)*, 2013.

[51] P. Wendell, J. W. Jiang, M. J. Freedman, and J. Rexford. DONAR: Decentralized server selection for cloud services. In *Proc. ACM SIGCOMM*, 2010.

[52] H. Xu, C. Feng, and B. Li. Temperature aware workload management in geo-distributed datacenters. In *Proc. USENIX ICAC*, 2013.

[53] H. Xu and B. Li. Joint request mapping and response routing for geo-distributed cloud services. In *Proc. IEEE INFOCOM*, 2013.

[54] R. Zhou, Z. Wang, A. McReynolds, C. Bash, T. Christian, and R. Shih. Optimization and control of cooling microgrids for data centers. In *Proc. IEEE ITherm*, 2012.

A Measurement-based Analysis of the Energy Consumption of Data Center Servers

Jordi Arjona Aroca[*], Angelos Chatzipapas[+,*], Antonio Fernández Anta[+], and Vincenzo Mancuso[+,*]

[*]University Carlos III of Madrid, Spain   [+]IMDEA Networks Institute, Madrid, Spain

{jorge.arjona, angelos.chatzipapas, antonio.fernandez, vincenzo.mancuso}@imdea.org

ABSTRACT

Energy consumption is a growing issue in data centers, impacting their economic viability and their public image. In this work we empirically characterize the power and energy consumed by different types of servers. In particular, in order to understand the behavior of their energy and power consumption, we perform measurements in different servers. In each of them, we exhaustively measure the power consumed by the CPU, the disk, and the network interface under different configurations, identifying the optimal operational levels. One interesting conclusion of our study is that the curve that defines the minimal CPU power as a function of the load is neither linear nor purely convex as has been previously assumed. Moreover, we find that the efficiency of the various server components can be maximized by tuning the CPU frequency and the number of active cores as a function of the system and network load, while the block size of I/O operations should be always maximized by applications. We also show how to estimate the energy consumed by an application as a function of some simple parameters, like the CPU load, and the disk and network activity. We validate the proposed approach by accurately estimating the energy of a map-reduce computation in a Hadoop platform.

Categories and Subject Descriptors

B.8.2 [**Performance and reliability**]: Performance Analysis and Design Aids ; C.4 [**Performance of systems**]: *Measurement techniques*.

General Terms

Measurement, Performance, Experimentation.

Keywords

Measurements; Power and energy consumption; DVFS; CPU; Network; Disk I/O.

1. INTRODUCTION

Massive data centers are becoming common nowadays. Large companies such as Google, Yahoo!, Amazon or Microsoft have deployed large data centers, housing tens of thousands of servers, and consuming a huge amount of energy every year. According to Van Heddeghem *et al.* [8], data centers' total energy consumption in 2012 was about 270 *TWh*, which corresponds to almost 2% of the global electricity consumption, and has an approximated annual growth rate of 4.3%. This trend has driven researchers all over the world to focus on energy efficiency in data centers. Examples of energy saving techniques proposed during the recent years are virtualization plus consolidation and scheduling optimization [12, 17]. However, industry requirements keep increasing, and more research is necessary.

In this paper, out of all possible components of a data center, e.g., servers, routers, switches, etc., we concentrate on the characterization of servers and the energy they consume. Indeed, in order to obtain full benefit of the aforementioned energy-efficient techniques, it is crucial to have a good characterization of servers in the data center, as a function of the utilization of the server's components. That is, it is necessary to know and understand the energy and power consumption of servers and how this changes under the different configurations. There is a large body of literature on characterizing servers' energy and power consumption. However, the existing literature does not jointly consider phenomena like the irruption of multicore servers and dynamic voltage and frequency scaling (DVFS) [21], which are key to achieve scalability and flexibility in the architecture of a server. With these new parameters, more variables come into play in a server configuration. Learning how to deal with these new parameters and how they interact with other variables is important since this may lead to larger savings.

It has been traditionally considered that the CPU is responsible for most of the power being consumed in a server, and that this power increases linearly with the load. Although the power consumed by the CPU is significant, we believe that the power incurred by other elements of the server, like disks and NICs (Network Interface Cards) are not negligible, and have to be taken into account. Moreover, we believe that the assumption that CPU power consumption depends linearly from the load in a server may be too simplistic, especially when the server has multiple cores and may operate at multiple frequencies. In fact, even the way load is expressed has to be carefully defined (e.g., it cannot be defined as a proportion of the maximal computational capacity of the CPU, since this value changes with the operational frequency). Therefore, more complex/complete models for the power consumed by a server are necessary. In order to be consistent, these models have to be based on empirical values. However, we found that there is a lack of empirical work studying servers energy behavior.

Our work tries to partially fill this void by proposing a measurement-based characterization of the energy consumption of a server components with DVFS and multiple cores. We evaluate here different server machines and evaluate what is the contribution to their power consumption of the CPU, hard drive disk, and network card (NIC). Our results support, for instance, our belief that more complex models than linear are required for CPU power consumption. From the measurements obtained from the servers we evaluate, we propose a holistic energy consumption characterization, that accounts for the power consumed by CPU, disk, and NIC. Our approach captures the influence of the processing frequency and the multiple cores, not only to the CPU power consumption, but also to that of disk input/output (I/O) and NIC activity.

Main results and contributions.

Our main contributions are of two kinds: (*i*) we propose a methodology for empirically characterizing the energy consumption of a server, and (*ii*) we provide novel insights on the power and energy consumption behavior of the most relevant server's components.

As concerns the methodology, we observe that *active CPU cycles per second* (ACPS) is a convenient metric of CPU load in architectures using multiple frequencies and cores. We show how to isolate the contribution to energy/power consumption due to CPU, disk I/O operations, and network activity by just measuring the total server power consumption and a few activity indicators reported by the operating system. We also show that the *baseline* power consumption of a server—i.e., the power consumed just because the server is on—has a strong weight on the total server consumption.

As concerns the components' characterization, we show that, besides the *baseline component*, the CPU has the largest impact among all components, and its power consumption is not linear with the load. Disk I/O operations are the second highest cause of consumption, and their efficiency is strongly affected by the I/O block size used by the application. Eventually, network activity plays a minor yet not negligible role in the energy/power consumption, and the network impact scales almost linearly with the network transmission rate. All other components can be accounted for in the *baseline* power consumption, which is subject to minor variations under different operational conditions.

The main results of our campaign of measurements and analysis can be listed as follows:

- The CPU consumption depends on the number of active cores, the CPU frequency, and the load (in ACPS units). Our measurements confirm that the power consumption with a single active core at constant frequency can be closely approximated by a linear function of the load. However, given a CPU frequency, the power consumption is a concave function of the load and can be approximated by a low-order polynomial. The power consumption for a fixed load is, in general, minimized by using the highest number of cores and the lowest frequency at which the load can be served. However, the minimum achievable power consumption is a piecewise concave function of the load.

- The power consumed by hard disks for reading and writing depends on CPU frequency and I/O block sizes. Both reading and writing costs increase slightly with the CPU frequency. While the consumption due to reading is not affected by block size, the power consumed when writing increases with the block size. The reading efficiency (expressed in MB/J) is barely affected by the CPU frequency, while writing efficiency is a concave function of the block size since it boosts the throughput of writing until a saturation value is reached.

- The power consumption and the efficiency of the NIC, both in transmission and reception, depends on the CPU frequency, the packet size, and the transmission rate. The efficiency of data transmission increases almost linearly with the transmission rate, with steeper slopes corresponding to lower CPU frequencies. Although a linear relation between transmission rate and efficiency holds for data reception as well, small packet sizes yield higher efficiency in reception.

- Overall, we provide a holistic energy consumption model that only requires a few calibration parameters for every different server that we want to evaluate (a universal power model will be too simplistic and inaccurate). We validate our model by means of a server computing the *pagerank* metric of a graph in a *Hadoop* platform, with bulky network activity, and we found that the error due our energy estimates is below 7%.

The power due to memory is not considered separately, but as part of the other components' consumption.

The rest of the paper is organized as follows. Section 2 describes the methodology we used for our experiments. Section 3 presents the measurements we collected for our tested servers, for every single component that we evaluated. Sections 4 is devoted to modeling the power consumption of the servers based on calibration parameters that we have found with our measurements. Section 5 discusses our findings and their implications. Section 6 provides information about related works and, finally, Section 7 concludes the paper.

2. METHODOLOGY

In this section we introduce the measurement techniques we used to characterize the power consumption of CPU activity, disk access (read and write operations), and network activity. Our measurements start characterizing the CPU power consumption, from where we obtain information about the baseline power consumption of the system. After CPU and baseline characterization, we follow with experiments for the other two components, namely, disk and network. Note that CPU and baseline measurements are of capital importance in order to evaluate the other components, because any operation run in a machine is like a puzzle with multiple pieces and we must know what is the contribution of each one of these pieces. Consider that, we are paying a cost just for having a server switched on and the operating system running on it. Similarly, every time we run a task in the system, some CPU cycles are needed in order to execute it as well as to use the component that has to perform the task. Hence, in order to understand the contribution of any component, we first need to identify the contribution of the CPU and compute the difference with respect to the aforementioned baseline.

To explore the possible parameters determining the power consumption of a server and to gain statistic consistency we run our experiments multiple times. Similarly, we run these experiments in different servers and architectures in order to validate our results and give consistency to our conclusions.

2.1 Collecting system data and fixing frequency parameters

One prerequisite for our experiments was having Linux machines due to the kind of commands and benchmarks we wanted to use and, mainly, because of the possibility of adding some kernel modules and utilities,[1] which allows us to change CPU frequencies at will. In a Linux system, CPU activity stats are constantly logged, so we can periodically read the core frequency and the number of *active* and *passive* CPU ticks at each core.[2] Once we have the number of ticks and the core frequency, since a tick represents a hundredth of second, cycles can be calculated as 100 *ticks/frequency*.

We use active cycles per second (ACPS) instead of CPU load percentage to characterize CPU load because the latter depends on the CPU frequency used, as the higher the frequency the more the work that can be processed. Hence, a percentage of load is not comparable when different frequencies are used, while the amount of ACPS that can be processed can be considered as an absolute magnitude. In order to get (set) information about the operative frequency of the system we used the `cpufrequtils` package.[3] With those tools, we can monitor the CPU frequency at which the system works and assign different frequencies to the cores. However, to limit the number of possible combinations to characterize, we fix the frequency to be the same for all cores.

2.2 CPU

In order to evaluate the CPU power consumption we prepared a script based on the benchmark application, namely `lookbusy`.[4] Note that `lookbusy` allows us to load one or more CPU cores with the same load. Our `lookbusy`-based experiment follows the next steps: we first fix the CPU frequency to the lowest possible frequency in the system; then we run `lookbusy` with fixed amount of load for one core during timeslots of 30 seconds, starting with the maximum load and then decreasing the load gradually. After the last `lookbusy` run we measure the power consumed during an additional timeslot with *no* `lookbusy` load offered. We register the active cycles and the power used during each timeslot.

After taking these different samples for one frequency we move to the immediately higher frequency (we can list and change frequencies thanks to `cpufrequtils`) and repeat the previous steps. After going through all the available frequencies, we restart the whole process but increasing by one

the number of active cores. We repeat this whole process until all the cores of the server are active. Note that when we change the frequency of the cores we change it in all of them, active or not, for consistency. Similarly, when we have more than one active core, the load for all the active cores will be the same.

Once explained the scheme of our experiments, we must clarify the meaning of running a timeslot with *no* load. Note that zero-load is clearly not possible as there is always going to be load in the system due to, e.g., the operating system. However, during the timeslot in which we do not run `lookbusy`, we measure the power corresponding to the operational conditions which are as close as possible to the ones of an idle system. Moreover, the decision of using timeslots of 30 seconds is to guarantee enough, yet not excessive, time for the measurements. In fact, as we start and stop `lookbusy` at the beginning and end of the timeslots, we need to ignore the first and the last few seconds of measurements in each timeslot to avoid measurement noise due to power ramps and operational transitions.

The measured values of load (in ACPS) and power in each timeslot are used to obtain a least squares polynomial fittings curve. These fittings characterize the CPU power consumption for each combination of frequency and number of active cores. We will use as *baseline power consumption* of each one of these configurations the zero-order coefficient of the polynomial of these fittings curves.

2.3 Disks

The power consumption of the hard drive was evaluated using 2 different scripts (for reading and writing) based on the `dd` linux command.[5] We chose `dd` as it allows us to read files, write files from scratch, control the size of the blocks we write (read), control the amount of blocks written (read) and force the commit of writing operations after each block in order to reduce the effect of operating system caches and memory. We combine this tool with flushing the RAM and caches after each reading experiment.

In both our scripts we perform write (read) operations for a set of different I/O block sizes and for different data volumes to be written (read). In each case we record the CPU active cycles, the total power and time consumed in each one of these operations for each combination of block size and available frequency.

Finally, we identify the contribution of the hard drive to the total power consumption by subtracting the contribution of both the baseline and the CPU consumption from the measured total power.

Disk I/O experiments shed light on the relevance of the block sizes when reading or writing as well as whether there is an influence of the frequency on these operations.

2.4 Network

In order to evaluate the contribution of the network to the power consumption of a server, we devised a set of experiments based on the `iperf`[6] tool as well as on our own UPD-client-server C script.

There are several aspects that we consider relevant in order to characterize the impact of the NIC on the total power consumption of a server and that led us to choose these two tools. The first is the ability of performing tests where the

---

[1] For instance cpufrequtils, acpi-cpufreq.

[2] File `/proc/stat` reports the number of ticks since the computer started devoted to *user*, *niced* and *system* processes, waiting (*iowait*), processing interrupts (i.e., *irq* and *softirq*), and *idle*. In our experiments we count both waiting and idle ticks as *passive* ticks, while we denote the aggregated value of the rest of ticks as *active*.

[3] `https://wiki.archlinux.org/index.php/CPU_Frequency_Scaling`

[4] `http://www.devin.com/lookbusy`.

[5] `http://linux.die.net/man/1/dd`.

[6] `http://iperf.fr/`

Table 1: Characteristics of the servers under study

Component	Servers		
	Survivor	Nemesis	Erdos
CPU (# cores)	4	4	64
# freqs	8	11	5
Freqs List	1.2 _GHz_, 1.333 _GHz_, 1.467 _GHz_, 1.6 _GHz_, 1.733 _GHz_, 1.867 _GHz_, 2 _GHz_, 2.133 _GHz_	1.596 _GHz_, 1.729 _GHz_, 1.862 _GHz_, 1.995 _GHz_, 2.128 _GHz_, 2.261 _GHz_, 2.394 _GHz_, 2.527 _GHz_, 2.666 _GHz_, 2.793 _GHz_, 2.794 _GHz_	1.4 _GHz_, 1.6 _GHz_, 1.8 _GHz_, 2.1 _GHz_, 2.3 _GHz_
RAM	4 _GB_	4 _GB_	512 _GB_
Disk	2 _TB_	2 + 3 _TB_	2 × 146GB 4 × 1 _TB_
Network	1 _Gbps_	3 × 1 _Gbps_	4 × 1 _Gbps_, 2 × 10 _Gbps_

computer under study acts as a server (sender) or as a client (receiver) of the communication, in order to observe its behavior when sending data or receiving it. For the sake of clarity, we will use, from now on, the terms _sender_, for the server injecting traffic to the network, and _receiver_ for the server accepting traffic from the network. The second aspect consists in the ability to change several parameters that we consider relevant for this characterization, namely, the packet size and the offered load, jointly with the frequency of the system.

Our experiments consist, then, on measuring the data rate achieved, the CPU active cycles and the total power consumption of the server under study acting as sender or receiver when using different packet sizes and different rates. We run each experiment multiple times for statistical consistency.

Finally, in order to isolate the consumption from the network, we characterize with the CPU active cycles measured in the experiment the consumption due to the CPU and the baseline and subtract them from our measurements.

3. MEASUREMENTS

3.1 Devices and Setup

In order to monitor and store the instantaneous power consumed by a server during the different experiments we used a Voltech PM1000+ power analyzer,[7] which is able to measure the total instantaneous power consumed by the server under test on a per-second basis. In order to take our measurements we connected the server being measured to the power analyzer and the latter to the power supply. In the experiments where the network was not involved (CPU and disk), we unplugged the network cable from the server, which has an impact on the power consumption as the port goes idle. In the network based experiments we established an Ethernet connection between the server under study and a second machine in order to study the server behavior, both as a receiver as well as as a sender.

We evaluated three different servers: Survivor, Nemesis, and Erdos. We will now present these servers although their main characteristics, including their sets of available CPU frequencies, can be also found in Table 1. Survivor has an

---

[7] http://www.farnell.com/datasheets/320316.pdf

Intel Xeon E5606 4-core processor, with 4 _GB_ of RAM, a 2 _TB_ Seagate Barracuda XT hard drive and a 1 _Gigabit_ Ethernet card integrated in the motherboard. Nemesis is a Dell Precision T3500 with an Intel Xeon W3530 4-core processor, 4 _GB_ of RAM, 2 hard drives (a 2 _TB_ Seagate Barracuda XT and a 3 _TB_ Seagate Barracuda), a 1 _Gigabit_ Ethernet card integrated in the motherboard, and a separate Ethernet card with two 1 _Gigabit_ ports. In this study we only evaluate the Seagate Barracuda XT disk and the integrated Ethernet card. Both Survivor and Nemesis use the Ubuntu Server edition 10.4 LTS Linux distribution. Finally, Erdos is a Dell PowerEdge R815 with 4 AMD Opteron 6276 16-core processors (i.e., 64 cores in total), 512 _GB_ of RAM, two 146 _GB_ SAS hard drives configured as a single RAID1 system (which is the "disk" analyzed here) and four 1 _TB_ Near-line SAS hard drives. It also includes four 1 _Gigabit_ and two 10 _Gigabit_ ports. Erdos is a high-end server and uses Linux Debian 7 Wheezy.

3.2 Baseline and CPU

As mentioned in the previous section, for each server we have measured the power it consumes without disk accesses nor network traffic. We assume that the power consumption observed is the sum of the baseline consumption plus the power consumed by the CPU. We have obtained samples of the power consumed under different configurations that vary in the number of active cores used, the frequency at which the CPU operates (all cores operate at the same frequency), and the load of the active cores (all active cores are equally loaded). The list of available and tested CPU frequencies and cores can be found in Table 1. We tune the total load ρ by using lookbusy, as described in the previous section. Each experiment lasts 30 s and it is repeated 10 times. Results are summarized in terms of average and standard deviation. Specifically, in the figures reported in this section, the power consumption for each tested configuration is depicted by means of a vertical segment centered on the average power consumption measured, and with segment size equal to two times the standard deviation of the samples.

The results of these experiments for each of the 3 servers are presented in Figure 1 (the measurements for some frequencies and some number of cores are omitted for clarity). Here, for each configuration of number of active cores, frequency, and load in ACPS, the mean and standard deviation of all the experiments with that configuration are presented. Also the least squares polynomial fitting curve for the samples is shown for each number of cores and frequency. The curves shown are for polynomials of degree 7, but we observed that using a degree 3 polynomial instead does not reduce drastically the quality of the fit (e.g., the relative average error of the fitting increases from 0.7% with 7-th degree polynomials to 1.5% with degree equal to 3 for Erdos, while it remains practically stable and below 0.7% for Nemesis). In general, we can use an expression like the following to characterize the CPU power consumption:

$$P_{BC}(\rho) = \sum_{k=0}^{n} \alpha_k \rho^k, \quad n \leq 7, \qquad (1)$$

where P_{BC} includes both the baseline power consumption of the servers and the power consumed by the CPU, and ρ is the load expressed in active cycles per second. Therefore, coefficient α_0 in Eq. 1 represents the consumption of

(a) Survivor

(b) Nemesis

(c) Erdos

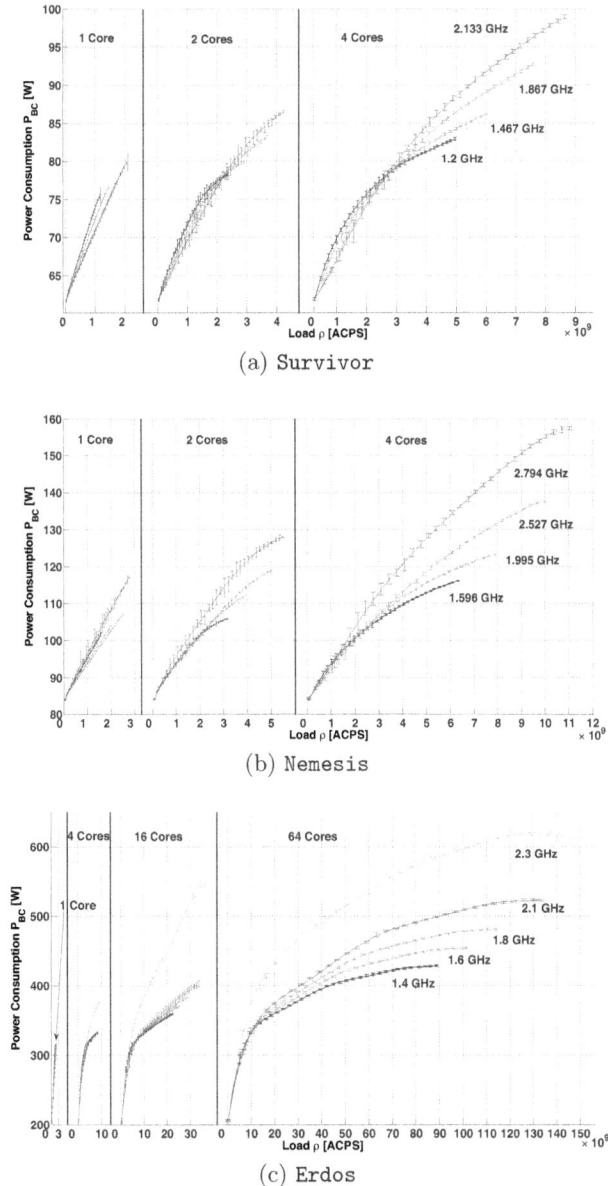

Figure 1: Power consumption of 3 servers (Survivor, Nemesis, and Erdos) for baseline and CPU characterization experiments.

(a) Minimal power.

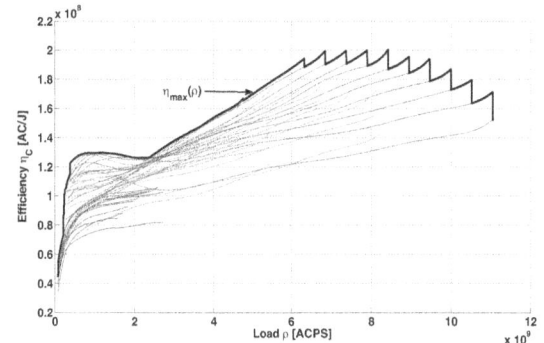

(b) Maximal efficiency.

Figure 2: CPU performance bounds of Nemesis.

the system when the CPU activity tends to 0, and we can thereby interpret α_0 as the baseline power consumption of the system. Note that the polynomial fitting, and hence the baseline power consumption α_0, depends on the particular combination of number of cores and frequency adopted. However, for sake of readability, we do not explicitly account for such a dependency in the notation.

A first observation of the fitting curves for each particular server in Figure 1 reveals that the power for near-zero load is almost the same in curves (e.g., for Nemesis this value is between 84 and 85 W). Observe that it is impossible to run an experiment in which the load of the CPU is actually zero to obtain the baseline power consumption of a server. However, all the fitting curves converge to a similar value

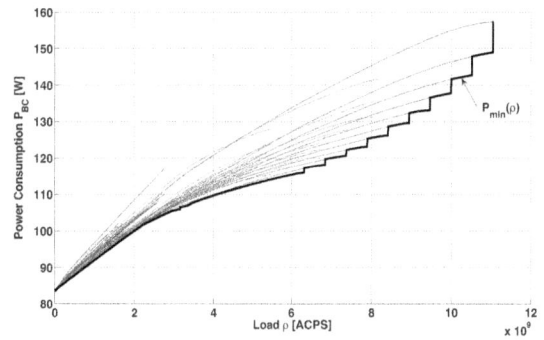

for $\rho \to 0$, which can be assumed to represent the baseline power consumption.

A second observation is that for one core the curves grow linearly with the load. However, as soon as two or more cores are used, the curves are clearly concave, which implies that for a fixed frequency the efficiency grows with the load (we will discuss later the efficiency in terms of number of active cycles per energy unit).

A third observation is that frequency does not significantly impact the power consumption when the load is low. In contrast, at high load, the consumption clearly increases with the CPU frequency. More precisely, the power consumption grows superlinearly with the frequency, for a fixed load and number of cores. This is particularly evident in the curves characterizing Erdos, which is the most powerful among our servers.

From the previous figures it emerges that the power consumption due to CPU and baseline can be minimized by selecting the right number of active cores and a suitable CPU frequency. Similarly, we can expect that the energy efficiency, defined as number of active cycles per energy unit, can be maximized by tuning the same operational parameters. We graphically represent the impact of operation parameters on power consumption and energy efficiency in Figures 2 and 3 respectively for Nemesis and Erdos (results for Survivor are similar to the ones shown for Nemesis and are omitted). In particular, Figures 2(a) and 3(a) report all possible fitting curves for the power consumption measurements, plus a curve marking the lowest achievable power consumption at a given load. We name such a curve "minimal power curve" $P_{\min}(\rho)$, and we observe that (i) it only

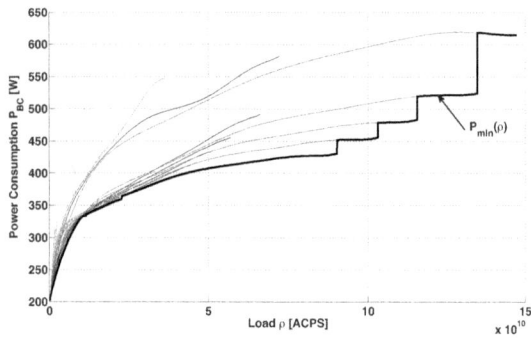

(a) Minimal power.

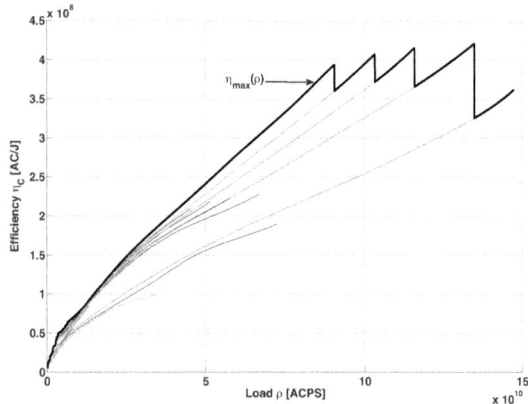

(b) Maximal efficiency.

Figure 3: CPU performance bounds of Erdos.

depends on the load ρ, and (ii) it is a piecewise concave function, which makes it suitable to formulate power optimization problems. Finally, to evaluate the energy efficiency of the CPU, we report in Figures 2(b) and 3(b) the number of active cycles per energy unit obtained from our measurements respectively for Nemesis and Erdos. We compute the power due to active cycles as the power $P_{BC} - \alpha_0$, i.e., by subtracting the baseline consumption from P_{BC}, and we obtain the efficiency η_C by dividing the load (in active cycles per second) by the power due to active cycles:

$$\eta_C = \frac{\rho}{P_{BC}(\rho) - \alpha_0}. \qquad (2)$$

Also in this case we show the curve that maximizes the efficiency at a given load, which we name "Maximal efficiency curve" $\eta_{\max}(\rho)$. Interestingly, we observe that (i) $\eta_{\max}(\rho)$ presents multiple local maxima, (ii) for a given configuration of frequency and number of active cores, the efficiency is maximized at the highest achievable load, (iii) all local maxima corresponds to the use of all available active cores, but (iv) the absolute maximum is *not* achieved neither at the highest CPU frequency nor at the lowest.

3.3 Disks

We now characterize the power and energy consumption of disk I/O operations. During the experiments, we continuously commit either read or write operations, while keeping the CPU load ρ as low as possible (i.e., we disconnect the

network and we do not run other tasks). Still, the power measurements obtained during the disk experiments contain both the power used by the disk and power due to CPU and baseline. Indeed, Figure 4 shows, for each experiment, the total measured power P_t, the power P_{BC} computed according to Eq. 1 at the load ρ measured during the experiment, and the power due to disk operations, computed as:

$$P_D^x = P_t - P_{BC}(\rho), \quad x \in \{r, w\}, \qquad (3)$$

where superscripts r and w refer to reading and writing operations, respectively. We test sequentially all the available frequencies for each server (see Table 1), and I/O block sizes ranging from 10 KB to 100 MB. Figure 4 shows average and standard deviation of the measures over 10 experiment repetitions. Results for Survivor are omitted since they are like Nemesis' results. Indeed, Survivor and Nemesis have similar disks and file systems, while Erdos is equipped with SAS disks with RAID. In all cases shown in the figure, the disk power is small but not negligible with respect to the baseline consumption. Furthermore, we can observe that the two servers presented behave differently. Indeed, while the power consumption due to writing is affected both by the block size B for both machines, we observe that Nemesis' disk writing power P_D^w is not affected by the CPU frequency, while Erdos' results show an increase with the frequency. Moreover, the results obtained with Erdos are affected by a substantial amount of variability in the measurements, which we believe is due to the caching operations enforced by the RAID mechanism in Erdos.

Similarly to what was described for the CPU, we now comment on the energy efficiencies η_D^r and η_D^w of disk reading and writing operations. Figure 5 reports efficiency as a function of the I/O block size, and shows one line per each CPU frequency. The efficiency is computed by subtracting the baseline power from the total power, and by measuring the volume V of data read or written in an interval T:

$$\eta_D^x = \frac{V}{P_D^x T}, \quad x \in \{r, w\}. \qquad (4)$$

We can observe that results are similar for all the servers. Specifically, reading efficiency is almost constant at any frequency and for each block size, while writing is more efficient with large block sizes. We also observe that the efficiency changes very little with the adopted CPU frequency. Another observation is that the efficiency saturates to a disk-dependent asymptotic value, which is due to the mechanical constraints of the disk (e.g., due to the non-negligible *seek* time, the number of read/write operations per second is limited). In addition, although not visible in the figure due to the log-scale adopted, η_D^w is a concave function of the block size B.

3.4 Network

The last server component that we characterize via measurements is the network card. Similarly to the cases described previously, we run experiments in which only the operating system and our test scripts are active. In this case, we run a script to either transmit or receive UDP packets over a gigabit Ethernet connection and count the system active cycles ρ. We measure the total power consumption P_t during the experiment, so that the power due to network activity can be then estimated as follows:

$$P_N^x = P_t - P_{BC}(\rho), \quad x \in \{s, r\}, \qquad (5)$$

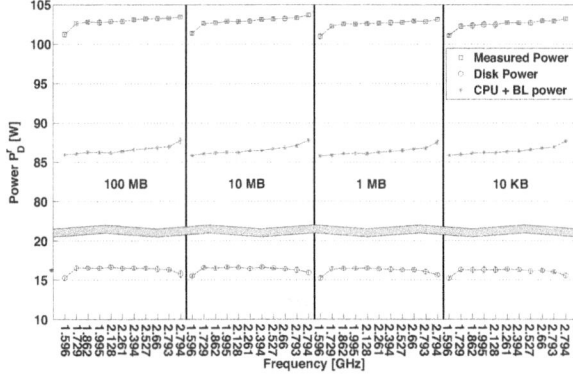

(a) Power consumption during reading (`Nemesis`).

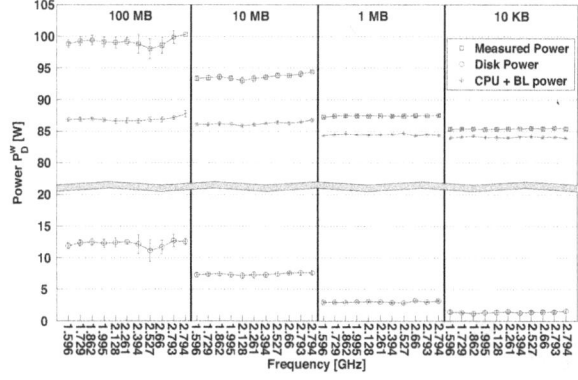

(b) Power consumption during writing (`Nemesis`).

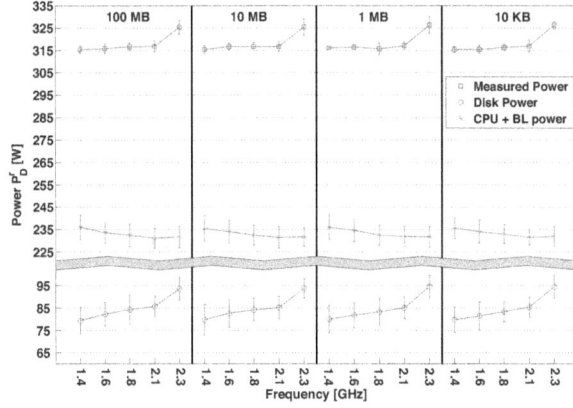

(c) Power consumption during reading (`Erdos`).

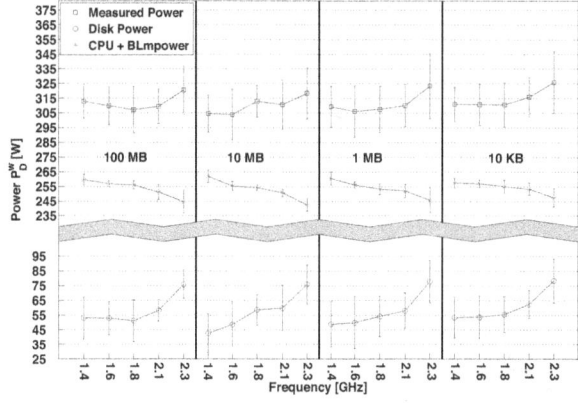

(d) Power consumption during writing (`Erdos`).

Figure 4: Instantaneous power consumption for a reading/writing operations. Results are presented for every frequency and for 4 different block sizes for each one of our servers.

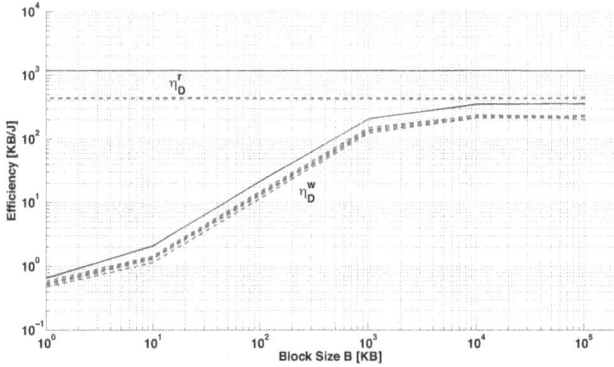

Figure 5: Disk reading and writing efficiencies for `Erdos` (red dotted lines) and `Nemesis` (blue solid lines).

where superscripts s and r refer to the sender and the receiver cases, respectively.

In the experiments, we sequentially test all the available frequencies for each server (see Table 1), and fix the packet size S and the UDP transmission rate within the achievable set of rates (which depends on the packet size, e.g., < 950 *Mbps* for 1470-B packets). We report results for the network energy in terms of efficiencies η_N^s and η_N^r (volume of data transferred per unit of energy). These efficiencies are computed as follows:

$$\eta_N^x = \frac{R}{P_N^x}, \quad x \in \{s, r\}, \tag{6}$$

where R is the transmission rate during the experiment.

Figure 6 shows the network efficiencies of `Nemesis` and `Survivor` averaged over 3 samples per transmission rate R.[8] For sake of readability, the figure only shows results for the extreme value used for the packet size, and for three CPU frequencies: the lowest, the highest, and an intermediate frequency in the set of available frequencies reported in Table 1 for `Nemesis` and `Survivor`. The figure also reports the polynomial fitting curves for efficiency, which we found to be at most of second order. Since the efficiency is represented

---

[8]Network results are obtained by using a point-to-point Ethernet connection between two controlled servers. Since `Erdos` is located in a different building with respect to `Nemesis` and `Survivor`, it was not possible to test the network efficiency of `Erdos`.

(a) Receiver network efficiency (**Survivor**).

(b) Receiver network efficiency (**Nemesis**).

(c) Sender network efficiency (**Survivor**).

(d) Sender network efficiency (**Nemesis**).

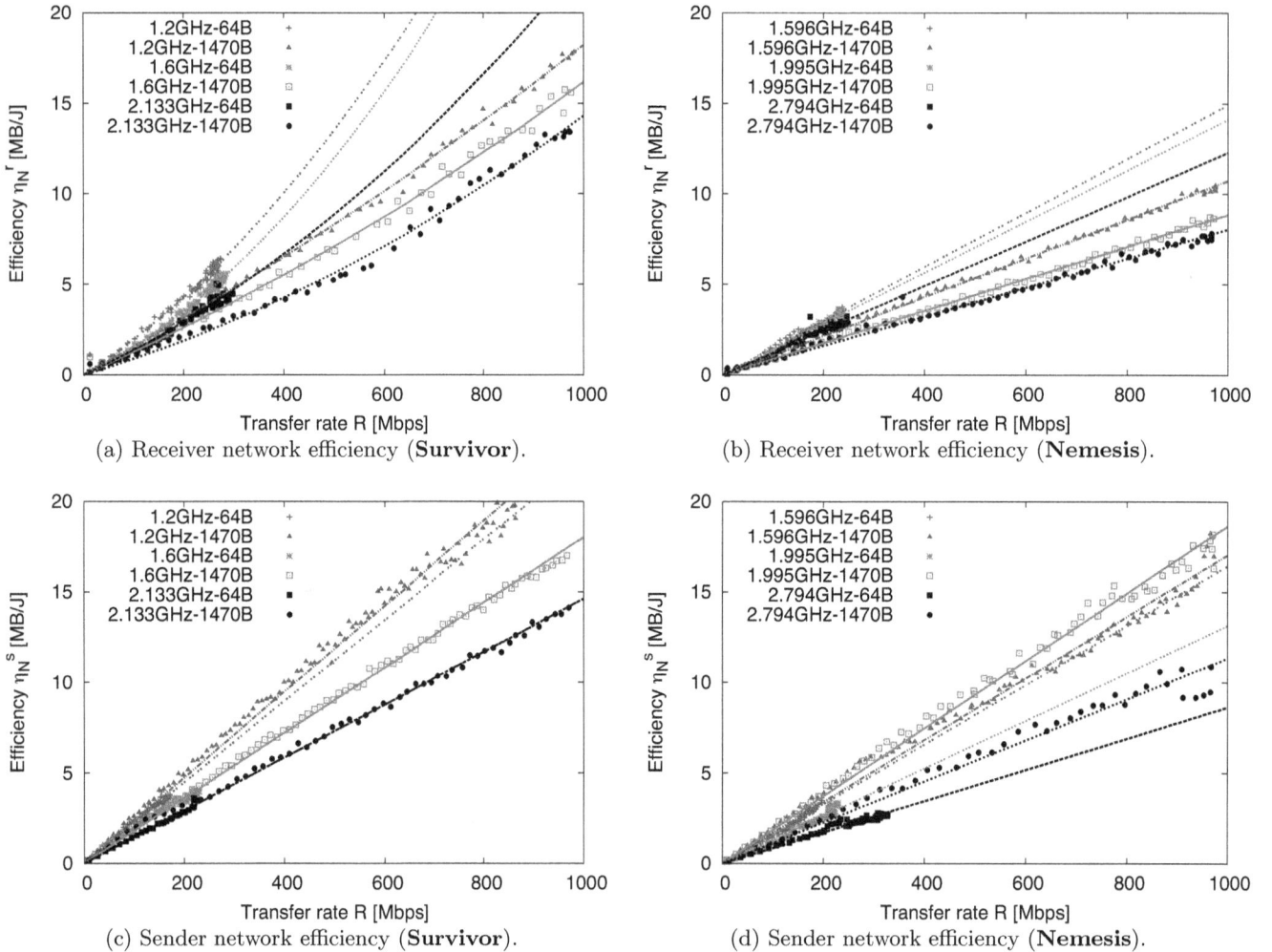

Figure 6: Network efficiencies for different frequencies and 64-B and 1470-B packets.

in terms of network activity only, in the fitting we force the zero-order coefficient of the polynomials to be 0. Therefore, we can use the following expression to characterize the network efficiencies of our servers:

$$\eta_N^x = \beta_1 R + \beta_2 R^2, \quad x \in \{s, r\}, \qquad (7)$$

where the β_i coefficients are computed by minimizing the least square error of the fitting. Table 2 gives the fitting coefficients for sending and receiving efficiencies for the cases shown in Figure 6 and for other tested configurations.

From both the figure and the table, we can observe that efficiencies are almost linear or slightly superlinear with the transfer rate, e.g., the receiving efficiency of Survivor exhibits an evident quadratic behavior. Indeed, our measurements show that the network power consumption is independent from the throughput, which is a well known result for legacy Ethernet devices. In fact, the NICs of our servers are not equipped with power saving features like, e.g., the recently standardized IEEE 802.3az [9].

In all cases, the efficiency is strongly affected by the selected CPU frequency. Moreover, efficiency is also affected by packet size, although the impact of packet size changes

from server to server, e.g., Survivor sending efficiency is only slightly affected by it.

Another observation is that, depending on the packet size and frequency used, sending can be more energy efficient than receiving at a given transmission rate, and using the highest CPU frequency is never the most efficient solution. Note also that the efficiency decreases with the packet size, although this effect is particularly evident at the receiver side, while it only slightly impacts the efficiency of the packet sender. However, network activity also causes non-negligible CPU activity, as shown in Figure 7 for a few experiment configurations for Nemesis. Overall, the lowest CPU frequency yields the lowest total power consumption during network activity periods.

4. ESTIMATING ENERGY CONSUMPTION

While the results presented in the previous sections are useful to understand the power consumption pattern of CPU, disk and network, we believe that a much more important use of these results is to estimate the energy consumption of applications. In this section we describe how this could be done from simple data about the application, and validate

Table 2: Polynomial fitting for network efficiency: empirically evaluated coefficients for Eq. 7 (coefficients β_1 are expressed in W^{-1}, while coefficients β_2 are in $W^{-1} \cdot bps^{-1}$).

		RECEIVER								
		Survivor					Nemesis			
	freq / pck size	1.2 GHz	1.6 GHz	1.867 GHz	2.133 GHz	freq / pck size	1.596 GHz	1.995 GHz	2.394 GHz	2.794 GHz
β_1 / β_2]	64 B	1.751e-2 / 1.904e-5	1.314e-2 / 2.160e-5	1.268e-2 / 1.395e-5	1.254e-2 / 1.031e-5	64 B	1.491e-2	1.410e-2	1.330e-2	1.227e-2
β_1 / β_2	500 B	1.736e-2 / 2.627e-6	1.386e-2 / 1.595e-6	1.144e-2 / 2.836e-6	9.962e-3 / 3.541e-6	500 B	1.565e-2	1.234e-2	1.107e-2	1.074e-2
β_1 / β_2	1000 B	1.560e-2 / 3.155e-6	1.296e-2 / 1.736e-6	1.132e-2 / 1.080e-6	1.029e-2 / 1.208e-6	1000 B	1.170e-2	9.451e-3	7.712e-3	7.448e-3
β_1 / β_2	1470 B	1.497e-2 / 3.231e-6	1.216e-2 / 4.006e-6	1.073e-2 / 3.533e-6	2.684e-2 / -4.746e-6	1470 B	1.072e-2	8.849e-3	8.207e-3	8.040e-3
		SENDER								
		Survivor					Nemesis			
	freq / pck size	1.2 GHz	1.6 GHz	1.867 GHz	2.133 GHz	freq / pck size	1.596 GHz	1.995 GHz	2.394 GHz	2.794 GHz
β_1	64 B	2.239e-2	1.802e-2	1.582e-2	1.462e-2	64 B	1.642e-2	1.313e-2	1.029e-2	8.625e-3
β_1	500 B	1.742e-2	1.576e-2	1.429e-2	2.205e-2	500 B	1.599e-2	1.130e-2	1.234e-2	1.014e-2
β_1	1000 B	1.784e-2	1.634e-2	1.454e-2	2.230e-2	1000 B	1.767e-2	1.781e-2	1.824e-2	1.179e-2
β_1	1470 B	1.801e-2	1.620e-2	1.461e-2	2.369e-2	1470 B	1.703e-2	1.863e-2	1.279e-2	1.134e-2

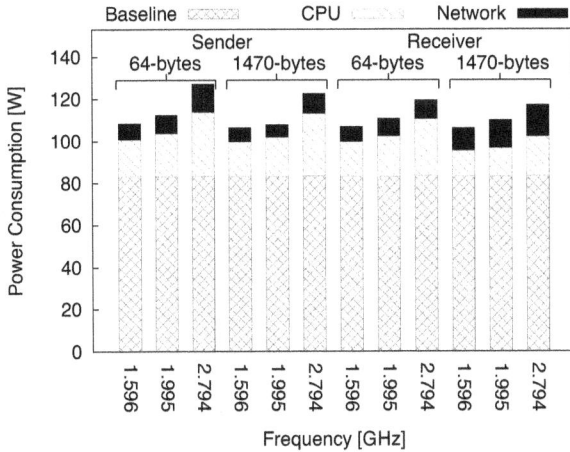

Figure 7: Power consumption with network activity for Nemesis (64-B experiments were run with a transmission rate $R = 150$ $Mbps$, while $R = 400$ $Mbps$ for the experiments with 1470-B packets).

the proposed process by estimating the energy consumed by map-reduce Hadoop computations.

4.1 Energy Estimation Hypothesis

The process we propose to estimate the energy consumed E_{app} by an application has as basic assumption that this energy is essentially the sum of the baseline energy E_B (the baseline power times the duration of the execution), the energy consumed by the CPU E_C, the energy consumed by the disk E_D, and the energy consumed by the network interface E_N. I.e.,

$$E_{app} = E_B + E_C + E_D + E_N. \qquad (8)$$

Hence, the process of estimating E_{app} is reduced to estimating these four terms. In order to estimate the first two terms, we need to know the total number of active cycles that the application will execute, C_{app}, and the load ρ_{app} (in ACPS) that the execution will incur in the CPU. From this, the total running time T_{app} can be computed as

$$T_{app} = C_{app}/\rho_{app}.$$

Then, once the number of cores and the frequency that will be used have been defined, it is also possible to estimate the baseline power plus CPU power, P_{BC}, from the fitting curves of Figure 1. This allows to estimate the sum of the first two terms of Eq. 8 as

$$E_B + E_C = P_{BC}T_{app} = P_{BC}C_{app}/\rho_{app}. \qquad (9)$$

The energy consumed by the disk is simply the energy consumed while reading and writing, i.e., $E_D = E_D^r + E_D^w$. To estimate these latter values, the block size to be used has to be decided, from which we can obtain an estimate of the efficiency of reading, η_D^r, and writing, η_D^w (see Figure 5). These, combined with the total volume of data read and written by the application, denoted as V_D^r and V_D^w respectively, allow to obtain the estimate energy as

$$E_D = \frac{V_D^r}{\eta_D^r} + \frac{V_D^w}{\eta_D^w}. \qquad (10)$$

Finally, to estimate E_N, the transfer rate R and packet size S has to be chosen, which combined with the frequency used, yield sending and receiving efficiencies η_N^s and η_N^r (see Figure 6). Then, if the total volume of data to be sent and received is V_N^s and V_N^r, respectively,

$$E_N = \frac{V_N^s}{\eta_N^s} + \frac{V_N^r}{\eta_N^r}. \qquad (11)$$

All is left to do to obtain the estimate E_{app} is to add up the values obtained in Equations 9, 10, and 11.

4.2 Empirical Validation

We test now the process and hypothesis presented above for the estimation of the energy consumed by an application. For that, we have chosen to execute in Nemesis a map-reduce Hadoop application that computes several iterations of the pagerank algorithm on an Erdos-Renyi random (directed) graph with 1 million nodes and average degree 5. Since the pagerank application does not use the network, while it is running we execute another process generating network traffic. This provides a richer experiment.

An execution of the pagerank application has three phases: preprocessing, map-reduce, and postprocessing. On its side, the map-reduce phase is a sequence of several homogeneous

(a) Sender side.

(b) Receiver side.

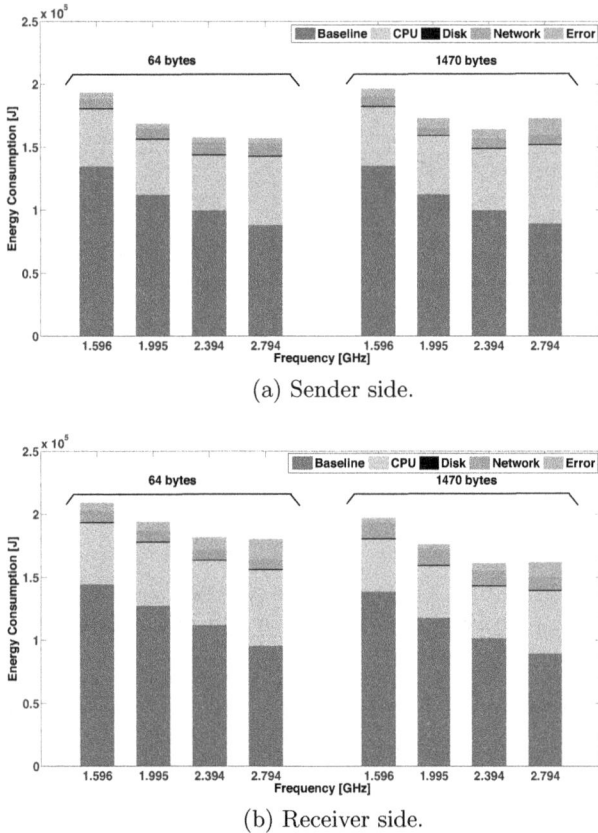

Figure 8: Comparison of the real versus estimated energy consumption values.

iterations of the pagerank algorithm. For simplicity, we only estimate the energy consumed during the map-reduce phase of the pagerank algorithm. In our experiments we run in Nemesis one instance of the pagerank application with 10 iterations in its map-reduce phase for each one of the 11 available frequencies. We run this experiment 4 times, each with different characteristics of the network traffic generated in parallel. In particular, we run experiments with Nemesis behaving as a sender and as a receiving, and using packets of 64 and 1470 bytes. Instead of estimating the energy for the whole sequence of 10 iterations, it is simpler to estimate the energy for every iteration separately. Then, for each iteration i we can register the total active cycles executed C_{app}^i, the time consumed T_{app}^i, and the volume of data read and written, $V_D^{r,i}$ and $V_D^{w,i}$, respectively, and the transfer rate R (the same for all iterations: 150 $Mbps$ for experiments with 64-B packets and 400 $Mbps$ for experiments with 1470-B packets).

Unfortunately, we cannot measure the instantaneous CPU load. Instead, we assume that the CPU load is the same during the execution for a given frequency and network configuration. Hence we estimate it as $\rho_{app}^i = C_{app}^i/T_{app}^i$. Then, from this value we obtain the estimate of the instantaneous power P_{BC}^i using the fitting curves as described above. Finally, using Eq. 9 we compute the estimate $E_B^i + E_C^i$.

In order to estimate the energy consumed by the disk operations, we use the fact that Hadoop uses a block size of 64 MB. This allows us to estimate the reading and writing

efficiencies, $\eta_D^{r,i}$ and $\eta_D^{w,i}$ (see Figure 5). Combining these values with the measured volume of data read and written ($V_D^{r,i}$ and $V_D^{w,i}$) as described in Eq. 10, we obtain E_D^i.

Finally, to estimate the network consumption in one iteration with Nemesis sending traffic (resp., receiving traffic), the sending efficiency η_N^s, (resp., receiving efficiency η_N^r) is obtained from the transfer rate R, and the frequency and packet size used (see Figure 6). The amount of data sent (reps., received) is obtained as the product of the rate R and the time T_{app}^i. Then, the energy of the network is obtained using Eq. 11.

Once we have computed the energy due to the different components in iteration i, the total energy E_{app}^i is obtained by adding them. Adding these values for the 10 iterations of an experiment we obtain the estimate E_{app}. The (approximate) total *real* energy $\hat{E}_{app}^i$ consumed by iteration i is computed by obtaining the average value of the power samples we registered with our power analyzer during the iteration, and multiplying it by T_{app}. Again, the total energy consumed by the experiment are obtained as $\hat{E}_{app} = \sum_{i=1}^{10} \hat{E}_{app}^i$. The estimation error for each experiment is then computed as $\hat{E}_{app} - E_{app}$.

We show the results obtained for four selected frequencies (the results for the rest are similar) in Figure 8(a), for the sender cases, and Figure 8(b) for the receiving cases. Each figure includes the results for the two packet sizes used. As can be seen, the error is very small (always below 7% of the total energy), being a bit more relevant in the case of the highest frequency.

5. DISCUSSION

We discuss now some of the implications of our results. We start with consolidation. It has been typically assumed that the best way of doing consolidation is to fill servers as much as possible, to reduce the total number of servers being used, hence proposing bin-packing based solutions [3, 15, 20] and not necessarily having frequency into account. However, the results presented in Figures 2(b) and 3(b) show that the highest frequency is not the most efficient one, and this has been found to be true for two different architectures (Intel and AMD). This implies that, by running servers at the optimal amount of load, and the right frequency, a considerable amount of energy could be saved.

A second relevant aspect is the baseline consumption of servers. The results presented for all 3 servers show that their baselines are within a 30-50% of the maximum consumption. Then, it is straightforward that more effort is to be done for reducing baseline consumption. For instance, a solution could consist in switching off cores in real time, not just disabling them, or in introducing very fast transitions between active and lower energy states, i.e., to achieve real *suspension* in idle state.

Finally, we refer to the CPU load associated to disk and network activity. It can be observed in Figure 4 that disks do not incur much CPU overhead. In fact, the power consumed by CPU plus baseline does not change much across the experiments. Instead, the energy consumed by CPU due to network operations is even larger than the energy consumed by the NIC (see Figure 7). Some works [7] have already pointed out that the way the packets are handled by the protocol stack is not energy efficient. Our results reinforce this feeling and point out that building a more efficient protocol stack would certainly reduce the amount of energy consumed due to the network.

6. RELATED WORK

There is a large body of work in the field of modeling server power consumption and its components, both theoretical and empirical. The consumption of servers has been assumed as linear e.g., by Wang *et al.* [20], Mishra *et al.* [15] or Beloglazov *et al.* [3], who assumed models where consumption depended mainly on CPU and linearly on its utilization, proposing bin-packing-like algorithms to reduce power consumption. Other works like the ones from Andrews *et al.* [1] or Irani *et al.* [10] proposed non-linear models, claiming that energy could be saved by running processes at the lowest possible speed.

Moving to the empirical field, we first classify works in two different groups, those who consider the effect of frequency on their analysis and those who do not consider it. We start with those not considering frequency. In this category we find articles proposing models where server components follow a linear behavior like [11, 14, 19] or more complex ones, like in [2, 5, 13]. In [14], Liu *et al.* propose a simple linear model and evaluate different hardware configurations and types of workloads by varying the number of available cores, the available memory, and considering also the contribution of other components such as disks. Vasan *et al.* [19] monitored multiple servers on a datacenter as well as the power consumption of several of the internal elements of a server. However, they considered that the behavior of this server could be approximated by a model based only on CPU utilization. Similarly, Krishnan *et al.* [11] explored the feasibility of lightweight virtual machine power metering methods and examined the contribution of some of the elements that consume power in a server like CPU, memory and disks. Their model depends linearly on each of these components. In [5], Economou *et al.* proposed a non-intrusive method for modeling full-system power consumption by stressing its components with different workloads. Their resulting model is also linear on the utilization of its components. Finally, Lewis *et al.* [13] and Basmasjian *et al.* [2] presented much more complex models which, apart from the contribution of different components of the server, considered extra parameters like temperature and cache misses as well as multiple cores. In particular, Lewis *et al.* [13] reported also an extensive study on the behavior of reading and writing operations in hard disk and solid state drives. In contrast, we show that linear models are not accurate and we complement the existing studies by showing the effect of different block sizes and frequencies, e.g., on network and individual read or write operations.

Now we move to the works which also considered frequency in their analysis. Miyoshi *et al.* [16] analyzed the runtime effects of frequency scaling on power and energy. Brihi *et al.* [4] presented an exhaustive study of DVFS using a `cpufrequtils` as we do. Main differences with our work were that they studied four different power management policies under DVFS and centered their study on the relationship between CPU utilization and power consumption. However, they also present interesting results about disk consumption that match partially our results, showing a flat consumption in reading operations and variations in the writing ones that they attribute to the size of the files being written. Although it was not the main objective of their

work, Raghavendra *et al.* [18] performed a per-frequency and core CPU power characterization of two different blade servers. However, they claimed that CPU power depends linearly on its utilization. The main difference with our analysis is that we consider that the load supported by a server increases with the number of active cores and, hence, this load should not be represented in percentage. Gandhi *et al.* [6] published an analysis of global power consumption versus frequency, based on DVFS and DFS and gave some intuition about the non-linearity of this relation. In contrast, we present a per-component analysis, which allows us to enter into deeper details on the power versus frequency analysis.

7. CONCLUSIONS

In this work we have reported our measurement-based characterization of energy and power consumption in a server. We have exhaustively measured the power consumed by CPU, disk, and NIC under different configurations, identifying the optimal operational levels, which usually do not correspond to the static system configurations commonly adopted. We found that, besides the *baseline component*, which does not changes significantly with the operational parameters, the CPU has the largest impact on energy consumption among all the three components. We observe that CPU consumption is neither linear nor concave with the load, i.e., the systems are not *energy proportional*. Disk I/O is the second larger contributor to power consumption, although performance changes sensibly with the I/O block size used by the applications. Finally, the NIC activity is responsible for a small but not negligible fraction of power consumption, which scales almost linearly with the network transmission rate. In general, most of the energy/power performance figures do not scale linearly with the utilization, in contrast to what is commonly assumed in the literature. We have then shown how to predict and optimize the energy consumed by an application via a concrete example using network activity plus pagerank computation in Hadoop. Our model achieves very accurate energy estimates, within 7% or less from the measured total power consumption.

8. ACKNOWLEDGMENTS

This research was partially supported by the Comunidad de Madrid grant S2009TIC-1692, the MICINN grant TEC2011-29688-C02-01, the National Natural Science Foundation of China grant 61020106002, and the Greek State Scholarships Foundation. The authors would like to thank Luis Núñez Chiroque, Philippe Morere, and Miguel Peón for their help with some experiments.

9. REFERENCES

[1] ANDREWS, M., ANTONAKOPOULOS, S., AND ZHANG, L. Minimum-cost network design with (dis)economies of scale. In *IEEE FOCS* (2010), pp. 585–592.

[2] BASMADJIAN, R., ALI, N., NIEDERMEIER, F., DE MEER, H., AND GIULIANI, G. A methodology to predict the power consumption of servers in data centres. In *ACM e-Energy* (2011), pp. 1–10.

[3] BELOGLAZOV, A., ABAWAJY, J., AND BUYYA, R. Energy-aware resource allocation heuristics for efficient management of data centers for cloud

computing. *Future Generation Computer Systems 28*, 5 (2012), 755–768.

[4] BRIHI, A., AND DARGIE, W. Dynamic voltage and frequency scaling in multimedia servers. In *IEEE AINA* (2013).

[5] ECONOMOU, D., RIVOIRE, S., KOZYRAKIS, C., AND RANGANATHAN, P. Full-system power analysis and modeling for server environments. In *Proceedings of Workshop on Modeling, Benchmarking, and Simulation* (2006), pp. 70–77.

[6] GANDHI, A., HARCHOL-BALTER, M., DAS, R., AND LEFURGY, C. Optimal power allocation in server farms. In *ACM SIGMETRICS* (2009), pp. 157–168.

[7] GARCIA-SAAVEDRA, A., SERRANO, P., BANCHS, A., AND BIANCHI, G. Energy consumption anatomy of 802.11 devices and its implication on modeling and design. In *ACM CoNEXT* (2012), pp. 169–180.

[8] HEDDEGHEM, W. V., LAMBERT, S., LANNOO, B., COLLE, D., PICKAVET, M., AND DEMEESTER, P. Trends in worldwide ICT electricity consumption from 2007 to 2012. *Computer Communications* (Submitted).

[9] IEEE STD. 802.3AZ. Energy Efficient Ethernet, 2010.

[10] IRANI, S., SHUKLA, S., AND GUPTA, R. Algorithms for power savings. *ACM TALG 3*, 4 (2007), 41.

[11] KRISHNAN, B., AMUR, H., GAVRILOVSKA, A., AND SCHWAN, K. VM power metering: feasibility and challenges. *ACM SIGMETRICS Performance Evaluation Review 38*, 3 (2011), 56–60.

[12] KUSIC, D., KEPHART, J. O., HANSON, J. E., KANDASAMY, N., AND JIANG, G. Power and performance management of virtualized computing environments via lookahead control. *Cluster computing 12*, 1 (2009), 1–15.

[13] LEWIS, A. W., GHOSH, S., AND TZENG, N.-F. Run-time energy consumption estimation based on workload in server systems. *HotPower'08* (2008), 17–21.

[14] LIU, C., HUANG, J., CAO, Q., WAN, S., AND XIE, C. Evaluating energy and performance for server-class hardware configurations. In *IEEE NAS* (2011), pp. 339–347.

[15] MISHRA, M., AND SAHOO, A. On theory of vm placement: Anomalies in existing methodologies and their mitigation using a novel vector based approach. In *IEEE CLOUD* (2011), pp. 275–282.

[16] MIYOSHI, A., LEFURGY, C., VAN HENSBERGEN, E., RAJAMONY, R., AND RAJKUMAR, R. Critical power slope: understanding the runtime effects of frequency scaling. In *ACM ICS'02* (2002), pp. 35–44.

[17] MOORE, J. D., CHASE, J. S., RANGANATHAN, P., AND SHARMA, R. K. Making scheduling "cool": Temperature-aware workload placement in data centers. In *USENIX annual technical conference, General Track* (2005), pp. 61–75.

[18] RAGHAVENDRA, R., RANGANATHAN, P., TALWAR, V., WANG, Z., AND ZHU, X. No power struggles: Coordinated multi-level power management for the data center. In *ACM SIGARCH Computer Architecture News* (2008), vol. 36, ACM, pp. 48–59.

[19] VASAN, A., SIVASUBRAMANIAM, A., SHIMPI, V., SIVABALAN, T., AND SUBBIAH, R. Worth their Watts? - An empirical study of datacenter servers. In *IEEE HPCA* (2010), pp. 1–10.

[20] WANG, M., MENG, X., AND ZHANG, L. Consolidating virtual machines with dynamic bandwidth demand in data centers. In *IEEE INFOCOM* (2011), pp. 71–75.

[21] WEISER, M., WELCH, B., DEMERS, A., AND SHENKER, S. Scheduling for reduced CPU energy. In *Mobile Computing*. Springer, 1996, pp. 449–471.

Balance your Bids before your Bits: The Economics of Geographic Load-Balancing

Jose Camacho
Universidad Carlos III de Madrid, Spain
jmc.camacho@gmail.com

Ying Zhang, Minghua Chen, Dah Ming Chiu
Dept. of Information Engineering
The Chinese University of Hong Kong
{zy013,minghua,dmchiu}@ie.cuhk.edu.hk

ABSTRACT

By routing workload to locations with cheaper electricity, geographic load-balancing (GLB) has been shown a promising mechanism to cut down the electricity bill of geo-distributed datacenters operated by the same organization. Most existing studies on GLB assume that the use of GLB has no impact on electricity prices, even though GLB increases local electricity demand variation. In practice, however, electricity prices are determined by how supply and demand are dynamically balanced by local electricity utilities, and thus may as well be affected by GLB. In this paper, in order to understand and unleash GLB's economic potential, we carry out a comprehensive study on how GLB interacts with electricity supply chains. In particular, we show that as GLB introduces extra uncertainty in local demand, utility companies may have to increase electricity prices to ensure certain profit margin in face of such demand uncertainty. Consequently, cloud service providers (CSP) doing GLB may end up getting minor cost reduction or even paying *higher* electricity bills than not doing GLB, as shown in our case study based on real-world traces. Then, motivated by the recent practice of large CSPs moving into electricity markets, we propose to allow CSPs to purchase electricity from markets through brokers. The advantage is that GLB no longer causes economic loss to utilities. Meanwhile, CSPs can still exploit their presence in multiple geo-locations to achieve desirable electricity cost reduction. Our case study using real-world traces shows that the solution can save CSPs up to 12% of the electricity cost.

Categories and Subject Descriptors

J.7 [**Computers in other systems**]: Industrial control
; G.1.6 [**Optimization**]: Stochastic Optimization

Keywords

smartgrid, datacenter, pricing, electricity market, auction, geographic load-balancing

1. INTRODUCTION

The flourishing Internet-scale cloud services are revolutionizing the landscape of human activity. The rapid growth of such services has triggered an increasing deployment of massive geo-distributed data centers worldwide.

As a result, energy consumption of data centers hosting these services has been skyrocketing. In 2010, data centers worldwide consumed an estimated 240 billion kilowatt-hours (kWh) of electricity [18], almost enough to power the entire Spain [31]. The corresponding worldwide data center annual electricity bill is around 16 billion US dollars [18]. Today, energy cost represents a large fraction of the data center operating expense [9], and the cost is increasing at an alarming rate of 12% annually [34]. Consequently, reducing energy cost has become a critical concern for data center operators.

There have been a significant amount of academic and industrial efforts on minimizing data center energy cost; see for instance [28, 30, 27] and a recent survey in [6]. Among them, in this paper we focus on the solutions that exploit "price-aware" geographic load-balancing (GLB) across geo-distributed data centers.

For cloud service providers (CSPs) that own data centers in different geographic locations, such as Google, Microsoft, and Amazon, routing user requests to locations with cheaper electricity has been shown a promising approach to cut down the electricity bill; see *e.g.*, [20, 36, 26, 33] and the references therein. These exciting studies suggest that GLB could achieve cost reduction (not necessary energy reduction) of 30-40%, depending on the flexibility of the service provider to shift traffic among locations.

Nevertheless, all existing works focus on addressing technical feasibility and revealing the abundant benefits of GLB, assuming the electricity prices are not affected by GLB, even though GLB increases local electricity demand variation.

In practice, however, the electricity prices are determined by how supply and demand are dynamically balanced by local utilities, and thus may as well be affected by GLB. In particular, the fact that the electricity is a non-storable commodity forces the utility to predict the demand and schedule its supply in advance. As GLB increases demand variation, it may incur extra errors in demand prediction. As we will show, these prediction errors will lead to over-/under-supply and consequently to economic loss of utilities. As a result, utilities may have to increase electricity prices to ensure certain profit margin in face of such extra economic loss caused by GLB.

Therefore, in order to understand and unleash GLB's economic potential, it is critical to understand the interaction between the GLB ability to alter electricity demand patterns, and the impact of this uncertainty on the electricity prices.

Before we turn to our focus and contributions, we note that *GLB can cause non-negligible demand variation for a utility*. For example, Facebook, Apple, Google and Amazon have built or will build

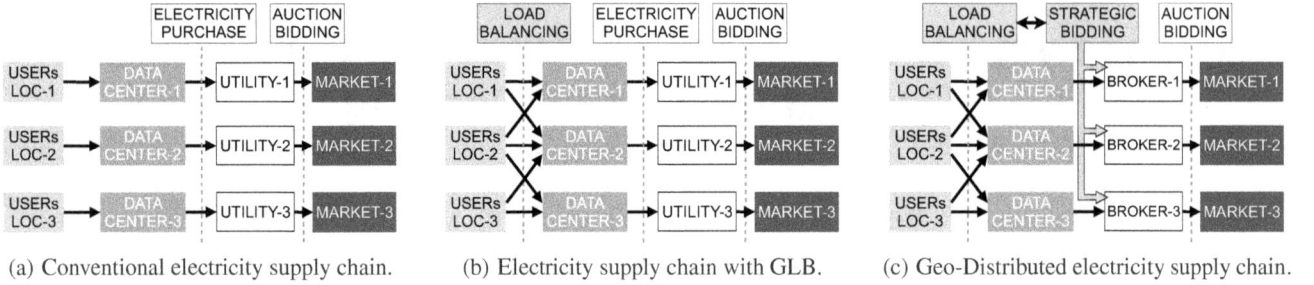

(a) Conventional electricity supply chain.　　(b) Electricity supply chain with GLB.　　(c) Geo-Distributed electricity supply chain.

Figure 1: Three electricity ecosystems studied in this paper.

large data centers in Prineville (Oregon, US) to leverage the chilly outdoor air for data center cooling at low cost. A fully-operated data center (*e.g.*, Google's data center in Oregon) is estimated to consume 90 MW power [5]. Power Pacific, a large utility serving Oregon including Prineville, sells 35 GWh daily [25]. Hence, these data centers once all in full operation could consume 8.6 GWh daily or 22% of Power Pacific sales today, and 33% in 4 years if we aggressively consider data center energy demand grows 15% annually as estimated in [18] while conventional demand remains steady. If data centers can shift 30% electricity demand away by doing GLB according to the estimate in [26], then GLB could lead to 10% demand variation for Power Pacific in 4 years.

Motivated by the above observations, we develop relevant models and carry out a comprehensive study of the impact of GLB on the electricity supply chain. Specifically, we analyze the intriguing interaction of GLB and utilities, revealing fundamental insights for the following two scenarios:

- **Current Model**: In this scenario (see Fig. 1(a)), electricity utilities purchase electricity from local electricity spot markets. Then, the utilities sell electricity like a commodity to data center owners to support their operation. The scenario evolves to Fig. 1(b) if GLB is used.

- **Broker Model**: In this scenario (see Fig. 1(c)), data center owners directly purchase electricity from local spot markets, either by obtaining a valid license[1] or through a broker (*e.g.*, utilities are ideal candidate for brokers).

In particular, we make the following contributions.

▷ We first give a brief overview of the electricity supply chain and introduce CSPs doing GLB as a *new* type of customers – they can make their local demand more *elastic* to prices by "shifting" electricity demand among geo-locations (Sec. 2). They are very different from conventional electricity customers whose demands are localized and inelastic.

▷ We provide a pricing model for the electricity sold by the utilities (Sec. 3). This model takes into account the increments in price to compensate the demand prediction errors and the price volatility from the market auctions.

▷ Then, motivated by the recent practice of large CSPs moving into electricity markets, we propose to allow CSPs to directly purchase electricity from markets through brokers (Sec. 4). By doing GLB and electricity procurement jointly, CSPs can eliminate the trading inefficiency between utilities and CSPs. Consequently, GLB no longer causes economic loss to utilities, and CSPs can still

exploit their presence in multiple geo-locations to achieve desirable electricity cost reduction. Specifically, CSPs can first bid in different spot markets, *i.e.*, *balance their bids*, and then depending on their purchase of electricity perform GLB to optimize the load distribution, *i.e.*, *balance their bits*.

▷ In the performance evaluation section, by analysis and case study using real-world traces, we investigate the interaction of GLB with the supply chain and its economic consequence (Sec. 5). We show that electricity utilities rely on accurate demand prediction to balance supply and demand efficiently. As GLB makes accurate demand prediction harder, it causes trading inefficiency between utilities and CSPs and subsequently economic loss to the utilities. As a result, utilities will have to increase retail prices to ensure certain profit margin in face of the economic loss. Consequently, CSPs doing GLB end up getting poor cost reduction or even paying higher electricity bills than not doing GLB – 1% higher in our case study. The second part of the section shows that the broker-assisted GLB solution can save CSPs up to 12% of the electricity cost, while avoid the issues risen by the conventional (non-coordinated) GLB.

After discussing the related work in Sec.6, we conclude the paper in Sec.7.

2. THE ELECTRICITY SUPPLY CHAIN

In this section, we provide a high-level introduction of the electricity supply chain. In general, electricity supply chains consist of four components:

- *Generating Companies* (GENCOs),

- *Electricity Wholesale Market* (Market),

- *Utility Companies* (Utilities),

- *Customers* (in particular, Cloud Services Providers (CSPs) that owns multiple geo-distributed data centers).

Their interaction is shown in Fig. 1(a) (or Fig. 1(b) if CSPs perform GLB). GENCOs run the generating units and sell electricity on the wholesale Market. Utilities buy from the Market and sell retail to CSPs. For our study, it suffices to consider three components in the supply chain: Market, Utilities, and CSPs.

In the common practice today, the supply is traded in multiple timescales to match the demand. For example, in the US, the most common are day-ahead and real-time trading in the supply chain. Our study focuses on the day-ahead trading, which is based on a forward market that determines largely the hourly supply available to the utilities in the next day. The hourly timescale aligns with the suggested time granularity for CSPs to perform GLB [26].

---

[1]As a real-world example, in February 2010 the Federal Energy Regulatory Commission authorized Google to buy and sell energy at market rates [14].

2.1 Electricity Spot Markets

In recent years, the landscape of electricity wholesale trading has completely shifted towards de-regularized *spot markets*, to allow renewable energy integration and improve trading efficiency to offer lower prices to end customers [4].

In every spot market, the electricity supply is auctioned[2]. The *sellers*, *i.e.*, GENCOs, submit (hourly) generation offers, and the *buyers*, *i.e.*, Utilities, submit (hourly) demand bids, all in the form of *<marginal price, quantity>*, to the Independent System Operator (ISO), *i.e.*, the *auctioneer*. In the offers, the GENCOs specify the amount of electricity they want to sell (resp. Utilities specify in the bids the amount they want to buy) and at which marginal price. Each seller (resp. buyer) is allowed to submit multiple offers (resp. bids) in the same auction with different prices and quantities.

The ISO matches the offers with the bids, typically using a well-established double auction matching mechanism. The mechanism is rather sophisticated in details (we refer interested readers to [19, 16] and focus on the necessary background here), but the outcome is that it determines a *market clearing price* (MCP) for all the traded units.

The MCP clears the market in the following sense. A selling offer (<marginal price, quantity>) with the marginal price below the MCP is successful – the specified amount of electricity is sold on the market at the MCP. Thus *successful sellers sell at prices at least as good as what they offered*. Meanwhile, a buying bid succeeds if the buying price is above the MCP; then, the specified amount of electricity is purchased from the market at the MCP and *buyers pay no more than what they bid*. Remaining selling offers fail as their marginal prices are above the MCP (resp. remaining buying bids fail as their marginal prices are below the MCP[3]).

The MCP is jointly determined by independent bids submitted by uncoordinated parties. Because of the gigantic amount of electricity and capital involved in the auction, no single buyer or seller should dominate the market and determine the MCP. In practice, MCP can be well modeled as a random number drawn from an empirical distribution built from historical data, *independent of individual bids*. See later Fig. 2 for the empirical MCP distribution (ranging from 35 \$/MWh to 130 \$/MWh) of three day-ahead spot markets in the US.

2.2 Electricity Utilities

Similar to the retailers in a generic supply chain, utilities buy commodity – electricity – from spot markets and sell to CSPs to power data centers. Utilities make profit by selling electricity at a proper retail price. A conservative estimate of the retail prices for data centers today is about 60 \$/MWh [26].

Meanwhile, utilities are unique retailers in two senses:

- utilities are trading a non-storable commodity (electricity) with very short "expiration time";

- utilities have to schedule electricity purchase one day before the demand arrives, by bidding in the day-ahead market.

---

[2]In the day-ahead market that we are interested in, electricity supply for each hour of the next day is auctioned. Without loss of generality, we focus on the auction for the electricity supply of a particular hour.

[3]Buyers that could not get their bids matched in the day-ahead market can attempt to get their supply in subsequent real-time markets. However, generating sources with short response-times, such as gas turbines, are expensive and they cannot be permanently running. As a result, the average MCP of real-time markets are likely to be more expensive and changing [2, 25].

These two facts force the utilities to *predict* precisely both the demand quantity and time-of-arrival, so as to *schedule* the purchase of the right amount of supply to be served at the right time. For example, a utility that predicts a data center needs 30MWh electricity tomorrow at 2-3pm needs to buy today, from the day-ahead market, the predicted amount of electricity for its dispatch tomorrow 2-3pm. If there are errors in the prediction, utilities will suffer from over-/under- supply. Over-/under- supply leads to either unmatched demand (to be compensated in more *volatile* markets) or unused electricity. Both immediately translates into economic loss for the utility.

Consequently, when setting the retail price, utilities have to take into account the potential economic loss due to demand prediction error. Larger demand uncertainty leads to larger prediction error, and thus higher economic loss. This observation is crucial in understanding the results in Sec. 3.

2.3 Cloud Services Providers (CSPs)

In this paper, we consider CSPs that operate energy-hungry geo-distributed data centers (*e.g.*, Google and Microsoft) to provide *computing-intensive* services (*e.g.*, search) to its users through the Internet. Depending on whether they perform GLB, CSPs' roles as electricity customers differ significantly.

- Without GLB, a CSP manages its geo-distributed data centers separately as shown in Fig. 1(a). Each data center only serves its regional workload, and it purchases electricity from local utilities for its energy needs. In this case, from the utilities' point of view, each data center is no different from traditional electricity customers (*e.g.*, commercial buildings).

- As shown in Fig. 1(b), CSPs can also perform GLB for various purposes, including but not limited to reducing the total electricity cost of its geo-distributed data centers. As long as the quality of service does not degrade, routing service requests to data centers at locations with cheaper electricity price can provide important cost reduction [26]. According to the widespread estimate in [23], the workload of a data center that can be geographically load-balanced corresponds to 20-30% of the data center electricity demand. In such scenario, CSPs represent a *new* type of electricity customers to local utilities, whose energy demand at a location is *elastic* (caused by CSPs moving their workload around).

There have been works studying the economic benefit of GLB to CSPs, under the assumption that the electricity prices seen by CSPs are not affected by GLB. However, as shown in the next section, as GLB introduces additional uncertainty in the local demand, utilities have to increase electricity prices to ensure certain profit margin in face of such demand uncertainty, cancelling the benefit of GLB. The alarming observation motivates us to consider a broker-assisted GLB solution as a clean alternative in Sec. 4.

3. ELECTRICITY PRICING MODEL

The electricity prices that CSPs pay are the result of the trading at each step of the supply chain. Any trading inefficiency along the chain reflects into the final prices. A well-known example is the extremely high electricity retail prices in California during 2001, which were due to inefficiencies coming from the spot markets [16]. Furthermore, inefficiencies may also arise between a utility and a CSP. Demand uncertainty may result in economic loss for the utility due to over-/under- estimation of the required supply.

In this section we present a model that shows how utilities have to increase retail prices in order to ensure certain profit margin in face of the economic loss caused by GLB. Consequently, CSPs doing GLB (as in Fig. 1(b)) actually may end up paying *higher* electricity bills than not doing GLB (as in Fig. 1(a)).

3.1 Prediction Error Increases Retail Price

We begin by showing how larger errors in demand prediction will lead to higher retail prices. Utilities make profit by determining a proper retail price for selling electricity. Let d be the actual demand for a particular hour in the next day and $\tilde{d}$ be the utility's prediction of d. Let w_b be the average (MCP) price at which the utility purchased $\tilde{d}$ amount of electricity for that hour from the day-ahead market.

Without prediction error, *i.e.*, $\tilde{d} = d$, given a price[4] p_0, the utility obtains a desired expected profit for the hour as

$$(p_0 - w_b)\, d. \tag{1}$$

With prediction error, the utility suffers economic loss as compared to the error-free case.

- In case of over-prediction, there is $\tilde{d} - d > 0$ amount of electricity surplus (and it cannot be stored). In today's practice, the utility can sell them back to a GENCO at an average marginal price denoted as w_s (usually $w_b > w_s$). The economic loss to the utility is $(w_b - w_s)\left(\tilde{d} - d\right)$.

- In case of under-prediction, there is $d - \tilde{d} > 0$ amount of unmatched demand to be urgently balanced by the utility to avoid power outage. In today's practice, the utility can purchase supply in the hour-ahead or real-time markets to satisfy urgent demand, but at a price higher than in day-ahead markets. Denote the average marginal price of buying electricity in urgency as w_u ($w_u > w_b$). The economic loss to the utility is then $(w_u - w_b)\left(d - \tilde{d}\right)$.

In order to compensate the economic loss of the utility due to prediction error, and to obtain the same expected profit in Eq. 1, the utility needs to set a retail price p *higher* than p_0 (the price for the error-free case) according to:

$$
\begin{aligned}
p = p_0 &+ (w_b - w_s)\, \mathbb{E}\left[\left(\tilde{d} - d\right)^+ / d\right] \\
&+ (w_u - w_b)\, \mathbb{E}\left[\left(d - \tilde{d}\right)^+ / d\right] > p_0.
\end{aligned}
\tag{2}
$$

In today's practice, prediction error is specified in terms of *mean absolute percentage error* (MAPE), defined as

$$\Delta d = \mathbb{E}\left[\left|\tilde{d} - d\right| / d\right]$$

With only MAPE available, the utility can define its price as

$$p = p_0 + (w_u - w_s)\, \Delta d. \tag{3}$$

3.2 Market Volatility Increases Retail Price

So far, we have considered that the MCP w_b is a value provided by the market. In practice, following the discussion in Sec. 2.1, this wholesale price depends on whether the bids that the utility places in the market auction are granted with supply. We model that in each location there are a day-ahead market and a real-time market,

---

[4]The process of how a utility determines its retail price can be highly involved (consideration factors include competition from other local utilities). A vital requirement that the price has to be high enough to guarantee the (expected) profit is larger than a minimum for the utility to stay in business.

which run for each hour (of the next day). We also assume that the utility places a single bid $(b, \tilde{d})$ in the day-ahead market; here b represents the bidding price, while $\tilde{d}$ is the bidding electricity quantity, which must match the predicted demand. If the bid fails to win in the auction, i.e., it is lower than the day-ahead MCP, then the electricity is purchased at the real-time MCP.

Denote w_t and w_u as the MCPs of the day-ahead and real-time markets, respectively. Then, the marginal electricity price for a particular hour is

$$
w_b = \begin{cases} w_t, & \text{if } b \ge w_t; \\ w_u, & \text{otherwise.} \end{cases}
\tag{4}
$$

Based on historical data, the MCP distribution for each market can be estimated. Denote f_t and f_u as the probability density functions of w_t and w_u, respectively. Then the average wholesale price $\overline{w}_b$ is given by,

$$\mathbb{E}\left[w_b\right] = \int_0^b x \cdot f_t(x)dx + \mathbb{E}\left[w_u\right] \int_b^\infty f_t(x)dx \tag{5}$$

Note the dependency on the bidding price. The right term of the equation, $\Delta w = \mathbb{E}\left[w_u\right] \int_b^\infty f_t(x)dx$, is an additional (marginal) cost due a wrong estimation of the MCP while choosing the bidding price. Following a similar development as for the demand prediction error, market volatility increases the average retail price like

$$p = p_0 + (w_u - w_s)\, \Delta d + \Delta w. \tag{6}$$

3.3 Discussion: Incentives for Coordination

Based on this electricity pricing model, demand and MCP prediction are critical for the operation of the utilities. Currently, demand prediction is negligible. Electrcity demand is rather predictable as it follows patterns that repeats daily, with seasonality during weekends and holidays.

Although its impact depends on the amount of routed electricity, GLB may introduce utterly different demand patterns. When used extensively, the difficulty for a utility to predict routed electricity demand is that the demand also depends on the prices in other locations, which may not be disclosed timely to the utility (unless the utility is a market participant in all the locations). Therefore, just by adapting local demand prediction methods to GLB may not be enough to yield accurate predictions. On the other hand, coordination does removes this demand-side uncertainty, it is possible the first incentive for the utilities to coordinate with CSPs.

The second incentive is related to Demand-Side Management (DSM) techniques. GLB and DSM are similar in the sense that they both make the demand elastic to prices. As prices increase for a particular time, users may decrease the demand. The difference resides in that, while DSM defers demand to off-peak hours *when* prices are cheaper, GLB routes demand to other locations *where* prices are cheaper.

Consequently, since demand elasticity depends on the prices in other locations, then (i) the demand may not be deferred to other hours as in conventional DSM, but consumed in other locations, possibly served by other utilities operating there and thus decreasing the local demand. (ii) Off-peak reduction may be more difficult to achieve in locations where prices are cheaper. Even if prices are increased to that end, they may still be cheaper than in other locations.

Summarizing, for utilities it is harder to deploy DSM unilaterally, having another incentive to coordinate with CSPs. In the next section, we introduce a cooperative model in which CSPs doing

GLB can exploit their positioning in multiple locations. In this scenario, if the CSP and utility cooperates, then demand uncertainty (Δd) is suppressed.

In addition, the fact that a part of the CSPs demand does not have to be attended locally, allows to purchase and consume the electricity in multiple locations. That implies having more opportunities to obtain that electricity, what immediately decreases the level of risk faced in the auctions and thus the market uncertainty (Δw).

As for the utilities, this model also present incentives to cooperate as they could retail at lower prices, avoid a potential operatonal losses when CSPs use GLB extensively and simplify their purchase of electricity in the markets, at least the supply corresponding to the datacenters.

4. A BROKER-ASSISTED GLB SOLUTION

Motivated by the recent practice of large CSPs moving into electricity markets and the deployment of *SmartGrid* infrastructure, we propose a cooperative scenario that is efficient with respect to the pricing model we just shown. In this scenario, CSPs purchase their electricity needs either directly from markets or through brokers. By doing GLB and electricity procurement jointly, CSPs can eliminate the trading inefficiencies we discussed in the previous section. Consequently, GLB can be used without causing economic losses to utilities, and CSPs can still exploit their presence in multiple geo-locations to reduce electricity cost.

Implicitly, this approach creates a "geo-distributed supply chain" illustrated in Fig. 1(c), in which a large CSPs like Google, which can buy and sell electricity directly from/to the spot markets since 2010 [14], can first bid in different spot markets, *i.e.*, *balance its bids*, and then it can balance its load across geo-distributed data centers according to the obtained electricity supply, *i.e.*, *balance its bits*.

4.1 Joint GLB and Electricity Procurement: Problem Formulation

In our broker-assisted solution, the CSP needs to solve a joint GLB and electricity procurement problem. We first present the setting and necessary notation. Without loss of generality, we consider the problem for a particular hour of a day. Consider a CSP that receives U_i amount of service requests from location i ($1 \leq i \leq m$), and it runs data centers at n locations where data center at location j has a capacity of C_j ($1 \leq j \leq n$). We assume the CSP, based on their service history, can estimate U_i ($1 \leq i \leq m$) accurately, which is aligned with the recent successes on using time series analysis for estimating user service requests [11].

We model the GLB quality of service constraint by defining $a_{ij} = 1$ if data center at location j serves requests at location i with satisfactory quality of service, $a_{ij} = 0$ otherwise.

Let z_{ij} be the corresponding network cost of serving one request from location i in the data center at location j. Let $u_{ij} \geq 0$ be the amount of requests from location i served by the data center at location j, then the total requests served by data center at location j is $\sum_{i=1}^{m} u_{ij} a_{ij}$. Let γ be the conversion ratio that maps the total requests to the amount of electricity needed to serve the requests[5], then the electricity demand for serving $\sum_{i=1}^{m} u_{ij} a_{ij}$ amount of requests is simply $\tilde{d} = \gamma \cdot \sum_{i=1}^{m} u_{ij} a_{ij}$.

We denote the expected wholesale price at location j as $\mathbb{E}\left[w_b^j\right]$. Recall this expected value is a function of the bidding price b_j, real-time expected price w_u^j and the probability density functions f_t^j and f_u^j (see Eq. 11).

[5]For example, as reported by Google [26], each search consumes 0.28 Watts-hour electricity in its data centers.

With the above notations, we can formulate the joint GLB and electricity procurement problem for a CSP as follows:

$$\min \sum_{j=1}^{n} \mathbb{E}\left[w_b^j\right] \cdot \sum_{i=1}^{m} u_{ij} a_{ij} + \sum_{i=1}^{m} \sum_{j=1}^{n} z_{ij} u_{ij} \quad (7)$$

$$\text{s.t.} \sum_{j=1}^{n} u_{ij} a_{ij} \geq U_i,\ 1 \leq i \leq m, \quad (8)$$

$$u_{ii} \geq \alpha \cdot U_i, 1 \leq i \leq m, \quad (9)$$

$$\sum_{i=1}^{m} u_{ij} a_{ij} \leq \min\left\{C_j, \frac{1}{\gamma}\tilde{d}_j\right\},\ 1 \leq j \leq n, \quad (10)$$

$$\mathbb{E}\left[w_b^j\right] = \int_0^{b_j} x \cdot f_t^j(x) dx + \mathbb{E}\left[w_u^j\right] \int_{b_j}^{\infty} f_t^j(x) dx,\ (11)$$

$$\text{var. } u_{ij} \geq 0, b_j \geq 0, \tilde{d}_j \geq 0, 1 \leq i \leq m, 1 \leq j \leq n.$$

In the above problem, the objective in Eq. 7 represents the total expected cost of energy procurement and network load balancing cost. The constraints in Eq. 8 say that the demand at every location i must be served. The constraints in Eq. 9 put a minimum on the percentage of the demand that must be served locally; here $0 \leq \alpha \leq 1$ is a pre-assigned constant. The constraints in Eq. 10 mean that the total allocated requests to data center at location j can exceed neither its physical capacity (*e.g.*, the number of total servers) nor the "effective" capacity determined by the purchased electricity $\tilde{d}_j$. Eq. 11 is the closed-form formula of $\mathbb{E}\left[w_b^j\right]$ expressed in b_j, f_t^j, and f_u^j (since $\mathbb{E}\left[w_u^j\right] = \int_0^{\infty} x \cdot f_u^j(x) dx$).

We propose the following algorithm to find the optimum value of this formulation.

4.2 An optimal algorithm

The approach we follow to solve the joint GLB and electricity procurement problem in Eq. 7-11 is based on the following observation. If $\left(b_j, \tilde{d}_j\right)$ ($1 \leq j \leq n$) are given, then $\mathbb{E}\left[w_b^j\right]$ and $\min\left\{C_j, \frac{1}{\gamma}\tilde{d}_j\right\}$ are fixed and the above problem in Eqs. 7-11 reduces to the standard GLB formulation in [26].

Thus the novelty of our problem resides in that the electricity must be obtained from the auctions, so that the electricity price and quantity are now random variables. Consequently, the GLB optimization becomes a stochastic optimization problem. So as to solve this problem, we use a two-stage technique used in stochastic programming. In our case, this means that first we try to obtain the optimal bids, denoted as $\left(b_j^*, d_j^*\right)$ ($1 \leq j \leq n$), and then in a second stage, once the outcome of the auctions is known, we solve the remaining GLB problem given $\left(b_j^*, d_j^*\right)$ ($1 \leq j \leq n$).

The first difficulty we find is that in our case the first stage is a non-convex problem, in general. The term $E[w_b^j]$ in the objective function is not convex in b_j due to the arbitrary form of $f_t^j(x)$. Although non-convex problems are difficult to solve and there are no standard techniques for solving them, we can solve the problem in Eq. 7-11 in a divide-and-conquer manner. Note that, the optimal bidding price b_j^* does not depend on the workload assignment u_{ij}.

Based on this observation, we can solve the non-convex problem sequentially. Hence, we have two stages and for the first stage we need to solve two sub-problems, **SP1-j** and **SP2**. Problem **SP1-j** provides the optimum bidding price b_j^* by minimizing the price expectation in each regional market. Afterwards, we use the outcome of **SP1-j** in **SP2** and we compute the bid quantities d_j^*.

Therefore, for any $1 \leq j \leq n$ we solve **SP1-j**

$$\textbf{SP1-j}: \qquad \min_{b_j} \quad E[w_b^j].$$

Even though **SP1-j** is still a non-convex problem, it reduces to compute the optimal bid in an auction with substitute items (all valued at the MCP). The optimal bidding strategy in this type of auctions is to bid at the *true price*. In our case in which we assume that the utility aims at profit zero, the true value is directly $b_j^* = E[w_u^j]$. That is because the CSP will always buy the electricity at the real-time (expected) price, as long as the bid fails in the day-ahead auction. Hence, the true price is the price expectation in the local real-time market.

Second, let the minimum expected price in **SP1-j** be $(w_b^j)^*$, then we solve **SP2** to determine the tentative workload assignment u_{ij}^* in the first stage.

$$\textbf{SP2}: \qquad \min \sum_{j=1}^n (w_b^j)^* \cdot \left[\sum_{i=1}^m u_{ij} a_{ij} \right] + \sum_{i=1}^m \sum_{j=1}^n z_{ij} u_{ij}$$

$$\text{s.t.} \ \sum_{j=1}^n u_{ij} a_{ij} \geq U_i, \ 1 \leq i \leq m,$$

$$u_{ii} \geq \alpha \cdot U_i, \ 1 \leq i \leq m,$$

$$\sum_{i=1}^m u_{ij} a_{ij} \leq C_j, \ 1 \leq j \leq n,$$

$$\text{var.} \ u_{ij} \geq 0, \ 1 \leq i \leq m, \ 1 \leq j \leq n.$$

SP2 is a linear programming problem and we can solve it to get its optimal solution u_{ij}^* by standard techniques. After that, we can calculate the bidding quantity d_j^* for the jth data center by

$$d_j^* = \gamma \sum_{i=1}^m u_{ij}^* a_{ij}, 1 \leq j \leq n. \qquad (12)$$

After the auctions are executed, depending on the outcome and the winning and non-winning bids, we get the final electricity price w_b^j and amount d_j. These values are used to solve the second and final stage, from which we obtain the final workload assignment u_{ij}. This workload is computed by replacing the expected values, $\mathbb{E}\left[w_b^j\right]$ and $\tilde{d}_j$, in Eqs. 7-11 by w_j and d_j.

Algorithm 1 Algorithm for *Broker-assisted GLB*

1: **for** $1 \leq j \leq n$ **do**
2:     $b_j^* \leftarrow E\left[w_u^j\right]$;
3:     $E[w_b^j]^* \leftarrow \int_0^{b_j^*} x \cdot f_t^j(x) dx + \mathbb{E}\left[w_u^j\right] \int_{b_j^*}^\infty f_t^j(x) dx$;
4: **end for**
5: Get the (optimal) tentative workload assignment $[u_{ij}^*]_{n \times m}$ by solving **SP2**;
6: **for** $1 \leq j \leq n$ **do**
7:     $d_j^* \leftarrow \gamma \sum_i u_{ij}^* a_{ij}$;
8:     bid with (b_j^*, d_j^*);
9: **end for**
10: Do conventional GLB with auction outcomes w_b^j and d_j to obtain the final optimal workload assignment u_{ij}

We summarize the above understandings into *Algorithm* 1 and show its optimality by *Theorem 1*. For $1 \leq i \leq m, 1 \leq j \leq n$,

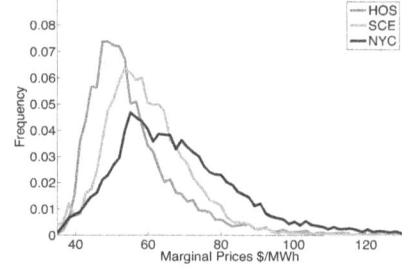

Figure 2: MCP distribution for San Diego (SCE), Houston (HOS) and New York City (NYC) in 2009 - 2012

Theorem 1. *The bids (b_j^*, d_j^*) and workload assignment u_{ij} obtained by Algorithm 1 are an optimal solution to the problem in Eq. 7-11.*

PROOF. see *Appendix 1* □

5. PERFORMANCE EVALUATION

We evaluate the performance of the broker-assisted GLB solution that we propose. First, we describe and characterize the dataset we use in the experiments. Part of this analysis serves as a validation of the incentive analysis and assumptions made about the workload. Second, we analyze the cost effectiveness and optimality of the solution.

Our evaluation is carried out in a scenario in which a (virtual) CSP operates three data centers, in San Diego, Houston, and New York City. We choose this scenario as it reflects the tendency of large CSPs, such as Google and Facebook, to deploy customized data centers in the East, Mid, and West part of the US. For this scenario we take into account the following considerations:

Ratio of workload eligible for GLB: As Eq. 9 shows, some portion of workload must be served locally while the rest is *eligible* for GLB. We denote the percentage of the workload that is eligible for GLB as β, and $\beta = 1 - \alpha$. The proportion between them is usually due to many factors that vary from one provider to another, e.g., response time requirement, resource and information availability, SLAs, etc. Therefore, we investigate the performances of our Broker-assisted GLB with different values of β.

Topology constraints: The same as in [26], we assume that eligible workload is re-routed maximum between two consecutive locations before seemingly degrading the quality of service. Therefore, the CSP can balance San Diego's eligible load between San Diego and Houston, New York's load between New York and Houston, and Houston's among the three locations.

Internet-related costs: Furthermore, in our simulation we do not consider the internet cost. It does not mean that we treat that kind of cost as negligible, yet we adopt this model as (i) large internet companies like Facebook or Google negotiate with carriers on a nationwide basis, therefore bandwidth prices are usually not geographically differentiated [26]; (ii) Internet transit costs are referred the maximum traffic during a time period or the so called 95-percentile of the bandwidth allocation [7]. Thus we assume that network related cost are similar regardless the use of GLB.

Data centers' capacity: The maximum workload that CSPs can re-route is estimated nowadays between $20 - 30\%$. Taking into account that not all load is eligible for GLB, we assume that data centers' capacity is large enough to cope with additional incoming load due to GLB. We justify this assumption using the fact that typically data center owners overdimension their capacity, typically, at least by 20% [1].

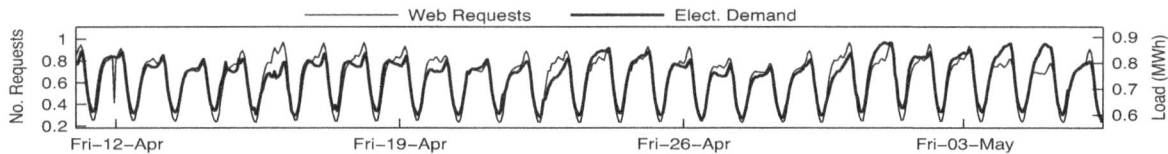

Figure 3: Evolution of the (aggregated) electricity demand and web workload between April 12th and May 6th 2013.

5.1 Dataset Characterization

Electricity demand and prices: To obtain the total electricity demand for each of the three local utilities, we crawl the hourly electricity demand from the spot markets in San Diego [10], CA, Houston [12], TX, and New York [24], NY for 2009-2012, and choose nodal demand until the data center demand represents to 30% of the utility's demand (following the back-of-the-envelope computation presented in the introduction). We also collect the hourly MCPs of the three spot markets for the same period. The empirical distributions of the MCP for the three markets are shown in Fig. 2.

Finally, to maximize their prediction accuracy, utilities take into account the weather conditions and daily activity patterns. We crawl the hourly weather conditions [35] in the three areas and the official holidays calendar for 2009 - 2012. We omit the weekends in all our experiments, due to the seasonality of the workload and electricity demand during these days.

CSP Workload: We use traces from the Akamai CDN as the user request workload of the (virtual) CSP in its three data centers. We crawl Akamai's Internet Observatory website [8] to obtain the number of HTTP requests per minute against the Akamai CDN in North America. Akamai CDN relies on co-location data centers that individually do not represent large electricity consumption. Nevertheless, using the conversion rate of $1kJ$ per query (0.28 $Watts \cdot h$) claimed by Google for its data centers [26], the crawled workload aggregately creates a power consumption of 125 MW, which may serve well to approximate the consumption of three Facebook's data centers at full utilization (according to [5, 3]).

Since Akamai does not dissect the information of its workload per location, we have run a preliminary experiment to make an educated approximation of the workload splitting for the three locations. We aggregate the electricity demand curves from the three locations into a time series, respecting the time difference between the aggregated time series of each location. We compare this (normalized) electricity demand aggregate with the time series of the (normalized) number of web requests against the Akamai CDN. The two series are displayed in Fig. 3.

The correlation coefficient of these aggregated curves is 0.92. Most differences appear during the morning and more noticeably in some weekends, what we associate with the industrial and commercial activity. If we take into account that the three areas we are using have similar development levels, then it is reasonable to assume that a random sample among the population of these three areas will provide similar results about the usage of electricity and web services (and the ratio between these two). Therefore, splitting the number web requests in each location according to the ratios of electricity demand among the locations should provide us with a good approximation.

5.2 GLB increases Utilities Prediction Error

As GLB dynamically allocates energy-intensive workload to data centers at different geo-locations, it increases electricity demand variation for the local utilities. According to Eq. 6, if this variation introduces prediction errors, it may result in higher retail prices. To

Table 1: MAPE and Prices vs. Balanced Load

GLB	San Diego		Houston		New York	
(%Load)	MAPE (%) & Avg. Price ($/MWh)					
0	3.0	47.9	2.7	43.9	3.0	70.2
15	6.8	49.3	3.5	45.5	6.4	70.8
30	8.2	49.8	7.3	47.2	7.6	71.0
45	10.7	50.8	10.5	48.7	8.6	71.2
60	14.3	52.2	14.8	50.8	10.7	71.6
MAPE/GLB	0.714		0.921		0.345	

assess such phenomenon, we carry out a case study based on our real-world dataset and analyze to what extent this extra demand variation will lead to larger errors in utilities' demand prediction.

We evaluate the prediction error of the utility. We change the demand corresponding to the allowed GLB workload between 0-30% of the total utility demand. We also extend the range up to 60% to evaluate a futuristic scenario reflecting the data center electricity demand growth. For each hour, the CSP solves a standard GLB cost-minimization problem as the one in [26] to allocate its allowed GLB workload optimally.

The evaluation is carried out assuming that utilities use commonly adopted *neural networks* (NN)-based demand forecast algorithms [32] to predict their electricity demand[6]. Utilities use NNs as a black-box, which require training with sample data. Once they are trained, for each hour, the NN takes as inputs the weather forecast, historical demand records, and whether it is a public holiday/weekend or not. Based on these input values, the NN predicts the demand for that particular hour, with a certain estimation error.

We train the NN with data from 2009-2011 and use the trained algorithm to perform hourly demand prediction during 2012. To this end, we use different training datasets, one for the case without GLB and one for each GLB eligible ratio that we study (for that we perform GLB on the training load as well). We compare the prediction and the actual demand, record the MAPE, and compute the retail prices with and without prediction errors according to Eqs. 1 and 3 with $p_0 = w_b$ (modeling an altruistic utility targeting zero expected profit in the error-free case).

Electricity Demand Prediction Error: The results of how GLB affects retail prices are summarized in Table 1. Each data center location has two associated columns. The first column shows the MAPE in the presence of varying GLB load (in percentage, increased at 15% resolution). The second column is the corresponding average retail prices according to Eq. 3. The last row shows the ratio MAPE per % of routable load to other locations.

Several interesting observations can be made. First, without GLB (corresponding to the third row of 0% GLB load), the NN algorithm can predict the actual demand pretty accurately – with a MAPE at most 3%. A closer look into the prediction accuracy of the NN al-

---

[6]For a real case, see http://www.mathworks.com/ tagteam/63938_91460v01_GasNaturalFenosa_ English_final.pdf.

gorithm for the San Diego site shows the hourly MAPE has a mean of 3% and a standard variation of 6%. These results show that without GLB, NNs can predict accurately the real-world electricity demand, justifying its widespread adoption in practice.

Second, as the GLB load percentage increases, MAPE of the NN algorithm becomes worse. For example, in Table 1, when the GLB load increases to 30%, the MAPE for San Diego increases to 8.15%, 2.7 times of that of no GLB. The standard deviation of MAPE is 11.3%, almost twice of that of no GLB. These results are in sharp contrast to the case of no GLB, and confirm our intuition that GLB introduces demand uncertainty and extra errors in the demand prediction.

Increment on the Electricity Bill for CSPs: Using the pricing model from Section 3, we can compute the increment in the retail prices corresponding to the economic loss of the utility. This is displayed also in Table 1; **the retail price for San Diego on average increases by 0.7% for every increment of 1% in the GLB load.**

We add to the pricing information the workload allocation to compute the cost. We do it for the cases where the CSP is able to move $\beta = 0\%, 15\%, 30\%$, and 60% of the total local utility demand. We study and compare the total electricity cost (sum of the three locations for the year 2012) between the baseline case, $\beta = 0\%$, and the rest (in percentage).

Results show that in the $\beta = 15\%$ case **the CSP actually ends up paying a total bill 1% higher than not doing GLB at all**. In the $\beta = 30\%$ case where the CSP can move up to 30% of its overall workload, the ability to aggressively move workload to low-price locations improves the results, despite the increase in the electricity prices due to higher degrees of uncertainty. However, there is still minor savings in the overall electricity bill, about 3%, while the CSP is already moving the full allowed GLB workload of its data centers. Finally, higher benefits could be achieved for large *allowed* GLB load. For the $\beta = 60\%$ case, the GLB effect provides 9% cost reduction. However, this case requires the CSP to move a workload that is beyond the *feasible* percentage in data centers nowadays (20-30% [26]).

5.3 Cost Reduction with Joint Procurement

We evaluate the performance of the Algorithm 1 in the scenario with three data-centers. We have implemented the algorithm in a simulator of market auctions, which we feed with our dataset.

We first assume that 30% of the workload can be routed freely for the broker-assisted GLB model, i.e. $\beta = 30\%$, and compute the average cost per hour for the CSP with or without GLB. The result is displayed in Fig. 4(a). Each bar represents, for each hour of the day, the average cost. The results show the day and night pattern of the web requests. From the figure we also identify two valleys at noon and around 5-7 pm, which we associate with lunch time and commuting after work and the peak hour around 8-9 pm.

The gray portion of the bars are the average cost for our broker-assisted solution. The darker portion of the bars represent the extra cost in average that the CSP pays in the $\beta = 0\%$ case, which is noticeable in most of the hours. The total electricity can be reduced by 12.8% in average on a daily basis.

Results on a yearly basis are shown in Fig. 5 (real workload curve). The tendency shows that larger values of β lead to higher cost reduction remains. The cost reduction ratio is 4.13% when $\beta = 5\%$ and increases steadily to 12.7% for $\beta = 30\%$.

5.4 Performance degradation by workload prediction error

One of the main assumptions behind the suitability of broker-assisted GLB solution is that, as a consequence of their geogra-

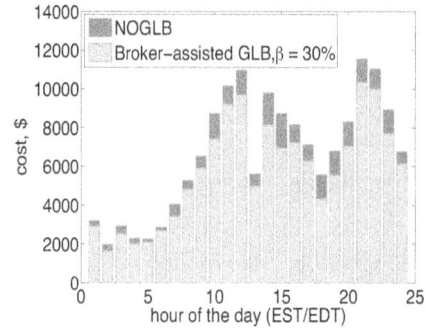

(a) Cost comparison between the $\beta = 0\%$ and broker-assisted with $\beta = 30\%$ case.

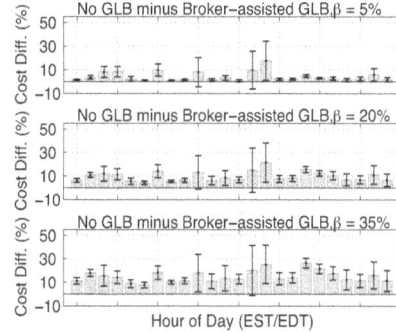

(b) Hourly cost difference between $\beta = 0\%$ and the three *Broker* cases, $\beta = 5\%, 20\%$ and 35% GLB.

Figure 4: CSP cost for each hour of the day as 4(a) average cost and 4(b) differential w.r.t. the $\beta = 0\%$ case.

phic diversification and ability to accommodate demand, CSPs do a more (economically) efficient use of the electricity supply-chain. Whether this assumption holds depends strongly on the ability of CSPs to predict workloads more efficiently than how utilities predict electricity demand.

In the simulations shown until now, we assumed that CSPs know the future workload exactly. We now re-compute the cost reduction ratio by executing Alg. 1 over predicted workload instead of real workload. For the predicted workload case, we sample the workload of the same hour and same day of the week in the previous 5 weeks and use the sample average as estimator. Results displayed in Fig. 5 show the impact of the workload prediction error. The cost reduction ratio is lower for all values of β when the predicted workload is used instead.

We also test the broker-assisted GLB's performance with different prediction errors (MAPE), while setting $\beta = 20\%$. Consistently, the curve in Fig. 6 shows that the bigger the prediction error, the more the performance degrades.

Finally, after showing that the workload MAPE does have an impact on the cost reduction ratio, we compare the CSPs' workload MAPE with the utilities' electricity demand MAPE. The prediction error distribution for each hour of the day during 2012 are shown for the workload MAPE in Fig. 7(a) and for the electricity demand MAPE in the San Diego market, cases $\beta = 0\%$ and $\beta = 30\%$, in Figs. 7(b)-7(c).

Although the prediction method used for the CSP workload, described above, is less elaborated than the NN we used for the utili-

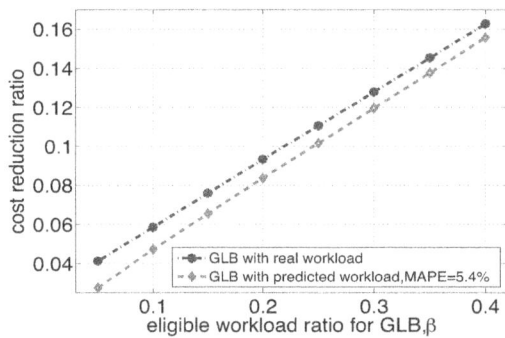

Figure 5: cost reduction ratio for GLB with real workload and predicted workload, as β increases from 5% to 40%

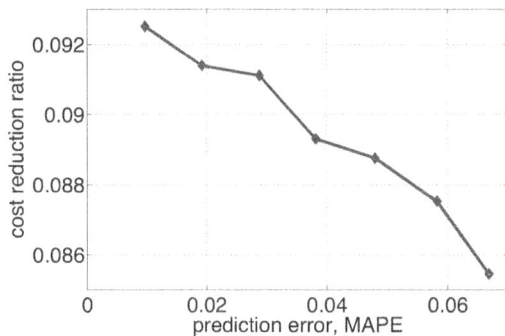

Figure 6: cost reduction ratio with different prediction errors, as $\beta = 20\%$

ties' demand prediction, it achieves only 5% MAPE, which is close to the 3% of the $\beta = 0\%$ and substantially more efficient than the MAPE for the $\beta = 30\%$ case. This results point out that if GLB is used, CSPs can do a more effective prediction of their demand than the utilities.

6. RELATED WORK

The seminal work suggesting the use of GLB to reduce the electricity bill of geo-distributed data-center owners is probably by Qureshi *et al.* [26]. Subsequent publications analyzed the technical feasibility and assess the possibilities of GLB [20, 36, 33, 22, 13]. All these works consider that GLB is innocuous to the electricity prices, what we show it is a strong assumption. We suggest that our broker-assisted model opens the possibility to exploit the advantages of these works without any undesired effects for the utility companies. More recently, other works start considering the potential of using spot markets information in data centers [17]. They show promising results, using markets information to defer energy consuming tasks in data centers while elevated prices are accused. Compared to our broker-assisted solution, they do not explore the benefits of a jointly scheduling of energy purchase and consumption.

Regarding this optimal procurement, cloud-providers are completely new players in the electricity markets. In fact, pricing models specific to datacenter demand response has been recently proposed [21]. These pricing models analyze the demand response of only one datacenter. We consider several datacenters instead,

showing that in contrast to the utilities, the CSP is able to bid more efficiently in markets in different locations. Finally, the optimization of those bids also provides a novel study case for the existing literature on strategic bidding [29, 15, 19].

7. CONCLUSIONS

We carry out a comprehensive study of the potential of GLB on reducing the electricity bills for CSPs that operate multiple geo-distributed data centers. By analysis and case study using real-world traces, we show that as GLB introduces extra uncertainty in local electricity demand, it causes trading inefficiency between local utilities and CSPs and subsequently economic loss to the utilities. As such, to ensure certain profit margin in face of such GLB-induced economic loss, utilities will have to increase electricity prices. This challenges the common assumption in existing studies that GLB has no impact on electricity prices. Our study reveals a perhaps surprising observation – CSPs doing GLB can see poor cost reduction or even pay more in electricity than not doing GLB. We then propose to allow CSPs to purchase electricity from markets through brokers. By doing GLB and electricity procurement jointly, CSPs eliminate the trading inefficiency between them and utilities and the economic loss to utilities. Meanwhile, CSPs can still exploit their presence in multiple geo-locations to reduce electricity bills – up to 12% less than not doing GLB, for our case study based on real-world traces.

8. ACKNOWLEDGEMENTS

This work was partially supported by National Basic Research Program of China (Project No. 2012CB315904 and 2013CB336700) and several grants from the University Grants Committee of the Hong Kong S.A.R., China (Area of Excellence Grant Project No. AoE/E-02/08, Theme-based Research Scheme Project No. T23-407/13-N, and General Research Fund Project No. 411011).

9. REFERENCES

[1] Data center knowledge archive. available at http://www.datacenterknowledge.com.
[2] Duke energy annual report 2011. http://www.duke-energy.com/pdfs/DukeEnergy_2011_AR-10k.pdf.
[3] Facebook's new 'cloud'. Technical report, ECONorthWest, 2011.
[4] 2012 state of the markets report. Technical report, Federal Energy Regulatory Commission, 2012.
[5] How clean is your cloud? Technical report, Greenpeace Climate, 2012.
[6] A. Beloglazov, R. Buyya, Y. C. Lee, and A. Zomaya. A taxonomy and survey of energy-efficient data centers and cloud computing systems. *Advances in Computers, vol. 82, pp. 47-111*, 2011.
[7] M. Adler, R. K. Sitaraman, and H. Venkataramani. Algorithms for optimizing the bandwidth cost of content delivery. *Computer Networks*, 55(18):4007–4020, December 2011.
[8] Akamai Internet Observatory website.
[9] L. Barroso and U. Holzle. The case for energy-proportional computing. *IEEE Computer*, 40(12):33–37, 2007.
[10] Caiso archive. available at http://www.caiso.com.
[11] G. Chen, W. He, J. Liu, S. Nath, L. Rigas, L. Xiao, and F. Zhao. Energy-aware server provisioning and load

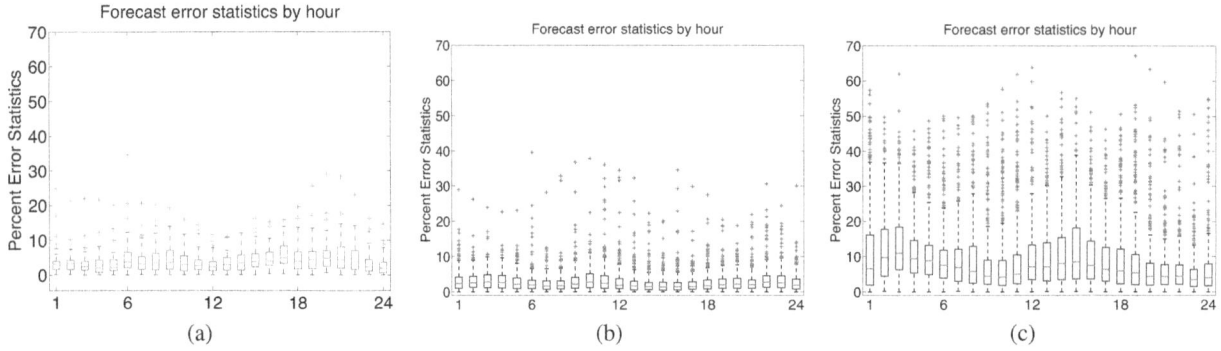

Figure 7: (a) MAPE for the CSP workload prediction error; (b) MAPE for the utility electricity demand prediction without GLB; (c) MAPE for the utility electricity demand prediction with GLB at 30%.

dispatching for connection-intensive internet services. In *Proc. USENIX NSDI*, 2008.

[12] Ercot archive. available at http://www.ercot.com.

[13] P. X. Gao, A. R. Curtis, B. Wong, and S. Keshav. It's not easy being green. In *Proceedings of the ACM SIGCOMM 2012*, pages 211–222, New York, NY, USA, 2012. ACM.

[14] Google energy wiki. http://en.wikipedia.org/wiki/Google_Energy.

[15] R. Herranz, A. Munoz San Roque, J. Villar, and F. Campos. Optimal demand-side bidding strategies in electricity spot markets. *Power Systems, IEEE Transactions on*, 27(3):1204 –1213, aug. 2012.

[16] P. Joskow. California's electricity crisis. *Oxford Review of Economic Policy*, 17(3):365–388, 2001.

[17] C. Kelly, A. Ruzzelli, and E. Mangina. Using Electricity Market Analytics to Reduce Cost and Environmental Impact. In *Proceedings of the 2013 IEEE Green Technologies Conference*, pages 414–421, 2013.

[18] J. G. Koomey. Growth in data center electricity use 2005 to 2010. *Oakland, CA: Analytics Press*, 2010.

[19] M. Liu and F. Wu. Risk management in a competitive electricity market. *International Journal of Electrical Power & Energy Systems*, 29(9):690–697, 2007.

[20] Z. Liu, M. Lin, A. Wierman, S. Low, and L. Andrew. Greening geographical load balancing. In *Proc. ACM SIGMETRICS*, pages 233–244, 2011.

[21] Z. Liu, I. Liu, S. Low, and A. Wierman. Pricing data center demand response. In *Proc. ACM SIGMETRICS '14*, Jun. 2014.

[22] J. Luo, L. Rao, and X. Liu. Data center energy cost minimization: a spatio-temporal scheduling approach. In *Proc. IEEE INFOCOM*, 2013.

[23] D. Meisner, B. Gold, and T. Wenisch. Powernap: eliminating server idle power. *ACM SIGPLAN Notices*, 2009.

[24] Nyiso archive. available at http://www.nyiso.com.

[25] 2011 Oregon Utility Statistics.

[26] A. Qureshi, R. Weber, H. Balakrishnan, J. Guttag, and B. Maggs. Cutting the electric bill for internet-scale systems. In *Proc. ACM SIGCOMM*, pages 123–134, 2009.

[27] R. Raghavendra, P. Ranganathan, V. Talwar, Z. Wang, and X. Zhu. No power struggles: Coordinated multi-level power management for the data center. In *ACM SIGARCH*, volume 36, pages 48–59, 2008.

[28] N. Rasmussen. Electrical efficiency modeling of data centers. *Technical Report White Paper*, 113, 2007.

[29] S. Sethi, H. Yan, J. Yan, and H. Zhang. An analysis of staged purchases in deregulated time-sequential electricity markets. *Journal of Industrial and Management Optimization*, 1(4):443–463, 2005.

[30] R. Sharma, C. Bash, C. Patel, R. Friedrich, and J. Chase. Balance of power: Dynamic thermal management for internet data centers. *IEEE Internet Computing*, 2005.

[31] Spain energy consumption. http://www.nationmaster.com/country/sp-spain/ene-energy.

[32] G. K. Tso and K. K. Yau. Predicting electricity energy consumption: A comparison of regression analysis, decision tree and neural networks. *Energy*, 32(9):1761–1768, 2007.

[33] R. Urgaonkar, B. Urgaonkar, M. Neely, and A. Sivasubramaniam. Optimal power cost management using stored energy in data centers. In *Proc. ACM SIGMETRICS*, pages 221–232, 2011.

[34] U.S. Environmental Protection Agency. Epa report on server and data center energy efficiency. *ENERGY STAR Program*, 2007.

[35] Weatherunderground. http://www.wunderground.com.

[36] P. Wendell, J. Jiang, M. Freedman, and J. Rexford. Donar: decentralized server selection for cloud services. In *Proc. ACM SIGCOMM*, volume 40, pages 231–242, 2010.

APPENDIX

Proof of *Theorem 1*

PROOF. There are three different variables b_j^*, d_j^* and u_{ij} for the Problem in Eq. 7-11, with $1 \leq i \leq m, 1 \leq j \leq n$. But since the definitive allocation u_{ij} is calculated in the second stage as a correction of the first stage, we need to show optimality of the cost expectation determined by b_j^* and d_j^*. We use the following notation

Notation	Description
$\mathbf{B} = [b_j]$	bidding vector
$\mathbf{U} = [u_{ij}]$	workload assignment matrix
$\mathbb{E}[w_b^j]$	electricity price expectation with b_j
$\mathbf{P} = [z_{ij} + \mathbb{E}[w_b^j]a_{ij}]$	price matrix for workload from the ith location to the jth location
$\mathcal{C}(\mathbf{B}, \mathbf{U})$	cost expectation with $\mathbf{B}$ and $\mathbf{U}$

By Eq. 7, we can obtain

$$\mathcal{C}(\mathbf{B}, \mathbf{U}) = \sum_{j=1}^{n} \mathbb{E}[w_b^j] \cdot \left[\sum_{i=1}^{m} u_{ij} a_{ij} \right] + \sum_{i=1}^{m} \sum_{j=1}^{n} z_{ij} u_{ij} \quad (13)$$

$$= \mathbf{U} \bullet [z_{ij} + \mathbb{E}[w_b^j] a_{ij}] \quad (14)$$

$$= \mathbf{U} \bullet \mathbf{P} \quad (15)$$

Suppose the solution by *Algorithm 1* is $\mathbf{B}^*$, $\mathbf{U}^*$, and the corresponding price matrix is $\mathbf{P}^*$. Let $\tilde{\mathbf{B}}, \tilde{\mathbf{U}}$ be another feasible solution and the corresponding price matrix is $\tilde{\mathbf{P}}$.

In fact, the optimal solution to **SP1** is $b_j^* = \mathbb{E}[w_u^j]$, which can be verified by

$$\begin{cases} \frac{d\mathbb{E}[w_b^j]}{db_j} \le 0, \text{when } b_j < \mathbb{E}[w_u^j] \\ \frac{d\mathbb{E}[w_b^j]}{db_j} \ge 0, \text{when } b_j > \mathbb{E}[w_u^j] \end{cases}$$

Since we obtain $\mathbf{B}^*$ by minimizing the electricity price expectation $\mathbb{E}[w_b^j]$ (**SP1**), and z_{ij} is constant, we can get

$$\mathbf{P}_{ij}^* \le \tilde{\mathbf{P}}_{ij}, \forall i, j$$

Then

$$\tilde{\mathbf{U}} \bullet \mathbf{P}^* \le \tilde{\mathbf{U}} \bullet \tilde{\mathbf{P}} \quad (16)$$

Furthermore, we obtain $\mathbf{U}^*$ by minimizing $\mathbf{U} \bullet \mathbf{P}^*$(**SP2**), i.e.

$$\mathbf{U}^* \bullet \mathbf{P}^* \le \tilde{\mathbf{U}} \bullet \mathbf{P}^* \quad (17)$$

With Eq. 16 and Eq. 17, we can get $\mathcal{C}(\mathbf{B}^*, \mathbf{U}^*) \le \mathcal{C}(\tilde{\mathbf{B}}, \tilde{\mathbf{U}})$.

$\square$

Understanding the Environmental Costs
of Fixed Line Networking

Louise Krug
BT PLC
Adastral Park, Ipswich
Suffolk, UK
+44 1473 629839
Louise.krug@bt.com

Mark Shackleton
BT PLC
Adastral Park, Ipswich
Suffolk, UK
+44 1473 629841
Mark.shackleton@bt.com

Fabrice Saffre
BT PLC
Adastral Park, Ipswich
Suffolk, UK
+44 1473 629840
Fabrice.Saffre@bt.com

ABSTRACT

In this paper, we calculate the power-per-line and the energy-per-bit associated with real-world communication networking. We highlight the key real-world network deployment issues, particularly legacy systems and utilization, which can have a strong bearing on the level of energy efficiency. We show how and why the real-world metric values differ from prior models of network energy use. We show how including embodied energy leads to the overall environmental impact being minimized only when legacy systems are maintained. We capture the full end to end impact of networking including an understanding of the data centre and home equipment. An accurate understanding is needed if claims around the potential carbon benefit of communications technologies are to be substantiated.

Categories and Subject Descriptors

C.2.3 [**Computer-Communication Networks**]: Network Operations

General Terms

Measurement, Performance.

Keywords

Network energy

1. INTRODUCTION

Reducing the likelihood of significant global warming leading to climate change and reducing energy dependence are key, inter-related problems for both industry and government [23]. It is claimed that communication products have the potential to provide a net carbon benefit– enabling customers to save up to five times the carbon emissions that provision of the product consumes [17]. For example, audio and video conferencing and teleworking lead to travel reduction, whilst electronic delivery of goods and services can also reduce the need to extract and process raw materials into end products. However, such benefits can only be achieved if the energy required to provide the alternative services is constrained. This paper therefore investigates the energy and carbon costs of communications based on the BT UK network.

BT, a major supplier of telecommunications services in the UK, uses over 0.7% of the UK's electricity supply and produces 316 thousand tonnes of CO_2e each year to operate its UK network [5]. This energy use is significant; it is of a similar scale to the energy used within data centres worldwide. [13]. However, unlike data centres, this energy use is less visible, as the energy is not consumed in a few large locations, rather relatively small amounts of energy are consumed in thousands of exchange buildings around the country. Another area of energy use that is not always immediately apparent is the so-called embodied energy associated with creating the electronic devices and fibre cabling needed for network operation.

To achieve the full potential of telecommunications networks to reduce the likelihood of significant climate change and to help tackle energy security issues, we need to ensure that the communications industry is not causing more problems than it is solving. To understand this we need accurate quantification of the actual energy use associated with communications networks.

In this paper we develop an end-to-end view of the energy and carbon impacts of a real-world network, based on measurement data available from BT's network. We develop an understanding of the key metrics of "power per line" and "energy per bit" applied to the fixed network based on observed data, highlighting key real-world network deployment issues that can have a strong bearing on the level of energy efficiency. We show how and why the real-world metric values differ from prior models of network energy use. To understand the full impact of communication networking, we need to look beyond the equipment within our own network and understand the impact of resources used in the home, in data centres and in other networks. Our main focus is on the electrical in-use energy, but we go beyond this to also consider the embodied energy and carbon impacts associated with networks and the services that they deliver.

2. BACKGROUND

In [4] the authors presented a model to estimate the energy impact of optical IP networks based on data from commercially available network equipment. The model network topology is a fair reflection of modern network structure and the model aims to capture practical implementation factors from the concentration that is applied as traffic shares resources through to the impact of cooling overheads. The model also shows how to evaluate the impact of changing equipment efficiency. The authors use this model to generate an expression of the power per access line of the Internet, as a function of access rate for various network access technologies. Such modeling capability is useful as it allows comparison between different architectural solutions without needing to rely on full implementation. They have then used their model to develop an understanding of cloud computing [6] – a technology that is often promoted as a green technology by centralizing computing resources and so enabling these resources to be efficiently managed. To achieve this, a proportion of the power per line is allocated to the specific cloud use – in particular a metric of "joules per bit" is used for shared network resources.

A broadly similar approach to modeling networks was used in [8] to compare different network architectures. This extended the analysis to include an estimate of the energy embodied within a network. This paper notes that the energy embodied in optical fibres is not insignificant, and so an architecture that minimises operational energy use may not minimise the total energy impact.

In the above models, the metrics of "power per line" and "joules per bit" are key. In this paper we consider how these metrics can be developed and used in a real-world, deployed network context.

In [15] the authors examine the question of the real-world cost of networking. They use a top down approach based on total electricity consumption of a number of network operators. An advantage of our study is that we can use the top down analysis to verify a bottom up analysis based on deployed equipment. This enables us to understand the relative impact of different service types. It is also easier for us to understand, for example, the impact of leased lines and virtual private networks.

Many attempts to understand carbon abatement could be seen to under-estimate the impact of the explosion in ICT equipment that has occurred over the last twenty years. It appears unlikely that we would have the growth in laptop and tablet devices if we did not have the network infrastructure to support them, so an end-to-end model of energy/carbon impacts should consider this aspect. We have estimated the total carbon footprint of equipment in the home that exists partially or totally as a result of the communications infrastructure. The purpose of this is to capture the potential rebound effects of networking more completely.

It should not be forgotten that, as noted earlier, ICT products have the potential to provide a significant net carbon benefit for customers [17], [14], [9]. The research presented in this paper will enable a more accurate estimate of potential net savings to be calculated and will also indicate how those savings can be maximized through improvements in communication system efficiency.

3. ENERGY USE IN TELECOMS

3.1 Network Platforms and Infrastructure

A real communications network that has been evolving for over 100 years is inevitably complex. Essentially, BT's network is a conglomeration of a range of different underlying network platforms. For example, the Public Switched Telephone network (PSTN) is the telephony network that provides services worldwide, and some of its supporting equipment has been installed and operational for several decades.

Of a similar age is a private circuit network that is used primarily for leased line and early Internet Access services. Although this supports many data services, the underlying technology is circuit based, so this network provides many features that until very recently have been unavailable within IP-based networks. For example, because of the need to have accurate timing data, many mobile base stations in the UK have a leased line for handover

signaling in addition to high speed IP/Ethernet connections for the data traffic. Typically, legacy networks remain in operation where they provide specific functionality or performance features that are not replicated by more modern network technologies. However, as customers gradually move to new ways of working supported by new technologies, the legacy networks will see steadily declining use, and steadily increasing under-utilization which has implications for energy efficiency of real-world network deployments to which we will return.

In recent years, we have deployed a range of access technologies including digital subscriber line (DSL), Asymmetric digital subscriber line 2 plus (ADSL2+), Fibre to the Cabinet (FTTC) and fibre-based Ethernet to provide ever greater access bandwidths to residential and businesses users.

The ADSL2+ , FTTC and Ethernet access networks have been supported by new (21C) backhaul, metro and core network infrastructure - a high speed network based on optical transmission, Ethernet switching and IP routing. Note that the BT infrastructure is used by many communication providers, so the Ethernet switching provides isolation between these different providers. Although the basic 21C network was deployed around 2005, it is seeing continual development to handle continuing traffic growth.

3.2 A Model of Energy Use

Energy costs BT over £250m per year, so is a significant expense. Saving energy brings both the environmental (carbon) benefits as well as the associated cost savings. The lion's share of energy use is due to the electricity consumed by BT's networks, which co-exist in around 6000 exchange buildings, for which electricity meter readings are available.

Given these drivers and the overall level of network complexity, it is important that BT has the ability to understand network energy use at a lower level of detail, so that usage hotspots and opportunities for energy reduction can be identified. We have therefore built an energy model that captures the electricity use of each network platform.

This model is primarily based upon records of deployed equipment with estimates of power use, supplemented with domain expert knowledge where necessary. The power estimates are usually based upon measurements made on sample equipment, either live or within network test facilities - this is particularly important for older equipment, where power data was traditionally provided solely for the purpose of power provision and so was typically a worst-case estimate. The model also estimates the energy overheads associated with equipment, such as the cooling required for the high density 21C core equipment. These estimates were made by first obtaining measurements at a small number of sites of the AC and DC loads at those sites. The DC load is solely associated with the network equipment. By comparing the AC and DC load, we can therefore quantify the overheads at those sites. These sites were chosen because they were of different types containing different ranges of equipment. The overheads were found to be platform dependent. The platform-specific overhead value was then applied to all equipment within each platform. The output of the model is then verified against electricity bills.

The energy model also includes an estimate of data centre energy, based on equipment records. Energy overheads are again estimated from a comparison of the AC and DC loads at each data centre.

The energy associated with running a business – offices and call centers is taken directly from billing information for each office building. Some buildings have shared use, for example office and telephone exchange. Where available, sub-meter readings have been used to quantify the office energy. This has provided data to enable us to estimate the split between office and exchange for buildings without such sub-meters. The model also includes overheads associated with network maintenance – IT systems to identify and monitor faults, the truck rolls to repair them, and the use of oil in generators to power the network during electricity failures. These factors are taken directly from fuel bills. Note that the model can also provide future projections based on network development plans.

3.3 Energy Use – the Big Picture

Figure 1 shows the energy footprint of BT's UK business based upon the BT energy model, providing the big picture of energy use in BT, dominated by in-use energy used to run the UK network infrastructure.

The figure could of course be translated into a carbon footprint using the relevant conversion factors. In fact BT has an agreement with its energy supplier that they will source 100% of BT's UK electricity from renewable sources, i.e. a matching number of units from renewable sources are fed back into the electricity grid for every unit BT consumes Thus the carbon emissions factor for BT's UK electricity use could be considered close to zero. However this does not negate the need for energy efficiency, since the UK faces electricity supply challenges nationally and energy prices will continue to rise steeply.

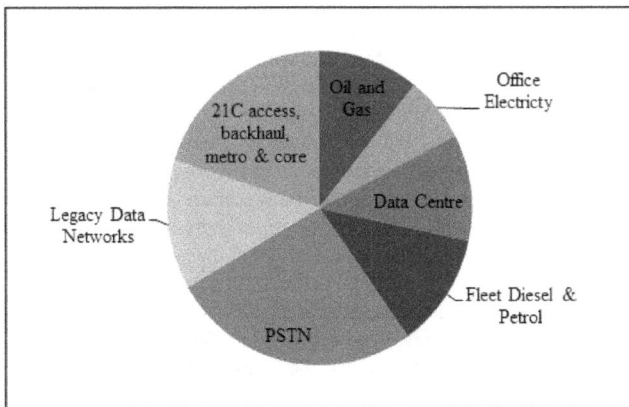

Figure 1 Energy Use within BT

3.4 Network Energy Efficiency Values

Typical network energy efficiency metrics that have proved useful are "power per line" (as used in [4]) and "energy per bit" (eg [24]). Power per line figures are an effective way to quantify the total environmental impact of networking whilst energy per bit is a generic metric that can be used to quantify the impact of specific services – for example a CD download which needs a known number of bits to be transmitted. Here we describe the method by which these metrics are calculated for our network, using the 21C network as the exemplar. Note that here we focus purely on network energy costs.

3.4.1 Power Per Line

The 21C network has three types of access port: ADSL2+, FTTC and Ethernet. There is one access port per line, thus the *power per access port* is easily calculated by dividing the total power of the relevant **access platform** (e.g. ADSL2+) by the total number of active lines it supports. Note that the platform energy, which is determined from the BT energy model, already includes all energy overheads such as AC to DC conversion losses and cooling. This method of calculating the power per line also fully captures the impact of any spare capacity.

Other types of resource, such as **backhaul or core network platforms**, are shared between users. Records are maintained that allow us to estimate the total provisioned bandwidth on each platform based upon the known number of users and the bandwidth provisioned per user. Typically, different types of user have different resources configured for them. For example, the backhaul bandwidth provisioned per FTTC user is greater than that provisioned per ADSL user. The energy consumption of such shared resources is allocated on the basis of the provisioned bandwidth per user divided by the total bandwidth provisioned on that platform. This most accurately reflects what drives growth in the network and therefore the energy use of the network, enabling an estimate of the power per line to be calculated.

It is normal to consider *essential* network equipment that is located physically within the home as part of the fixed network. We consider that the home energy of broadband lines includes the equipment used to terminate the access line and a wireless home router (these are often integrated into one unit). The energy use of the home router may depend upon its usage profile as some elements within more modern routers use less energy when not actively connected to the network. Colleagues [McDonald, personal communication] have measured the power draw of typical BT supplied home devices for each state of operation and also the typical activity levels (over multiple lines at one local exchange) and determined that on average a home router is actively connected to the network for 7 hours a day. This lets us estimate the weighted average power consumption of the home router – for example 6W for the ADS2+ modem. Note that the home energy associated with a PSTN user is assumed to be zero, since a basic phone is reverse-powered from the exchange.

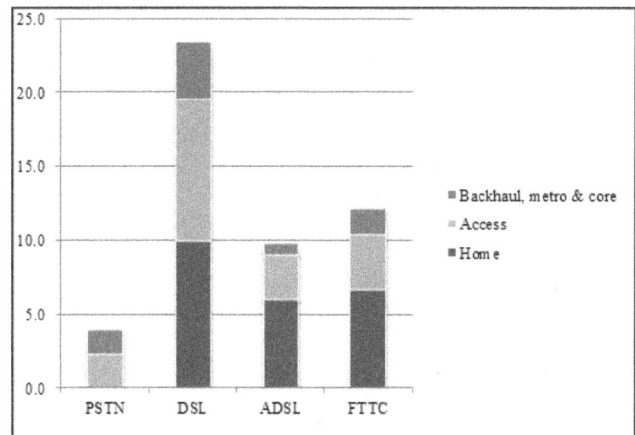

Figure 2 Power per line (W) for key access technologies

Figure 2 shows the power per line calculated as above for four key access technologies. We use data from the energy model for 2016, as at this time deployment of FTTC will be more established and the metric values therefore more stable – currently the power per line for FTTC is changing rapidly due to the high rate of network deployment and rapid increase in user base. (This choice of year does not materially impact the power per line calculated for the other technologies).

3.4.2 Energy Per Bit

To calculate the "energy per bit" metric, we need traffic statistics. Focusing on residential broadband customers, traffic measurements by colleagues [Soppera, personal communication], [Cathcart, personal communication] quantify the amount of data that is downloaded per line and how that depends upon line access type. We can then use this data to calculate the *energy per bit* for each of the different platforms. The energy per bit can be calculated as: the power per line multiplied by the number of seconds in a month divided by the bits per line in a month. Results are as shown in table 1.

Table 1. Energy-per-bit for various access types.

μ joules / bit	PSTN	DSL	ADSL	FTTC
Home	0	183	56	35
Access	1716	176	29	20
Backhaul, metro and core	1200	70	8	9

We present an energy per bit metric that is time averaged over actual traffic load rather than maximum capacity. This gives a more realistic indication of the actual energy involved in communication. It can be seen that the energy per bit is actually minimized when traffic load is at its highest. This might imply that the most energy efficient way of using a network is to add load at peak times. On a longer timescale however, such behavior would drive the network provider to add more capacity, increasing the energy costs. The instantaneous cost of using the network off-peak is higher than average, but the long term cost is less. Hence we use a time averaged energy per bit value.

The PSTN and DSL access lines are connected to legacy backhaul, metro and core networks, hence they are less efficient as more recently-deployed equipment efficiency has improved over time.

The energy per bit used within the 21C backhaul, metro and core region is virtually identical for ADSL and FTTC customers, even though the latter has a higher power per line in that region. This is because the higher level of provisioning (and so energy) for the latter is compensated by higher usage (more bits), i.e. the provisioning is proportionate to usage. This is unsurprising since similar Quality of Service expectations exist.

Assuming similar usage and quality of service profiles across different types of network user, then we would expect all services using the 21C backhaul, metro and core network to have broadly similar energy per bit figures. Similarly, we would expect other services using the oldest circuit-switched network to have energy per bit figures similar to that of the PSTN.

The aggregated energy per bit for the broadband networks is 113 μj/bit which, assuming download speeds of nearly 15Mbps [20], is approximately ten times greater than some prior models have suggested for communication across the Internet [4]. Before we consider additional costs (outside of BT) we first identify why communication costs in a live network may be higher than modeled costs.

3.5 Issues Affecting Energy Efficiency

There are a number of reasons why the power per line and energy per bit figures of real-world deployed networks are higher than might be otherwise estimated by models, including issues associated with legacy networks, provisioning and utilization.

3.5.1 Legacy Momentum

The effects of efficiency improvements take a long time to be fully incorporated into the network. Equipment remains in the network for as long as it is needed. For example, DSL equipment which is now being removed has been in place for around ten years or more, whilst the PSTN equipment is over twenty five years old. Whilst specific network devices may be replaced to provide increased capacity, if the old equipment is still viable, it is likely to be re-used elsewhere within the network. Note that this reduces the impact of embodied energy which can be an important factor in overall energy/carbon footprint (discussed later).

BT has been monitoring its network energy use for many years and can make traffic estimates for its network over the same period. These estimates are based upon usage patterns (the typical call times per voice line and the average data volume downloaded per broadband line) for each particular year. Where the data is not available (such as for private networks) we make the assumption that the utilization levels will be similar to those on other networks. This has allowed us to estimate our observed aggregated network efficiency as shown in Figure 3, which here excludes the home element. This shows that network efficiency does indeed improve over time. This improvement occurs because new equipment needs to be added to the network to address traffic growth. To support the higher data rates that are needed because of traffic growth, each new generation of network equipment is implemented with silicon that has a smaller gate size, with a fortuitous reduction in energy. Historically, a two times increase in speed caused by a decrease in gate size is accompanied by a 1.4 times increase in power consumption. Since speed doubles approximately every 18 months, the energy per bit for equipment reduces by about 0.8 a year [16].

The observed network efficiency improvement rate is around 0.16 - slightly slower than the technology efficiency improvement noted by [16]. We note also that by the time equipment is deployed it is inevitably already behind the most efficient systems.

3.5.2 Provisioning and Utilization

Traffic levels vary tremendously during the day, as can be seen in figure 4 which shows average traffic as downloaded by ADSL and FTTC broadband users. Further, as users migrate to new networks, this effect is getting stronger, i.e. the difference between average demand and peak demand is increasing.

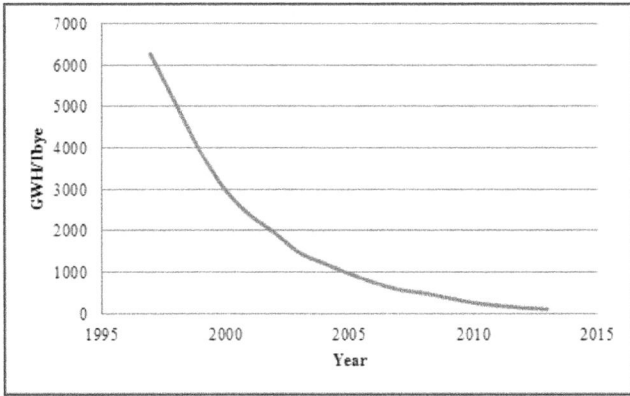

Figure 3 Observed network efficiency

There is a lack of adaptation within most network equipment to enable it to respond to variable traffic levels, i.e.the power drawn does not typically go down as traffic decreases. Based on a comparison of peak bandwidth and actual utilization levels, we estimate that if the energy consumption of the network were able to fully track the utilization, then we would save 55% of network energy.

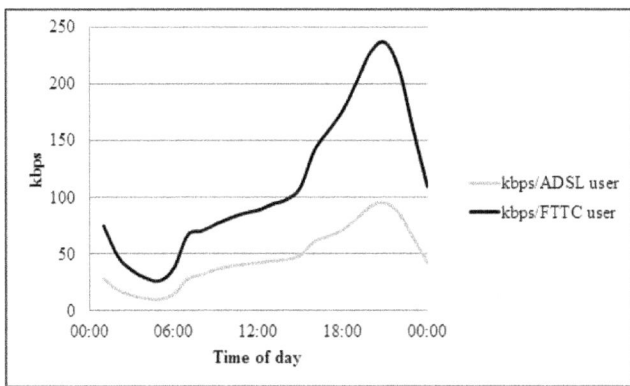

Figure 4 average traffic by time of day from residential broadband users

Note that traffic with a less variable demand level could achieve a significantly lower *energy per bit* value, as relatively fewer resources would need to be provisioned to support the same quality of service and total volume of traffic (since peak demand drives the level of provisioning), but at present we see no evidence to support a suggestion that smoother traffic profiles are commonplace within our network.

The provisioned resources will be greater than the peak required bandwidth in order to ensure that there is sufficient headroom to ensure good quality of service. Further, because it can take time to provision new resources, there will be sufficient headroom to ensure that the quality of service does not degrade as traffic grows – current rate of growth is observed to be around 25-30% a year within the UK. Finally, to maintain reliability levels, most resources have a level of redundancy associated with them.

3.5.3 Rollout of New Access Technologies

Utilisation can also be low because of the effects of granularity associated with the rollout of new access technologies. Take for example a typical VDSL cabinet. For a cabinet serving between 1 and 48 VDSL users, it must be provisioned with a 48-port line card. Even with lower power modes operational for ports that are not connected the power for one user is over 100W, falling to 2.2W as number of users rises to 48.

Then, the utilisation of any fibre gigabit Ethernet (GE) links back to the exchange will be significantly less than 100 percent, even at peak times. If there is only one use on a cabinet, with a service of up to 80Mbps being provided, a whole GE link must be provided. This difficulty in matching link bandwidth or switching capability to the required capacity continues through the network.

3.5.4 Regulatory Constraints

BT's network supports many different communication providers via a range of wholesale and access line products in a manner defined by regulation. This has led to a network design that contains additional electronic switching points at regulated points of interconnect. Today, as competition becomes established within the UK, some of these switches may be removed if they are no longer providing interconnect.

3.5.5 Summary of Energy Efficiency Issues

Figure 5 shows our cumulative estimate of the impact of all of the above factors on the network (excludes home impact).

The first bar shows the aggregate network efficiency today; the second bar shows the efficiency of the most modern FTTC/21C platform (from Table 1).

We separated "adaptation to redundancy and granularity" from "adaptation to utilization", since any adaptation to these will take place on different timescales. Adaptation to changes in utilization levels would need to take place in nano-second timescales to avoid impacting network quality of service, whereas reaction to, for example, network failure, can occur in a milli-second timescale. We estimated earlier that complete adaptation to utilization would save up to 55% of network energy use. Similarly, we can estimate the maximum savings that can be made with slower adaptation based on the number of spare access ports that are available and the amount if capacity that is provided for redundancy purposes.

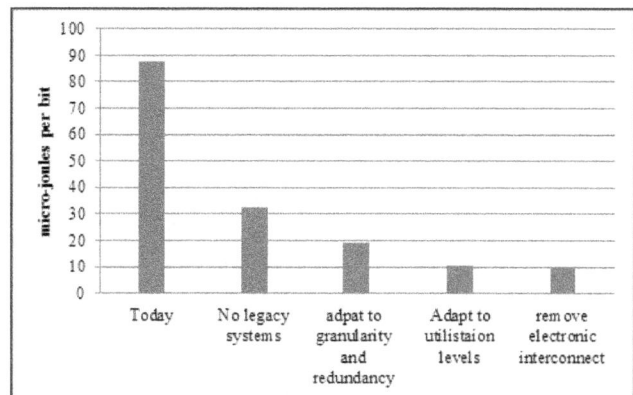

Figure 5: Impact of real-world on network efficiency

We note that legacy networks have the biggest impact; these are today also the networks with the greatest number of users. However the ability to adapt the network energy use to traffic load could have a significant impact on network energy consumption and so is an interesting area for further research.

3.6 Energy Use Beyond BT's Network

As we wish to understand the full end-to-end energy impacts of networks and network services, it is also important to consider those elements that lie beyond BT's own network, but which are required for a network service. These are discussed below.

3.6.1 Internet Energy Use

The total energy cost of communications needs to include the energy in other parts of the Internet network, beyond BT's own network. Analysis of our traffic suggests that around 80-90% percent of traffic on our network is coming from data centres which are external to BT [Soppera, personal communicaton]. These data centers are typically those which are providing video, news or host e-commerce sites.

To estimate the energy costs associated with networking (beyond BT's network) to the data centre we first make the assumptions that it exhibits similar efficiency to BT's network and that the energy use of the network is proportional to the number of IP switching hops within it. We have then used traceroute to examine the routes most commonly taken by traffic that terminates on our network to estimate the number of hops both on and off the BT network. As an example, 20% of traffic for our residential customers is from YouTube; this requires only an additional three IP hops to reach the data centre server after the exit from BTs network (a total of 17 IP hops including the home router).

We found that for many popular (in terms of either traffic volume or web page hits) sites the traffic is traversing only a few hops outside of the BT infrastructure. Whilst some popular sites have noticeably longer routes, these tend to be responsible for relatively low amounts of actual traffic. Typically we find that the routes that are heavily used are short.

Based on the average IP hop count of the sample of routes investigated, we can estimate the additional energy needed to connect from the BT network to the data centre. Using a simple pro-rata approach based on this hop count, we estimate that about three quarters of the energy used to transmit data from the data centre to a BT customer is used within the BT network. Note that we exclude the energy associated with the home router in this calculation. Note also that this result will differ between service providers.

3.6.2 Data Centre Energy Use

The energy used within the data centre itself should cover devices to manage connectivity between the internet and the data centre (including Ethernet access termination for example) and internal networking energy, as well as energy for servers and storage. At present we have only been able to sample the energy costs associated with data centres, gathering data from three major data centres: Facebook as an example of a social media provider, Google which provides search engine and YouTube video and Akamai, a content distributor which supports a wide range of sites such as for news and internet shopping sites.

Facebook estimates that it uses 532GWH a year [10]. It is estimated that it is responsible for between 1.3 and 3 percent of Internet traffic [21]. We assume that the total Internet traffic is 31339 PBytes a month, as given by [7] for 2012. This implies of order 20 to 50 µj per bit.

Similarly, Google is responsible for around 20% of all traffic (YouTube plus other services, [21]) and uses 3,325 GWH a year [11]. This leads to an estimate of around 20µj per bit.

Finally, Akamai estimates its energy use as 216 GWH a year [2] and that it delivers 15% to 30% of Internet traffic [1]. This leads to an estimate of 0.9 to 1.7 µjoules per bit.

This suggests a large range in the performance of data centres, from 1 to 50 micro-joules per bit from any particular data centre. At first glance it is likely that this is linked to the general complexity of the data center.

To estimate the power cost per line associated with data centres in general, we use the fact that traffic analysis suggests that 80 to 90 percent of traffic on any one line is coming from a data centre. Since the weighted-average traffic over broadband lines is of order 300Gbits a month per line, thus we can estimate that the users on a single broadband line use between 243 and 13680 kjoules per month in data centre energy (across all data centres touched by the user). This is equivalent to 0.1 to 5 W per access line.

3.7 Embodied Energy of Networks

The energy embodied in the network includes the energy used in the fabrication of optical fibres and routers, as significant components.

A study on behalf of BT by Small World Consulting estimated that the carbon footprint of BT's supply chain is around 64% of the total BT carbon footprint [22]. This is based on an Environmentally Extended Economic Input-Output (EEIO) analysis – thus it is based upon BTs spending levels in different industry categories. This approach uses knowledge of the direct emissions associated with each category of industry and assumes that every unit of expenditure in any industry category has the same emissions intensity. The approach used is in fact a hybrid Environmentally Extended Input Output (EEIO) method, in that corrections have been made where the assumption can be proven to be invalid.

An alternative analysis has been carried out using a "process sum" approach to estimate embodied energy in a network [8]. This is a bottom-up approach which aims to estimate the emissions that take place at each stage of product manufacture. This again suggests that the embodied energy within a network is around twice the in-use energy.

Given the high embodied energy costs of networking, it may be considered that the net environmental impact of a network may be minimized if legacy systems were maintained. Figure 6 shows the cumulative energy used for a router replaced every year, eight years and 25 years. It uses the data for a CSR1 router from [8] assuming that equipment efficiency improves at 20% a year [16], with no change in embodied energy or equipment capacity.

The figure shows that the cumulative energy is lowest when equipment is replaced every eight years. This suggests that the optimal lifetime for network equipment is around eight years. Re-running the calculations with the assumption that the capacity of the equipment when replaced will need to be upgraded to handle traffic growth of 30% a year, the optimal lifetime increases to around twelve years. An optimization model is left for future work.

It is worth maximizing the life of fibre as this requires no in-use energy but has a high embodied energy cost. Fibre lifetimes of twenty five years are not uncommon. Using the data from [8], two routers would have a total embodied energy of 1.3 TJ and use 0.9 TJ per year. If these routers were interconnected by 40km of fibre, the embodied energy of the fibre would be 7 TJ. The EEIO analysis of [22] also shows the embodied energy associated with cables and fibre to be higher than that of the electronic equipment. A network is therefore minimizing its total environmental footprint when it is not constantly being upgraded, driven by a desire to minimize its in-use energy consumption.

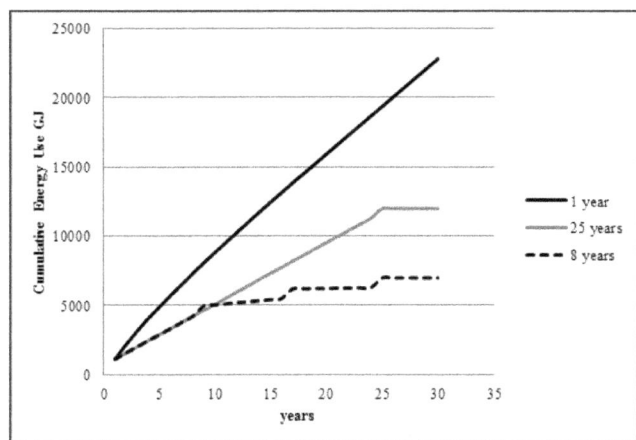

Figure 6. Cumulative energy used for a router with different replacement strategies

We observe however that the understanding of embodied energy of networks is still somewhat in its infancy and therefore currently lacks consensus.

4. HOME NETWORK EQUIPMENT

As we are seeking to develop a full end-to-end view of the energy and carbon impacts of real-world networks, it is necessary to consider the impacts of home equipment associated with telecommunications networks. The devices that we consider important to include are laptops, PCs, smartphones, games consoles, e-readers and tablet computers.

We do not include TVs and various TV-related set top boxes or music players in this analysis, since it appears that these devices have been subject primarily to substitution, as opposed to a growth in devices triggered by new network based services. For example, an internet-enabled music player often replaces a portable cassette or CD player.

We have gathered data on the penetration of different device types within the home [18], typical power consumption, lifetime energy use and embodied energy for each of these device types [3][25]. Because of the inherent uncertainty in much of the data, to build an understanding of the energy and carbon impact of networked

home devices, Monte-Carlo simulation was used as a modelling tool.

We have allocated a share of the in-use and embodied energy as a network cost, the share being device dependent. For laptops and PCs, we have compared the total device use time (which we calculated from lifetime energy use and typical energy consumption) to the time spent on the network [18]. For devices such as an e-readers, 100% of the cost is allocated against the network as these devices fundamentally rely upon the network connectivity. A smartphone is 50% allocated to the fixed network and 50% allocated to a mobile network.

Table 2 shows the key parameters used in the model. The model output does depend strongly on these parameter values and on the expected lifetime of devices (we assume 4 years for the larger devices and 3 for the smaller devices). Figure 7 then shows our estimate of the likely carbon impact of home networking in an average UK household, in kg CO2 per household (the sum of in-use and embodied carbon per year). Based on the estimates of in-use and embodied carbon in Table 2, the model also generates separate results for in-use and embodied carbon as 54 ±16 kg CO2 and 104± 24 kg CO2 respectively. *We note that, due to the data available on the environmental impact of home electronics, we have switched from considering "energy" to "carbon" in this model.*

To convert these carbon figures to an average power per household and average energy per bit figures (for ease of comparison to the data in the other sections), we assume a global average of 0.0858 tCO2 = 1 GJ, based on worldwide energy use and carbon emissions [12].

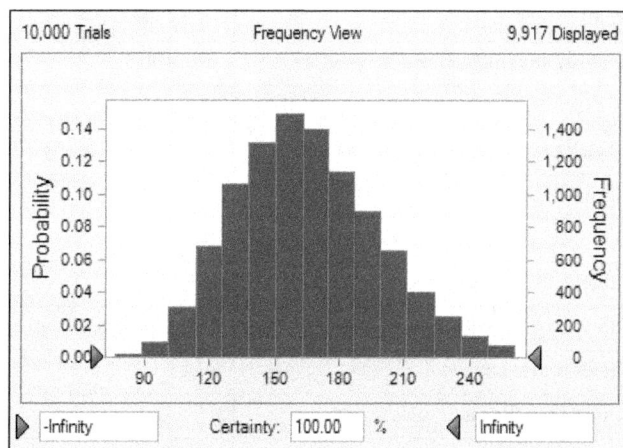

Figure 7 Model results for environmental costs of home networked devices, kg CO2 per year per home

This gives the effective in-use power draw of home equipment as around 20W per household. This number may appear small given the number of devices often simultaneously in-use, but reflects the large improvements in energy efficiency especially in battery powered devices, usage patterns and the assumption that the devices will otherwise be switched off or in energy saving modes [13].

Table 2 Home network energy model parameters

Parameter	Value per year
Laptop Device Penetration	61 %
Laptop embodied carbon	97 kg CO2 ± 30
Laptop in-use carbon	24 kg CO2 ± 10
% of laptop allocated to network	52 – 100%
Games machine Device Penetration	52%
Games machine embodied carbon	102 kg CO2± 10%
Games machine in-use carbon	59 kg CO2± 10%
% of games machine allocated to network	35 – 100%
PC Device Penetration	44 %
PC embodied carbon	108 kg CO2 ± 40
PC in-use carbon	99 kg CO2 ± 40
% of PC allocated to network	26 – 100 %
Smartphone Device Penetration	39 %
Smartphone embodied carbon	19 kg CO2 ± 6
Smartphone in-use carbon	4 kg CO2 2
% smartphone allocated to network	50%
Small games Device Penetration	32 %
Small games device embodied	13 kg CO2 ± 4
Small games in-use carbon	1 kg CO2 ± 0.4
% of small games allocated to network	47 – 100 %
E-reader Device Penetration	14 %
E-reader embodied carbon	13 kg CO2 ± 4
E-reader in-use carbon	1kg CO2 ± 0.4
% of e-reader allocated to network	100%
Tablet Device Penetration	18 %
Tablet embodied carbon	35 kg CO2 ± 10
Tablet in-use carbon	9 kg CO2 ± 4
% of tablet allocated to network	47 – 100 %

Using average data volumes as before, we can then estimate the (in-use) energy per bit as 174 μjoules. The embodied energy is found to be almost twice the in-use energy. We note that this is an average across all device types. Portable devices in particular can be seen to have a much higher ratio of embodied to in-use energy than wired devices. We further note, as highlighted in [13], embodied energy estimates are still uncertain.

5. CONCLUSIONS

ICT has the potential to provide a net carbon benefit, enabling users to save more carbon through activities such as video-conferencing than the provision of ICT services uses. However, the energy and carbon cost of networking is not trivial - BT alone uses around 0.7% of the UKs electricity.

To achieve the full potential of telecommunications networks to reduce the likelihood of significant climate change and to help tackle energy security issues, we need to ensure that the ICT industry is not causing more problems than it is solving. To understand this we need accurate quantification of the actual energy use associated with communications networks.

In this paper, we calculate the power-per-line and the energy-per-bit associated with real-world communication networking. These parameters give us an overall understanding of the total energy cost of networking, and a means to calculate the energy use of any specific service.

Table 3 shows the in-use energy impact of fixed line networking. The figures for broadband represent an average across the different network types, weighted by the number of users of each system.

Additionally, we have examined the information currently available on embodied energy costs. Within the home environment it appears that (using current equipment lifetimes) embodied energy is approximately twice the in-use energy. Within the fixed network electronic equipment, cumulative in-use energy and embodied energy are approximately equivalent if systems are replaced every eight to twelve years. The total environmental impact of a network is minimized if systems are maintained for eight to twelve years, even though this means that the in-use energy will be significantly higher than might be estimated from state of the art equipment. Network lifetimes of twelve to twenty-five years are currently not unusual, with copper and fibre cable lifetimes often significantly longer. The embodied energy costs associated with the cable infrastructure is not insignificant. The net effect is that the environmental impact of the fixed network could be four times the in-use estimate. However, as noted earlier this needs to be treated with caution as there is not currently consensus on the level of embodied carbon in networks.

We showed that the typical in-use energy per bit figures for real networks are often higher than those predicted by modelling alone. The primary reasons for this are firstly that the impact of legacy systems is not fully recognized and secondly that network utilization is much lower than often assumed within a model. Low utilization is driven equally by the need for redundancy, to ensure quality-of-service and the need to provision for peak traffic load. The impact of low utilization could be addressed if equipment could adapt its energy consumption to the current traffic level.

Table 3 Typical figures for network energy use

	Energy, μjoules / bit	Power, W / line
Home Devices	174	20
Legacy Network	2916	4
Broadband Access (including network termination in home)	116	11
Broadband Core (including access to data centre)	17	1.5
Data Centre	1 - 50	0.1 – 5

We note that the impact of the equipment in the home is limited. This can be attributed to rapid improvements in the energy efficiency of home equipment over the last few years. Of course the rapid update of home electronics carries an embodied energy implication.

We also see that although data centres receive significant, often negative, publicity about their energy consumption, the energy consumption of other elements in the communication chain can be as significant. These figures suggest that remote location of data centres (for example to enable access to a low-carbon energy source) may not always be effective, end-to-end. This is because it would increase the network distance traversed, typically requiring more network routing and additional fibre lengths.

We conclude that to understand the full environmental impact, the full end-to-end implications need to be understood. Although data on embodied energy is still poorly understood, the evidence suggests nevertheless that any end-to-end energy estimation needs to take embodied energy into account. Future work therefore should seek to understand the embodied aspects more thoroughly, considering not only equipment manufacture but also the equipment decommissioning. An optimization could then be made between in-use and embodied energy to understand the system lifetime that minimizes environmental impacts. Additionally, further research is needed to understand how to make a network adapt its energy use to the actual traffic demand as this would have a significant impact on operational energy use in a practical deployment.

6. ACKNOWLEDGMENTS

We wish to thank Camanoe Associates for their assistance building the home devices model.

7. REFERENCES

[1] AKAMAI. 2013. Facts & Figures. Available from http://www.akamai.com/html/about/facts_figures.html

[2] AKAMAI. 2013. CDP 2013 Investor CDP 2013 Information Request. Available from http://www.akamai.com/dl/sustainability/CDP_2013_Investor_Climate_Change_Information_Request.pdf

[3] APPLE. 2013. Apple and the environment http://www.apple.com/uk/environment/reports/

[4] Baliga, J, Ayre,R, Hinton,K, Sorin, W, , and Tucker, R. 2009. Energy consumption in optical IP Networks, *Journal of Lightwave Technology*, Vol. 27, Issue 13

[5] BT. 2012. Carbon Emissions Statement 2012. http://www.btplc.com/Betterfuture/NetGood/Ourownoperations/Ourcarbonemissions/BT_carbon_emissions_statement_2013.pdf

[6] CEET University of Melbourne. 2013. The power of wireless cloud. Available from http://www.ceet.unimelb.edu.au/pdfs/ceet_white_paper_wireless_cloud.pdf

[7] CISCO. 2013. Cisco Visual Networking Index: Forecast and Methodology, 2012–2017. Available from http://www.cisco.com/en/US/solutions/collateral/ns341/ns525/ns537/ns705/ns827/white_paper_c11-481360_ns827_Networking_Solutions_White_Paper.html

[8] Dong,X, Lawey,A, El-Gorashi,T, Elmirghani.J. 2012. Energy Efficient Core networks. *16th Int Conf on optical Network Design and Modelling,*. http://dx.doi.org/10.1109/ONDM.2012.6210196

[9]   Edwards,J, McKinnon,A, Cullinane, S. 2010 Comparative analysis of the carbon footprints of conventional and online retailing: A "last mile" perspective. *International Journal of Physical Distribution & Logistics Management*, Vol. 40 Issue 1/2. http://dx.doi.org/10.1108/09600031011018055

[10] Facebook. 2012. Sharing our footprint. Available from https://newsroom.fb.com/News/412/Sharing-Our-Footprint

[11] Google. Data for 2012 available from http://www.google.com/green/bigpicture/

[12] International Energy Agency. Key World Energy Statistics. http://www.iea.org/publications/freepublications/publication/KeyWorld2013.pdf

[13] Koomey, Berard, Sanchez and Wong. 2011. "Implications of historical trends in the electrical efficiency of computing" *IEEE Annals of the History of Computing*

[14] Koomey,J. 2011. Growth in data center electricity use 2005 to 2010. http://www.analyticspress.com/datacenters.html,

[15] Lambert,S, Van Heddeghem,W, Vereecken,W, Lannoo,B, Colle,D and Pickavet,M. 2012, "Worldwide electricity consumption of communication networks", *Optics Express*, Vol. 20, Issue 26, pp. B513-B524

[16] Neilson,D, Holmdel, N. 2006. Photonics for switching and routing, *IEEE J. Sel. Topics Quantum Electronics* vol. 12, no. 4. http://dx.doi.org/10.1109/JSTQE.2006.876315

[17] Neves, L Krajewski,J, Jung,P, Bockemuehl, M. 2012. GESI SMARTer 2020: The Role of ICT in Driving a Sustainable Future. http://gesi.org/SMARTer2020

[18] OFCOM. 2012. Communications Market Report. http://stakeholders.ofcom.org.uk/binaries/research/cmr/cmr12/CMR_UK_2012.pdf

[19] OFCOM. 2013. Average UK Broadband speeds hit double figures. Available from http://consumers.ofcom.org.uk/2013/03/average-uk-broadband-speeds-hit-double-figures/

[20] Ofcom, August 2013, Average UK broadband speed continues to rise available from http://media.ofcom.org.uk/2013/08/07/average-uk-broadband-speed-continues-to-rise/

[21] Sandvine. 2013. Global internet phenomena report 2013. Available from https://www.sandvine.com/downloads/general/global-internet-phenomena/2013/2h-2013-global-internet-phenomena-report.pdf

[22] Small World Consulting. 2013. BT's supply chain carbon emissions – a report on the approach and methodology. Available from http://www.btplc.com/Betterfuture/NetGood/OurNetGoodMethodology/SWC_BT_supplychainemissions.pdf

[23] Thomas, L. 2009. Green ICT. http://www.jisc.ac.uk/media/documents/publications/bpgreenictv1.pdf

[24] Tucker,R.S. 2008. "Optical packet-switched WDM networks: a cost and energy perspective", *Optical Fiber Communications* (OFC'08), Paper OMG1, San Diego,

[25] University of Pennsylvania accessed 2013 Computer Power Usage https://secure.www.upenn.edu/computing/resources/category/hardware/article/computer-power-usage

When Mice Consume Like Elephants:
Instant Messaging Applications

Ekhiotz Jon Vergara, Simon Andersson, Simin Nadjm-Tehrani
Department of Computer and Information Science
Linköping University, Sweden
ekhiotz.vergara@liu.se, siman481@student.liu.se, simin.nadjm-tehrani@liu.se

ABSTRACT

A recent surge in the usage of instant messaging (IM) applications on mobile devices has brought the energy efficiency of these applications into focus of attention. Although IM applications are changing the message communication landscape, this work illustrates that the current versions of IM applications differ vastly in energy consumption when using the third generation (3G) cellular communication. This paper shows the interdependency between energy consumption and IM data patterns in this context.

We analyse the user interaction pattern using a IM dataset, consisting of 1043370 messages collected from 51 mobile users. Based on the usage characteristics, we propose a message bundling technique that aggregates consecutive messages over time, reducing the energy consumption with a trade-off against latency. The results show that message bundling can save up to 43% in energy consumption while still maintaining the conversation function. Finally, the energy cost of a common functionality used in IM applications that informs that the user is currently typing a response, so called typing notification, is evaluated showing an energy increase ranging from 40-104%.

Categories and Subject Descriptors

C.2.1 [**Computer Communication Networks**]: Wireless communication; C.4 [**Performance of Systems**]: Measurement techniques

General Terms

Design, Measurement

Keywords

instant messaging; transmission energy; UMTS; mobile devices; typing notification

e-Energy'14, June 11–13, 2014, Cambridge, UK.
ACM 978-1-4503-2819-7/14/06.
http://dx.doi.org/10.1145/2602044.2602054.

1. INTRODUCTION

Instant messaging (IM) applications have emerged as the substitute for Short Message Service (SMS) and have gained wide popularity. These applications offer the possibility of sending text messages (1-to-1 or to a group) as well as other multimedia messages (e.g., images, audio or video). Applications such as WhatsApp or QQ have already 400 and 800 million online users respectively [3, 4], and recently, IM has overtaken the traditional SMS text messages [1]. Given the widespread use of IM, even home appliance manufacturers envision its usage for controlling their equipment [2].

While this might seem a blessing to the user, IM text messages are an example of a type of traffic with low bandwidth requirement, which leads to high energy consumption. The exchange of a couple of text messages can consume as much as sending an image due to the radio resource allocation of cellular networks. From the cellular network operator perspective, the signalling overhead created by IM is very high given their intermittent and small data transmissions.

IM applications provide more functionalities than regular SMS, such as online presence awareness, typing notification or status updates. Application developers may unfortunately integrate these features without studying the potential impact on energy consumption. A recent study analysed more than 9 million comments from the Google Play Store and showed that more than 18% of all commented applications have negative comments regarding energy consumption [28].

The result is that different applications delivering similar function consume completely different amounts of transmission energy. We selected 6 of the most popular IM applications from the Play Store on 15th January 2013 as an illustrative example, and sent the same 2 minutes conversation between two smartphones connected via 3G using the different applications. The energy consumption for each application was computed using EnergyBox [26], our tool that is described briefly in section 6.2.

Fig. 1 (top and bottom-right) shows a great diversity regarding the amount of energy spent and data sent by the different applications when performing the short conversation. The most consuming application (Messenger) consumes 153% more energy than the least consuming one (GTalk) to transmit the same conversation. Fig. 1 (bottom-left) shows a significant diversity in the packet size for the 3 selected applications, which impacts the transmission pattern, and thus the radio resource allocation and energy consumption. For example, WhatsApp employs smaller packets than GTalk, but performs transmissions more often leading

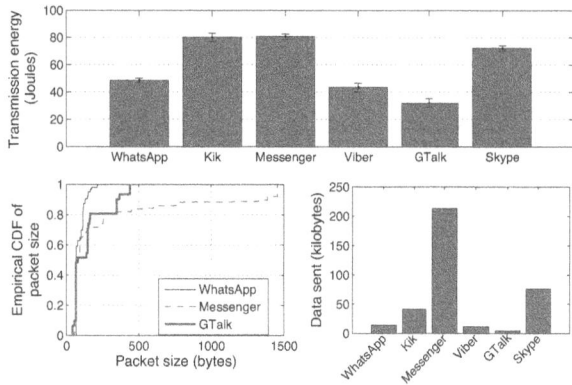

Figure 1: Average transmission energy, amount of data sent and empirical CDF of packet size for different Instant Messaging applications exchanging a short conversation.

to higher energy consumption. Kik, Messenger and Skype transmit more data than the others, making the 3G interface consume more. Using the least energy-efficient application could substantially shorten the battery lifetime of a device, by a factor of 2.5, and reduce the quality of experience (QoE) for the user.

The transmission pattern of IM is mainly determined by user interactions, where interactive traffic is generated by a sequence of exchanged messages. Thus, the complexity of designing energy-efficient transmissions increases given the a priori unpredictability of the users. However, studying current usage patterns can reveal inefficient ways of performing transmissions since neither the users nor the applications are aware of the energy footprint characteristics.

The contributions of our work, which aims to significantly reduce the energy consumption of IM for mobile devices, are threefold:

- We collect, analyse and provide an IM text message dataset[1] of 1043370 messages from 51 mobile users that describes users' diverse usage patterns.

- We demonstrate the high energy cost of a networking functionality, typing notification, that most IM applications implement amounting to additional energy consumption between 40-104%.

- Informed by the usage patterns found in our dataset, a message bundling algorithm is proposed showing that aggregating consecutive messages from the same user saves up to 43% energy.

The paper is organised as follows: section 2 explains the background and describes the related works. Section 3 analyses the IM dataset of real user messages. Section 4 describes the proposed message bundling technique, followed by the algorithm applied to the typing notification feature in section 5. The evaluation methodology is presented in section 6, and section 7 and 8 present the results. Finally, the conclusions and future work are presented in section 9.

---

[1]http://www.ida.liu.se/~rtslab/energy-efficient-networking

2. BACKGROUND AND RELATED WORKS

We begin by providing an overview on the communication energy footprint for the third generation Universal Mobile Telecommunications System (UMTS) at the user equipment (UE) side. The main related works are presented in section 2.2.

2.1 Energy footprint of 3G

The energy consumption of the UE when connected to a 3G UMTS network is mostly influenced by the radio resource management performed at the network operator side by the Radio Network Controller (RNC). The RNC employs the Radio Resource Control (RRC) and Radio Link Control (RLC) of the UMTS Wideband Code Division Multiple Access protocols to perform the radio resource management of the UE [11].

According to the RRC, the UE implements a state machine where the different states have different power consumption and performance in terms of maximum data rate and latency. The UE states are CELL_DCH or Dedicated Channel (DCH), CELL_FACH or Forward Access Channel (FACH), and URA_PCH or Paging Channel (PCH), sorted from highest to lowest power drain and performance in terms of data rate and response time. Since the states URA_PCH and CELL_PCH result in similar energy consumption, we consider them as PCH for simplicity.

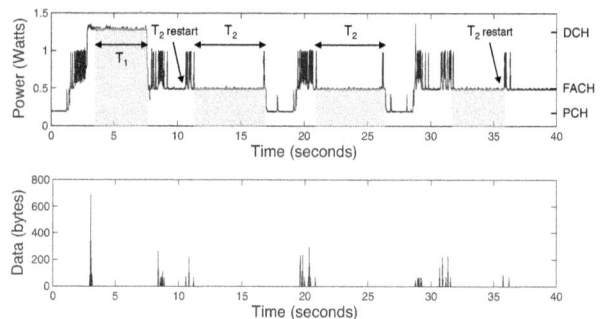

Figure 2: Example power profile for 3G using a mobile broadband module (Ericsson F3307) and Skype as instant messaging application.

Fig. 2 shows the observed power consumption levels of the different states at one location for the state machine implemented by the operator TeliaSonera in Sweden. The bottom graph shows the packets when they were captured at the network interface of the UE. In PCH, the UE cannot transmit any data, but it can be paged with the lowest energy drain. When the UE starts generating or receiving traffic, some signalling is required to establish the connection and move the UE from PCH to DCH before sending any data.

The RNC employs the RLC protocol to evaluate the allocation of resources and control state transitions to higher performance states. The UE reports the observed traffic volume to the RNC, which re-allocates the UE state if the RLC buffer data occupancy of the UE exceeds some fixed RLC thresholds. These thresholds control the PCH-DCH and PCH-FACH state transitions. When the PCH-DCH threshold is exceeded, the UE is moved to DCH (3 s in Fig. 2). In DCH, the UE is allocated a dedicated physical channel (uplink and downlink) providing the highest data rates. The first packet is a downlink transmission, and thus the signalling occurs before the data is received at the UE.

The RRC state machine uses inactivity timers to down switch the UE to lower performance states. The UE is moved to FACH after T_1 when there is small or no data transmission (8 s in Fig. 2). In FACH, the UE is assigned a default common or shared transport channel where only low-speed transmission can be performed. Finally, the transition from FACH to PCH is controlled by the inactivity timer T_2.

Inactivity timers create energy overheads known as energy *tails* since the UE remains in a high energy consuming state while not transmitting anything [6, 25]. Fig. 2 shows that the data pattern (inter-packet interval and packet size) clearly influences the energy consumption driven by the RRC state machine, where even small transfers of data can trigger state transitions to DCH (e.g., in the case of a small chat message) or the restart of the inactivity timers.

To sum up, this illustrates that the RRC state machine and the above mechanisms impact the energy consumption of the UE through the data pattern in a complex way.

2.2 Related works

We categorise the related works into two different groups: IM and energy consumption of cellular data transfers at the user end.

IM: Even though IM has a great popularity and a large number of users, little work has been done to understand its energy consumption at the user end. Most IM related works focus either on users' social interactions [10], security [22] or analysing the IM traffic generated in desktop-oriented machines [13,15,30].

While presence updates have been studied in desktop-oriented machines [27,30] and in the mobile context [7,8,17], the cost of the typing notification feature or the impact of consecutive messages has not attracted attention so far.

Cellular communication energy: Several works address the general problem of high energy consumption of cellular communication at the user end. The readers interested in other aspects than transmission energy are referred to the survey by Vallina-Rodriguez et al. [24].

EnergyBox [26] is developed to study the energy consumption of 3G and WiFi transmission energy. ARO is a similar tool that at the time of its publication [21] was not available to other researchers. Pathak et al. [18] propose Eprof, a system-call-based energy profiling tool for smartphones, and show that transfers of advertisements in free applications have a great energy cost.

Periodic transfers and background traffic of mobile applications are known to incur great energy consumption. Some proposals [5,9] employ the Fast Dormancy (FD) mechanism introduced in the 3GPP Release 8 as a radio resource control technique to move the UE to PCH before the expiration of the inactivity timers. Traffic shaping techniques [6, 12, 14, 16, 20] are common. These shift transmissions over time (e.g., batching background traffic) to minimise the transmission cost. For example, our previous work [25] schedules background data transfers considering the inactivity timers and the RLC data buffers in combination.

While the above works attempt at reducing energy footprint for a generic class or a subset of application flows, this work explores tailor-made solutions for IM using application indicators and the user interaction knowledge obtained from

our dataset. We also show, by analysing the cost of added functionalities (typing notification), that developers can rethink the inclusion of the function or providing the option to disable them.

3. COLLECTED IM DATASET

Analysing the way users write text messages using IM applications can reveal current inefficiencies in terms of energy consumption. We are interested in the user input, which is translated to network traffic by the applications. Thus, we study a dataset of user text messages collected at the application layer in this section.

The messages were collected from one of the most widely used IM applications (WhatsApp) during a period between 23rd of January 2011 and 8th of January 2014. Note that the logs from different users have different starting time. We agreed on collecting the usage data with the users after they were created (from past logs), thus the data reflects the normal behaviour of the users. The users employ WhatsApp as their primary IM application.

A parser was developed to obtain the messages from the logs of WhatsApp in each user device. Every text message is represented by its timestamp (UNIX time), the message length in characters, the direction (in/out), the user number, the chat type (single chat or group chat) and the chat number. A *chat* is a sequence of messages exchanged with a user (1-to-1 single chat) or a group of users (group chat) over the duration of collection. By *conversation* we will denote a subsequence of all the messages belonging to one of these chats. The user name and the actual content of the message are obfuscated for privacy reasons. The focus of this work is on text conversations, and therefore we do not consider multimedia messages, which are left for extensions of this work.

The dataset currently contains 1043370 messages collected from 51 users. The age of the users is different: 34 users between 25-30 years, 12 users between 30-35 years, and 5 users above 45 years. Regarding the country, most users are from Spain (33) and Sweden (13), whereas the rest are from Belgium (2), Germany (1), USA (1) and Mexico (1). The messages appear in 1815 conversations with other users (2089 users in total).

While selection of representative subset of all messaging patterns in the world would require a careful analysis, we believe that the current dataset provides an interesting subset since (1) it has a diverse user base, and (2) it shows a great diversity in terms of number of messages sent per day as well as used chat types (single or group chat).

The timestamp and message size are the most interesting values from the transmission pattern perspective. We start by analysing the message distribution according to their origin (in/out) and conversation type.

3.1 Message origin

Single chats are the most common type of conversation (83% against 17% for group chats). The larger fraction of messages is originated from single chats (59% of all the messages), whereas the rest (41%) is from group chats. Table 1 shows the number of messages per chat type and direction. The input messages dominate in the dataset (65%).

We observe that there is a great diversity in the above numbers across the different users of the dataset. Fig. 3

Table 1: Message origin per direction and chat type.

	In	Out	Total
Single chat	29%	30%	59%
Group chat	36%	5%	41%
Total	65%	35%	

shows the message classification per user (the users are sorted by the number of single chat messages).

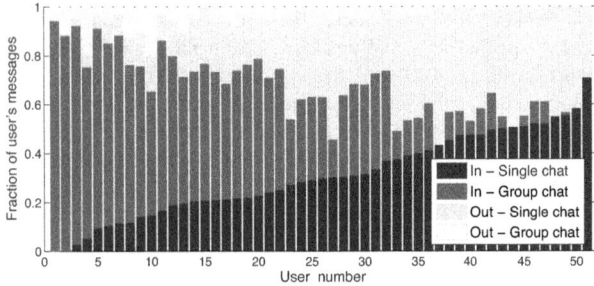

Figure 3: Message classification per user.

Most of the users are shown to have all the message classes, but in different proportion. For example, user 10 has a much larger proportion of group chat input messages compared to user 40 (50% against 5%), meaning that half of the messages received by user 10 are from group chats. However, user 40 has a larger proportion of single chat in and out messages, meaning that the user mostly uses single chats. Some users do not even use group chats (e.g., user 37 or 44).

Regarding the number of chats per user, the average and variance are 35±23 chats. For an arbitrary user, the greatest proportion of messages is typically concentrated in a few chats: On average, 50% of the messages of a user belong to only 2 of her chats (and these are typically single chats). Fig. 4 (left) shows a number of selected users (one curve per each user) according to the message distribution over the chats sorted by message volume in order to illustrate the diversity across the users. The average number of users in group chats is 7. However, larger groups are also present (up to 26 users) but less common. Only 11% of the groups are larger than 12 users.

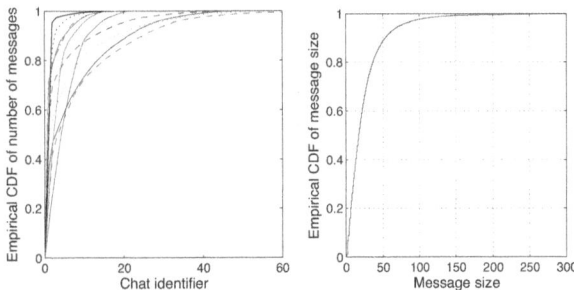

Figure 4: Message distribution of selected users over chat (left) and overall message size distribution (right).

To summarise, the great diversity among users makes the usage depend much on the type of chat they employ. Differentiating these cases is interesting to employ different techniques to save energy. For example, some users might receive many messages from group chats while not using their device, leading to high energy consumption. A downlink message batching policy could reduce the energy consumption for this type of users.

3.2 Message size

Regarding message size, we observe that short messages are predominant. The average message size is 26 characters. Fig. 4 (right) shows that messages shorter than 40 characters comprise 83% of all the messages. Small messages lead to small packets, making it very inefficient to send each message in a separate packet. For example, if the transmission of these small messages is performed over TCP/IP (i.e., the most common case), the overhead created by the packet headers (40 bytes) is the same size as the payload (i.e., the message).

In order to understand which message sizes produce more traffic we multiply the message size by the number of messages. Fig. 5 shows the distribution of the total traffic over the message size and the proportion of the different origins (single/group chat and in/out). The small packets generate most of the traffic.

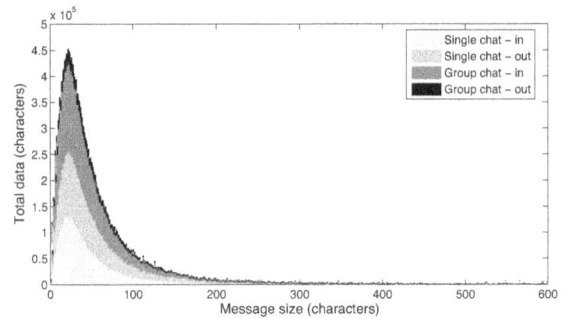

Figure 5: Distribution of the total data sent.

Various works show the benefit of compression for transmitting less network data and thus reducing the energy cost [19, 29]. We analysed the compression performance of the default compression strategy in Android[2] on the actual messages from the collected WhatsApp logs. Since most of the messages are short messages with few recurring patterns, we found that only 2.3% of the messages of our dataset would benefit from compression.

3.3 Temporal properties

Fig. 6 (top-left) shows the distribution of messages appearing in the collected dataset. As expected, the users tend to exchange more messages during the afternoon and the evening. Looking at the aggregates, the number of messages gradually grows during the day and peaks at 20:30 in the evening.

Fig. 6 (bottom) suggests that there is no clear weekly pattern in contrast to the cellular traffic observed in other works [23], where the daily peaks observed on the weekdays

---

[2]http://www.gzip.org/algorithm.txt

are higher than during weekends. Every day of the week shows a similar trend.

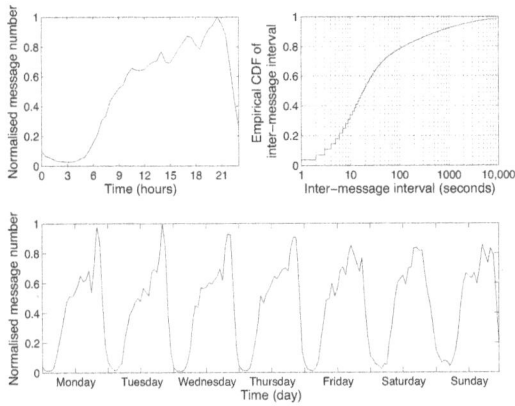

Figure 6: Normalised number of messages over hours in a day (top-left), empirical CDF of inter-message interval (top-right) and normalised number of messages during different days of a week (bottom).

Fig. 7 shows the average and standard deviation of the number of messages sent per day and user. There is a great diversity across the dataset, from very active users (more than 200 messages) to users that exchange few messages. The large standard deviation describes the variation for the same user between days, which makes it difficult to predict the IM traffic only based on the transmitted messages in the past.

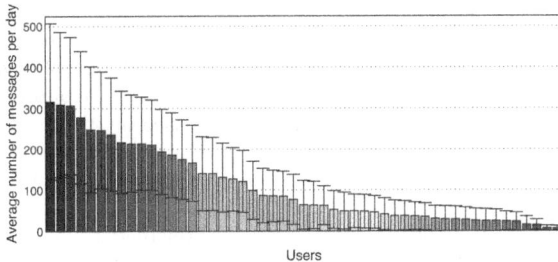

Figure 7: Average and standard deviation of messages per day per user.

The empirical CDF of inter-message interval (IMI) of the dataset is shown in Fig. 6 (top-right). We observe that messages with short IMI are predominant, where 73% of the messages have an IMI shorter than 1 minute. The long tail describes the distinct idle periods of the users.

We have observed that users generally write more than one message in a row before receiving any answer. This type of message is hereafter referred to as *consecutive* message. 48% of the messages in the dataset show this characteristic. From the energy perspective, consecutive messages are wasteful since the inactivity timers of the cellular interfaces restart leading to higher energy consumption. If the elapsed time is greater than the inactivity timer, the UE consumes another energy tail. The short IMI of most messages, their small size and the significant presence of consecutive

messages suggest that these could be coalesced to extend the idle time. In this paper we explore this option and present an algorithm that aggregates them in section 4.

Finally, two types of conversations (i.e., a chunk of the whole chat) can be identified over time. Based on the number of messages sent and their closeness in time, we can distinguish two different types of conversations over time: *sparse* and *dense* conversation periods. Sparse conversation periods have their messages more separated in time (i.e., higher IMI), while the dense ones represent intensive periods of interaction with shorter IMIs. This knowledge is used later on to select the evaluation traces.

To sum up, the dataset provides valuable insights for studying the message exchange characteristics of different users and efficiency of transmissions.

4. BUNDLING OF MESSAGES

Bundling aggregates consecutive messages by sending them together, ideally in the same packet. The potential benefits are the following:

- Less protocol overhead: Since the small messages predominate the IM text traffic, sending the messages in the same packet payload instead of sending them in separate packets would reduce the amount of protocol overhead.

- Extended idle state time: Reducing the number of transmissions by aggregating messages in the same bundle allows the UE to extend its idle state time, and therefore the energy consumption.

- Opportunity for better compression: We conjecture that aggregating messages would improve the compression results. However, the impact of compression is not studied in this paper.

Even though the benefits of message bundling are convincing, the main drawback is that the technique delays messages in order to send them together. Nevertheless, it is unclear whether introducing delay for consecutive messages is detrimental for the QoE when the other user is not active in the conversation.

Algorithm 1 Message Bundling

Require: Q_M (initially $\emptyset$), BundleTime
1: **Upon:** send button pressed
2:     m $\leftarrow$ text area content
3:     $Q_M \leftarrow$ m
4:     BundleTimer $\leftarrow$ BundleTime
5: **Upon:** text input area changed
6:     BundleTimer $\leftarrow$ BundleTime
7: **Upon:** BundleTimer = 0
8: **if** $Q_M \neq \emptyset$ **then**
9:     Transmit Q_M
10:     $Q_M \leftarrow \emptyset$
11:     BundleTimer $\leftarrow$ BundleTime
12: **end if**

In order to investigate the potential energy savings of message bundling and the impact on QoE in terms of message delay, we propose an event-based algorithm, which uses information from the graphical user interface. Algorithm 1 describes the operation of message bundling. The intuition behind the algorithm is that when the user presses the *send button* the message is not directly sent over the network. Instead, a *BundleTimer* is started (or restarted if it is already running). The content of the *text input area* (i.e., the message m) is queued in the message queue Q_M.

Whenever the text input area is changed, it means that the user is typing the next message. Therefore, the Bundle-Timer is restarted every time the user changes the text, so that the new message can be bundled too. This prevents the Q_M contents to be transmitted while the user is typing, thus recognises consecutive messages.

However, if the user never stops typing, the messages will never be sent. We argue that if the user keeps typing, the messages can be considered as the same one and QoE will not suffer from sending them together, no matter the length of the message. Therefore, we consider this case to be a pathological case.

The BundleTimer is a statically configured countdown timer, with the *BundleTime* as an input parameter. Whenever it expires, the messages in Q_M are transmitted over the network, Q_M is emptied and the BundleTimer is restarted.

The proposed BundleTime parameter provides flexibility: a short BundleTime decreases the sending delay for single messages. A longer BundleTime would allow text over several consecutive messages to be aggregated. Since the "text input area changed" event requires the screen to be switched on, we do not consider more general indicators such as screen for simplicity.

5. TYPING NOTIFICATION

The typing notification is a common feature implemented by most IM applications. The mechanism notifies the (receiving) user when the other (sending) user in the conversation is typing, creating a notion of presence and interactivity. Users can use this information to decide whether they should remain in the conversation.

In order to study the cost of this mechanism, we develop an algorithm, which emulates its operation in a simple IM application. The notify updates should be triggered when the user types a character in the text input area on the graphical user interface. However, it is up to the implementation to decide the frequency of these events resulting in a network packet being sent to the receiving user as a notification. The typing notification feature increases the amount of packets transmitted, and potentially the energy consumption.

Algorithm 2 employs a countdown timer named Notify-Timer to restrict the rate of notify messages. The NotifyTimer is statically configured with a NotifyTime value in seconds. When the user is typing, a text input area changed event is triggered. If the NotifyTimer is not running (i.e., NotifyTimer = 0), the algorithm will send a notification packet to the network and start the NotifyTimer. The next time the user types, the NotifyTimer will avoid a new packet being sent to the network. Thus, if the user is continuously typing the algorithm performs only a single notification transmission every NotifyTime.

When the other user receives the typing notification, the receiving end of the application will show the receiving user the notification in the screen. For example, we observe that WhatsApp uses approximately a 3 seconds timer for the NotifyTime.

Algorithm 2 Typing notification
Require: NotifyTimer (initially NotifyTime)
1: **Upon:** text input area changed
2: **if** NotifyTimer $= 0$ **then**
3:     Transmit notification
4:     NotifyTimer $\leftarrow$ NotifyTime
5: **end if**

---

6. EVALUATION METHODOLOGY

This section describes the methodology and the evaluation environment used to quantify energy consumption of the typing notification and message bundling.

The general methodology is as follows: a predefined set of real conversations is automatically replayed between a pair of clients using a prototype IM application running on commodity devices. The conversations are transformed to network transmissions (i.e., packet traces) by our prototype application. The transmission is performed using the real 3G network described in section 2, and the resulting packet traces are captured. The energy is calculated using Energy-Box from the captured real packet traces.

First, the energy consumption of each conversation is calculated as a baseline (without typing notification nor message bundling). Second, the conversations are replayed with only message bundling enabled (Algorithm 1), and the energy savings are calculated and compared against the baseline. Third, the conversations are replayed with only the typing notification enabled (Algorithm 2), and the extra energy cost is calculated by comparing the resulting energy against the baseline.

First, we briefly describe the evaluation environment as well as the evaluation conversations and EnergyBox.

6.1 Evaluation environment

The client application provides the chat functionality between two Android devices and implements the logic of Algorithms 1 and 2. The implementation of the message bundling and the typing notification feature are based on instances of the Async Task class provided by Android, where the Async Task represents the timers that can be cancelled, reset and started again.

We selected the Message Queueing Telemetry Transport (MQTT) protocol as the transport protocol for the following reasons: it is a lightweight application protocol, some IM applications officially use it (e.g., Facebook Messenger), and the Mosquitto open source project provides easy to set up public servers that accelerate the development phase. MQTT is a publish/subscribe protocol, where the subscribers are instantaneously notified whenever a publisher generates a new event.

Fig. 8 shows the general architecture of the application and the test environment. The IM clients are able to communicate using MQTT through the server that hosts the MQTT broker. Each user subscribes to her nickname. The conversation partners send a message by publishing the message to the nickname (in publish/subscribe terms, the topic) of the recipient. The MQTT broker keeps track of the topic subscriptions.

Since the IM applications tested in section 1 are black boxes, we cannot compare the results obtained from our prototype application against them in a fair way. However, for the interested reader, the basic energy cost of the prototype

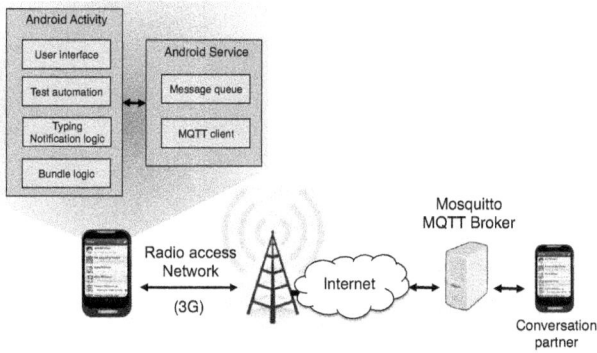

Figure 8: Architecture of the IM prototype implementation and the test environment.

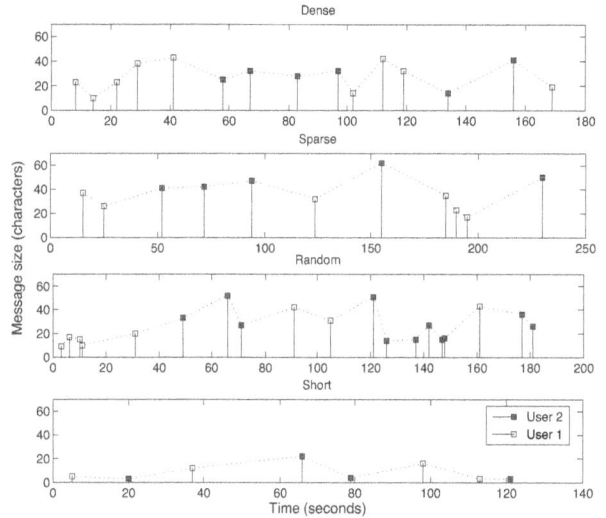

Figure 9: Test conversations.

application for the same conversation as shown in section 1 is lower than the rest (18 Joules).

6.2 Test traces and parameter settings

This section describes the parameter settings and the conversations used to study the energy characteristics of the typing notification and the message bundling.

Test conversations: Four different test conversations are selected for the tests based on the different patterns observed in section 3. Two conversations (*Dense* and *Sparse*) were randomly selected from the dataset, representing intensive conversations (short IMIs) and slow-paced ones (longer IMIs). *Random* is a synthetic conversation generated by randomly selecting messages from the dataset not considering the resulting conversation's dense/sparse characteristics. By randomly selecting the messages we aim at obtaining messages of different sizes. The selection follows the following rules: Message pairs in the resulting conversation have an IMI of shorter than 30 s since larger IMIs are uninteresting from the energy perspective (greater than the typical inactivity timers). Moreover, if a selected message appears in a sequence of consecutive messages, then the other messages belonging to that sequence are also selected to keep the realistic consecutive message relations from the dataset. Finally, *Short* is the same conversation used in the introduction to compare the different IM applications. It characterises a trace containing short messages, a single consecutive message, and IMIs between the Sparse and Dense conversations. The four categories have different number of consecutive messages, which is interesting to test the message bundling.

The test conversations used are shown in Fig. 9. The duration of the selected conversations is below 250 s. We believe these are representative conversations for IM. Since our dataset did not delimit conversations (the users were always logged in and no distinction of different conversations were made within the chats), we base our reasoning about duration on earlier work [30], where 9900 of approximately 10000 conversations were shorter than 250 s. Note that in Fig. 9 the conversations do not start from 0 since the time to write the message is also considered, and the difference in their length is not important since the results are studied per conversation.

Writing speed parameters: In order to simulate the user typing and automate the tests, the prototype application is instrumented to automatically write characters at a parametrised writing speed. For each message of a given conversation, the characters of the message are written using a constant typing speed. The automation logic starts writing in the input text field so that the message is sent in its correct timestamp. The time to start writing the message is calculated using the message length and the average writing speed.

For simplicity, the typing speed is set to a constant of 287 ms delay per character. This number was experimentally obtained by averaging the measured time to write 160 characters (i.e., a SMS) for 6 different people.

Computing the transmission energy: While replaying the sequence of messages of the test conversations, the packet traces are captured in the device of the user 1 using *tcpdump* for every test, later used for computing the energy consumption. Only the traffic of the IM application is allowed using a firewall to block the rest of the traffic.

Next, the transmission energy consumption for each test is calculated from the gathered traces using the EnergyBox. EnergyBox has been evaluated against physical energy consumption measurements showing an accuracy of 98% [26]. Given the 3G network parameters specified at operator level, EnergyBox derives the 3G states of the UE employing trace-based iterative packet-driven simulation. The RRC state machine is captured by a finite state machine that simulates state transitions using the inactivity timers or exceeding the RLC buffer thresholds. The state machine is forced to go through transitions by an iterative packet-driven simulation mechanism, which uses the inter-packet interval, the size and the direction (uplink/downlink) of the data traffic trace. The energy consumption of a given packet trace for the given network parameters is calculated by associating the UE-specific power levels with the emulated intervals in each state, and integrating them over time.

The parameters of EnergyBox are set as follows: We set the 3G network settings that correspond to the operator TeliaSonera (the operator used for the tests) measured in our local (experiment) area. The inactivity timers T_1 and T_2 are set to 4.1 s and 5.6 s respectively. The RLC buffer thresholds correspond to: $B_1^u = 1000$ and $B_2^u = 294$ bytes for uplink, and $B_1^d = 515$ and $B_2^d = 515$ bytes for downlink. The time to perform the different state transitions are set to 1.7 s, 0.65 s and 0.435 s for PCH-DCH, FACH-DCH and PCH-FACH respectively. The UE power values for the different RRC states are based on earlier measurements: DCH = 612 mW, FACH = 416 mW. We set PCH = 0 W in order to quantify only the energy spent for data transmission.

The evaluation methodology and environment are employed to analyse the potential energy savings of the message bundling and the cost of the typing notification in the next sections.

7. DOES MESSAGE BUNDLING PAY OFF?

Next, we quantify the energy savings that message bundling can provide at the cost of an introduced delay due to aggregating messages.

7.1 Energy savings and bundling results

Each test conversation is tested with the following BundleTimes: 1, 3, 5 and 7 s. The results are normalised to the base energy consumption with the message bundling disabled (32.63, 26.68, 32.81 and 17.81 Joules for Dense, Sparse, Random and Short respectively). The results are based on 3 repetitions of each unique test. Additional repetitions are run when large standard deviation is observed.

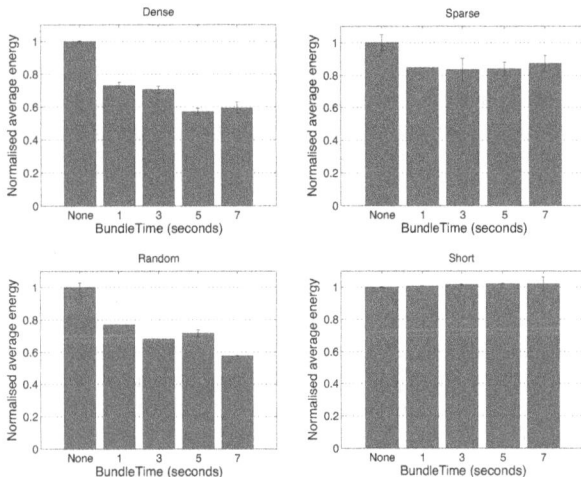

Figure 10: Normalised average energy and standard deviation for message bundling.

Energy savings: Fig. 10 shows the energy savings for the different test conversations. The message bundling provides energy savings when the algorithm successfully performs at least one bundle. The energy savings vary between the conversations, and thus we describe them separately in this section.

The energy savings due to bundling range from 27% to 43% for the Dense test conversation. Since it contains many consecutive messages and these are often close in time (i.e., the user starts writing soon after a previous message is sent), even a short BundleTime of 1 s can achieve 27% savings.

The results for Sparse are different. The message bundling achieves 16% energy savings with a BundleTime of 1 s. However, increasing the timer value does not increase the energy

savings. The IMI of the consecutive messages is long for the Sparse conversation, thus the short BundleTime values do not allow performing most of the possible bundles.

Regarding the Random conversation, the energy savings range from 24% to 42% for the different BundleTimes. The shortest timer provides again significant energy savings.

There is only one consecutive message in the Short conversation. No bundle is created since its inter-message interval is longer than the BundleTimes, and the message length is short (i.e., the typing time is short).

Bundling results: Tables 2 and 3 show the achieved number of bundles and the messages per bundle for the different BundleTimes using the Dense and Sparse conversations. *Possible bundles* refers to the number of distinct bundles where each bundle is a sequence of consecutive messages with the maximum length appearing in the conversation.

Table 2: Number of bundles and bundles per message for the Dense conversation.

BundleTime (s)	Bundles	Messages per bundle
1	3	3, 3, 2
3	3	4, 3, 2
5	4	5, 3, 3, 2
7	4	5, 3, 3, 2
Possible bundles	4	5, 4, 3, 2

For Dense, the BundleTime of 1 s creates 3 bundles out of the 4 possible bundles (i.e., 4 groups of consecutive messages). Only one more message is aggregated for the 3 s BundleTime. All the possible bundles are performed when the BundleTime is increased to 5 s achieving the maximum energy savings. Similar results are obtained for 5 and 7 s, i.e., no additional messages are bundled even increasing the BundleTime.

Table 3: Number of bundles and bundles per message for the Sparse conversation.

BundleTime (s)	Bundles	Messages per bundle
1	1	3
3	2	2, 3
5	2	2, 3
7	2	2, 3
Possible bundles	3	2, 3, 3

For Sparse, the BundleTime of 1 s leads to a single bundle out of the 3 possible bundles. The other BundleTimes only create an additional bundle of 2 messages.

Protocol overhead: The message bundling also provides less TCP/IP header overhead. The number of packets sent in the Random conversation was reduced from 40 to 16 when using a BundleTime of 7 s. Thus, the messages are sent in the same packet reducing the TCP/IP overhead.

To sum up, our results show that even a short BundleTime can lead to significant energy savings. The next section studies the potential drawback of bundling.

7.2 Message delay

Even though the bundle technique is desirable from the energy perspective, one needs to also consider its negative impact on per-message delay. The bundle technique delays each message by a minimum of the BundleTime value. The delay of the held messages increases when the user continues typing a consecutive message since the BundleTimer is restarted every time the user types a character.

The per-message delay is computed for the Dense and Sparse test conversations for different BundleTimes. The application is instrumented in order to obtain the delay between the moment of pressing the sending button and the time that the message is actually sent to the network. The minimum delay for each BundleTime is the BundleTime itself, representing the case that a message was not bundled. The bundled messages are typically delayed more than the minimum, depending on the IMI, the BundleTime and the number of characters in the next message.

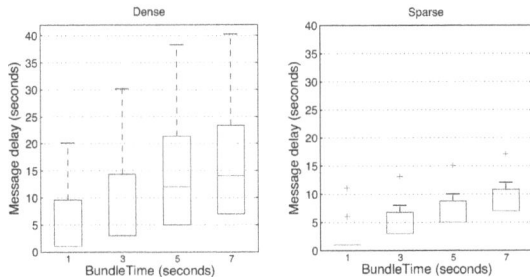

Figure 11: Box plot of the delay experienced by the different messages for Sparse and Dense conversations.

Fig. 11 shows the delay introduced by bundling in the Dense and Sparse conversations. The median delay for the Dense conversation with the BundleTimes 1 and 3 s is the BundleTime since most messages are just delayed by the minimum delay. These are the last messages added to a bundle or the messages that were not bundled. As expected, the bundled messages experience greater delay.

Fig. 11 shows that the maximum delay for the BundleTimes 1 and 3 s is 20 and 30 seconds in the Dense scenario. The maximum delay for 3 s BundleTime increases because it bundles an additional message. The more messages in the bundle, the higher is the maximum delay of the first bundled message. However, increasing the BundleTime leads to a great increase of the per-message delay, especially the messages that are bundled. In Dense, even though the Bundle-Times 5 and 7 s form exactly the same bundles, the messages experience an extra delay with no extra energy saving.

The results for the Sparse conversation show that the median delay is the minimum experienced delay. The long IMI of the Sparse conversation make the bundle technique to create a single bundle of 3 messages for the 1 s BundleTime (the outliers of 6 and 11 s in Fig. 11), and an additional bundle of 2 messages for the rest. Thus, the per-message delay is shorter due to the smaller number of bundles than for the Dense conversation.

Comparing the energy savings and the introduced per-message delay, we observe that a short BundleTime of 1 s leads to significant energy savings while not causing huge delays. This indicates that simply keeping track of the user typing is enough for a simple bundle policy. Longer BundleTime values can increase the energy savings for dense conversations at the cost of higher delay. However, Sparse

conversations with sporadic messages should not use long timers.

Finally, the message delay does not always have a negative impact on the QoE. When the user is not engaged in an active conversation, the reception of the non-delayed messages or a bundle of delayed messages can be argued to be the same. However, from the energy perspective, the latter drastically reduces the energy consumption.

8. COST OF TYPING NOTIFICATION

Aggressive notification policies can lead to wasting energy. This section studies the additional energy cost incurred by the typing notification functionality for the different test conversations. The results are based on 3 repetitions of each unique test. An additional 2 repetitions are run if large standard deviation is observed in the results.

For each conversation, we compute the energy consumption with the typing notification functionality disabled as a baseline. We select 3, 5 and 10 s as NotifyTime values for the different tests. These values are representative of the parameters used in real typing notification mechanisms.

Since the focus is on the additional cost, we normalise all the values to the average energy consumed by the baseline for each conversation (30.65, 26.99, 33.36 and 18.47 Joules for the Dense, Sparse, Random and Short respectively), i.e., the energy cost with no typing notification.

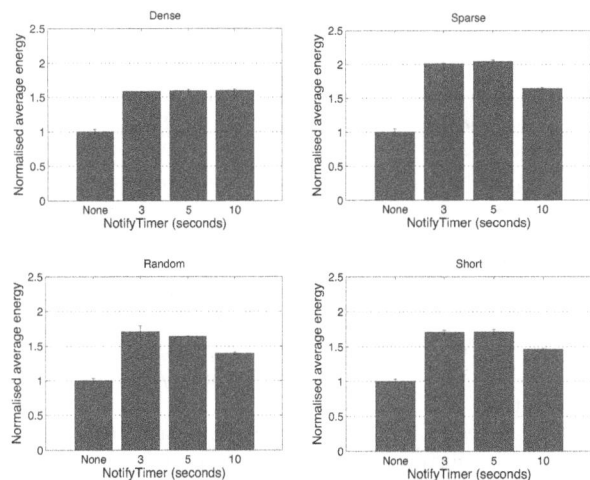

Figure 12: Normalised average energy and standard deviation of the typing notification feature for the different conversations.

Fig. 12 shows that in general the additional energy cost of the typing notification feature is large, varying from 1.4 to 2 times the base energy consumption (40-104% more energy). Since the functionality sends packets whenever the user is typing, it keeps the 3G interface in an active state for almost the whole duration of the test. The results for each conversation are explained next.

For the Dense conversation, the energy consumption for the different NotifyTime values is similar. Even though a longer NotifyTime implies sending fewer notify packets, when the device enters a high energy RRC state, sending more data does not incur higher energy cost. Most of the energy consumption is due to resetting the inactivity timers by the operator, and thus the message pattern of the conversation greatly influences the consumed energy. Since the conversation is dense, the impact of the typing notification is not as high as in the Sparse conversation.

The additional energy cost for the Sparse conversation is higher than the Dense one. The Sparse conversation has periods of time where the device is in PCH between message sendings. However, the typing notification messages greatly reduce the idle time. Since the 3 and 5 s NotifyTimes are shorter than the inactivity timer T_2, the T_2 timer is reset before it has expired. When the NotifyTime is 10 s, T_2 expires, which results in higher idle time. However, the energy cost is still 64% more than the baseline. The Sparse conversation is characterised by having slightly longer messages, and thus the time to type for the user is longer and more notify packets per message are sent.

The results for the different NotifyTimes for the Random and Short are similar to the Sparse conversation. The Short and Random conversations contain mostly short messages. When NotifyTime is 10 s, less notify messages are sent since the user spends less time typing the messages.

To sum up, the typing notification functionality results in a high additional cost for an IM application. Even though a longer NotifyTime avoids excessive usage of the 3G interface, the cost is still high.

9. CONCLUSION AND FUTURE WORK

When developing energy-efficient solutions for application data transmission, there is a trade-off between adding application features that perform network transmissions and energy conservation. There is a need to quantify the extra energy cost and the perceived functionality benefit from the user side.

The typing notification functionality employed by most IM applications quantified in our work was shown to have a tremendous energy cost. According to our results, this functionality can increase the energy consumption of an IM application by 40-104% from the basic message exchange functionality. Quantifying the cost of a functionality can allow the developers to rethink the need for the functionality or provide the option to dynamically enable/disable it (e.g., at low battery levels).

When the traffic is directly generated by user interaction, the network transmissions can easily result in energy waste. In our work we collected and studied an IM dataset from mobile users to create a better understanding of the user inputs that trigger network transmissions. Based on our study with collected real usage data, we observe that IM application users currently tend to write consecutive messages, which increases the active time of the wireless interface.

We show that bundling can be used to reduce transmissions while the user continues typing, and send them at one go. Our results show energy savings up to 43% depending on the message pattern of the conversation. Given the high percentage of the consecutive messages, this is a promising result. However, using longer timers for the bundle technique can lead to high delays for some messages. Thus, the bundle technique can be dynamically activated for sparse conversations, or when the receiving end of a chat is offline or away.

Our work can be extended by moving message bundling to the server side, which appears very interesting for group chats that usually have denser conversations. The current study can also be made more extensive by creating sets of synthetic data as well as employing further real traces, and confirming the trends observed above. Studying the user interaction changes given the different functionalities (e.g., adding bundling or removing typing notification) is left for future works.

More sophisticated bundling techniques are feasible leveraging knowledge of user activity (e.g., the screen is off, the user switched the focus to another application), message content parsing (e.g., conversational closings such as "talk to you later"), context information (e.g., built-in sensors) or presence information from other users. Distinguishing between periods of sparse and dense conversations is interesting to dynamically activate the bundle technique (e.g., moderately using the typing notification). Considering multimedia messages is also a future direction.

Acknowledgements

This work was supported by the Swedish national graduate school in computer science (CUGS). The authors wish to thank the support of Ericsson AB, and in particular B-O Hertz, Pär Emanuelsson and Claes Alströmer for providing the measurement kit which has been used in validating the EnergyBox and facilitating the measurement gathering phase. We would also like to thank the instant messaging users that shared their data, and the anonymous reviewers for their many insightful comments and suggestions.

10. REFERENCES

[1] BBC. Chat app messaging overtakes SMS texts, Informa says, accessed 20th February, 2014. http://www.bbc.co.uk/news/business-22334338.

[2] CNET. LG shares its plans for home appliance evolution, accessed 20th February, 2014. http://www.cnet.com/news/lg-shares-its-plans-for-home-appliance-evolution/.

[3] The Verge. WhatsApp now has over 400 million monthly users, accessed 20th February, 2014. http://www.theverge.com/2013/12/19/5228656/whatsapp-now-has-over-400-million-monthly-users.

[4] Tencent. About Tencent, accessed 20th February, 2014. http://www.tencent.com/en-us/at/abouttencent.shtml.

[5] P. K. Athivarapu, R. Bhagwan, S. Guha, V. Navda, R. Ramjee, D. Arora, V. N. Padmanabhan, and G. Varghese. Radiojockey: mining program execution to optimize cellular radio usage. In *Proceedings of the 18th Annual International Conference on Mobile Computing and Networking*, Mobicom '12, pages 101–112. ACM, 2012.

[6] N. Balasubramanian, A. Balasubramanian, and A. Venkataramani. Energy consumption in mobile phones: a measurement study and implications for network applications. In *Proceedings of the 9th ACM SIGCOMM conference on Internet measurement conference*, IMC '09, pages 280–293. ACM, 2009.

[7] Y. W. Chung. An improved energy saving scheme for instant messaging services. In *Wireless Advanced, 2011*, pages 278–282. IEEE, 2011.

[8] Y. W. Chung. Investigation of energy consumption of mobile station for instant messaging services. In *Proceedings of the 2011 Tenth International*

Symposium on Autonomous Decentralized Systems, pages 343–346, IEEE. 2011.

[9] S. Deng and H. Balakrishnan. Traffic-aware techniques to reduce 3G/LTE wireless energy consumption. In *Proceedings of the 8th International Conference on Emerging Networking Experiments and Technologies*, CoNEXT '12, pages 181–192. ACM, 2012.

[10] R. E. Grinter, L. Palen, and M. Eldridge. Chatting with teenagers: Considering the place of chat technologies in teen life. *ACM Transactions on Computer-Human Interaction (TOCHI)*, 13(4):423–447, Dec. 2006.

[11] H. Holma and A. Toskala. *WCDMA for UMTS: HSPA Evolution and LTE*. Wiley Online Library: Books. John Wiley & Sons, 2010.

[12] J. Huang, F. Qian, Z. M. Mao, S. Sen, and O. Spatscheck. Screen-off traffic characterization and optimization in 3G/4G networks. In *Proceedings of the 2012 ACM Internet Measurement Conference*, IMC '12, pages 357–364. ACM, 2012.

[13] E. Isaacs, A. Walendowski, S. Whittaker, D. J. Schiano, and C. Kamm. The character, functions, and styles of instant messaging in the workplace. In *Proceedings of the 2002 ACM Conference on Computer Supported Cooperative Work*, pages 11–20. ACM, 2002.

[14] H. A. Lagar-Cavilla, K. Joshi, A. Varshavsky, J. Bickford, and D. Parra. Traffic backfilling: subsidizing lunch for delay-tolerant applications in UMTS networks. *SIGOPS Operating Systems Review*, 45(3):77–81, ACM. Jan. 2012.

[15] J. Leskovec and E. Horvitz. Planetary-scale views on a large instant-messaging network. In *Proceedings of the 17th International Conference on World Wide Web*, WWW '08, pages 915–924. ACM, 2008.

[16] H. Liu, Y. Zhang, and Y. Zhou. Tailtheft: leveraging the wasted time for saving energy in cellular communications. In *Proceedings of the Sixth International Workshop on MobiArch*, pages 31–36. ACM, 2011.

[17] L.-S. Meng, D.-S. Shiu, P.-C. Yeh, K.-C. Chen, and H.-Y. Lo. Low power consumption solutions for mobile instant messaging. *IEEE Transactions on Mobile Computing*, 11(6):896–904, June 2012.

[18] A. Pathak, Y. C. Hu, and M. Zhang. Where is the energy spent inside my app?: Fine grained energy accounting on smartphones with Eprof. In *Proceedings of the 7th ACM European Conference on Computer Systems*, EuroSys '12, pages 29–42, 2012.

[19] F. Qian, J. Huang, J. Erman, Z. M. Mao, S. Sen, and O. Spatscheck. How to reduce smartphone traffic volume by 30%? In *Proceedings of the 14th International Conference on Passive and Active Measurement*, IMC '13, pages 42–52. Springer-Verlag, 2013.

[20] F. Qian, Z. Wang, Y. Gao, J. Huang, A. Gerber, Z. Mao, S. Sen, and O. Spatscheck. Periodic transfers in mobile applications: network-wide origin, impact, and optimization. In *Proceedings of the 21st International Conference on World Wide Web*, WWW '12, pages 51–60. ACM, 2012.

[21] F. Qian, Z. Wang, A. Gerber, Z. Mao, S. Sen, and O. Spatscheck. Profiling resource usage for mobile applications: A cross-layer approach. In *Proceedings of the 9th International Conference on Mobile Systems, Applications, and Services*, MobiSys '11, pages 321–334. ACM, 2011.

[22] S. Schrittwieser, P. Frühwirt, P. Kieseberg, M. Leithner, M. Mulazzani, M. Huber, and E. R. Weippl. Guess who's texting you? evaluating the security of smartphone messaging applications. In *19th Annual Network and Distributed System Security Symposium (NDSS)*, ISOC. 2012.

[23] M. Z. Shafiq, L. Ji, A. X. Liu, and J. Wang. Characterizing and modeling internet traffic dynamics of cellular devices. In *Proceedings of the ACM SIGMETRICS Joint International Conference on Measurement and Modeling of Computer Systems*, pages 305–316. ACM, 2011.

[24] N. Vallina-Rodriguez and J. Crowcroft. Energy management techniques in modern mobile handsets. *Communications Surveys Tutorials, IEEE*, 15(1):179–198, 2013.

[25] E. J. Vergara and S. Nadjm-Tehrani. Energy-aware cross-layer burst buffering for wireless communication. In *Proceedings of the 3rd International Conference on Future Energy Systems: Where Energy, Computing and Communication Meet*, e-Energy '12. ACM, 2012.

[26] E. J. Vergara, S. Nadjm-Tehrani, and M. Prihodko. Energybox: Disclosing the wireless transmission energy cost for mobile devices. *Sustainable Computing: Informatics and Systems*, Elsevier. Accepted for publication. 2014.

[27] D. Wang, J. McNair, and A. George. A smart-NIC-based power-proxy solution for reduced power consumption during instant messaging. In *Green Technologies Conference, IEEE*, pages 1–10, 2010.

[28] C. Wilke, S. Richly, S. Götz, C. Piechnick, and U. Aßmann. Energy Consumption and Efficiency in Mobile Applications: A User Feedback Study. In *International Conference on Green Computing and Communications*, pages 134–141. IEEE, 2013.

[29] L. Xiang, J. Luo, and C. Rosenberg. Compressed data aggregation: Energy-efficient and high-fidelity data collection. *IEEE/ACM Transactions on Networking*, 21(6):1722–1735, 2013.

[30] Z. Xiao, L. Guo, and J. Tracey. Understanding instant messaging traffic characteristics. In *Proceedings of the 27th International Conference on Distributed Computing Systems*, pages 51–59. IEEE, 2007.

Experimental Evaluation and Comparative Study on Energy Efficiency of the Evolving IEEE 802.11 Standards

Stratos Keranidis⊕, Giannis Kazdaridis⊕, Nikos Makris⊕,
Thanasis Korakis⊕, Iordanis Koutsopoulos⊎ and Leandros Tassiulas⊕
○Department of Electrical and Computer Engineering, University of Thessaly, Greece
⁺Centre for Research and Technology Hellas, CERTH, Greece
⊎Department of Computer Science, Athens University of Economics and Business, Greece
{efkerani, iokazdarid, nimakris, korakis, leandros}@uth.gr, jordan@aueb.gr

ABSTRACT

Over the last decade, the IEEE 802.11 has emerged as the most popular protocol in the wireless domain. Since the release of the first standard version, several amendments have been introduced in an effort to improve its throughput performance, with the most recent one being the IEEE 802.11n extension. In this paper, we present experimentally obtained results that evaluate the energy efficiency of the base standard in comparison with the latest 802.11n version, under a wide range of settings. To the best of our knowledge, our work is the first to provide such a detailed comparative analysis on the performance of both standards. The followed power measurement methodology is based on custom-built hardware that enables online energy consumption evaluation at both the wireless transceiver and the total node levels. Based on in-depth interpretation of the collected results, we remark that the latest standard enables significant improvement of energy efficiency, when combined with standard compliant frame aggregation mechanisms. Our detailed findings can act as guidelines for researchers working on the design of energy efficient wireless protocols.

1. INTRODUCTION

IEEE 802.11 is currently considered as the default solution for implementing wireless local area network communications. The wide adoption of this standard by vendors of wireless devices offers high interoperability, which in combination with the provided ease of use and low deployment cost have resulted in its unprecedented market and everyday life penetration. While the base version of the standard was released in 1997, subsequent amendments have been proposed throughout the years, such as the widely adopted 802.11b, 802.11a and 802.11g. In 2007, the current standard IEEE 802.11-2007 [1] was released and merged several amendments with the base version.

In an effort to improve throughput performance of the base standard, the IEEE 802.11 standard working group started in 2003 to develop the IEEE 802.11n high-throughput (HT) extension of the base standard that was finally published in 2009. The most important improvement of the 802.11n on the Physical layer (PHY) is the ability to combine multiple antenna elements to achieve higher PHY bit rates and increased link reliability. In order to increase medium utilisation and exploit from the increased PHY bit rates, efficient Medium Access Control layer (MAC) frame aggregation mechanisms [2] are also supported. Several recent studies [3, 4] in the field of wireless networking have experimentally verified the improved channel efficiency and throughput performance that the 802.11n is able to deliver in comparison with 802.11a/g systems.

On the other hand, the recent penetration of 802.11n compatible chipsets in "smart" mobile devices has raised concerns regarding the energy efficient operation of the HT protocol. As the dramatically increased PHY bit rates, require the activation of multiple RF chains and complex baseband processing as well, 802.11n compatible chipsets induce significantly higher power consumption that grows with the number of active RF chains. Our experimental results that match other relevant studies [5, 6] as well, show that a modern 802.11n 3x3 MIMO compatible chipset is able to draw up to 2.45 W, in the case that all the various chipset components are constantly activated and the highest PHY bit rate performance is achieved. Especially in the case of smartphone platforms, the energy greedy profile of the supported state-of-the-art wireless technologies may induce up to 50% of the total platform power consumption [7], under typical use case scenarios. As the focus of researchers is usually on network performance, only a few works have presented detailed experimental results that characterise the energy consumption of 802.11n chipsets [5, 6, 8]. The work in [5] is restricted in characterising the power consumption profile of commercial 802.11n chipsets, while the rest two studies [6, 8] experimentally investigate the impact of standard compliant power saving mechanisms on the operation of 802.11n protocol.

In this work, we take a step further than relevant studies and characterise the energy efficiency of 802.11 compliant protocols, in comparison with the achievable network performance they are able to offer. Our study is not restricted in evaluating the performance of 802.11n chipsets, but presents detailed experimentally obtained measurements that compare the performance of the legacy 802.11a/g standard with the latest 802.11n version. The impact of various MAC layer enhancements, both vendor specific and standard compliant

e-Energy'14, June 11–13, 2014, Cambridge, UK.
Copyright 2014 ACM 978-1-4503-2819-7/14/06 ...$15.00.
http://dx.doi.org/10.1145/2602044.2602069.

ones, is also considered in the performance evaluation of both protocols. The obtained results are collected in realistic scenarios and under a wide range of settings, considering varying application-layer traffic loads, frame payload lengths and different network topologies that offer varying channel conditions as well. Finally the impact of the default 802.11 Power Saving Mechanism (PSM) on the performance of both protocols during periods of activity has also been investigated.

Accurate energy efficiency evaluation under real world scale and settings, is a rather complex task that requires the application of detailed evaluation methodologies, in combination with advanced power monitoring platforms. The followed power measurement methodology is based on custom-built hardware that was developed in our previous work [9] and enables online energy consumption evaluation at both the Network Interface Card (NIC) and the total wireless node levels. In-depth analysis of the extensive list of obtained measurements aided in identifying factors that affect energy consumption on commodity 802.11 hardware. Our detailed findings that can act as guidelines towards designing energy efficient wireless protocols, are summarised as follows:

- Activation of additional RF chains that enable MIMO communications results in remarkably increased power consumption (up to 2.5x) at the NIC level. However, our experiments have shown that the resulting increased PHY bit rates of 802.11n are able to increase energy efficiency at the NIC level by 33% during transmission (63% in reception), in comparison with the rates of 802.11a/g. Moreover, we observed that proper activation of the required number of RF-chains for each specific rate configuration can aid towards saving energy.

- Application of MAC-layer aggregation mechanisms is able to deliver substantially increased throughput, while also resulting in considerable energy savings. Power consumption experiments that consider consumption at the total node level have shown that the aggregation assisted 802.11n can improve energy efficiency by more than 80%, in comparison with the performance of the 802.11a/g standard.

- While transmitting MAC frames of low payload length and under high-SNR conditions, 802.11n increased energy efficiency at the node level by 90%, in comparison with 802.11a/g. This observation is related to the fact that the supported by 802.11n aggregation mechanisms enable delivery of high throughput performance (>100 Mbps), even when transmitting frames of 300 bytes payload.

- Considering low-SNR conditions, the Spatial Diversity mode of 802.11n offers increased MAC-layer Frame Delivery Rate (FDR) and throughput improvement by a factor of 4.6x, as observed in our experiments. In addition, we remark that the monitored throughput improvement did not induce significant energy costs, as the energy efficiency at the NIC level also increased by 58%.

- Experimentation with the default 802.11 PSM mechanism has shown that 802.11n is able to provide significant energy savings (> 75%), across varying traffic loads and without sacrificing application-layer throughput or jitter performance.

This paper is organized as follows. In Section 2 we present the evolution of the base 802.11 standard over the last years. Section 3 details the experimental setup and the followed power measurement methodology that is used in our experimental evaluation. In Section 4, we characterise the power consumption profiles of the two wireless chipsets that are used in our experiments, while in Section 5 we present extensive experiments that compare the performance of the 802.11a/g and 802.11n protocols in terms of network performance and energy consumption. Finally, in Section 6 we point out the conclusions reached through this work.

2. EVOLUTION OF IEEE 802.11

The aforementioned versions of IEEE 802.11 use different PHY layer specifications, but all follow the MAC architecture of the base protocol. The mandatory access scheme that has been specified by the legacy IEEE 802.11 standard is implemented through the distributed coordination function (DCF), which is based on the carrier sense multiple access with collision avoidance (CSMA/CA) mechanism. The large PHY and MAC layer overheads that are associated with the DCF process, result in a reduction of more than 50% of the nominal link capacity, which effect is more pronounced for higher PHY bit rates, as shown in [10]. The work in [11] has analyzed the throughput and delay limits of the IEEE 802.11 standard and has shown that for infinitely high PHY bit rate and a frame payload size of 1024 bytes, the maximum achievable throughput is upper bounded to 50.2 Mbps. Such observations highlighted that MAC layer enhancements need to be applied, in order to reduce the impact of the PHY and MAC layer overheads of the base standard.

In an effort to improve throughput performance, vendors of wireless products started integrating innovative techniques into their products, as early as 2003. Such techniques include the "Atheros Fast Frames" (FF) [12], which improves 802.11a/b/g performance, by combining two MAC frames into the payload of a single aggregated frame. However, application of vendor-specific techniques has been reported to result in hardware incompatibilities, or at least degraded performance for standard compliant devices, as presented in [13].

Along the same direction, the IEEE 802.11 standard working group introduced the 802.11n extension that offers both PHY and MAC layer enhancements over legacy 802.11 systems. Through the combination of multiple antenna elements and complex MIMO processing, 802.11n is able to achieve higher PHY bit rates (in Spatial Multiplexing mode) and increased link reliability through the exploitation of multipath transmissions and antenna diversity (in Spatial Diversity mode) [14]. Another significant feature is the application of channel bonding, which increases the channel bandwidth from 20 MHz to 40 MHz and thus doubles the theoretical capacity limits. Moreover, the available Modulation and Coding Schemes (MCS) were extended through the introduction of the new coding rate of 5/6, as well as through the decrease of the OFDM guard interval from 0.8 μs to 0.4 μs. Finally, the number of OFDM data subcarriers was increased from 48 to 52, towards improving spectral efficiency. Application of the aforementioned enhancements is able to deliver the remarkably increased PHY bit rate of 600 Mbps (when using 4 antennas), resulting in performance improvement of more than 10x compared to legacy 802.11a/g systems.

In order to increase medium utilisation and exploit from the increased PHY bit rates, two different types of frame aggregation are provided, namely A-MSDU and A-MPDU aggregation. The former combines multiple higher layer packets into a single MAC layer frame with maximum size of 7935 bytes, while the latter combines multiple MAC layer frames to form an aggregated frame that cannot exceed the 65.536 bytes. In general, A-MPDU aggregation outperforms A-MSDU, which technique results in considerably degraded performance under low quality channel conditions and high PHY bit rates, as it was shown in [15]. Both frame aggregation mechanisms are enhanced by a block acknowledgment mechanism, which further reduces protocol overhead.

3. MEASUREMENT SETUP

In this section, we present the measurement setup that is used in the detailed experimental evaluation that aims at deriving a comparative performance analysis between the 802.11a/g and 802.11n standards. We start by describing the exact experimental setup, which is based on commercial wireless NICs that are representative of the state-of-the-art of each standard. In addition, we detail the followed power measurement procedure and the underlying hardware that are used to characterise the energy consumption performance of the considered protocols. The experimental setup that is used as the basis of our evaluation, consists of a single communicating pair of nodes that both feature the specifications listed in Table 1.

Component	Type
Motherboard	Commell LE-575X
CPU	Intel Atom D525 (1.8 GHz)
RAM	Kingston HYPERX DDR3 - 4GBs
Hard Drive	Samsung SSD - 64 GBs
Power Supply	60W - 12V
OS	Ubuntu 13.04
Wireless cards	Atheros 9380 / 5424
Wireless Drivers	madwifi-0.9.4 / backportsv3.12.1

Table 1: Node Specifications

Wireless communication is enabled through the Atheros AR5424 and AR9380 chipsets that implement the 802.11a/g and 802.11n protocols and are configured through the use of the *Mad-WiFi* [16] and *ath9k* [17] open source drivers accordingly. The wireless nodes are closely located in an indoor office environment at the University of Thessaly premises and are configured to operate in infrastructure mode, on the RF-isolated channel 36 of the 5 GHz band, in order to constantly guarantee un-interfered communication. We setup two different topologies, by keeping the AP node at the same physical location, while we move the STA between the two locations that are depicted in Fig. 1.

We use the Iperf [18] tool to generate traffic and collect network performance statistics. A typical experimental setup for experiments considering downlink transmissions, would be to run an Iperf client at the AP node, having also an Iperf server residing at the STA, receiving the traffic and collecting statistics. Moreover, we also exploit from the statistics that the applied Rate Adaptation algorithm of

each wireless driver is able to export, in order to measure link reliability in terms of MAC-layer FDR, as calculated per each configured PHY-layer rate.

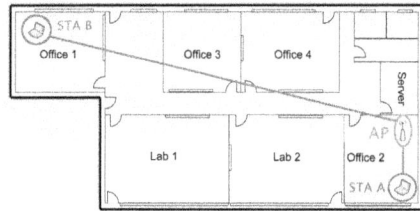

Figure 1: Experimental Topology

3.1 Experimental Setup

We first place the STA at location A to establish a line-of-sight high-SNR link (Signal to Noise Ratio (SNR) ~ 35 dB), by configuring the transmission power of both nodes at the maximum level of 20 dBm. Towards executing experiments under low-SNR (SNR ~ 15 dB) channel conditions, we move the STA to location B and reduce the transmission power of both nodes to the minimum available level of 0 dBm. The aforementioned SNR values correspond to the 802.11a/g link, while the 3x3 MIMO configuration of the 802.11n link provides approximately 5dB gain in each setup, by exploiting spatial diversity at the receiver through the Maximal-ratio Combining (MRC) technique [19].

Towards providing for a proper comparison setup between the two standards, we configure both transceivers to use the same channel bandwidth of 20 MHz and OFDM guard interval of 0.8 μs. Under this setup, we execute each discrete experiment in two phases, where in each phase either the 802.11a/g or the 802.11n protocols are configured through the use of the corresponding transceivers. As the AR9380 chipset is also able to operate in the 802.11a/g mode, we measure its performance under this configuration, across the various considered cases as well. Under these settings, the 802.11n compatible chipset supports the maximum PHY bit rate values of 65 Mbps, 130 Mbps and 195 Mbps for single, double and triple spatial stream configurations accordingly, while the 802.11a/g compatible chipsets support PHY bit rate values between 6 Mbps and 54 Mbps.

3.2 Power Measurement Methodology

In order to accurately measure the instantaneous power consumption, we follow a widely adopted power measurement procedure, which requires the placement of a high-precision, low impedance current-shunt resistor (R) of a known resistance value, in series with the power source and the power supply pin of the device to be measured. The exact measurement setup described above is presented in Fig. 2(a). By consistently measuring the voltage ($V_R(t)$) across the current-shunt resistor through proper voltage metering equipment, we are able to extract the instantaneous current draw of the device, based on Ohm's law. The instantaneous power consumption can be calculated as the product of the input voltage V_{IN} and the measured current draw:

$$P(t) = V_{IN}\frac{V_R(t)}{R} \qquad (1)$$

Estimation of the total energy consumption during a specific experiment, necessitates the accurate sampling of the instantaneous power consumption during the total experiment duration. Total energy consumption can be calculated

(a) Power Measurement setup   (b) Modified mini PCI-e adapter   (c) NITOS ACM card

Figure 2: NITOS ACM card and the accompanying hardware and software components

as the integral of the power consumption over the specified duration ($Dt = t_1 - t_0$), as follows:

$$E(Dt) = \frac{V_{IN}}{R} \int_{t_0}^{t_1} V_R(t)dt \qquad (2)$$

However it should be made clear that through the voltage sampling equipment, only a finite number of samples of $V_R(\cdot)$ are acquired over $[t_0, t_1]$ at discrete time instances.

In our study, we consider power consumption at both the total node level, as well as at the level of the wireless NIC. As a result, we decided to equip both nodes with appropriate current shunt resistors that have been placed in series with the power supply of the NIC and the Atom-based node accordingly. In order to ease the interception of the NIC power supply pins and refrain from modifying each different type of card, we decided to insert the current-shunt resistor on a PCI-e to mini PCI-e adapter card that is compatible with both wireless cards. Fig. 2(b) illustrates the modified adapter card that is attached with a high-precision current-shunt resistor of 0.1 Ω. We also modified the nodes' power supplies by inserting a current-shunt resistor of 0.01Ω in series between the power supply and the node's motherboard. In order to accurately measure the voltage drop across the resistors, we used the NITOS ACM card that was introduced in our previous work [9]. The developed card, which is presented in Fig. 2(c), supports the high sampling rate of 63 KHz and features up to three input channels, thus providing for online power consumption monitoring at both the NIC and the total node level, in a joint way.

4. POWER CONSUMPTION PROFILING

This initial set of experiments has been designed to clearly describe the power consumption profile of each chipset and set the basis for the realistic performance evaluation that follows in Section 5. Based upon the high-SNR setup, we characterize the instantaneous power consumption of the two NICs across various operational modes and present the obtained results in Table 2.

We clearly observe that the later manufactured AR9380 chipset is highly optimised for energy efficiency, as it consumes far less than 50% power than the AR5424 chipset, under all operational modes in the single antenna configuration. While considering MIMO operation, we notice that the activation of additional RF chains remarkably increases power consumption, as several hardware components need to be activated, in order to provide for the complex baseband processing that MIMO communications require. However, it is interesting to note that only in the case that 3x3 MIMO transmissions are executed by the AR9380, its power consumption increases above the consumption levels

Chipset	AR5424	AR9380		
Antennas	1x1	1x1	2x2	3x3
Mode	Power Consumption (Watts)			
Sleep	-	0.12		
Idle	1.47	0.49	0.56	0.69
Receive	1.52	0.62	0.74	0.85
Transmit	1.97	0.98	1.75	2.45

Table 2: Power consumption of AR5424 and AR9380 NICs across different operational modes

of the AR5424 chipset. Considering the power consumption in the sleep mode of operation, we remark that the *MadWiFi* driver does not support the activation of the *Power Saving Mode (PSM)* for the 802.11a/g compatible chipset. On the other hand, the PSM mode can be activated for the AR9380 NIC through the *ath9k* driver and set the card in a low-power state (82% less than in idle mode), by disabling most of the NIC's circuitry.

In order to assess the impact of varying PHY bit rates on NIC energy efficiency, we next proceed by characterising the energy consumption per transmitted bit of information (E_B), under the various PHY bit rate configurations that each protocol supports. We calculate E_B, expressed in Joules/bit, as the division of the resulting power consumption (Joules/sec) under each operational mode, by the specified PHY bit rate value expressed in bits/sec. In Figures 3(a) and 3(b), we plot the obtained E_B across the available IEEE 802.11a/g compatible PHY bit rate configurations, for the AR5424 and the AR9380 chipsets accordingly. In the case that the AR9380 chipset is configured to operate in the IEEE 802.11a/g mode, we manually disable the excess RF chains and use the single mode antenna of operation, thus resulting in the significantly reduced E_B values. Based on the obtained results, we remark that instantaneous power consumption of both chipsets does not significantly vary between different PHY bit rate settings. On the other hand, as plotted in Figures 3(a) and 3(b), higher PHY bit rate settings always result in lower E_B, mainly due to the decreased duration of the transmission or reception operations.

We next proceed to the characterization of the power consumption profile of the 802.11n compatible AR9380 chipset, which offers a wider range of available MCS configurations, as it features three RF-chains and supports up to 3x3 MIMO mode of operation. In Fig. 4(a), we plot the obtained E_B across the 23 available MCS configurations, in the case that all RF-chains are constantly enabled. We clearly notice that MCS configurations significantly impact power consumption, as imposed by the calculated E_B, which ranges from 47.1 nJ/bit (MCS0) to 1.53 nJ/bit (MCS23). This finding indicates the huge potential of energy expenditure minimi-

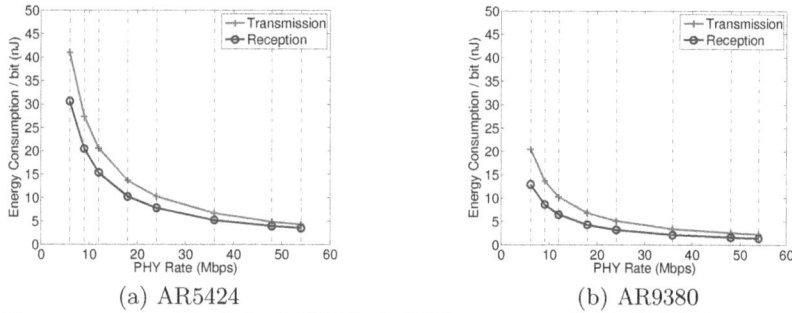

(a) AR5424   (b) AR9380

Figure 3: Energy consumption/bit of 802.11a/g NICs across available PHY bit rate configurations

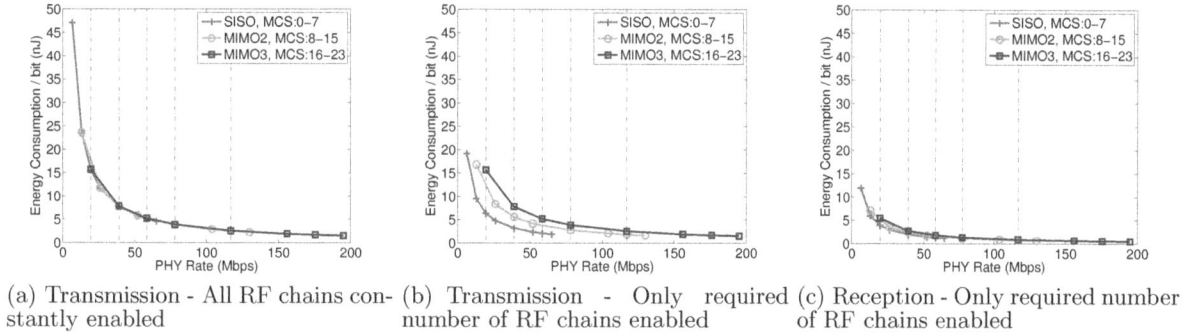

(a) Transmission - All RF chains con- (b) Transmission - Only required (c) Reception - Only required number
stantly enabled   number of RF chains enabled   of RF chains enabled

Figure 4: Energy consumption/bit of 802.11n NIC across available PHY bit rate configurations

sation (up to 97%), through proper adaptation of MCS configurations, as employed in similar studies [20].

In the case that all RF-chains are continuously enabled and while operating in the SISO and MIMO2 modes, the excess antennas do not contribute to the PHY bit rate increase, but are only used to provide increased link reliability. However, under ideal channel conditions, the excess antennas are no longer required to improve link reliability and thus can be deactivated, towards reducing energy expenditure. Figures 4(b) and 4(c) present E_B measurements for transmission and reception accordingly, in the case that only the required number of RF-chains are enabled for each configured SS setting. We notice that proper activation of the required number of RF-chains (SISO, MIMO2) can significantly increase energy savings up to 60% for transmission (27% for reception), as for the MCS0 case, where E_B reduces to 19.15 nJ/bit (11.92 nJ/bit). Considering the 802.11n configuration of the AR9380 chipset, we observe that its instantaneous power consumption does not significantly vary between different MCS indexes within the same SS configuration. Based on this fact, we infer that the high diversity of E_B values that is plotted in Figures 4(b) and 4(c), is mainly due to the increased power consumption that activation of additional RF-chains results in.

Based on direct comparison of the E_B values plotted in Figures 3(b), 4(b) and 4(c), we aim at quantifying the energy savings that 802.11n can offer in contrast to the earlier 802.11a/g protocol. Considering the power consumption performance of the AR9380 chipset at the highest configurable PHY rates of each protocol (54 Mbps for 802.11a/g and 195 Mbps for 802.11n), we observe that energy savings of up to 33% can be attained during transmission (63% during reception), as E_B reduces from 2.27 nJ/bit to 1.53 nJ/bit (1.44 nJ/bit to 0.54 nJ/bit in reception). Concluding, we note that the remarkably higher rates of 802.11n protocol can offer significant energy savings when combined with

proper adaptation of antenna modes, in comparison with the energy consumption performance of the earlier 802.11a/g protocol. However, the power consumption profile characterisation is only based on static PHY bit rate configurations and does not consider protocol overheads, MAC-layer parameters, such as aggregation, or link performance and their impact on energy efficiency. In the following section, we proceed by comparatively evaluating the performance of the two standards under realistic throughput experiments, considering various protocol parameters as well.

5. REALISTIC EXPERIMENTATION

In this section, we take a step further from characterising energy consumption under fixed modes of operation and conduct extensive realistic experiments to compare the performance of the two standards, by jointly considering application-layer performance and energy efficiency as well. We start by configuring the high-SNR setup to investigate the impact of varying application-layer traffic rate and frame payload length on the performance of each protocol. The obtained results are analyzed in Sections 5.1 and 5.2, for each scenario accordingly. In both scenarios, we manually configure the maximum available PHY bit rates of each standard and guarantee that these rates can be supported by the prevailing channel conditions, by constantly monitoring the achievable FDR and assuring that it never drops below 95% in all the conducted experiments.

Under these conditions, we start by measuring the throughput performance of each protocol without enabling any form of aggregation, while we next repeat the same experiments by explicitly enabling the FF and A-MPDU aggregation mechanisms. In each experiment, we also monitor the power consumption at both the NIC and the total node level, in order to assess the impact of the various configured settings on energy consumption. Next, in Section 5.2.2, we configure the low-SNR experimental setup to conduct series of

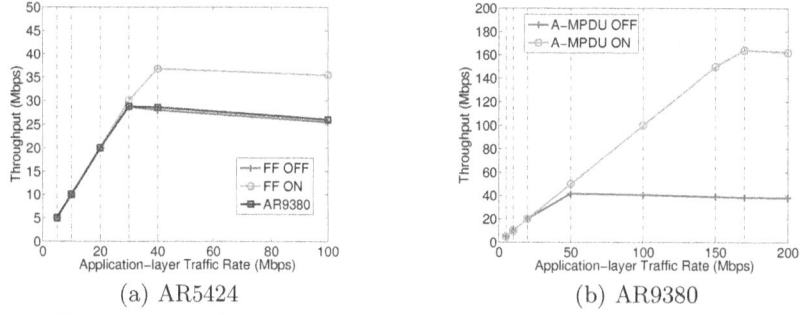

(a) AR5424   (b) AR9380

Figure 5: Throughput performance per NIC across varying Application-Layer Traffic load

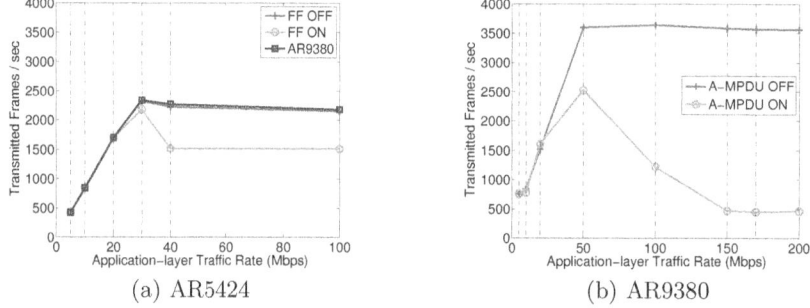

(a) AR5424   (b) AR9380

Figure 6: MAC-layer Frame Transmission rate per NIC across varying Application-Layer Traffic load

experiments under varying frame payload size and investigate the impact on performance of both protocols, under low link quality conditions. Finally, in section 5.3, we assess the potential energy savings that the application of the PSM mechanism is able offer, under varying application-layer traffic rates.

5.1 Varying Application-Layer Traffic load

We start by measuring the throughput performance under perfect channel conditions and across varying application layer traffic loads. The obtained results for the 802.11a/g and 802.11n protocols are illustrated in Figures 5(a) and 5(b) accordingly. In Fig. 5(a), we observe that below channel saturation, throughput performance is similar for both chipsets, while we also notice that the *FF* mechanism does not induce any impact. On the other hand and as soon as the load approaches 40 Mbps, we observe that the application of the *FF* mechanism offers approximately 31.4% increase in the maximum achievable throughput from 28 Mbps (*FF* disabled) to 36.8 Mbps (*FF* enabled). Based on detailed study of the *Mad-WiFi* driver code, we concluded that *FF* is only activated when the driver detects that the channel is approaching saturation through inspection of the transmission queue levels. We also verified our findings by monitoring the number of MAC-layer frames that are being transmitted in each time instant. In Fig. 6(a), we plot the collected results and observe that in the 40 Mbps load case, the frame transmission rate decreases from 2150 to 1510 frames/sec (30% decrease).

Based on the 802.11n compatible setup, we repeat identical experiments and plot the collected results in Figures 5(b) and 6(b) accordingly. In the case that A-MPDU aggregation is disabled, channel reaches the saturation point as soon as traffic load equals 50 Mbps, while in the A-MPDU enabled case, saturation is only reached at the traffic load of 170 Mbps. Similar observations were made regarding the activation of A-MPDU aggregation, which is only activated when the channel approaches saturation (˜50 Mbps). Consid-

ering the 170 Mbps load case, we observe that A-MPDU aggregation increases throughput from 38.3 Mbps to 164 Mbps (4.3x increase) and decreases the MAC frame transmission rate from 3562 to 465 frames/sec. Our findings clearly verify that MAC layer improvements need to be applied, in order to exploit from the increased PHY bit rates that 802.11n offers.

Having extensively evaluated the throughput performance improvement that the 802.11n protocol can offer across the various considered traffic loads, we next investigate how the monitored improvement is related with the resulting energy consumption. Figures 7(a) and 7(b) illustrate the average power consumption of both the 802.11a/g compatible chipsets and the total Atom node across the various configured traffic load values. As expected, average power consumption at both the NIC and total node level increases at higher traffic loads, due to the increased frequency of frame transmissions at the NIC level and the increased rate of frames that are being processed at the node level. In Fig. 7(a), we observe that the NIC consumes between 1.55 W and 1.73 W, in both the *FF* enabled and disabled case, as the *FF* mechanism is not yet activated. As soon as the traffic load increases above 30 Mbps, *FF* is activated and average power consumption for the *FF* enabled case increases above the average monitored consumption for the *FF* disabled case, till it reaches the maximum value of 1.79 W. This observation comes due to the fact that in the *FF* enabled case, the NIC consumes more power on average as it operates in transmit mode for longer duration. Considering the power consumption of the total Atom node, we observe that the two different 802.11a/g based setups consume different amounts of power on average, due to the use different wireless chipsets and drivers. However, both setups witness an increase of approximately 0.5 W, as the traffic load increases from 5 Mbps to 30 Mbps. In the case of the *FF* enabled 802.11a/g setup, we observe that average power consumption at the total node level is decreased between the 30 Mbps (22.56 W) and the 40 Mbps (22.53 W), in spite of the through-

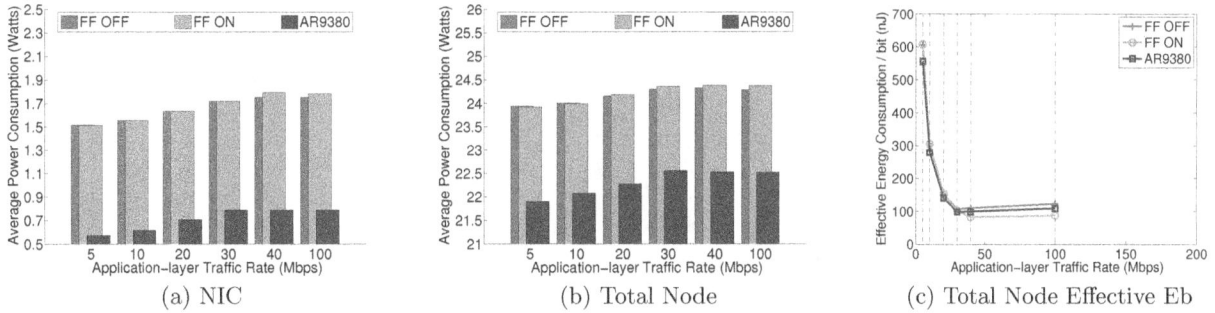

Figure 7: Energy efficiency characterisation of 802.11a/g setup across varying Application-Layer Traffic load

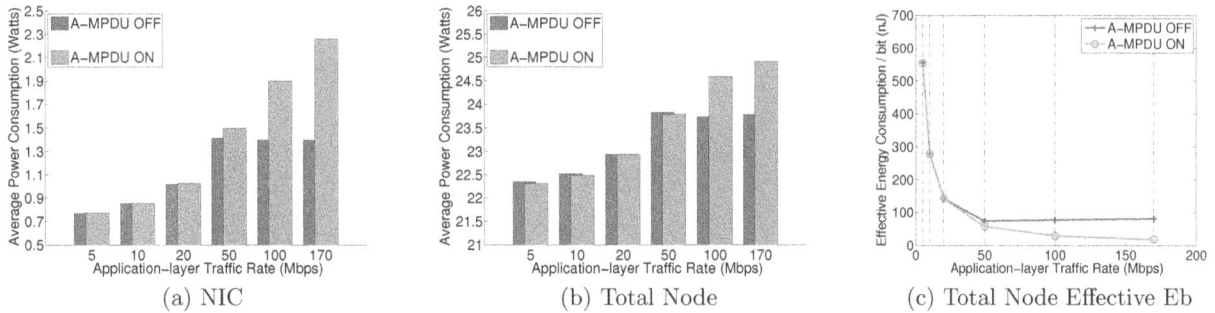

Figure 8: Energy efficiency characterisation of 802.11n setup across varying Application-Layer Traffic load

put performance increase. This observation is related with the activation of the *FF* aggregation mechanism, which efficiently reduces the rate of MAC-layer frames that are being processed by the driver. Our findings are summarised in the Effective E_B representation in Fig. 7(c), which characterises the total node power consumption as a function of the resulting throughput and not as a function of the configured PHY bit rate. The obtained results clearly show that *FF* is able to reduce energy expenditure at the Atom-based node level, even up to 28% in the 40 Mbps case (119.5 nJ/bit FF OFF - 85.51 nJ/bit FF ON). Regarding the performance of the AR9380 equipped wireless node, we remark that in spite of its low power consumption profile, the resulting Effective E_B values are higher than the levels achieved by the application of the *FF* mechanism.

Similar results are obtained while evaluating the impact of A-MPDU aggregation on the power consumption of the AR9380 NIC and the Atom node, which are plotted in Fig. 8(a) and Fig. 8(b) accordingly. We clearly observe that A-MPDU aggregation results in significantly higher average power consumption, for traffic loads above 100 Mbps, both at the NIC as well as at the total node level, as a result of the achievable throughput gains. Comparing the consumption of the Atom node, as plotted in Figures 7(b) and 8(b), we observe that under low traffic loads (< 50 Mbps) both protocols result is similar power consumption behaviour. This comes due to the fact the A-MPDU mechanism is not yet activated and as the high PHY rates of 802.11n are only able to reduce the average power consumption at the NIC level, the consumption of the total node is only minimally impacted. However, while considering traffic loads above 100 Mbps, we notice that the remarkably increased throughput performance that A-MPDU aggregation results in does not come at much higher energy costs. The Effective E_B representation in Fig. 8(c), summarises the above results

and shows that A-MPDU aggregation can increase energy efficiency up to 78%. Finally, direct comparison of E_B values at the corresponding saturation points of each standard shows that 802.11n offers more that 80% reduction of E_B compared with the AR9380 based 802.11a/g standard.

5.2 Varying Frame Payload Length

Extensive throughput experiments were also conducted under varying frame payload lengths, in order to investigate how varying Payload size affects throughput performance and energy expenditure. In order to enable delivery of frames longer than 1500 bytes to the MAC layer, we configured the wireless NIC's Maximum Transmission Unit (MTU) size to the maximum supported value of 2304 bytes. We have to mention that in cases where the *FF* mechanism is enabled, aggregation of frames longer than 1700 bytes could not be handled by the driver, as the transmission duration exceeded the threshold of 4 ms that the 802.11 standard specifies as the maximum acceptable frame transmission duration. Having investigated the impact of varying frame payload length on performance under high SNR conditions, we next proceed by conducting identical experiments in the low-SNR experimental setup. The full list of obtained results are detailed in the corresponding sections that follow.

5.2.1 High SNR conditions

The throughput performance of the 802.11a/g and 802.11n protocols are illustrated in Figures 9(a) and 10(a) accordingly. We observe that under high-SNR conditions, increasing frame length values consistently result in improved throughput performance for both protocols. The throughput improvement between the lowest (300) and highest (2200) considered payload lengths varies between the factors of 3x and 5x for all the considered cases, except for the A-MPDU assisted 802.11n scenario, where the improvement is restricted

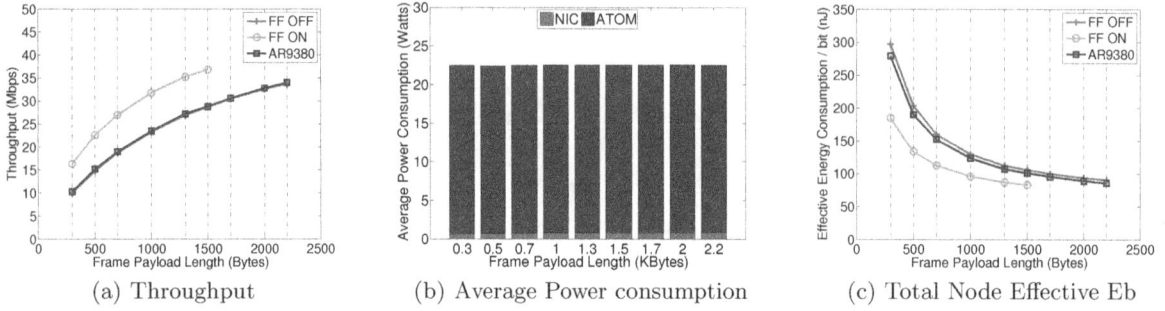

(a) Throughput   (b) Average Power consumption   (c) Total Node Effective Eb

Figure 9: Performance of 802.11a/g across varying Frame Payload Length values under high-SNR conditions

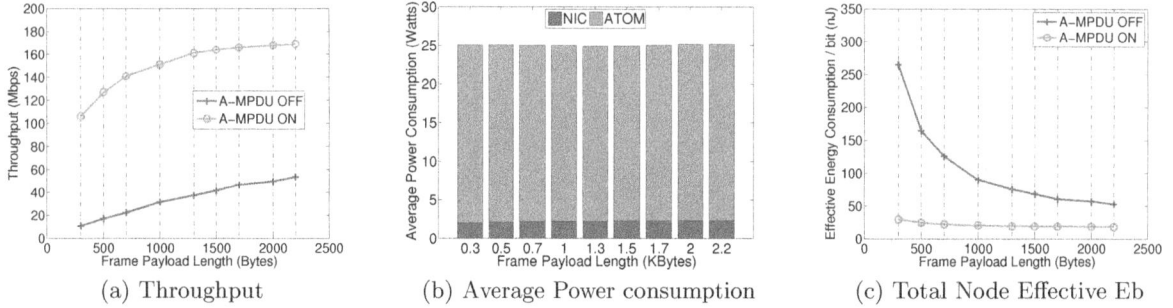

(a) Throughput   (b) Average Power consumption   (c) Total Node Effective Eb

Figure 10: Performance of 802.11n across varying Frame Payload Length values under high-SNR conditions

in the order of 1.6x. This observation is related to the fact that A-MPDU aggregation enables 802.11n to deliver high throughput performance (>100 Mbps) even at the lowest payload length, as A-MPDU frame size is only limited by the maximum number of subframes (64) and maximum A-MPDU length (65.535 bytes).

Figures 9(b) and 10(b) plot the power consumption of the AR9380 based setup, as it resulted during the operation of the 802.11a/g and A-MPDU-assisted 802.11n protocols accordingly. The full list of presented measurements have been collected using only the AR9380 based setup, in order to provide for direct comparison between the two protocols. Considering the minimum and maximum payload lengths for both protocols, we observe an increase of approximately 0.18 W in the consumption of the 802.11a/g configured NIC (0.3W 802.11n). The observed increase is directly related with the longer duration that the NIC remains in transmission mode, while achieving higher throughput. Regarding the consumption at the node level, in general we did not observe any significant consumption variation across varying payload lengths, which fact comes in contrast with the results obtained in the previous section, where even minor throughput improvement resulted in consumption increase at the total node level. In Fig. 10(b), we even observe that the average power consumption decreases when the frame payload size increases from 300 bytes (25.1W) to 1300 bytes (24.88 W), Considering also that the NIC's average power consumption is also increased between these two cases, we remark that the consumption increase at the total node level approximates 0.5 W. As a result, we reach the conclusion that considerable amounts of energy are consumed while each frame crosses the protocol stack and verify the findings of the work in [21]. This observation in combination with the high throughput gains that payload increase results in,

indicate that the use of longer frames is preferable in both terms of network performance and energy efficiency.

Our findings are summarised in the Effective E_B representation in Figures 9(c) and 10(c). In comparison with the AR9380 based 802.11a/g setup, we remark that the A-MPDU assisted 802.11n is able to reduce the Effective E_B at the node level, from 279 nJ/bit to 29 nJ/bit (-90%) and also from 86 nJ/bit to 18 nJ/bit (-80%), when transmitting frames of 300 and 2200 bytes accordingly. Recent studies [22] of the packet size distributions in Internet traffic have shown that the most common packet lengths are of 576 bytes size, which fact highlights even more the energy savings that can be attained through the application of the 802.11n protocol. In addition, we remark that low frame lengths are usually preferable in the wireless domain, as they are able to provide increased FDR, especially when using complex modulation schemes that are susceptible to low-SNR conditions. This observation yields interesting insights and motivates further investigation regarding the performance of 802.11n across varying frame payload lengths and low-SNR conditions.

5.2.2 Low SNR conditions

Towards executing identical experiments under low link quality conditions, we establish the low-SNR experimental setup. In the following experiments, we measure the performance of 802.11a/g considering only the AR9380 setup and compare it against the A-MPDU assisted 802.11n case. Under this setup, the 802.11a/g configuration is able to sustain the PHY bit rate of 18 Mbps, while the 802.11n setup is able to use up to the MCS6 configuration in the Spatial Diversity mode. In addition, we measure the performance of less complex modulation schemes and more specifically the rates of 9 Mbps and 12 Mbps for the 802.11a/g configuration, while MCS4 and MCS5 are also configured for the 802.11n protocol. Characteristics of the various configured modulation schemes are listed in Table 3.

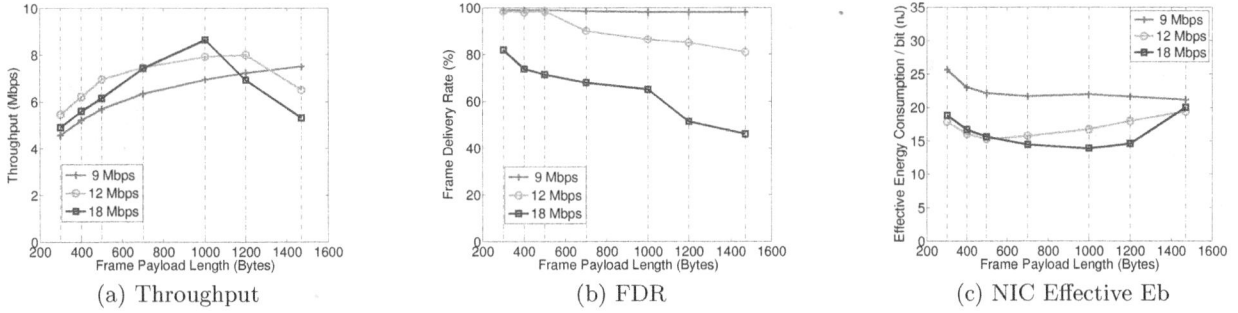

| (a) Throughput | (b) FDR | (c) NIC Effective Eb |

Figure 11: Performance of 802.11a/g across varying Frame Payload Length values under low-SNR conditions

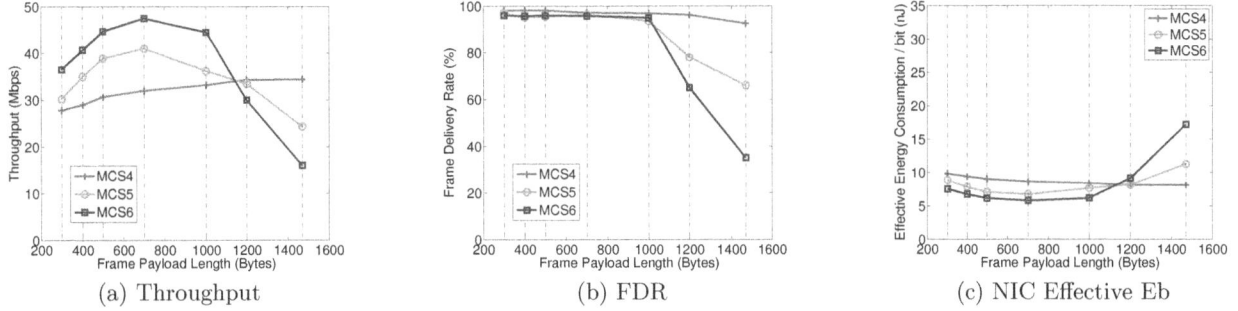

| (a) Throughput | (b) FDR | (c) NIC Effective Eb |

Figure 12: Performance of 802.11n across varying Frame Payload Length values under low-SNR conditions

MCS	PHY Rate (Mbps)	Modulation	FEC
9 Mbps	9	BPSK	3/4
12 Mbps	12	QPSK	1/2
18 Mbps	18	QPSK	3/4
MCS4	39	16-QAM	3/4
MCS5	52	64-QAM	2/3
MCS6	58.5	64-QAM	3/4

Table 3: Characteristics per configured MCS

We start by measuring the throughput performance across varying frame payload lengths, between 300 and 1500 bytes, which is the default MTU size for the wireless chipsets under consideration. In Figures 11(a) and 12(a), we illustrate the throughput performance that is achieved by each protocol. We clearly observe that in the default MTU case, the 802.11n protocol is able to deliver significantly higher throughput of 34.4 Mbps than the 7.5 Mbps of 802.11a/g (4.6x increase), by enabling the use of more complex and efficient modulation schemes. Moreover, we notice that only the lowest rate configurations of each protocol consistently provide higher throughput performance for increasing payload length, while in the rest configurations the maximum throughput is achieved under lower frame lengths. Detailed study of the throughput plots shows that proper payload length adaptation is able to provide up to 15% (8.64 Mbps - 1000 bytes payload) increase in the throughput performance of the 802.11a/g protocol and 38% (47.5 Mbps - 700 bytes payload) increase in the performance of 802.11n. The improved throughput performance is related to the increased FDR that lower payload length configurations are able to result in. In Figures 11(b) and 12(b), we depict the FDR performance of each protocol and highlight its relation with the complexity of each modulation type.

Energy consumption measurements were also conducted, in order to evaluate the energy efficiency of each protocol across varying payload lengths. Considering the fact that

the AR9380 card is characterised by a totally different power consumption profile in the two setups, along with the highly varying FDR and throughput performance, we conclude that deriving the most energy efficient payload size per case is a rather complex task. Towards deriving concrete conclusions, we plot the Effective E_B representation at the NIC level in Figures 11(c) and 12(c) for each protocol. Regarding the Effective E_B at the NIC level as obtained between the two setups, we notice that the 802.11n setup is able to reduce energy consumption down to 5.78 nJ/bit (MCS6 - 700 bytes) and offer reduction of 58% in comparison with the 13.89 nJ/bit (18 Mbps - 1000 bytes) that the 802.11a/g can offer at best. The obtained results show that payload lengths between 500 and 1200 bytes are preferable in terms of energy efficiency for the operation of the 802.11a/g protocol, while in the case of 802.11n even lower frame sizes between 300 and 1000 bytes can further reduce energy expenditure. Concluding, we remark that it is important to design automated algorithms that jointly adapt the MAC frame payload length and the PHY bit rate, towards achieving higher throughput and lower energy consumption.

5.3 Experimentation with 802.11 PSM

Through this experiment, we aim at quantifying the potential energy savings of the 802.11 PSM during periods of network activity, by experimenting in network setups that are based on both protocols under consideration. The 802.11 PSM mechanism is designed to set the wireless NICs of stations (STAs) in a low-power state during periods of inactivity and periodically activate them to fetch cached data from the access point (AP). Considering an active network, the useful period during which the STA's NIC can remain de-activated, is directly determined by the inter-packet arrival time of traffic flows that are destined to the STA. While the STA's NIC is in sleep mode, all cached frames at the AP are being delayed till the next *Beacon Interval*.

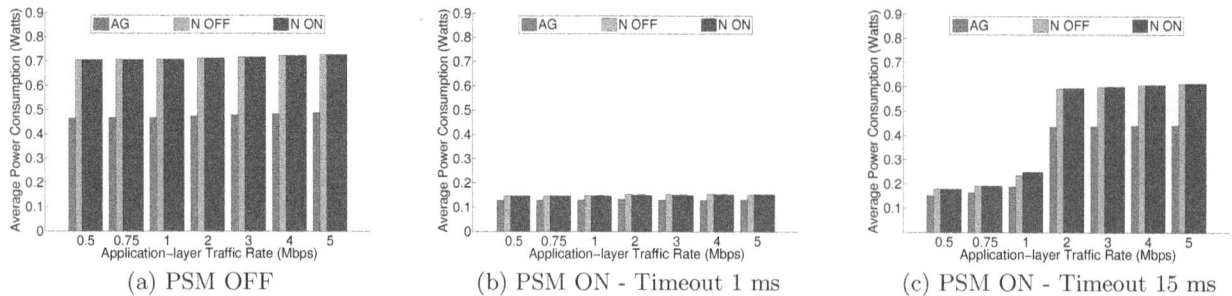

(a) PSM OFF   (b) PSM ON - Timeout 1 ms   (c) PSM ON - Timeout 15 ms

Figure 13: Power consumption of AR9380 NIC across varying PSM configurations

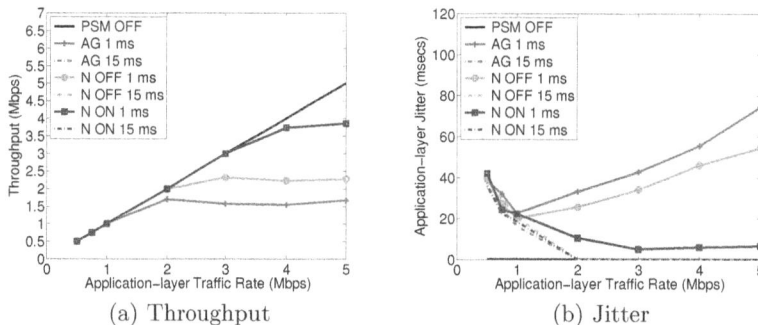

(a) Throughput   (b) Jitter

Figure 14: Network performance of AR9380 NIC across varying PSM configurations

As the PSM mechanism is only able to affect the consumption of STAs, in this experiment we consider downlink transmissions and measure the impact of PSM on the energy efficiency of STAs (receivers), while also evaluating network performance metrics. We configure the high-SNR experimental setup that was described in Section 3 and equip both nodes with the AR9380 chipset that supports the 802.11 PSM mechanism. We also assign the default *Beacon Interval* of 100 ms at the AP node. Towards stressing the operation of the 802.11 PSM mechanism, we exploit the ability of the *ath9k* driver to tune the Timeout Period (*TP*) parameter, which configures the interval before the NIC goes back to sleep mode, in order to control the tradeoff between the induced delay and energy savings. In this experiment we vary the *TP* between the minimum value of 1 ms and 15 ms and investigate the impact of PSM on application-layer performance and NIC energy efficiency.

We start by measuring performance in the case that the PSM is deactivated and proceed with the next two phases, where the 1 ms and 15 ms TP intervals are configured. In each phase, we vary the application-layer traffic rate at the AP side, by configuring values between 0.5 Mbps and 5 Mbps and measure the network performance in terms of throughput and jitter, while also monitoring the energy consumption of the STA's NIC. Figures 13(a), 13(b) and 13(c) present the average power consumption of the STA's NIC in each phase, considering the application of each protocol accordingly. In the case that the 802.11n protocol is applied, we also distinguish between the A-MPDU assisted (N ON) and the non-assisted case (N OFF). We observe that the 1 ms *TP* configuration provides significant energy savings, in comparison with the PSM disabled case, that approximate at maximum 74% for the 802.11a/g setup (AG) and 79% for the 802.11n setup (N ON) . Considering the 15 ms *TP* configuration, a minimal reduction of energy savings is observed, across traffic load values below 2 Mbps. In the case that the traffic

load exceeds the 2 Mbps value, the NIC rarely falls in sleep mode across all the considered cases, thus resulting in lower energy savings (not exceeding 15%).

Next, we characterise the impact of PSM on application layer performance, considering throughput and jitter, as plotted in Figures 14(a) and 14(b) accordingly. In general, we observe that the 15 ms *TP* configuration poses no impact on throughput and only minimal impact on jitter performance, thus not sacrificing network performance for saving energy. On the other hand, the 1 ms *TP* configuration that stresses the operation of the 802.11 PSM mechanism, provides more interesting results that clearly highlight the impact of the 802.11n's high PHY bit rates and A-MPDU aggregation on network performance. As depicted in Fig. 14(a), the increased PHY bit rates of the 802.11n improve throughput in comparison with the 802.11a/g setup, when considering traffic loads above 2 Mbps. Moreover, we observe that the application of A-MPDU aggregation further increases throughput performance, by combining several cached at the AP frames into a single A-MPDU frame, thus efficiently reducing frame losses due to buffer overflows at the transmitter. The impact of the 802.11n's increased PHY bit rates and A-MPDU aggregation in jitter performance are highlighted in Fig. 14(b), where we observe that the A-MPDU assisted protocol constantly enables on time frame delivery and results in remarkably reduced jitter.

Concluding, we remark that this last experiment has clearly demonstrated that the 802.11n protocol is able to provide both increased network performance and significant energy savings through the application of the PSM mechanism, during periods of network activity. Moreover, our results have shown that scheduling of sleep intervals in an adaptive to the prevailing traffic conditions and protocol parameters way, is able to bridge the gap between high network latency and low energy savings, as shown in [23].

6. CONCLUSIONS

In this work, we presented detailed experimentally obtained results that evaluate the energy efficiency of the base 802.11 standard in comparison with the latest 802.11n version, under a wide range of settings. In-depth analysis of the collected results has shown that the advanced features of the latest standard enable significant reduction of energy expenditure, across all the various considered scenarios. We envision that our findings will provide valuable insights to researchers working on the design of energy efficient wireless protocols.

7. ACKNOWLEDGEMENTS

The research leading to these results has received funding from the European Union's Seventh Framework Programme (FP7/2007-2013) under grant agreement n. 258301 (CREW IP project). I. Koutsopoulos, N. Makris and G. Kazdaridis also acknowledge the support of ERC08-RECITAL project, co-financed by Greece and the European Union (European Social Fund) through the Operational Program Education and Lifelong Learning - NSRF 2007-2013. S. Keranidis specifically acknowledges the support of AGILENET Marie Curie IRSES project.

8. REFERENCES

[1] IEEE 802.11-2007 Wireless LAN Medium Access Control and Physical Layers Specifications.

[2] D. Skordoulis, Qiang Ni, Hsiao-Hwa Chen, A.P. Stephens, Changwen Liu, and A. Jamalipour. IEEE 802.11n MAC frame aggregation mechanisms for next-generation high-throughput WLANs. *Wireless Communications, IEEE*, 15(1):40–47, 2008.

[3] K. Pelechrinis, T. Salonidis, H. Lundgren, and N. Vaidya. Experimental characterization of 802.11n link quality at high rates. In *Proceedings of ACM WiNTECH*, 2010.

[4] L. Kriara, M.K. Marina, and A. Farshad. Characterization of 802.11n wireless LAN performance via testbed measurements and statistical analysis. In *Proceedings of SECON*, 2013.

[5] D. Halperin, B. Greenstein, A. Sheth, and D. Wetherall. Demystifying 802.11n power consumption. In *Proceedings of SIGOPS HotPower*, 2010.

[6] I. Pefkianakis, Chi-Yu L., and Songwu L. What is wrong/right with IEEE 802.11n Spatial Multiplexing Power Save feature? In *Proceedings of ICNP*, 2011.

[7] N. Balasubramanian, A. Balasubramanian, and A. Venkataramani. "energy consumption in mobile phones: A measurement study and implications for network applications". In *Proceedings of IMC*, 2009.

[8] M. Tauber and S.N. Bhatti. The Effect of the 802.11 Power Save Mechanism (PSM) on Energy Efficiency and Performance during System Activity. In *Proceedings of IEEE GreenCom*, 2012.

[9] S. Keranidis, G. Kazdaridis, V. Passas, T. Korakis, I. Koutsopoulos, and L. Tassiulas. Online Energy Consumption Monitoring of Wireless Testbed Infrastructure Through the NITOS EMF Framework. In *Proceedings of ACM WiNTECH*, 2013.

[10] G. Bhanage, R. Mahindra, I. Seskar, and D. Raychaudhuri. Implication of MAC frame aggregation on empirical wireless experimentation. In *Proceedings of GLOBECOM*, 2009.

[11] Y. Xiao and J. Rosdahl. *Throughput and delay limits of IEEE 802.11, IEEE Communications Letters, 2002.*

[12] "Vendor Specific Improvements", http://goo.gl/ti8cxT.

[13] "Wireless Incompatibilities", http://goo.gl/5c1cHq.

[14] IEEE 802.11n-2009, Amendment 5: Enhancements for Higher Throughput., 2009.

[15] B. Ginzburg and Kesselman A. Performance analysis of A-MSDU and A-MPDU aggregation in IEEE 802.11n. In *Proceedings of IEEE SARNOFF*, 2007.

[16] "Mad-WiFi Wireless driver", http://madwifi-project.org/.

[17] "Ath9k Wireless driver", http://goo.gl/VrHtj.

[18] "Iperf", http://dast.nlanr.net/Projects/Iperf/.

[19] "Maximal-ratio combining", http://goo.gl/ABj8PY.

[20] C. Li, C. Peng, S. Lu, and X. Wang. "Energy-based rate adaptation for 802.11n". In *Proceedings of Mobicom*, 2012.

[21] A. Garcia-Saavedra, P. Serrano, A. Banchs, and G. Bianchi. "Energy consumption anatomy of 802.11 devices and its implication on modeling and design". In *Proceedings of CoNEXT*, 2012.

[22] "Packet size Distributions in Internet traffic", http://goo.gl/cBLxq6.

[23] K. Jang, S. Hao, A. Sheth, and R. Govindan. "Snooze: energy management in 802.11n WLANs". In *Proceedings of CoNEXT*, 2011.

Energy Demand Forecasting: Industry Practices and Challenges

Mathieu Sinn
IBM Research

Abstract

Accurate forecasting of energy demand plays a key role for utility companies, network operators, producers and suppliers of energy. Demand forecasts are utilized for unit commitment, market bidding, network operation and maintenance, integration of renewable energy sources, and for novel dynamic pricing mechanisms, e.g., demand response. In order to achieve accurate forecasts with high spatial and temporal resolution, data from various sources needs to be integrated: Smart meters, SCADA, weather forecasts, physical, statistical and geographical models.

In this talk I will give an overview of recent work within IBM Research on an intelligent large-scale energy demand forecasting solution which provides forecasts at different aggregation levels, quantifies uncertainty in demand, and estimates the amount of distributed renewable energy behind the meters. The solution can be seamlessly integrated with external applications for network planning and decision support, and has been validated with leading electric utility companies world-wide.

Categories and Subject Descriptors

G.3 PROBABILITY AND STATISTICS --- Multivariate statistics; J.2 PHYSICAL SCIENCES AND ENGINEERING --- Engineering

Keywords

Smart grids; Smart meters; Renewable energy sources; Energy demand forecasting; Analytics; Machine Learning

Short Bio

Mathieu Sinn is an Advisory Research Staff Member and Manager at the IBM Research Smarter Cities Technology Center in Dublin, Ireland, where he leads the Exploratory Predictive Analytics team and manages several research projects in Smarter Energy. Prior to joining IBM, he was working as a Postdoctoral Research Fellow at the David R. Cheriton School of Computer Science at the University of Waterloo, Canada.

Dr. Sinn has more than 10 years of research experience in Statistics, Data Mining, Machine Learning, and various applications such as computational physiology and biology, health informatics, finance, intelligent transportation and energy systems. His current research interests include scalable algorithms for robust statistical regression models, variable selection and feature extraction methods for high-dimensional data, transfer learning, and systems for exploring and reasoning about large numbers of predictive models. Dr. Sinn has authored over 35 peer-reviewed papers and served as reviewer and program committee member for leading conferences in the field.

Dr. Sinn received his B.S./M.Sc. in Computer Science in 2006 and his PhD in Mathematics in 2009 from the University of Lübeck, Germany. His research has been funded by the DFG (German Research Foundation), MITACS and the Canadian Bureau for International Education.

e-Energy'14, June 11–13, 2014, Cambridge, UK.
ACM 978-1-4503-2819-7/14/06.
http://dx.doi.org/10.1145/2602044.2602086

Hot, Cold and In Between: Enabling Fine-Grained Environmental Control in Homes for Efficiency and Comfort

Neil Klingensmith
University of Wisconsin
1210 West Dayton Street
Madison, WI, USA
naklingensmi@wisc.edu

Joseph Bomber
University of Wisconsin
1210 West Dayton Street
Madison, WI, USA
bomber@wisc.edu

Suman Banerjee
University of Wisconsin
1210 West Dayton Street
Madison, WI, USA
suman@cs.wisc.edu

ABSTRACT

Forced-air heating and cooling systems frequently perform poorly in multi-story homes. Long, leaky ducts running from the heater or air conditioner to the rooms of the house can impede airflow to second story rooms, creating dramatic temperature differentials between different spaces in the house. Such temperature discrepancies can lead not only to occupant discomfort, but also to energy waste since the thermostat would have to be set higher to achieve the desired temperature in some rooms. In this work, we propose a decentralized platform for heating and cooling systems in medium-sized homes that aims to independently control the temperature of each room. The goal of this approach is to provide heating and cooling necessary for poorly conditioned individual rooms to reach the required comfort level. By heating and cooling different rooms to different setpoints at different times, we can leverage our understanding about the way spaces in the home are actually used in order to fine-tune the environmental settings. We show that our techniques can both increase the residents' comfort and decrease the energy used by the house's heating and cooling system. In our primary test home, we estimate that our techniques could reduce natural gas consumption by roughly 18% during the coldest months of the heating season while increasing the temperature in the most-used living spaces by 2-5°F.

Categories and Subject Descriptors

C.3 [**Special-Purpose and Application-Based Systems**]: Real-time and embedded systems

Keywords

Smart Energy; Temperature Sensing; HVAC; Sensor Platforms

1. INTRODUCTION

Residential heating and cooling systems frequently have trouble maintaining a constant temperature distribution throughout the building, particularly in multi-story homes. Homes heated by forced air systems are often the most difficult to control because conditioned air is not always distributed equally among all rooms in the house. In general, the farther away a room is from the furnace, the less conditioned air it will get. However, most residential furnaces have a single, centralized point of control – the thermostat – which controls delivery of conditioned air to the entire house. Thermostats are often located close to the furnace – generally on the first floor of a two story house – in rooms that receive a relatively high flow of conditioned air from the furnace or air conditioner.

Since there is generally only one point of sensing and control in most residential heating and cooling systems, the heating and cooling system can have an incomplete view of the temperature distribution in the house. Furthermore, residential HVAC[1] systems do not have the ability to fine-tune the temperatures on a room-by-room basis because there is no way to selectively heat or cool a subset of the rooms even if the thermostat knew that there were temperature disparities in some rooms. Because they do not have fine-grained control for multiple rooms, residential HVAC systems often spend a lot of energy to condition unoccupied areas of the home. For example, the bedrooms are frequently located on the second floor of a two-story house. These spaces are often too hot during the summer months and too cold during the winter months because they are not receiving enough conditioned air from the HVAC system. At night, the temperature in the bedrooms can be high or low by as much as ten degrees Fahrenheit, making it difficult to sleep, while the unoccupied areas such as the kitchen and living room are relatively comfortable.

To address this problem, some larger houses can be outfitted with multi-zone HVAC systems. In these systems, the home is divided into regions or zones that each have independent sensing and control. This is often done by outfitting each zone with an independent furnace, air conditioner, and duct system. For new construction, multi-zone HVAC systems are much more expensive to operate than single-zone systems because multiple furnaces and air conditioners may need to be installed and maintained. It is also extremely expensive and intrusive to retrofit an existing home with a

---

[1]Heating, ventilation, and air conditioning

multi-zone HVAC system because in addition to equipment costs, ductwork needs to be redone, requiring drywall to be torn out. The additional installation and maintenance costs put multi-zone systems out of reach for most homeowners.

Inefficiencies in residential heating and air conditioning systems can lead to discomfort in the home and excessive energy consumption. Since approximately 70% of US homes are conditioned by forced-air AC systems, and approximately 62 % of US homes feature some form of warm air furnace, these problems have broad reach across many people [5]. Furthermore, the US Department of Energy estimates that more than half of the energy consumed by buildings in the United States is used for space heating and cooling [6]. For this reason, small inefficiencies in a single type of system — the furnace or air conditioner — can have a massive effect on the country's energy consumption, while low energy prices insulate individual consumers.

To address these problems, we augment existing forced-air heating and cooling systems with a few additional components to provide localized control over the temperature of individual rooms. The relevant system components are depicted in Figure 1.

1. **Network-connected temperature sensors** located in every room of the home that measure environmental conditions and report to an off-site database server.

2. **Register booster fans** increase airflow from the heating and cooling systems to rooms that are too cold in the winter or too hot in the summer.

3. **Space heaters** locally augment the central heating system in rooms that are particularly cold.

4. **Network-connected smart power strips** with embedded relays that can control each register booster or space heater by switching its power on or off.

5. **Intelligent server-side control software** that analyses data reported by the environmental sensors and sends control messages to the smart power strips to regulate the temperatures of each room in the home.

Using these components, we can make residents more comfortable by individually controlling the temperature of small areas of the home. This is beneficial to homeowners and occupants in two ways. First, localized environmental control allows us to eliminate hot or cold regions of the home by selectively conditioning individual rooms. Second, we can avoid over-conditioning regions of the home that are not actively used.

Fortunately, heating and cooling systems lend themselves well to technological solutions for controlling energy consumption because users are accustomed to these systems being under automatic control. A reasonable approach to this problem would therefore be to develop control techniques that take energy consumption into consideration. By taking a global view of the temperature distribution in the home, we seek to control the temperature in a building on a per-room basis. This will allow building occupants to condition spaces in a way that is more closely aligned with the way the space is actually used.

The approach proposed in this paper allows homeowners to cheaply and easily retrofit an existing house that has single zone HVAC with fine-grained multi-zoned control. Our

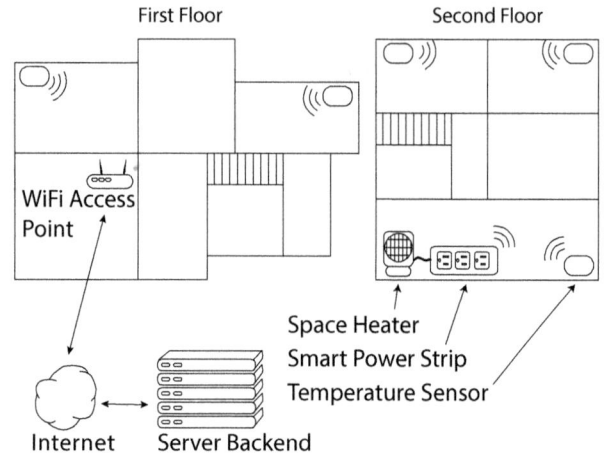

Figure 1: Floorplan of Home A in our study, showing the placement of temperature sensors throughout the building. Each sensor connects to the Internet through an existing WiFi access point. A remote server collects the data and controls local heating and cooling appliances through network-connected smart power strips.

system is much easier to deploy than multi-zone HVAC because it can be installed by homeowners without the burden and expense of hiring a contractor. Furthermore, it can effect control of the HVAC system on a much finer granularity than multi-zone HVAC.

We demonstrate that local temperature control is practical for average-sized two-story single family houses. To our knowledge, previous work in this area has focused primarily on small single-story houses, which generally do not have large temperature disparities between different areas of the building.

The goals of this work are to identify the sources of inefficiency in existing forced air heating and air conditioning systems and develop technical solutions to mitigate these problems. To this end, we have identified two related objectives. First, we need to make sure that the heating and air conditioning systems are correctly performing the tasks they set out to accomplish. If a user sets the thermostat to 70 degrees, we need to make sure that the temperature is actually 70 degrees. Using a decentralized sensing and control system, we are able to individually adjust the temperatures of the rooms in a building to ensure occupant comfort. This is important because we want to discourage residents from overcompensating for local temperature discrepancies (in a single room for example) with global corrections like turning the temperature setpoint up several degrees in the entire house.

Second, we wish to reduce the energy consumed by HVAC systems by intelligently conditioning spaces in the home based on the occupants' needs. For example, rooms that are heavily used should be tightly controlled at a comfortable temperature, while rooms that are not as frequently used may be allowed to drift. By combining these two techniques, we expect that it would be possible to set back the global thermostat settings while selectively conditioning rooms that are heavily used. In doing so, we can save energy and make the residents more comfortable.

The primary contributions of this work are as follows:

- We develop and deploy a distributed environmental sensing platform that can monitor the temperatures of each room in a home and report those measurements to a central controller.

- We use measurements taken by this system in *several homes over the course of six months* to identify sources of inefficiency in the HVAC systems. We observe consistent variations on the order of 5-10°F in second-story rooms among the houses we studied.

- Using feedback control on a room-by-room basis, we show that it is possible to simultaneously optimize the temperature distribution in a home while reducing the energy consumed by the HVAC system. In our testbed, we estimate that homeowners can reduce their natural gas consumption by 18% while reducing temperature variations in the rooms they use most.

2. UNDERSTANDING EXISTING HEATING AND COOLING SYSTEMS

In this section, we discuss the way existing heating and cooling systems operate in the homes we studied. For this work, we deployed temperature monitoring equipment in each room of three homes, which we call Homes A, B, and C. The homes we studied for this work were all two story single-family houses with single-zone forced air HVAC systems whose owners complained of temperature discrepancies between the first and second floors.

2.1 Shortcomings of Centrally-Controlled Heating And Cooling Systems

Each home we studied exhibited roughly the same types of behavior with respect to its heating and air conditioning system. Each had a 6-10°F temperature difference between the first and second floors during the warmest and coolest months of the year. We found that the airflow from the HVAC system was dramatically different on the first and second floor. Table 1 shows our measurements of airflow coming from the vents on the first and second floors of each home. Each had about a 50% reduction in airflow coming from the vents on the second floor, resulting in a commensurate reduction in conditioned air mass available to heat or cool the rooms. The difference in airflow between the two floors is a plausible explanation for the temperature differences.

Every house we studied had its thermostat in the dining room on the first floor. In two of the three houses, the residents did not even use the dining room on a regular basis, so it made little sense for the HVAC control system to be taking its only temperature measurements in that location. Since the point of measurement was on the first floor close to the central HVAC system, the whole first floor in all three houses roughly followed the schedule that the residents programmed into their thermostat. However, the second floor consistently had 5-10°F temperature variations. In order to keep the second story comfortable, the thermostat would have to be programmed to over-heat or over-cool the first floor. To compensate, the residents generally chose to program the thermostat with some middle ground settings that kept the first floor slightly over-conditioned while the second floor was under conditioned, but liveable. For example,

Home	1st Floor	2nd Floor
A	2.9 m/s	1.4 m/s
B	3.1 m/s	1.6 m/s
C	2.8 m/s	1.4 m/s

Table 1: Airflow measurements taken at each of the three homes in our study. In each building, there was roughly a 50% decrease in conditioned airflow to the second floor.

the programmable thermostat in Home C was set to 68°F during the evening hours while the residents were working in the second story office. The residents reported that they were comfortable between 60-65°F, but they increased the setpoint throughout the home in order to be comfortable on the second floor.

Figure 8 shows temperature measurements taken over the course of an average day in December for Home C. We refer to the difference between the setpoint of the thermostat and the actual temperature in a room as the *temperature error*. On the second floor, the master bedroom is consistently 6-8°F cooler than the dining room on the first floor during the time period shown, making that space uncomfortable for the residents.

Rooms on the first floor can also suffer the effects of unequal airflow. Spaces located near the furnaces tend to receive disproportionately high air flow, resulting in highly variable temperatures. This is because conditioned air from the furnace or air conditioner has to travel through a shorter length of duct which puts less back pressure on the air flowing to these spaces.

Since gas fired furnaces produce conditioned air at temperatures of 130-160°F, rooms close to the furnace can receive high volumes of extremely warm air that has not lost heat while travelling through ducts. The result can be uncomfortably warm and highly variable conditions in these rooms. Figure 2 shows a plot of the air temperature in a room that is close to the furnace and receives a lot of over-conditioned air. The measurements shown in the figure were taken on the opposite side of the room from the HVAC register, so the sensor experiences the same hot and cold fluctuations as the rest of the room.

In this work, we seek to identify the reasons for large temperature errors and to take steps to correct those errors in places where they cause the residents discomfort. More specifically, our goals are to

- Provide additional heating and cooling to rooms with large temperature errors in order to make those spaces more comfortable.

- Allow the user to set different setpoints for different rooms at different times of the day so the living space is conditioned to meet the user's needs.

For example, we found that residents will often heat or cool their entire house so they can be comfortable in just one or two rooms. This represents an enormous waste of energy that can be avoided by ensuring that the actual temperature in a room adheres to the desired setpoint schedule.

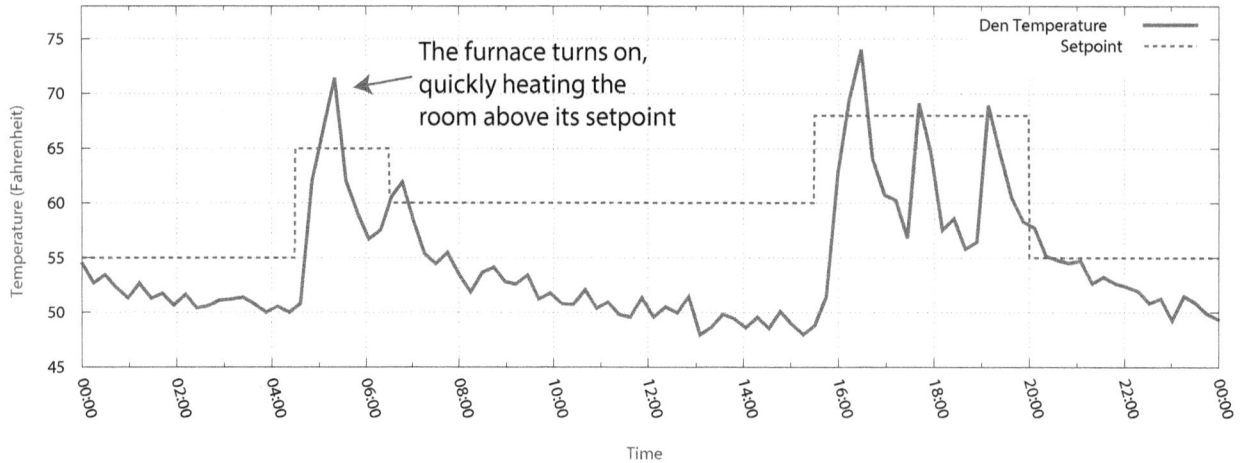

The furnace turns on, quickly heating the room above its setpoint

Figure 2: Without correction, even rooms close to the furnace or air conditioner can experience wildly fluctuating temperatures. In the den of Home C, high-temperature air from the furnace quickly heats the room above its setpoint. When the furnace turns off, heat leaks away through the three exterior walls.

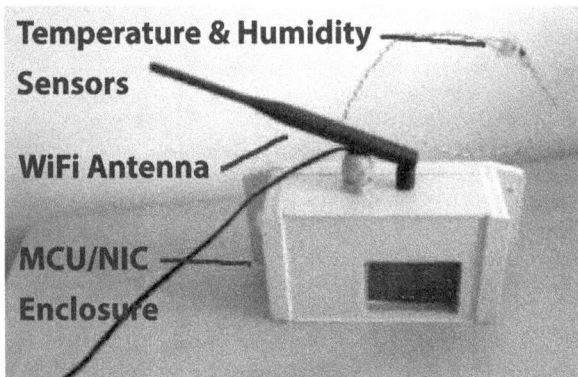

Figure 3: Photograph of temperature sensors used to monitor the environmental conditions in each room.

2.2 A Distributed Environmental Sensing System

In order to understand the temperature discrepancies between rooms' setpoints and their actual temperatures, we developed and deployed embedded temperature and humidity sensors in each room of several single-family houses during the course of a six month period. We chose to develop our own hardware platform because it is cheaper and much more configurable than commercial off the shelf components. Figure 3 shows a photo of the sensors as they were deployed. The hardware and software are variants of the Emonix platform [8], which is a flexible network-connected sensor platform that can be easily reconfigured for various distributed sensing applications.

Each sensor connects to the Internet through the home WiFi network and reports its readings to a central controller at one-minute intervals. We chose to connect our sensors to the Internet using WiFi because it is widely available in residential environments. By contrast, many embedded sensor networks use an intelligent bridge to facilitate communication between a low-end sensor network (eg. Zigbee) and an

off-site controller. While this approach can slightly simplify the embedded nodes, it has the disadvantage of increasing the complexity of the overall deployment by adding a new point of failure (the intelligent bridge).

Our nodes collect temperature readings once per minute and transmit them to a centralized off-site controller. The controller logs each temperature reading in a database and returns an application-level acknowledgement to the sensor. Sensor readings are stored locally on the sensor nodes, and messages are retransmitted in case of packet loss.

3. AUGMENTING THE CENTRAL HVAC SYSTEM WITH LOCALIZED CONTROL

In order to reduce temperature error in second-story rooms, we added local temperature controls to a subset of the rooms on the second floor of Home C that were most heavily used by the residents. In addition to setting a global (house-wide) temperature schedule on their programmable thermostat, we were able to provide per-room temperature schedules in these rooms. We assume that occupancy data and analysis techniques are available to evaluate the residents' habits and construct a thermostat schedule that meets their needs. Several existing pieces of work — including commercial products — address this problem [3, 9, 11].

For this work, we allow the thermostat to maintain control over the global temperature settings for the home, and we install additional devices to augment the central HVAC system on a per-room basis. Each room in the home that has localized control installed can have an independent thermostat schedule separate from the main HVAC system's schedule. This requires minimal installation on the part of the homeowner, in keeping with our goal of making it possible for homeowners to do the installation themselves.

We used several techniques to locally adjust the temperatures in each room: register damper control, register booster fans, space heaters, and window air conditioners. Register dampers can be closed to shut off air to areas of the home that are properly conditioned. Likewise, register booster fans can help push air through the ducts into rooms that are not receiving enough air flow to help pull air from the duct system. Space heaters can be used in rooms where the central HVAC system can not sufficiently heat or cool the space, even with the addition of localized register controls.

Except for the register dampers, each of these techniques uses a device that can be controlled by an Emonix smart power strip. The smart power strip has two key components used by our controller. First, the controller can use an internal relay in the smart power strip to actuate the devices that draw power through it. This allows us to easily turn electrical equipment on or off by simply sending a command over the Internet to the power strip. Second, the controller can log the power consumed by the devices connected to the power strip. This allows us to monitor the energy used by our system for the purposes of assessing energy efficiency. Each technique is discussed in detail below.

Control Algorithm

The goal of our control algorithm is to minimize the temperature error in rooms that have local control equipment. Our controller takes as input a temperature schedule for each room in a single family house as well as a set of temperature measurements taken in the room. Two example temperature schedules are shown in Table 2. Based on the room's average temperature measured over the last five minutes, the controller can either turn on or turn off a power strip which controls the registers, space heater, etc. in the room. The controller has $2°C$ of hysteresis around the setpoint.

If the measured temperature in a room under local control is more than $2°C$ below its local setpoint[2], the central server turns on a space heater or register booster in that room. If the temperature is more than $2°C$ above the room's local setpoint, the controller turns off the local control devices. The localized heating in the room will not turn back on until the room stabilizes at $2°C$ below the setpoint.

The temperature in each room under local control is re-evaluated once every minute during the early morning and evening hours. These are the times when the residents in the home are most likely to be using the second story space. During the middle of the day and at night, the local control mechanisms are turned off because the residents are either asleep or away from the house. While the local control mechanisms are turned off, the central furnace system is responsible for maintaining all spaces in the home at a global setpoint. Control actions such as turning space heaters on or off can also be taken once per minute in response to each new temperature reading, but in practice the switching is much less frequent.

3.1 Register Control

Our first approach to provide localized control for the HVAC system in a home was to selectively close registers that feed parts of the house that are already well-conditioned. A similar approach is commonly used by multi-zone HVAC systems, in which a damper[3] is used to shut off air flow to entire lengths of ductwork that feed sections of the home. In this work, we chose not to use dampers because they are expensive and intrusive to install.

We believed that since all rooms on the first floor of the test houses in our deployment were receiving adequate air supply from the furnace and air conditioner, we could redi-

---

[2]The local setpoint in a room may be different from the main thermostat's global setpoint.

[3]A damper is a valve that controls airflow through a duct.

Data: Temperature Readings
Result: Device state for local heating
foreach *room under local control* **do**
    if *during household's normal occupancy hours* **then**
        read temperature;
        if *temperature below setpoint* **then**
            turn heater on;
        else
            turn heater off;
        end
    else
        relinquish control to thermostat;
    end
end

Algorithm 1: Localized temperature control, run once per minute on the controller.

rect air to the under-served second floor. We tried closing the registers on the first floor manually using the levers on the vents, and in some cases, we used cardboard and duct tape to seal off the duct. Similar techniques have been shown to work in smaller single story homes by other studies [12]. However, this did not have a detectable effect on second story air flow or temperature in any of the three homes we studied. Since our primary goal was to improve airflow and temperature variations in second story living spaces, we could not rely on register control alone.

In some cases, register control was useful to temper the wide variations we observed in first story rooms. As depicted in Figure 2, first-story rooms can often experience dramatic variability in temperature, particularly in rooms located near the furnace. By closing some vents in strategic locations on the first floor, we were able to reduce many of these variations.

We believe that the ducting system in these houses had leaks that allowed air to escape from the system before it reached the second story rooms. The US Department of Energy estimates that between 25-40% of conditioned air in average forced air heating systems escapes through leaks in the ducts [1]. In fact, they estimate that even well-sealed ducts will leak up to 20% of the conditioned air that flows through them. Since the ducts feeding rooms on the second floor are physically longer than those feeding the first floor, there is more opportunity for conditioned air to escape on its way to the register. Furthermore, friction between air and the wall of the pipe causes the air to slow down as it passes through a long pipe.

The perils of closing off the registers that feed large portions of a home are well-known to HVAC contractors and academics alike [13]. Increased back pressure caused by closing off registers can damage some components of the system. The resulting decreased airflow can also reduce the HVAC system's ability to heat or cool the house — decreasing airflow to one portion of the house does not necessarily increase flow to other areas. For this reason, systems that rely exclusively on dampers to direct conditioned air to specific areas in the building may have to allow some air to flow to spaces that do not need it in order to avoid excessive back pressure in the ducts.

Because we were not able to satisfactorily improve temperature discrepancies using register control alone, we tried using other measures.

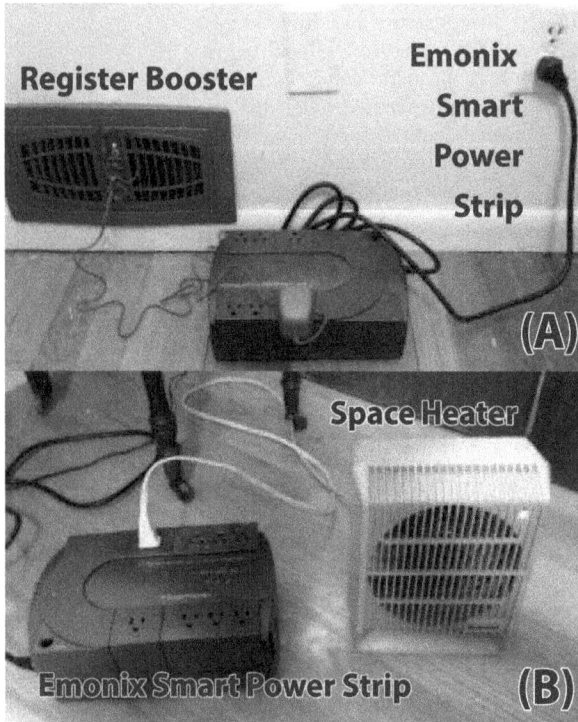

Figure 4: Photographs of our control equipment. (a) A register booster fan is controlled using an Emonix smart power strip by an off-site controller. (b) An Emonix network-connected power strip controls a space heater that provides additional heat in rooms that are too cold during the winter months.

3.2 Register Booster Fans

In a second attempt to increase air flow to poorly-conditioned rooms, we installed booster fans in the registers of some rooms. Figure 4 (A) shows a photo of a booster fan installed in Home C. These fans pull air out of the registers, selectively creating lower pressure at the output of the duct system in places where conditioned air was needed. The booster fans we used take only about five minutes to install, and the only tool required to do the job is a screwdriver.

The booster fans we used increased the air flow to second story rooms to roughly 2.5 m/s while drawing only about 5 Watts of electric power. As a result, we observed a corresponding improvement in temperature in rooms that had register boosters.

One drawback of using register booster fans is that they can only work while the central furnace or air conditioner is on. This is also true of damper actuators as employed by multi-zone HVAC systems. Decentralized HVAC control systems that rely only on damper or register controllers would have a difficult time heating or cooling a small portion of a home.

We tested booster fans in two rooms of Home C. The guest bedroom, which has only one small section of exterior wall and its own return, responded well to the boosters. The master bedroom, with three large outside walls and no cold air return, did not benefit from boosters. Figure 6 shows a box plot of the temperatures errors in the guest bedroom

Figure 5: The internals of an Emonix smart power strip include a relay to switch power to the plugs it serves and an analog adapter board to sense the power consumption of the connected appliances. The main CPU sits beneath the analog adapter board along with its WiFi interface that directly connects to the home's network. This allows energy measurements to be relayed to an off-site controller.

during the first half of the month of December, before and after register boosters were installed.

Figure 7 shows a histogram of the temperature error in the guest bedroom before and after booster fans were installed. Before installation of register booster fans on the 8th day of the month, the temperature was on average 2.5°C below the setpoint in the guest bedroom. Ideally, our goal was to increase the temperature in the guest bedroom so the mean deviation from the setpoint is zero. This would mean the histogram in Figure 7 would center around 0. After installation, the average temperature deviation was about 1.1°C below setpoint. This improvement corresponds to about 50% of the achievable goal. Intuitively, an increase of 1.4°C as we saw in the guest bedroom has a noticeable effect on comfort.

The standard deviation of temperature errors also increased after installing register boosters. This is likely because the air coming out of the registers is much warmer than the air in the room. Before installing register boosters, there was less airflow from the vents, and that air was not mixing well with the air in the room because it was moving slowly as it exited the vent. After adding register boosters, the warm air would mix more with the room's air, and the temperature in the room would fluctuate up and down as the furnace cycles on and off through the course of the day.

Unfortunately, register booster fans do not work well for all rooms. If a room is poorly insulated or particularly far away from the furnace or air conditioner, the additional airflow they provide may not be enough to correct temperature disparities. The master bedroom in Home C is one such case. Not only is it poorly insulated and physically far away from the furnace, it also lacks a cold air return. Cold air returns are used to evacuate stale air from the space so that excessive pressure does not build up, allowing air to circulate more freely throughout the house. Thus, the lack of a cold air return can lead to inefficiencies in the HVAC system.

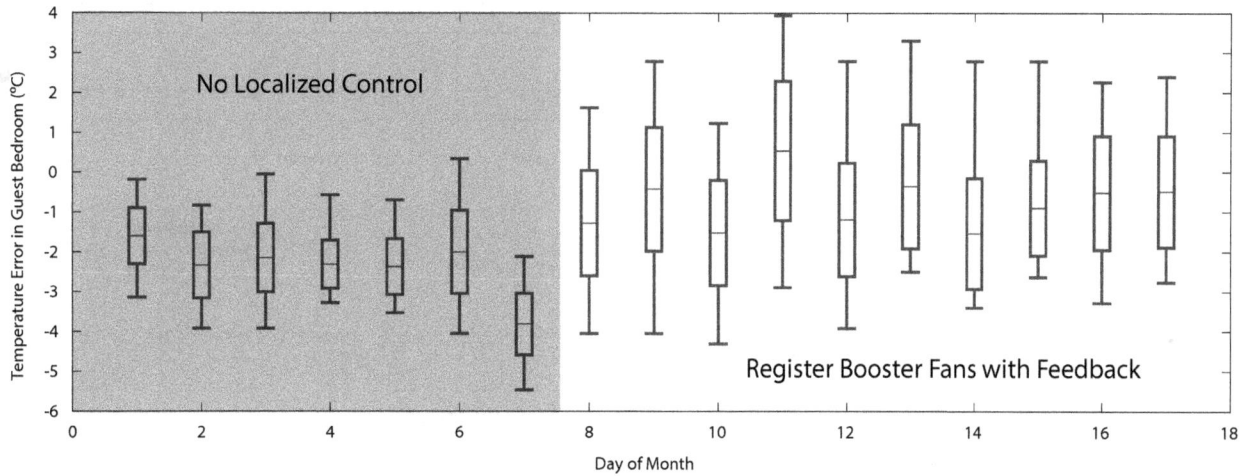

Figure 6: Deviations from the setpoint temperature in the guest bedroom of Home C. Before installing register booster fans, the room was on average 2.5°C below the thermostat's setpoint. Booster fans decreased the average deviation to 1.1°C below setpoint.

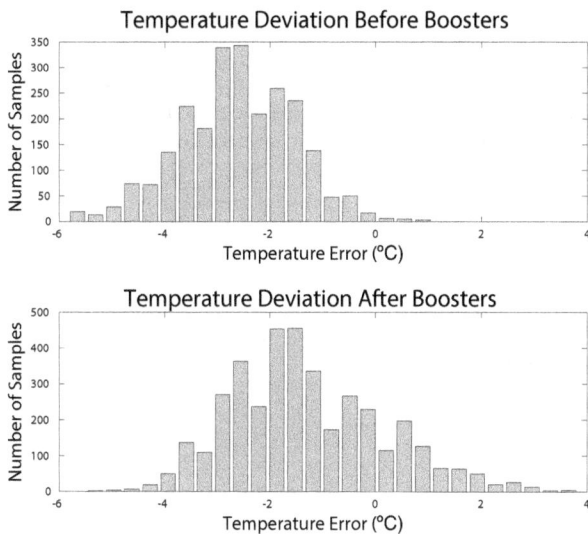

Figure 7: Histogram of temperature deviations from the setpoint in the guest bedroom of Home C before and after the installation of register booster fans. The use of register booster fans decreases the magnitude of the average temperature error by 1.4°C.

Time Period	Before	After
5:00 AM - 8:00 AM	65 °F	60 °F
8:00 AM - 4:30 PM	60 °F	55 °F
4:30 PM - 10:00 PM	68 °F	60 °F
10:00 PM - 5:00 AM	55 °F	55 °F

Table 2: Set points of the programmable thermostat in Home C before and after adding localized control.

3.3 Space Heater

For additional heating capacity in the winter, we added a small space heater in the master bedroom that could be controlled by a smart power strip. If the controller detects that the the temperature in the master bedroom drifts below its setpoint, it can turn the space heater on by sending an asynchronous control message to the power strip. This system could be logically extended to also control actuation of an air conditioning (cooling) unit in the hot summer months.

Figure 4 shows a prototype of this configuration as deployed in Home C. The final system would be more compact, with the control and communication for the space heater embedded in the heater itself. In-wall space heaters could also be used to save space and reduce cord clutter, though this would require more complex installation.

Figures 8 and 9 illustrate the improvements in temperature errors in the master bedroom from using localized control. Figure 8 shows the temperature profile of the master bedroom over the course of a typical day before installing local control in the master bedroom. The temperature in the master bedroom is roughly 5°F below the dining room (where the thermostat is located) and it is 10°F below the setpoint for most of the evening hours. Figure 9 depicts the situation after adding localized control. During two crucial periods — early morning and mid evening — the master bedroom temperature is still slightly below setpoint, but it is actually warmer than the dining room.

4. ANALYSIS

In Home C, we used localized techniques to make the second story rooms more comfortable. We chose Home C as the primary subject for active control, because out of all homes we studied, Home C best exemplified the common problems associated with current HVAC systems. Our main goal was to regulate the temperature in the master bedroom between 60-65°F in the evening while the rest of the house cooled down. This is the room where the occupants spend most of their time in the evening, and it was also the room that had the biggest temperature errors when controlled only by the central heating system. In this work, we assume that a suitable thermostat setpoint schedule can be established either manually or using automated techniques that take account

	Heating °C Days	Natural Gas Usage	Electric Heating
Furnace Only	804	107 Therms	0 kWh
Local Control	659	87 Therms	54 kWh
Improvement	18%	20 Therms = 586 kWh (**18.7%**)	(54 kWh)

Table 3: Energy savings that resulted from the use of localized control in Home C.

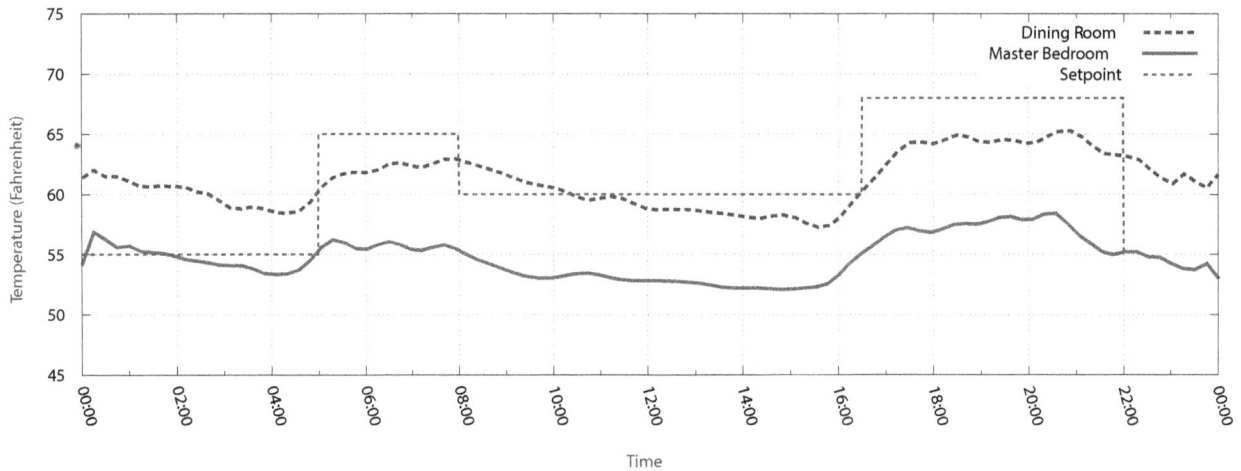

Figure 8: Observed room temperatures for two rooms on an average day in December 2013. The x-axis is the time of day, and the y-axis is the measured temperature. The master bedroom is located on the second floor and receives less air flow from the furnace, resulting in dramatic temperature reductions.

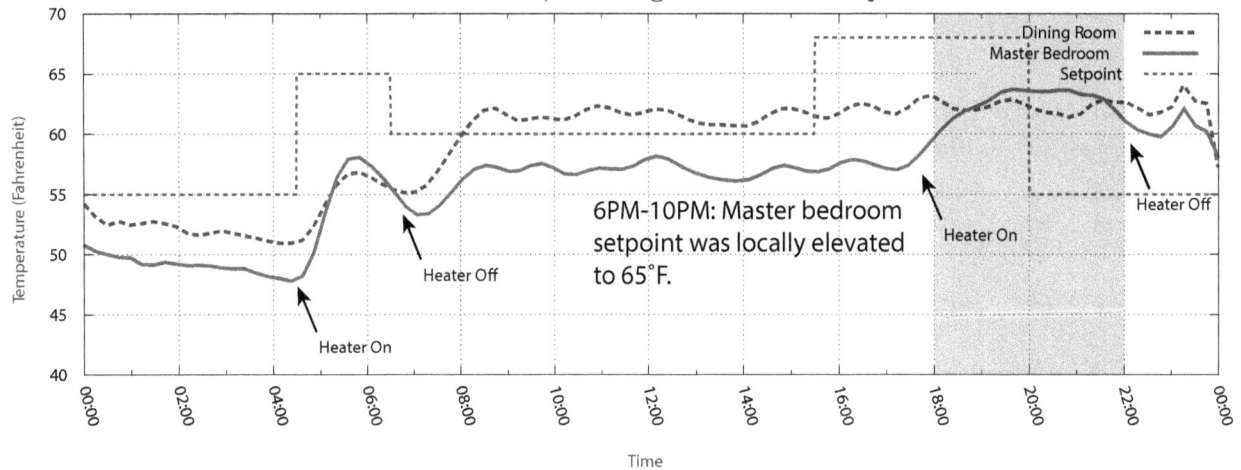

Figure 9: Observed room temperatures for the master bedroom and dining room after adding localized control to master bedroom. The x-axis is the time of day, and the y-axis is the measured temperature. A space heater is used to increase the master bedroom temperature from 6PM-10PM and from 4:30AM-6:30AM. For the rest of the day, the temperature in the master bedroom is allowed to drift away from its setpoint.

of occupancy data as well as user input. Several pieces of work have demonstrated that this is feasible [7, 9, 11].

Prior to adding localized control, the master bedroom had been so cold that the residents only used it for sleeping. This was inconvenient because it also served as an office, so the residents had to move their computers, desk, and files to other areas of the house that were more comfortable.

After adding localized control to target temperature variations on the second floor in Home C, the occupants were able to turn the global thermostat settings down by roughly 10°F during the second half of the month of December. Figure 8

shows the temperature in two rooms as a function of time before adding localized control. Clearly, the temperature in the second-story master bedroom is several degrees below the setpoint of the furnace's thermostat, making that room uncomfortable. Figure 9 shows a plot of the temperatures of the same two rooms as a function of time after adding localized control and setting back the thermostat. In this plot, the temperature in the master bedroom is higher during the hours between 6:00 PM and 10:00 PM. The invariant between Figures 8 and 9 is the temperature setpoint in the master bedroom between 6:00-10:00 PM.

We estimate that Home C used roughly 18% less natural gas after turning the thermostat down. Table 3 shows our estimates of the energy savings in Home C if the setback had been done for the entire month of December. The 20 therm reduction in natural gas consumption during the month of December in Home C is equivalent in terms of energy to 586 kWh of electric power — *more than 10 times the additional energy we expended to locally heat the master bedroom*[4].

To generate the projections shown in Table 3, we used a metric known as *heating degree days* (HDD) to estimate the natural gas used by the furnace. The number of heating degree days for some time interval is the number of degrees the furnace must heat the house above outside temperature multiplied by the length of the time interval in days. A heating degree day over some interval T is defined as

$$HDD = \int_T (T_{room}(t) - T_{ambient}(t)) \mathrm{d}t \quad (1)$$

Where $T_{room}(t)$ is the room temperature defined by the thermostat's setpoint, and $T_{ambient}(t)$ is the outside air temperature[5]. For example, if the outside temperature was 20 degrees cooler than the thermostat's setpoint for one day, we would count this as 20 heating degree days.

For each thermostat schedule shown in Table 2, we computed the number of heating degree days for the month of December using the integral in Equation 1. The number of heating degree days is different for the two schedules because the setpoint $T_{room}(t)$ is different, while $T_{ambient}(t)$ was the same for both schedules.

Our local utility (Madison Gas and Electric) models the energy usage of a furnace as a linear function of heating degree days [10]. Under this assumption, the natural gas usage of the furnace should also decrease by 18% because the furnace is the only gas-fired appliance in the house. This model gives a good first-order approximation of the energy usage of a heating or cooling system. By setting the thermostat back in Home C, we were able to achieve an 18% reduction in heating degree days during the month of December while maintaining thermostat schedule in the spaces used most by the residents.

Another important result of this work is that it incentivizes people to use less energy by providing additional benefit: increased comfort. Since the user's point of interaction with the system is the setpoint for the given room, logically users will maximize their comfort by defining a setpoint to suit their needs. Thus, our goal in this work is to optimize the residents' comfort by minimizing the temperature error in targeted areas of the house during time periods when we knew those areas would be occupied. In this way, we improve the efficiency of the HVAC system by conditioning the rooms in accordance with the user's desire, while reducing energy wasted by conditioning rooms that are not in use.

5. RELATED WORK

Network-connected controllers for residential HVAC systems have been introduced in various forms. The Nest thermostat [3] and the Bay Web Thermostat [2] are both com-

mercial examples of so-called "smart thermostats." Both of these devices use a single point of measurement and a single point of control for the HVAC system without providing fine-grained control on a room-by-room basis.

RoomZoner is an academic system that uses distributed sensors to adjust the temperatures of individual rooms in a single-family house [12]. In this work, the authors use damper actuators to selectively cut off airflow to rooms that have reached their desired setpoints. The authors found that dampers worked well for a relatively small single-story house. However, in our experiments we found that this approach did not scale well to larger multi-story buildings.

PreHeat [11] and the Smart Thermostat [9] use occupancy data to establish a thermostat schedule that adapts to building occupants' use of their space. Thermovote [7] uses a crowd-sourcing or participatory sensing approach to establish an optimal temperature setting in an occupied space. In our work, we assume that an optimal thermostat schedule is available, and we focus on finding ways to fit local room temperatures to that schedule.

6. CONCLUSION

In this work we developed new techniques for correcting the shortcomings of single-zone HVAC systems in multi-story homes. We found that single-zone systems do not always serve second-story rooms well primarily because the duct system causes reduced airflow into those spaces. Furthermore, they have no way to identify or correct any temperature disparities resulting from impeded airflow because they lack the sensing and actuation systems required to do so.

In our work, we provide room-by-room sensing and actuation which allows us to maintain tight control over the environmental conditions in each space of the house. We use equipment that can be quickly and easily installed by the average homeowner without using special tools. We have shown that these techniques can both make the living spaces in the home more comfortable and reduce the overall energy consumption of the heating and cooling systems.

Currently, our techniques require the homeowner to program the thermostat and the sensing system with settings that they believe will make the living spaces comfortable most of the time. However, we recognize that these settings may not always be optimal. If the occupants change the way they use the spaces in the home, the settings may need to be adjusted.

For this reason, we believe that our work could benefit greatly from real-time occupancy sensing and prediction techniques. Knowing occupancy information, we may be able to eliminate the need for homeowners to program their thermostats. Such a system would be able to infer reasonable setpoints for the spaces in the home without intervention of the homeowner.

7. ACKNOWLEDGMENTS

We would like to thank our shepherd Sebastian Lehnhoff and the anonymous reviewers whose comments helped us to finalize the presentation of our ideas. Also, we thank Steve and Rachel Perlman for allowing us to conduct experiments in their home. Without their cooperation and enthusiasm, this project would not have been possible.

---

[4]1 Therm = 100,000 BTU US, and 1 kWh = 3412 Btu, therefore 1 Therm $\approx$ 29.30 kWh and 20 Therms $\approx$ 586 kWh [4].
[5]By this definition, it is possible to have a fractional number of HDD because the time interval T could be a fractional number of days.

All the authors are supported in part by the following awards of the US National Science Foundation: CNS-1040648, CNS-0916955,CNS-0855201,CNS-0747177, CNS-1064944, CNS-1059306, CNS-1343363, and CNS-1230751.

This research was also supported in part by the Department of Energy (DOE) Office of Energy Efficiency and Renewable Energy (EERE) Building Technologies Program (BTP) under the BTP Innovators Program administered by the Oak Ridge Institute for Science and Education (ORISE) for the DOE. ORISE is managed by Oak Ridge Associated Universities (ORAU) under DOE contract number DEAC05-06OR23100. All opinions expressed in this paper are the author's and do not necessarily reflect the policies and views of NSF, DOE, ORAU, or ORISE.

8. REFERENCES

[1] Air distribution system installation and sealing: Proper duct installation increases efficiency, 2003. US Department of Energy Building Technologies Office.

[2] Bay Web Thermostat, 2014. http://www.bayweb.com.

[3] Nest, 2014. http://www.nest.com.

[4] American Physical Society. Energy Units, 2014. http://www.aps.org/policy/reports/popa-reports/energy/units.cfm.

[5] U. S. Department of Energy. Residential Energy Consumption Survey (RECS), 2009. http://www.eia.gov/consumption/residential/data/2009/index.cfm.

[6] U. S. Department of Energy. Buildings Energy Data Book, 2012. http://buildingsdatabook.eren.doe.gov.

[7] V. L. Erickson and A. E. Cerpa. Thermovote: Participatory sensing for efficient building HVAC conditioning. In *Proceedings of the Fourth ACM Workshop on Embedded Sensing Systems for Energy-Efficiency in Buildings*, BuildSys '12, pages 9–16, New York, NY, USA, 2012. ACM.

[8] N. Klingensmith, D. Willis, and S. Banerjee. A distributed energy monitoring and analytics platform and its use cases. In *Proceedings of the 5th ACM Workshop on Embedded Systems For Energy-Efficient Buildings*, BuildSys'13, pages 36:1–36:2, New York, NY, USA, 2013. ACM.

[9] J. Lu, T. Sookoor, V. Srinivasan, G. Gao, B. Holben, J. Stankovic, E. Field, and K. Whitehouse. The smart thermostat: Using occupancy sensors to save energy in homes. In *Proceedings of the 8th ACM Conference on Embedded Networked Sensor Systems*, SenSys '10, pages 211–224, New York, NY, USA, 2010. ACM.

[10] Madison Gas and Electric. Degree day information, 2014. http://www.mge.com/customer-service/billing/about-bill/degree-day-info.htm.

[11] J. Scott, A. Bernheim Brush, J. Krumm, B. Meyers, M. Hazas, S. Hodges, and N. Villar. Preheat: Controlling home heating using occupancy prediction. In *Proceedings of the 13th International Conference on Ubiquitous Computing*, UbiComp '11, pages 281–290, New York, NY, USA, 2011. ACM.

[12] T. Sookoor and K. Whitehouse. RoomZoner: Occupancy-based room-level zoning of a centralized HVAC system. In *Proceedings of the ACM/IEEE 4th International Conference on Cyber-Physical Systems*, ICCPS '13, pages 209–218, New York, NY, USA, 2013. ACM.

[13] I. S. Walker. Register closing effects on forced air heating system performance. Technical report, Lawrence Berkeley National Laboratory, January 2003.

An Occupant-participatory Approach for Thermal Comfort Enhancement and Energy Conservation in Buildings

Abraham Hang-yat Lam[*][§] , Yi Yuan[*] and Dan Wang[*]
Department of Computing, The Hong Kong Polytechnic University[*]
The Hong Kong Polytechnic University Shenzhen Research Institute
Building Integration Perfection Ltd.[§]
MEGA Automation Ltd.
{cshylam,csyiyuan,csdwang}@comp.polyu.edu.hk

ABSTRACT

Commercial building is one of the major energy consumers worldwide. Among the building services, the heating, ventilating and air-conditioning (HVAC) system dominates the total energy consumption. Recent studies have proposed various approaches to audit, automate and optimize energy usage of the HVAC system. Nevertheless, these schemes seldom discuss human thermal comfort. To minimize complaints, the current practice of the facility management is to adopt very conservative temperatures, leading to massive waste of energy.

In this paper, we actively take thermal comfort into consideration. We propose a participatory approach allowing the occupants provide feedback regarding their comfort levels. A major challenge for a participatory design is to reduce intrusiveness of the system. To this end, we develop a temperature comfort correlation model that can build a profile for each occupant. The decision of setpoint temperature can be primarily model-driven, requiring minimal inputs of the occupants. We validated our model with field experiments. Besides, we developed a setpoint optimization algorithm to handle the diverging thermal requirements of multiple occupants in same room, and examined the model with simulations. We implemented our design and conducted field experiments in a University and a commercial office. Results showed that our algorithm can successfully maintain high thermal comfort, while reducing 18% of energy consumption.

Categories and Subject Descriptors

H.1.2 [**Models and Principles**]: User/Machine Systems

Keywords

Participatory Thermal Comfort, Energy Conservation, Smart Building

e-Energy'14, June 11–13, 2014, Cambridge, UK.
Copyright 2014 ACM 978-1-4503-2819-7/14/06 ...$15.00.
http://dx.doi.org/10.1145/2602044.2602067.

1. INTRODUCTION

In recent years, people have been paying more attentions to energy conservation around the world. The largest sectors of energy consumption are commercial buildings, residential houses, transportation, and manufactory industry. In Hong Kong, where the industry sectors are small, commercial buildings account for more than 65% of energy consumption of the city [1]. In a typical building, the HVAC (heating, ventilation, and air conditioning) system dominates the energy expenses. It is reported in the Office Segment of Hong Kong 2013 that 53% energy have been consumed in room conditioning [1]. As a result, numbers of recent studies have proposed the idea of energy conservation by intelligently managing the HVAC systems [2][3].

Energy conservation is on one end of the spectrum. Clearly, we can simply turn-off all the air-conditioning, thus maximizing energy saving[1]. Nevertheless, the HVAC systems are designed to provide a comfort indoor environment for occupants in buildings. However, complaint minimization, rather than energy conservation, is the top priority of buildings and building operators. Therefore, it is important to take human thermal comfort into consideration.

The current practice of supporting human thermal comfort by building operators is to apply a fixed setpoint temperature. These temperatures are derived from large-scaled field surveys or laboratory experiments. Such recommendation provides building operators with a benchmark in temperature settings and assists them to cope with complaints. To minimize the number of complaints, these recommended temperatures are usually very conservative (i.e., the setting is on the low temperature side) and uniformly apply to the entire building unless special requests are made. However, this traditional practice has led to massive waste of energy. In addition, a lower temperature does not necessarily reflect better human thermal comfort. What is more, it is difficult for occupants to adjust the temperature on their own in many high-end buildings with the installation of the centralized HVAC system.

As opposed to such fixed setpoint strategy, there are proposals on dynamical control of the HVAC systems. One direction is to detect human presence. If a room is not occupied, the air-conditioning of the room will be turned-off.

---

[1]To ease our presentation, in this paper, we use air-conditioning to represent the HVAC systems. In the context of air-conditioning, setting a lower temperature means more energy has to be consumed.

Various detection objectives and solutions have been proposed in previous studies [4][5].

In this paper, we explore another direction on dynamic control of the HVAC systems. Rather than passively detecting human presence or comfort levels, we take a participatory approach in which occupants can provide inputs. More specifically, occupants can actively provide feedback on the comfort level with the use of their smartphones. The idea is simple, yet for a participatory design to succeed, we face several challenges: 1) the incentives of occupants are important. The design should be as non-intrusive as possible. Requesting occupants to provide feedback via their phones every time they stay in a room will possibly discourage participation of people. Besides, it is of great importance to protect one's privacy; 2) occupants are insensitive to the numerical expression of temperature [6]. For instance, one may not be able to differentiate the actual differences between 22.5°C and 24.5°C. However, current building management system (BMS) requires numerical values for calculation and comparison. Therefore, it is necessary to have a context-aware translation; 3) it is possible to have multiple occupants in a room, thus an optimized aggregation of different comfort levels is needed; 4) it is necessary to develop a system consisting of data collection, smartphone application, interaction with building controls for air-conditioning adjustment, etc. Many of these challenges are similar to those of typical participatory sensing systems [7][8], but are specific in the building environment.

To handle these challenges, we first made use of the comfort index in linking the human thermal comfort with numerical values. We then developed a temperature-comfort correlation model to create a profile for each individual occupant. In that sense, the air-conditioning adjustment decisions are primarily model-driven, substantially reducing human feedback. Our model has referred to the thermal comfort model from the inter-discipline of built environment, where they require to collect different kinds of data with the use of special equipment. We made careful simplification on the models that the required parameters are available in a typical BMS of buildings. We developed a setpoint optimization algorithm to cater the comfort requirements for multiple occupants, and conducted a series of real-world experiments to validate our temperature-comfort correlation model. It is showed that our model has a high accuracy in predicting the occupants' thermal preference. A comprehensive set of simulations have been utilized to study thermal comfort levels and energy conservation. We implemented our design with a smartphone application, a wireless sensing system to collect necessary environmental data and a system that interacts with the BMS. We have also conducted experiments in our university and a commercial office and achieved a 18% of energy saving. The result indicates the effectiveness of our participatory approach.

2. BACKGROUND AND RELATED WORK

Recently, there are many studies from computer science researchers on smart buildings. The studies start from energy auditing systems using wireless sensor networks [9][10], provding fine-grained data regarding energy usage. In addition, there are studies on smart wireless systems for better automation and control of building equipment [11]. Numerous studies have also been proposed on human detection [12][5][13] of which lighting and air-conditioning can

be turned-off in a smarter way. There are also studies on more intelligent arrangement of human activities such as meetings and classes with the objective in minimizing energy or electricity bills [14][4]. However, these studies have not considered human thermal comfort, which is the gap of the existing studies we seek to fill in this paper. One possible difficulty is that human thermal comfort is not immediately quantitative to computer scientists.

As a matter of fact, there are tons of studies on human thermal comfort in built environment. These studies can be summarized into two approaches [15]: the heat-balanced approach and the adaptive approach. The heat-balanced approach, first studied by Fanger in 1970 [16], observes the linkage between thermal comfort and physiological factors such as skin temperature and sweat rate. It establishes a thermal comfort model with factors such as air temperature, clothing insulation, metabolic rate, etc. To average the comfort level of all people, a predicted mean vote (PMV) model is proposed. The adaptive approach considers such factors as adaptations, e.g., behavioural and psychological adaptations [15], social and cultural background towards the thermal expectations, and also physical stimuli in response to the changing indoor and outdoor temperatures [17]. The objective of these studies is to derive a comfort temperature to the occupant, either in his activity and physiological perspective, or from his behavior, cultural background and physical environment perspective. With the objectives to improve the predictability of the models, the state-of-the-art models require many associated parameters that are complicated to obtain [18]. Besides, these experiments have heavily relied on advanced equipment for measurement. The heat-balance approach conducts experiments in laboratory with climate chamber to simulate different combination of environmental conditions, whereas adaptive approach conducts massive field studies in different regions and countries. Noted that these studies are not easy to be implemented in daily life and hence discrete from the actual operation of BMS.

As a result, there is a clear separation where the advances of smarter and more fine-grained building automation and control system seldom take human thermal comfort into consideration, and the studies of such modeling development are isolated from the control-loop of the room air-conditioning. In this paper, we jointly consider the two issues. From a high level point of view, our design considers the thermal feedback of occupants during the decision of setpoint temperature is made to the room. There are a few similar work, e.g., Thermovote [6] and SPOT+ [19]. However, there are two common problems in their studies. Firstly, they usually rely on an existing thermal comfort model from built environment (e.g., PMV). As discussed, some parameters of these models are not easy to be obtained in daily life. Therefore, they rely on prior-obtained fixed settings of these parameters, leading to error-prone results. Secondly, these studies usually require occupants to keep providing their feedback every time he stays in each room (when the occupant is not comfort). While it may improve the accuracy at that moment, it may also adversely discouraged the incentives of the participants in long run, which is a common problem encountered in participatory sensing systems [20][6]. Of course, the objectives of these studies differ from ours. In this paper, we propose a participatory approach addressing these two problems.

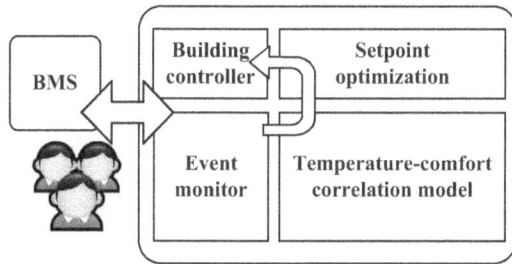

Figure 1: Overview of OPTC

3. OCCUPANT-PARTICIPATORY THERMAL COMFORT (OPTC): AN OVERVIEW

In this paper, we developed a smartphone application for occupants to provide their feedback (or in other words, to vote) regarding their thermal sensations to the indoor environment of buildings. The smartphone application is able to directly communicate with the BMS and thus the room setpoint temperature is adjusted accordingly. Each vote of the occupants will be recorded along with the current environmental data, e.g. indoor room temperature and outdoor temperature, to formulate that occupant's thermal comfort model. The temperature adjustment of the room can thus be model-driven most of the time with minimizing the intrusiveness to the occupant, therefore, the occupant is not expected to keep submitting their votes all the time.

In our system, we have a OPTC server to store the data collected from each occupant, including his thermal comfort profile. We first clarify the possible privacy concerns in this regard. In our design, each occupant is required to register an account with his email address and agrees a set of rules, e.g., allow us to collect his thermal comfort information. If one does not register, his thermal preference will not be taken into the consideration of our temperature adjustment. Based on our experiments, we found that all occupants have registered. Our post-experiment survey revealed that people in our experiments were not so much concerned about their thermal preferences being recorded. Instead, they were more concerned that they would be left out in our setpoint adjustment in a room of multiple people.

We have developed an Occupant-Participatory Thermal Comfort (OPTC) framework as shown in Fig. 1. There are four main modules: (1) Temperature-comfort correlation (TCC) model: the objective of TCC model is to establish a correlation (or profile) between the indoor and outdoor temperature with the comfort index of each individual occupant; (2) Setpoint optimization module: based on the TCC model, setpoint optimization computes the optimal setpoint temperature for occupant(s), especially for multiple occupants; (3) Event monitor module: the event monitor module collects data from the existing environment (e.g., indoor, outdoor temperature) and occupants information for two purposes: to trigger decision making in setpoint optimization, and to gradually train the TCC model; (4) Building controller module: After setpoint optimization module makes an adjustment decision, the building controller module communicates with the BMS to change the setpoint of the room.

Our TCC model is developed interdisciplinary with the field of built environment. However, the thermal comfort models in built environment are complicate and difficult to be implemented in real environment. Besides, the traditional thermal comfort models require tremendous field tests or laboratory experiments, which special equipment like climate chamber to simulate different climatic conditions are used. On the contrary, our model is designed to rely on daily collectable data only, e.g., indoor and outdoor temperature, and additionally occupants feedback regarding the thermal preference, though with the expectation that more feedback will be collected in the times of feeling discomfort. The feedback of each user is saved into his own profile for modeling, hence the setpoint temperature adjustment can be model-driven most of the time. Details are shown in Section 4.

The setpoint optimization module determines the setpoint adjustment. For example, when some specified events happen (e.g., indoor/outdoor temperature change and occupants' comfort index are collected, etc.), the setpoint optimization module is then triggered. It translates the inputs from event monitor module and the TCC model into a decision for room setpoint adjustment. More importantly, we have developed an algorithm to compute the optimized setpoint temperature when there are multiple occupants sharing the same space/room. The details are demonstrated in Section 5.

Event monitor module collects all the required data and responses accordingly. To collect the thermal preference of one, we have developed a smartphone application based on the comfort index as shown in Table 1. We have translated the fuzzy preference into computable numerical values. We elaborate the details in Section 7.

In building controller module, decisions made by the setpoint optimization module are passed to the BMS, which is discussed in Section 7.

The remaining part of the paper is organized as follows. The TCC model is discussed in Section 4, and we validated our TCC model by conducting a series of field experiments with the occupants. We then present our setpoint optimization algorithm in Section 5. In Section 6, we show a comprehensive set of simulations using our model. We have also evaluated a large sets of occupants with different physical characteristics, and evaluated the energy saving with various room configurations and sets of simulated occupants. We then present the implementation of our system in Section 7. In Section 8, we conducted two sets of experiments, one in a university and the other one in a commercial office. These experiments serve to validate our simulation results.

4. TEMPERATURE-COMFORT CORRELATION (TCC) MODEL

In essence, we need a model indicating the levels of comfort of a person, given the indoor and outdoor temperature at a specified time are known. We can then determine the setpoint temperature accordingly. As discussed before, there are many models from the discipline of built environment [21][22][23][24][16], but the accuracy of these models largely rely on real-time measurement of the occupants and the surrounding environment, where special equipment are needed.

Our choice is that we build an initial model following the rudimental laws of metabolism. Clearly, this model is still based on the discipline of built environment. In this model, we carefully categorize three different sets of parameters: 1) parameters that we can collect in one time, e.g., the age, gender, height, weight, etc of the occupant. This informa-

Table 1: 7-point thermal comfort index

Point	Sensation
+3	Hot
+2	Warm
+1	Slightly Warm
0	Neutral
-1	Slightly Cool
-2	Cool
-3	Cold

	Men	Women
Sedentary	1.0	1.0
Active	1.25	1.27

Table 2: Physical activity factor

tion are one-off and we collect them at the time of registration, 2) parameters that change, but can be collected by non-intrusive sensors, e.g., indoor or outdoor temperatures; 3) parameters that are hard to collect using daily sensors; and we train these parameters collectively by the votes and other parameters.

In the following parts, we first link the thermal comfort with quantifiable (numerical) values. We then develop user's thermal preference with our model. Finally we validate our model using real-world experiments.

4.1 Thermal Comfort Metric

To quantify thermal comfort, we adopt a seven-point *thermal comfort index* from the American Society of Heating, Refrigerating and Air-conditioning Engineers (ASHRAE). This index scales from -3 to 3 and links the thermal comfort from cold to hot as shown in Table 1.

From the occupants perspective, this index is easily comprehensible to reflect his thermal sensation, i.e. he can vote either hot or cold. From the built environment perspective, a value of 0 indicates that an occupant reaches *thermal neutrality*, meaning the heat generation and heat loss of the occupant is in the state of equilibrium. A negative index means that the occupant losses more heat than his body produces so that he feels cool or cold. The smaller the index, the more uncomfortable the occupant feels. When the index of an occupant is between -1 (Slightly Cool) and 1 (Slightly Warm), the occupant is regarded as comfort. This index range $(-1, 1)$ is defined as the *comfort zone* [25].

4.2 Model Development

As explained, we first build an initial model. In this model, the thermal comfort is a function of indoor temperature T_i of room i, outdoor temperature T_o and the elapsed time t a person stays at the space/room. The thermal sensation is determined by the balance of heat gain and loss of human body. Let $G(t)$ be the heat gain and $L(T_i, T_o)$ be the heat loss. Thus, the thermal comfort $C(T_i, T_o, t)$ is:

$$C(T_i, T_o, t) = G(t) + L(T_i, T_o) \quad (1)$$

In what follows, we will first present the high level ideas, followed by the details of model $G(t)$ and $L(T_i, T_o)$.

In general, the amount of heat generated is primarily settled by metabolic rate. It is also affected by the physical activity (PA) of people [26], e.g., a person has a higher metabolic rate during walking, whereas lower rate after staying sedentary. When the PA of a person changes, e.g., sit down after running, his metabolic rate changes accordingly. Thus, the occupant experiences a change of thermal sensations in the same environment. Moreover, the speed of metabolic rate change differs among individuals. In $G(t)$,

we consider metabolic rate changes as elapsed time t after occupant enters a room.

The amount of heat lost is determined by indoor temperature and clothes insulation. In operation, information of clothes insulation is difficult to access. However, from results of field studies [27], it is showed that the effect of clothes insulation can be reflected by outdoor temperature. Intuitively, when the outdoor temperature is higher, occupants are likely wearing less clothes, and hence prone to a higher rate of heat loss. In this regard, they prefer a warmer indoor temperature. Thus, we use indoor temperature and outdoor temperature as determining variables in $L(T_i, T_o)$.

4.2.1 Heat Generation Modeling

According to [28, 29], heat production is proportional to physical activity, whereas metabolic rate adjusts according to physical activity. To estimate metabolic rate of an occupant, we adopt the Estimated Energy Requirement (EER) model [30], which is first proposed by the Institute of Medicine (IOM) that used to estimate a person's daily average of dietary energy intake to maintain his energy balance. It considers the factors of gender, age, height, weight as well as the physical activity of users. EER is shown as follows:

$$EER = k_1 - k_2 \times Age + [PA \times (k_3 \times W + k_4 \times H)] \quad (2)$$

Here, k_1 is a constant related to gender and age. k_2 is a constant related to age. k_3 and k_4 are constants related to weight (W) and height (H) respectively. The PA coefficient is related to the physical activity and varies with genders. As we are interested in the change of metabolic rate of a person from outdoor to indoor, we consider the coefficients of two physical activities: *active* and *sedentary*. The coefficients of active and sedentary for male and female are shown in Table 2. The details of other coefficients can be found in [30].

According to [26][25], metabolic rate changes smoothly after physical activity changes. To obtain the corresponding EER at time t, we formulate the EER into:

$$EER(t) = \begin{cases} \frac{(EER_s - EER_e)}{t_c}(t_c - t) + EER_e & t < t_c \\ EER_e & t \geq t_c \end{cases} \quad (3)$$

Here, EER_s and EER_e are EER of a person at active state and sedentary state respectively. t_c is the time required by a person to recover from active to sedentary. Beyond t_c, EER is assumed to remain as the metabolic rate becomes steady. Fig. 2 shows the EER of a male and a female with different ages, heights and weights.

Noted that t_c is a parameter that is difficult to obtain from daily sensors. It differs from person to person as well. Intuitively, even if two people have the same weight, they still differ from muscle-fat ratio. In built environment, this is a factor of research and there are ways to estimate t_c using laboratory equipment. As mentioned, we train t_c using the votes from occupants.

Table 3: Category of BMI

Category	BMI Range
Underweight	<18.5
Normal	18.5-25
Overweight	>25

As described, heat production is proportional to EER. Thus we have:

$$G(t) = a_1 \times EER(t) + b_1 \qquad (4)$$

Here, a_1 is the activity sensitivity and is associated to t_c, and b_1 is stable comfort preference. To make our presentation concise, we put the derivation of these two parameters into the Appendix.

4.2.2 Heat Loss Modeling

For heat loss, there are comprehensive recent findings from field studies [17][23] showing a noticeable relationship between the outdoor temperature and human thermal comfort. The correlation is formulated as $T_c(T_o) = a_2 + b_2 \times T_o$, where T_c is the comfort temperature function of outdoor mean temperature, a_2 is a constant related to comfort temperature and b_2 is the correlation between outdoor temperature change and comfort temperature change. Intuitively, this model says that if the outdoor temperature increases, the occupants prefer higher indoor temperature. In this paper, we applied the model in [31], where a_2 is set to 17.8 and b_2 is set to 0.31.

As specified in the standard [25], temperature range for comfort zone is $7°C$. This means that when indoor temperature increases from $T_c(T_o) - 3.5°C$ to $T_c(T_o) + 3.5°C$, the comfort index thus changes from -1 to 1. Since $L(T_i, T_o)$ is a linear function of T_i, k can be computed as $k = 7/2$. Thus, R can be calculated as $R = 3 \times k = 10.5°C$, which is the boundaries for the comfort zone of a person. The heat loss model is thus:

$$L(T_i, T_o) = \begin{cases} 3 & T_i - T_c(T_o) \geq R \\ k(T_i - T_c(T_o)) & -R < T_i - T_c(T_o) < R \\ -3 & T_i - T_c(T_o) \leq -R \end{cases}$$
$$(5)$$

4.3 Model Validation

We conducted a series of field experiments to validate our model. One experiment was conducted in a commercial office for five consecutive days, and 13 occupants were invited to participate in this experiment. We built the profile of each occupant using the TCC model and trained for three consecutive days. For the remaining two days, we compare

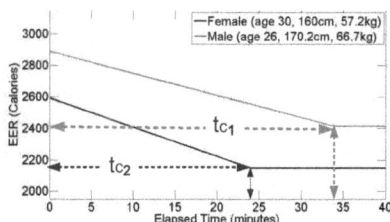

Figure 2: The EER example of two people

the comfort index from our TCC model with the actual feedback of occupants.

Referring to the World Health Organization (WHO) [32], we classify the occupants into three categories according to their body mass index (BMI): i) underweight (UW), ii) normal (NL), and iii) overweight (OW). The formula of BMI is as follows, and the BMI index of each group is shown in Table 3.

$$BMI = \frac{Weight(kg)}{(Height(m))^2} \qquad (6)$$

In our experiment, 3 of the occupants were UW, 8 were NL and 2 were OW. Each round of training was carried out in the time when occupants arrived the office from outside environment. In each round of training, we assigned a fixed setpoint temperature, and occupants were asked to submit their feedback at a 5-minute interval. We adjusted the setpoint (indoor) temperature from 20 °C to 25°C, with 0.5 °C increment in each training.

The key parameters of our model for training are a_1, b_1 and t_c of each occupant. We use linear regression that obtained from the training period and we estimate the comfort index of each occupant from our TCC model. The comparisons between the TCC model and the actual feedback of occupants are shown in Fig. 4. The accuracy for OW is 78%, NL is 75% and UW is 67%. The maximum error of the comfort index is only 1. The result indicates that our TCC model is capable to estimate the comfort index of the three occupants.

Here we explain our model in details. Noted that the heat loss is primarily determined by the clothes of an occupant, and in our model, this is determined by the outdoor temperature (which is translated into approximately the clothing of an occupant). The heat generation, however, depends on the metabolic rate of an individual and this differs across different occupants (one may recall our three training parameters a_1, b_1 and t_c are all for heat generation). We look into EER in more details. Fig. 3a shows one of the trainings, where one occupant is selected from each BMI group: occupant A from OW, occupant B from NL and occupant C from UW. Their change of EER are shown in Fig. 3b. Fig. 3a and 3b indicate that there is a strong correlation between the change of EER with the comfort index of occupants. More specifically, occupants A, B and C have diverging comfort indices at the beginning: A and B are warm and slightly warm respectively, and C is neutral. Their differences can be explained by the EER_s values, which are 3100, 2350 and 2100. Noted that the thermal sensations of occupants change with time, e.g., occupant A becomes neutral after 30 minutes, whereas B and C are both slightly cool after 40 and 25 minutes respectively. It is worth noticing that the thermal sensations of B and C are close to each other as their EER_e are close to each other. The result verifies the connection between EER and comfort index of a person.

5. THE SETPOINT OPTIMIZATION ALGORITHM

The objective of the setpoint optimization algorithm (SOA) is to find out the optimal setpoint temperature to a group of occupants in a specific room, thus maximizing the overall thermal comfort of all occupants, where a certain percentage of occupants are staying within the comfort zone. Our

(a) Comfort index

(b) EER

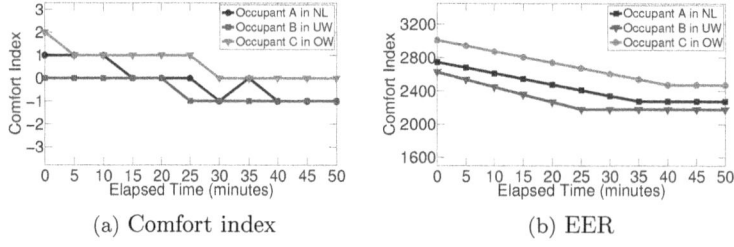

Figure 3: Connection between EER and Comfort index

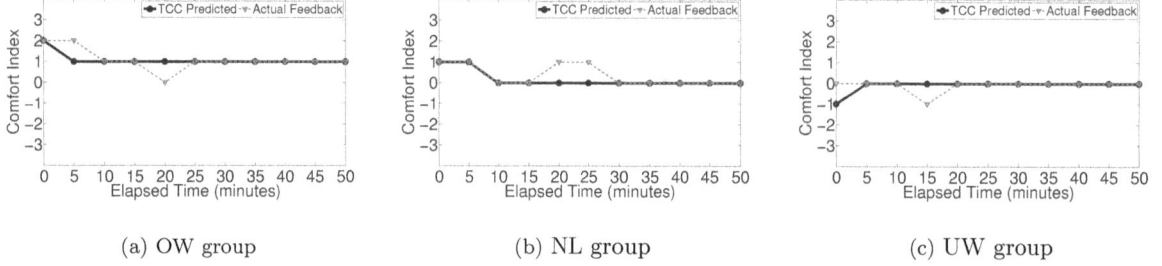

(a) OW group

(b) NL group

(c) UW group

Figure 4: TCC model validation under different BMI groups

algorithm is shown in Algorithm 1. There are three input parameters: $\mathbb{O}$, r, T_o. $\mathbb{O}$ is the set of occupants in a room; r is the threshold percentage of occupants within the comfort zone (e.g., 80%); and T_o is the outdoor temperature. For every occupant $j \in \mathbb{O}$, there is a corresponding TCC model C_j and a elapsed time t_j after occupant j enters the room.

Our algorithm first identifies the comfort temperature of each occupant. Then we compute the optimized setpoint temperature iteratively for all occupants. In each iteration, we determine a candidate of setpoint temperature and check whether this temperature satisfies the thermal comfort requirement of all occupants. If it fails, we adjust the set of occupants and proceed next iteration. In other words, we first calculate a candidate of setpoint temperature T^* by minimizing the sum of comfort index of all occupants. Then we count the numbers of occupants who feel comfortable, denoted as N. If the target requirement (more than $r|\mathbb{O}|$ occupants are satisfied) is met, the optimized setpoint T^* is found. Otherwise, we eliminate an occupant whose preferred temperature is the farthest from the candidate setpoint temperature since we try to satisfy as many occupants as possible.

6. SIMULATION

6.1 Simulation Setup

We evaluated our system in two different scales. Firstly, we simulated a classroom with different occupants' profiles. Secondly, we adopted the academic calendar from The Hong Kong Polytechnic University (denoted PolyU thereafter) to evaluate our system in a large scale. We compare our system with fixed setpoint strategy.

In our simulation, we created the occupant profiles based on the results from our experiment in model validation. We picked one occupant from each BMI category. The profile of an occupant is denoted as $[a_1, b_1, t_c]$. Thus, profiles from occupant in OW category, NL category and UW category

---

Algorithm 1 The Setpoint Optimization Algorithm

Input: $\mathbb{O}$, r, T_o
Output: T^*
1: $T^* \leftarrow \emptyset$;
2: **for** $\forall j \in \mathbb{O}$ **do**
3:     $T_j^* = \arg\min_T |C_j(T_o, T, t_j)|$;
4: **end for**
5: **while** 1 **do**
6:     $T^* = \arg\min_T \sum_{j \in \mathbb{O}} |C_j(T_o, T, t_j)|$;
7:     $N = 0$;
8:     **for** $\forall j \in \mathbb{O}$ **do**
9:         **if** $|C_j(T_o, T^*, t_j)| \leq 1$ **then**
10:             $N = N + 1$;
11:         **end if**
12:     **end for**
13:     **if** $N \geq r|\mathbb{O}|$ **then**
14:         break;
15:     **else**
16:         $\mathbb{O} \leftarrow \mathbb{O} \setminus \{\arg\max_{j \in \mathbb{O}} |T^* - T_j^*|\}$;
17:     **end if**
18: **end while**

---

are [0.0027, -4.99, 30], [0.0041, -7.08, 40] and [0.002, -2.5325, 25] respectively.

For the simulation in a classroom, we created two groups of occupants, named as group A and group B. Each group had 100 occupants. The ratio of OW:NL:UW in group A was 1:7:2, whereas group B was 1:1:3. The outdoor temperature was set to $30°C$. The class in each group lasted for an hour. The temperature under the fixed setpoint was $22°C$.

For the PolyU data, there were over 950 classes in every weekday. We evaluated our system with one whole year, and the classes were repeated every week. We adopted the outdoor temperature data of Hong Kong in 2013 from The Hong Kong Observatory [33] as the system input. From our field measurement, PolyU applied a fixed setpoint temperature of $22°C$ in summer period (May to October) and $24°C$ in winter period.

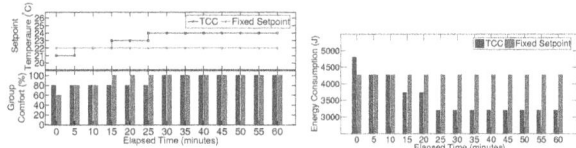

(a) Group comfort   (b) Energy consumption

Figure 5: Group A simulation results

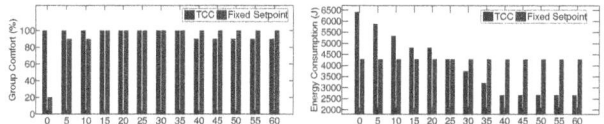

(a) Group comfort   (b) Energy consumption

Figure 6: Group B simulation results

To compare the energy consumption, we adopted the energy-temperature correlation model $P = |\frac{\lambda}{M}(T_i - T_o)|$ in [14]. We define P as the energy consumed by HVAC system in one-second, λ as the conductivity of that particular classroom. Intuitively, the larger the λ, the less the heat preservation being trapped into the room. M is energy transformation ratio of HVAC system, which is used to indicate the energy efficiency to the HVAC system. Again, T_i is the actual room temperature, and T_o is the average outdoor temperature. The model assumes that in a given room, $\frac{\lambda}{M}$ is fixed, and thus more energy is consumed when the room setpoint temperature is far away from the outdoor temperature. The values of λ and M for classrooms at PolyU are same as [14], where M is 0.14 for all classrooms. There are 155 classrooms in PolyU main campus, and the details are summarized in Table 4. For the simulation in a classroom, we took the parameters of the classroom with a capacity of 100 seats.

Table 4: Classroom at PolyU

Seats	No.	Size ($L \times W \times H, m$)	λ ($J/s \cdot K$)
20	8	$4 \times 5 \times 3$	70.5
40	42	$8 \times 5 \times 3$	118.5
60	67	$6 \times 10 \times 3$	162
80	10	$8 \times 10 \times 3$	201
100	4	$10 \times 10 \times 3.3$	249
150	17	$10 \times 15 \times 4$	375
200	5	$15 \times 14 \times 5$	533
300	2	$15 \times 20 \times 6$	765

6.2 Simulation Results

6.2.1 Classroom simulation result

Figure 5 shows the result of group A. With the starting setpoint calculated by OPTC at 21°C, it progressively increases with time and higher than the fixed setpoint, which is 22 °C after 15 minutes. We can see that OPTC achieves group thermal comfort requirement($\geq 80\%$) all the time, while fixed setpoint fails to meet the requirement in the first few minutes.

The energy consumption is shown in Fig. 6b. Since fixed setpoint does not changes its setpoint, its energy consumption is steady. For OPTC, when the setpoint is changed, the energy consumption drops dramatically. For the last 40 minutes, OPTC consumes only 35% of the energy of fixed setpoint. As a whole, there is a reduction of 16.5% energy consumption under OPTC.

The result of group B is shown in Fig. 6. Compared to that of group A, the group thermal comfort under fixed setpoint is far from satisfaction when the class begins. Only 20% of the students are within the comfort zone. In contrast, OPTC brings all the students stay within the comfort zone

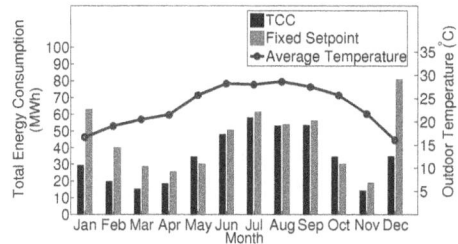

Figure 7: Energy consumption in one year

for more than 60% of the time, and it maintains 90% of group comfort for the students in class. From the results, beside the large differences of energy consumption between OPTC and fixed setpoint, it is obvious that group B saves even more energy. It can be explained by the ratio of UW is more than the OW in group B, which the setpoint temperatures from OPTC are generally higher than group A.

6.2.2 Simulation of annual energy consumption

The results of monthly energy consumption are shown in Fig. 7. The maximum and minimum averaged monthly temperature are 14°C and 31.1°C respectively. OPTC outperforms the fixed setpoint in 10 months with an exception in May and October. During summer period, the difference between OPTC and fixed setpoint are approximately 5%. However, such differences enlarged rapidly when the outdoor temperature drops, especially at its bottom in January and December, the fixed setpoint consumes more than twice of the energy than OPTC. When compared with the fixed setpoint, OPTC saves 23.1% annual energy consumption.

7. IMPLEMENTATION DETAILS

We implemented a prototype of OPTC in buildings. The system workflow is shown in Fig. 8. The system is deployed in an OPTC server. The event monitor module in OPTC server collects data from the environment and occupants. After the optimal setpoint temperature is calculated, the building control module requests BMS to adjust the room temperature. To collect data from occupants, we developed a mobile application. The occupants provide their thermal feedback and base rooms to the OPTC server via the mobile application. Besides collecting data from the occupants, the OPTC server communicates with the BMS for two objectives: 1) to collect the indoor temperature and the outdoor temperature; 2) to control the indoor temperature of a room. We discuss each part in details as follows.

7.1 A Mobile Application for Occupants

The mobile application collects the following information:

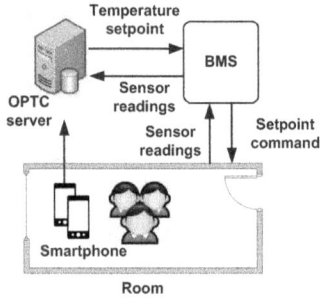

Figure 8: The system workflow of OPTC

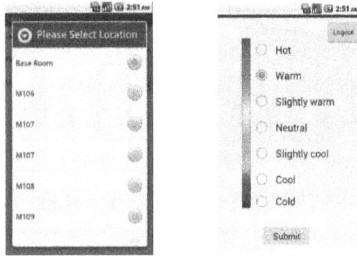

(a) Location selection (b) Voting screen

Figure 9: The mobile application for occupants

1) Occupant identity information; as explained before, our system requests occupant registration. This registration is one-off and collects data such as weight, age, gender, etc of the occupants. Recalled from Section 4, this information are needed for our TCC model.

2) The occupants are required to register their base rooms as shown in Fig. 9a; This registration is also one-off. If the occupant has only one base room, all the computation and adjustment will be based on this room. Noted that in this situation, the setpoint temperature still requires adjustments from time to time, and primarily non-intrusive. If the room hosts multiple occupants, the setpoint optimization algorithm needs to be applied. If an occupant has multiple base rooms, we need to obtain his location from time to time. To minimize the inputs from the occupant, the location can be obtained either from his meeting schedule, or a location detection algorithm can be applied. In a commercial office setting, an occupant usually has few numbers of base rooms. This makes the challenge for the location detection algorithm reasonable. The detailed location detection algorithm is out of the scope of our paper. In Section 8, our experiment is solely confined to the single room case.

3) Occupants thermal sensation (i.e., their votes); when our model-driven adjustment is not able to satisfy occupant's comfort, the occupant can provide feedback using the mobile application as shown in Fig. 9b, which follows the 7-point thermal comfort index design as explained in Section 4.3.

7.2 Data Collection and Temperature Control in Building

In a typical HVAC system, there are thousands of sensors to monitor the equipment status and condition feedback from the serving areas [11]. The temperature sensors are normally mounted on walls or at the ceiling of room. There are also sensors installed outside the buildings to col-

lect outdoor sensors data. Both of these data are sent to BMS through a network. Our OPTC requires the indoor and outdoor temperature. Since these data are available in the existing BMS, we retrieve such data directly from the BMS [18].

Besides the data collection at BMS, we also need to control the setpoint temperature of rooms. This function is realized through the Building Automation and Control Networks (BACnet) protocol [34] in our OPTC framework [35]. Given that BACnet is the most dominant communication protocol in BMS today, we believe our system can be widely adopted into different buildings.

8. EXPERIMENT

8.1 Experiment Setup

We conducted experiments in our university and a A-class commercial office. In our university, the air-conditioning of lecture theaters were controlled by the BMS, and the lecture theatre in our experiment had a capacity of 130 people at the building of Y-core.

For the commercial office in our experiment, the provision of air-conditioning was 24/7, the floor plan and the size of rooms are shown in Fig. 13. There were 5 individual rooms (room A to E) and 3 meeting rooms (room 1 to 3).

We set up our OPTC server on campus and connected both the BMSes of campus and office using virtual private network (VPN) since the campus network was located at Intranet. To collect the votes of students, we designed the mobile application as discussed in Sec. 7.1.

We evaluate our scheme through three performance metrics: 1) the improvement of thermal comfort of occupants; 2) the missing rate in satisfying group thermal comfort. We adopt a threshold of 80% following the ASHRAE standard; and 3) energy conservation.

8.2 Experiment results in our university

We conducted our experiment during a three-hour lecture in our university. 87 students were participated in the experiment, and the outdoor temperature was 31.4°C. From our pre-measurement, the university has a fixed setpoint temperature of 21.5°C. We divided the lecture into two one-hour sessions, where we experimented the fixed setpoint approach in the first session, and TCC approach in the second session.

Before the class, students were guided to install our smartphone application. They were instructed to provide feedback regarding their thermal sensations (as shown in Table 1) at an interval of 10 minutes. To develop the TCC model of each student, we also collected student's age, height and weight respectively.

Results of different group comfort under the fixed setpoint and our TCC modeled setpoint are shown in Fig. 10. The

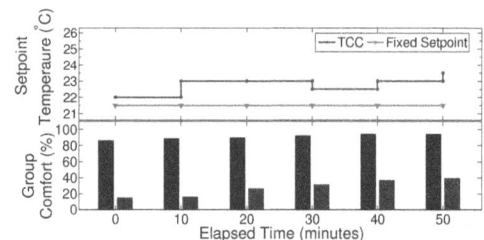

Figure 10: Setpoint temperature and group comfort

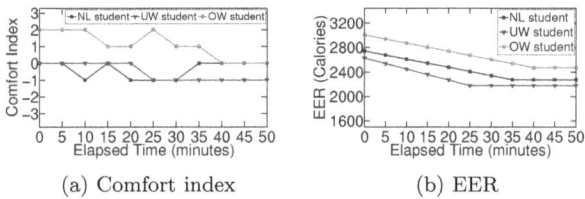

(a) Comfort index   (b) EER

Figure 11: Students from different BMI groups

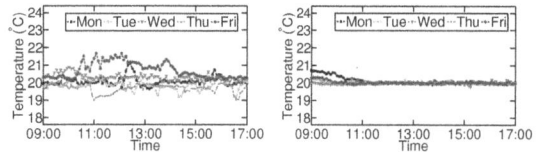

(a) Room B   (b) Room E

Figure 12: Temperature of two office rooms

x-axis is the elapsed time starting from the students arriving at the lecture theater. The y-axis of the upper part of the figure is the corresponding setpoint given by the fixed setpoint approach and our TCC approach; and the y-axis of the lower part of the figure is the overall feedback of students.

We compare the two setpoint approaches. In the experiment on fixed setpoint approach, more than 85% of the students were not at a comfort condition when they were just arrived the lecture theatre. In other words, their comfort indices were outside the comfort zone. 25 students even voted 3, and only 5 students voted thermal neutrality. At the time of 40 minutes, fixed setpoint has achieved its highest group comfort, which is still only about 40% of the students.

We then applied our model by first creating their profile using the TCC model with the given data. We categorized the students into three groups according to their BMIs. We selected one student from each group and showed their comfort indices and EER in Fig. 11a and 11b respectively. It was not surprised that students in OW group had a higher EER_s, followed by the student in NL group, who had a relatively mild change of EER with time. The student in the UW group had both the highest and least EER_s and EER_e respectively among the other groups.

To compare the improvement brought by our TCC model, we started to adjust the setpoint temperature of the lecture theater via our OPTC server after the 10-minute break at our second-hour experiment session. Students were again told to vote at every 10 minutes. Again, in Fig. 10, when the elapsed time was between 0 and 10 minutes, the TCC setpoint ($22°C$) was slightly higher than the fixed setpoint, and the difference enlarged between 10 to 30 minutes. The result showed that there was a great improvement to their conditions of thermal comfort as compared with the default fixed setpoint at $21.5°C$. Only 9 students (10.3%) were not at the comfort zone in the first 20 minutes, and later reduced to 5 students (5.7%) after 30 minutes. Our TCC approach was able to achieve 80% group comfort throughout the whole period. As compared with the group comfort before the TCC model was applied, there was an average of 63% thermal comfort improvement to the students in our experiment.

8.3 Experiment results in a commercial office

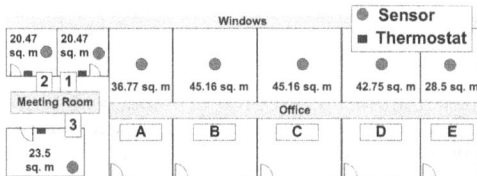

Figure 13: Floor plan of office

In this part, we discuss the experiment conducted in a commercial office. To study the existing indoor temperature and occupants comfort, we initially deployed three temperature sensors at different rooms for three weeks aiming to study the trend of temperature change under different outdoor temperatures. We then carried out two five-day sessions, one for the fixed setpoint approach and one for our TCC approach.

Before going into the analysis, we first present several interesting observations. Firstly, rooms with more people (e.g., room B with 13 people), experienced more significant temperature changes than rooms with less people (e.g., room E with 2 people). Fig.12a and 12b illustrate this phenomenon in room B and E respectively from one sample day during working hours.

Secondly, we observed that the temperature differences in a room can be as much as $2.5°C$; such differences may contribute to occupant discomfort. We traced the reasons and found that areas with printer and computers were the main culprits for a warmer temperature; and during noon time, the areas near windows were affected by the sunlight and thus created a small warm zone.

These findings show that the placement of temperature sensors have a direct effect to the control accuracy of BMS and thus the room temperature. The number of sensors and location should be carefully considered; otherwise, occupants will be modeled with bias.

Surprisingly, we also observed that it took approximately 4.5 minutes in average for a room to reach a setpoint temperature. From our discussion with building services engineers, it takes time for the setpoint adjustment since the chilled water and the air flow from the air-conditioning terminal units (e.g., fan coil unit and variable air volume box) need time to work together to attain the desired setpoint. This time-lag varies with building designs and air-conditioning systems. As such, in our experiment, the setpoint temperature was determined by the TCC model at every 5-minute.

Room B was chosen in our experiment as it has the highest and most steady occupancy. Two smart sensors TelosB were additionally deployed in room to provide a finer temperature measurement. The default setpoint temperature was fixed at $22°C$ (summer period) by the facility management of the building. We carried out two 5-day (Monday to Friday) measurements. We studied the fixed setpoint approach in the first measurement. Occupants were invited to provide feedback using our smartphone application anytime when they felt there was an obvious change to the thermal sensation.

We finally collected a total of 403 votes, which were fairly distributed from the 13 occupants. The results are shown in Fig. 14a. The central red line is the median, and the height of the box is the inter-quartile range of the votes, where the top and bottom of the boxes are the 75th and 25th percentile

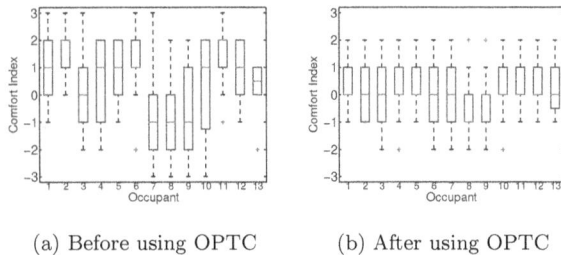

(a) Before using OPTC (b) After using OPTC

Figure 14: Feedback from office experiment

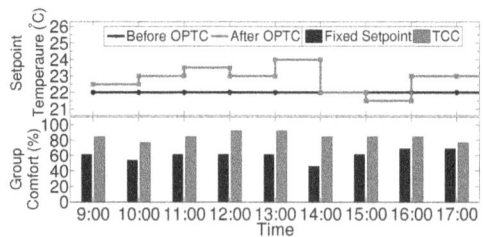

Figure 15: Setpoint and group comfort in office

of the votes. Extreme data that are considered outliers is shown using the "whiskers", i.e., with a "plus" sign.

There were dissatisfactions from the occupants to their existing fixed setpoint temperature. Around 45% of the votes were outside the comfort zone, and 7 votes (7.4%) were even at the extreme comfort index (-3 or 3).

We then deployed our OPTC for comparison. With the previous feedback and information of occupants (i.e., age, weight and height), we built the TCC model for each occupant. We conducted another 5-day experiment, and collected 334 votes.

The results are shown in Fig.14b. There was a major improvement of the occupant thermal comfort. 89% of the votes were within the comfort zone and no votes was in the extreme range (-3 or 3). There were 115 votes with thermal neutrality and they were fairly distributed from the 13 occupants. 12 occupants had a median of comfort neutrality, compared with 1 in our first week experiment. The overall improvement was 33.8%.

We further display one of the experiment days in the timeline format as shown in Fig. 15. There are two parts in the figure. The upper part shows the setpoint adjustment under fixed setpoint approach and our TCC approach. The lower part shows the group thermal comfort from the votes of occupants. The average outdoor temperature was 30.52°C during the day of experiment, with a diurnal difference of 3.17°C. Obviously, our TCC model has maintained a higher level of thermal comfort to the occupants than the fixed setpoint as shown in the group comfort percentage. Noted that the fixed setpoint failed to meet the target of group comfort during that experiment (i.e., 80%), whereas our TCC model was able to achieve 70% of the time meeting the requirement.

Beside the improvement of thermal comfort, there is also better energy performance. With the baseline of setpoint temperature at 22°C, there was an average of 1.75°C setpoint increment during the experiment period. Studies indicate that one-degree setpoint difference yields around 10% difference on energy use [36]. More specifically, we consider the energy input for the air-conditioning terminal units (kWh),

$$\sum_{i=1}^{n}\left\{\left(\frac{\dot{m}_i c \Delta T_i}{\eta_i \cdot COP} + P_{f_i}\right)hr_i\right\}, \qquad (7)$$

where $\dot{m}$ is the air mass flow rate (kg/s), c is the specific heat capacity of air (kJ/kgK), ΔT is the difference between supply and return air temperature (K), η is the heat transfer efficiency of the air-conditioning unit using chilled water, P_f is the operating fan motor power, COP is the coefficient of

performance of the central chiller plant and hr is the cooling duration (hours).

We calculate the energy input by using the operating logs of BMS every 5-minute interval (i.e., $hr = 1/12$). By assuming that the operating conditions were the same during the experiment, we can derive that our OPTC scheme was able to save 18% of energy consumption of the air-conditioning terminal units.

9. CONCLUSION

In this paper, we present an occupant-participatory thermal comfort framework. This framework incorporates occupants feedback into the loop of air-conditioning adjustment decisions. In the core of this framework, we developed a temperature-comfort correlation (TCC) model, capturing users favorite temperatures non-intrusively from their daily environment. Our model adopts the spirits of traditional P-MV index and the adaptive approach developed from built environment. Nevertheless, to make sure that the model can fit in daily usage, we make certain modifications where the model input data can be easily collected so that the occupant has incentives to participate. We also developed an algorithm which resolves diverging comfort requirements of multiple people. We have a full set of field validations, comprehensive simulations and real world experiments. The results showed that we can maintain thermal comfort while reducing energy consumption for 18%.

Acknowledgements

This work is supported in part by National Natural Science Foundation of China (No. 61272464), RGC/GRF PolyU 5264/13E, HK PolyU G-YM06, A-PK95, 1-ZVC2.

10. REFERENCES

[1] Electrical and Mechanical Service Department (EMSD), Hong Kong,
http://www.emsd.gov.hk/emsd/eng/pee/edata_1.shtml.
[2] A. Aswani, N. Master, J. Taneja, D. Culler, and C. Tomlin. Reducing transient and steady state electricity consumption in hvac using learning-based model predictive control. 100(1):240–253, 2012.
[3] Carl Ellis, James Scott, Mike Hazas, and John C. Krumm. Earlyoff: Using house cooling rates to save energy. In Proc. ACM BuildSys '12.
[4] Y. Agarwal, B. Balaji, S. Dutta, R. Gupta, and T. Weng. Duty-cycling buildings aggressively: The next frontier in hvac control. In Proc. ACM/IEEE IPSN'11.
[5] Y. Agarwal, B. Balaji, R. Gupta, J. Lyles, M. Wei, and T. Weng. Occupancy-driven energy management for smart building automation. In Proc. ACM BuildSys '10.

[6] Varick L. Erickson and Alberto E. Cerpa. Thermovote: participatory sensing for efficient building hvac conditioning. In *Proc. ACM BuildSys '12*.

[7] Xinlei Wang, Wei Cheng, P. Mohapatra, and T. Abdelzaher. Artsense: Anonymous reputation and trust in participatory sensing. In *Proc IEEE INFOCOM 13'*.

[8] Delphine Christin, Andreas Reinhardt, Salil S. Kanhere, and Matthias Hollick. A survey on privacy in mobile participatory sensing applications. *Journal of Systems and Software*, 84(11):1928 – 1946, 2011.

[9] Xiaofan Jiang, Stephen Dawson-Haggerty, Prabal Dutta, and David Culler. Design and implementation of a high-fidelity AC metering network. In *Proc. ACM IPSN '09*.

[10] Stephen Dawson-Haggerty, Steven Lanzisera, Jay Taneja, Richard Brown, and David Culler. @scale: insights from a large, long-lived appliance energy WSN. In *Proc. ACM IPSN '12*.

[11] Stephen Dawson-Haggerty, Andrew Krioukov, Jay Taneja, Sagar Karandikar, Gabe Fierro, Nikita Kitaev, and David Culler. BOSS: building operating system services. In *Proc. USENIX NSDI '13*.

[12] Marija Milenkovic and Oliver Amft. An opportunistic activity-sensing approach to save energy in office buildings. In *Proc. ACM e-Energy '13*.

[13] Jiakang Lu, Tamim Sookoor, Vijay Srinivasan, Ge Gao, Brian Holben, John Stankovic, Eric Field, and Kamin Whitehouse. The smart thermostat: using occupancy sensors to save energy in homes. In *Proc. ACM SenSys '10*.

[14] Yi Yuan, Dawei Pan, Dan Wang, Xiaohua Xu, Yu Peng, Xiyuan Peng, and Peng-Jun Wan. A study towards applying thermal inertia for energy conservation in rooms. *ACM Trans. Sen. Netw.*, 10(1):7:1–7:25, December 2013.

[15] Nol Djongyang, Ren Tchinda, and Donatien Njomo. Thermal comfort: A review paper. *Renewable and Sustainable Energy Reviews*, 14(9):2626 – 2640, 2010.

[16] Fanger PO. *Thermal comfort, analysis and application in environmental engineering*. Copenhagen: Danish Technical Press, 1970.

[17] de Dear, G. Brager, and D. Cooper. Developing an adaptive model of thermal comfort and preference. *ASHRAE Trans.*, V.104(1a)(1a):145–167, 1998.

[18] Hang-Yat Lam Abraham and Dan Wang. Carrying my environment with me: A participatory-sensing approach to enhance thermal comfort. In *Proc. ACM BuildSys '13*.

[19] Peter Xiang Gao and S. Keshav. Optimal personal comfort management using spot+. In *Proc. ACM BuildSys '13*.

[20] Farrokh Jazizadeh and Burcin Becerik-Gerber. Toward adaptive comfort management in office buildings using participatory sensing for end user driven control. In *Proc. ACM BuildSys '12*.

[21] A.P. Gagge, J.A.J. Stolwijk, and B. Saltin. Comfort and thermal sensations and associated physiological responses during exercise at various ambient temperatures. *Environmental Research*, 2(3):209 – 229, 1969.

[22] T. Goto, J. Toftum, R. Dear, and P.O. Fanger. Thermal sensation and thermophysiological responses to metabolic step-changes. *International Journal of Biometeorology*, 50(5):323–332, 2006.

[23] J. F. Nicol and M. A. Humphreys. New standards for comfort and energy use in buildings. *Building Research & Information*, 37(1):68–73, 2009.

[24] A.P. Gagge, A.P. Fobelets, and L.G. Berglund. *A standard predictive index of human response to the thermal environment*. Jan 1986.

[25] ASHRAE standard 55-2010:Thermal Environmental Conditions for Human Occupancy. ASHRAE, 2010.

[26] Innova Air Tech Instruments. *Thermal Comfort*. Innova Air Tech Instruments, 2002.

[27] Craig Morgan and Richard de Dear. Weather, clothing and thermal adaptation to indoor climate. *Climate Research*, 24(3):267–284, 2003.

[28] K Krauchi and ANNA Wirz-Justice. Circadian rhythm of heat production, heart rate, and skin and core temperature under unmasking conditions in men. *American Journal of Physiology-Regulatory, Integrative and Comparative Physiology*, 267(3):R819–R829, 1994.

[29] John R Speakman. Body size, energy metabolism and lifespan. *Journal of Experimental Biology*, 208(9):1717–1730, 2005.

[30] Institute of Medicine. *Dietary Reference Intakes for Energy, Carbohydrate, Fiber, Fat, Fatty Acids, Cholesterol, Protein, and Amino Acids (Macronutrients)*. The National Academies Press, 2005.

[31] G.S. Brager and R.J. de Dear. Climate, comfort & natural ventilation: A new adaptive comfort standard for ashrae standard 55. In *Proc. Moving Thermal Comfort Standards into the 21st Century 01'*.

[32] World Health Organization. www.who.int/bmi/, 2014.

[33] Hong Kong Observatory. www.hko.gov.hk/contente.htm, 2014.

[34] ASHRAE standard 135-2010:A Data Communication Protocol for Building Automation and Control Networks. ASHRAE, 2010.

[35] Qinghua Luo, A.H.-Y. Lam, Dan Wang, D.W.-T. Chan, Yu Peng, and Xiyuan Peng. Demo abstract: Towards a wireless building management system with minimum change to the building protocols. In *Proc. ICCPS '12*.

[36] Office of Environment and Heritage (OEH), NSW, www.ehp.qld.gov.au/sustainability/sector-guides/energy-use.html.

Appendix

We discuss the approach to compute a_1 and b_1 in Section 4.2.1. We use linear regression to process data in period $t \in [0, t_c]$. Combined with Eq. 4, Eq. 1 can be written as:

$$C(T_i, T_o, t) = a_1 \times EER(t) + b_1 + L(T_i, T_o)$$

With Eq. 3, we have:

$$C(T_i, T_o, t) = \hat{a} \times t + \hat{b} + L(T_i, T_o) \qquad t \in [0, t_c] \qquad (8)$$

where $\hat{a} = -a_1(EER_s - EER_e)/t_c$ and $\hat{b} = a_1 \times EER_s + b_1$.

From Eq. 5, $L(T_i, T_o)$ is computed given the values of T_i and T_o. Thus $C(T_i, T_o, t) - L(T_i, T_o)$ is linear to t because the unknown parameters $(\hat{a}, \hat{b})$ in Eq. 8 are constants. When an occupant votes, we record T_i, T_o, t and the voted thermal comfort index v. Ideally, the predicted index from our model equals to the voted index from occupant, which means that we expect $C(T_i, T_o, t) = v$. We can then use the linear regression technique with collected data $\langle T_i, T_o, t, v \rangle$ to obtain $\hat{a}$ and $\hat{b}$. Finally, a_1 and b_1 can be computed from $\hat{a}$ and $\hat{b}$ since EER_s, EER_e and t_c are known.

An In-depth Study of Forecasting Household Electricity Demand using Realistic Datasets

Chien-Yu Kuo
Department of Computer
Science and Information
Engineering
National Taiwan Normal
University
60047072s@ntnu.edu.tw

Ming-Feng Lee
Green Energy and
Environment Research Lab
Industrial Technology
Research Institute
mingfenglee@itri.org.tw

Chia-Lin Fu
Green Energy and
Environment Research Lab
Industrial Technology
Research Institute
fjlstar@itri.org.tw

Yao-Hua Ho
Department of Computer
Science and Information
Engineering
National Taiwan Normal
University
yho@ntnu.edu.tw

Ling-Jyh Chen
Institute of Information
Science
Academia Sinica
cclljj@iis.sinica.edu.tw

ABSTRACT

Data analysis and accurate forecasts of electricity demand are crucial to help both suppliers and consumers understand their detailed electricity footprints and improve their awareness about their impacts to the ecosystem. Several studies of the subject have been conducted in recent years, but they are either comprehension-oriented without practical merits; or they are forecast-oriented and do not consider per-consumer cases. To address this gap, in this paper, we conduct data analysis and evaluate the forecasting of household electricity demand using three realistic datasets of geospatial and lifestyle diversity. We investigate the correlations between household electricity demand and different external factors, and perform cluster analysis on the datasets using an exhaustive set of parameter settings. To evaluate the accuracy of electricity demand forecasts in different datasets, we use the support vector regression method. The results demonstrate that the medium mean absolute percentage error (MAPE) can be reduced to 15.6% for household electricity demand forecasts when proper configurations are used.

Categories and Subject Descriptors

H.4 [**Information Systems Applications**]: Miscellaneous

Keywords

Electricity demand forecast; household electricity demand; data analysis

1. INTRODUCTION

With recent advances in the Internet of Things (IoT) and smart grid technologies, smart electricity meters have been developed and are now widely deployed. Unlike conventional electricity meters that require labor-intensive reading, smart electricity meters exploit modern data communication techniques to transmit their readings to remote data centers periodically. The resulting automated meter reading (AMR) infrastructure provides more insightful information about electricity demand at a finer granularity. The information enables power suppliers to improve their electricity services, such as electricity billing, pricing, provisioning, and real-time demand responses. Moreover, it allows consumers to monitor their electricity consumption continuously, and it induces behavior changes that save energy and lead to more environmentally friendly lifestyles [2, 19, 25].

Several attempts have been made to analyze AMR data for value-added and advanced electricity services in recent years [6, 8, 10, 11, 12, 14, 15, 22, 25, 27]. These works can be categorized into two types based on their objectives, namely, *comprehension-oriented* studies and *forecast-oriented* studies. While the former focus on gaining a thorough understanding of the intrinsic properties of AMR data, the latter go one step further and forecast the demand for electricity. The drawback of existing works is that they only consider regional scenarios (e.g., commercial buildings, cities, and country areas) without considering the scenarios on a per-household basis. In fact, forecasting household electricity demand is regarded as challenging because it must take various human factors into account (e.g., income levels, activities, and lifestyles). A large-scale in-depth study of forecasting electricity demand in a household-based setting is therefore highly desirable.

In this study, we investigate the research problem of large-scale AMR data analysis with the objective of improving the accuracy of forecasting household electricity demand. Using the realistic datasets compiled by the Pilot Smart Meter

Deployment Project in Taiwan, as well as data on weather conditions recorded by the weather stations near the deployment areas, we analyze the AMR data and investigate its correlations with various external factors, such as the temperature, the number of the floor where the smart meter is located, and different time scales. Then, we use the support vector regression (SVR) method [26] to evaluate the accuracy of electricity demand forecasts under different parameter settings. The contribution of this work is three-fold.

1. We conduct in-depth analysis using realistic smart electricity meter datasets and investigate the correlations between electricity demand and several external factors, such as the time, temperature, and number of the floor where the meter is located. The datasets are large-scale (i.e., 1,296 meters), and cover a long period (i.e., more than two years). They are also diverse in terms of household types (i.e., apartments and houses) and locations (i.e., entirely residential areas and mixed residential/commercial areas).

2. We perform cluster analysis on the datasets under an extensive set of parameter settings (e.g., under different distance measurement methods, clustering algorithms, and cluster validity indices). In addition, we exploit a decision mechanism based on the Memetic Algorithm [20] to determine the optimal number of clusters for each configuration.

3. To evaluate the accuracy of forecasting household electricity demand, we apply the SVR method on different datasets under different parameter settings, and analyze the results in detail.

Based on our research findings, we draw the following conclusions.

1. There is a *turning temperature*, which means the daily household electricity demand and the daily average temperature have a positive correlation when the temperature is greater than the turning temperature; otherwise, they have a negative correlation.

2. There is a significant drop in the daily household electricity demand on non-working weekdays (holidays), but there are no significant variations in the demand on weekdays or weekends.

3. The datasets exhibit a *lifestyle diversity*, and the best forecast performance of each dataset occurs under different parameter settings. Overall, the medium MAPE of the best forecast achieved was 15.6% when proper configurations were used in this study.

The remainder of this paper is organized as follows. Section 2 contains a review of recent studies on smart meter data analysis. In Section 3, we describe the three datasets used in this study; and in Section 4, we analyze the datasets and their correlations with different external factors. In Section 5, we conduct cluster analysis on the datasets, and also describe the Memetic Algorithm-based approach used to determine the optimal number of clusters for each dataset under different parameter settings. In Section 6, we evaluate the accuracy of forecasting electricity demand forecast with the three datasets, and present a detailed analysis on the results. Section 7 contains some concluding remarks.

2. RELATED WORK

There have been a number of competitions to determine the best way to forecast demand. One of the most notable was the Electricity Load Competition hosted by EUropean Network Intelligent TEchnologies for Smart Adaptive Systems (EUNITE) in 2001 [1]. The contest utilized a dataset provided by the East-Slovakia Power Distribution Company with 578,082 take-off points in the Eastern Slovakian Region. The dataset contains the per-30-minute electricity loads and the daily average temperature between January 1997 and December 1998. Based on the dataset, the competitors were asked to predict the maximum daily electricity load for January 1999.

In the contest, several competitors observed that there was a strong correlation between the temperature and the electricity load. However, it has been found that the temperature feature is not useful in forecasting the electricity load unless the temperature forecast is accurate [8, 12, 14, 15]. Moreover, the electricity load is higher on weekends than on weekdays [10, 14]. The variation between weekdays and weekends can be exploited to improve the accuracy of electricity load forecasts [6, 8, 22]

Jain and Satish [11] conducted an electricity load forecast study using a 2-year dataset that contained the per-30-minute regional electricity load, the daily average temperature, and the day of week (DOW). They divided the dataset into several clusters based on arbitrary thresholds and used the SVR approach to make forecasts. Specifically, SVR predicted the electricity loads (i.e., 48 thirty-minute loads) based on the previous 48 thirty-minute loads, the previous day's average temperature, the DOW of the previous day, and the temperature forecast for that day.

Shen et al. [25] proposed a Pattern Forecasting Ensemble Model (PFEM) that combines the Pattern Sequence-based Forecasting (PSF) algorithm [17] with five clustering models (namely, K-Means, K-Medoids, Self-Organizing Map, Hierarchical Clustering, and Fuzzy C-Means) with different weights to derive more accurate electricity load predictions. The model was evaluated on three publicly available electricity demand datasets compiled by the New York Independent System Operator (NYISO), the Australian National Electricity Market (ANEM), and Ontario's Independent Electricity System Operator (IESO), respectively. The evaluation results showed that PFEM could provide more accurate and reliable forecasts than PSF with a single clustering method.

Finally, Solomom et al. [27] conducted a study to forecast the electricity demand of a large commercial building at 345 Park Avenue in Manhattan. Approximately 5,000 people work in the building and there are about 1,000 visitors every day. The authors used a dataset of the electricity demand in the building over fifteen months, The forecast, which was SVR-based, predicted the electricity demand for the next week based on previous electricity demands, daily average temperatures, dew point temperatures, and wind speed data.

3. DATASET

In this section, we present the datasets used in the current study and discuss their basic properties. The datasets were obtained from the Pilot Smart Meter Deployment Project in Taiwan, which was launched in 2010 with the support of the

Table 1: Summary of the dataset collected from the different deployment sites

Dataset (Site)	Type	Area	# of smart meters		Period (days)
			w/o floor info.	w/ floor info.	
Taipei	apartments	residential/commercial	715	540	992 (2010/11/08 - 2013/07/26)
Hsinchu	apartments	residential	419	240	999 (2010/11/01 - 2013/07/26)
Tainan	houses	residential	162	162	262 (2012/11/07 - 2013/07/26)

Taiwan Power Company and the Bureau of Energy, Ministry of Economic Affairs, Taiwan. The deployment started in the cities of Taipei and Hsinchu in the north of Taiwan; and in 2012, another deployment was added in Tainan, a city in the south of Taiwan.

The Taipei dataset comprises 715 smart electricity meters deployed in the Minsheng Community, which is a mixed-use area of residential and commercial properties in the east of Taipei City. Each smart meter corresponds to one household, and it reports the householdÕs electricity demand every fifteen minutes via different techniques (e.g., Wi-Fi and power line communication). Of the 750 smart meters listed in the dataset, 540 show the full postal address of the household (including the floor number) where they are installed. They are categorized into LOW floors (1F-5F with 464 meters); MIDDLE floors (6F-10F with 48 meters); and HIGH floors (11F-16F with 26 meters).

The Hsinchu dataset comprises 419 smart electricity meters deployed in the Siangshan Community in the southwest of Hsinchu County; again, each smart meter is associated with one household. The Siangshan Community is an entirely residential area, where most of the residents are either students or they work in nearby companies. The smart meters have similar configurations to those deployed in Taipei city including the sample rate and communication techniques. Of the 419 smart meters in the dataset, 240 show the complete postal addresses where they are located. There are 150 meters on LOW floors (1F-5F), 50 meters on MIDDLE floors (6F-10F), and 40 meters on HIGH floors (11F-18F), respectively.

The Tainan dataset only contains 162 smart meters, each of which is associated with one floor of a three-floor household (i.e., there are 54 households in the dataset). The complete postal addresses of the participating households are available. All the houses are located in the same community and have the same design: the living room is on the first floor (LOW floor), the kitchen and one bedroom are on the second floor (MIDDLE floor), and another two bedrooms are on the third floor (HIGH floor). Most of the residents are workers and students in nearby areas. The smart meters are configured to use the same sample rate and communication techniques as those in the Taipei and Hsinchu sites.

The deployment project was implemented in an incremental manner. In the early phase, the number of *concurrently alive meters* varied significantly over time due to meter failures and unreliable wireless communications. To resolve the problem, all the smart meters have been upgraded to use power line communications to transmit data, and the smart meters installed in the early phase of the project have been replaced with new models. Moreover, we designed a simple filter to remove obvious outliers from the datasets, such as negative electricity demands and extremely large demands (i.e., more than 100 kilowatt-hours) in a 15-minute time slot. Table 1 summarizes the datasets used in this study, and Figure 1 shows the number of the *concurrently alive meters* over time in the datasets.

To investigate the correlation between environmental factors and household electricity demand, we downloaded weather condition data from the weather station at Mingchuan elementary school, which is about one kilometer from the deployment site. For the Hsinchu and Tainan sites, we purchased weather condition data from the Taiwan Central Weather Bureau. We also obtained data from two weather observation stations that are about ten kilometers from the Hsinchu site and the Tainan site respectively.

4. DATA ANALYSIS

Next, we analyze the intrinsic properties of the three datasets; and then evaluate the correlations between electricity demand and various external factors.

Figure 2 shows the cumulative distribution function (CDF) of the data instances (i.e., *per-15-minute* electricity demand) in the three datasets. The curve of the Taipei dataset is always on the right of the other curves, indicating that the households in Taipei generally consume more energy than those in Hsinchu and Tainan. There are two reasons for this phenomenon: 1) some of the smart meters in the Taipei dataset are installed in premises used for commercial activities, which consume more power than strictly residential activities; and 2) the income level of households in Taipei is higher than that in the other two cities, so the residents tend to consume more energy [4]. In addition, we observe that 58% of the data instances in the Hsinchu dataset have extremely low values (i.e., less than 0.05kWh). This is because most of the households in the Hsinchu site are either single-person or dual-income-no-kids (DINK) entities. The residents tend to work long hours, even at weekends, in high-tech companies in the nearby Hsinchu Science Park; hence, the demand for electricity is extremely low.

Figure 3 compares the per-15-minute electricity demand of LOW, MIDDLE, and HIGH floor households over a day in the three datasets. We make the following observations.

1. Overall, electricity demand is highest at night and lowest in the early morning. The reason is simple: the demand is highly correlated to people's household activities at different times of the day.

2. In the Taipei dataset, LOW-floor households consume more power than the other groups around noon (11am - 1pm); while HIGH-floor households consume more power than the other groups in the evening (8pm - 9am). The former can be explained by the fact that some LOW-floor premises are used for business, and they are busier during the lunch period than at other times. The reason for the latter finding is that the temperatures in Taipei households on HIGH floors usually differ substantially from those on LOW floors due to the basin effect in Taipei. Thus, people on HIGH floors

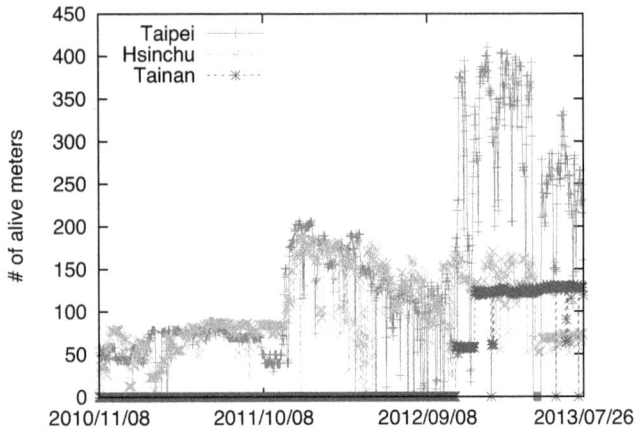

Figure 1: The number of the *concurrently alive meters* over time in the three datasets

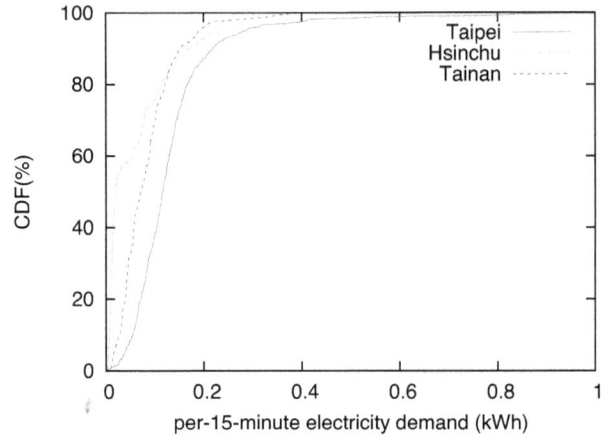

Figure 2: The CDF of the *per-15-minute* electricity demand in the three datasets

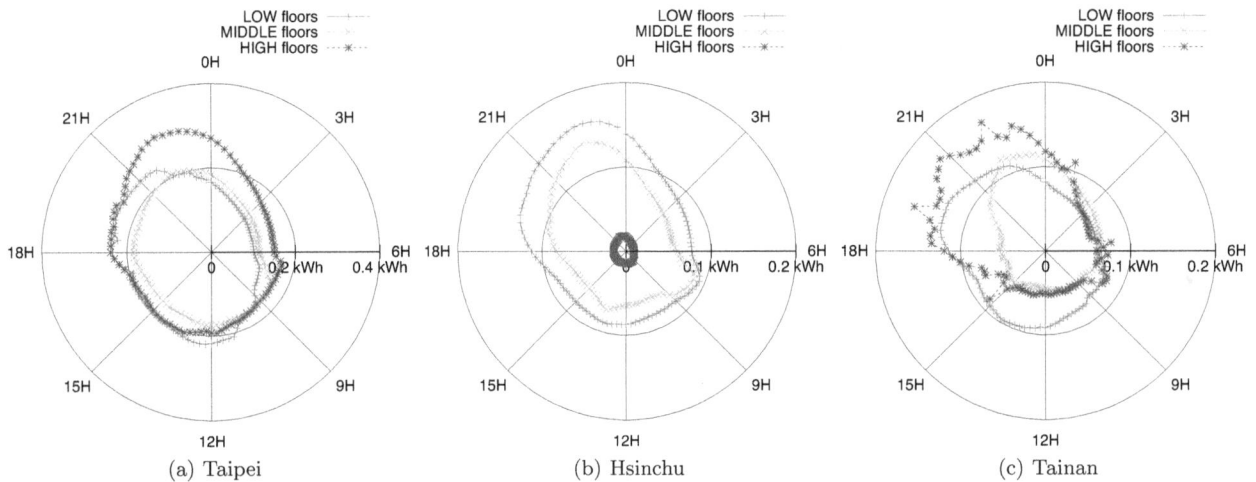

(a) Taipei (b) Hsinchu (c) Tainan

Figure 3: Comparison of the per-15-minute electricity demand on the LOW/MIDDLE/High floors in a day at the three sites

tend to use air conditioners more often in summer, and turn on heaters and dehumidifiers more often in winter.

3. In the Hsinchu dataset, LOW-floor households consume more energy than MIDDLE-floor premises over a day; while HIGH-floor households consume the least amount. The reason is that the deployment is located in a new residential area and many premises are not currently occupied. Interestingly, higher floors have more vacancies than middle and lower floors.

4. In the Tainan dataset, first-floor households consume the most electricity during the day, while third-floor households have the highest demand at night. The finding shows that people usually spend most of their time in the living room (1F) during the day, while the bedrooms (2F and 3F) are used mostly at night.

We also evaluate the correlations between the per-15-minute electricity demand and different types of day, i.e., working weekdays, weekends, and non-working weekdays (i.e., holidays). The results in Figure 4 show that electricity demand

on non-working weekdays is lower than on the other days. This is because most people go out (or go away) on those days. Moreover, the electricity demand on working weekdays is comparable to that on weekends in the three datasets. The reason is that people may also go out on weekends (e.g., for leisure instead of work), so their household life patterns are the same on working weekdays and weekends.

In addition, we investigate the impact of the daily average temperature on the daily electricity demand registered by each smart meter. From the results shown in Figure 5, we observe that the distribution forms a *V shape* in all three datasets. More precisely, there is a *turning temperature* in each dataset (i.e., the valley of the V shape); the greater the difference between the daily average temperature and the turning temperature, the higher the electricity consumption. The reason is that people tend to turn on air conditioners in summer and heaters in winter. Thus, the turning temperature is deemed to be the ideal temperature for most people (i.e., they feel comfortable) so there is no need for air conditioners/heaters. Specifically, the results in Figure 5 show

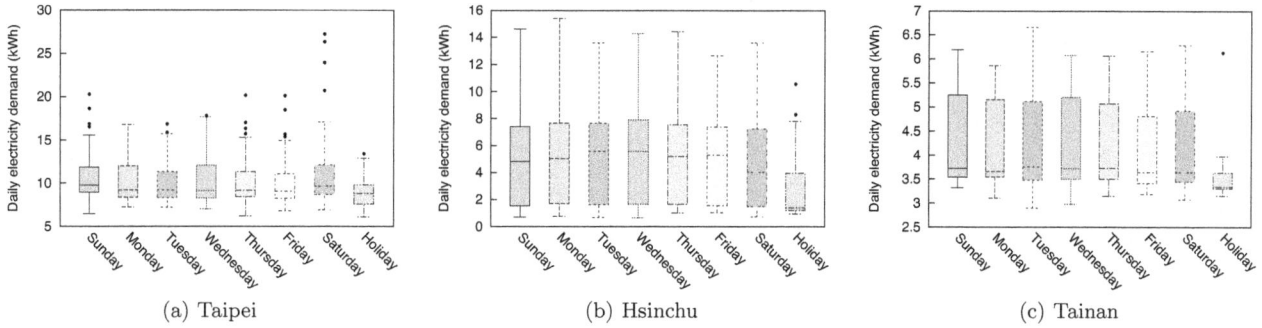

(a) Taipei   (b) Hsinchu   (c) Tainan

Figure 4: Comparison of the per-15-minute electricity demand on working weekdays, weekends, and non-working weekdays (i.e., holidays) in the three datasets

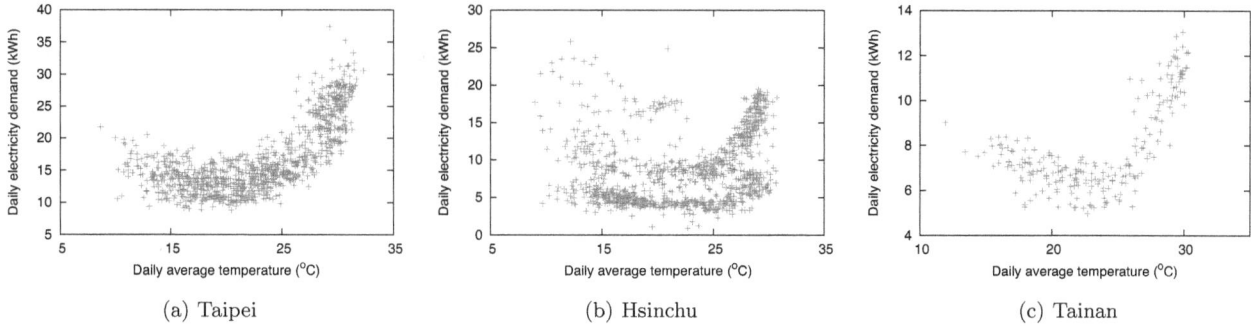

(a) Taipei   (b) Hsinchu   (c) Tainan

Figure 5: Illustration of the distribution of the daily electricity demand under different daily average temperatures in the three datasets

that the turning temperatures are $20^{\circ}C$, $25^{\circ}C$, and $25^{\circ}C$ in the Taipei, Hsingchu, and Tainan datasets respectively.

Finally, using the turning temperature in Figure 5, we evaluate the correlations between the daily average temperature and the daily electricity demand for households on different floors (i.e., HIGH/MIDDLE/LOW floors) under different weather conditions (i.e., above/below the turning temperature). The results in Table 2 show that, when the temperature is higher than the turning temperature, the correlation is strongly positive in the Taipei and Tainan datasets, and moderately positive in the Hsinchu dataset. In contrast, when the temperature is lower than the turning temperature, the correlation is weakly negative except for those household on MIDDLE and HIGH floors in the Taipei and Tainan datasets, which have moderately negative correlations. The reason is that heaters are not always needed during winter in the three cities because the climate in Taiwan ranges from subtropical in the north to tropical in the south. Thus, the correlation is moderate to weak when the daily average temperature is lower than the turning temperature.

5. CLUSTER ANALYSIS

We use cluster analysis to identify households with similar lifestyle patterns in the three datasets. In the analysis, we use the *daily* electricity demand, instead of per-15-minute consumption, because it is more representative of the seasonal changes in people's household lifestyle patterns. Moreover, we evaluate different parameter settings (e.g., distance measures, clustering algorithms, and cluster metrics) and implement a Memetic Algorithm-based approach to deter-

Table 2: Correlations between the daily average temperature and the daily electricity demand for smart meters on different floors and under different weather conditions in the three datasets

		LOW floors	MIDDLE floors	HIGH floors
Taipei	$\geq 20^{\circ}C$	0.780	0.823	0.783
	$< 20^{\circ}C$	-0.227	-0.654	-0.392
Hsinchu	$\geq 25^{\circ}C$	0.572	0.331	0.590
	$< 25^{\circ}C$	-0.288	-0.198	-0.094
Tainan	$\geq 25^{\circ}C$	0.831	0.869	0.757
	$< 25^{\circ}C$	0.194	-0.583	-0.655

mine the optimal number of clusters under each parameter setting. We present the detailed analysis in the following subsections.

5.1 Data Preprocessing

Two issues must be resolved before performing cluster analysis on the three datasets: 1) *data dependency*: the daily electricity demand is the combined result of people's lifestyle patterns and external factors, such as the temperature (as shown in Table 2); and 2) *data scaling*: different households may have similar behavior patterns in terms of daily electricity demand, but on different scales. The demand depends on the number (and the models) of the appliances used in different households. Thus, it is necessary to preprocess the datasets in order to mitigate the effects of the two issues. The data preprocessing phase involves two steps:

- *Data Separation*
  Using the turning temperatures discussed in Section 4,

we divide each dataset into two subsets: (1) the *warm subset*, which contains data instances for the months in which the average temperatures were higher than the turning temperature; and (2) the *cold subset*, which contains the rest of the data instances in the original dataset. In this study, the warm seasons are defined as April to November for the Taipei dataset, May to October for the Hsinchu dataset, and April to October for the Tainan dataset.

- *Data Standardization*

  To resolve the data scaling issue, we exploit the classic data *standardization* approach to convert the daily electricity demand from its raw form into a *standard score (z-Score)* [3]. Specifically, we let $X_k^{i,j}$ be the electricity demand recorded by the i-th smart meter in the k-th time slot of the j-th day in the dataset. The standard score of $X_k^{i,j}$ is

  $$Z_k^{i,j} = \frac{X_k^{i,j} - \mu(X_*^{i,j})}{\sigma(X_*^{i,j})}, \tag{1}$$

  where $\mu(X_*^{i,j})$ is the mean electricity demand of the i-th household on the j-th day, and $\sigma(X_*^{i,j})$ is the standard deviation of the electricity demand recorded by the i-th smart meter for all time slots on the j-th day.

5.2 Parameter Settings

In this subsection, we consider the different parameter settings used in the cluster analysis, including distance measures, clustering algorithms, and cluster validity indices. We discuss the possible settings of each parameter and the rationale for each one in the following subsections.

5.2.1 Distance Measure

Let $Z_k^{i,j}$ be the standardized electricity demand recorded by the i-th smart meter in the k-th time slot of the j-th day, and let n be the number of time slots in a day. We consider two distance functions to measure the distance between $Z_*^{i_1,j_1}$ and $Z_*^{i_2,j_2}$.

- *Euclidean distance:* The Euclidean distance represents the ordinary distance between two points in geometry, and it is widely used to measure the distance between two samples in a multi-dimensional space. In this study, we derive the Euclidean distance between $Z_*^{i_1,j_1}$ and $Z_*^{i_2,j_2}$ by computing the square root of the sum of the squares of the differences between two standardized electricity demands, i.e.,

  $$D^{Euclid}(Z_*^{i_1,j_1}, Z_*^{i_2,j_2}) = \sqrt{\sum_{k=1}^{n}(Z_k^{i_1,j_1} - Z_k^{i_2,j_2})^2}. \tag{2}$$

- *Dynamic Time Warping (DTW) Distance:* The DTW distance [13] is commonly used to measure the similarity between two time sequence data events that may vary in time and speed. To calculate the DTW distance between $Z_k^{i_1,j_1}$ and $Z_k^{i_2,j_2}$, we first identify four time slots (as shown in Figure 6):

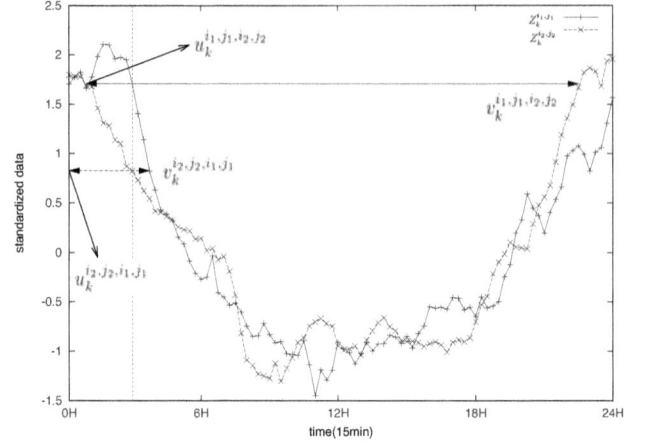

Figure 6: Illustration of the Dynamic Time Warping (DTW) distance

1. $u_k^{i_1,j_1,i_2,j_2}$: the nearest backward slot of $Z_*^{i_1,j_1}$ such that its value is equal to $Z_k^{i_2,j_2}$. i.e.,

   $$u_k^{i_1,j_1,i_2,j_2} = \max\left(0, \underset{1 \le k' < k}{\mathrm{argmax}}\,(Z_{k'}^{i_1,j_1} = Z_k^{i_2,j_2})\right). \tag{3}$$

2. $v_k^{i_1,j_1,i_2,j_2}$: the nearest forward slot of $Z_*^{i_1,j_1}$ such that its value is equal to $Z_k^{i_2,j_2}$, i.e.,

   $$v_k^{i_1,j_1,i_2,j_2} = \min\left(0, \underset{k < k' \le n}{\mathrm{argmin}}\,(Z_{k'}^{i_1,j_1} = Z_k^{i_2,j_2})\right). \tag{4}$$

3. $u_k^{i_2,j_2,i_1,j_1}$: the nearest backward slot of $Z_*^{i_2,j_2}$ such that its value is equal to $Z_k^{i_1,j_1}$, i.e.,

   $$u_k^{i_2,j_2,i_1,j_1} = \max\left(0, \underset{1 \le k' < k}{\mathrm{argmax}}\,(Z_{k'}^{i_2,j_2} = Z_k^{i_1,j_1})\right). \tag{5}$$

4. $v_k^{i_2,j_2,i_1,j_1}$: the nearest forward slot of $Z_*^{i_2,j_2}$ such that its value is equal to $Z_k^{i_1,j_1}$, i.e.,

   $$v_k^{i_2,j_2,i_1,j_1} = \min\left(0, \underset{k < k' \le n}{\mathrm{argmin}}\,(Z_{k'}^{i_2,j_2} = Z_k^{i_1,j_1})\right). \tag{6}$$

Then, the directional DTW distance between $Z_k^{i_1,j_1}$ and $Z_k^{i_2,j_2}$ (i.e., $\overrightarrow{D}^{DTW}(Z_k^{i_1,j_1}, Z_k^{i_2,j_2})$) and the distance in the opposite direction (i.e., $\overrightarrow{D}^{DTW}(Z_k^{i_2,j_2}, Z_k^{i_1,j_1})$) are obtained by

$$\overrightarrow{D}^{DTW}(Z_k^{i_1,j_1}, Z_k^{i_2,j_2})$$
$$= \min\left(k - u_k^{i_1,j_1,i_2,j_2}, v_k^{i_1,j_1,i_2,j_2} - k\right), \text{ and} \tag{7}$$

$$\overrightarrow{D}^{DTW}(Z_k^{i_2,j_2}, Z_k^{i_1,j_1})$$
$$= \min\left(k - u_k^{i_2,j_2,i_1,j_1}, v_k^{i_2,j_2,i_1,j_1} - k\right). \tag{8}$$

Finally, the DTW distance between $Z_*^{i_1,j_1}$ and $Z_*^{i_2,j_2}$ is determined by considering either the mean directional distance of each corresponding pair (as shown in Eq. 9) or the minimum directional distance of each corresponding pair (as shown in Eq. 10).

$$D_{mean}^{DTW}(Z_k^{i_1,j_1}, Z_k^{i_2,j_2}) = \sum_{k=1}^{n} \frac{\overrightarrow{D}^{DTW}(Z_k^{i_1,j_1}, Z_k^{i_2,j_2}) + \overrightarrow{D}^{DTW}(Z_k^{i_2,j_2}, Z_k^{i_1,j_1})}{2}. \quad (9)$$

$$D_{min}^{DTW}(Z_k^{i_1,j_1}, Z_k^{i_2,j_2}) = \sum_{k=1}^{n} \min(\overrightarrow{D}^{DTW}(Z_k^{i_1,j_1}, Z_k^{i_2,j_2}), \overrightarrow{D}^{DTW}(Z_k^{i_2,j_2}, Z_k^{i_1,j_1})). \quad (10)$$

5.2.2 Clustering Algorithms

We exploit two clustering algorithms in the analysis: the K-Means algorithm [16] and the K-Medoids algorithm [24]. The K-Means algorithm is one of the most popular methods used in data mining. It partitions the data space into several Voronoi cells such that the distance between a data point and the geometric center of its own Voronoi cell is less than the distance to the centers of any other cells.

Specifically, given K as a priori information, the K-Means algorithm clusters the daily electricity demand dataset as follows:

Step 1: It selects K data instances at random from the dataset as the cluster centers.

Step 2: For the rest of the data instances in the dataset, it uses Eq. 2 to calculate the Euclidean distance from each data instance to each cluster center. Then, it associates each data instance with the closest cluster center.

Step 3: It calculates the geometric center of each cluster, and updates the cluster centers accordingly.

Step 4: It repeats Step 2 and Step 3 until no further changes can be made.

The K-Medoids algorithm is implemented in a similar way to the K-Means algorithm, except that: 1) in Step 2, it utilizes the DTW distance (Eq. 9 and Eq. 10) instead of the Euclidean distance to measure the distance between two data instances in the dataset; and 2) in Step 3, it chooses one of the samples as the new cluster center, such that the sum of the distances between the new cluster center and the other data instances in the same cluster is the minimum. Depending on the distance function used, the K-Medoids algorithm has two variants: K-Medoids-mean (i.e., using Eq. 9) and K-Medoids-min (i.e., using Eq. 10).

5.2.3 Cluster Validity Index

Instead of using an arbitrary number K as a priori number of clusters, we exploit two cluster validity indices, the PBM index [21] and the Davies-Bouldin (DB) index [9], to determine the optimal number of clusters for data clustering. Let K be the number of clusters; C_i be the i-th cluster; c_i be the center of the i-th cluster; and $z_{i,j}$ be the j-th data instance in the i-th cluster. We calculate the two cluster validity indices as follows.

- *PBM Index:* The *intra-cluster* distance between data instances belonging to the same cluster and the *inter-cluster* distance between two cluster centers are derived by Eq. 11 and Eq. 12 respectively; where $|C_i|$

denotes the number of data instances belonging to the i-th cluster, and D^* is the distance function used.

$$E_K = \sum_{i=1}^{K} \sum_{j=1}^{|C_i|} D^*(z_{i,j}, c_i). \quad (11)$$

$$F_K = \max_{1 \le i \ne j \le K} D^*(c_i, c_j). \quad (12)$$

Then, given a cluster number K, the PBM index is obtained by

$$PBM(K) = (\frac{1}{K} \times \frac{E_1}{E_K} \times F_K)^2, \quad (13)$$

where E_1 is the sum of the distances of all data instances to the center of the dataset. The larger the value of $PBM(K)$, the more stable will be the clustering results. The optimal number of clusters K is obtained when the value of $PBM(K)$ is maximal.

- *DB Index:* We derive the intra-cluster distance for the i-th cluster by Eq. 14. Then, we calculate the *goodness-of-fit* of the i-th cluster by finding the best partner cluster that can maximize the ratio of the intra-cluster distance over the inter-cluster distance, as shown in Eq. 15.

$$S_i = \frac{1}{|C_i|} \sum_{j=1}^{|C_i|} D^*(z_{i,j}, c_i). \quad (14)$$

$$R_i = \max_{1 \le j \le K; j \ne i} \frac{S_i + S_j}{D^*(c_i, c_j)}. \quad (15)$$

The DB index is obtained by calculating mean goodness-of-fit value of the K clusters, as shown in Eq. 16. In contrast to the PBM index, the optimal number of clusters K is obtained when the value of $DB(K)$ is minimal.

$$DB(K) = \frac{1}{K} \sum_{i=1}^{K} R_i. \quad (16)$$

5.3 Clustering Results

It has been shown that the cluster initialization issue influences the clustering results of many clustering algorithms [5, 28]. We address the issue as follows. Given a fixed number of clusters K, we utilize the Memetic-based algorithm [20] to combine *local search* and *genetic algorithms* to find the optimal clustering results. Figure 7 shows the flowchart of the algorithm.

There are eight steps:

- *Initial Population:* The algorithm selects K data instances at random as the initial cluster centers. Then, it repeats the process N_1 times to form N_1 sets of initial cluster centers.

- *Local Search:* For each set of cluster centers, the algorithm uses the selected clustering algorithm to analyze the dataset and yields K clusters.

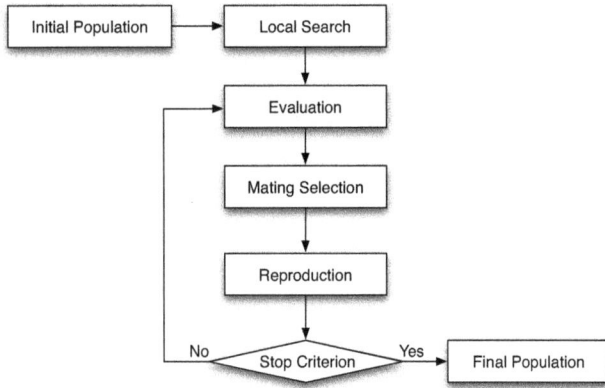

Figure 7: The flowchart of the Memetic-based algorithm used for cluster initialization

- *Evaluation*: The algorithm uses the selected cluster validity index to calculate the index value of the clustering results of each set of cluster centers.

- *Mating Selection*: The algorithm uses the *Tournament Selection* method [18] to select N_2 sets of cluster centers at random ($N_2 < N_1$), and reports the top two sets of clustering results (i.e., those that yield the maximal PBM index value or the minimal DB index value).

- *Reproduction*: Using the two sets of cluster centers derived by the *Mating Selection* step, the algorithm creates two sets of offspring by *one-point order crossover* [23] without mutation.

- *Environmental Selection*: The algorithm selects the best N_1 sets of cluster centers (from the initial N_1 sets and the two sets of offspring) as the new initial population for the next generation.

- *Stop Criterion*: The algorithm stops when it has iterated T times.

- *Final Population*: The algorithm outputs the best clustering results from the latest population.

Using the Memetic Algorithm with $N_1 = 10$, $N_2 = 4$, and $T = 20$, we performed cluster analysis on the three datasets under different parameter settings with different K values. Then, we obtain the optimal K value that yields the optimal cluster validity index value under each parameter setting for all the clusters. Table 3 shows the optimal K values under different clustering algorithms, distance measures, cluster validity indices and weather conditions in the three datasets.

6. FORECAST PERFORMANCE

Next, based on our analysis, we evaluate the accuracy of forecasts of the daily electricity demand for each smart meter. We use the ε-support vector regression (ε-SVR) method [26, 29] provided by the open source machine learning library, LIBSVM [7], as the forecasting tool. Specifically, in ε-SVR, the width of the ε-insensitive tube is set at 0.14286 (the default value suggested by the LIBSVM library); and the cost of errors is set at 4,096 for the Hsinchu dataset, 32 for the Taipei dataset, and 32 for the Tainan dataset.

Table 3: The optimal number of clusters suggested for each dataset under different clustering algorithms, distance measures, cluster validity indices and seasons

		PBM Index		DB Index	
		warm season	cold season	warm season	cold season
Taipei	K-Means	3	3	3	3
	K-Medoids-mean	2	2	4	3
	K-Medoids-min	5	5	3	4
Hsinchu	K-Means	3	3	3	3
	K-Medoids-mean	2	4	2	8
	K-Medoids-min	4	3	3	8
Tainan	K-Means	2	3	2	4
	K-Medoids-mean	3	2	5	3
	K-Medoids-min	4	5	2	5

Table 4: The number of smart meters suitable for forecast evaluations, when $d = 7$, in the three datasets

		Taipei	Hsinchu	Tainan
warm season	LOW floors	412	119	51
	MIDDLE floors	48	41	33
	HIGH floors	26	31	33
	Total	486	191	117
cold season	LOW floors	423	133	52
	MIDDLE floors	44	43	28
	HIGH floors	19	34	29
	Total	486	210	109

In addition, we perform *three-fold cross validation* for each dataset under different clustering parameter settings; and we use the mean absolute percentage error (MAPE) as the evaluation metric to measure the forecast accuracy for each smart meter. The MAPE value of the i-th smart meter is derived by

$$MAPE_i = 100 \times \frac{1}{p} \times \sum_{j=1}^{p} \frac{\left| V_{i,j} - \widehat{V_{i,j}} \right|}{V_{i,j}}; \qquad (17)$$

where $V_{i,j}$ is the true result of the j-th forecast on the i-th smart meter, $\widehat{V_{i,j}}$ is the j-th forecast value on the i-th smart meter, and p is the number of forecasts made for the i-th smart meter. The distribution of the MAPE values is skewed due to extreme values in general. Therefore, in the following discussion, we consider the 50% (i.e., median) and 80% MAPE values of all smart meters under different parameter settings.

6.1 Feature Selection

We use the *immediate last d contiguous days* of data instances (including the electricity demand and the other external factors) as the selected features for SVR forecasting. Intuitively, there exists a tradeoff in deciding the d value. The higher the value of d, the greater will be similarity between the lifestyles of the instances matched and the one to be forecast. However, using a large d value may reduce the number of matched instances, resulting in a failed or biased forecast.

In Figure 8, we compare the accuracy of forecasts of the daily electricity demand for households in the Taipei dataset with different d values, clustering algorithms, and cluster

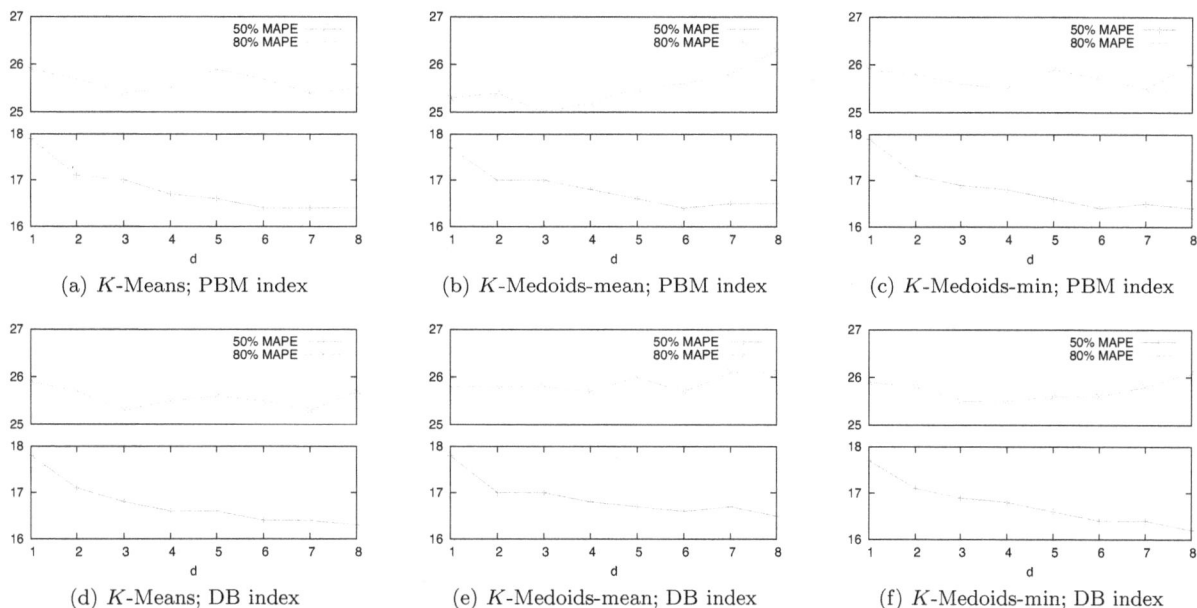

(a) K-Means; PBM index   (b) K-Medoids-mean; PBM index   (c) K-Medoids-min; PBM index

(d) K-Means; DB index   (e) K-Medoids-mean; DB index   (f) K-Medoids-min; DB index

Figure 8: Comparison of the 50% and 80% MAPE results of forecasting daily household-based electricity demand using the Taipei dataset with different d values, clustering algorithms, and cluster validity indices

validity indices. We observe that when $d = 7$, the medium (50%) MAPE value is either the first or the second minimal value among the d values in all test cases. The 80% MAPE value is also approximately minimal when $d = 7$. The observations also apply to the Hsinchu and Tainan datasets, but we do not provide the MAPE values here due to the page limitation. Therefore, we set $d = 7$ in the following evaluation. Using the d value, Table 4 shows the number of smart meters in each dataset that have eight contiguous days of electricity demand and are eligible for the following evaluation.

6.2 Forecast Results

In addition to the daily electricity demand, we consider the following three external factors in the evaluation of the forecast performance: the temperature, the floor number, and the type of day. When the temperature feature is considered, we append the daily average temperature record to each daily electricity demand instance in the dataset. We also include this feature in the SVR training set and test set. When the floor number feature is considered, we divide the dataset into three subsets based on the floor type (i.e., HIGH, MIDDLE, or LOW) of each smart meter in the dataset. Moreover, when the type of day feature is considered, we divide the dataset into two subsets based on whether the measurement was obtained on regular days (working weekdays and weekends) or holidays (non-working weekdays).

Table 5 shows the 50% and 80% MAPE results of forecasting daily electricity demand using the three datasets with different cluster parameter settings and different feature combinations. Each feature is labeled either T (true) or F (false) based on whether it is considered, and the labels of the three features are concatenated in the following order: temperature, floor number, and day type. For instance, 'TFF' refers to a case where we only consider the tempera-

ture, and 'FTF' refers to a case where we only consider the floor number feature.

The results in Table 5 show that, for the Taipei and Hsinchu scenarios, the accuracy of the forecasts derived by the PBM and DB indices is comparable; the best forecast performance is achieved when the K-Means clustering algorithm and the Euclidean distance are used together. However, for the Taipei scenario, the best forecast performance only occurs when the type of day feature is considered (i.e., FFT). This result seems to contradict our earlier findings (discussed in Section 4) that the demand for electricity is highly correlated to the temperature. There are three reasons for this phenomenon:

1. Although the earlier analysis showed a strong correlation between electricity demand and the temperature feature, the distribution per temperature value spans a wide range of electricity demands (c.f., Figure 5), so forecasting demand is a difficult task.

2. The earlier analysis was performed by dividing the dataset into the warm season subset and the cold season subset. This procedure cannot be used to forecast electricity demand because the daily average temperatures in a contiguous d-day period may not belong to the same season subset.

3. Some of the smart meters in the Taipei dataset are located in premises used for commercial activities, which are more responsive to holidays. By contrast, the other two datasets only contain residential properties.

As a consequence, the temperature feature does not improve the accuracy of forecasts of the daily electricity demand in the Taipei scenario.

The results in Table 5 also show that the best forecast performance for the Hsinchu scenario is only achieved when

Table 5: The 50% and 80% MAPE results of forecasting daily electricity demand using the three datasets with different cluster parameter settings and different feature combinations

			FFF	FFT	FTF	FTT	TFF	TFT	TTF	TTT
Taipei	PBM Index	K-Means	16.4/25.4	*16.4/25.2*	16.6/26.3	16.9/26.1	16.6/26.2	17.1/26.4	17.2/27.3	17.7/27.9
		K-Medoids-mean	16.5/25.8	16.5/26.0	16.8/26.5	16.8/26.8	16.9/26.3	17.2/26.4	17.1/27.2	17.7/27.4
		K-Medoids-min	16.5/25.5	16.6/25.8	16.7/26.4	17.0/27.1	16.8/26.7	17.4/27.1	17.5/27.3	18.2/28.8
	DB Index	K-Means	16.4/25.3	*16.4/25.2*	16.5/25.9	16.8/25.9	16.6/25.9	17.0/25.9	17.1/26.9	17.7/27.7
		K-Medoids-mean	16.7/26.1	16.6/26.2	16.9/26.5	16.9/26.9	16.7/26.6	17.2/27.3	17.2/27.4	17.7/28.3
		K-Medoids-min	16.4/25.8	16.4/25.8	16.8/26.2	16.8/26.6	16.5/26.0	17.0/26.5	17.1/26.9	17.5/27.8
Hsinchu	PBM Index	K-Means	21.9/39.3	22.4/38.3	*21.9/37.7*	23.0/40.0	33.3/64.0	29.3/54.3	30.4/60.1	34.1/75.1
		K-Medoids-mean	22.0/38.9	22.4/39.3	22.3/39.1	22.8/38.0	32.0/63.7	28.1/46.5	33.6/68.1	33.8/59.3
		K-Medoids-min	22.2/39.0	22.7/38.6	22.4/38.0	23.2/38.8	32.2/62.4	30.6/60.1	32.6/60.0	34.6/75.4
	DB Index	K-Means	21.9/39.3	22.4/38.3	*21.9/37.7*	23.0/40.0	33.3/64.0	29.3/54.3	30.4/60.1	34.1/75.1
		K-Medoids-mean	22.0/38.9	22.4/39.3	22.3/39.1	22.8/38.0	32.0/63.7	28.1/46.5	33.6/68.1	33.8/59.3
		K-Medoids-min	21.9/37.8	22.2/38.4	22.1/38.4	23.2/37.0	33.5/59.0	30.0/51.7	35.0/66.1	36.2/68.3
Tainan	PBM Index	K-Means	*20.1/32.3*	21.4/36.9	21.0/33.3	22.6/35.9	21.8/32.7	23.9/36.8	21.9/34.8	24.3/37.2
		K-Medoids-mean	20.5/33.3	21.2/35.8	21.3/34.1	22.8/35.8	22.2/34.0	23.0/33.1	23.0/33.5	23.7/35.5
		K-Medoids-min	20.8/36.0	21.0/36.7	22.3/35.6	23.3/37.9	21.2/35.7	23.5/36.0	23.4/35.8	25.2/37.9
	DB Index	K-Means	21.3/33.6	21.3/36.7	21.0/34.1	22.4/36.5	22.0/33.4	22.9/36.5	22.3/34.8	24.6/38.3
		K-Medoids-mean	21.3/33.8	22.3/36.7	22.6/33.6	24.3/35.1	22.5/32.9	23.3/36.1	24.1/34.0	24.9/36.2
		K-Medoids-min	21.1/34.2	21.4/35.7	21.9/34.4	22.1/36.2	21.3/33.3	23.6/36.2	23.1/33.9	25.4/39.1

Table 6: The 50% and 80% MAPE results of forecasting daily electricity demand using the Tainan dataset with different features and cluster parameter settings

		FXF	FXT	TXF	TXT
PBM Index	K-Means	15.9/21.1	16.9/21.2	17.8/21.9	18.1/24.9
	K-Medoids-mean	*15.6/20.9*	16.0/21.2	16.9/21.3	18.4/24.3
	K-Medoids-min	15.7/22.2	16.9/22.7	17.7/21.5	18.7/24.2
DB Index	K-Means	18.2/24.9	19.8/30.1	19.3/27.6	19.5/29.9
	K-Medoids-mean	18.6/23.6	21.0/31.8	19.3/26.5	20.1/31.7
	K-Medoids-min	18.2/25.2	21.4/31.6	18.0/25.0	20.9/29.7

the floor number feature is considered (i.e., FTF). This is because there are many vacancies on the HIGH floors of properties in the Hsinchu dataset, so the floor number feature has a strong influence on the forecasts of electricity demand. Moreover, we observe that the 80% MAPE values are greater than 46.5% when the temperature feature is considered (i.e., TFF, TFT, TTF, and TTT). One of the reasons is that the correlation of the electricity demand and the temperature is between weak and moderate in the Hsinchu dataset, and the misuse of the temperature feature degrades the prediction accuracy significantly.

With regard to the Tainan dataset, the best forecast performance is achieved when the K-Means algorithm and the PBM index are used, but none of the three features are considered. The reasons are as follows.

1. Tainan has a tropical climate, which means the temperatures are relatively high throughout the year. Thus, the temperature feature has less impact on forecasts of electricity demand.

2. Unlike the other two datasets, the Tainan dataset shows the electricity demand for each floor of a three-floor house. Therefore, the per-floor electricity demand depends more on the lifestyles of the household's residents than the floor number (i.e., LOW, MIDDLE, or HIGH).

3. The Tainan site is located in a purely residential area, so holidays have less effect on daily electricity demands.

We also evaluated the forecast accuracy by considering the total household electricity demand in the Tainan dataset (i.e., the electricity demand of the three floors in a building). The evaluation results are shown in Table 6, where 'X' means "don't-care" of the corresponding feature. The best forecast performance occurs when the parameter settings are the same as those in the per-floor case; however, the 50%/80% MAPE values improve significantly in the per-household results (15.6/20.9 compared to 20.1/32.3 in the per-floor case). The results confirm that there exists a lifestyle factor in the per-floor-based dataset. Nevertheless, by aggregating the electricity demand of floors in the same building, it is possible to derive accurate forecasts of electricity demand in the Tainan scenario.

7. CONCLUDING REMARKS

We have conducted in-depth data analysis and forecast of household electricity demand using three realistic datasets of different household lifestyles. The analysis shows that household electricity demand is highly correlated to the temperature, the floor number, and the type of day in all the datasets at different scales. Moreover, using various parameter settings for data clustering and the SVR method, we evaluate the accuracy of forecasts of daily electricity demand in the three datasets. The results demonstrate that there exists a life style diversity between the three datasets, and the best forecast performance of each dataset is derived under different parameter settings. Specifically, the medium MAPE of the best forecast achieved is 15.6%. Research on finer-grained forecasts of household electricity demand is ongoing. We hope to report the results in the near future.

8. ACKNOWLEDGEMENTS

This research was partially supported by the National Science Council (NSC 101-2628-E-001-004-MY3) and the Bureau of Energy of the Ministry of Economic Affairs, Taiwan.

9. REFERENCES

[1] Electricity load forecast using intelligent adaptive technology. http://neuron-ai.tuke.sk/competition/, 2001.

[2] Assessment of demand response and advanced metering. FERC Staff Report, October 2013.

[3] AERA, APA, and NCME. *Standard for Educational and Psychological Testing*. American Educational Research Association, 1999.

[4] N. Atamturk, M. Zafar, and P. Clanon. Electricity use and income: A review. Technical report, Policy and Planning Division Literature Review, California Public Utilities Commission, June 2012.

[5] S. Bubeck, M. Meila, and U. von Luxburg. How the initialization affects the stability of the k-means algorithm. *ESAIM: Probability and Statistics*, 16:436–452, January 2012.

[6] E. Castillo, B. Guijarro, and A. Alonso. Electricity load forecast using functional networks. In *EUNITE Symposium - Competition on Electricity Load Forcast Using Intelligent Technologies*, 2001.

[7] C.-C. Chang and C.-J. Lin. LIBSVM - A Library for Support Vector Machines. http://www.csie.ntu.edu.tw/ cjlin/libsvm.

[8] B.-J. Chen, M.-W. Chang, and C.-J. Lin. Load forecasting using support vector Machines: a study on EUNITE competition 2001. *IEEE Transactions on Power Systems*, 19(4):1821–1830, November 2004.

[9] D. L. Davies and D. W. Bouldin. A Cluster Separation Measure. *IEEE Transactions on Pattern Analysis and Machine Intelligence*, PAMI-1(2):224 – 227, April 1979.

[10] D. Esp. Adaptive logic networks for east slovakian electrical load forecasting. In *EUNITE Symposium - Competition on Electricity Load Forcast Using Intelligent Technologies*, 2001.

[11] A. Jain and B. Satish. Clustering based Short Term Load Forecasting using Support Vector Machines. In *IEEE Bucharest Power Tech Conference*, 2009.

[12] W. Kowalczyk. Averaging and data enrichment: two approaches to electricity load forecasting. In *EUNITE Symposium - Competition on Electricity Load Forcast Using Intelligent Technologies*, 2001.

[13] J. B. Kruskal and M. Liberman. *Time Warps, String Edits, and Macromolecules - The Theory and Practice of Sequence Comparison*, chapter The Symmetric Time-Warping Problem: from Continuous to Discrete, pages 125–161. Reading. Addison-Wesley Publishing Co., Massachusetts, September 1983.

[14] A. Lewandowski, F. Sandner, and P. Protzel. Prediction of electricity load by modeling the temperature dependencies. In *EUNITE Symposium - Competition on Electricity Load Forcast Using Intelligent Technologies*, 2001.

[15] A. Lotfi. Application of Learning Fuzzy Inference Systems in Electricity Load Forecast. In *EUNITE Symposium - Competition on Electricity Load Forcast Using Intelligent Technologies*, 2001.

[16] J. MacQueen. Some methods for classification and analysis of multivariate observations. In *Berkeley Symposium on Mathematical Statistics and Probability*, 1967.

[17] F. Martinez-Alvarez, A. Troncoso, J. C. Riquelme, and J. S. AguilarRuiz. Energy Time Series Forecasting Based on Pattern Sequence Similarity. *IEEE Transactions on Knowledge and Data Engineering*, 23(8):1230–1243, August 2011.

[18] B. L. Miller and D. E. Goldberg. Genetic Algorithms, Tournament Selection, and the Effects of Noise. *Complex Systems*, 8:1930212, 1995.

[19] A. K. Mishra, D. E. Irwin, P. J. Shenoy, J. Kurose, and T. Zhu. Smartcharge: Cutting the electricity bill in smart homes with energy storage. In *ACM e-Energy*, 2012.

[20] P. Moscato. On Evolution, Search, Optimization, Genetic Algorithms and Martial Arts: Towards Memetic Algorithms. C3P Report 826. California Institute of Technology,, 1989.

[21] M. K. Pakhira, S. Bandyopadhyay, and U. Maulik. Validity index for crisp and fuzzy clusters. *Pattern Recognition*, 37(3):487–501, March 2004.

[22] E. Pelikan. Middle-Term Electric Load Forecasting by Time Series Decomposition. In *EUNITE Symposium - Competition on Electricity Load Forcast Using Intelligent Technologies*, 2001.

[23] R. Poli and W. B. Langdon. Genetic Programming with One-Point Crossover. In *Soft Computing in Engineering Design and Manufacturing*, 1997.

[24] A. P. Reynolds, G. Richards, and V. J. Rayward-Smith. The Application of K-medoids and PAM to the Clustering of Rules. In *International Conference on Intelligent Data Engineering and Automated Learning*, 2004.

[25] W. Shen, V. Babushkin, Z. Aung, and W. L. Woon. An ensemble model for day-ahead electricity demand time series forecasting. In *ACM e-Energy*, 2013.

[26] A. J. Smola and B. Scholkopf. A tutorial on support vector regression. *Statistics and Computing*, 14(3):199–222, August 2004.

[27] D. M. Solomon, R. L. Winter, A. G. Boulanger, R. N. Anderson, and L. L. Wu. Forecasting Energy Demand in Large Commercial Buildings Using Support Vector Machine Regression. Technical Report CUCS-040-11, Department of Computer Science, Columbia University, 2011.

[28] P.-N. Tan, M. Steinbach, and V. Kumar. *Introduction to Data Mining*. Addison-Wesley, 2006.

[29] V. N. Vapnik. *Statistical Learning Theory*. Wiley-Interscience, 1st edition, September 1998.

The Cost of Virtue: Reward As Well As Feedback Are Required to Reduce User ICT Power Consumption

Yi Yu
School of Computer Science
University of St Andrews
St Andrews, Fife, KY16 9SX, UK
yy235@st-andrews.ac.uk

Saleem N. Bhatti
School of Computer Science
University of St Andrews
St Andrews, Fife, KY16 9SX, UK
saleem@st-andrews.ac.uk

ABSTRACT

We show that students in a school lab environment will change their behaviour to be more energy efficient, when appropriate incentives are in place, and when measurement-based, real-time feedback about their energy usage is provided. Rewards incentivise 'non-green' users to be 'green' as well as encouraging those users who already claim to be 'green'. Measurement-based feedback improves user energy awareness and helps users to explore and adjust their use of computers to become 'greener', but is not sufficient by itself. In our measurements, weekly mean group energy use as a whole reduced by up to 16%; and weekly individual user energy consumption reduced by up to 56% *during active use*. The findings are drawn from our longitudinal study that involved 83 Computer Science students; lasted 48 weeks across 2 academic years; monitored a total of 26778 hours of active computer use; collected approximately 2TB of raw data.

Categories and Subject Descriptors

J.m [**Computer Applications**]: Miscellaneous

Keywords

user behaviour; energy usage; energy efficiency; energy monitoring; energy feedback; green ICT

1. INTRODUCTION

ICT systems consume significant and increasing amount of energy on the planet, with estimated total CO_2 comparable to the aviation industry [18]. As the use of ICT grows, it is increasingly important to improve energy efficiency in the use of ICT systems.

Forrester Research [21] and Gartner [11] reported that there were over 1 billion PCs in use worldwide by the end of 2008, and the total will surpass 2 billion by 2010. Gartner predicted [12] that consumer ICT devices, including PCs,

e-Energy'14, June 11–13, 2014, Cambridge, UK.
Copyright 2014 ACM 978-1-4503-2819-7/14/06 ...$15.00 .
http://dx.doi.org/10.1145/2602044.2602063.

tablets and mobile phones, will increase by a total of 2.4 billion units in 2013, reaching over 2.9 billion by 2017.

However, the aggregated energy waste due to inefficient *usage* is still high. For instance, it is estimated that US$2.8 billion was wasted in 2009 in the US by ~108 million office PCs left on when not in use [1]. While technical solutions for managing such desktop systems continue to mature, *modest energy savings from the user would scale up and yield significant impact.* How can we motivate users to improve energy efficiency in their use of ICT systems? What changes in their use of ICT systems are they willing to make?

1.1 Motivation and Approach

We take the position that: (i) there is the potential to reduce users' energy wastage; and (ii) it is possible to motivate users to improve energy efficiency, both through encouraging change in user behaviour, and not just relying on systems-level (hardware and software) interventions.

People using portable devices (e.g. smart phones, tablets, laptops) conserve battery power to achieve longer use by adjusting the ways they operate their devices. Common power saving techniques include setting device screen to auto turn off sooner when idle; dimming the screen brightness when possible; keeping WiFi, Bluetooth and/or other wireless communication interfaces off when not in use; using some kind of task manager to auto kill inactive background processes on smart phones (although this technique is proven unnecessary in modern mobile operating systems). In contrast, people using desktop computers, do not have concerns for battery life, and might not be incentivised to employ energy efficient behaviour. Unlike portable devices, desktop computers may not have even the most basic power usage indicators to help users self-assess their power usage.

Our objective was to find out, without changing users' objectives or their tools (lab computers):

- if ICT users can change their behaviour in using computers and improve energy efficiency;

- what level of effort they are willing to make to improve energy efficiency;

- how feedback on energy usage and incentives (rewards) help them to improve their energy efficiency.

1.2 Contribution and Structure of This Paper

We show that within a university computer teaching lab, feedback on users' individual power use coupled with some small financial rewards produce energy savings. We observed a mean of 16% group energy saving, and up to 56%

individual energy saving. The specific novelty of our study is to consider *what change in behaviour users are willing to accept and what actions they are willing to take whilst they are using the computers*. This is complementary to existing work that considers system-level interventions and mechanisms that are designed to function without the cooperation or knowledge of users, when computers are *not in use*, e.g. send computers to sleep when not in use [2].

Incentives together with feedback about energy usage were required to sustain energy-saving behaviour: feedback alone was not sufficient, as personal preferences of completing work, convenience and/or certain workstation configuration have overwhelming priority over energy saving. We observed that there was much room for improvement amongst users who thought they were already 'green', and that the additional information we gave through a simple desktop feedback application helped them become 'greener'.

We first present some related work in Section 2 covering well-known power management techniques in the industry, previous research on using feedback to reduce power wastage in household environments, and some relevant behavioural studies. We then describe our experiment design in Section 3. In Section 4 and 5 we present our observations and discuss their implications. Limitations of our work are discussed in Section 6. We conclude with a summary and indications for future work in Section 7.

2. RELATED WORK

We made passive observations of user behaviour, and examined the impact of *feedback* about their energy usage with the role of *incentives*. Our intention was to observe behaviour and what impacts the behaviour of users, rather than effect permanent behaviour change with respect to energy usage.

2.1 User Behaviour

Demand Side Reduction, or Demand Side Management (DSM), is a technique primarily used in the electric power industry to reduce consumers' demand for energy. Various methods, including financial incentives and education to encourage consumers, are used to reduce energy usage during peak hours and shift the power demanding jobs to off-peak periods such as night time [4]. It demonstrates reduction in energy usage by changing user behaviour, rather than focusing solely on improving the energy efficiency of hardware.

Kollmuss et. al. [14] showed that people are concerned about the environment, but this does not always translate into protective actions. There are social, cognitive and behavioural factors explaining why many people have not yet adopted changes to help reduce energy consumption.

Fogg's behaviour model [9] suggests three crucial factors that are required to change human behaviours: *sufficient motivation*, *sufficient ability* and an *effective trigger*. In most cases, people rarely have completely no motivation or ability towards a reasonable target behaviour. Effective persuasive techniques will help to boost their motivation and/or ability, followed by the right trigger to realise the desired behaviour.

The UK Cabinet Office Behavioural Insights Team [5] presented three of the most significant insights from behavioural economics and psychology grounded by academic evidence: *Discounting the future*. People may prefer a small discount or reward today rather than a larger reward in the future [16] – this is the reason why people do not always pay now to get more saving in the future.

Social norms. Behavioural studies show that people are greatly influenced by what others around them are doing. *Defaults*. Behavioural economics tells us that individuals tend to go with the default options/settings, often regardless of whether it maximises individual or collective well-being.

So, in our study, we tested what changes users were prepared to make in order to be more energy efficient. We wanted to see what simple information and/or education they would respond to. We used prizes as incentives and surveys as triggers to remind users of their tasks. Also, by focussing on a whole class, even though we wanted to measure individual users, we were ensuring that such behaviour would be known to all users, (even those that eventually chose not to participate in the study), and so a social norm was established for that context.

2.2 Power Usage Feedback

Use of indirect energy feedback in household environments, e.g. frequent billing showing historical usage and a detailed listing of energy consumption, has been proven effective in promoting energy awareness and energy saving behaviours by a Norwegian power supplier in 1999 [20]. Also, psychologists, power providers and the UK government also conducted experiments and determined direct power feedback was useful for energy savings in household environments [3,7]. They used small desktop displays to show realtime and/or historical energy usage, as well as the estimated electricity costs in households. The results showed that most people paid attention to such information, and achieved 5-15% power savings by reducing their energy wastage in the use of air conditioning systems, lighting, etc. [6].

It has been observed in both domestic and office environments, that users have strong impact on energy demand and usage [15,17]. Through surveys, people expressed that realtime and historical data of their energy use helped them to reflect on the impacts of their activities on energy consumption and possible wastage [17]. However, raw data without annotations provide little information to non-expert users, but finely annotated data may pose privacy concerns [17] and lead to resistance towards energy saving by feedback.

Yun et al. [22] conducted several similar studies in 2013 with a total of 22 people across a university lab, a university office and a government research lab. Their results showed that up to 40% overall energy savings can be achieved based on 6 people's performances at the university office, provided users are (1) educated to save energy; (2) given energy saving advice whenever applicable; (3) allowed to self-monitor power usage; (4) able to compare their performances to others; (5) given easy and simple ways to control electric appliances around them; (6) given rewards for achieving target energy saving behaviour.

In our study, we have also used the 6 points identified by Yun et al. [22]. We created a simple graphical application that gave feedback to the users. We also provided energy saving 'tips' for users, as well as a briefing session for all users. We informed users of the way in which the workstation configuration could be modified for energy efficiency. We also held competitions with prizes as incentives to save energy. However, the study by Yun et al. [22] was concerned with the whole office and lab environment, and did not consider the sue of the computer systems in detail as we have.

3. A 2-YEAR MEASUREMENT STUDY

We measured the use of energy and the activities of undergraduate users on the teaching lab workstations at the School of Computer Science, University of St Andrews. Over the teaching periods in academic years 2011/12 and 2012/13, we conducted the same experiment once in each year, with a few small modifications in the second year. In the rest of this paper, we use the labels shown in Table 1 to refer to different periods of the 2-year study.

Table 1: Labels used for periods of study and for the datasets collected from those periods.

Academic Year	Semester	Label
2011/12	1	Y1S1
	2	Y1S2
	1+2	Y1
2012/13	1	Y2S1
	2	Y2S2
	1+2	Y2

Guided by Fogg's design process of creating persuasive technologies [10], we adapted both Fogg's behaviour model for persuasive design [9] and Geller's behaviour-change model [13]. Each run of the experiment was divided into four stages, involving three types of actions that help participants to move onto the next stage. Measurement of system usage was in progress throughout the period to determine actual energy usage, with user surveys to determine intent, motivation and perception of users during the study.

Stage 1. Unconscious incompetence, where participants do not save energy because they do not think or know about the energy issue. The first survey in the series was designed to gather general background of each participant so we know which stages the participants considered themselves at.

Action 1. After the first survey, S1, some general information on the negative impacts of electricity generation and six energy saving tips were given to the participants so they learnt (1) how to reduce energy consumption on lab computers; (2) why it is environmentally important to do so.

Stage 2. Conscious incompetence, where participants have been educated but still do not take many actions to save energy due to lack of motivation. We designed the second survey, S2, to find out how many of them have moved onto this stage.

Action 2. A 4- to 5-week energy efficiency 'competition', with multiple prizes (vouchers and USB memory sticks), was run to encourage participants to reduce their energy usage in their use of lab computers. Over selected periods during and after the competition, individual's real-time power usage feedback was displayed via an on-screen applet on each lab computer.

Stage 3. Conscious competence, where participants are not only aware of why and how to save energy, but also take actions to save energy on lab computers.

Action 3. Energy efficiency competition ends. Real-time energy usage feedback remains available at all times on all lab computers. Survey S3 recorded user attitudes.

Stage 4. Unconscious competence, where participants try to reduce power consumption without the incentive of prizes. Survey S4 recorded user attitudes.

Table 3 in Appendix D shows a detailed experiment timeline over two years.

At the beginning of each year, over 40 participants (first and second year undergraduate students) were recruited for our study. An individual user's power consumption and activities on the workstations – 24" iMac units – were recorded. Measurements used the iMac's built-in power sensors along with some standard software (such as *ps*), with some of our own software for orchestration, management and collection (Appendix B). We also gathered participants' attitudes and motivations towards energy saving via 4 surveys (S1 to S4) through the first semester of each year for qualitative analysis and cross reference against measurements.

A control group was not used because: 1) there is no group interaction or collaboration, and so individual users may behave differently; 2) the focus is on potential changes of individual behaviour; 3) users do not have exactly the same workload or habits of using lab computers, therefore it did not make sense to compare one group against another. As a result, at the beginning of each academic year, we used 2 weeks to gather baseline measurements of individual participants. This baseline was then used in the subsequent weeks of the study to determine individuals' changes in computer usage. (Appendix A details about the participant group.)

During the study, participants' identities were automatically anonymised, from both their survey submissions and automatically collected workstation measurements, using a one-way hash algorithm to protect their privacy, and guarantee the uniqueness of individual user's data.

3.1 Power Usage Feedback for Users

We used a simple application – a menu bar applet (power applet) – to provide information about power usage to the users. In Y1, our power applet showed very simple numerical screen brightness levels, real-time power reading and cumulative energy usage of the current session – see Figure 1. Users were able to change the display unit of cumulative energy usage to Watt-hour, mass of carbon footprint (grams), volume of CO_2 emission (litres) or the cost of electricity (pennies). Although many participants liked it and found it useful (27 out of 31 participants), we also received some suggestions and requests for improvements.

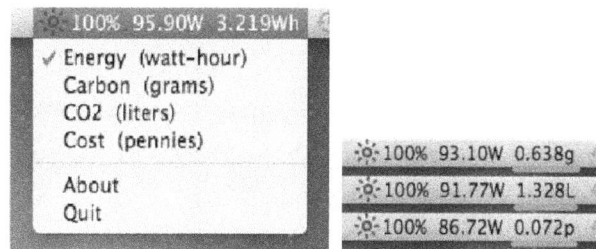

Figure 1: The menu bar power applet used in Y1. Users were able to select the display unit of total session energy consumption from 4 options.

In Y2, we improved the power applet with new features including colour-coded graphical indicators – see Figure 2. We added: green/amber/red 'smiley' faces for low/moderate/high power consumption levels with predefined thresholds based on observations in Y1; live plots of real-time and historical power usage; rate of cost and carbon emissions, in addition to power usage.

To distinguish the effect of incentives (prizes of vouchers and some USB sticks for completing the surveys) and the power applet, we deployed and removed the power applet at certain times from week 8 to 12 in Y1S1, and kept the power applet on in Y1S2 and Y2S2 to compare between Y1S1 and Y2S1, respectively.

3.2 Power and System Usage Monitoring

Using iMac's built-in power sensors and standard Unix utilities, we were able to implement a single, lightweight program that collects, anonymises, and uploads both computer power measurements and participants' computer usage (more details in Appendix B). The collected data are described in Section 4.1.

3.3 Surveys

Four surveys were conducted during the experiment. In every survey, we asked our participants to self-evaluate their current awareness and attitude toward energy saving by choosing one out of six options that best described themselves. From this, we derived what stages in the behavioural model that each participant was at, and monitored the transitions between different stages of the behavioural model.

Background survey (S1): we recorded the general understanding, knowledge, awareness, habits and attitudes of users towards energy- saving at both home and school. We asked users: how motivated they were to save energy; what could motivate them to save energy; their thoughts on what level of information and feedback on energy usage could help them to save energy.

Survey on energy saving tips (S2): we recoded how users responded to the energy-saving tips that we gave them. We wanted to compare their declared motivation with their use of energy-saving tips, and what demotivated them from carrying out these energy-saving tips.

Energy efficiency competition feedback survey (S3): we recorded if the prizes had motivated the participants to save energy, and in what ways if the feedback application was useful to them.

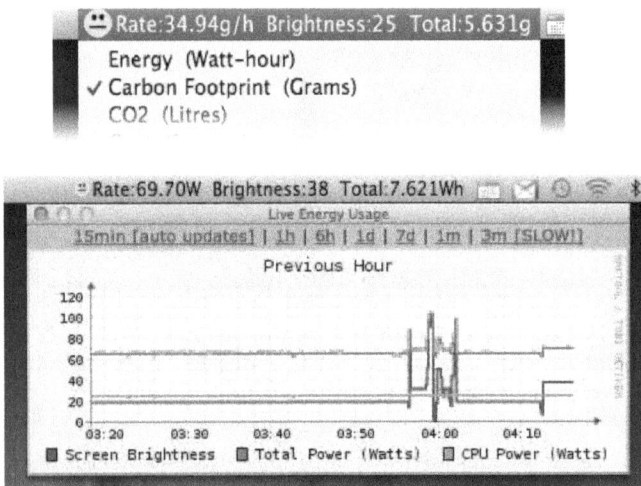

Figure 2: The improved power applet used in Y2, with a colour indicator, rate of power consumption in selected unit, and the option of viewing live plots of historical power usage.

Final survey (S4): the final survey recorded if participants' motivations to save energy had changed after the experiment, and how significant the menu bar power applet was as a reminder to save energy.

4. RESULTS AND OBSERVATIONS

Both qualitative and quantitative data show that our users changed their behaviour. We observed that 'non-green' users became 'green', and saw that 'green' users become 'greener'. We also observed a few exceptions. We refer to the behavioural Stages listed in Section 3.

4.1 Collected Data

Our monitoring tool captured one snapshot of computer power measurements and process status every 1s during active user sessions, and every 10s while the computer was idling. Table 2 shows the metadata of these collected data.

Table 2: Metadata of our experiment and collected data.

	Y1	Y2	Unit
Users	45	47	person
- In both Y1 and Y2	9	9	person
- First year student	28	26	person
- Second year student	13	17	person
- Other	4	4	person
Monitored Hosts	72	72	iMac 10,1
Collection Duration	24	24	week
	4032	4032	hour
User Sessions	9500	7150	session
- Duration	15388.9	11388.9	hour
- Samples	55.4	41.0	million
Collected Data	860	1220	GB
- User data	443.9	690.5	GB

4.2 Individual User's Self-Assessments

A user's change in attitude was determined by tracing their responses to the series of surveys in each year. If a user missed out one or more surveys, his/her data were considered incomplete and excluded from the analysis, so we only consider continuous, progressive trends and changes. So, another challenge was to keep users engaged throughout our experiment.

In all surveys, high percentages of users considered themselves to have good awareness and attitudes about energy saving. Based on the model in Section 3, users considered themselves already at Stage 3 or better. There were few users at Stage 2 (aware of the issue and possible solutions, but lacking motivation to act). Overall, the self assessment results were much more positive than we had expected. No user in our study was averse to saving energy, or at Stage 1.

Overall, the attitudes of users were stable, but on an individual basis, some self-assessments moved between Stage 2 and 3+. Figure 3 illustrates the changes between surveys. While 40% or more of users assessed themselves as being consistent throughout the study, the rest felt their attitude had either improved or worsened, with individual positive and negative responses cancelling each other out, hence little change observable in overall distributions for the group as a whole. Although up to 30% of users had expressed their

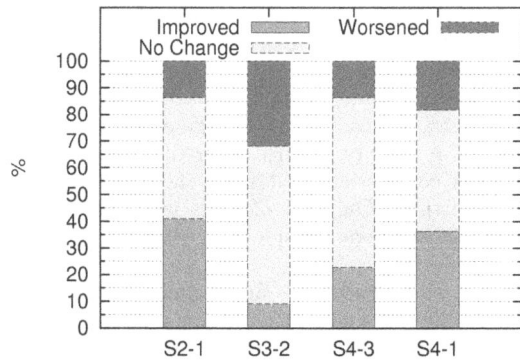

Self-Evaluation Changes - Y1S1 (22 participants)

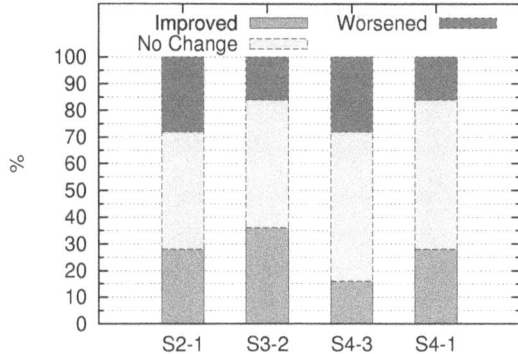

Y2S1 (25 participants)

Figure 3: Attitude changes between surveys. Data presented are from those who completed all four surveys during our experiment. 'Sn-m' on the X axis stands for comparison of response to survey n compared to survey m.

attitudes or behaviours to be less positive in between surveys, they were still at Stage 2 or higher, meaning they were at least all aware of the energy issue, but perhaps lacked motivation to be more energy efficient.

Even though the sequences of changes in both years were statistically insignificant, we were able to tell that the vast majority of our users considered themselves energy-conscious throughout our study. However, as we see in the next section, their measured behaviour did not always match their self-assessments.

4.3 Exceptional Observations

Although most users' self-assessments matched their measured computer and power usage, a few contradictory exceptions were observed.

Better attitude but worse power efficiency – one participant, P65 (a pseudonym), reported improved motivation and attitude towards energy saving in Y2S1. However, the measured power changes for that user showed the opposite. Neither reward nor feedback motivated P65 to reduce power consumption.

Worse attitude but better power efficiency – user P03 had shifted his/her self-assessment from Stage 3 towards Stage 2 over Y1S1. However, we found P03's energy saving improvement (> 10%) was consistent over the period. Similarly, self-assessments of participant P12 worsened over time, but his/her measured energy-efficiency improved.

4.4 Initial Survey – User Motivation

From S1 (background survey) we found our users in Y1S1 and Y2S1 were reasonably consistent in terms of how motivated they were to save energy (see Appendix C). The majority of them expressed they were already motivated to save energy at the beginning of the study in each year. Approximately half of users claimed they actively engaged in energy saving actions in other parts of their daily lives. However, similar numbers of users lacked the motivation to save energy. They did not always remember to apply energy-saving techniques, therefore could potentially be responsive to test if our on-screen power applet could act as a reminder to save energy at later stages of our experiment.

In Y1S1, every user claimed to be motivated to save energy. Only one of them admitted not knowing how to save energy. In Y2S1, although two users expressed no motivation to save energy, they were open to receive more information on this issue.

At the start of both years, participants generally behaved differently at their residence and in the lab. At this stage, some of the users who saved energy at their residence also gave other motivations: *pressure from other flat mates to save on energy bills, which is separate from my own desire to save money; to prevent the predicted energy crisis that will cause blackouts within the next 2 decades; to prevent global warming; moral conscience;* or simply *to protect electronic devices.*

4.5 Energy Saving Tips

Six energy-saving tips were given to users in order to help them more effectively reduce energy consumption when they used lab computers. Not all tips were easy to carry out, and we deliberately used these to observe how much effort the users were willing to make in order to save energy in the lab.

The six tips (in abbreviated form) are listed below. Brief explanations on how and why these tips could reduce energy wastage were given to users.

1. Reduce screen brightness.

2. Use 'lightweight' applications (with reduced CPU and disk usage).

3. Reduce the use of streaming audio and video, e.g. Flash media players embedded in web pages.

4. Block unwanted web content with a browser add-on.

5. Quit unused applications completely rather than leaving them in the background.

6. Turn off the computer after use.

Figure 4 shows the feedback on energy-saving tips gathered from both survey S2 (pre-competition) and survey S3 (post-competition). Ideally, an overall balanced pentagon shape is expected for each tip given, meaning the user finds the tip understandable (U), sensible (S), easy (E) to carry out, is motivated (M) to use it, and would actively (A) practice it. (Note that this is irrespective of how effective such tips are.) We found that only Tips 1 and 5 were successful in this respect. Tip 2 was the least successful (smallest pentagon): although it was understandable and seemed sensible, it was somewhat difficult to carry out, hence low popularity. Tips 3, 4 and 6 gained reasonably high and balanced votes

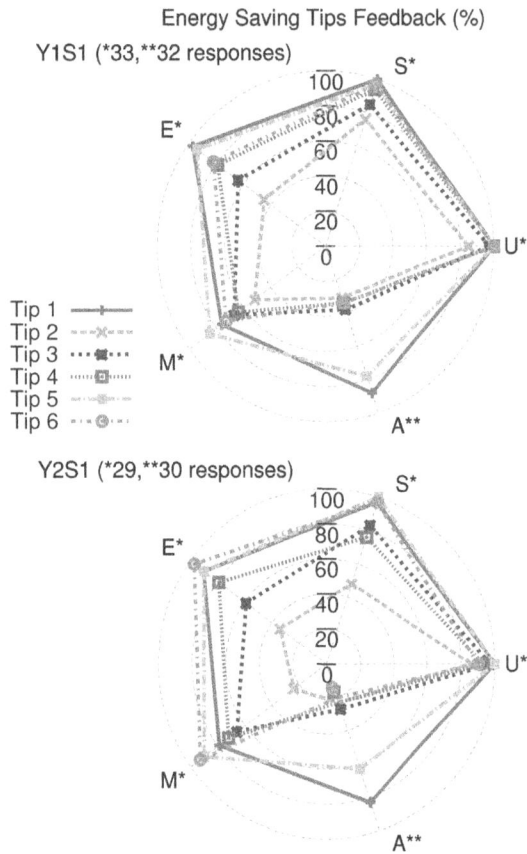

Figure 4: Feedback on energy-saving tips for Y1S1 and Y2S1. U: understandable; S: sensible; E: easy to carry out; M: motivated to use; A: actively practised during competition.

in U, S, E and M, but did not get practised much during the competition (see Section 5.1). Note that Tip 6 is periphery to our study, as our key aim was to find what actions and behaviour change users would accept *whilst using the computers*.

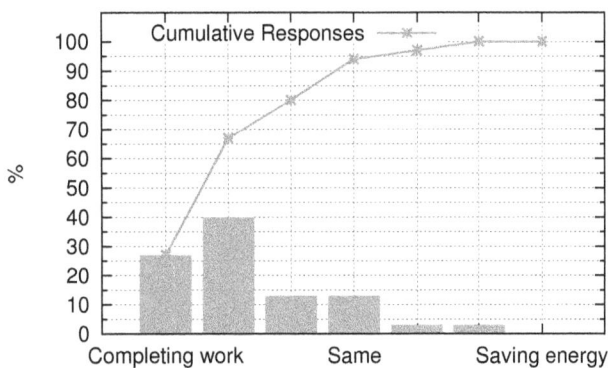

Figure 5: Distribution of users' personal preferences of completing their work vs saving energy in Y2S1. (33 responses)

Based on user's performances and feedback in Y1S1, we asked users in Y2S1, after the energy efficiency competition, a new question on the balance between completing their work and saving energy on a 7-point Likert Scale. As Figure 5 shows, despite being educated, energy aware and given incentives to save energy, as high as 80% of the 33 respondents gave more preference to getting their work done. 13% consider completing their work and saving energy are equally important. Only 6% of users were biased towards energy saving, but none considered saving energy to be the most important.

Our users made reasonable and balanced choices on the adoption of different energy saving tips over time. Figure 6 shows the evolution of the adoption rates of tips from survey S2 to S4. After high adoption rates during the 'try-out' period (before S2), use of tips dropped.

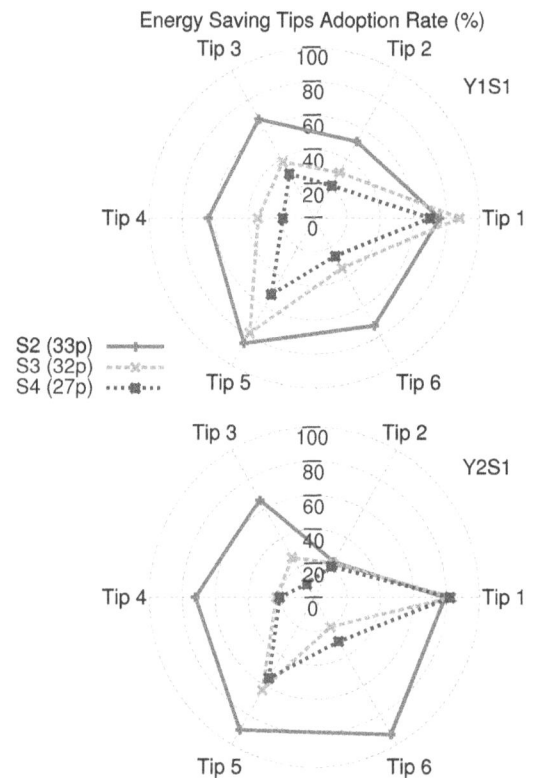

Figure 6: Adoption rates of energy saving tips by users who were motivated to save energy, recoded in surveys S2, S3 and S4. The overall rates decreased over time due to personal preferences, practicability and school/system restrictions. Tip 1 and 5 retained high adoption rates because they were the easiest to carry out.

4.6   Feedback is Welcomed and Helps Users

Measurement-based feedback is the most accurate and straightforward way to make users aware of their energy usage and potentially help improve energy efficiency.

In Y1S1, 97% of 39 users thought information on personal energy usage would help them to save energy in the lab. Also considered to be helpful was information on the School's energy usage as a whole (82% of users), and their peers' energy usage (77% of users), as well as more information on how to save energy (79% of users). Users suggested that a reward programme would make a significant difference.

Similar responses were received in Y2S1 (32 responses). 94% considered information on personal energy usage would help them to save energy at school; 78% wanted information on the School's energy usage as a whole and their peers' energy usage. 63% asked for more information on how to save energy (a reduction on the previous year, due to an energy-saving campaign at the beginning of the semester organised by the University and not part of our study).

By the end of Y2S1, 87% out of 30 users who submitted feedback on the power applet liked the enhanced version of the applet.

4.7 Measured Changes in Power Consumption

While almost every user reported themselves 'green' with no significant attitude change in surveys, there were significant changes in their measured power consumptions over the 2-year period. Over 75% of users in Y1S1 and over 85% in Y2S1 had a trend of decreasing power consumption when they used the lab computers. Many users were not as 'green' as they thought, and they had become 'greener' through participation in the experiment. (More discussion in Section 5.5.)

Trends of power consumptions per semester were identified by mechanically producing the best-fit gradient from a series of percentage changes (Δ) in mean weekly power consumption, compared against the baseline:

$$\Delta = \frac{WeeklyAveragePower - BaselinePower}{BaselinePower} \times 100\%$$

Potentially, we might expect 4 types of patterns: (1) a series of overall decreasing measurements; (2) a series of overall increasing measurements; (3) a series of measurements with big, arbitrary variations; (4) a series of measurements with small, arbitrary variations. After eliminating incomplete data, we visually inspected each user's data per semester and saw no indication of patterns (3) or (4). Therefore, we were able to summarise our observation in one simple plot (Figure 7).

From Figure 7, an overall positive result was observed in Y1S1 and Y2S1. A reduction of power usage can be observed through the competition periods when the feedback and information were both provided, and sustained till the end of the semester (Figure 8).

In the second semester of each year, the feedback (power applet) was available, but there was no incentive (no competition with prizes). As high as 65% of users Y1S2 and 75% of users in Y2S2 seemed to forget about saving energy and gradually increased their power consumption towards the end of semester.

5. ANALYSIS AND DISCUSSION

5.1 Choosing Effective Energy Saving Tips

During the competition (Figure 4), Tips 1 and 5 gained significant popularity in both years due to their simplicity and ease of use. Other tips were only practised by around 30% to 40% of users in Y1S1 and even fewer in Y2S1, despite incentives provided. These numbers were much lower than those who claimed to be motivated to want to adopt

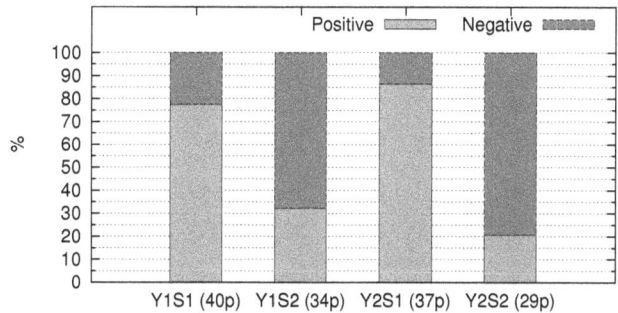

Figure 7: Proportions of positive (decreasing power consumption) and negative (increasing power consumption) trends in users' power usage. In both years, Semester 1 did have a competition (incentives) but Semester 2 did not.

energy saving actions prior to the competition. The primary reasons why users may be averse to using the tips varied.

Tip 1 (Reduce screen brightness.) Personal preference of bright, high contrast screens over energy saving.

Tip 2 (Use lightweight applications.) In both years, this was voted the most difficult tip to carry out. One example we gave was to use a simple text editor to write programmes instead of using complex, graphical IDEs. The users have argued that (a) they did not have a choice since first and second year students are required to use Eclipse, a relatively heavyweight IDE, to complete their coursework; (b) personal preference of tools/software that is most appropriate or convenient for the task, as it is believed that power could also be saved if the task was completed quicker. (c) There is no standard metric to tell which programs are more lightweight than others. Our power applet does not provide sufficiently fine-grained feedback per application to assist users to make such choices.

Tip 3 (Reduce use of audio and video.) Personal preference of online entertainment services. Some users did not often stream audio or video in labs anyway hence this tip did not apply to them.

Tip 4 (Block unwanted web content.) (a) Some users mistook that if they installed a browser add-on on a lab computer, other users who use this machine would be affected, hence were reluctant to do so out of goodwill. (b) It was troublesome to install browser add-ons on lab computers, or the installation would not succeed due to system configuration restrictions. However, we found out that 60% to 80% of users were willing to make such efforts to save energy. (c) General unpleasant experience with browser add-ons, hence rejecting all of them. (d) Unwillingness to block advertisements, in order to support websites, developers and free online services that rely on revenue from advertisements.

Tip 5 (Quit unused applications.) Personal preference for quick access to background applications (i.e. work efficiency) over energy saving (see Figure 5).

Tip 6 (Turn off computer after use.) This was periphery to our study, as we were concerned with energy savings during use of the computers. However, it is interesting to note the large impact it can have, as has been observed by others, e.g. [2]. Some users did not want to cause inconvenience for other lab users out of goodwill, although we

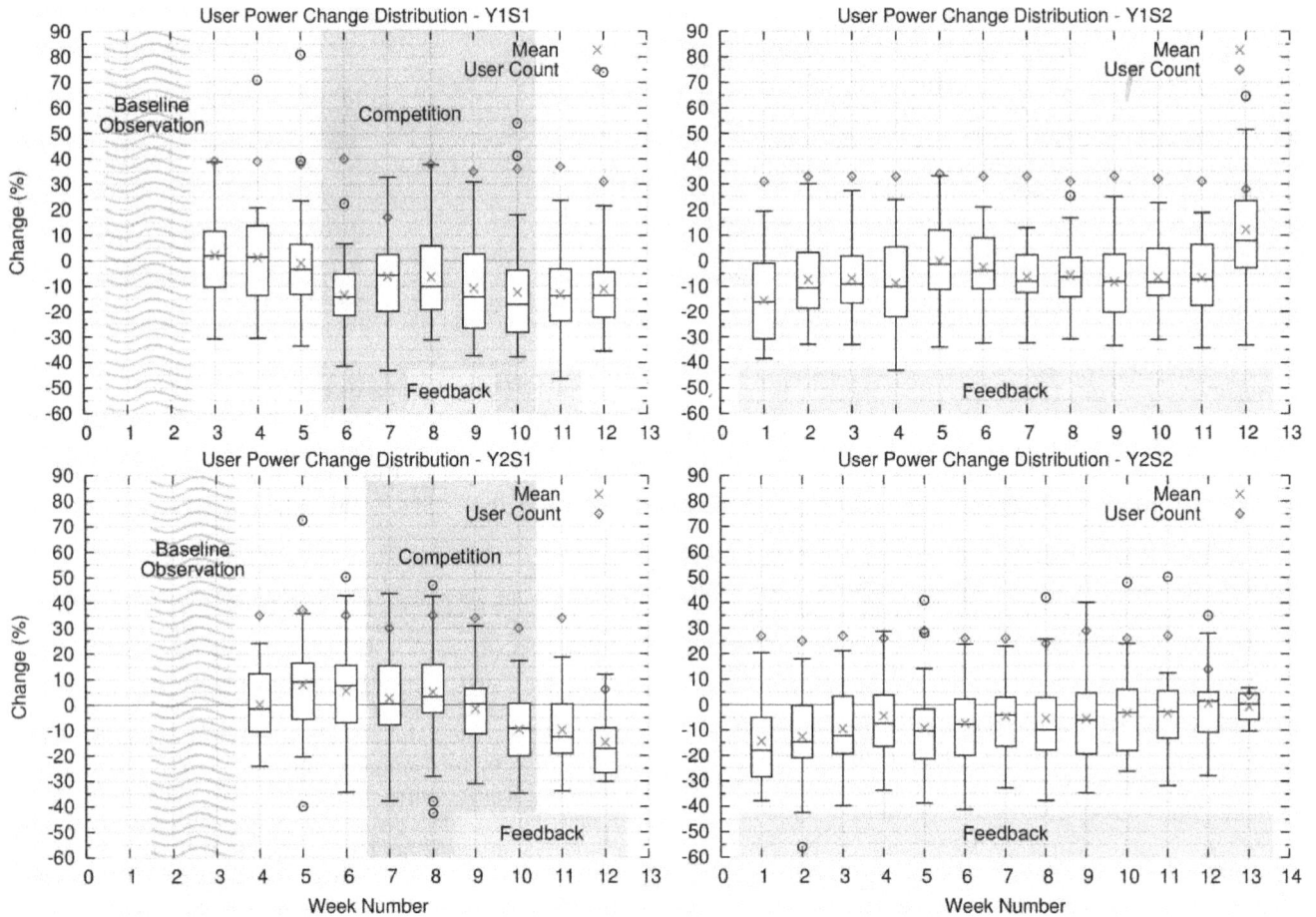

Figure 8: Distributions of users' power changes per week per semester using boxplot. A user's power change in a given week is calculated using the equation and description in Section 4.7 (the mean values taken over the duration of individual user sessions). The 'Change (%)" on the vertical axes are with respect to the baseline measurements in the first semester. Both range and mean of power usage in Y1S2 week 12, Y2S1 week 12 and Y2S2 week 13 were atypical due to the way the semester is organised (coursework deadlines, upcoming exams and low user counts in the labs). Therefore, these three figures (plotted for the sake of completeness) should be ignored in considering trends.

made it clear that the iMac in the lab only takes about 50 seconds from being powered-down to read-to-use. Approximately two thirds of lab computers were kept on between 8am (auto-powered on) and 6pm (auto-powered off). The rest were kept on 24/7 because they were in use at 6pm and did not automatically power off. This gives a total of 822,528 'iMac-on-hours' (including both stand by and in use hours) in two academic years. Our experiment participants (approximately one third of all students who used the lab) utilised a total of 26,777.8 iMac-hours, which makes an estimated total of 80,333.4 hours of active use by all lab users. This only accounts for ~9.8% of total iMac-on-hours for the lab. So, an estimate of at least 16,328.3 KWh[1] could have been saved from our lab over the two years if the iMacs did not automatically power-on daily, and every student turned off the computer immediately after use.

---

[1] An iMac's minimal standby (not in use) power is ~22 Watts, with screen automatically turned off.

5.2 Rewards Are Good Incentives

During the first two weeks of the energy efficiency competition, the following pattern was observed in both years (Y1S1 week 6-7, Y2S1 week 7-8): (1) average power use in both weeks was lower than the week before the competition started. This indicates the competition and prizes worked well in motivating users to save energy. However, (2) average group power usage started to increase in the second week of the competition. We consider this an indication that the effectiveness of prizes was not long-lived, as users soon started to prioritise other factors or 'forget' about the competition.

The gradients of power changes decline from the third week of the competition until the end of the competition in both years. The overall energy consumption during the competition was significantly lower than pre-competition usage. Approximately 65% of users in each year reported they were motivated to save energy during competitions because of the prizes, so we conclude that rewards do encourage energy saving behaviours.

However, from Figure 5, we also see that users prioritise completing their work. How can we move users' priority from completing work towards saving energy? Offering bigger prizes may attract more attention on saving energy. However, is it worth trading off work efficiency of students (or employees in an organisation) for energy savings? A balance must be found so that the value of the compromise made does not exceed the gains of saved energy.

5.3 Feedback Helps Reduce Power Usage

Per host live power feedback was displayed via an on-screen menu bar applet from the second half of the energy efficiency competitions (see Figure 8). A decrease in group mean power usage was observed compared to the previous week, when the applet was not in use. So, power usage feedback helped users to further lower their power usage.

In the second semester of each year, having feedback alone without incentives (the competition) still helped users to keep their mean power usage lower than without the feedback, although the average power consumptions slowly and steadily increased from week 1 (lowest) till week 12 (highest) in both years. We consider this good evidence that our energy feedback promotes energy saving behaviour and delays the resumption of non-energy efficient computer use. It also shows that feedback alone is insufficient to sustain energy saving behaviour in this context.

We also observed that 75% of users in Y2S2 performed slightly better than those in Y1S2. In Figure 8, the variation of mean and the 75th percentile are similar. As the only major difference in the experiment between Y1S2 and Y2S2 was the design of the power applet, this is a good indication that improved feedback was more useful in promoting energy saving behaviour. However, as the experiments ran in consecutive years, there were 9 students in the second year that had already undertaken the experiment in the first year. This potential bias is checked by observing that their baseline measurements at the start of Y2 were similar to Y1's, i.e. the 9 students demonstrated no permanent behaviour change from their previous participation in the experiment.

5.4 Rewards & Feedback Together are Better

As discussed in Section 5.2 and 5.3, although helpful, none of rewards or feedback alone yields sustainable energy saving behaviour. However, consistent decreasing and low power power consumptions were observed in Y1S1 weeek 8-9 and Y2S1 week 9-10, when both rewards and feedback were present. Although it is desirable to provide both rewards and feedback for longer periods to obtain more convincing trends of change, what we have observed so far are still good indications that rewards and feedback together produced the most effective energy saving.

5.5 Inflated Self-Assessments

In Section 4.2, we presented our users' very positive self-assessments. Later, by evaluating their real computer and energy usage, it appeared that about 70% participants (out of 23 who completed all four surveys in either year of study) had over- estimated their abilities and/or energy saving practices. They either became 'greener' while they have considered themselves already the 'greenest', or our measurements showed they were not energy efficient, even though they had considered themselves as 'green'.

This type of cognitive bias towards mistakenly over-rating one's ability higher than average is known as the Dunning-Kruger effect [8]. It is frequently observed among human subjects, which makes self-assessment on its own unreliable. As a result, it is important to collect both qualitative and quantitative data in this type of study to be able to draw more accurate conclusions.

5.6 Potential Energy Savings During Use

With a mean group saving of 16% and a mean power usage of approximately 60 Watts, over 10 Watts could be saved on each iMac during use. Over our 2-year experiment, an estimated saving of 248.177 KWh was achieved by our users *during the use of iMacs*, excluding any saving by powering off the computers when not in use. If all first and second year students had participated in our experiment (we had volunteers and some of the class chose not to participate), the saving would have been approximately double this amount.

We can translate this saving to a global scale in the spirit of a Fermi estimate. Bloomberg[2] reported that Apple iMacs sales in 2012 were expected to reach 3.8 million, according to the research firm DisplaySearch[3]. Again, based on the estimate of 10 Watts power saving per iMac during active use (excluding savings by turning off the computer), over 38,000 KWh saving per hour could be achieved from all of the iMacs sold worldwide in 2012. OFCOM[4] estimates that the average time spent using computers to access the Internet at home is ∼5.5 hours per week per person in the UK and USA in 2012 (which is probably a conservative estimate). This makes an estimated annual saving of 10,906,000 KWh. An average UK household consumes about 4,226 KWh of electricity annually [19], which means the energy saving from the iMacs worldwide is enough to power approximately 2581 homes in the UK for a year. In is equivalent to approximately GBP 14.6 million[5] (USD 24.1 million[6])). Note that this is only for new iMacs sold in 2012, and does not include any other iMacs, or other desktop computers: the potential total global savings are significant.

6. LIMITATIONS AND IMPROVEMENTS

Although we have seen satisfying outcomes from this study, we discuss a number of limitations, biases and potential improvements.

The scope of this study is limited to an institutional environment with a group of frequent users all performing similar work: users did not have exactly the same tasks to accomplish, so their individual behaviour is not directly comparable. It would be worthwhile carrying out a similar study in a more diverse environment. However, the set of users represents a typical set for our institution, and perhaps other similar institutions, so is usefully indicative.

Due to considerations of personal privacy and constraints from our ethical approval, it was not possible to distinguish between cohorts of students – first year or second year students. There is a possibility that the two cohorts behaved

---

[2] http://goo.gl/zc7Z4D
[3] http://www.displaysearch.com
[4] Independent regulator and competition authority for the UK communications industries: http://goo.gl/6JUxsY
[5] Based on British Gas standard electricity price at 13.38 pence per KWh in 2013. http://www.britishgas.co.uk/
[6] At exchange rate of GBP 1 = USD 1.65

differently. A more detailed tracking of usage may yield finer-grained analysis, at the risk of reduced privacy and so the risk of fewer volunteers.

MacOS 10.6 was installed on the iMacs used for our experiment in Y1, and then upgraded to MacOS 10.7 in Y2. While there was no significant difference in energy consumption between Mac OS 10.7 and 10.6 observed with respect to our study, we still used normalised percentage power changes rather than raw measurements in our analyses to reduce any bias caused by either the operating system or individuals.

Lack of user control of the workstations due to institutional system administration policy reduced possibilities of even greater energy saving by allowing more control of the lab computers. Indeed, our institutional policy implicitly and indirectly prioritises systems security, system integrity, and operational stability, over energy efficiency.

The power applet consumed approximately 0.77 Watts of power (mean) during active sessions (See Appendix B for more details). Given that the iMac consumes ~32.9 Watts power during an active session when idling with lowest screen brightness, the overhead of power monitoring accounts for up to 2.3% of total power. This percentage figure is much lower during users' normal use of an iMac. Although possible, we did not optimise the power monitor in terms of power efficiency for this study because we needed frequent measurements (once a second) to best gather detailed data for our experiment. Users achieved a mean of 16% group power saving (and up to 56% individual power saving) with our monitor executing. In summary, we achieved a mean saving of (just over) 10 Watts per user, even with the power applet running, so the 0.77 Watt used by the power applet is considered an acceptable cost.

In terms of the energy saving tips given to the users, our intention was to see specifically which tips the users, through their own preferences, would want to employ. For example, would being green have a greater importance for them than the possible inconvenience using a particular tip to save energy? Another way of presenting the tips would have been to provide some quantitative information about the energy saving potential. For example, reducing screen brightness has the greatest impact on energy usage, unless very CPU-intensive jobs were running. However, this may have biased a user's behaviour: the screen brightness tip was the easiest to perform, as well as having the highest impact, and so users may not have tried other tips that had lower impact. Our unbiased presentation of the tips let us discover what the the users which tips the users would gravitate to naturally.

There has also been work in considering system level interventions, which can also result in large savings (e.g. [2]) and complements our study. Clearly, it would be useful to investigate and understand the compatibility between different user interventions and system-level interventions when used together.

7. CONCLUSIONS AND FUTURE WORK

In our 2-year study of energy usage in a University Computer Science teaching lab, we have found that when users are given a combination of incentives and measured feedback of their energy usage, they can be motivated to improve their energy efficiency. We find that incentives or feedback alone is not sufficient, but incentives with feedback produces and sustains energy-efficient practices. We show the possi-

bility for, and quantify the gains from, having users save energy while the computers are in use, in complement to other systems controls and interventions when the computers are not in use. Our study also showed that some users, even if self-motivated by altruistic or environmental factors, still respond better when both feedback and incentives are present. However, we also find that users do prioritise the tasks they have to perform over energy savings.

As future work, we would like to conduct similar experiments in more diverse environments, where users may (a) be able to gain more control of the ICT equipment they use (e.g. install or remove software); (b) carry out similar tasks therefore comparable with each other; (c) have other social backgrounds than students. It was clear that no one complained that the information we provided was too much. It is therefore desirable to improve our power monitor and provide more information, e.g. per application power profiles, preferably with lower overhead. A natural extension of this work is also to investigate the compatibility between our approach and previous work that investigates system-level interventions, to see which could be used together to gain energy savings, both when desktop computers are in use and when they are not in use.

Acknowledgements

We are grateful to the anonymous reviewers and our paper shepherd, Prof Amarjeet Singh, who have helped us to improve the quality of this paper. Amazon UK kindly sponsored Amazon vouchers for use as rewards in our study. This work was partly supported by the IU-AC project, funded by grant EP/J016756/1 from the Engineering and Physical Sciences Research Council (EPSRC).

8. REFERENCES

[1] 1E. PC Energy Report 2009. http://goo.gl/8Ilr7i, 2009. Last access: Jan 2014.

[2] Y Agarwal, Stefan Savage, and R Gupta. Sleepserver: A software-only approach for reducing the energy consumption of pcs within enterprise environments. In *The 2010 USENIX conference on USENIX annual technical conference (USENIXATC'10)*, 2010.

[3] D. Allen and K. Janda. The effects of household characteristics and energy use consciousness on the effectiveness of real-time energy use feedback: a pilot study. *ACEEE Summer Study on Energy Efficiency in Buildings*, pages 1–12, 2006.

[4] Balijepalli, V.S.K.M. and Pradhan, V. and Khaparde, S.A. and Shereef, R.M. Review of demand response under smart grid paradigm. In *Innovative Smart Grid Technologies, India, 2011 IEEE PES*, pages 236–243, 2011.

[5] Cabinet Office and Behavioural Insights Team. Behaviour Change and Energy Use: behavioural insights team paper. 2011. Last access: Jan 2014.

[6] S. Darby. The Effectiveness of Feedback on Energy Consumption. In *Report for DEFRA, by the Environmental Change Institute, University of Oxford*. Environmental Change Institute (ECI) - Oxford University, 2006.

[7] Department of Energy & Climate Change, UK Government Department. Energy Metering: a

consultation on smart metering for electricity and gas, Consultation, May 2009.

[8] D. Dunning, K. Johnson, J. Ehrlinger, and J. Kruger. Why people fail to recognize their own incompetence. *Current Directions in Psychological Science*, 12(3):83–87, June 2003.

[9] B.J. Fogg. A behavior model for persuasive design. In *Proc. 4th Intl. Conf. on Persuasive Technology - Persuasive '09*, page 1, New York, New York, USA, 2009. ACM Press.

[10] B.J. Fogg. Creating persuasive technologies: an eight-step design process. In *Proc. of the 4th Intl. Conf. on Persuasive Technology*, 2009.

[11] Gartner. Forecast: PC Installed Base, Worldwide, 2004-2012. *Market Analysis and Statistics: G00157113*, 10 Apr 2008.

[12] Gartner. Press Release: Gartner Says Worldwide PC, Tablet and Mobile Phone Combined Shipments to Reach 2.4 Billion Units in 2013. goo.gl/Z2mv5q, Apr 2013. Last access: Jan 2014.

[13] E.S. Geller. The challenge of proenvironmental behavior. In *Betchel, R.B., Churchman, A. (eds.) Handbook of Environmental Psychology*, pages 525–540, 2002.

[14] A. Kollmuss and J. Agyeman. Mind the Gap : why do people act environmentally and what are the barriers to pro-environmental behavior? *Environmental Education*, 8(3), 2002.

[15] L Liikkanen. Extreme-user approach and the design of energy feedback systems. In *Intl. Conf. on Energy Efficiency in Domestic Appliances and Lighting*, 2009.

[16] G. Loewenstein and R.H. Thaler. Anomalies : Intertemporal Choice. *The Journal of Economic Perspectives*, 3(4):181–193, 1989.

[17] S. Taherian, M. Pias, G. Coulouris, and J. Crowcroft. Profiling energy use in households and office spaces. *Proc. of the 1st Intl. Conf. on Energy-Efficient Computing and Networking - e-Energy '10*, page 21, 2010.

[18] The Climate Group and GeSI. Smart 2020: Enabling the low carbon economy in the information age. 2008. Last access: Jan 2014.

[19] UK Government. Energy consumption in the uk (2013): Chapter 3 domestic energy consumption in the uk between 1970 and 2012. http://goo.gl/UABGhi, Jul 2013. Last access: Jan 2014.

[20] H. Wilhite, A. Hoivik, and J. Olsen. Advances in the use of consumption feedback information in energy billing: the experiences of a Norwegian energy utility. In *Proc., European Council for an Energy-Efficient Economy*, 1999.

[21] S. Yates, E. Daley, B. Gray, J.P. Gownder, and R. Batiancila. Forrester Research, Worldwide PC Adoption Forecast, 2007 To 2015: Abstract. http://goo.gl/SrnUiC, Jun 2007.

[22] R. Yun, B. Lasternas, A. Aziz, V. Loftness, P. Scupelli, A. Rowe, R. Kothari, F. Marion, and J. Zhao. Toward the design of a dashboard to promote environmentally sustainable behavior among office workers intervention techniques for sustainability. In *Proc. 8th Intl. conference on Persuasive Technology*, pages 246–252. Springer-Verlag, 2013.

APPENDIX

A. PARTICIPANTS

Our experiment participants (users) were all undergraduate Computer Science students, and broadly shared the following characteristics:

1. They frequently used the school computer lab for their day-to-day work and assignments.

2. They were enthusiastic young individuals who were eager to learn and experiment with new ideas.

3. They had sufficient computer skills and knowledge to be able to apply the energy-savings tips that they were given, and make informed choices about their individual choices of computer usage.

4. They do not pay directly for their electricity usage at school.

5. They were responsive to material rewards (free food, gifts, coupons, etc.).

Among these characteristics, number 1 was verified by our measurements; numbers 2, 3 and 5 were educated assumptions which were later verified via surveys; number 4 was a known fact.

B. DATA COLLECTION

Our data collection was performed by a python script that incorporated the following information and then uploaded to a collection sink.

In line with our ethics approval, user Unix IDs were anonymised with HMAC keyed-hashing, as we were required to anonymise all data collection.

System usage information was collected using:

```
ps axo "user stat etime time pcpu pmem vsize rss tt pid comm"
```

Our ethics approval required that command-line arguments to programs and processes were not recorded to preserve users' privacy.

Various other system information, including screen brightness and power consumption, was collected using the Apple System Management Control (SMC) Tool v0.01. The decoding and parsing methodology for which is available upon email request to the authors.

The SMC allowed us to collect two types of data. The first type is the raw power measurements and screen brightness. The raw power measurements include total computer power, CPU power and North Bridge (data IO) power. These were read from the built-in power sensors in each iMac. The screen brightness was measured through an operating system API, ranging from level 0 (lowest brightness setting, but not off) to 100 (highest brightness setting).

All the information above was captured as a sample (a snapshot of system/power usage). Every 30 samples were compressed and cached locally in an archive. The power monitor uploaded all cached samples at a random interval between 32 and 100 seconds to: 1) avoid network congestion; 2) avoid data loss; 3) achieve near-real-time data collection. User historical usage was displayed via power applet or the Web front end on demand. Real-time power feedback was always displayed in the menu bar via applet using local measurements. As future work, we intend to implement a round-robin local storage for displaying historical usage

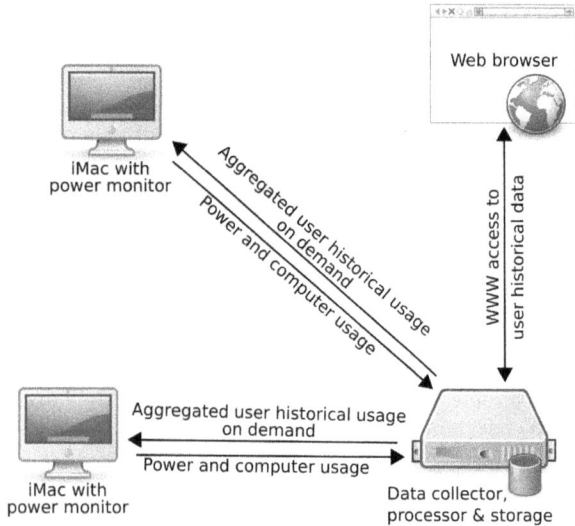

Figure 9: A sketch of power monitor-feedback model.

without contacting the collection server to enable off-line viewing, reduce network traffic and server load.

During an active user session, the power monitor took a sample every second, and consumed a mean of 0.77 Watts of power. When the machine was not in use, a sample was taken every 10 seconds to lower the power overhead to ∼0.08 Watts. If not for our experiment, the power monitor would only need to execute during active user sessions to provide feedback, and would not be operational otherwise.

B.1 Screen Power

Screen power was not available from the built-in power sensors, so we measured the total power of an idle iMac at every possible screen brightness setting (level 0 to 100), subtracting the iMac's total idle power when the screen is turned off (22 Watts), and obtained a mapping table from screen brightness level to its power consumption for our reference – see Figure 10.

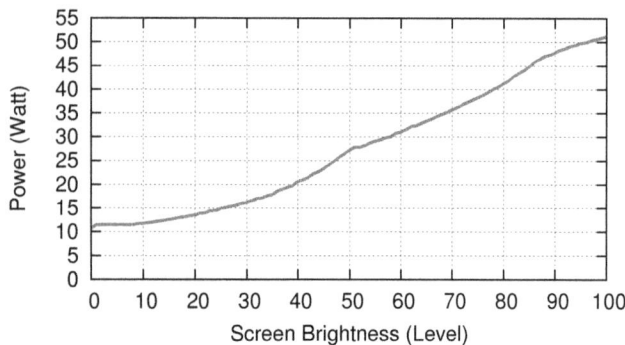

Figure 10: Screen brightness level to power consumption mapping by measurements.

C. HOW MOTIVATED TO SAVE ENERGY

Figure 11 shows participants' self-assessments in S1 on how motivated they were to save energy. Similar and overall positive results were observed in both years.

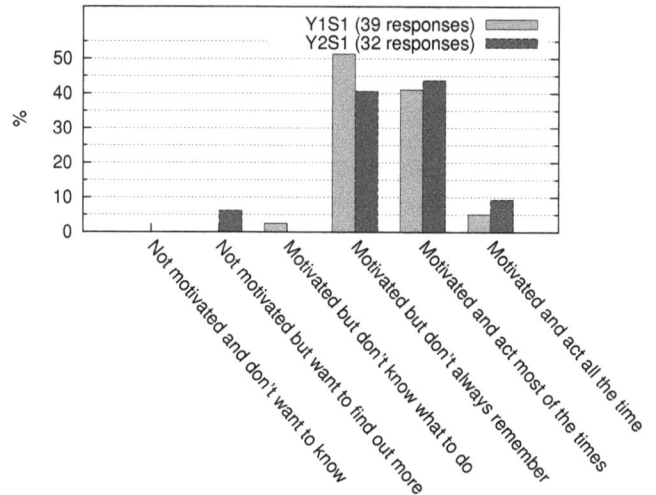

Figure 11: Participants' self-assessments on how motivated they were to save energy at the beginning of our experiment.

D. EXPERIMENT PLAN

As described in Section 3, below is the detailed, week-by-week breakdown of when the various activities ran.

Table 3: Experiment design over 2 academic years. Week 7 in Y1S1 was Reading Week (no teaching or coursework deadline), therefore significantly less use of the lab computers was observed. This could have led to biased results, but no obvious difference was observed. Vacation and exams periods were excluded from our observation due to low and inconsistent lab usage. A tick/check indicates in which week the relevant activity was in progress. In the 'Survey' row, S1, S2, S3, and S4 denote the four user surveys that were conducted. Note that in Y1S1, week 12 was followed by a vacation. This was changed to exams in Y2S1. As a result, atypical usage was observed in 3 out of 4 last-week-of-semester (Y1S2 week 12, Y2S1 week 12, Y2S2 week 13) due to pressure from the coursework deadlines and upcoming exams (see Figure 8).

	Y1S1													Y1S2												
Week	1	2	3	4	5	6	7	8	9	10	11	12	Vac.	1	2	3	4	5	6	7	Vac.	8	9	10	11	12	Exams
Recruitment	✓	✓																									
Baseline Obs.	✓	✓																									
Power Monitoring	✓	✓	✓	✓	✓	✓	✓	✓	✓	✓	✓	✓		✓	✓	✓	✓	✓	✓	✓		✓	✓	✓	✓	✓	
Usage Monitoring	✓	✓	✓	✓	✓	✓	✓	✓	✓	✓	✓	✓		✓	✓	✓	✓	✓	✓	✓		✓	✓	✓	✓	✓	
Tips				✓																							
Survey			S1			S2					S3		S4														
Competition						✓	✓	✓	✓	✓																	
Power Feedback								✓	✓		✓			✓	✓	✓	✓	✓	✓	✓		✓	✓	✓	✓	✓	

	Y2S1													Y2S2													
Week	1	2	3	4	5	6	7	8	9	10	11	12	Exams	1	2	3	4	5	6	7	Vac.	8	9	10	11	12	13	Exams
Recruitment	✓	✓																										
Baseline Obs.		✓	✓																									
Power Monitoring		✓	✓	✓	✓	✓	✓	✓	✓	✓	✓	✓		✓	✓	✓	✓	✓	✓	✓		✓	✓	✓	✓	✓	✓	
Usage Monitoring		✓	✓	✓	✓	✓	✓	✓	✓	✓	✓	✓		✓	✓	✓	✓	✓	✓	✓		✓	✓	✓	✓	✓	✓	
Tips						✓																						
Survey				S1		S2				S3		S4																
Competition							✓	✓	✓	✓																		
Power Feedback								✓	✓	✓	✓			✓	✓	✓	✓	✓	✓	✓		✓	✓	✓	✓	✓	✓	

Impact of Demand-Response on the Efficiency and Prices in Real-Time Electricity Markets*

Nicolas Gast[†]
IC-LCA2
EPFL, Switzerland
nicolas.gast@epfl.ch

Jean-Yves Le Boudec
IC-LCA2
EPFL, Switzerland
jean-yves.leboudec@epfl.ch

Dan-Cristian Tomozei
IC-LCA2
EPFL, Switzerland
dan-cristian.tomozei@epfl.ch

ABSTRACT

We study the effect of Demand-Response (DR) in dynamic real-time electricity markets. We use a two-stage market model that takes into account the dynamical aspects of generation, demand, and DR. We study the real-time market prices in two scenarios: in the former, consumers anticipate or delay their flexible loads in reaction to market prices; in the latter, the flexible loads are controlled by an independent aggregator. For both scenarios, we show that, when users are price-takers, any competitive equilibrium is efficient: the players' selfish responses to prices coincide with a socially optimal policy. Moreover, the price process is the same in all scenarios. For the numerical evaluation of the properties of the equilibrium, we develop a solution technique based on the Alternating Direction Method of Multipliers (ADMM) and trajectorial forecasts. The forecasts are computed using wind generation data from the UK. We challenge the assumption that all players have full information. If the assumption is verified, then, as expected, the social welfare increases with the amount of DR available, since DR relaxes the ramping constraints of generation. However, if the day-ahead market cannot observe how elastic loads are affected by DR, a large quantity of DR can be detrimental and leads to a decrease in the welfare. Furthermore, the DR operator has an incentive to under-dimension the quantity of available DR. Finally, we compare DR with an actual energy storage system. We find that storage has a faster response-time and thus performs better when only a limited amount is installed. However, storage suffers from charge-discharge inefficiency: with DR, prices do concentrate on marginal cost (for storage, they do not) and provide a better welfare.

Categories and Subject Descriptors

C.4 [**Performance of Systems**]: Modeling techniques.;
G.3 [**Probability and Statistics**]: Stochastic processes.

---

*This work is partially supported by the EU project QUAN-TICOL, 600708.
†Nicolas Gast is currently affiliated with Inria, France.

e-Energy'14, June 11–13, 2014, Cambridge, UK.
ACM 978-1-4503-2819-7/14/06.
http://dx.doi.org/10.1145/2602044.2602052 .

Keywords

Electricity Pricing; Demand-response; Market Efficiency; Energy Economics.

1. INTRODUCTION

Electricity markets are developing worldwide, replacing tightly regulated systems by decentralized control mechanisms [20]. Demand-response (DR) mechanisms have emerged in order to take advantage of flexible demand in a system where demand is traditionally considered as inflexible [17]. DR can compensate mismatches between production and consumption, thus increasing the potential deployment of renewable generation by reducing the necessity for regulation reserve. It can be implemented by having consumers react to prices [14] or to congestion signals [13].

The authors of [19] present a model of real-time electricity market that incorporates the dynamic constraints of generation and the uncertainties dues to forecast errors. The system is composed of two market actors (a supplier and a consumer) that exchange energy at a spot price. They show that there exists a competitive equilibrium, *i.e.*, a price process such that market actors agree on the quantity of energy exchanged. This market is efficient: for any competitive equilibrium, the selfish decisions of both market actors coincide with the hypothetical decisions taken by a social planner that aims to maximize the sum of every actor's utility. However, the equilibrium price exhibits large fluctuations and is never equal to the marginal production cost.

We extend [19] to model a two-stage electricity market that features generation constraints, inelastic loads, and elastic loads corresponding to a set of DR appliances. Our elastic load model captures several key-features of controllable thermostatic loads. The loads are elastic in the sense that it is possible to perform price arbitrage by delaying or anticipating the consumption of each load, but an appliance's consumption cannot be arbitrarily reduced by augmenting prices. Each appliance has an internal state representing, *e.g.*, its temperature. A load that is delayed for too long reaches an undesirable state. For thermostatic loads, this corresponds to having the temperature outside a given deadband. We add a second dimension to the state space: a counter indicates the waiting time before the appliance is allowed to respond to DR signals, thus modeling mini-cycle avoidance (an appliance that has just been switched on cannot be switched off immediately). In our numerical evaluations we use a mean-field model to keep track of the empirical distribution of the appliances' states.

We consider two market scenarios. In Scenario 1, the flexible appliances are controlled by the consumer who reacts to real-time prices. She takes advantage of price difference by anticipating or delaying the consumption. In Scenario 2 a DR operator controls all the flexible appliances. She charges a fixed rate to users and makes a profit by price arbitrage: scheduling the appliances when the market price is low. We show that in both cases, the market is efficient, *i.e.*, the selfish decisions of players coincide with the ones of a hypothetical social planner.

We develop a numerical methodology based on the Alternating Direction Method of Multipliers (ADMM) to compute the market equilibrium for a realistic forecast error model. The forecast errors are modeled using multiple trajectories [15], generated from multivariate Gaussian random variables. The correlation matrices are derived from traces of data from the UK.

We study numerically the system as a function of the DR capacity, which is the aggregate maximal power of flexible appliances. Our results show that, when the DR capacity is low, the gain obtained by using demand-response is almost linear in the capacity. For large capacity, if the state of the appliances can be observed by all players, the gain saturates to a value that does not depend on the appliances' nature. However, if the states cannot be observed by the day-ahead market, increasing the capacity of DR can be detrimental: after a certain capacity, it decreases the social welfare, as the consumption of DR appliances is harder to predict. Finally, we also show that DR operators have an incentive to undersize the DR capacity.

We also compare DR with classical energy storage [9]. We find that, at low capacity, a storage system offers better performance than DR because it reacts faster. However, for large capacities of installed DR, DR behaves similarly to a perfectly efficient storage. As such, for large capacities, DR outperforms energy storage systems, since these have a charge-discharge efficiency of $70-90\%$.

Roadmap. We discuss related work in Section 2. We present the model, the assumptions, and the main definitions in Section 3, and the social welfare theorem in Section 4. We describe our statistical model of error and our numerical methodology in Section 5. Finally, we give the numerical parameters and present the numerical evaluation of the model in Section 6. We conclude in Section 7.

2. RELATED WORK

The authors of [1] present an overview of DR programs and their integration within the electricity market. They compare price-based and incentive-based programs and present their benefits (peak reduction, bill savings, reliability) and drawbacks (deployment cost, rescheduling, metering infrastructure). New market models tailored for DR have also been investigated. For example, the authors of [18] develop a new market-clearing mechanism for load-shifting. However, it assumes perfect forecast and is limited to a small number of players. Hence, a key research topic is the means of presenting DR as a service transparent to use via smart home controllers or by having a DR operator with direct control of appliances. Multiple models are proposed, using response to prices [14] or to congestion signals [13].

Demand response fatigue and rebound effect are a large concern for the DR operator and the grid regulator, in particular because it leads to observability problem. In [12], the authors use a simplified model and find that when the state of flexible appliances is not taken into account in the control, a large accumulated delayed load may manifest unexpectedly and randomly. In this paper we model the internal states of each appliance in detail and, in Section 6.3 study whether such an effect continues to occur.

Our appliance model is similar to [10, 13], who also consider thermostatic controllable loads. A difference with our model is that we add a second dimension for modeling mini-cycle avoidance. We also take into account the undesirable states that could be reached in blackout conditions. Moreover, we consider that the elastic loads can be anticipated or delayed, but that in the long run they consume a fixed amount of energy, *e.g.*, the average consumption of a heater or cooler. This is not the case in [13]. In many papers about demand-response in electricity markets, it is often considered that higher prices result in reduced consumption [1].

Our work builds on various papers about efficiency in electricity markets (*e.g.*, [19, 9] and the reference therein). One key contribution of the current paper is that we are able to handle a more realistic forecast model in our numerical methodology. The numerical results produced in [19, 9] were performed by assuming that the forecast error can be represented by a Brownian motion with stationary increments. We use a non-stationary model of error that is becoming a standard for wind forecast. It uses a probabilistic forecast developed by Pinson et al. [15], where the errors are represented by a finite number of possible trajectories.

We consider a system with a large number of flexible appliances. In order to keep the model tractable, we use a mean-field approximation to approximate their dynamics. More details about these models and their relations with stochastic optimal control are presented in [2, 7, 8].

3. SYSTEM MODEL

We consider a two-stage electricity market (day-ahead and real-time) with three actors: the consumer, the supplier, and the DR operator. The supplier has two roles: she generates the bulk of the electricity determined via the day-ahead scheduling and she provides regulation electricity to compensate for mismatches in real-time. The consumer aggregates the consumption of a population of end-users. The controllable demand of end-users is managed by the DR operator who uses the flexibility of the controllable appliances as a means to perform arbitrage on the real-time electricity market. The role of the DR operator can be assumed by the consumer, or by an independent actor. In Section 6, we will explore two types of controllable loads: fridges and boilers.

3.1 Two-stage Electricity Markets

Two-stage electricity markets are used to determine the price of electricity supplied to the consumers. In the day-ahead stage, the actors use forecasts of consumption and of renewable production to schedule the bulk production for the next day. In the real-time stage, last-minute decisions are taken to compensate mismatches.

We start from the day-ahead market of [5]. The forecast demand for the next day at time t is used to set the scheduled production $g^{da}(t)$. The scheduled production incorporates both renewable energy (volatile) and conventional energy sources. The forecast demand has two components: the non-controllable demand $d^{da}(t)$ and the controllable (flexible) demand $f^{da}(t)$. An additional fixed quantity r^{da} is produced as a precaution against forecast errors. Thus, in the day-ahead market the actors agree to trade an amount $g^{da}(t)+f^{da}(t)$ the next day at time t at a price $p^{da}(t)$, where $g^{da}(t):=d^{da}(t)+r^{da}$.

The real-time market deals with the inevitable mismatches that arise from forecast errors. Thus, at time t the end-users express a total aggregated non-controllable demand $D^a(t) = d^{da}(t) + D(t)$ and controllable (flexible) demand $F^a(t) = f^{da}(t) + F(t)$. The quantities $D(t)$ and $F(t)$ are the real-time components of the demand, and they can be positive or negative. While $D(t)$ is given by nature, $F(t)$ can be controlled to some extent, depending on the state of the controllable appliances and on the control signal decided by the DR operator.

The supplier deploys real-time production $G(t)$ in order to compensate for mismatches. This part of the generation comes from conventional sources, and is subject to ramping constraints. The total amount of produced electricity at time t is thus $G^a(t) = f^{da}(t) + g^{da}(t) + \Gamma(t) + G(t)$, where $\Gamma(t)$ is the forecast error of renewable sources (i.e., the difference between actual and forecast production). The energy produced in real-time is traded at price $P(t)$ at time t.

In this paper, we study the effect of demand-response on the real-time market. We assume that the market actors are price takers: they strategically define their actions based on prices, but they cannot influence these prices. Moreover, we assume that the market actors base their decisions at time t on the knowledge of past data and actions (up to time t) and the statistics of future data. This knowledge is shared by all actors, unless otherwise specified. In our mathematical model, this means that there exists a filtration $(\mathcal{F}_t)$ such that the decision processes are adapted to this filtration.

3.2 Controllable Appliance Model

We consider N appliances that can be controlled via demand-response. Their maximum aggregated power consumption is denoted P_{on}. At any time step, each appliance is fully characterized by its state $i = (s, x, y) \in \mathcal{M}$. The state space is defined as $\mathcal{M} = \{\text{on}, \text{off}\} \times \mathbb{Z} \times \{0, \dots, Y_{max}\}$, where

- $s \in \{\text{on}, \text{off}\}$ indicates whether the appliance is on, in which case it consumes a power P_{on}/N, or whether it is off, in which case it consumes 0; if $s = \text{on}$ then we denote by $\bar{s} = \text{off}$ and vice-versa;
- $x \in \mathbb{Z}$ reflects the internal state of the appliance, e.g., the temperature in the case of a fridge;
- $y \in \{0, \dots, Y_{max}\}$ represents the amount of time that needs to pass before the device can react to demand-response. The device can be switched from on to off (or vice-versa) only if $y = 0$. Moreover, as soon as the state is switched as a result of a demand-response action, the value y jumps from 0 to Y_{max}. By accounting for y, we avoid operation in mini-cycles which might damage the appliance.

In Figure 1, we represent the Markov chain that gives the evolution of the state of an appliance. Each node on the diagram corresponds to a possible state, with

- $s = \text{on}$ for the nodes in the upper rectangle and $s = \text{off}$ for the ones in the lower rectangle,
- x is given by the position on the x-axis, and
- y is given by the corresponding y-axis.

Any state $i = (s, x, y)$ has a horizontal transition to a neighboring state $(\text{on}, x + 1, y)$ if $s = \text{on}$ and $(\text{off}, x - 1, y)$ if $s = \text{off}$. The probability of this horizontal transition is

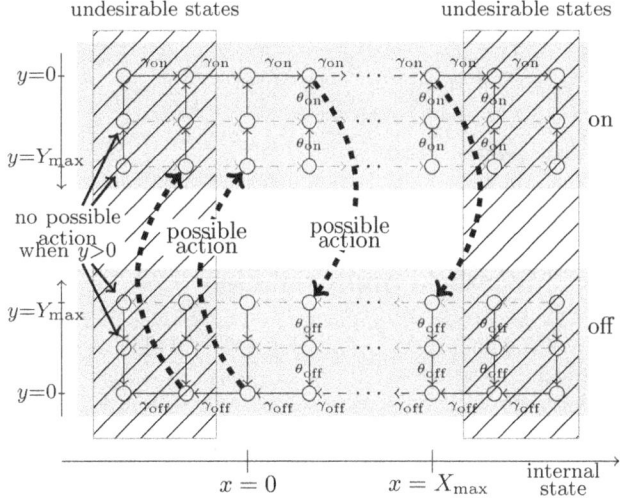

Figure 1: Markov model of an appliance. Each state is characterized by a tuple (s, x, y), with $s \in \{\text{on}, \text{off}\}$. The x-axis represents the internal state (e.g., temperature). The y-axis is the time before the device can be switched on or off.

γ_s if $y > 0$, or $(1 - a_i)\gamma_s$ if $y = 0$. We consider that γ_{on} is typically larger than γ_{off}. This allows to model the different speed at which the internal state of the appliance evolves when it is on or off (e.g., a fridge spends less time on than off). When $y > 0$, we add a vertical transition to a state $(s, x, y - 1)$, which decreases the y counter with a certain probability θ_s.

We partition the state space into "responsive" states $\mathcal{M}_1 \overset{\text{def}}{=} \{(s, x, y) : y = 0\}$ and "non-responsive" states $\mathcal{M}_2 = \mathcal{M} \setminus \mathcal{M}_1$. A demand-response action is defined as a vector of probabilities $a = (a_i)_{i \in \mathcal{M}}$ indexed on the states. For a state $i = (s, x, y)$, a_i is the probability that an appliance switches its s state:

- If the appliance is in the responsive state $(s, x, 0)$, its state becomes the non-responsive state $(\bar{s}, x, Y_{max})$.
- If the state is non-responsive, the action has no effect.

We consider that if the same action a is sent to two appliances, their transitions are independent. Moreover, the effect of the actions is applied after the horizontal transitions. The actions are represented as thick dotted transitions in Figure 1.

The appliance remains in the same state with the probability that none of the transitions previously described occur: $1 - \gamma_s$ if $y = 0$ and $1 - \gamma_s - \theta_s$ if $y > 0$. These self-transitions are not represented in Figure 1 for the sake of readability. The transition probability of an appliance from state i to state j can be written:

$$\pi(i, j, \alpha) = \mathbb{P}(m(t+1) = j | m(t) = i, a_i(t) = \alpha)$$
$$= (1 - \alpha)\pi(i, j, 0) + \alpha\pi(i, j, 1). \quad (1)$$

Some states of the appliance are undesirable, e.g., if the internal temperature of a fridge is too high or too low. We model this by associating a penalty with certain values of x. Specifically, as long as $x \in \{0 \dots X_{max}\}$, this penalty is 0. When $x < 0$ or $x > X_{max}$, the penalty is proportional to the gap between x and the desirable states. Explicitly, we define a penalty vector $\kappa = (\kappa_i)_{i \in \mathcal{M}}$ indexed by the states

$i = (s, x, y)$:

$$\kappa_i = \begin{cases} 0 & \text{if } x \in \{0, \ldots, X_{\max}\} \\ -\delta \cdot x / X_{\max} & \text{if } x < 0 \\ \delta \cdot (x - X_{\max}) / X_{\max} & \text{if } x > X_{\max} \end{cases}$$

for some positive constant $\delta > 0$.

When there is no DR, the appliance automatically switches *on* or *off* just before it reaches an undesirable state. In this specific scenario there is no penalty.

3.3 Mean-field Approximation

The role of each DR appliance is symmetrical. Hence, the state of the appliances is fully characterized at time t by an occupancy measure $M^N(t) = (M_i^N(t))_{i \in \mathcal{M}}$, where $M_i^N(t)$ is the fraction of appliances that are in state i at time t. We represent $M^N(t)$ as a row vector (of infinite dimension). Unless otherwise specified, all actors know $M^N(0) = M_0$.

We consider that the number of flexible appliances N is large. It is shown in [7, Section 3.1] that, as N grows, the $M^N(t)$ goes to $M(t)$, which evolves as:

$$M_j(t+1) = \sum_{i \in \mathcal{M}} M_i(t) \pi(i, j, a_i(t)). \tag{2}$$

Moreover, as N goes to infinity, the optimal control for the mean field limit M is asymptotically optimal for the system with a finite number of appliances [7, 8].

We denote by Π^0 and Π^1 the two matrices:

$$\Pi^0(i, j) = \pi(i, j, 0) \text{ and } \Pi^1(i, j) = \pi(i, j, 1) - \pi(i, j, 0).$$

Using Equation (1), the evolution of the occupancy measure is

$$M_j(t+1) = \sum_{i \in \mathcal{M}} M_i(t) \Pi^0(i, j) + \sum_{i \in \mathcal{M}} M_i(t) a_i(t) \Pi^1(i, j).$$

In what follows we assume that the occupancy measure $M(t)$ can be fully observed at t. Thus, we replace $a(t)$ by a more convenient control $U(t)$, $U_i(t) = M_i(t) a_i(t)$. Formally, we define the set X_U of processes $(U(t))$ such that $M(0) = M_0$ and for all t:

$$M(t+1) = M(t)\Pi^0 + U(t)\Pi^1, \tag{3}$$

$$U_i(t) \in [0; M_i(t)] \quad \forall i \in \mathcal{M} \tag{4}$$

The two controls a and U are equivalent in the following sense: a process $(M(t), M(0) = M_0)$ describing the evolution of the occupancy measure can be obtained via (2) using a control process $(a(t))$ if and only if there exists $U \in X_U$ such that $U_i(t) = M_i(t) a_i(t)$ for all t, i. These equations remain valid if the same actions $a(t)$ are sent to all appliances, or if each individual received an action. In that case, $a(t)$ is the average over all actions. See the discussion in [7, Section 5.1].

Finally, the power consumption and penalty, defined in §3.2, can be expressed as scalar products[1] with $M(t)$:

- The power consumption of flexible appliances is

$$F^a(t) = f^{da}(t) + F(t) = P_{\text{on}} M(t) \cdot \varsigma^\top, \tag{5}$$

where the row vector $\varsigma = (\varsigma_i)_{i \in \mathcal{M}}$ is such that $\varsigma_i = 1$ if i is an *on* state and $\varsigma_i = 0$ otherwise.

- The total penalty at time t is

$$M(t) \cdot \kappa^\top. \tag{6}$$

---

[1] For two row vectors x and y, $y^\top$ denotes the transpose of y and $x \cdot y^\top$ is the scalar product between x and y.

3.4 Market Actors

We now describe the market actors and their objectives in two different scenarios. In the first scenario, the consumer also manages the flexible demand. Based on the current or anticipated market prices and on the blackout cost she decides whether to anticipate or delay a flexible load. The amount of flexible load close to undesirable states also influences this decision. In the second scenario, the DR operator is a stand-alone market actor that directly buys energy from the market.

3.4.1 Scenario 1: Consumer Controls DR Actions

The consumer controls the quantity of energy $E_D(t)$ purchased on the real-time market at time t. In this scenario, she also manages the the flexible demand $F(t)$ by influencing the state of the flexible appliances. The payoff of the consumer at time t is a sum of three terms:

- We consider linear utilities of satisfied non-controlled consumption $v \min\{D^a(t), E_D(t) + g^{da}(t) - F(t)\}$ and of satisfied controlled consumption $v' F^a(t)$.

- The disutility of a blackout is expressed as a sum of two terms: a linear term in the amount of unsatisfied non-controllable demand $-c^{bo}(D^a(t) + F(t) - E_D(t) - g^{da}(t))^+$ and a penalty of pushing controllable demand in undesirable states $-M(t) \cdot \kappa^\top$ defined in (6). As the consumer aggregates many individuals, she may curtail only part of their demand. For example, this corresponds to interrupting the service for a neighborhood in case of insufficient resources, rather than interrupting an entire city. We treat controllable demand differently, since it is actively interrupted or encouraged to consume.

- The amount of money spent on buying energy on the two markets at prices $P(t)$ and $p^{da}(t)$ is captured as $-P(t)E_D(t) - p^{da}(t)(g^{da}(t) + f^{da}(t))$.

To summarize, the total payoff of the consumer is

$$W_D^{tot}(t) := v \min\{D^a(t), E_D(t) + g^{da}(t) - F(t)\} + v' F^a(t)$$
$$- c^{bo}(D^a(t) + F(t) - E_D(t) - g^{da}(t))^+ - M(t) \cdot \kappa^\top$$
$$- P(t)E_D(t) - p^{da}(t)(g^{da}(t) + f^{da}(t)).$$

We strip away all the terms that are not controllable in real-time. Taking into account (5) and (6), the real-time component of the payoff is:

$$W_D(t) = M(t) \cdot (v' P_{\text{on}} \varsigma - \kappa)^\top - P(t)E_D(t) \tag{7}$$
$$- (v + c^{bo})(E_D(t) - D(t) - P_{\text{on}} M(t) \cdot \varsigma^\top + f^{da}(t) + r^{da})^-.$$

where $x^- = \max(-x, 0)$, for any real number x.

In the real-time market the consumer maximizes her expected payoff over the duration T of a day, given the scheduled day-ahead decisions. Her objective is

$$\underset{\substack{E_D, U \in X_U \\ (\mathcal{F}_t)-\text{adapted}}}{\arg\max} \ \mathcal{W}_D, \text{ where } \mathcal{W}_D := \mathbb{E}\left[\sum_{t=0}^{T} W_D(t)\right].$$

The supplier sells a quantity $E_S(t)$ on the real-time market, and produces $G(t)$ subject to the following constraints at each time t:

1. the sold quantity cannot exceed the produced quantity, i.e., $E_S(t) \leq G(t) + \Gamma(t)$,

2. the real-time production has ramping limitations $\zeta^- < 0$ and $\zeta^+ > 0$: $\zeta^- \leq \frac{G(t')-G(t)}{t'-t} \leq \zeta^+$, $\forall t' > t$.

We denote the set of processes $(E_S(t), G(t))$ that satisfy these constraints by X_S. Thus, taking into account the marginal generation cost of the day-ahead production c^{da} and that of the real-time production c, the payoff of the supplier is:

$$W_S^{tot}(t) = (p^{da}(t) - c^{da})(f^{da}(t) + g^{da}(t)) + P(t)E_S(t) - cG(t).$$

Removing the terms that are not controllable in real-time, this payoff becomes

$$W_S(t) = P(t)E_S(t) - cG(t). \tag{8}$$

Finally, the supplier maximizes her expected payoff

$$\underset{\substack{(E_S, G) \in X_S \\ (\mathcal{F}_t)-\text{adapted}}}{\arg\max} \; \mathcal{W}_S, \text{ where } \mathcal{W}_S := \mathbb{E}\left[\sum_{t=0}^{T} W_S(t)\right].$$

Dynamic Competitive Equilibrium. We recall the notion of dynamic competitive equilibrium [5, 19].

DEFINITION 1. *A dynamic competitive equilibrium* $(P^e, E_D^e, E_S^e, G^e, U^e)$ *is a set of* $(\mathcal{F}_t)$*-adapted price and control processes that satisfy:*

$$(E_D^e, U^e) \in \underset{E_D, U \in X_U}{\arg\max} \; \mathcal{W}_D, \tag{9}$$

$$(E_S^e, G^e) \in \underset{(E_S, G) \in X_S}{\arg\max} \; \mathcal{W}_S, \tag{10}$$

$$E_D^e = E_S^e. \tag{11}$$

In the above definition, (9) means that (E_D^e, U^e) constitutes an optimal control from the selfish consumer's perspective. Similarly, (10) states that (E_S^e, G^e) is optimal from the supplier's perspective. Finally, (11) is the market constraint. Note that in (9), the consumer is not subject to the supplier's constraints and vice-versa for (10). See [5] for a discussion.

3.4.2 Scenario 2: Standalone DR operator

In this scenario, we consider that end-users are charged at two different retail prices per energy unit: one for the non-controllable appliances, and another one for the controllable appliances. The bill for the controllable appliances is collected by the DR operator. The rationale of the DR operator is that controllable appliances (e.g., fridges, boilers) are always operational and that they consume roughly a constant (predictable) quantity of energy per day. Hence, from the DR operator's viewpoint, it is as if consumers pay a constant subscription fee per month for a provided service (e.g., to keep the fridge cool). The DR operator has the possibility of performing arbitrage on the real-time market thanks to the flexibility of the appliances.

The consumer controls only the quantity of purchased real-time energy $E_D(t)$ for serving the non-controllable demand. In this scenario, her payoff at each time t is:

$$W_D^{tot}(t) := v \min(D^a(t), E_D(t) + g^{da}(t)) + - c^{bo}(D^a(t) - E_D(t) - g^{da}(t))^+ - [P(t)E_D(t) + p^{da}(t)g^{da}(t)].$$

The real-time component of the consumer's payoff is

$$W_D(t) = -(v+c^{bo})(E_D(t) - D(t) + r^{da})^- - P(t)E_D(t). \tag{12}$$

The DR operator is an independent actor that controls the real-time consumption of controllable demands $F(t)$. On the real-time market, when $F(t) < 0$, she acts as a virtual energy supplier and gets payed for generating "nega-Watts". She generates revenue via arbitrage on the real-time market. Her payoff function is

$$W_F^{tot}(t) = -p^{da}(t)f^{da}(t) - P(t)F(t) + v'F^a(t) - M(t) \cdot \kappa^\top.$$

By Equation (5), $F(t) = P_{on}M(t)\kappa^T - f^{da}(t)$. Hence, her real-time controllable payoff is

$$W_F(t) = -P(t)P_{\text{on}}M(t) \cdot \varsigma^\top + M(t) \cdot (v'P_{\text{on}}\varsigma - \kappa)^\top \tag{13}$$

The DR operator maximizes her expected payoff subject to $(\mathcal{F}_t)$-adapted feasible controls $U \in X_U$, specifically:

$$\underset{\substack{(U) \in X_U \\ (\mathcal{F}_t)-\text{adapted}}}{\arg\max} \; \mathcal{W}_F, \text{ where } \mathcal{W}_F := \mathbb{E}\left[\sum_{t=0}^{T} W_F(t)\right].$$

The supplier behaves the same way as in the previous scenario and has the same payoff (8).

A similar definition of a dynamic competitive equilibrium can be written in this scenario. A competitive equilibrium is now the tuple $(P^e, E_D^e, F^e, E_S^e, G^e, U^e)$. The difference with respect to the previous case is that the consumer who was adjusting the amount of bought energy via the real-time flexible demand F^e now needs to pay for $F^e(t) = P_{\text{on}}M^e(t) \cdot \varsigma^\top - f^{da}(t)$ at the price of the real-time market as a form of virtual energy generation. The market constraint (11) becomes

$$E_S^e(t) = E_D^e(t) + F^e(t) \text{ for all } t. \tag{14}$$

4. SOCIAL WELFARE THEOREM

In both presented scenarios we compute the social welfare as the sum of the actors' payoffs when the market clearing constraint is satisfied. In the case of a standalone DR operator (Scenario 2), the total payoff is the sum of Equations (8), (12) and (13). It is equal to

$$W_{\text{tot}}(t) := -(v+c^{bo})(E_D(t) - D(t) + r^{da})^- - cG(t) \tag{15}$$
$$+ M(t) \cdot (v'P_{\text{on}}\varsigma - \kappa)^\top + P(t)(E_S(t) - E_D(t) - F(t)).$$

When the market constraints (14) are satisfied, the bought energy is equal to the sold energy at each time step. Hence, the price disappears from the total welfare.

A socially optimal allocation maximizes the total expected payoff. As $W_{\text{tot}}(t)$ is increasing in $E_S(t)$, we can further simplify (15). Taking into account the constraints on $E_S(t)$, we get that $E_S(t) = G(t) + \Gamma(t)$ maximizes $W_{\text{tot}}(t)$. Using (14) to express E_D and denoting the random (uncontrolled) component of the social welfare by $Z(t) := \Gamma(t) - D(t) + f^{da}(t) + r^{da}$, a socially optimal allocation maximizes the total expected payoff:

$$W_{\text{tot}}'(t) = -(v+c^{bo})(G(t) + Z(t) - P_{\text{on}}M(t) \cdot \varsigma^\top)^- + M(t) \cdot (v'P_{\text{on}}\varsigma - \kappa)^\top - cG(t). \tag{16}$$

We call (G^*, U^*) a *socially optimal* allocation if it is a solution to the following problem:

$$\underset{G \in X_S, \, U \in X_U \text{ are } (\mathcal{F}_t)-\text{adapted}}{\arg\max} \; \mathbb{E}\left[\sum_{t=0}^{T} W_{\text{tot}}(t)\right] \tag{17}$$

A direct computation shows that the total welfare is the same in Scenario 2. This implies that the socially optimal allocations are the same in both scenarios.

The following result holds. It is proved in Appendix A.

THEOREM 1. *If $(P^e, E_D^e, E_S^e, G^e, U^e)$ is a dynamic competitive equilibrium in Scenario 1, then the allocation (G^e, U^e) is socially optimal.*

Similarly, if $(P^e, E_D^e, F^e, E_S^e, G^e, U^e)$ is a dynamic competitive equilibrium in Scenario 2, then the allocation (G^e, U^e) is socially optimal.

5. NUMERICAL SOLUTION OF THE PROBLEM

In the rest of this paper we compute numerically the equilibrium prices and welfare given by Theorem 1. To this end we use a specific model for the random component $Z(t)$ that is both tractable and realistic.

5.1 Branching Trajectory Forecasts

We use discrete time and evaluate our model over a period of 24h. Each time slot represents a five minute interval [16]. Hence, the real-time market lasts for $T = 288$ time slots.

Inspired by the methodology of Pinson *et al.* [15], we assume that the forecast error process Z can be represented by a finite number of 2^τ trajectories. For a trajectory $\omega \in \{1 \dots 2^\tau\}$, the value of the forecast error at time t is denoted $Z^\omega(t)$. To model the fact that the forecast for the near future (*e.g.*, the next hour) is more accurate than the forecast for a distant future (*e.g.*, 12 hours from the present), we consider that the possible trajectories for the forecast error coincide initially before separating in distinct branches at certain moments $\{t_1 \dots t_\tau\}$. Thus, over time the number of branches increases exponentially: between times t_{k-1} and time t_k, there are 2^k possible such branches of the forecast errors. We consider that initially, between times $t_0 = 0$ and t_1, there are two equally likely branches: the odd trajectories and the even trajectories.

At each time t_k, each group of trajectories separates into two equiprobable groups of trajectories. Formally, between t_{k-1} and t_k, all trajectories ω that have the same remainder modulo 2^k share the same values:

$$\forall \omega < 2^\tau - 2^k, \forall t \in [t_{k-1}; t_k] : Z^\omega(t) = Z^{\omega+2^k}(t). \quad (18)$$

An example of trajectory is represented in Figure 2. For more clarity, we only represent eight trajectories. In the rest of the paper, the numerical evaluations use 512 trajectories. On this figure, we see that before $t_1 := 4.5h$, there are two possible forecast errors (the "odd" and "even" trajectories) Between t_1 and $t_2 = 12h$, there are four branches. After t_2, all trajectories are distinct.

These trajectories are generated using the covariance of real forecast errors in the UK. The methodology and the algorithm used will be described in §6.1.

5.1.1 Observability assumptions

We assume that at each of the branching instants t_k, players can observe the forecast error and can know on which branch the system is evolving at t_k. However, they cannot predict which branch the forecast errors will follow after t_k. For example, a time $t_1 = 4.5h$, players can observe if the forecast error is one of the four odd (Z^1, Z^3, Z^5, Z^7) or one

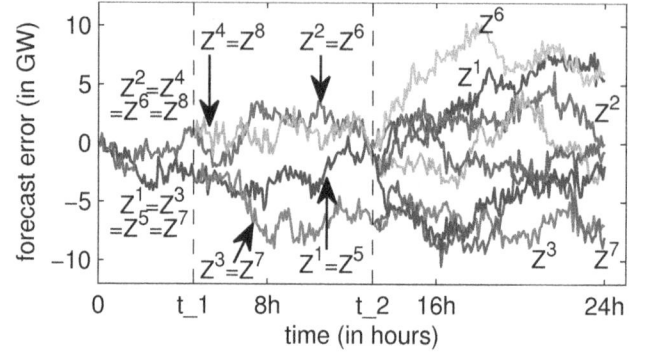

Figure 2: Possible trajectories of the forecast errors. To ease the presentation, this example has only eight trajectories. The numerical results of Section 6 use 512 trajectories. These trajectories are generated using data from the UK (see §6.1).

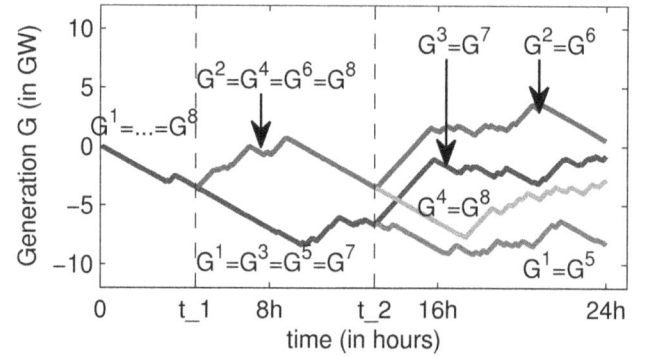

Figure 3: Example of an admissible control for G corresponding to the forecast errors of Figure 2.

of the four even trajectories. The only information about the future that they have is that each trajectory is *equiprobable*.

The set of control variables $(G, U, \dots)$ is restricted to the set of admissible controls, which are the sequence of causal decisions: a decision taken at time t can use the information available at time t as well as the statistics about future trajectories but not the exact future realization of the forecast errors. Using our observation model, this means an admissible control for G and U is a sequence of values $G^\omega(t)$ and $U^\omega(t)$ that satisfies the generation and DR constraints (3) such that for all $\omega < 2^\tau - 2^k$ and all $t \in [t_k; t_{k+1}]$:

$$G^\omega(t) = G^{\omega+2^k}(t); \quad U^\omega(t) = U^{\omega+2^k}(t). \quad (19)$$

For example, if the forecast error is represented by the trajectories of Figure 2, an example of admissible control for G is depicted in Figure 3. This control is causal. At time $t_0 = 0$ it knows that the forecast error may follow one of the two branches. The chosen control for the interval $[0; t_1]$ is a compromise that yields the best average performance. At the observation point t_1, players observe whether the branch that was followed was that of an odd or of an even trajectory. Since each branch separates again in two branches, there are two causal sequences of controls for the interval $[t_1; t_2]$ that can be applied, depending on the observations made at time t_1. Similarly, at time t_2 the four possible observations lead to four possible decisions.

5.2 Casting the Stochastic Problem into Coupled Deterministic Problems using ADMM

To compute the equilibrium, we use an optimization algorithm called the *alternating direction method of multipliers* (ADMM) [3]. ADMM is an iterative process to solve deterministic constrained maximization problems with concave[2] objective and linear constraints:

$$\max_{x \in \mathbb{R}^d, z \in \mathbb{R}^e} f(x) + g(z) \text{ subject to } Ax + Bz = c, \quad (20)$$

where f and g are two concave functions that take real values or $-\infty$; A and B are two matrices of size $d \times d_x$ and $d \times d_z$; and c is a vector of size d.

Let $\rho > 0$. For each $(x, z, \lambda) \in \mathbb{R}^{d_x + d_z + d}$, the augmented Lagrangian $L_\rho(x, z, \lambda)$ is defined as:

$$L_\rho(x, z, \lambda) = f(x) + g(z) - \frac{\rho}{2} \|Ax + Bz + \lambda - c\|^2. \quad (21)$$

ADMM performs the following iterations at step $k + 1$:

$$x^{k+1} := \arg\max_x L_\rho(x, z^k, \lambda^k) \quad (22)$$

$$z^{k+1} := \arg\max_x L_\rho(x^{k+1}, z, \lambda^k) \quad (23)$$

$$\lambda^{k+1} := \lambda_k + Ax^{k+1} + Bz^{k+1} - c, \quad (24)$$

where x^1, z^1 and λ^1 have been initialized to any vector of the proper size.

It is shown in [3] that under very general assumptions, the ADMM iterations converge to a solution of the optimization problem (20), regardless of the initial conditions. ADMM also converges when f or g are not strictly concave and when they take infinite values.

The social maximization problem (17), is a stochastic optimization problem where the expectation is taken over all possible forecast processes. As we assume that the forecast errors can be represented by a finite number of trajectories, this problem can be written

$$\arg\max_{G, U \in \text{admissible}} \sum_\omega W_{tot}(G^\omega, U^\omega).\text{proba}(\omega), \quad (25)$$

where the set admissible controls G, M denotes controls that satisfy generation constraints X_S, DR constraints X_U, as well as causality constraints (19).

In particular, Equation (19) implies that the decisions taken at a time t depend only on the information up to time t. As such, they are a compromise between the possible optimal decisions taken by a hypothetical omniscient controller that can observe the future.

5.3 Equilibrium Computation using ADMM

The formulation of ADMM, given by Equation (20), requires the optimization space to be partitioned into two groups of variables with no objective functions that depends on both groups, like $h(x, z)$. To perform this separation, we enlarge our optimization space. In addition to the original variables $G^\omega(t)$, $M^\omega(t)$ and $U^\omega(t)$, we add, for each $t < T$ and ω, the variables $\overline{M}^\omega(t)$, $\overline{G}^\omega(t)$, $\underline{G}^\omega(t)$, $E_D(t)$, $E_F^\omega(t)$, $E_S^\omega(t)$, $\underline{U}^\omega(t)$, $\overline{U}^\omega(t)$ and the linear constraints given by Equation (19) and

$$M(t+1) = \overline{M}(t)\Pi^0 + U(t)\Pi^1; \quad M(t) = \overline{M}(t); \quad (26)$$

---

[2] ADMM is usually presented as a solution to solve convex minimization problems. In this paragraph, we keep the concave maximization formulation of Section 3.

$$\underline{U}(t) = U(t); \overline{U}(t) = \overline{M}(t) - U(t); E_F(t) = P_{on}M(t) \cdot \varsigma^\top \quad (27)$$

$$\overline{G}(t) = G(t) = \underline{G}(t); \quad G(t) = E_S(t). \quad (28)$$

The first group of variables (the "X variables") contains the variables $M^\omega(t)$, $\underline{U}^\omega(t)$ and $\overline{U}^\omega(t)$, $G^\omega(t)$. The corresponding objective function $f(M, \underline{U}, \overline{U}, G)$ is:

$$\sum_{t,\omega} M^\omega(t) \cdot (v'P_{on}\varsigma - \kappa)^\top - cG^\omega(t) + \text{Pos}(\underline{U}^\omega, \overline{U}^\omega), \quad (29)$$

where $\text{Pos}(x, x') = 0$ if all coordinates of the vectors x and x' are non-negative and $-\infty$ otherwise.

The second group of variables contains the variables $\overline{M}$, U, $\overline{G}$, $\underline{G}$, E_D, E_F, E_S. The corresponding objective function $g(U, \overline{M}, \overline{G}, \underline{G}, E_D, E_F, E_S)$ is equal to:

$$\sum_{t,\omega} -(v + c^{bo})E_D(t)^- + \text{Pos}(\varsigma^+ - \underline{G}^\omega(t+1) + \overline{G}^\omega(t))$$

$$+ \text{Pos}(\underline{G}^\omega(t+1) - \overline{G}^\omega(t) - \varsigma^-)$$

$$+ \text{Equal0}(E_S^\omega(t) + Z^\omega(t) - E_D^\omega(t) - E_F^\omega(t)) \quad (30)$$

where $\text{Equal0}(x) = 0$ if all coordinates of x equal 0 and $-\infty$ otherwise.

5.4 Analysis of the ADMM Algorithm

When the constraints given by Equations (26-27) and the two terms $\text{Pos}(\cdot)$ of Equation (29) are satisfied, the evolution of $M(t)$, given by Equation (3) is respected. Similarly, the constraints given by (28) and the two term $\text{Pos}(\cdot)$ of Equation (30) ensure that the ramping constraints of G are satisfied.

This implies that our algorithm converges to the set of socially optimal allocations. Moreover, it also computes competitive equilibria. The following theorem summarizes these results. It is proved in Appendix B.

THEOREM 2. *Let E_D^k, E_S^k, G^k, U^k be the values after the kth iteration and let $(\lambda_G^k)^\omega(t)$ be the multipliers associated with the constraints $E_S^\omega(t) = G^\omega(t)$. Then:*
(i) There exists P such that $\lim_{k \to \infty} \rho(\lambda_G^k)^\omega(t) = P^\omega(t)$.
(ii) Any subsequence of E_D^k, E_S^k, G^k, U^k has a subsequence that converges. Let $E_D^\infty, E_S^\infty, G^\infty, U^\infty$ be its limit. Then
  - *$(P, E_D^\infty + E_F^\infty, E_S^\infty, G^\infty, U^\infty)$ is a competitive equilibrium for Scenario 1.*
  - *$(P, E_D^\infty, E_F^\infty, E_S^\infty, G^\infty, U^\infty)$ is a competitive equilibrium for Scenario 2.*
As a consequence, G^∞, U^∞ is socially optimal.
(iii) If the maximization algorithm has a unique solution, the algorithm converges to this solution. If there are multiple optimal solutions, they form a convex set and the algorithm converges to this set (for the Euclidean distance).

Remark. Even if we consider piecewise-linear objective functions, ADMM only requires the objective to be concave. Hence, the same algorithm can be applied to more general cost functions and Theorem 2 also holds.

6. NUMERICAL EVALUATIONS

6.1 Parameters and Trajectory Generation

As in [9], we use $\varsigma^+ = 1$GW/h, $\varsigma^- = 3\varsigma^+$. We set the ratio between the blackout cost and the generation cost to $(v + c^{bo})/c = 10$. The values of v, c^{bo} and c are normalized so the flexibility provided by *fridges* L parametrized below leads to a welfare gain of 100 when P_{on} is large.

We compare three cases of appliances [11]:

- **Fridges L** (large inertia fridges) – the *on* period is set to $X_{\max}/\gamma_{on} = 60$min and the off period is 120min, with a mini-cycle prevention period $Y_{\max}/\theta_{on}=0$ or 20min. It corresponds to $X_{\max}=6$, $\gamma_{on}=\theta_{on}=\theta_{off}=0.5$, $\gamma_{off}=0.25$.
- **Fridges S** (small inertia fridges) – same as *Fridges L* but with $X_{\max} = 3$. The only difference is that the *on* period lasts 30min and the *off* period lasts 60min.
- **Boilers** – the *on* period is $4h$ and the *off* period is $20h$. It corresponds to $X_{\max} = 12$, $\gamma_{on} = 0.25$, $\gamma_{off} = 0.05$ and $\theta_{on} = \theta_{off} = 0.5$.

The random transitions of our model of appliance account for various random evolutions of the internal temperature, *e.g.*, due to fridge doors opening. The second fridge model corresponds to a fridge with a smaller inertia. It consumes the same average power but has less flexibility, typically because the temperature deadband is narrower. The ratio between the duration of *off* and *on* periods is 2 for fridges and 5 for boilers. Our numerical evaluation shows that, qualitatively, the behaviors of the three models are the same.

6.1.1   Trajectory Generation using UK Data

To construct wind forecast errors, we use wind production and day-ahead wind production forecast in the time interval from June 2009 to April 2012, obtained from the BMRA data archive (**elexonportal.co.uk**). We normalize the values of production and forecast to maintain a constant wind capacity[3] of 26GW all throughout the 1300 days. We obtain 1300 samples of forecast error trajectories $\{\varepsilon_d(t)\}$. $\varepsilon_d(t)$ is the error for the day $d \in \{0 \dots 1300\}$ at time $t \in [0; 24h]$.

A generic method to generate forecast error trajectories has been introduced in [15]. To generate one trajectory, the authors compute the covariance Σ of the process ε_d (a 288×288 matrix in our case) and then generate a multivariate normal vector of covariance Σ. We adapt their method to our case of branching forecast. Algorithm 1 generates a set of trajectories such that each one has covariance Σ, and such that two trajectories that share a branching point depend on each other only via their values before the branching point.

Input: Covariance matrix Σ, sequence $t_1, \dots, t_{\tau-1}$
Output: Trajectories $Z^1, \dots, Z^{2^\tau}$
1 $A \leftarrow$ lower Cholesky decomposition of Σ; $t_0 \leftarrow 0$;
2 $N_1 \leftarrow$ vector of T *i.i.d.* normal random variables;
3 **for** $k \leftarrow 0$ **to** $\tau - 1$ **do**
4   **for** $\omega \leftarrow 1$ **to** 2^k **do**
5         $N^{\omega+2^k} \leftarrow [N^\omega(1\dots t_k); \hat{N}^{\omega+2^k}]$, where $\hat{N}^{\omega+2^k}$ is a vector of $T - t_k$ *i.i.d.* normally distributed random variables;
6   **end**
7 **end**
8 **for** $\omega \leftarrow 1$ **to** 2^τ **do**
9      $Z^\omega \leftarrow A \times N^\omega$;
10 **end**

Algorithm 1: Generation of 2^τ branching trajectories satisfying Theorem 3. The notation $N^\omega(1\dots t_k)$ denotes the first t_k elements of the vector N^ω. All vectors are column vectors. $[A; B]$ is the concatenation of two column vectors to form one column vector.

---

[3]This scenario is envisioned for the UK in 2020, where 20% of the total electricity consumption is covered by wind.

These properties are summarized in Theorem 3.

THEOREM 3. *Assume that Σ has full rank. Then, Algorithm 1 generates a set of trajectories such that:*
(i) individually, each trajectory Z^ω is a multivariate normal vector of covariance Σ;
(ii) If a subset of trajectories $Z^{i_1} \dots Z^{i_k}$ is fixed, then the distribution of another trajectory Z_i is the distribution of a multivariate normal vector of covariance Σ subject to respecting Equation (18).

This theorem is proved in Appendix C. The proof can be adapted if Σ is not full rank but it is more technical.

As a consequence, all trajectories $Z^1 \dots Z^{2^\tau}$ are equally likely. Moreover, as τ grows, the process obtained by following the branching trajectories "approaches" a normally distributed random process with covariance Σ.

6.2   Impact of DR Capactiy and of the Nature of Elastic Loads

For a given power flexibility P_{on}, we denote $\mathcal{W}^*(P_{on})$ the optimal value of social welfare in Equation (17). $\mathcal{W}^*(0)$ corresponds to the social welfare without DR. For $P_{on} > 0$, the optimal welfare $\mathcal{W}^*(P_{on})$ depends on the type of appliance, while $\mathcal{W}^*(0)$ does not.

In Figure 4 we plot the "relative" social welfare, *i.e.*, the difference $\mathcal{W}^*(P_{on}) - \mathcal{W}^*(0)$ as a function of P_{on}. We compare the three types of appliances. For *fridges L*, we plot both the case without mini-cycle avoidance ($Y_{\max} = 0$) and with mini-cycle avoidance ($Y_{\max} > 0$). As expected, the welfare is then increasing and concave in P_{on}. We observe that, as P_{on} grows, the social welfare increases and tends to stabilize at the value 100, regardless of the appliance type or the value of $Y_{\max}$, although for a fixed capacity of DR, increasing the mini-cycle avoidance parameter $Y_{\max}$ diminishes its benefits. Moreover, for a given appliance type, the gain of using demand-response is almost linear in P_{on} for small values of the installed capacity P_{on}. In view of the similarity of the appliance responses, for the rest of the numerical evaluation we only show the results for the *fridges L*.

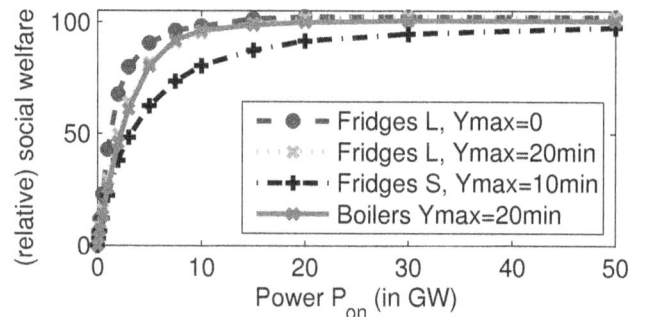

Figure 4: Relative social welfare $\mathcal{W}^*(P_{on}) - \mathcal{W}^*(0)$ as a function of P_{on} – the available power capacity of DR – for the three types of appliances.

6.3   Non-Observability of DR

The previous figure assumes that the day-ahead market is able to predict without error the consumption of demand-response appliances. In practice, this can be done because each appliance evolves mainly independently of the others.

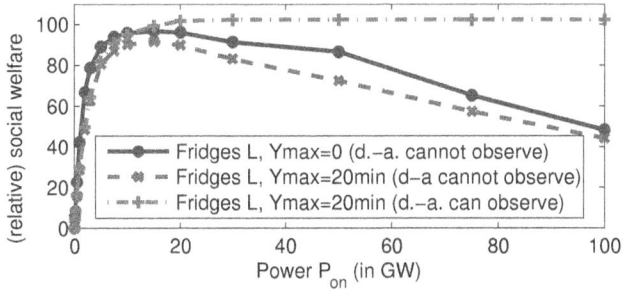

Figure 5: Relative social welfare $\mathcal{W}^*(P_{on}) - \mathcal{W}^*(0)$ as a function of available power flexibility P_{on} when the day-ahead market cannot observe DR's initial state, compared to the case when the day-ahead can observe this initial state. The x-axis is between 0 and 100GW.

As a results, the relative error of current load-prediction techniques is less than 1% [6]. However, one of the concerns of demand-response is that the presence of a large player that controls many appliances will introduce synchronization between devices, which will make the behavior of the system less predictable. For example, a small congestion can cause lots of DR loads to be delayed, which can cause a bigger problem in the future because these delayed loads were not forecast at this date [12].

In this section, we show that when the day-ahead market cannot fully observe the demand-response state, adding too much demand-response can be harmful, even if the real-time market has full information about the states of appliances. More precisely, we assume that:

- the day-ahead market cannot observe $M(0)$, the state of the demand-response at time 0. It assumes that $f^{da}(t)$ is equal to the overall average consumption of all demand-response appliances and plans the day-ahead generation $g^{da}(t)$ accordingly.
- the actor that controls flexible loads can observe the states of all DR appliances in real time.

We plot the relative social welfare $\mathcal{W}^*(P_{on}) - \mathcal{W}^*(0)$ for this scenario in Figure 5. When the flexible power is small ($P_{on} < 10$GW), the benefit of demand-response is close to the one with full information. However, when the power flexibility is large, adding more demand response decreases the total welfare. The non-observability problem is probably hidden today as the power flexibility of DR is small but this is a threat for the future. The results for *fridges S* and *boilers* are very similar and are not shown here.

6.4 Comparison with Energy Storage Systems

Demand-response is often viewed as a virtual energy storage system, which is potentially cheaper than real storage systems such as batteries. Instead of charging and discharging a battery, DR allows to anticipate or delay the consumption of appliances. In this section, we compare energy storage and flexible loads. We highlight two differences: for low capactiy, storage provides more flexibility because it reacts faster. However, at high capactiy, storage is less efficient because of the energy losses at each charging/discharging cycle.

We consider a storage model like in [9]: the storage has an energy capacity of B_{max} and a maximum charging and

discharging power capacity C_{max} and D_{max}. The cycle efficiency is η: only a fraction η of the stored energy can be retrieved. To perform a fair comparison of DR and storage, we consider a storage system that has the same flexible power: we set $C_{max} = D_{max} = P_{on}/2$. We chose B_{max} to reflect the quantity of the energy stored in DR appliances. Recall that when an appliance is *on*, its internal state x increases with probability γ_{on}. When *off*, its internal state decreases with probability γ_{off}. Thus, the average consumption of the DR appliances is $P_{on}\gamma_{off}/(\gamma_{on} + \gamma_{off})$. The internal state of an appliance that avoids the undesirable states oscillates between 0 and X_{max}. We set B_{max} equal to the difference in consumption between the case where all DR appliances have an internal state of X_{max} and the case where they are all in state 0. Hence, we take:

$$B_{max} = \frac{P_{on}X_{max}}{\gamma_{on} + \gamma_{off}} \times 5\text{min} \qquad (31)$$

With the *fridges L* model, this implies $B_{max} = \frac{P_{on}}{2}$GWh.

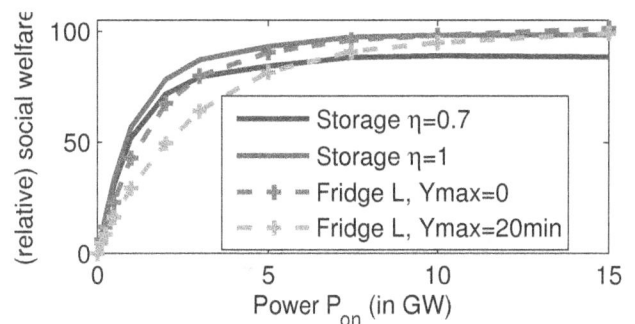

Figure 6: Social welfare as a function of available capacity of demand-response P_{on} or of storage. The storage flexibility is similar to the one of DR: $C_{max} = D_{max} = P_{on}/2$ and $B_{max} = (P_{on}/2)$GWh.

We adapt our ADMM algorithm of §5.3 for the case where a storage system replaces DR. The results are reported in Figure 6. We plot the welfare as a function of the flexible power P_{on} in four scenarios: presence of DR but no storage (two dashed curves); or presence of storage but no DR (two solid curves).

We observe that, at low power capacities, storage provide higher gain than DR. Two reasons explain this:

- the fatigue effect: because of internal state constraints, some appliances cannot be switched anymore.
- the mini-cycle effect $Y_{max} > 0$: appliances that have just been switched cannot be switched instantaneously.

For large capacities, the situation is reversed. The welfare of DR and that of idealized storage saturate at the same value. This value is strictly larger than the one of 70%-efficient storage. For large power capacity, DR outperforms realistic storage (typical efficiency $70 - 90\%$).

6.5 Price Equilibrium

When there is no demand-response or storage, it has been shown in [19] that the price process oscillates between 0 and the choke price $v + c^{bo}$. In this case it is never equal to the marginal production cost. The situation is different in the presence of storage. In [9], we exhibit two different situations, depending on the charge-discharge efficiency of storage η:

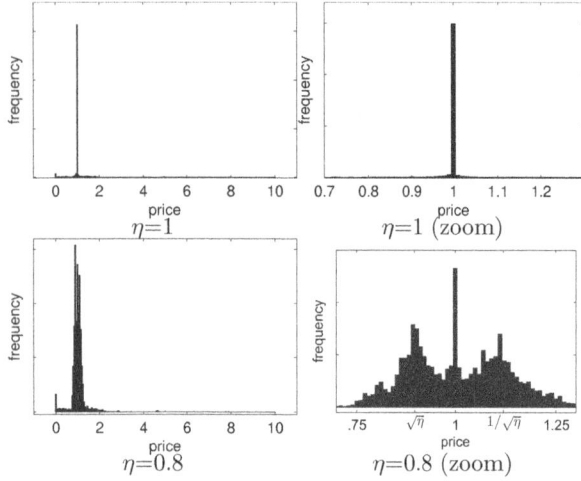

Figure 7: Distribution of prices for a system equipped with storage of capacity $C_{\max} = 5\text{GW}$, $B_{\max} = 5\text{GWh}$ and charge-discharge efficiency $\eta = 1$ or 0.8. For readability, we scale the values c, v and c^{bo} to $c = 1$.

a) When $\eta = 100\%$ (perfect storage), the prices do in fact concentrate on the marginal production cost c as the quantity of storage gets large.
b) When $\eta < 100\%$ (realistic storage), the prices do not concentrate on c, but exhibit two modes around $c\sqrt{\eta}$ and $c/\sqrt{\eta}$.

These results were obtained assuming that the forecast error is stationary and can be represented by a Brownian motion with stationary increments. We simulate the same scenarios using our more realistic non-stationary branching forecast model and our ADMM implementation. The price distributions are reported in Figure 7. They confirm that the results of [9] are robust to the forecast model: for $\eta = 1$, the prices concentrate on $c = 1$. For $\eta < 1$, the price distribution exhibit two modes around $\sqrt{\eta} \approx 0.89$ and $1/\sqrt{\eta} \approx 1.12$.

This price spread is explained by the fact that only a fraction η of the stored energy can be retrieved. As a consequence, a storage owner will store energy only if it can be sold at a $1/\eta$ times larger price. In the case of DR, the energy is virtually stored or retrieved by delaying or anticipating consumption. The corresponding prices are reported in Figure 8. It confirms that the system behaves like a 100% efficient storage system (like in §6.4): even when $Y_{\max} > 0$, the prices concentrate on the marginal production cost c.

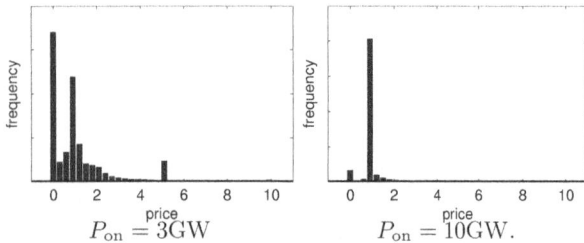

Figure 8: Distribution of prices for a system equipped with DR appliances *Fridges L* with $Y_{\max} = 20\text{min}$. For readability, we scale the values c, v and c^{bo} to $c = 1$.

6.6 Incentive to Install Demand Response

The storage/demand-response operator makes money via price arbitrage. An independent storage operator buys cheap energy and resells it when prices rise. Similarly, a demand-response operator tries to shift the appliances' consumption to when the energy is inexpensive. The flexibility brought by demand-response or by storage results in more concentrated prices. In [9], we have shown that, to maximize their revenue, independent storage operators will underdimension their storage system. In this section, we show that this also holds for DR operators.

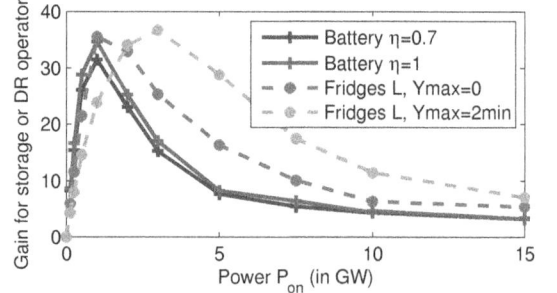

Figure 9: Revenue for the DR or storage operator as a function of the installed capacity. The studied scenarios are the same as in Figure 6.

We simulate the same scenarios as in Figure 6 and we compute the expected revenue of the DR operator or of the storage operator as a function of the flexible power capacity. In all cases, this gain reaches a maximum and then decreases. This maximum is attained at $P_{\text{on}} \approx 1\text{GW}$ for batteries and *fridges L* with $Y_{\max} = 0$. When $Y_{\max} = 20\text{min}$, this maximum is reached at $P_{\text{on}} \approx 3\text{GW}$. More problematically, the maximum is attained at a value that is far from optimal for the social welfare: This entails that even if we disregard installation costs, the operator seeking to maximize her revenue will not deploy more than 1GW (or 3GW) of DR capacity. In Figure 4, we observe that these values of P_{on} lead to a gain of only $40-60\%$ of the potential welfare benefit of DR/storage. Hence, to maximize her revenue, a DR operator will deploy a suboptimal capacity from a social perspective.

7. CONCLUSION

In this paper we studied the effects of demand-response in a real-time electricity market. We modeled a population of flexible appliances that can anticipate or delay their consumption. This model accounts for fatigue via undesirable states and enforces mini-cycle avoidance via an additional dimension in the state space. We showed that when demand-response is traded by price-taking actors, the dynamic competitive equilibrium is socially efficient. We considered a realistic and tractable trajectorial forecast error model where trajectories separate into branches over time. We parametrized the model using real wind forecasts from the UK and solved numerically the model by using ADMM. We showed that if the appliance states are unknown, too much demand-response can be detrimental. We compared demand-response to an energy storage system and concluded that a sufficiently large amount of demand-response is as beneficial as a perfect storage system. Demand-response relaxes the ramping constraints of generation and smooths prices, that concentrate around the marginal generation cost.

APPENDIX

A. PROOF OF THEOREM 1

We give the proof for Scenario 1. The proof for Scenario 2 is similar, with three actors instead of two. It is similar to the proof of [9, Theorem 2] and [19].

Let $\mathcal{W}(G, U)$ be the social welfare. For a given price P, we denote $\mathcal{W}_D(E_D, U, P)$ the welfare of the consumer when she takes the decisions E_D, U and by $\mathcal{W}_S(E_S, G, P)$, the welfare of the supplier for the decisions E_S, G. We consider the social optimization problem (17) and we relax the constraint $E_S = E_D$. Denoting the corresponding Lagrange multiplier by P, the Lagrangian $\mathcal{L}(E_D, E_S, U, G, P)$ is equal to:

$$\mathcal{W}(G, U) + \mathbb{E}\left[\sum_{t=0}^{t} P(t)(E_D(t) - E_S(t))\right]$$
$$= \mathcal{W}_D(E_D, U, P) + \mathcal{W}_S(E_S, G, P).$$

When the constraint $E_D = E_S$ is respected, the social welfare $\mathcal{W}(G, U)$ equals $\mathcal{W}_D(E_D, U, P) + \mathcal{W}_S(E_S, G, P)$.

If $(E_D^e, E_S^e, G^e, U^e, P^e)$ is a competitive equilibrium, then

$$\sup_{G,U} \mathcal{W}(G, U) = \sup_{\substack{G,U,E_S,E_D \\ \text{s.t. } E_S = E_D}} \mathcal{L}(E_D, E_S, G, U, P^e)$$
$$\leq \sup_{G,U,E_S,E_D} \mathcal{L}(E_D, E_S, G, U, P^e)$$
$$= \sup_{E_D,U} \mathcal{W}_D(E_D, U, P^e) + \sup_{E_S,G} \mathcal{W}_S(E_S, G, P^e)$$
$$= \mathcal{W}(E_D^e, U^e, P^e) + \mathcal{W}_S(E_S^e, G^e, P^e)$$
$$= \mathcal{W}(G^e, U^e).$$

The last equality holds because a competitive equilibrium implies $E_D^e = E_S^e$. The one before last equality holds because each player maximizes his social welfare.

Hence, the allocation (G^e, U^e) is socially optimal. $\square$

B. PROOF OF THEOREM 2

B.1 Convergence of ADMM

The problem formulated in §5.3 is a maximization problem with a concave objective and linear constraints. Moreover, there exists a allocation such that all constraints are satisfied (for example $G^\omega(t) = G(0)$, and $M^\omega(t+1) = M^\omega(t)\Pi^1$). Hence, the Slater's conditions are satisfied and the unaugmented Lagrangian has a saddle point [4, Chapter 5].

We use the generic notation of §5.2 and denote the variables after iteration k by x^k, z^k, λ^k. By [3, §3.2.1], the existence of the saddle point implies:

(I) x^k, z^k approach feasibility: $\lim_{k\to\infty} Ax^k + Bz^k = c$.
(II) λ^k converges to a dual optimal point λ^∞.
(III) $f(x^k) + g(z^k)$ converges to the optimal value of the social optimal problem:

$$\lim_{k\to\infty} f(x^k) + g(z^k) = \sup_{x,z \text{ s.t.} Ax+Bz=c} f(x) + g(z)$$

The augmented Lagrangian $L_\rho(x, z, \lambda)$ goes to infinity as x or z goes to infinity. Hence, the iterations x^k, z^k are bounded and any subsequence x^k, z^k has converging subsequence. Let x^∞, z^∞ be its limit. By (I), (x^∞, z^∞) is a feasible allocation. Moreover, by (III), it is socially optimal allocation. This shows *(i)* and *(iii)*. Since λ^∞ is a dual optimal point, $(x^\infty, z^\infty, \lambda^\infty)$ is a saddle point. In particular, (x^∞, z^∞) is a maximizer of $L_\rho(x, z, \lambda^\infty)$.

B.2 Definition of the Price as a Multiplier

In our ADMM formulation of §5.3, the augmented Lagrangian $L_\rho(x, z, \lambda)$, is equal to:

$$\sum_{t,\omega} -(v+c^{bo})E_D^\omega(t)^- -cG^\omega(t) + \text{Pos}(\underline{U}^\omega)+\text{Pos}(\overline{U}^\omega)$$
$$+ \text{Pos}(\zeta^+ -\underline{G}^\omega(t+1)+\overline{G}^\omega(t))+\text{Pos}(\underline{G}^\omega(t+1)-\overline{G}^\omega(t)-\zeta^-)$$
$$+ \text{Equal0}(E_S^\omega(t) + Z^\omega(t) - E_F^\omega(t) - E_D^\omega(t))$$
$$- \frac{\rho}{2}\|Ax + Bz - c + \lambda\|^2,$$

where the linear equation $Ax + Bz = c$ represents all linear constraints (26,27,28) and (19).

Let $(\lambda_G^k)^\omega(t)$ and $(\lambda_F^k)^\omega(t)$ be the multipliers after the kth iteration of the ADMM, corresponding to the constraints $E_S^\omega(t) = G^\omega(t)$ and $E_F(t) = F(t)$ respectively. The values of E_S^{k+1} and E_F^{k+1} after the kth iteration maximize

$$-\frac{\rho}{2}(\|E_S-G^{k+1}+\lambda_G^k\|^2 + \|E_F-F^{k+1} + \lambda_F^k\|^2)-(v+c^{bo})E_D(t)^-, \quad (32)$$

subject to $E_S + Z - E_F - E_D = 0$.

A necessary condition for that is that $E_S^{k+1} - G^{k+1} + \lambda_G^k = -(E_F^{k+1} - F^{k+1} + \lambda_F^k)$. By Equation (24), the multipliers λ_G^{k+1} and λ_F^{k+1} are $\lambda_G^{k+1} := \lambda_G^k + E_S^{k+1} - G^{k+1}$ and $\lambda_F^{k+1} := \lambda_F^k + E_F^{k+1} - F^{k+1}$. Hence, this implies that after this iteration, the two multipliers λ_G^{k+1} and λ_G^{k+1} are opposite (for all t, ω).

Let $(\lambda_G^\infty)^\omega(t)$ be the limit of $(\lambda_G^k)^\omega(t)$ as k grows. We define the price process $P^\omega(t)$ as $P^\omega(t) = \rho(\lambda_G^\infty)^\omega(t)$.

B.3 This Price Leads to an Equilibrium

We now show that this price leads to a competitive equilibrium for Scenario 2. The proof is similar for Scenario 1. We denote the limiting values of λ^k, x^k, z^k and by $\lambda^\infty, x^\infty = (M^\infty, \underline{U}^\infty, \overline{U}^\infty, G^\infty), z^\infty = (\overline{M}^\infty, U^\infty, \overline{G}^\infty, \underline{G}^\infty, E_D^\infty, E_F^\infty, E_S^\infty)$.

Supplier's problem – We first show that G^∞ is an optimal schedule for the supplier's – The vector (x^∞, z^∞) maximizes $L_\rho(x, z, \lambda^\infty)$. Hence, $(G^\infty, \overline{G}^\infty, \underline{G}^\infty)$ maximizes

$$\sum_{t,\omega} -cG^\omega(t) - \frac{\rho}{2}[E_S^\omega(t) - G^\omega(t) + \lambda_G^\omega(t)]^2 \quad (33)$$
$$+ \text{Pos}(\zeta^+ -\underline{G}^\omega(t+1)+\overline{G}^\omega(t))+\text{Pos}(\underline{G}^\omega(t+1)-\overline{G}^\omega(t)-\zeta^-)$$
$$- \frac{\rho}{2}[G^\omega(t)-\overline{G}^\omega(t)+\lambda_{\overline{G}}^\omega(t)]^2 - \frac{\rho}{2}[G^\omega(t)-\underline{G}^\omega(t)+\lambda_{\underline{G}}^\omega(t)]^2$$

The quantity $\frac{\rho}{2}\|E_S^\omega-G^\omega+\lambda_G^\omega\|^2$ rewrites as $P^\omega \cdot (E_S^\omega-G^\omega)^\top + \frac{\rho}{2}(\|\lambda_G^\omega\|^2+\|E_S^\omega-G^\omega\|^2)$. Since G^∞ maximizes (33) and satisfies $G^\infty = \overline{G}^\infty = \underline{G}^\infty$, it also maximizes $f_\rho(G)$, where

$$f_\rho(G) = \sum_{t,\omega}(P^\omega(t) - c)G^\omega(t) - \frac{\rho}{2}\|E_S^\omega(t)-G^\omega(t)\|^2.$$

Let G_S be an optimal schedule for the supplier and let us show that G^∞ also optimal for the supplier.

For $\theta \in [0; 1]$, we define an allocation $G_\theta := \theta G_S + (1 - \theta)G^\infty$ and $g_0(\theta) = f_0(G_\theta)$ and $g_\rho(\theta) = f_\rho(G_\theta)$. As $G^\infty = E_S$ we have

$$g_0(\theta) = \sum_{t,\omega}(P^\omega(t) - c)G_\theta^\omega(t); \quad (34)$$

$$g_\rho(\theta) = \sum_{t,\omega}(P^\omega(t) - c)G_\theta^\omega(t) - \theta^2\frac{\rho}{2}\|G_S-G^\infty\|^2. \quad (35)$$

As G_θ is a convex combination of two feasible allocation. Hence, it also satisfies the generation constraints. As G_S is optimal for the supplier, the function $g_0(\theta)$, attains its maximum in $\theta = 1$. Moreover, this function is concave in θ and therefore, it has a right derivative in $\theta = 0$ that satisfies $g_0'(0) \geq 0$. Similarly, the function g_ρ is concave and attains its maximum in $\theta = 0$. Hence, it has a right derivative in $\theta = 0$ that satisfies $g_\rho'(0) \leq 0$.

It should be clear from the expressions of g_0 and g_ρ, given by Equations (34) and (35), that $g_0'(0) = g_\rho'(0)$. This implies that $g_0'(0) = 0$. Hence, $\theta = 0$ is also an optimum for g_0, which implies that G^∞ is optimal for the supplier.

DR operator's problem – We showed in §B.2 that the multipliers for $E_F = F$ and for $E_S = G$ are opposite. Hence, the optimality of E_F^∞, U^∞ for the DR operator under the price P follows from the same approach as for the supplier (by comparing the situations $\rho = 0$ and $\rho > 0$).

Demand's problem – Replacing E_S by $E_D + E_F - Z$, maximizing Equation (32) on E_D subject to $E_S + Z - E_D - E_F = 0$ is equivalent to maximizing without constraint:

$$-\frac{\rho}{2}(\|E_D + E_F - Z - G^{k+1} + \lambda_G^k\|^2 + \|E_F - F^{k+1} + \lambda_F^k\|^2) - (v + c^{bo})E_D(t)^-.$$

As the second term does not depend on E_D, it maximizes

$$-\frac{\rho}{2}\|E_D + E_F - Z - G\|^2 - P(t)E_D(t) - (v + c^{bo})E_D(t)^-.$$

Hence, the optimality of E_D for the Demand under the price P follows from the same approach as for the supplier (by comparing $\rho = 0$ and $\rho > 0$).

C. PROOF OF THEOREM 3

The matrix Σ is the covariance of the forecast error process ε. As such, Σ is a positive-definite symmetric matrix of size $T \times T$ and has real entries. Thus, there exists a real matrix A of size $T \times T$ such that $\Sigma = A \times A^\top$ and A is a lower-triangular matrix, i.e., for all $t \in \{1, \ldots, T\}$ and $s \in \{t+1, \ldots, T\}$, $A_{t,s} = 0$. A is called the lower Cholesky decomposition of Σ. It also exists when Σ is not full rank.

Let Z^ω be a trajectory. By construction, the vector N^ω is a vector of T i.i.d. normally distributed random variables. Moreover, we have $Z^\omega(t) = \sum_s A_{t,s} N^\omega(s)$. Hence, the covariance $\mathbb{E}[Z^\omega(t) Z^\omega(t')]$ is equal to $AA' = \Sigma$, which implies that property *(i)* holds.

Let us fix a sub-set of trajectories $Z^{\omega_1} \ldots Z^{\omega_k}$ and let Z^ω be another trajectory. Let τ be the largest branching time of Z^ω shared with one of these trajectories. By construction, $Z^\omega = AN^\omega$. The matrix A and the vector N^ω can be decomposed as:

$$A = \begin{bmatrix} B & 0 \\ C & D \end{bmatrix} \text{ and } N^\omega = \begin{bmatrix} N_1 \\ N_2 \end{bmatrix},$$

where the matrices B, C and D have size $\tau \times \tau$, $(T - \tau) \times \tau$ and $(T - \tau) \times (T - \tau)$ and N_1 has size τ.

By construction, the distribution of Z^ω given trajectories $Z^{\omega_1}, \ldots, Z^{\omega_k}$ is the distribution of Z^ω given $N^\omega(1), \ldots, N^\omega(\tau)$. Let $z = B.[N^\omega(1), \ldots, N^\omega(\tau)]$. Because A has full rank, B has also full rank and is invertible. Hence, the distribution of Z^ω conditioned on $Z^\omega(t) = z_t$ for $t \leq \tau$ is the same as the distribution of Z^ω given $N^\omega(1) \ldots N^\omega(\tau)$. The former is the conditional distribution of a multivariate Gaussian random variable of covariance Σ subject to Equation (18). $\square$

D. REFERENCES

[1] M. H. Albadi and E. El-Saadany. A summary of demand response in electricity markets. *Electric Power Systems Research*, 78(11):1989–1996, 2008.

[2] M. Benaim and J.-Y. Le Boudec. A class of mean field interaction models for computer and communication systems. *Performance Evaluation*, 65(11):823–838, 2008.

[3] S. Boyd, N. Parikh, E. Chu, B. Peleato, and J. Eckstein. Distributed optimization and statistical learning via the alternating direction method of multipliers. *Foundations and Trends® in Machine Learning*, 3(1):1–122, 2011.

[4] S. P. Boyd and L. Vandenberghe. *Convex optimization.* Cambridge university press, 2004.

[5] I. Cho and S. Meyn. Efficiency and marginal cost pricing in dynamic competitive markets with friction. *Theoretical Economics*, 5(2):215–239, 2010.

[6] E. A. Feinberg and D. Genethliou. Load forecasting. In *Applied mathematics for restructured electric power systems*, pages 269–285. Springer, 2005.

[7] N. Gast and B. Gaujal. A mean field approach for optimization in discrete time. *Discrete Event Dynamic Systems*, 21(1):63–101, 2011.

[8] N. Gast, B. Gaujal, and J.-Y. Le Boudec. Mean field for markov decision processes: from discrete to continuous optimization. *Automatic Control, IEEE Transactions on*, 57(9):2266–2280, 2012.

[9] N. Gast, J.-Y. Le Boudec, A. Proutière, and D.-C. Tomozei. Impact of storage on the efficiency and prices in real-time electricity markets. In *Proceedings of the fourth international conference on Future energy systems*, pages 15–26. ACM, 2013.

[10] S. Koch, J. L. Mathieu, and D. S. Callaway. Modeling and control of aggregated heterogeneous thermostatically controlled loads for ancillary services. In *Proc. PSCC*, pages 1–7, 2011.

[11] G. Koutitas and L. Tassiulas. A delay based optimization scheme for peak load reduction in the smart grid. In *Proceedings of the 3rd International Conference on Future Energy Systems: Where Energy, Computing and Communication Meet*, page 7. ACM, 2012.

[12] J.-Y. Le Boudec and D.-C. Tomozei. Stability of a Stochastic Model for Demand-response. *Stochastic Systems*, 3(1):11–37, 2013.

[13] S. Meyn, P. Barooah, A. Busic, and J. Ehren. Ancillary service to the grid from deferrable loads: the case for intelligent pool pumps in Florida. *ACE (GW)*, 100(50):50, 2013.

[14] A.-H. Mohsenian-Rad and A. Leon-Garcia. Optimal residential load control with price prediction in real-time electricity pricing environments. *Smart Grid, IEEE Transactions on*, 1(2):120–133, 2010.

[15] P. Pinson, H. Madsen, H. A. Nielsen, G. Papaefthymiou, and B. Klöckl. From probabilistic forecasts to statistical scenarios of short-term wind power production. *Wind energy*, 12(1):51–62, 2009.

[16] Pjm operational data, 2013. http://www.pjm.com/markets-and-operations/energy/real-time/lmp.aspx.

[17] K. Spees and L. B. Lave. Demand response and electricity market efficiency. *The Electricity Journal*, 20(3):69–85, 2007.

[18] C.-L. Su and D. Kirschen. Quantifying the effect of demand response on electricity markets. *Power Systems, IEEE Transactions on*, 24(3):1199–1207, 2009.

[19] G. Wang, M. Negrete-Pinetic, A. Kowli, E. Shafieepoorfard, S. Meyn, and U. Shanbhag. Dynamic competitive equilibria in electricity markets. In *Control and Optimization Theory for Electric Smart Grids*. Springer, 2011.

[20] R. Wilson. Architecture of power markets. *Econometrica*, 70(4):1299–1340, 2003.

iDR: Consumer and Grid Friendly Demand Response System[*]

Vikas Chandan[#1], Tanuja Ganu[#1], Tri Kurniawan Wijaya[#2†], Marilena Minou[#3],
George Stamoulis[#3], George Thanos[#3], Deva P. Seetharam[#1]

[#1]IBM Research India, [#2]EPFL, Switzerland, [#3]Athens University of Economics and Business, Greece

ABSTRACT

Peak demand is a major challenge for power utilities across the world. Demand Response (DR) is considered to be effective in addressing peak demand by altering consumption of end consumers, so as to match supply capability. However, an efficient DR system needs to respect end consumer convenience and understand their propensity of participating in a particular DR event, while altering the consumer demand. Understanding such preferences is non-trivial due to the large-scale and variability of consumers and the infrastructure changes required for collecting essential (smart meter and/or appliance specific) data.

In this paper, we propose an inclusive DR system, *iDR*, that helps an electricity provider to design an effective demand response event by analyzing its consumers' house-level consumption (smart meter) data and external context (weather conditions, seasonality etc.) data. *iDR* combines analytics and optimization to determine optimal power consumption schedules that satisfy an electricity provider's DR objectives - such as reduction in peak load - while minimizing the inconvenience caused to consumers associated with alteration in their consumption patterns. *iDR* uses a novel context-specific approach for determining end consumer baseline consumptions and user convenience models. Using these consumer specific models and past DR experience, *iDR* optimization engine identifies -(i) when to execute a DR event, (ii) who are the consumers to be targeted for the DR, and (iii) what signals to be sent. Some of *iDR*'s capabilities are demonstrated using real-world house-level as well as appliance-level data.

Categories and Subject Descriptors

H.4 [**Information Systems Applications**]: Miscellaneous

[*]Supported by European Union's Seventh Framework Programme (FP7/2007-2013) 288322, WATTALYST.

[†] This work was done during the author's internship at IBM Research, India

General Terms

User preferences, Human Factors, Optimal Scheduling

Keywords

Demand Response, Energy Consumption Scheduling, User Preferences, Smart Grids, Smart Meters

1. INTRODUCTION

Demand Response (DR) programs aim to alleviate the peak demand problem and provide higher system reliability by altering consumer demand in response to the power grid's supply and economic conditions. Various evaluation studies indicate that DR can be an effective mechanism for addressing the challenges of growing energy demand and related supply-demand imbalances [1–3]. A staff report by Federal Energy Regulatory Commission [4] estimates that the feasibility of peak demand reduction in the United States can be up to 20% by using DR technologies with full participation. As per another study [5], DR programs alone could achieve up to half of the European Union's 2020 targets concerning energy savings and CO2 emissions. Additionally, many electricity suppliers around the world are deploying smart meters to gather fine-grained spatio-temporal consumption data, and to provide a bi-directional communication mechanism [6]. This infrastructure enhancement is a significant enabler for bringing DR vision to reality.

However, the success of DR programs essentially depends upon the end consumers' participation. Various evaluation studies [7, 8] based on results of DR pilots and surveys of participants indicate that *discomfort/inconvenience* caused during a DR event is a key factor that adversely affects DR participation. Additionally, it was found that demographic attributes such as family size, income level, participants' activity structure, etc. are relevant factors for DR participation. Hence, any effective DR system needs to understand the end consumers' electricity usage preferences and their demographic attributes while choosing the right set of consumers for a DR contract and/or for a particular DR event.

Energy suppliers/aggregators offer various types of DR contracts to the end consumers, such as Time of Use (ToU) Rates, Capacity Biding Programs (CBP), Demand Biding Programs (DBP) and Peak Day Pricing (PDP) [9]. Any particular DR program needs to confer *fairness* amongst consumers under the same DR contract. Additionally, it should also take into account adverse side-effects of DR, such as rebound effect [10]. Considering above mentioned challenges, it is non-trivial to determine - (i) the *time window* for executing a DR event, considering supply conditions and predicted consumer demand, (ii) the *right set of consumers to be targeted* for a particular DR event considering factors such as end consumers' preferences, DR contracts and DR participation history, (iii) *target reduction per consumer* and *expected DR outcome*.

To address the afore-mentioned challenges, in this paper, we present *iDR*, an inclusive DR planning system, that helps energy suppliers design effective DR events, while taking into account consumers' preferences and fairness of the system with respect to the DR contracts. The key contributions of this paper are:

1. A novel context-based method to determine baseline consumption and quantify inconvenience caused to consumers (in the form of utility functions), using smart meter data.

2. A novel and simple context-based approach to determine inconvenience (in the form of utility functions) using appliance-level data, if available.

3. A stochastic optimization framework that uses the above utility functions to determine when to execute DR events, which consumers to target, and what signals to send.

4. A mechanism to ensure fairness amongst multiple consumers with same type of DR contract while planning DR events.

The remainder of this paper is organized as follows. In Section II, we provide an overview of the related work. In Section III, we describe our context based approaches for determining end consumers' preferences of electricity usage. In Section IV, we define an optimization framework for optimal and fair DR scheduling. We showcase the evaluation of *iDR* on a real-world dataset in Section V, and finally, in Section VI, we conclude our work and discuss avenues for future work.

2. RELATED WORK

Determining consumer preferences for individual appliance usage and using these preferences for optimal appliance scheduling is well studied in literature. In [11], the authors consider optimal household appliance scheduling for dynamic pricing. They propose a system, *Yupik* that determines preferred time of use for individual appliances and generates appliance usage schedules to minimize both a household's energy costs and potential lifestyle disruptions. [12] presents a methodology to schedule appliances taking into account cost, scheduling preferences and climactic comfort requirements. In [13], authors propose an approach for determining consumer preferences for appliance use by categorizing household appliances into four types and deriving different utility functions for each of these types. Further, they propose an optimal DR strategy based on utility maximization, where dual objectives are formulated for cost minimization from the utility provider's perspective, and social welfare maximization from the consumers' perspective. [14] extends this work for computation time reduction by proposing load consolidation and a LP framework.

Though the existing literature provides various approaches for modeling and determining consumer preferences and optimal scheduling for demand response events or dynamic pricing, their practical usefulness is somewhat limited because of the underlying complexity associated with the use of appliance level utility models only. For example, a utility provider might not have access to appliance level consumption information for all its consumers. This motivates the need for a DR planning methodology which is not dependent on fine-grained appliance-level information, but works well with house-level (smart meter) consumption data only. In this paper, we present a novel approach for determining consumer preferences using smart meter data only, and/or appliance level data, if available. Additionally, the existing work mainly considers automatic demand response scenarios and hence proposes the direct control or scheduling of individual home appliances. On the contrary, we consider a more practical and widely prevalent demand response scenario wherein the utility provider sends DR signals to consumers, and thereafter consumers can accept or decline the signals and determine appliance schedules as per their convenience. In this context, this paper presents a *stochastic optimization* approach to determine when to send DR signal (optimal DR timeslots), whom to send it (selecting the right set of consumers) and how much reduction to target.

There is also an increasing interest in obtaining useful DR related insights from smart meter data such as application specific consumer segmentation or baseline load forecasting for individual consumers. For example, smart meter data has been used for consumer segmentation in [15] and [16]. A body of literature also exists on baseline consumption estimation. KEMA Inc. [17] and EnerNOC [18] provide excellent overviews of the baseline estimation methods employed by utilities in the United States. The above-mentioned references serve as enablers or background for our approach of optimal DR using smart meter data. However, existing work has not used smart meter data for understanding consumer preferences and subsequent DR planning. The proposed work addresses these gaps by providing a methodology to plan and schedule DR events based on smart meter data alone as well as combining appliance-level data, if available.

3. DETERMINING CONSUMER PREFERENCES

In this section, we present methodologies to model the utility (benefit) derived by a consumer as a function of her consumption. These models form the basis of the optimization framework presented in section 4. We propose two utility modeling frameworks - one at the aggregate house level (using smart meter data), and another which uses appliance level consumption data if such high resolution sensing infrastructure is available. The common nomenclature used in this paper is shown in Table 1.

3.1 Preference mining using smart meter data

Analysis of historical consumption data for a consumer over time can provide information on her consumption preferences. We use two quantities - baseline and utility - to quantify such preferences. Baseline is defined as an estimate of the electrical load drawn by a consumer in the absence of any DR related curtailment actions. Utility is defined as the 'benefit' obtained by a consumer corresponding to a given amount of consumption. The objective of preference mining in this work using smart meter data is to determine baselines and utilities for each consumer. The underlying methods are explained below.

Symbol	Description
d	General notation to represent a day
i	General notation to represent a consumer
t	General notation to represent a timeslot
T	Number of timeslots in a day d
N	Number of consumers served by a utility company
$Q_{i,t,d}$	Consumption in kWh by consumer i during timelot t in day d
$Q_{i,t,d}^b$	Baseline consumption in kWh by consumer i during timelot t in day d
$U_{i,t,d}(.)$	Utility function associated with consumer i during timelot t in day d
$Q_{t,d}^s$	Maximum amount of energy in kWh that the utility can supply during timelot t in day d
n_t	Maximum number of consumers that the utility decides to target for DR during timelot t
η_{max}^t	Maximum reduction in consumption as a fraction of baseline consumption
$\nu_{i,t,d}$	Boolean variable representing whether consumer i should be targeted for DR during timelot t in day d
$\Delta Q_{i,t,d}$	Reduction in consumption (kWh) from baseline by consumer i during timelot t in day d

Table 1: Nomenclature of common symbols

3.1.1 Baseline estimation

Existing methods for baseline estimation involve averaging [17], regression [19] and time series analysis [20]. In this work, we obtain baselines by first identifying appropriate consumer contexts. A context is defined as a combination of external and internal factors that influence a consumer's consumption decisions. For instance, at a month level, influencing contexts could be season of a year (summer, autumn, winter or spring) or at a finer resolution month of the year (January, February, etc.). Similarly, at a day level, possible contexts are weekday/weekend or day of the week(Monday, Tuesday, etc.).

Multiple contexts may be associated with a particular day. As an example, October 17th, 2013 can be represented by contexts such as {Autumn}, {Autumn, weekday}, {October, Thursday}, etc. To choose the most appropriate context, and obtain the corresponding baseline consumptions, we proceed as follows:

1. We denote the day for which baselines are to be estimated by d. We assume that this day is divided into T discrete timeslots. We first identify the set $C(d)$ consisting of all contexts and their combinations that explains the day d.

2. Based on the historical data, we find the context $C^* \in C(d)$, whose consumption has lowest dispersion. Here dispersion can be quantified using statistical measures such as standard deviation or inter-quartile range.

3. The baseline consumption for each timeslot $t \in \{1, 2, ..., T\}$ is then determined by a measure of central tendency - such as mean or median - applied to historical consumption data at timeslot t on previous days in the context C^*.

In obtaining the baseline consumption as described above, historical data can be used in several different ways. The simplest method is to use a static time window, where consumption data from all previous days in the context are used,

irrespective of how far in the past these days are from the day d. On the other hand, a moving window approach only uses consumption data from N_{prev} most recent days. An exponentially moving average approach is a variation of the moving window approach, where a weighted average is performed with more importance (higher weights) being given to the more recent days.

Figure 1 provides an evaluation of the proposed context based baseline estimation method with respect to existing approaches based on average mean absolute error (MAE) across consumers for residential consumer [21] and commercial consumer [22] datasets. Our proposed approach performs better than existing approaches on both datasets. For a more detailed comparative analysis of various methods for baseline prediction, the user is directed to the study [17].

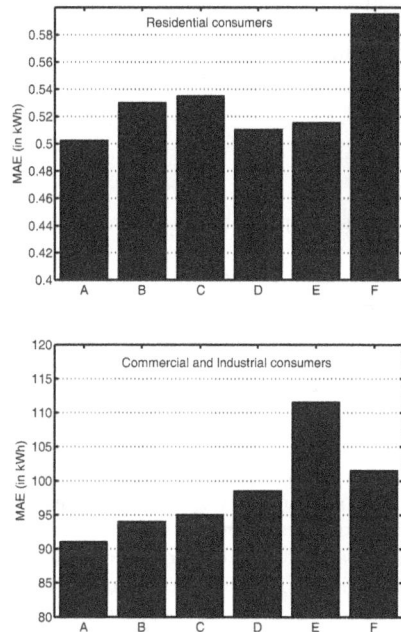

Figure 1: Evaluation of the proposed baseline estimation method with respect to existing approaches based on average mean absolute error (MAE) across all consumers for Residential consumers [21] and Commercial Consumers [22] datasets. Approaches A and B present our proposed context-based baselining method with (A) using Enlarged window with exponentially moving average and (B) using Enlarged window. Approaches C to F present existing methods [17] - (C) CAISO, (D) ISONE, (E) Low5Of10 and (F) NYISO.

3.1.2 Utility quantification

To express the utility derived by a consumer as a function of her consumption, we make the following assumptions:

1. A consumer derives maximum utility when her consumption equals baseline, since by definition the baseline represents the preferred level of consumption.

2. Any deviation from baseline - either above or below - results in a reduction of utility.

In order to satisfy the above assumptions, we propose the use of probability distribution of consumption during the specific timeslot (on the past consumption data filtered by optimal context C^*) to quantify utilities. However, it should be noted that the use of probability distribution reflects a specific choice, among several candidate methods for quantifying utilities that can potentially satisfy the above assumptions.

The probability associated with a consumption of q kWh, reflects the consumer's preference for consuming an amount of energy q KWh during the specified slot and under the context C^*. To make this setting more formal, we introduce the concept of utility functions.

The utility function is defined as follows: Consider a consumer i, and a timeslot t in the day, where $i \in \{1, 2, ..., N\}$, and $t \in \{1, 2, ..., T\}$ and d is the day in consideration for DR planning. Let C^* be the optimal context for the triplet $\{i, t, d\}$ based on the method discussed in Section 3.1.1 and $Q^b_{i,t,d}$ be the corresponding estimated baseline consumption. For any particular consumption $Q_{i,t,d}$ by the consumer at this time slot of the day, associated utility function $U_{i,t,d}(.)$ is expressed as:

$$U_{i,t,d}(Q_{i,t,d}) = \frac{p^{C^*}(Q_{i,t,d})}{p^{C^*}(Q^b_{i,t,d})} \quad (1)$$

where $p^{C^*}(q)$ gives the probability of consumption q in the past data under optimal context C^*. The consumer preferences - captured via baselines and utility functions as described above - are inputs that are used to set up the optimization frameworks presented in Section 4.

3.2 Preference mining using appliance data

So far, we have presented an approach for quantifying consumer preferences using aggregated, household level, consumption data. Nevertheless, assuming that appliance level data is available, for example where AMIs are in place, there is an evident potential to leverage this information in order to form a more detailed and accurate depiction of user's preferences. This section presents a methodology for achieving that. The proposed methodology is based on mining utility (benefit) derived from each monitored appliance. More specifically, it estimates the importance that each consumer places on a specific appliance via calculating a corresponding "weight". These weights constitute a measure of how flexible (elastic) the consumers are in altering the typical use of each appliance, for example in the case of a DR event.

Our methodology follows three distinct phases. At first, by using statistical analysis, we derive the utility values of each appliance in order to formulate the consumption profile of each household. Next, we fit the derived utility values from phase 1 to those resulting from the utility functions of [13], thus also validating the results from our approach against a more theoretic one that assumes the knowledge of utility functions. Finally, exploiting the fitted utility functions we mine the weights that reflect consumer's preferences regarding the usage of appliances, under specific realistic assumptions.

As a prerequisite, our work adopts the categorisation of household devices that is proposed in the widely cited work [13]. According to this reference, the typical household appliances can be classified into four types. The first type includes appliances such as refrigerator and air-conditioner which control temperature. The second type includes appliances such as washing machine where the consumer only cares about whether a task is completed before a certain

time. The third category includes appliances such as lighting that must be ON for a certain period of time. The fourth type includes appliances such as TV or computer that the consumer uses for entertainment. Each type is characterized by a utility function $U_{i,\alpha}(q_{i,\alpha})$ that models how much consumer i values the consumption vector $q_{i,\alpha}$ and a set of linear constraints on $q_{i,\alpha}$.

To experimentally evaluate our approach, we use real consumption data from 6 households in India. The available data comprises of sensor readings at a granularity of ten seconds for four different appliances: air-conditioner, fridge, washing machine and television (TV). These readings are extracted for a given context C, that is weekdays in July and correspond to three of the four appliance categories proposed by [13] (Type 1, 2 and 4), as the fridge and the air-conditioner both belong to the same, Type 1 category. This is because sensor readings for Type 3 appliances (e.g. lighting) were not available.

For conciseness, we present application details of our proposed methodology to only one of the three categories of devices (Type 4). However, the same approach was used for the other three devices.

3.2.1 Phase 1: Derivation of utility values from appliance level data

In Phase 1, the utility values for the respective devices are empirically estimated using statistical analysis. We now explain this process for Type 4 devices. Type 4 category includes appliances such as TV, video games, and computers that a consumer uses for entertainment. In this case, the consumer's utility depends on two factors: how much power is consumed at each time she wants to use them, and how much total power is consumed over the entire day. At each time, $t \in \{1, 2, ..., T\}$, we assume that the consumer i attains a utility $U_{i,t,\alpha}(q_{i,t,\alpha})$ from energy consumption $q_{i,t,a}$ on appliance α.

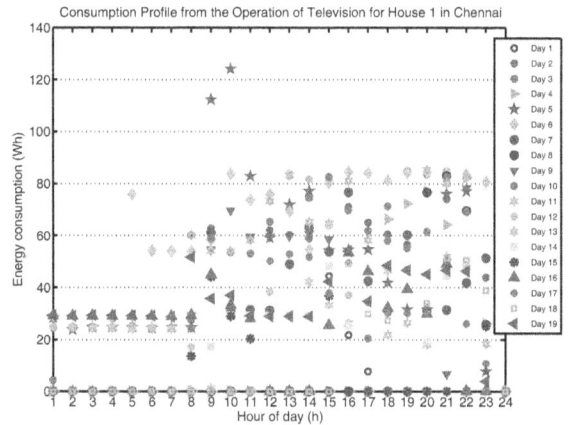

Figure 2: Hourly consumption of TV operation of House 1 during weekdays in July in Chennai, India. The figure shows the behavior of a specific consumer (House 1) over a specific appliance under specific context (weekdays in July).

By constructing the histograms of the consumption vector $Q_{i,d,\alpha} := \{q_{i,t,\alpha}, t \in \{1, 2, ..., T\}\}$, over all timeslots, as shown in Figure 2, we can analyse the consumer behavior i.e. the timeslots when their appliances are operated and the associated consumption level. For this type of appliances we can assume that higher the consumption, the greater the satisfaction experienced by the consumers, which in economic theory is expressed as a "utility value". At this point, as we do not have any knowledge of the function that expresses the relationship between the consumption values and the obtained utility values, the latter can be approximated by the empirical cumulative distribution function for given consumer i, appliance α, timeslot t and context, as follows:

$$U_{i,t,\alpha}(q_{i,t,\alpha}) = \begin{cases} 0, & \text{if } q_{i,t,\alpha} < q_{i,t,\alpha}^{min} \\ eCDF_{i,t,\alpha}(q_{i,t,\alpha}), & \text{if } q_{i,t,\alpha} \in [q_{i,t,\alpha}^{min}, q_{i,t,\alpha}^{max}] \\ 1, & \text{if } q_{i,t,\alpha} > q_{i,t,\alpha}^{max} \end{cases} \quad (2)$$

Here, $q_{i,t,\alpha}^{min}$ and $q_{i,t,\alpha}^{max}$ are minimum and maximum consumption observed in timeslot t, respectively in the given context, and $eCDF_{i,t,\alpha}(x)$ represents the value of the empirical cumulative distribution function for consumer i when operating appliance α at power level x at timeslot t. In particular, given the range of observed consumption values $[q_{i,t,\alpha}^{min}, q_{i,t,\alpha}^{max}]$, and by assuming that the utility is an increasing function of consumption and thus monotonic, we define the utility value associated with a consumption x as the cumulative frequency of consumption values $\leq x$ in this range.

Note that, when calculating the probability of a consumption value to be less than a certain value, the eCDF takes into consideration situations of zero consumption, i.e. when no utility is gained. Therefore, we do not explicitly take such situations into account in deriving the utility values.

Next, to define the utility value $U_{i,d,\alpha}(Q_{i,d,\alpha})$ for a specific day d, a given consumer i, and a given appliance α, where

$$Q_{i,d,\alpha} = [q_{i,1,\alpha}, q_{i,2,\alpha}, ..., q_{i,T,\alpha}]^T,$$

we estimate it as the median - weighted sum:

$$U_{i,d,\alpha}(Q_{i,d,\alpha}) = \frac{\sum_{t=1}^{t=T}(median_{i,t,\alpha} \times U_{i,t,\alpha}(q_{i,t,\alpha}))}{\sum_{t=1}^{t=T} median_{i,t,\alpha}}, \quad (3)$$

where, $median_{i,t,\alpha}$ is the median of consumption data of appliance α in timeslot t for a consumer i and given context, and it is used in order to avoid the analysis to be skewed in favour of very high or very low consumption values.

3.2.2 Phase 2: Fitting the estimated utility values to the utility functions of [13]

In the next step, our approach uses the utility functions of the different types of appliances from [13] represented as continuously differentiable concave functions of the total consumption in timeslot t and day d. Our objective is to approximate these coefficients such that the resulting utility values match those statistically estimated in Phase 1. This can be achieved by minimizing the distance of the curve formed from the utility values, i.e. the eCDF curve at the points of evaluation, from the curve of the utility functions in [13].

We adopt the utility functions as well as the initialization data defined in the experimental section of [13]. In particular, for Type 4 appliances, the utility function takes the form of:

$$U_{i,t,\alpha}(q_{i,t,\alpha}) = C_\alpha - (b_\alpha - \frac{q_{i,t,\alpha}}{\overline{q}_\alpha})^{-1.5} \quad (4)$$

where $C_\alpha \geq 0$, $b_\alpha \geq 0$ and $\overline{q}_\alpha > 0$ are the variables to be fitted. In this case, the fitting is executed at each timeslot t due to the nature of the appliance and corresponds to a non linear regression problem.

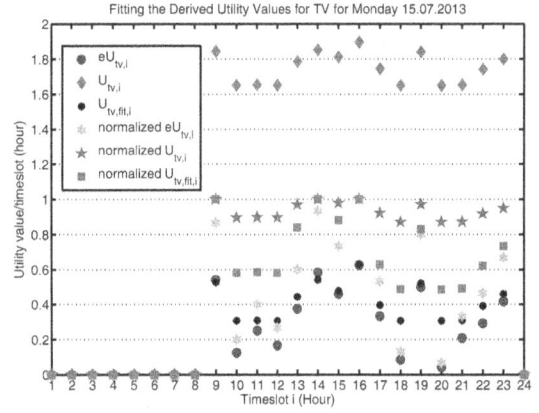

Figure 3: TV - Fitting the derived utility values to utility values based on [13] for Monday - Jul 15, 2013

Figure 3 presents the results for a particular consumer and a particular day, while the notation follows the nomenclature in Table 2. The day was divided into 4 timeslots, that is $T = 4$. The coefficients obtained using least squares fit are $C_{TV} = 2.2953$, $b_{TV} = 0.5786$ and $\overline{q}_{TV} = 7.5397 \times 10^3$. From Fig. 3, we observe that the normalized utility values ($U_{TV,fit,t}$), after fitting are close to the normalized values of $U_{TV,t}$ from the utility functions.

Symbol	Description
$eU_{\alpha,t}$	Estimated utility values derived in Phase 1 for appliance α during timeslot t
$U_{\alpha,t}$	Utility values resulting from utility functions in [13] for appliance α during timeslot t
$U_{\alpha,fit,t}$	Utility values resulting from applying fitted coefficient values to the utility functions for appliance α during timeslot t
normalized $eU_{\alpha,t}$	is calculated as $\frac{eU_{\alpha,t}}{\max(eU_{\alpha,t})}$
normalized $U_{\alpha,t}$	is calculated as $\frac{U_{\alpha,t}}{\max(U_{\alpha,t})}$
normalized $eU_{\alpha,fit,t}$	is calculated as $\frac{U_{\alpha,fit,t}}{\max(U_{\alpha,fit,t})}$

Table 2: Nomenclature of symbols used in Figure 3

In general, the results from the fitting methodology for all appliances imply that our approach of statistically deriving the consumers preferences, in terms of utility values, with use of detailed consumption data and without any knowledge about the utility functions has small deviations from the case where full knowledge is available, as in [13].

3.2.3 Phase 3: Mining the weights of each appliance

To derive the weights of each appliance that reflect the consumer's preferences, we use the assumption that given two different days of the same context, e.g. two weekdays, the consumption profile might vary, but the total Net Benefit (NB) obtained (i.e. the utility gained minus the monetary cost) is the same. This implies that for both days if the energy tariff scheme is known - a valid assumption in our case - each consumer chooses that consumption, which maximizes her total NB. To apply this assumption to our methodology, we calculate one respective weight per timeslot for the TV (type 4 appliance), fridge (type 1 appliance) and air-conditioner (type 1 appliance) and one per day for the washing machine (type 2 appliance). We use only one weight for the washing machine as we are interested only in the total consumption of the appliance after each operation, since the respective load (in one washing cycle) can be interrupted by the consumer and shifted to subsequent timeslots, which cannot be the case, for example, in the use of an air-conditioning device.

Thereby, given a set of appliances $\alpha \in A, A := \{AC, FR, WM, TV\}$, the weights $w_{i,\alpha}, \alpha \in A$ and the same context for each day $d, d \in C$, the NB is of the following form:

$$NB_{i,d} = \sum_{\alpha \in A} w_{i,\alpha} U_{i,d,\alpha}(Q_{i,d,\alpha}) - C_{i,d}(\sum_{\alpha \in A} Q_{i,d,\alpha}), \quad (5)$$

where $Q_{i,d,\alpha} = [q_{i,1,\alpha}, q_{i,2,\alpha}, q_{i,3,\alpha}, q_{i,4,\alpha}]$, and $C_{i,d}(\sum_{\alpha \in A} Q_{i,d,\alpha})$ are the cost functions based on which the consumer is charged for electricity consumption. Note that in this phase we consider all type 1 appliances of consumer i as a single appliance for simplicity. Thus, by equating the NB formulas for all the combinations of days from the available set of days C and applying linear least squares optimization, we derive the weights presented in Table 3.

Timeslot	$w_{i,Type4}$	$w_{i,Type1}$
1	0.0004	29.7085
2	0.0013	0.4750
3	4.6355	0.6577
4	0.5947	0.0007
$w_{i,Type2}$		
7.0732		

Table 3: Values of appliances' weights using NB

The results indicate that consumers are rather inelastic to changes in the consumption of type 1 appliances (i.e. their corresponding weights exhibit the greatest values amongst all), which is rational due to the fact that the use of such appliances (for e.g. cooling devices) in the given context of July weekdays is of paramount importance to them. We also observe that the weights that correspond to type 4 appliances can take mostly smaller values than those of type 1 and type 2 appliances respectively. This implies that this type of load can be curtailed at a specific time period or shifted to another time period, without causing significant inconvenience to consumers.

On the other hand, we observe that type 2 appliances are more elastic in terms of the time of their operation. This means that their load cannot be curtailed or shifted before a specific task is finished but they can operate at anytime during the day, which explains why the resulting value shown in Table 3 is greater than the values of type 4. Generally, the conclusions one can deduce about the importance of the appliances in the consumers' everyday life are consistent with the respective bibliography about the categorization of appliances in terms of shiftable and curtailment load. An energy provider can therefore leverage our methodology to quantify each consumer's personal preferences, and use them in order to predict their behaviour in the case of a DR signal being sent to them.

To conclude, although we have presented two frameworks for understanding and quantifying consumers' preferences, in the remainder of this paper we use the framework based on smart meter data alone (Section 3.1) for further development of iDR. This is because the rapid penetration of smart meters in today's grids have allowed utility companies access to consumers' aggregate consumption data at the household level. Therefore, we believe that at the current state of metering infrastructure, the framework based on smart meter data is more universally applicable than that based on appliance level data. However, we recommend the use of appliance level preference mining, wherever possible, as we believe it is a more accurate representation of consumers' consumption patterns.

4. OPTIMIZATION FRAMEWORK

In this section, we present a methodology that can be used by the utility provider for planning DR events. In particular, for a given day, we seek to determine the following in advance: (i) when should DR events be conducted, (ii) which consumers should be targeted, and (iii) what DR signals should be sent to each such consumer. Our approach involves solving an optimization problem, which uses consumers' preferences quantified in Section 3.1. The goal of the optimization is to plan DR response events such that the inconvenience caused to consumers is minimized while the utility provider's targets with regard to reduction in consumption are achieved. In the presentation of this methodology, we do not make any specific assumption on the form of the utility function. Therefore, it can be applied to any candidate utility function deemed appropriate by the reader. An example of such a utility function was provided in (1).

Before a formal presentation of the framework, we first define the underlying nomenclature. The number of consumers served by the utility is denoted by N. The day for which DR planning is to be performed is denoted by d. It is divided into T timeslots. Consider a consumer i, and a timeslot t in the day, where $i \in \{1, 2, ..., N\}$, and $t \in \{1, 2, ..., T\}$. For the triplet $\{i, t, d\}$, the best matching context C^* can be obtained using the methodology described in Section 2. Using this context, a baseline consumption $Q_{i,t,d}^b$ and the corresponding utility function $U_{i,t,d}(.)$ are determined.

We assume that for each timeslot t in the day d under consideration, the utility provider determines, in advance, the maximum amount of energy, $Q_{t,d}^s$ to be supplied. Such a determination can be made based on a combination of the provider's power procurement schedule from power generating companies for that day, and economics associated with power purchase. For instance, if it is known that buying electricity during certain time periods (e.g. peak demand periods) would be more expensive than during other periods, the utility provider may choose to limit the amount of energy procured during those time periods.

Given the above setting, we first determine the set T_{DR} of timeslots when DR events should be conducted. This set consists of timeslots when the expected (baseline) consumption, added across consumers exceeds the desired supply, and is more formally expressed as:

$$T_{DR} = \left\{ t : \sum_{i=1}^{N} Q_{i,t,d}^b \geq Q_{t,d}^s, t \in \{1, 2, ...T\} \right\}. \quad (6)$$

Next, to determine the consumers to be targeted for DR and the DR signals to be sent, we propose the following optimization frameworks. The first framework assumes that the targeted consumers would always participate in the DR event. The second framework assumes that these consumers would participate only with some pre-determined probability. Two design variables - n_t and η_{max}^t - are used in these

188

frameworks. The former represents the maximum number of consumers that the utility would like to target during timeslot t for participation in a DR event, whereas the latter represents the maximum reduction in consumption, expressed as a fraction of the baseline consumption $Q_{i,t,d}^b$ for each consumer, that the utility provider can request during a DR event at timeslot t. The use of n_t as a design variable is motivated by the need to reduce the computational requirements associated with the optimization. For example, in a realistic scenario, a utility provider can cater to millions of consumers, but might like to involve only a few thousand consumers at any given time for DR.

4.1 Deterministic framework

For all $t \in T_{DR}$, the following optimization problem is solved:

$$\{\nu_{i,t,d}^*, \Delta Q_{i,t,d}^*\} =$$

$$\underset{\{\nu_{i,t,d}, \Delta Q_{i,t,d}\}}{\text{argmax}} \quad J_d := \sum_{i=1}^{N} U_{i,t,d} \left(Q_{i,t,d}^b - \nu_{i,t,d} \Delta Q_{i,t,d} \right) \quad (7)$$

Subject to:

$$\sum_{i=1}^{N} \left(Q_{i,t,d}^b - \nu_{i,t,d} \Delta Q_{i,t,d} \right) \leq Q_{t,d}^s, \quad (8)$$

$$\nu_{i,t} \in \{0, 1\} \quad \text{for all} \quad i \in \{1, 2, ..., N\}, \quad (9)$$

$$\sum_{i=1}^{N} \nu_{i,t} \leq n_t, \text{ and} \quad (10)$$

$$0 \leq \Delta Q_{i,t,d} \leq \eta_{max}^t Q_{i,t,d}^b \quad \text{for all} \quad i \in \{1, 2, ..., N\}. \quad (11)$$

The objective of the above optimization, expressed by (7) is to maximize the aggregated utility obtained by the consumers during a DR event. In other words, we seek to minimize the inconvenience caused to the consumers resulting from reduction in consumption. The decision variables in the framework are as follows: (i) for each $i \in \{1, 2, ..., N\}$, the Boolean variable $\nu_{i,t,d}$ represents whether consumer i should be targeted for DR during timeslot t, indicated by a value of 1, and 0 otherwise; (ii) for each $i \in \{1, 2, ..., N\}$, the variable $\Delta Q_{i,t,d} \geq 0$ represents the target reduction in consumption for consumer i during the DR timeslot t. The constraint (8) restricts the aggregate consumption during each DR timeslot $t \in T_{DR}$ to be within the consumption bound $Q_{t,d}^s$ imposed by the utility provider. The DR design variables n_t and η_{max}^t, explained earlier, appear in constraints (10) and (11), respectively.

4.2 Stochastic framework

We denote the probability of user i responding to a DR event at timeslot t in day d by $p_{i,t,d}$. This probability can be determined, for instance, by analyzing the user's response history to previous DR signals sent to her on days and timeslots which correspond to the context C^*.

Next, we introduce a random boolean variable $\alpha_{i,t,d}$, which indicates the ith consumer's decision to participate, when the utility provider targets that consumer for a DR event. This setting can be mathematically expressed using the following equations:

$$\alpha_{i,t,d} \in \{0, 1\} \quad \text{for all} \quad i \in \{1, 2, ..., N\}, \quad \text{and} \quad (12)$$

$$P\left(\alpha_{i,t,d} = 1 | \nu_{i,t,d} = 1\right) = p_{i,t,d}. \quad (13)$$

A modified objective function J_s is defined as shown below, where $E(.)$ is the expected value operator.

$$J_s := E \left(\sum_{i=1}^{N} U_{i,t,d} \left(Q_{i,t,d}^b - \alpha_{i,t,d} \nu_{i,t,d} \Delta Q_{i,t,d} \right) \right). \quad (14)$$

The stochastic version of the constraint (8) is given by

$$E \left(\sum_{i=1}^{N} \left(Q_{i,t,d}^b - \alpha_{i,t,d} \nu_{i,t,d} \Delta Q_{i,t,d} \right) \right) \leq Q_{t,d}^s \quad (15)$$

The stochastic optimization framework, therefore seeks to maximize J_s given by (14), subject to the constraints (9) to (11), and the constraints (12), (13) and (15). Hence it represents a chance-constrained mixed integer program. The expected values appearing in equations (14) and (15) can be evaluated using (13), resulting in deterministic versions of these equations given by (16) and (17), respectively. It should be noted that by setting $p_{i,t,d}$ to 1, we recover the deterministic framework presented in Section 4.1.

$$J_s = \sum_{i=1}^{N} \left[U_{i,t,d} \left(Q_{i,t,d}^b \right) - \nu_{i,t,d} p_{i,t,d} X \right]$$

$$\text{where } X = \left\{ U_{i,t,d} \left(Q_{i,t,d}^b \right) - U_{i,t,d} \left(Q_{i,t,d}^b - \Delta Q_{i,t,d} \right) \right\}. \quad (16)$$

$$\sum_{i=1}^{N} \left(Q_{i,t,d}^b - \nu_{i,t,d} p_{i,t,d} \Delta Q_{i,t,d} \right) \leq Q_{t,d}^s. \quad (17)$$

The use of a stochastic framework can also allow the utility provider to ensure fairness on the basis of DR contract. For example, if the contract specifies a maximum number of DR signals $N_{DR,i}^{max}$ to be sent to a consumer i in a given time slot t, the probabilities $p_{i,t,d}$ can be iteratively adjusted (e.g. once every day) as shown below:

$$p_{i,t,d} = 1 - \frac{N_{DR,i}^{curr}}{N_{DR,i}^{max}} \quad (18)$$

Here, $N_{DR,i}^{curr}$ denotes the total number of times the consumer i has been selected at time slot t since the beginning of the contract upto the current iteration. We observe that (18) results in probabilities of participation which are monotonically decreasing functions of the number of times the consumer has been targeted for DR. When the consumer has been selected $N_{DR,i}^{max}$ number of times, $p_{i,t,d}$ becomes zero, which ensures that she would not be targeted for DR any further.

4.3 Feasibility condition

In this section, we prove a necessary and sufficient condition for feasibility of the afore-mentioned optimization framework, and determine a feasible point that can be used as a candidate initial point to solve it.

Theorem 1: *Without loss of generality, we assume that for a given $t \in T_{DR}$, the consumers indexed by $i \in \{1, 2, ..., N\}$ are arranged in the increasing order of $p_{i,t,d} Q_{i,t,d}^b$. The problem of maximizing J_s given by (16) subject to the constraints (17) and (9) to (11) admits a feasible solution if and only if the following inequality is satisfied:*

$$\sum_{i=1}^{N} Q_{i,t,d}^b - Q_{t,d}^s \leq \eta_{max}^t \sum_{i=N-n_t+1}^{N} p_{i,t,d} Q_{i,t,d}^b. \quad (19)$$

If the condition (19) *is satisfied, decision variables obtained by the assignments* (20) *and* (21) *are feasible.*

If $i \in \{1, 2, ..., N - n_t\}$, $\nu_{i,t,d} = 0$, $\Delta Q_{i,t,d} = 0$, and $\quad$ (20)

If $i \in \{N - n_t + 1, ..., N\}$, $\nu_{i,t,d} = 1$, $\Delta Q_{i,t,d} = \eta_{max}^t Q_{i,t,d}^b$. $\quad$ (21)

PROOF. We first prove the 'necesssay' part. If for all $i \in \{1, 2, ..., N\}$, $\nu_{i,t,d}$ and $\Delta Q_{i,t,d}$ are such that they satisfy (17) and (11), they also satisfy:

$$\sum_{i=1}^{N} Q_{i,t,d}^b - Q_{t,d}^s \le \sum_{i=1}^{N} \nu_{i,t,d} p_{i,t,d} \Delta Q_{i,t,d}$$

$$\le \eta_{max}^t \sum_{i=1}^{N} \nu_{i,t,d} p_{i,t,d} Q_{i,t,d}^b. \quad (22)$$

Since the set $\{1, 2, ..., N\}$ is sorted in the increasing order of $p_{i,t,d} Q_{i,t,d}^b$, the expression in the RHS of (22) attains a maximum value of $\eta_{max}^t \sum_{i=N-n_t+1}^{N} p_{i,t,d} Q_{i,t,d}^b$ due to the remaining constraints (9) and (10). Therefore, (22) can be satisfied only if: $\sum_{i=1}^{N} Q_{i,t,d}^b - Q_{t,d}^s \le \eta_{max}^t \sum_{i=N-n_t+1}^{N} p_{i,t,d} Q_{i,t,d}^b$.

To prove the 'sufficient' part, we assume that the condition (19) is satisfied. It can be easily verified that the decision variables obtained by assignments (20) and (21) satisfy the following relationship for all $i \in \{1, 2, ..., N\}$.

$$\nu_{i,t,d} p_{i,t,d} \Delta Q_{i,t,d} = \eta_{max}^t \nu_{i,t,d} p_{i,t,d} Q_{i,t,d}^b. \quad (23)$$

Using (19) and (23), we establish that the above chosen decision variables also satisfy the constraint (17). Since these decision variables also satisfy (9), (10) and (11), we conclude that this choice of decision variables is feasible, that is it satisfies all underlying constraints. Hence the condition (19) leads to a feasible choice of decision variables, given by (20) and (21). □

Note that if the condition (19) is not satisfied for a particular choice of design parameters, either η_{max}^t or n_t or both might have to be increased until it is satisfied.

5. EXPERIMENTAL EVALUATION

In this section, we perform simulation experiments using a real world consumption data set to evaluate the DR planning methodology presented in Section 4. We compare and evaluate the performance of three approaches - (i) deterministic optimization (Section 4.1), (ii) stochastic optimization (Section 4.2), and (iii) a rule based approach presented later in Section 5.5. The goal of these experiments is to understand and explain the results of the proposed optimization frameworks using intuition, and to quantify the efficacy of these frameworks by comparing with the rule-based approach. Each of these experiments is performed in two steps. In the first step, only 10 consumers are included to facilitate an easy understanding of the results. In the second step, the optimization is repeated on the complete set of consumers to demonstrate the scalability of *iDR*. Lastly, we also include an experiment, where we investigate the impact of the fairness strategy proposed in (18).

5.1 Data collection and pre-processing

We use consumption data available in the CER Ireland dataset [21]. This dataset contains approximately 5000 consumers, both residential and small and medium enterprises.

Measurements were obtained using smart meters for a period of 1.5 years, from July 2009 to December 2010. Since the dataset was collected as a part of a dynamic pricing trial, we select consumers who are in a single control group. In addition, we choose residential consumers with no missing data, thereby resulting in $N = 500$ consumers. For each day, and for each consumer, the recorded data is used to obtain consumption in kWh for each one hour time slot ($t \in \{1, 2, ..., 24\}$) during the day. In this way, we obtain the consumption $Q_{i,t,d}$ corresponding to each triplet $\{i, t, d\}$, where i is the consumer index ($i \in \{1, 2, ..., N\}$), t represents a slot in the day ($t \in \{1, 2, ..., 24\}$), and d refers to a day in the dataset.

5.2 Parameters for optimization

In the simulation experiments reported in this section, we choose the day d_{DR} for DR planning as April 1, 2011, which represents the first day of summer in 2011. We select the optimal context C^*, such that $d_{DR} \in C^*$, for each consumer as described in Section 3.1.1. Let d_C be the set of days belonging to context C^* for the given consumer. For simplicity and computational efficiency, we assume Gaussian distribution of consumption over the set d_C to calculate utility functions using (1). Thus, on day d_{DR}, for each pair $\{i, t\}$, where $i \in \{1, 2, ..., N\}$ and $t \in \{1, 2, ..., 24\}$, we determine the baseline consumption $Q_{i,t,d_{DR}}^b$ and the utility function $U_{i,t,d_{DR}}(.)$ using equations (24) and (25).

$$Q_{i,t,d_{DR}}^b = \mu_{i,t,d_C}, \quad (24)$$

$$U_{i,t,d_{DR}}(Q_{i,t,d_{DR}}) = \exp\left\{-\frac{\left(Q_{i,t,d_{DR}} - Q_{i,t,d_{DR}}^b\right)^2}{2\sigma_{i,t,d_C}}\right\}. \quad (25)$$

Here, μ_{i,t,d_C} and σ_{i,t,d_C} denote the mean and standard deviations, respectively, of the set $\{Q_{i,t,d} : d \in d_C\}$. Equation (24) sets the baseline consumption for a consumer in any timeslot to her mean consumption in that timeslot observed on days which lie in the appropriate context C^*. Equation (25) uses a Gaussian function to describe a utility value between 0 and 1 for consumption in each timeslot, ensuring that the maximum utility of 1 is obtained when consumption equals baseline consumption. Note that (25) satisfies the assumptions in Section 3.1.2.

As the first step in DR planning, we determine the set of timeslots in the day, T_{DR} to be targeted for DR. The sum $\sum_{i=1}^{N} Q_{i,t,d_{DR}}^b$ of baseline consumptions for all consumers, corresponding to each hourly timeslot in the day is plotted in Figure 4. The utility provider's assumed target energy delivery schedule is also shown in Figure 4. From a comparison of these plots, we determine, using (6) that the set of timeslots to be targeted for DR is $T_{DR} = \{13, 22\}$. To solve the mixed integer nonlinear optimization problems (MINLP) appearing in Sections 4.1 and 4.2, we use the NOMAD algorithm [23] implemented in the OPTI toolbox in MATLAB [24]. NOMAD is a mesh-adaptive direct search algorithm with the potential to find global solutions to MINLPs. It should be noted that the objective of this work is not to determine the best available solution method for the MINLP considered. Hence our use of NOMAD should be treated as one of the choices among several possible solvers, and the interested reader is free to use any other solver to perform these experiments. To analyze and understand the results of the optimization, the baseline consumptions $Q_{i,t,d_{DR}}^b$ and the standard deviations σ_{i,t,d_C} for each consumer for the DR timeslots $t = 13$ and $t = 22$ are shown in Tables 4 and 5, respectively. Given the aforementioned setup and parameters, we now describe various simulation experiments to evaluate the proposed DR planning methodology.

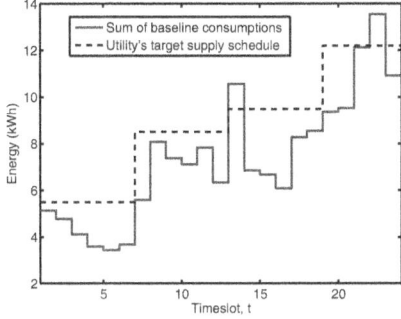

Figure 4: Comparison of the sum of baseline consumptions and the utility provider's power delivery schedule over the day d_{DR}.

Consumer number	$Q^b_{i,t,d_{DR}}$ (kWh)	σ_{i,t,d_c} (kWh)	$p_{i,t,d_{DR}}$ (for experiment 2)
1	3.143	2.685	0.9
2	0.393	0.373	0.9
3	0.305	0.287	0.9
4	0.417	0.449	0.9
5	1.077	1.268	0.9
6	1.928	1.752	0.1
7	0.164	0.251	0.1
8	1.140	1.324	0.1
9	1.440	1.495	0.1
10	0.680	0.982	0.1

Table 4: Baseline consumptions ($Q^b_{i,t,d_{DR}}$), standard deviations (σ_{i,t,d_c}) and probabilities of participation ($p_{i,t,d_{DR}}$) chosen for timeslot $t = 13$. These parameters are used to run the simulation experiments.

5.3 Approach 1: Deterministic case

In the first aprroach, we assume that each consumer's probability of participation in a DR event is unity, i.e. for each $t \in T_{DR}$, and for each $i \in \{1, 2, ...N\}$, $p_{i,t,d_{DR}} = 1$. The DR design parameters n_t and η^t_{max} which are required by the optimization framework presented in Section 4.1 are set to 3 and 0.25 respectively. It can be easily verified that this choice of these parameters satisfies the feasibility criterion (19) obtained earlier.

5.4 Approach 2: Stochastic case

In the second approach, we assign non-unity probabilities of participation $p_{i,t,d_{DR}}$ in a DR event for each consumer. Since DR participation information was not reported in the data set being used, we assign these probabilities as shown in Tables 4 and 5. With this choice of probabilities, the feasibility condition (19) is not satisfied. To address this, we increase n_t from 3 to 4.

5.5 Approach 3: Rule based strategy

In the third approach, we investigate a rule based strategy (Algorithm 1) for determination of which consumers should

Consumer number	$Q^b_{i,t,d_{DR}}$ (kWh)	σ_{i,t,d_c} (kWh)	$p_{i,t,d_{DR}}$ (for experiment 2)
1	0.675	0.357	0.9
2	0.988	0.626	0.9
3	0.729	0.491	0.9
4	1.060	0.962	0.9
5	3.116	2.261	0.9
6	1.079	1.062	0.1
7	0.388	0.594	0.1
8	1.701	1.304	0.1
9	1.723	0.966	0.1
10	1.275	1.153	0.1

Table 5: Baseline consumptions ($Q^b_{i,t,d_{DR}}$), standard deviations (σ_{i,t,d_c}) and probabilities of participation ($p_{i,t,d_{DR}}$) chosen for timeslot $t = 22$. These parameters are used to run the simulation experiments

be targeted for DR and what DR signals should be sent. In the absence of appropriate ground truth information, we use results obtained from this rule based scheme as the reference to test the value added by the DR planning methodology presented in Section 4. It identifies a set of n_t consumers which achieve the targeted reduction in demand by navigating through the set of consumers in the increasing order of their reduction in utility (steps 2, 3 and 4). Once a set of such consumers is obtained, it then assigns the demand reduction target for each of those consumers in such a way that their percentage reduction over their baseline consumption is the same (step 5). Such an assignment is performed to ensure a 'fair' DR strategy across the target consumers.

Algorithm 1: Rule based strategy for DR planning at timeslot $t \in T_{DR}$

STEP 1: For each consumer i, determine the reduction in utility $\Delta U^{max}_{i,t,d_{DR}}$ and the absolute expected reduction in consumption $\Delta Q^{max}_{i,t,d_{DR}} := p_{i,t,d_{DR}} \eta^t_{max} Q^b_{i,t,d_{DR}}$ from baseline consumption corresponding to a percentage reduction of η^t_{max}.

STEP 2: Sort consumers in ascending order of $\Delta U^{max}_{i,t,d_{DR}}$. We refer to this sorted set by S_t. Set m = 1.

STEP 3: Set the 'current decision set' D_t to consumers $\{m, m+1, ..., m+n_t-1\}$ in S_t. Set m = m + 1.

STEP 4: Repeat step 3 until the total expected reduction in consumption corresponding to D_t, $\sum_{i \in D_t} \Delta Q^{max}_{i,t,d_{DR}}$ is greater than or equal to the targeted reduction $\sum_{i=1}^{N} Q^b_{i,t,d} - Q^s_{t,d}$.

STEP 5: The final set of consumers to be targeted is given by D_t. The target reduction for each consumer $i \in D_t$, is then set to: $\Delta Q_{i,t,d_{DR}} = \dfrac{\left(\sum_{j=1}^{N} Q^b_{j,t,d} - Q^s_{t,d}\right) Q^b_{i,t,d_{DR}}}{\sum_{j \in D_t} p_{j,t,d_{DR}} Q^b_{j,t,d_{DR}}}$.

5.6 Results

The decision variables obtained using the three approaches described above are presented and compared in Figures 5 and 6. The consumers selected for DR during timeslots $t = 13$ and $t = 22$, are shown in Figure 5. The corresponding DR signals (targeted consumptions in kWh) are shown in Figures 6.

Due to the choice of the utility function in (25), for the same reduction over baseline consumption, a consumer with

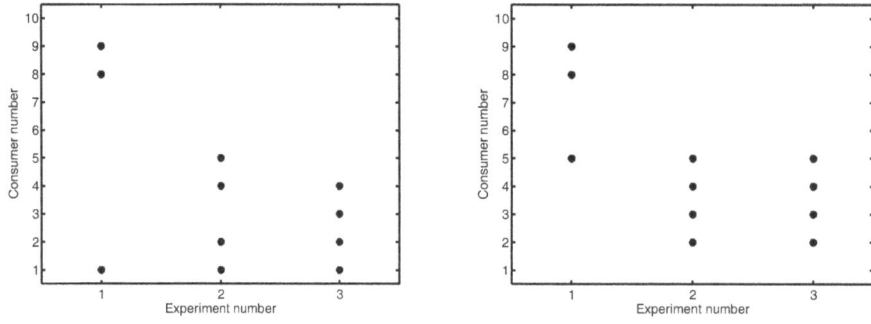

Figure 5: Comparison of consumers selected for DR using three approaches during time slots $t = 13$ (left) and $t = 22$ (right). Note that at $t = 13$, the stochastic case results in certain non-intuitive choice of consumers (e.g. 2 and 4 which have small baselines, but higher participation probabilities.) Similarly, at $t = 22$, the stochastic case results in certain non-intuitive choice of consumers (e.g. 2 and 3 which have small standard deviations)

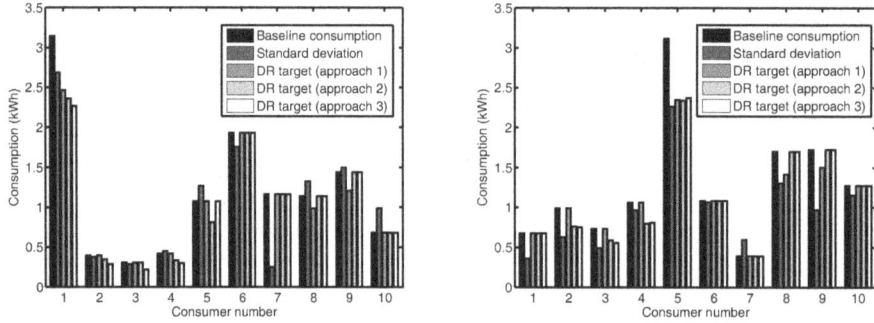

Figure 6: Comparison of DR target consumptions for consumers during time slots $t = 13$ (left) and $t = 22$ (right) using the first three optimization approaches. The baseline and standard deviation based on historical data are also shown for reference. Note that at $t = 13$, while consumers with small baseline and standard deviation (e.g. 2 and 4) are never targeted in the deterministic case (approach 1), they can be targeted in the stochastic case (approach 2) due to their higher participation probabilities.

larger standard deviation, σ_{i,t,d_C} would be subjected to a smaller reduction in utility than a consumer with smaller standard deviation. Also, for the same percentage reduction over baseline consumption, consumers with higher baseline consumption provide higher curtailment of demand than consumers with lower baseline consumption. As a result of these observations, we expect that consumers with large standard deviation and high baseline consumption should be chosen for DR in approach 1. From Figure 5, it can be verified that the optimal choice of consumers for DR indeed conforms to the above intuition.

The intuition stated above also holds for approach 2, after taking into account the probabilities of participation: we expect that consumers with large standard deviation, high baseline consumption and high probability of participation should be targeted for DR. It is difficult to apply this intuition directly, since a set of n_t consumers satisfying all the above 3 criterion does not exist. Therefore, in Figure 5, while we observe that some consumers satisfying these criterion (consumers 1 and 5 at $t = 13$) are selected, the selection of remaining consumers (2 and 4) is non-trivial. This supports the use of a systematic optimization framework - such as the one proposed in this work - since intuition might be limited and inadequate.

Next, we compare the results of approach 1 and approach 2 to the results of the the rule based strategy (approach 3). We first compare the expected reduction in aggregate con-

sumption $\left(\Delta Q_{\text{expected}}^t \right)$ obtained using these approaches, which is computed using the following equation:

$$\Delta Q_{\text{expected}}^t = \sum_{i=1}^{N} p_{i,t,d_{DR}} \Delta Q_{i,t,d_{DR}} \qquad (26)$$

The expected reduction in consumption in each of these approaches during timeslot $t = 13$ is 1.069 kW which exactly matches the desired reduction ($\sum_{i=1}^{N} Q_{i,t,d_{DR}}^b - Q_{t,d}^s$). The same observation was made for DR at timeslot $t = 22$. Therefore, we conclude that the consumpting mitigation objective of DR is met in all these approaches. We also quantify the inconvenience caused to consumers in each of these approaches. This is done by computing the expected reduction in utility from the maximum value of 1 for each consumer chosen to participate in DR, and adding it over all such consumers. The inconvenience caused to consumers for each of these approaches and during each DR timeslot, as obtained using this methodology, is shown in Figure 7. We observe that for DR during timeslot $t = 13$, approach 3 results in almost twice as much inconvenience as that caused in approach 2. For timeslot $t = 22$, the inconvenience caused is about 9% more in approach 3 than approach 2. From these results, we conclude that the rule based strategy is at best suboptimal and reinforces the importance of using a systematic optimization framework, such as the one pro-

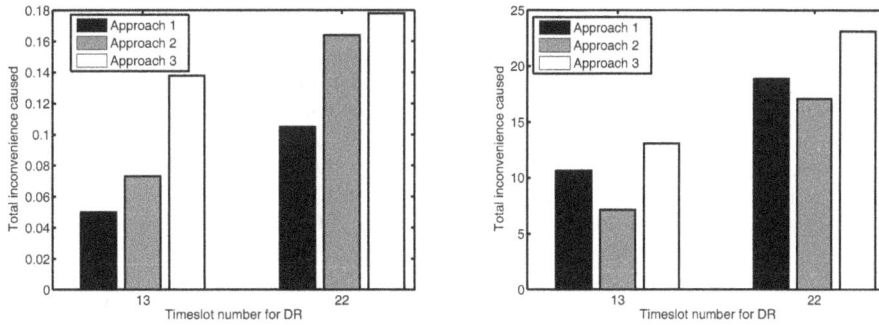

Figure 7: Comparison of inconvenience caused (total reduction in utility over all consumers) using the three approaches, when number of consumers is 10 (left) and when number of consumers is 500 (right). Note that for DR at timeslot $t = 13$, the inconvenience caused using heuristic rule-based DR strategy (approach 3) is almost twice that of iDR (approach 2).

posed, over heuristic rule based strategies for DR planning. Note that we do not perform a comparison of approaches 1 and 3 because they represent two different setups, the latter corresponds to a stochastic setting whereas the former is deterministic.

Lastly, we re-run the afore-mentioned experiments for the larger set of $N = 500$ consumers. The probabilities $p_{i,t,d_{DR}}$ were assigned arbitrarily, and we assume that the timeslots corresponding to DR are still $t = 13$ and $t = 22$, when the utility's desired supply power $Q^s_{t,d_{DR}}$ falls short of the expected demand $\sum_{i=1}^{N} Q^b_{i,t,DR}$ by 10%. The DR design variables η^t_{max} and n_t are set to 0.25 and 167 respectively. The observations made were similar to those reported above for 10 consumers. The targeted DR reduction was achieved in all these approaches and the inconvenience comparison is presented in Figure 7.

5.7 Fairness assessment

The objective of this experiment is to evaluate the fairness strategy proposed in (18). For simplicity, we create 10 identical clones of consumer 1 used in the previous three experiments, resulting in a group of consumers with similar consumption preferences. The parameters n_t in (10) and $N^{max}_{DR,i}$ in (18) are both set to 5, and the timeslot $t = 13$ is chosen for simulations.

Figure 8 shows the number of times each consumer is targeted, as DR iterations progress. It is observed that after the end of a sufficiently large number of iterations (in this case 10), all consumers have been chosen an equal number of times. This verifies that the proposed DR planning strategy is 'fair' across all consumers in the group.

6. DISCUSSIONS AND FUTURE WORK

In this paper, we presented iDR, a planning methodology that helps electricity providers in designing effective demand response events. In summary, iDR helps answer three important questions: (i) when to plan DR events, (ii) which consumers to target, and (iii) what signals to send. The proposed approach involved the estimation of baseline consumptions using historical consumption data obtained from smart meters, and then the development of utility functions using smart meter data to gauge the inconvenience associated with consumers shifting their demand from baselines. These utility functions were then used in the solution of a chance constrained, mixed integer nonlinear program. The approach was tested in simulation using data from a public

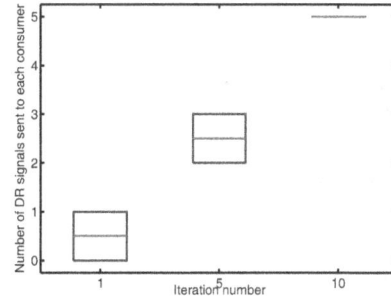

Figure 8: Progression of consumer selection as a function of DR iterations, shown as a box plot. Note that each consumer has been selected equal number of times at the end of 10 iterations, ensuring fairness

data source. Results indicated that the DR objectives were achieved, and iDR resulted in lower inconvenience than a heuristic rule based approach.

Based on the work presented in this paper, we identify the following avenues of future research involving iDR. The optimization framework presented in Section 4 and evaluated in Section 5 corresponds to the utility mining framework based on aggregate consumption (Section 3.1). An important area of investigation in future is the development of a DR planning methodology, analogous to that presented in Section 4, but based on appliance level utility functions (Section 3.2), if appliance level consumption information is available. Comparison of the results of these two optimization frameworks is expected to provide deeper insights towards establishing optimal consumption schedules for effective DR planning. A Gaussian utility function was used in the simulation experiments reported in Section 5. As an alternative, empirically derived utility functions from the consumption dataset can also be implemented. However, the potentially additional computational overhead introduced would need to be balanced against the value added by the use of such an empirical, purely data driven approach. The relationship between DR participation probabilities and incentives also needs detailed investigation. This can enable an augmentation of the existing capabilities of iDR. For example, it can enable the development of appropriate incentives in order to alter the participation probabilities of a set of consumers, such as those with poor DR participation history. In general, the use of participation probabilities in the framework provides a handle for the electricity providers to achieve other DR objectives besides demand mitigation, such as the development of effective DR contracts. The mitigation of unwanted outcomes such as rebound effects [10] can be included in the optimization framework to increase its practical value. Also, extensions of the proposed approach to plan DR for consumer groups instead of individual consumers can result in potential advantages such as a reduction in computational overhead. Previous work in the area of consumer segmentation such as [16] can be used in this context. Experimental results were not reported in this paper. However, we identify the real-world testing of *iDR* through pilot studies to gauge its true potential as a DR planning tool as an important final step in its development. Such pilot studies are being planned as a part of the European Union funded WATTA-LYST project [25], which would involve user studies to test the accuracy of the utility models developed in Section 3, effect of consumer participation in DR execution, as well as the efficacy of the DR planning methodology proposed in Section 4. Additionally, we plan to test *iDR* in simulation on a larger dataset than the one currently used, for a detailed scalability analysis.

7. REFERENCES

[1] N. Armaroli and V. Balzani, "The future of energy supply: challenges and opportunities," *Angewandte Chemie International Edition*, vol. 46, no. 1-2, pp. 52–66, 2007.

[2] U.S. Department of Energy, "Benefits of demand response in electricity markets and recommendations for achieving them," http://eetd.lbl.gov/ea/emp/reports/congress-1252d.pdf, 2006.

[3] K. Spees and L. Lave, "Impacts of responsive load in pjm: Load shifting and real time pricing," *The Energy Journal*, vol. 29, no. 2, pp. 101–122, 2008.

[4] Federal Energy Regulatory Commission, "A National Assessment of Demand Response Potential," http://www.ferc.gov/legal/staff-reports/06-09-demand-response.pdf, 2009.

[5] A. Chardon, O. Almen, P. E. Lewis, J. Stromback, and B. Chateau, "Demand Response: a decisive breakthrough for Europe. How Europe could save Gigawatts, Billions of Euros and Millions of tons of CO2." Capgemini, Tech. Rep., June 2008.

[6] Smart Metering Project in the United Kingdom, "Smart Metering Projects Map," http://bit.ly/GSs1o5, 2013.

[7] Peak Load Management Alliance (PLMA), "Demand Response: Design Principles for Creating Customer and Market Value," http://www.peaklma.com, November 2002.

[8] US Department of Energy, "Benefits of demand response in electricity markets and recommendations for achieving them," Feb. 2006.

[9] F. Yoo and C. Riker, "PG&E Automated Demand Response Program: IDSM Lessons Learned," http://energyefficiencysmartgrid.org/presentations.

[10] D. P. Seetharam, A. Agrawal, T. Ganu, J. Hazra, V. Rajaraman, and R. Kunnath, "Hidden costs of power cuts and battery backups," in *Proceedings of the fourth international conference on Future energy systems.* ACM, 2013, pp. 39–50.

[11] T. Bapat, N. Sengupta, S. K. Ghai, V. Arya, Y. B. Shrinivasan, and D. Seetharam, "User-sensitive scheduling of home appliances," in *Proceedings of the 2nd ACM SIGCOMM workshop on Green networking.* ACM, 2011, pp. 43–48.

[12] A. Agnetis, G. de Pascale, P. Detti, and A. Vicino, "Load scheduling for household energy consumption optimization," *IEEE Transactions on Smart Grid*, vol. 4, no. 4, pp. 2364–2373, Dec 2013.

[13] N. Li, L. Chen, and S. H. Low, "Optimal demand response based on utility maximization in power networks," in *2011 Power and Energy Society General Meeting.* IEEE, 2011, pp. 1–8.

[14] M. Kanakakis, M. Minou, C. Courcoubetis, G. D. Stamoulis, and G. Thanos, "A practical iterative price-based approach for optimal demand-response," in *proceedings of The Third International Conference on Smart Grids, Green Communications and IT Energy-aware Technologies*, 2013.

[15] A. Albert, R. Rajagopal, and R. Sevlian, "Segmenting consumers using smart meter data," in *Proceedings of the Third ACM Workshop on Embedded Sensing Systems for Energy-Efficiency in Buildings.* ACM, 2011, pp. 49–50.

[16] T. K. Wijaya, T. Ganu, D. Chakraborty, K. Aberer, and D. P. Seetharam, "Consumer segmentation and knowledge extraction from smart meter and survey data," in *SIAM International Conference on Data Mining (SDM14)*, 2014.

[17] K. Inc., "Pjm empirical analysis of demand response baseline methods," *White Paper*, 2011.

[18] EnerNOC, "The demand response baseline," *White Paper*, 2011.

[19] W. Charytoniuk, M. Chen, and P. Van Olinda, "Nonparametric regression based short-term load forecasting," *IEEE Transactions on Power Systems*, vol. 13, no. 3, pp. 725–730, 1998.

[20] W. Shen, V. Babushkin, Z. Aung, and W. L. Woon, "An ensemble model for day-ahead electricity demand time series forecasting," in *Proceedings of the fourth international conference on Future energy systems.* ACM, 2013, pp. 51–62.

[21] CER, "Electricity customer behaviour trial," http://www.ucd.ie/issda/data/commissionforenergyregulationcer/, 2012.

[22] "Enernoc: Open data to facilitate research and development," http://open.enernoc.com/data/, 2013.

[23] S. Le Digabel, "Algorithm 909: Nomad: Nonlinear optimization with the mads algorithm," *ACM Transactions on Mathematical Software (TOMS)*, vol. 37, no. 4, p. 44, 2011.

[24] Opti Toolbox - A free MATLAB toolbox for optimization, http://www.i2c2.aut.ac.nz/Wiki/OPTI/.

[25] "WATTALYST," http://www.wattalyst.org.

Cascading Failures in Power Grids – Analysis and Algorithms

Saleh Soltan
Electrical Engineering
Columbia University
New York, NY
saleh@ee.columbia.edu

Dorian Mazauric
Laboratoire d'Informatique
Fondamentale de Marseille
Marseille, France
dorian.mazauric@lif.univ-mrs.fr

Gil Zussman
Electrical Engineering
Columbia University
New York, NY
gil@ee.columbia.edu

ABSTRACT

This paper focuses on *cascading line failures in the transmission system of the power grid*. Recent large-scale power outages demonstrated the limitations of percolation- and epidemic-based tools in modeling cascades. Hence, we study cascades by using computational tools and a linearized power flow model. We first obtain results regarding the Moore-Penrose pseudo-inverse of the power grid admittance matrix. Based on these results, we study the impact of a *single line failure* on the flows on other lines. We also illustrate via simulation the impact of the distance and resistance distance on the flow increase following a failure, and discuss the difference from the epidemic models. We use the pseudo-inverse of admittance matrix to develop an efficient *algorithm to identify the cascading failure evolution*, which can be a building block for cascade mitigation. Finally, we show that finding the set of lines whose removal results in the minimum yield (the fraction of demand satisfied after the cascade) is NP-Hard and introduce a simple heuristic for finding such a set. Overall, the results demonstrate that using the resistance distance and the pseudo-inverse of admittance matrix provides important insights and can support the development of efficient algorithms.

Categories and Subject Descriptors

C.4 [**Performance of Systems**]: Reliability, availability, and serviceability; G.2.2 [**Discrete Mathematics**]: Graph Theory—*Graph algorithms, Network problems*

Keywords

Power Grid; Pseudo-inverse; Cascading Failures; Algorithms

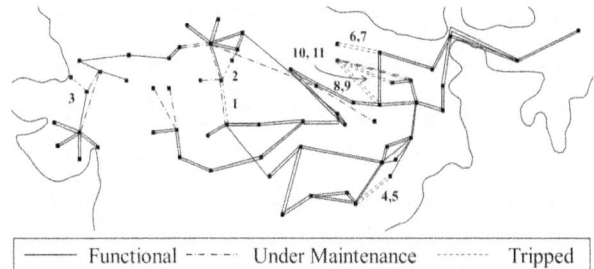

Figure 1: The first 11 line outages leading to the India blackout on July 2012 [2] (numbers show the order of outages).

1. INTRODUCTION

Recent failures of the power grid (such as the 2003 and 2012 blackouts in the Northeastern U.S. [1] and in India [2]) demonstrated that large-scale failures will have devastating effects on almost every aspect in modern life. The grid is vulnerable to natural disasters, such as earthquakes, hurricanes, and solar flares as well as to terrorist and Electromagnetic Pulse (EMP) attacks [43]. Moreover, large scale cascades can be initiated by sporadic events [1, 2, 42].

Therefore, there is a need to study the vulnerability of the power *transmission* network. Unlike graph-theoretical network flows, power flows are governed by the laws of physics and there are *no strict capacity bounds on the lines* [10]. Yet, there is a *rating threshold* associated with each line – if the flow exceeds the threshold, the line will eventually experience thermal failure. Such an outage alters the network topology, giving rise to a different flow pattern which, in turn, could cause other line outages. The repetition of this process constitutes a *cascading failure* [19].

Previous work (e.g., [17, 18, 45] and references therein) assumed that a line/node failure leads, with some probability, to a failure of nearby nodes/lines. Such epidemic based modeling allows using percolation-based tools to analyze the cascade's effects. Yet, in real large scale cascades, a failure of a specific line can affect a remote line and *the cascade does not necessarily develop in a contiguous manner*. For example, the evolution of the cascade in India on July 2012 appears in Fig. 1. Similar non-contiguous evolution was observed in a cascade in Southern California in 2011 [11, 42] and in simulation studies [11, 12].

Motivated by this observation, we study the effects of edge failures and introduce algorithms to identify the cascading failure evolution and vulnerable lines. We employ the (linearized) *direct-current (DC) power flow model*,[1] which is a practical relaxation of the alternating-current (AC) model, and the *cascading failure model* of [25] (see also [11–14]). Specifically, we first review the model and the Cascading Failure Evolution (CFE) Algorithm that has been used to identify the evolution of the cascade [13,14,19] (its complexity is $O(t|V|^3)$, where $|V|$ is the number of nodes and t is the number of cascade rounds).

Then, in order to investigate the impact of a single edge failure on other edges, we use matrix analysis tools to study the properties of the admittance matrix of the grid[2] and *Moore-Penrose Pseudo-inverse* [4] of the admittance matrix. In particular, we provide a rank-1 update of the pseudo-inverse of the admittance matrix after a single edge failure.

We use these results along with the *resistance distance* and *Kirchhoff's index* notions[3] to study the impact of a *single edge failure* on the flows on other edges. We obtain upper bounds on the flow changes after a single failure and study the robustness of specific graph classes. We also illustrate via simulations the relation between the flow changes after a failure and the distance (in hop count) and resistance distance from the failure in the U.S. Western interconnection as well as Erdős-Rényi [26], Watts and Strogatz [44], and Barábasi and Albert [9] graphs. These simulations show that there are cases in which an edge flow far away from the failure significantly increases. These observations are clearly in contrast to the epidemic-based models.

Once lines fail, there is a need for low complexity algorithms to control and mitigate the cascade. Hence, we develop the low complexity *Cascading Failure Evolution – Pseudo-inverse Based (CFE-PB) Algorithm* for identifying the evolution of a cascade that may be initiated by a failure of *several* edges. The algorithm is based on the rank-1 update of the pseudo-inverse of the admittance matrix. We show that its complexity is $O(|V|^3 + |F_t^*||V|^2)$ ($|F_t^*|$ is the number of edges that eventually fail). Namely, if $t = |F_t^*|$ (one edge fails at each round), the complexity of the CFE-PB Algorithm is $O(\min\{|V|, t\})$ times lower than that of the CFE Algorithm. The main advantage of the CFE-PB Algorithm is that it leverages the special structure of the pseudo-inverse to identify properties of the underlying graph and to recompute an instance of the pseudo-inverse from a previous instance.

Finally, we prove that the problem of finding the set of initial failures of size k that causes a cascade with the minimum possible yield (the fraction of demand satisfied after the cascade) is NP-hard. We introduce a very simple heuristic termed the Most Vulnerable Edges Selection – Resistance distance Based (MVES-RB) Algorithm. We numerically show that solutions obtained by it lead to a much lower yield than the solutions obtain by selecting the initial edge failures randomly. Moreover, in some small graphs with a single edge failure, it obtains the optimal solution.

The main contribution of this paper is the development of new tools, based on matrix analysis, for assessing the impact of a single edge failure. Using these tools, we (i) obtain upper bounds on the flow changes after a single failure, (ii) develop

a fast algorithm for identifying the evolution of the cascade, and (iii) develop a heuristic algorithm for the minimum yield problem.

This paper is organized as follows. Section 2 reviews related work. Section 3 describes the power flow, cascade model, metrics, and the graphs used in the simulations. In Section 4, we derive the properties of the admittance matrix of the grid. Section 5 presents the effects of a single edge failure. Section 6 introduces the CFE-PB Algorithm. Section 7 discusses the hardness of the minimum yield problem and introduces the MVES-RB Algorithm. Section 8 provides concluding remarks and directions for future work. The proofs appear in the Appendix.

2. RELATED WORK

Network vulnerability to attacks has been thoroughly studied (e.g., [3, 30, 37] and references therein). However, most previous computational work did not consider power grids and cascading failures. Recent work on cascades focused on probabilistic failure propagation models (e.g., [17,18,45], and references therein). However, real cascades [1,2,42] and simulation studies [11,12] indicate that the cascade propagation is different than that predicted by such models.

In Sections 4 and 6, we use the admittance matrix of the grid to compute flows. This is tightly connected to the problem of *solving Laplacian systems*. Solving these systems can be done with several techniques, including Gaussian elimination and LU factorization [27]. Recently, [20] designed algorithms that use preconditioning, to provide highly precise approximate solutions to Laplacian systems in nearly linear time. However, this approach only provides approximate solutions and is not suitable for analytical studies of the effects of edge failures.

In Section 5, we obtain upper bounds on the flow changes after a single failure and study the robustness of graph classes based on *resistance distance* and *Kirchhoff's index* [16,29]. Recently, these notions have gained attention outside the Chemistry community. For instance, they were used in network science for detecting communities within a network, and more generally the strength of the connection between nodes in a network [34,35]. Moreover, [22] recently used the resistance distance to partition power systems into zones.

The problem of *identifying the set of failures with the largest impact* was studied in [13, 14, 32, 38]. In particular, [14] studies the $N - k$ problem which focuses on finding a small cardinality set of links whose removal disables the network from delivering a minimum amount of demand. A broader network interdiction problem in which all the components of the network are subject to failure was studied in [41]. A similar problem is studied in [38] using the alternating-current (AC) model. However, none of the previous works consider the cascading failures. Moreover, while the optimal power flow problem has been shown to be NP-hard [31], the complexity of the cascade-related problems was not studied yet.

Finally, for the simulations, we use *graphs that can represent the topology of the power grid*. The structure of the power grids has been widely studied [5, 6, 9, 18, 23, 24, 44]. In particular, Watts and Strogatz [44] suggested the small-world graph as a good representative of the power grid, based on the shortest paths between nodes and the clustering coefficient of the nodes. Barabási and Albert [9, 18] showed that scale-free graphs are better representatives

---

[1]The DC model is commonly used in large-scale contingency analysis of power grids [13, 14, 38].

[2]An $n \times n$ admittance matrix represents the admittance of the lines in a power grid with n nodes.

[3]These notions originate from Circuit Theory and are widely used in Chemistry [29].

based on the degree distribution. However, [23] indicated that none of these models can represent U.S. Western interconnection properly. Following these papers, we consider the Erdős-Rényi graph [26] in addition to these graphs.

3. MODELS AND METRICS

3.1 DC Power Flow Model

We adopt the linearized (or DC) power flow model, which is widely used as an approximation for the more accurate non-linear AC power flow model [10]. In particular we follow [11–14] and represent the power grid by an undirected graph $G = (V, E)$ where V and E are the set of nodes and edges corresponding to the buses and transmission lines, respectively. p_v is the active power *supply* ($p_v > 0$) or *demand* ($p_v < 0$) at node $v \in V$ (for a *neutral node* $p_v = 0$). We assume *pure reactive* lines, implying that each edge $\{u, v\} \in E$ is characterized by its *reactance* $x_{uv} = x_{vu} > 0$.

Given the power supply/demand vector $P \in \mathbb{R}^{|V| \times 1}$ and the reactance values, a *power flow* is a solution (f, θ) of:

$$\sum_{v \in N(u)} f_{uv} = p_u, \ \forall \ u \in V \tag{1}$$

$$\theta_u - \theta_v - x_{uv} f_{uv} = 0, \ \forall \ \{u, v\} \in E \tag{2}$$

where $N(u)$ is the set of neighbors of node u, f_{uv} is the power flow from node u to node v, and θ_u is the phase angle of node u. Eq. (1) guarantees (classical) flow conservation and (2) captures the dependency of the flow on the reactance values and phase angles. Additionally, (2) implies that $f_{uv} = -f_{vu}$. *Note that the edge capacities are not taken into account in determining the flows.* When the total supply equals the total demand in each connected component of G, (1)-(2) has a unique solution [14, lemma 1.1].[4] Eq.(1)-(2) are equivalent to the following matrix equation:

$$A\Theta = P \tag{3}$$

where $\Theta \in \mathbb{R}^{|V| \times 1}$ is the vector of phase angles and $A \in \mathbb{R}^{|V| \times |V|}$ is the *admittance matrix* of the graph G, defined as follows:

$$a_{uv} = \begin{cases} 0 & \text{if } u \neq v \text{ and } \{u, v\} \notin E \\ -1/x_{uv} & \text{if } u \neq v \text{ and } \{u, v\} \in E \\ -\sum_{w \in N(u)} a_{uw} & \text{if } u = v. \end{cases}$$

If there are k multiple edges between nodes u and v, then $a_{uv} = -\sum_{i=1}^{k} 1/x_{uv_i}$. Notice that when $x_{uv} = 1 \ \forall \{u, v\} \in E$, the admittance matrix A is the *Laplacian matrix* of the graph [15]. Once Θ is computed, the power flows, f_{uv}, can be obtained from (2).

Throughout this paper $\|.\|$ denotes the *Euclidean norm* of the vector and the *operator matrix norm*. For matrix Q, q_{ij} denotes its ij^{th} entry, Q_i its ith row, and Q^t its transpose.

3.2 Cascading Failure Model

The Cascading Failure Evolution (CFE) Algorithm described here is a slightly simplified version of the cascade model used in [12, 14, 25]. We define $f_e = |f_{uv}| = |f_{vu}|$ and assume that an edge $e = \{u, v\} \in E$ has a predetermined power capacity $c_e = c_{uv} = c_{vu}$, which bounds its flow (that is, $f_e \leq c_e$). The cascade proceeds in rounds. Denote by

---

Algorithm 1 - Cascading Failure Evolution (CFE)

Input: A connected graph $G = (V, E)$ and an initial edge failures event $F_0 \subseteq E$.
1: $F_0^* \leftarrow F_0$ and $i \leftarrow 0$.
2: **while** $F_i \neq \emptyset$ **do**
3:     Adjust the total demand to equal the total supply within each connected component of $G = (V, E \setminus F_i^*)$.
4:     Compute the new flows $f_e(F_i^*) \quad \forall e \in E \setminus F_i^*$.
5:     Find the set of new edge failures $F_{i+1} = \{e | f_e(F_i^*) > c_e, \ e \in E \setminus F_i^*\}$. $F_{i+1}^* \leftarrow F_i^* \cup F_{i+1}$ and $i \leftarrow i + 1$.
6: **return** $t = i - 1$, $(F_0, \ldots, F_t)$, and $f_e(F_t^*) \ \forall e \in E \setminus F_t^*$.

$F_i \subseteq E$ the set of edge failures in the ith round and by $F_i^* = F_{i-1}^* \cup F_i$ the set of edge failures until the end of the ith round ($i \geq 1$). We assume that before the initial failure event $F_0 \subseteq E$, the power flows satisfy (1)-(2), and $f_e \leq c_e \ \forall e \in E$. Upon a failure, some edges are removed from the graph, implying that it may become disconnected. Thus, within each component, the total demand is adjusted to be equal to the total supply by decreasing the demand (supply) by the same factor at all demand (supply) nodes (Line 3). This corresponds to the load shedding/generation curtailing process. For any set of failures $F \subseteq E$, we denote by $f_e(F)$ the flow along edges in $G' = (V, E \setminus F)$ after the shedding/curtailing.

Following an initial failure event F_0, the new flows $f_e(F_0)$, $\forall e \in E \setminus F_0$ are computed (by (1)-(2)) (Line 4). Then, the set of new edge failures F_1 is identified (Line 5). Following [12, 14, 25], we use a deterministic outage rule and assume, for simplicity, that an edge e fails once the flow exceeds its capacity: $f_e(F_0^*) > c_e$.[5] Therefore, $F_1 = \{e : f_e(F_0^*) > c_e, e \in E \setminus F_0^*\}$.

If the set F_1 of new edge failures is empty, then the cascade is terminated. Otherwise, the process is repeated while replacing the initial event $F_0^* = F_0$ by the failure event F_1^*, and more generally replacing F_i^* by F_{i+1}^* at the ith round (Line 5). The process continues until the system *stabilizes*, namely until no edges are removed. Finally, we obtain the sequence $(F_0, F_1, \ldots, F_t)$ of the sets of failures associated with the initial event F_0, and the power flows $f_e(F_t^*)$ at stabilization, where t is the number of rounds until the network stabilizes. Since solving a system of linear equations with n variables, requires $O(n^3)$ time [27], the output can be obtained in $O(t|V|^3)$ time.

An example of a cascade can be seen in Fig. 2. Initially, the flows are $f_e = 0.5$ for all edges. The initial set of failures (F_0) disconnects a demand node from the graph. Hence, intuitively, one may not expect a cascade. However, this initial failure not only causes further failures but also causes failures in all edges except for two. This example can be generalized to a graph with $2n$ nodes where with the same set of initial failures, all the edges fail except for two.

For simplicity, when the initial failure event contains a single edge, $F_0 = \{e'\}$, we denote the flows after the failure by $f_e' \equiv f_e(\{e'\})$ and the flow changes by $\Delta f_e = f_e' - f_e \ \forall e \in E \setminus \{e'\}$.

3.3 Metrics

To study the effects of a *single edge (e') failure after one round*, we define the ratio between the change of flow on an edge, e, and its original value or the flow value on the failed edge, e':

---

[4]The uniqueness is in the values of f_{uv}-s rather than θ_u-s (shifting all θ_u-s by equal amounts does not violate (2)).

[5]Note that [12, 14, 25] maintain moving averages of the f_e values to determine which edges fail.

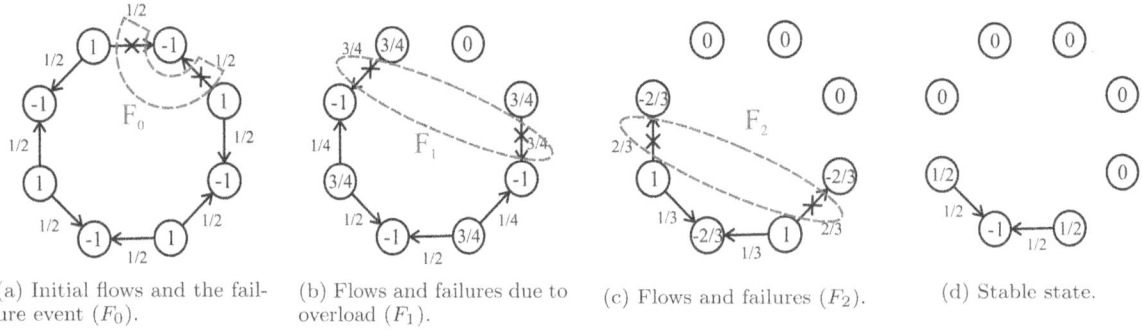

(a) Initial flows and the failure event (F_0).

(b) Flows and failures due to overload (F_1).

(c) Flows and failures (F_2).

(d) Stable state.

Figure 2: An example of a cascading failure initiated by outages of the edges connecting a demand node to the network. The edge capacities and reactance values are $c_e = 0.6$, $x_e = 1$. Numbers in nodes indicate power supply or demand (p_v), numbers on edges indicate flows (f_e), and arrows indicate flow direction.

Edge flow change ratio: $S_{e,e'} = |\Delta f_e/f_e|$.

Mutual edge flow change ratio: $M_{e,e'} = |\Delta f_e/f_{e'}|$.

Below, we define a metric related to the evaluation of the *cascade severity* for a given instance G, an initial failure event $F_0 \subseteq E$, and an integer $k \geq 1$. An instance is composed of a connected graph G, supply/demand vector P, capacities and reactance values c_e, x_e $\forall e \in E$. For brevity, an instance is represented by G.

Yield (the ratio between the demand supplied at stabilization and the original demand): $Y(G, F_0)$, $Y(G, k) = \min_{F_0 \subseteq E, |F_0| \leq k} Y(G, F_0)$.

3.4 Graphs Used in Simulations

The simulation results are presented for the graphs described below. All graphs have 1,374 nodes to correspond the subgraph of the Western interconnection. The parameters are as indicted below, unless otherwise mentioned.

Western interconnection: 1708-edge connected subgraph of the U.S. Western interconnection. The data is from the Platts Geographic Information System (GIS) [39].

Erdős-Rényi graph [26]: A random graph where each edge appears with probability $p = 0.01$.

Watts and Strogatz graph [44]: A small-world random graph where each node connects to $k = 4$ other nodes and the probability of rewiring is $p = 0.1$.

Barábasi and Albert graph [9]: A scale-free random graph where each new node connects to $k = 3$ other nodes at each step following the preferential attachment mechanism.

4. ADMITTANCE MATRIX PROPERTIES

In this section, we use the *Moore-Penrose Pseudo-inverse* of the admittance matrix [4] in order to obtain results that are used throughout the rest of the paper. Specifically they are used in Section 5 to study the impact of a single edge failure on the flows on other edges and in Section 6 to introduce an efficient algorithm to identify the evolution of the cascade. We prove several properties of the Pseudo-inverse of the admittance matrix A, denoted by A^+.[6] A^+ always exists regardless of the structure of the graph G. Some proofs and results that are used in the proofs appear in the Appendix.

Observation 1 shows that the power flow equations can be solved by using A^+.

OBSERVATION 1. *If (3) has a feasible solution, $\hat{\Theta} = A^+ P$ is a solution for (3).*[7]

PROOF. According to Theorem A.1, $\hat{\Theta} = A^+ P$ minimizes $\|P - A\Theta\|$. On the other hand, since (3) has a solution, $\|P - A\hat{\Theta}\| = \min_{\Theta} \|P - A\Theta\| = 0$. Thus, $\hat{\Theta} = A^+ P$ is a solution for (3). $\square$

Jointly verifying whether an edge is a cut-edge and finding the connected components of the graph takes $O(|E|)$ (using Depth First Search [21]). The following two Lemmas show that by using the precomputed pseudo-inverse of the admittance matrix, these operations can be done in $O(1)$ and $O(|V|)$, respectively. The algorithm in Section ?? uses the results to check if the pseudo-inverse should be recomputed. Moreover, Lemma 1 is crucial for the proof of the Theorem 1, below.

LEMMA 1 (BAPAT [8]). *Given $G = (V, E)$ and A^+, all the cut-edges of the graph G can be found in $O(|E|)$ time. Specifically, an edge $\{i, j\} \in E$ is a cut-edge if, and only if, $a_{ij}^{-1} - 2a_{ij}^+ + a_{ii}^+ + a_{jj}^+ = 0$.*

LEMMA 2. *Given $G = (V, E)$, A^+, and the cut-edge $\{i, j\}$, the connected components of $G \setminus \{i, j\}$ can be identified in $O(|V|)$.*

In the following, we denote by A' the admittance matrix of the graph $G' = (V, E \setminus \{i, j\})$ and by P' the power vector after removing an arbitrary edge $e' = \{i, j\}$ from the graph G and conducting the corresponding load shedding/generation curtailing.

Lemma 3 shows that after the removal of a cut-edge, A^+ can be used to solve (3) and A'^+ is not required.

LEMMA 3. *Given graph $G = (V, E)$, A^+, and a cut-edge $\{i, j\}$, then $\hat{\Theta} = A^+ P'$ is a solution of (3) in G'.*

The following theorem gives an analytical rank-1 update of the pseudo-inverse of the admittance matrix. Using Theorem 1 and Corollary 1, in Section 5 we provide upper bounds on the mutual edge flow change ratios ($M_{e,e'}$). We note that a similar result to Theorem 1 was independently proved in a very recent technical report [40].

THEOREM 1. *Given graph $G = (V, E)$, the admittance matrix A, and A^+, if $\{i, j\}$ is not a cut-edge, then,*

$$A'^+ = (A + a_{ij} X X^t)^+ = A^+ - \frac{1}{a_{ij}^{-1} + X^t A^+ X} A^+ X X^t A^+$$

in which X is an $n \times 1$ vector with 1 in i^{th} entry, -1 in j^{th} entry, and 0 elsewhere.

---

[6]$A^+ = \lim_{\delta \to 0} A^t (AA^t + \delta^2 I)^{-1}$ [4]. For more information regarding the definition, see Appendix.

[7]Recall from Section 3 that (1)-(2) have a unique solution with respect to power flows but not in respect to phase angles. Therefore, the solution to (3) may not be unique.

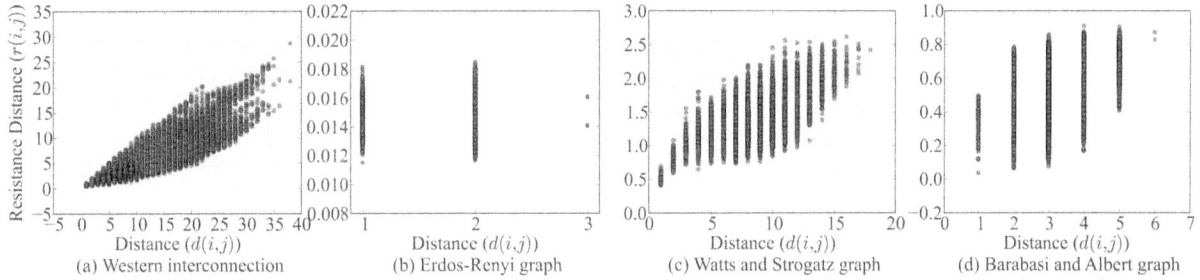

Figure 3: Scatter plot showing the distance versus the resistance distance between nodes in the graphs defined in Subsection 3.4.

For the following, recall from Section 3 that $A^+ = [a_{rs}^+]$.

COROLLARY 1.

$$f'_{rs} = f_{rs} - \frac{a_{rs}}{a_{ij}} \frac{(a_{ri}^+ - a_{rj}^+) - (a_{si}^+ - a_{sj}^+)}{a_{ij}^{-1} - 2(a^+)_{ij} + (a^+)_{ii} + (a^+)_{jj}} f_{ij}.$$

Finally, Lemma 4, gives the complexity of the rank-1 update provided in Theorem 1. This is used in the computation of the running time of the algorithm in Section 6.

LEMMA 4. *Given graph* $G = (V, E)$, A^+, *and an edge* $\{i, j\}$, *which is not a cut-edge of the graph,* A'^+ *can be computed from* A^+ *in* $O(|V|^2)$.

We now define the notion *resistance distance* [29]. In resistive circuits, the resistance distance between two nodes is the equivalent resistance between them. It is known that the resistance distance, is actually a measure of distance between nodes of the graph [8]. For any network, this notion can be defined by using the pseudo-inverse of the Laplacian matrix of the network. Specifically, it can be defined in power grid networks by using the pseudo-inverse of the admittance matrix, A^+.

DEFINITION 1. *Given* $G = (V, E)$, A, *and* A^+, *the resistance distance between two nodes* $i, j \in V$ *is* $r(i, j) := a_{ii}^+ + a_{jj}^+ - 2a_{ij}^+$. *Accordingly, the resistance distance between two edges* $e = \{i, j\}, e' = \{p, q\}$ *is* $r(e, e') = \min\{r(i, p), r(i, q), r(j, p), r(j, q)\}$.

When all the edges have the same reactance, $x_{ij} = 1 \ \forall \{i, j\} \in E$, the resistance distance between two nodes is a measure of their connectivity. Smaller resistance distance between nodes i and j indicates that they are better connected. Fig. 3 shows the relation between the distance and the resistance distance between nodes in the graphs defined in Subsection 3.4 (notice that $x_{ij} = 1 \ \forall \{i, j\} \in E$).[8] As can be seen, there is no direct relation between these two measures in Erdős-Rényi and Barábasi-Albert graphs. However, in the Western interconnection and Watts-Strogatz graph the resistance distance increases with the distance.

In Chemistry, the sum over the resistance distances between all pairs of nodes in the graph G is referred to as the *Kirchhoff index* [16] of G and denoted by $Kf(G)$. We use this notion in Subsection 5.2.2 to study the robustness of different graph classes to single edge failures.

DEFINITION 2. *Given* $G = (V, E)$ *and* A, *the Kirchhoff index of* G *is* $Kf(G) = \frac{1}{2} \sum_{i,j \in V} r(i, j)$.

---

[8]While in the Western interconnection the reactance values depend on the line characteristics (see values in [12]), for comparison and consistency, we used $x_{ij} = 1 \ \forall \{i, j\} \in E$ in all the graphs.

5. EFFECTS OF A SINGLE EDGE FAILURE

In this section we provide upper bounds on the flow changes after a single edge failure and study the robustness of different graph classes. For simplicity, in this section, we assume that $x_e = 1 \ \forall e \in E$, unless otherwise indicated. As mentioned in Section 3, in this case the *admittance matrix* of the graph, A, is equivalent to the *Laplacian matrix* of the graph. However, all the results can be easily generalized.

5.1 Flow Changes

5.1.1 Edge Flow Change Ratio

In order to provide insight into the effects of a single edge failure, we first present simulation results. The simulations have been done in Python using NetworkX library. Fig. 4 shows the edge flow change ratios ($S_{e,e'}$) as the function of distance ($d(e, e')$) from the failure for over 40 different random choices of an initial edge failure, e'. The power supply/demand in the Western interconnection is based on the actual data. In other graphs, the power supply/demand at nodes are i.i.d. Normal random variables with a slack node to equalize the supply and demand. Notice that if the initial flow in an edge is close to zero, the edge flow change ratio on that edge can be very large. Thus, to focus on the impact of an edge failure on the edges with reasonable initial flows, we do not illustrate the edge flow change ratios for the edges with flow below 1% of the average flow. Yet, we observe that such edges that experience a flow increase after a single edge failure, are within any arbitrary distance from the initial edge failure.

Fig. 4 shows that after a single edge failure, there might be a very large increase in flows (edge flow change ratios up to 80, 14, 50, and 24 in Fig. 4-(a), (b), (c), and (d), respectively) and sometimes far from the initial edge failure (edge flow change ratio around 10 for edges 11- and 4-hops away from the initial failure in Fig. 4-(a) and (c), respectively). Moreover, as we observed in all of the four graphs, there are edges with positive flow increase from zero, far from the initial edge failure.

Finally, we show that by choosing the parameters in a specific way, the edge flow change ratio can be arbitrarily large.

OBSERVATION 2. *For any* $x_{e_1}, x_{e_2} \in \mathbb{R}^+ \backslash \{0\}$, *there exists a graph* $G = (V, E)$ *and two edges* $e_1, e_2 \in E$ *such that* $S_{e_2, e_1} = x_{e_2}/x_{e_1}$.

5.1.2 Mutual Edge Flow Change Ratio

We use the notion of *resistance distance* to find upper bounds on the mutual edge flow change ratios ($M_{e, e'}$). The following Lemma provides a formula for computing the flow changes after a single edge failure based on the resistance

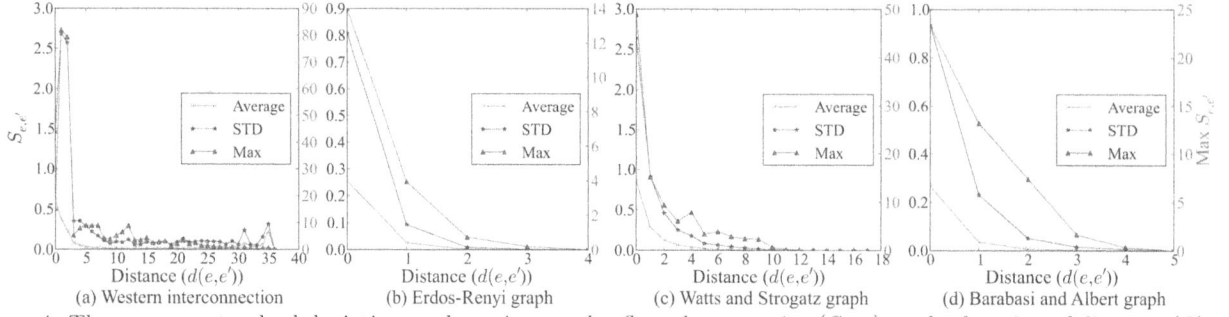

Figure 4: The average, standard deviation, and maximum edge flow change ratios ($S_{e,e'}$) as the function of distance ($d(e, e')$) from the failure. The right y-axis shows the values for the maximum edge flow change ratios (max $S_{e,e'}$). The data points are obtained for 40 different random choices of an initial edge failure.

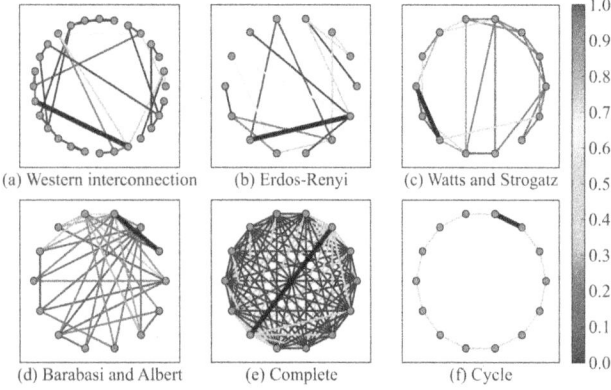

Figure 5: The mutual edge flow change ratios ($M_{e,e'}$) after an edge failure (represented by black wide line) in different graph classes. All the graphs have 14 nodes, except for (a) which has 28 nodes. In (b) $p = 0.1$.

distances. It is *independent* of the power supply/demand distribution.

LEMMA 5. *Given $G = (V, E)$, A, and A^+, the flow change and the mutual edge flow change ratio for an edge $e = \{i, j\} \in E$ after a failure in a non-cut-edge $e' = \{p, q\} \in E$ are,*

$$\Delta f_{ij} = \frac{1}{2} \frac{-r(i, p) + r(i, q) + r(j, p) - r(j, q)}{1 - r(p, q)} f_{pq},$$

$$M_{e,e'} = \frac{1}{2} \frac{-r(i, p) + r(i, q) + r(j, p) - r(j, q)}{1 - r(p, q)}.$$

PROOF. It is an immediate result of Corollary 1. □

Fig. 5 illustrates the mutual edge flow change ratios after an edge failure. Recall that $M_{e,e'}$ describes the distribution of the flow that passed through e' on the other edges. These values are differently distributed for different graph classes. In the next subsection, we study in detail the relation between the mutual edge flow change ratios and the graph structure.

The following Corollary gives an upper bound on the flow changes after a failure in a non-cut-edge $\{p, q\} \in E$ by using the triangle inequality for resistance distance and Lemma 5.

COROLLARY 2. *Given $G = (V, E)$, A, and A^+, the flow changes in any edge $e = \{i, j\} \in E$ after a failure in a non-cut-edge $e' = \{p, q\} \in E$ can be bounded by,*

$$|\Delta f_{ij}| \leq \frac{r(p, q)}{1 - r(p, q)} |f_{pq}|, \quad M_{e,e'} \leq \frac{r(p, q)}{1 - r(p, q)}.$$

With the very same idea, the following corollary gives an upper bound on the flow changes in a specific edge $\{i, j\} \in E$ after a failure in the non-cut-edge $\{p, q\} \in E$.

COROLLARY 3. *Given $G = (V, E)$, A, and A^+, the flow changes in an edge $e = \{i, j\} \in E$ after a failure in a non-cut-edge $e' = \{p, q\} \in E$ and the mutual edge flow change ratio $M(e, e')$ can be bounded by,*

$$|\Delta f_{ij}| \leq \frac{r(e, e')}{1 - r(p, q)} |f_{pq}|, \quad M_{e,e'} \leq \frac{r(e, e')}{1 - r(p, q)}.$$

Corollary 3 directly connects the resistance distance between two edges ($r(e, e')$) to their mutual edge flow change ratio ($M_{e,e'}$). It shows that the resistance distance, in contrast to the distance, can be used for assessing the influence of an edge failure on other edges.

We present simulations to show the relations between the mutual flow change ratios and the two distance measures. Figs. 6 and 7 show the mutual edge flow change ratio ($M_{e,e'}$) as the function of distance ($d(e, e')$) and resistance distance ($r(e, e')$) from the failure, respectively. The figures show that increasing number of edges (increasing p in Erdős-Rényi graph and increasing k in Watts and Strogatz, and Barábasi and Albert graphs) affects the $M_{e,e'}$-$r(e, e')$ relation more than the $M_{e,e'}$-$d(e, e')$ relation. This suggests that the resistance distance better captures the information hidden in the structure of a graph. Both figures show a monotone relation between the mutual edge flow change ratios and the distances/resistance distances. However, this monotonicity is smoother in the case of the distance.

Moreover, Fig. 6, unlike Fig. 4, shows that after a single edge failure, the mutual edge flow change ratios decrease as the distance from the initial failure increases. Thus, it suggests that probabilistic tools may be used to model the mutual edge flow change ratios ($M_{e,e'}$) better than the edge flow change ratios ($S_{e,e'}$).

5.2 Graph Robustness

We now use the upper bounds provided in Corollaries 2 and 3 to study the robustness of some well-known graph classes to single edge failures. We use the average mutual edge flow change ratio, $M_{e,e'}$, as the measure of the robustness. The small value of $M_{e,e'}$ indicates that the flow changes in edges after a single edge failure is small compared to the original flow on the failed edge. In other words, the network is able to distribute additional load after a single edge failure uniformly between other edges.

We show that (i) graphs with more edges are more robust to single edge failures and (ii) the Kirchhoff index can

200

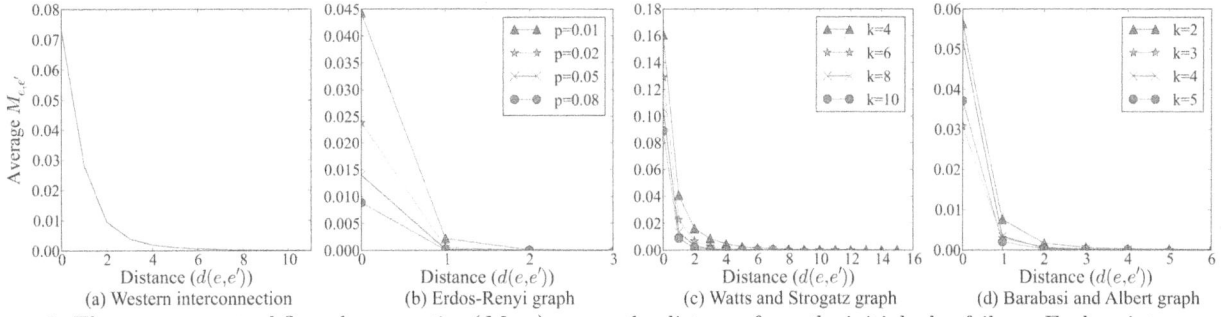

Figure 6: The average mutual flow change ratios ($M_{e,e'}$) versus the distance from the initial edge failure. Each point represents the average of 40 different initial single edge failure events.

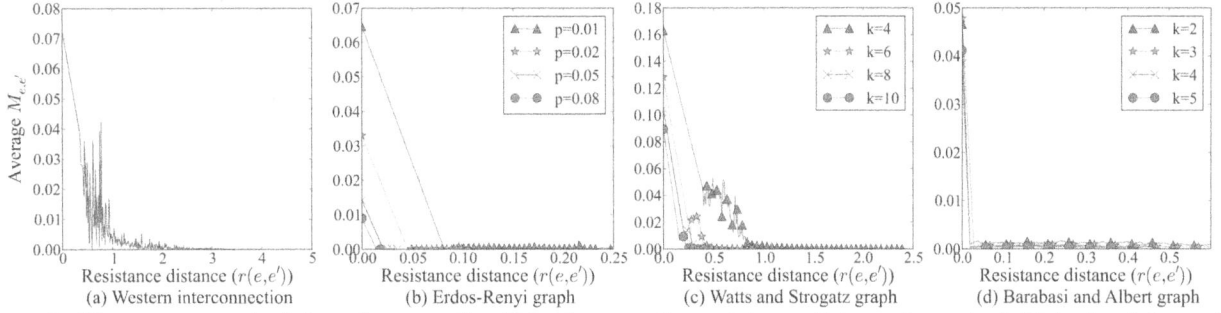

Figure 7: The average mutual flow change ratios ($M_{e,e'}$) versus the resistance distance from the initial edge failure. Each point represents the average of 40 different initial single edge failure events. For clarity, the markers appear for every 5 data points.

be used as a measure for the robustness of different graph classes.

5.2.1 Robustness Based on Number of Edges

Using Corollary 2, it can be seen that a failure in an edge with small resistance distance between its two end nodes leads to a small upper bound on the mutual edge flow change ratios, $M_{e,e'}$, on the other edges. Thus, the average $r(i,j)$ for $\{i,j\} \in E$ is relatively a good measure of the average mutual edge flow change ratio. The following Observation shows that graphs with more edges have smaller average $r(i,j)$ for $\{i,j\} \in E$, and therefore, smaller average mutual edge flow change ratio.

OBSERVATION 3. *Given $G = (V, E)$, the average $r(i,j)$ for $\{i,j\} \in E$ is $\frac{|V|-1}{|E|}$.*

Observation 3 implies that for a fixed number of nodes, the average resistance distance gets smaller as the number of edges increases. Therefore, graphs with more edges are more robust against a single edge failure.

5.2.2 Robustness Based on the Graph Class

Another way of computing the average mutual edge flow change ratio is to use Corollary 3 which implies that graphs with low average resistance distance over all pairs of nodes have the small average mutual edge flow change ratios. On the other hand, recall from Definition 2 that the average resistance distance over all pair of nodes is equal to Kirchhoff index of the graph divided by the number of edges. Hence, table 1 summarizes the Kirchhoff indices and corresponding average mutual edge flow change ratios for some well-known graph classes. To complete the table, in the following lemma we compute the Kirchhoff index of the Erdős-Rényi graph as a function of p.

Table 1: The Kirchhoff indices and the average mutual edge flow change ratios ($M_{e,e'}$) for some well-known graphs. The values that were previously known [33] are highlighted by grey cells.

Graph Class	Kirchhoff index	Average mutual edge flow change ratio ($M_{e,e'}$)
Complete graph	$n-1$	$O(\frac{1}{n})$
Complete bipartite graph	$4n-3$	$O(\frac{1}{n})$
Complete tripartite graph	$\frac{1}{2}(9n-5)$	$O(\frac{1}{n^2})$
Cycle graph	$\frac{1}{12}(n-1)n(n+1)$	$O(n^2)$
Cocktail party graph	$\frac{2n^2-2n+1}{n-1}$	$O(\frac{1}{n})$
Erdős-Rényi graph	$\Theta(\frac{n}{p})$	$O(\frac{1}{np^2})$

LEMMA 6. *For an Erdős-Rényi random graph, $G(n,p)$, $Kf(G)$ is of $\Theta(\frac{n}{p})$, and therefore the average resistance distance between all pairs of nodes is of $\Theta(\frac{1}{np^2})$.*

This Lemma shows that the average resistance distance between all pairs of nodes of an Erdős-Rényi graph is related to $1/p^2$. Since as p grows, the average number of edges in a Erdős-Rényi graph increases, this Lemma also suggests that graphs with more edges are more robust to a single edge failure. Thus, the results in this subsection are aligned with the result in Subsection 5.2.1 indicating that graphs with more edges are more robust to a single edge failure.

6. EFFICIENT CASCADING FAILURE EVOLUTION COMPUTATION

Based on the results obtained in Section 4, we present the Cascading Failure Evolution – Pseudo-inverse Based (CFE-PB) Algorithm which identifies the evolution of the cascade. The CFE-PB Algorithm uses the *Moore-Penrose Pseudo-*

Algorithm 2 - Cascading Failure Evolution – Pseudo-inverse Based (CFE-PB)

Input: A connected graph $G = (V, E)$ and an initial edge failures event $F_0 \subseteq E$.
1: Compute A^+, $F_0^* \leftarrow F_0$ and $i \leftarrow 0$.
2: **while** $F_i \neq \emptyset$ **do**
3:     **for** each $\{r, s\} \in F_i$ **do**
4:        **if** $\{r, s\}$ is a cut-edge (see Lemma 1) **then**
5:           Find the connected components after removing $\{r, s\}$. (see Lemma 2)
6:           Adjust the total demand to equal the total supply within each connected component.
7:        **else** update A^+ after removing $\{r, s\}$. (see Lemma 4)
8:     Compute the phase angles $\hat{\Theta} = A^+ P$ and compute new flows $f_e(F_i^*)$ from the phase angles.
9:     Find the set of new edge failures $F_{i+1} = \{e | f_e > c_e, \ e \in E \setminus F_i^*\}$. $F_{i+1}^* \leftarrow F_i^* \cup F_{i+1}$ and $i \leftarrow i + 1$.
10: **return** $t = i - 1$, $(F_0, \ldots, F_t)$, and $f_e(F_t^*) \ \forall e \in E \setminus F_t^*$.

---

inverse of the admittance matrix for solving (3). Computing the pseudo-inverse of the admittance matrix requires $O(|V|^3)$ time. However, the algorithm obtains the pseudo-inverse of the admittance matrix in round i from the one obtained in round $(i - 1)$, in $O(|F_i||V|^2)$ time. Moreover, in some cases, the algorithm can reuse the pseudo-inverse from the previous round. Since once lines fail, there is a need for low complexity algorithms to control and mitigate the cascade, the CFE-PB Algorithm may provide insight into the design of efficient cascade control algorithms.

We now describe the CFE-PB Algorithm. It initially computes the pseudo-inverse of the admittance matrix (in $O(|V|^3)$ time) and this is the only time in which it *computes A^+ without using a previous version of A^+.* Next, starting from F_0, at each round of the cascade, for each $e \in F_i$, it checks whether e is a cut-edge (Line 4). This is done in $O(1)$ (Lemma 1). If yes, based on Lemma 3, in Lines 5 and 6, the total demand is adjusted to equal the total supply within each connected component (in $O(V)$ time). Else, in Line 7, A^+ after the removal of e is computed in $O(|V|^2)$ time (see Lemma 4). After repeating this process for each $e \in F_i$, the phase angles and the flows are computed in $O(|V|^2)$ time (Line 8). The rest of the process is similar to the CFE Algorithm.

The following theorem provides the complexity of the algorithm (the proof is based on the Lemmas 1–4). We show that the algorithm runs in $O(|V|^3 + |F_t^*||V|^2)$ time (compared to the CFE Algorithm which runs in $O(t|V|^3)$). Namely, if $t = |F_t^*|$ (one edge fails at each round), the CFE-PB Algorithm outperforms the CFE Algorithms by $O(\min\{|V|, t\})$.

THEOREM 2. *CFE-PB Algorithm runs in $O(|V|^3 + |F_t^*||V|^2)$ time.*

We notice that a similar approach (the step by step rank-1 update) can also be applied to other methods for solving linear equations (e.g., LU factorization [27]). However, as we showed in Section 5, using the pseudo-inverse allows developing tools for analyzing the effect of a single edge failure. Moreover, it supports the development of an algorithm for finding the most vulnerable edges.

7. HARDNESS AND HEURISTIC

In this section, we prove that the decision problem associated with the minimum yield is NP-complete. Using the results from Section 5, we introduce a heuristic algorithm for the problem of finding the set of initial failures of size

Algorithm 3 - Most Vulnerable Edges Selection – Resistance distance Based (MVES-RB)

Input: A connected graph $G = (V, E)$ and an integer $k \geq 1$.
1: Compute A^+.
2: Compute the phase angles $\hat{\Theta} = A^+ P$ and compute flows f_e from the phase angles.
3: Compute the resistance distance $r(i, j) = r(e) \ \forall e = \{i, j\} \in E$.
4: Sort edges $e_1, e_2, \ldots, e_{|E|}$ such that $p \leq q$ iff $f_{e_p} r(e_p) \geq f_{e_q} r(e_q)$.
5: **return** $e_1, e_2, \ldots, e_k$.

---

k that causes a cascade resulting with the minimum possible yield (*minimum yield problem*). We numerically show that solutions obtained by the heuristic algorithm lead to a much lower yield than the solutions obtain by selecting the initial edge failures randomly. Moreover, in some small graphs with a single edge failure, this algorithm obtains the optimal solution.

First, we show that deciding if there exists a failure event (of size at most a given value) such that the yield after stabilization is less than a given threshold, is NP-complete.

LEMMA 7. *Given a graph G, a real number y, $0 \leq y \leq 1$, and an integer $k \geq 1$, the problem of deciding if $Y(G, k) \leq y$ is NP-complete.*

We now present a heuristic algorithm for solving this problem. We refer to it as the Most Vulnerable Edge Selection – Resistance distance Based (MVES-RB) Algorithm. From Corollary 2, it seems that edges with large $r(i, j) \times |f_{ij}|$ have greater impact on the flow changes on the other edges. Based on this result, the MVES-RB Algorithm selects *the k edges with highest $r(i, j) \times |f_{ij}|$ values as the initial set of failures.*

The MVES-RB Algorithm is in the same category as the algorithms that identify the set of failures with the largest impact (i.e., algorithms that solve the $N - k$ problem [14, 32, 38]). However, none of the previous works focusing on the $N - k$ problem, considers cascading failures. The MVES-RB Algorithm is simpler than most of the algorithms proposed in the past. However, it is not possible to compare its performance to that of algorithms in [14, 32, 38, 41] since they use different formulations of the power flow problem.

We first compare via simulation the MVES-RB Algorithm to the optimal solution in small graphs and for a single initial edge failure. Fig. 8 shows the yield after stabilization when selecting a single edge failure based on the MVES-RB Algorithm, randomly, and optimally. All the graphs have 136 nodes. For all the edges the reactance, $x_e = 1$,[9] and the capacity $c_e = 1.1 f_e$,[10] where f_e is the initial flow on the edge. At each point, equal number of power supply and demand nodes are randomly selected and assigned values of 1 and -1. As can be seen, the MVES-RB Algorithm obtains the optimal solution in Erdős-Rényi and Barábasi-Albert graphs. However, it does not achieve the optimal solution in the Western interconnection and Watts-Strogatz graph.

Finding the optimal solution for the minimum yield problem in the general case is impossible in practice. Therefore,

---

[9] While in the Western interconnection the reactance values depend on the line characteristics (see values in [12]), for comparison and consistency, we used $x_{ij} = 1 \ \forall \{i, j\} \in E$ in all the graphs.

[10] Following [12], we assume that the capacities are K times the initial flows on the edges. K is often referred to as the *Factor of Safety (FoS)* of the grid. Here, $K = 1.1$ as in [12].

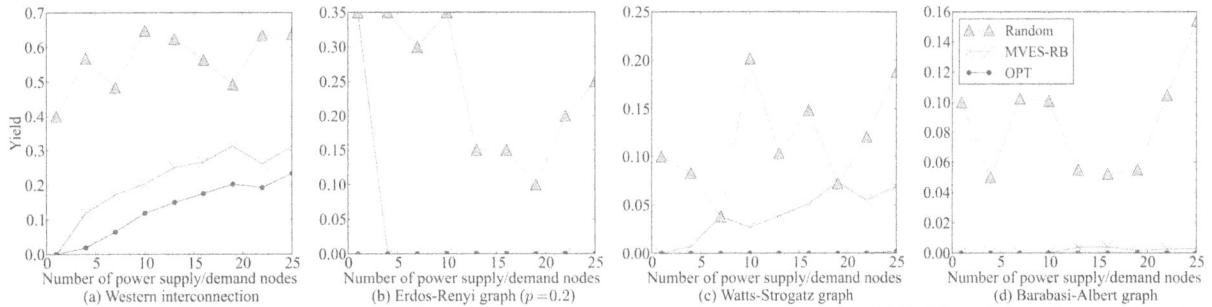

Figure 8: The yield after stabilization when selecting a single edge failure based on the MVES-RB Algorithm, randomly, and optimally. All graphs have 136 nodes. Every data point is the average over 20 trials, each composed of a different set of supply/demand nodes.

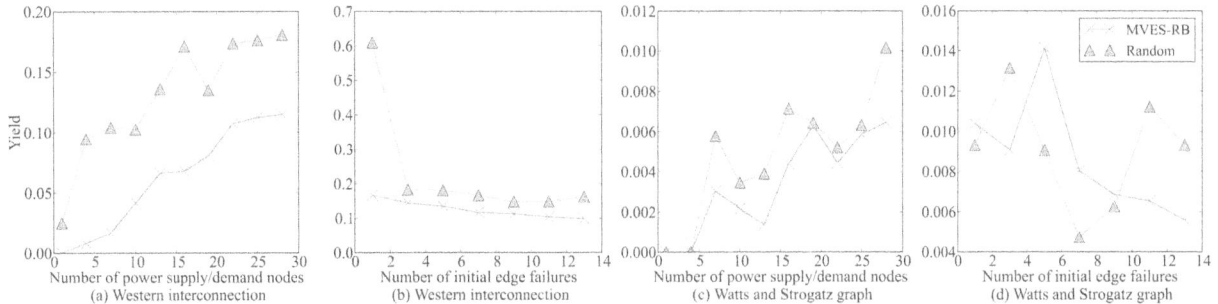

Figure 9: The yield after stabilization when selecting an initial set of edge failures randomly and based on the MVES-RB Algorithm. In (a) and (c) number of edge failures is 10, and in (b)and (d) the number of supply/demand nodes is 20. Every data point is the average over 20 trials, each composed of a different set of supply/demand nodes.

to get better insight into the performance of the MVES-RB Algorithm, we compare it with the case that k edges are selected randomly. As can be seen in Fig. 8, the MVES-RB Algorithm outperforms the random selection most of the time. Fig 9 depicts this comparison for larger initial failures in the Western interconnection and the Watts-Strogatz graph. The power supplies and demands, the reactances, and the capacities are as above. It can be seen that the MVES-RB Algorithm can perform significantly better than the random selection (Fig. 9-(a) and (b)), and in some cases obtains similar performance to the random selection (Fig. 9-(c) and (d)). Notice that in these cases, both methods perform relatively good (lead to yield less than 0.02).

To conclude, despite the simplicity and low complexity of the MVES-RB Algorithm, simulations indicate that it outperforms the random selection and in simple cases obtains the optimal solution.

8. CONCLUSIONS

We studied properties of the admittance matrix of the grid and provided analytical tools for studying the impact of a single edge failure on the flows on the other edges. Based on these tools, we derived upper bounds on the flow changes after a single edge failure and discussed the robustness of different graph classes against single edge failures. We illustrated via simulations the impact of a single edge failure. Then, we introduced a pseudo-inverse based efficient algorithm to identify the evolution of the cascade. Finally, we proved that the minimum yield problem is NP-hard and introduced a simple heuristic algorithm to detect the most vulnerable edges.

This is one of the first steps in using computational tools for understanding the grid resilience to cascading failures.

Hence, there are still many open problems. In particular, we plan to study the effect of failures on the interdependent grid and communication networks. Moreover, while due to its relative simplicity, most previous work in the area of grid vulnerability is based on the DC model, this model does not capture effects such as voltage collapse that may occur during a cascade. Hence, we plan to develop methods to analyze the cascades using the more realistic AC model.

Acknowledgement

This work was supported in part by CIAN NSF ERC under grant EEC-0812072, NSF grant CNS-1018379, and DTRA grant HDTRA1-13-1-0021.

9. REFERENCES

[1] U.S.-Canada Power System Outage Task Force. report on the August 14, 2003 blackout in the United States and Canada: Causes and recommendations. https://reports.energy.gov, (2004).
[2] Report of the enquiry committee on grid disturbance in Northern region on 30th July 2012 and in Northern, Eastern and North-Eastern region on 31st July 2012, Aug. 2012. http://www.powermin.nic.in/pdf/GRID_ENQ_REP_16_8_12.pdf.
[3] P. Agarwal, A. Efrat, S. Ganjugunte, D. Hay, S. Sankararaman, and G. Zussman. The resilience of WDM networks to probabilistic geographical failures. *IEEE/ACM Trans. Netw.*, 21(5):1525–1538, 2013.
[4] A. Albert. *Regression and the Moore-Penrose pseudoinverse*, volume 3. Academic Press, 1972.
[5] R. Albert, I. Albert, and G. L. Nakarado. Structural vulnerability of the North American power grid. *Phys. Rev. E*, 69(2):025103, 2004.
[6] L. A. N. Amaral, A. Scala, M. Barthélémy, and H. E. Stanley. Classes of small-world networks. *PNAS*, 97(21):11149–11152, 2000.
[7] T. Aura, M. Bishop, and D. Sniegowski. Analyzing single-server network inhibition. In *IEEE Proc. Computer Security Foundations Workshop (CSFW-13)*, 2000.

[8] R. Bapat. *Graphs and matrices*. Springer, 2010.

[9] A.-L. Barabási and R. Albert. Emergence of scaling in random networks. *Science*, 286(5439):509–512, 1999.

[10] A. R. Bergen and V. Vittal. *Power Systems Analysis*. Prentice-Hall, 1999.

[11] A. Bernstein, D. Bienstock, D. Hay, M. Uzunoglu, and G. Zussman. Sensitivity analysis of the power grid vulnerability to large-scale cascading failures. *ACM SIGMETRICS Perform. Eval. Rev.*, 40(3):33–37, 2012.

[12] A. Bernstein, D. Bienstock, D. Hay, M. Uzunoglu, and G. Zussman. Power grid vulnerability to geographically correlated failures - analysis and control implications. In *Proc. IEEE INFOCOM'14*, Apr. 2014.

[13] D. Bienstock. Optimal control of cascading power grid failures. *Proc. IEEE CDC-ECC*, Dec. 2011.

[14] D. Bienstock and A. Verma. The $N - k$ problem in power grids: New models, formulations, and numerical experiments. *SIAM J. Optimiz.*, 20(5):2352–2380, 2010.

[15] N. Biggs. *Algebraic graph theory*. Cambridge university press, 1994.

[16] D. Bonchev, A. T. Balaban, X. Liu, and D. J. Klein. Molecular cyclicity and centricity of polycyclic graphs. i. cyclicity based on resistance distances or reciprocal distances. *Int. J. Quantum Chem.*, 50(1):1–20, 1994.

[17] S. Buldyrev, R. Parshani, G. Paul, H. Stanley, and S. Havlin. Catastrophic cascade of failures in interdependent networks. *Nature*, 464(7291):1025–1028, 2010.

[18] D. P. Chassin and C. Posse. Evaluating North American electric grid reliability using the Barabási–Albert network model. *Phys. A*, 355(2-4):667 – 677, 2005.

[19] J. Chen, J. S. Thorp, and I. Dobson. Cascading dynamics and mitigation assessment in power system disturbances via a hidden failure model. *Int. J. Elec. Power and Ener. Sys.*, 27(4):318 – 326, 2005.

[20] P. Christiano, J. A. Kelner, A. Madry, D. A. Spielman, and S.-H. Teng. Electrical flows, Laplacian systems, and faster approximation of maximum flow in undirected graphs. In *Proc. ACM STOC'11*, June 2011.

[21] T. H. Cormen, C. E. Leiserson, R. L. Rivest, and C. Stein. *Introduction to algorithms*. MIT press, 2009.

[22] E. Cotilla-Sanchez, P. Hines, C. Barrows, S. Blumsack, and M. Patel. Multi-attribute partitioning of power networks based on electrical distance. *IEEE Trans. Power Syst.*, 28(4):4979–4987, 2013.

[23] E. Cotilla-Sanchez, P. D. Hines, C. Barrows, and S. Blumsack. Comparing the topological and electrical structure of the North American electric power infrastructure. *IEEE Syst. J.*, 6(4):616–626, 2012.

[24] P. Crucitti, V. Latora, and M. Marchiori. A topological analysis of the Italian electric power grid. *Phys. A*, 338(1):92–97, 2004.

[25] I. Dobson, B. Carreras, V. Lynch, and D. Newman. Complex systems analysis of series of blackouts: cascading failure, critical points, and self-organization. *Chaos*, 17(2):026103, 2007.

[26] P. Erdős and A. Rényi. On random graphs. *Publicationes Mathematicae Debrecen*, 6:290–297, 1959.

[27] G. H. Golub and C. F. Van Loan. *Matrix Computations*. Johns Hopkins Studies in Mathematical Sciences, 4th edition, 2012.

[28] I. Gutman and B. Mohar. The quasi-wiener and the Kirchhoff indices coincide. *J. Chem. Inf. Comput. Sci.*, 36(5):982–985, 1996.

[29] D. J. Klein and M. Randić. Resistance distance. *J. Math. Chem.*, 12(1):81–95, 1993.

[30] J. Kleinberg, M. Sandler, and A. Slivkins. Network failure detection and graph connectivity. In *Proc. ACM-SIAM SODA'04*, Jan. 2004.

[31] J. Lavaei and S. Low. Zero duality gap in optimal power flow problem. *IEEE Trans. Power Syst.*, 27(1):92–107, 2012.

[32] X. Liu, K. Ren, Y. Yuan, Z. Li, and Q. Wang. Optimal budget deployment strategy against power grid interdiction. In *Proc. IEEE INFOCOM'13*, Apr. 2013.

[33] I. Lukovits, S. Nikolić, and N. Trinajstić. Resistance distance in regular graphs. *Int. J. of Quantum Chem.*, 71(3):217–225, 1999.

[34] B. H. McRae. Isolation by resistance. *Evolution*, 60(8):1551–1561, 2006.

[35] M. E. Newman and M. Girvan. Finding and evaluating community structure in networks. *Phys. rev. E*, 69(2):026113, 2004.

[36] J. L. Palacios and J. M. Renom. Bounds for the Kirchhoff index of regular graphs via the spectra of their random walks. *Int. J. Quantum Chem.*, 110(9):1637–1641, 2010.

[37] C. Phillips. The network inhibition problem. In *Proc. ACM STOC'93*, May 1993.

[38] A. Pinar, J. Meza, V. Donde, and B. Lesieutre. Optimization strategies for the vulnerability analysis of the electric power grid. *SIAM J. Optimiz.*, 20(4):1786–1810, 2010.

[39] Platts. GIS Data. http://www.platts.com/Products/gisdata.

[40] G. Ranjan, Z.-L. Zhang, and D. Boley. Incremental computation of pseudo-inverse of Laplacian: Theory and applications. *arXiv:1304.2300*, Apr. 2013.

[41] J. Salmeron, K. Wood, and R. Baldick. Analysis of electric grid security under terrorist threat. *IEEE Trans. Power Syst.*, 19(2):905–912, 2004.

[42] The Federal Energy Regulatory Comission (FERC) and the North American Electric Reliability Corporation (NERC). Arizona-Southern California Outages on September 8, 2011. http://www.ferc.gov/legal/staff-reports/04-27-2012-ferc-nerc-report.pdf.

[43] U.S. Federal Energy Regulatory Commission, Dept. of Homeland Security, and Dept. of Energy. Detailed technical report on EMP and severe solar flare threats to the U.S. power grid, Oct. 2010.

[44] D. J. Watts and S. H. Strogatz. Collective dynamics of small-world networks. *Nature*, 393(6684):440–442, 1998.

[45] H. Xiao and E. M. Yeh. Cascading link failure in the power grid: A percolation-based analysis. In *Proc. IEEE Int. Work. on Smart Grid Commun.*, June 2011.

APPENDIX

A. PRELIMINARIES AND PROOFS

In this appendix we restate results related to the Moore-Penrose pseudo-inverse of matrix and the proofs for the results in Sections 4, 5, 6, and 7.

In the following, matrices I and J denote the identity and the all-1 matrices, respectively.

THEOREM A.1 (MOORE-PENROSE [4]). *For any $n \times m$ matrix H, Moore-Penrose pseudo-inverse of H,*

$$H^+ = \lim_{\delta \to 0}(H^t H + \delta^2 I)^{-1} H^t = \lim_{\delta \to 0} H^t(HH^t + \delta^2 I)^{-1}$$

always exists. And for any n-vector z, $\hat{x} = H^+ z$ is the vector of minimum norm among those which minimize $\|z - Hx\|$.

THEOREM A.2 (ALBERT [4]). *For any matrices U, V,*

$$(UU^t + VV^t)^+ = (CC^t)^+ + [I - (VC^+)^t]$$
$$\times [(UU^t)^+ - (UU^t)^+ V(I - C^+ C)KV^t(UU^t)^+]$$
$$\times [1 - VC^+]$$

where C and K are defined as follows

$$C = [I - (UU^t)(UU^t)^+]V$$

$$K = \{I + [(I - C^+ C)V^t(UU^t)^+ V(I - C^+ C)]\}^{-1}.$$

PROOF OF **Lemma 2**. Suppose that $\{i, j\}$ is a cut-edge of the connected graph G, and $G\backslash\{i, j\} = G_1 \cup G_2$. Assume that $i \in G_1$ and $j \in G_2$. We show below that for any $\{r, s\} \in G\backslash\{i, j\}$, $a_{ir}^+ - a_{jr}^+ = a_{is}^+ - a_{js}^+$. Moreover, for any $r \in G_1$ and $s \in G_2$, $a_{ir}^+ - a_{jr}^+ \neq a_{is}^+ - a_{js}^+$. Suppose that $\{r, s\} \in G\backslash\{i, j\}$ is an arbitrary edge. Then, the solution to (1)-(2) for the power vector $\hat{P}$ with $\hat{p}_r = -\hat{p}_s = 1$ and zero elsewhere is $f_{rs} = -f_{sr} = 1$ and zero elsewhere. Therefore, $f_{ij} = 0$. On the other hand, from Observation 1, $\hat{\Theta} = A^+ \hat{P}$ is a solution to the equivalent matrix equation (3). Since the solution with respect to power flows is unique, $0 = f_{ij} = -a_{ij}(\hat{\theta}_i - \hat{\theta}_j) = -a_{ij}(A_i^+ \hat{P} - A_j^+ \hat{P}) \Rightarrow 0 = (a_{ir}^+ - a_{is}^+ - a_{jr}^+ + a_{js}^+) \Rightarrow a_{ir}^+ - a_{jr}^+ = a_{is}^+ - a_{js}^+$. From this and since $a_{ii}^+ - a_{ji}^+ \neq$

$a_{ij}^+ - a_{jj}^+$ (Lemma 1), for any $r \in G_1$ and $s \in G_2$, $a_{ir}^+ - a_{jr}^+ \neq a_{is}^+ - a_{js}^+$. Thus, by using the precomputed pseudo-inverse of the admittance matrix, computing $A_i^+ - A_j^+$, and dividing the entries into two groups with equal values, the connected components of $G \setminus \{i, j\}$ can be identified. This process requires $O(|V|)$ time. $\square$

PROOF OF **Lemma 3**. First, from Observation 1, $\hat{\Theta} = A^+ P'$ is a solution to (3) for the power vector P' in the graph G. Since the solution to (1)-(2) with respect to power flows is unique, if $f_{ij} = 0$, then $\hat{\Theta} = A^+ P'$ is also a solution to (3) for the power vector P' in the graph G'. Therefore, we only need to prove that $\hat{\theta}_i = \hat{\theta}_j$ from $\hat{\Theta} = A^+ P'$. To prove this, we prove that $\hat{\theta}_i - \hat{\theta}_j = (A_i^+ - A_j^+) P' = 0$. However, from the proof of Lemma 2, since $\{i, j\}$ is a cut-edge, the entries of $A_i^+ - A_j^+$ have equal values at the entries in the same connected component. On the other hand, since P' is the power vector after load shedding/generation curtailing, then the sum of the supplies and demands at each connected component is zero. Thus, $(A_i^+ - A_j^+) P' = 0$. $\square$

PROOF OF **Theorem 1**[11]. First we show that if G is connected, then $AA^+ = I - \frac{1}{n} J$. A is a real and symmetric matrix, therefore there exist an orthogonal and unitary matrix U such that $A = U^t D U$, in which $D = \text{diag}(\lambda_1, \lambda_2, \ldots, \lambda_n)$ is the diagonal matrix of eigenvalues of A and U_i is the normalized eigenvector related to eigenvalue λ_i. It is well-known that when G is connected and unweighted, then the multiplicity of eigenvalue 0 of the Laplacian matrix is 1 [15]. Exactly the same result with the same approach can be obtained for weighted graph, therefore we can assume that $\lambda_1 = 0$ and all other eigenvalues are nonzero. In this case $U_1 = [\frac{1}{\sqrt{n}}, \frac{1}{\sqrt{n}}, \ldots, \frac{1}{\sqrt{n}}]$. On the other hand, $A^+ = U^t D^+ U$, therefore

$$
\begin{aligned}
AA^+ &= U^t DU U^t D^+ U = U^t D D^+ U \\
&= U^t \text{diag}(\lambda_1 \lambda_1^+, \lambda_2 \lambda_2^+, \ldots, \lambda_n \lambda_n^+) U \\
&= U^t (I - \text{diag}(1, 0, \ldots, 0)) U \\
&= I - U^t [U_1^t | 0] \ldots | 0]^t = I - \frac{1}{n} J
\end{aligned}
$$

in which $[U_1^t | 0] \ldots | 0]^t$ is an $n \times n$ matrix with U_1 in the first row and 0 elsewhere.

Similarly we show that if G has k connected components with $m_1, m_2, \ldots, m_k$ nodes, then $AA^+ = I - J_k$ in which

$$
J_k = \text{diag}(\frac{1}{m_1} J_{m_1 \times m_1}, \frac{1}{m_2} J_{m_2 \times m_2}, \ldots, \frac{1}{m_k} J_{m_k \times m_k})
$$

is a block matrix with matrices on the diagonal entries (with proper node indexing). Suppose G has $k \leq n$ connected components. Again it is well-known that when G is unweighted, multiplicity of eigenvalue 0 of the Laplacian matrix is equal to the number of connected components of graph G [15]. With exactly the same reasoning it can be shown that it is also the case for weighted graph. Therefore, in this case $\lambda_1 = \lambda_2 = \cdots = \lambda_k = 0$. Suppose m_i is the size of the ith connected component. With a proper indexing of nodes, it is easy to verify that $U_i = [0, \ldots, 0, \frac{1}{\sqrt{m_i}}, \ldots, \frac{1}{\sqrt{m_i}}, 0, \ldots, 0]$, in which $u_{ij} = \frac{1}{\sqrt{m_i}}$ for

$\sum_{k=1}^{i-1} m_k < j \leq \sum_{k=1}^{i} m_k$, and zero elsewhere. Now similar to previous part,

$$
AA^+ = I - U^t [U_1^t | U_2^t | \ldots | U_k^t | 0] \ldots | 0]^t = I - J_k.
$$

Now we can prove the theorem. A is a real and symmetric matrix, therefore there exist an $n \times n$ matrix B such that $BB^t = A$. Now using Theorem A.2,

$$
\begin{aligned}
(A + a_{ij} XX^t)^+ &= (CC^t)^+ + [I - (\sqrt{a_{ij}} XC^+)^t] \\
&\times [A^+ - a_{ij} A^+ X (I - C^+ C) KX^t A^+] \\
&\times [1 - \sqrt{a_{ij}} XC^+].^{12}
\end{aligned}
$$

Therefore, all we need to compute is matrices C and K. Using previous part,

$$
C = [I - AA^+] X = [I - I + J_k] X = J_k X.
$$

Since $\{i, j\} \in E$, nodes i and j should be in the same connected component of G. Therefore, from the structure of J_k, $J_k X = 0$ and so $C = 0$. Using this,

$$
\begin{aligned}
K &= \{I + a_{ij} [(I - C^+ C) X^t A^+ X (I - C^+ C)]\}^{-1} \\
&= \{I + a_{ij} [I X^t A^+ X I]\}^{-1} = \{1 + a_{ij} X^t A^+ X\}^{-1}.
\end{aligned}
$$

Notice that X is an $n \times 1$ vector, therefore $X^t A^+ X$ is an scaler and I in the second equation is 1×1. This is why it is written 1 instead of I in the last equation. Since $\{i, j\}$ is not a cut edge, from Lemma 1 we have, $1 + a_{ij} X^t A^+ X = a_{ij} [a_{ij}^{-1} - 2(a^+)_{ij} + (a^+)_{ii} + (a^+)_{jj}] \neq 0$, therefore K is well-defined. Replacing K and C,

$$
\begin{aligned}
&(A + a_{ij} XX^t)^+ \\
&= A^+ - a_{ij} A^+ X \{1 + a_{ij} X^t A^+ X\}^{-1} X^t A^+ \\
&= A^+ - \frac{1}{a_{ij}^{-1} + X^t A^+ X} A^+ XX^t A^+
\end{aligned}
$$

which is what we wanted to prove. $\square$

PROOF OF **Corollary 1**. It is easy to see from Theorem 1,

$$
A_r'^+ = A_r^+ - \frac{(a_{ri}^+ - a_{rj}^+)}{a_{ij}^{-1} - 2(a^+)_{ij} + (a^+)_{ii} + (a^+)_{jj}} (A_i^+ - A_j^+).
$$

Using this in $f'_{rs} = -a_{rs}(A_r'^+ - A_s'^+) P$ completes the proof. $\square$

PROOF OF **Lemma 4**. Based on Corollary 1, after the removal of a non-cut edge $\{i, j\}$, each entry of the pseudo inverse of the admittance matrix can be updated in $O(1)$ time. Thus, computing A'^+ from A^+ takes $O(|V|^2)$ time. $\square$

PROOF OF **Observation 2**. We construct the graph $G = (V, E)$ as follows, $V = \{s, t\}$, $P_s = -P_t = 1$, and there are two parallel edges e_1 and e_2 between s and t. Set the capacities $c_{e_1} = c_{e_2} = 1$. Assume the reactances x_{e_1}, x_{e_2} are such that $0 < x_{e_1} < x_{e_2}$.

By Eq. (1)-(2), we get $f_{e_1} = \frac{x_{e_2}}{x_{e_2} + x_{e_1}}$ and $f_{e_2} = \frac{x_{e_1}}{x_{e_1} + x_{e_2}}$. If $F_0 = \{e_1\}$, then $f_{e_2}(F_0) = 1$ and $S_{e_2, e_1} = \frac{x_{e_2}}{x_{e_1}}$. $\square$

PROOF OF **Corollary 2**. Using triangle inequality for resistance distance, we can write,

$$
\begin{aligned}
-r(i, p) + r(i, q) &\leq r(p, q) \\
r(j, p) - r(j, q) &\leq r(p, q).
\end{aligned}
$$

Apply these to Lemma 5 completes the proof. $\square$

---

[11]The proof provided could be simplified, if the form of the A'^+ was known in advance. However, the proof shows the derivation of A'^+.

---

[12]$\sqrt{a_{ij}}$ might be an imaginary number.

PROOF OF **Corollary 3**. Notice that $r(\{i,j\},\{p,q\}) = \min\{r(i,q), r(i,p), r(j,q), r(j,p)\}$. The proof is exactly the same as the proof of Corollary 2. □

PROOF OF **Observation 3**. From [8, Lemma 9.9], we have $\sum_{\{i,j\}\in E} r(i,j) = |V| - 1$ [8]. □

PROOF OF **Lemma 6**. It is known that the Kirchhoff index of the graph G can be written in terms of the eigenvalues of the Laplacian matrix of the graph as $Kf(G) = n\sum_{i=1}^{n-1}\frac{1}{\lambda_i}$ [28]. On the other hand,

$$n^2 \leq \left(\sum_{i=1}^{n-1}\frac{1}{\lambda_i}\right)\left(\sum_{i=1}^{n-1}\lambda_i\right) = \left(\sum_{i=1}^{n-1}\frac{1}{\lambda_i}\right)\mathrm{tr}(A).$$

However, when n is relatively big, then each node has the degree equal to $\Theta(np)$, therefore $\mathrm{tr}(A) = \Theta(n^2 p)$. Combining this with the equations above, we can easily see that $Kf(G) = \Omega(n/p)$. Thus, the average resistance distance is of $Kf(G)/|E| = \Omega(\frac{1}{np^2})$.

As for the upper bound, it is shown in [36] that for a d-regular graph H with n nodes, $Kf(H) \leq \frac{3n^2}{d}$. Using this bound for Erdős-Rényi graph, we can write $Kf(G) = O(n/p)$. Thus, the average resistance distance is of $O(\frac{1}{np^2})$. □

PROOF OF **Theorem 2**. Finding the pseudo inverse of the matrix requires $O(|V|^3)$ time. Therefore, Line 1 takes $O(|V|^3)$ time. Lines 5 and 6 in the algorithm take $O(|V|)$ time and Line 7 takes $O(|V|^2)$, therefore the whole **for** loop takes at most $O(|F_i||V|^2)$ time at each step. Using A^+ computed in the **for** loop, Lines 8 and 9 take $O(|V|^2)$ time. Thus, the total running time of the algorithm is at most $O(|V|^3) + O((|F_0|+|F_1|+\cdots+|F_t|)|V|^2) = O(|V|^3) + O(|F_t^*||V|^2)$. □

PROOF OF **Lemma 7**. Consider following problem:

PROBLEM 1. *Suppose $G = (V, E)$ is an instance of the classical flow problem, with a single source node $\{s\}$ and set of sink nodes T. Assume demands are equal to 1 and lines have unbounded capacity ($O(|V|)$). Does a subset of edges $\mathcal{A} \subseteq E$ with $|\mathcal{A}| \leq k$ exist such that $|T_{fail}| \geq m$? (T_{fail} is set of sink nodes which get disconnected from the source node s after removing set of edges $\mathcal{A}$.)*

It is proved in [7, Theorem 7], that problem 1 is NP-complete. We want to use this result to proof Lemma 7. For this reason we provide a polynomial time reduction from problem above to minimum yield problem.

PROBLEM 2. *Suppose $G = (V, E)$ is an instance of the power flow problem, with set of supply node $S = \{s\}$ and set of demand nodes T. Assume $P_t = -1$ for all $t \in T$, and $P_s = |T|$. Assume all the lines have capacities equal to $|T|$ and reactances equal to 1. Is $Y(G, k) \leq 1 - \frac{m}{|T|}$?*

CLAIM 1. *Suppose the graphs in problems 1 and 2 are the same, then the answer to problem 1 is yes if, and only if, the answer to problem 2 is yes.*

Proof. ($\Rightarrow$) Assume the answer to problem 1 is *yes*. It means that there exists a set of edges $\mathcal{A} \subseteq E$ with $|\mathcal{A}| \leq k$ such that their removal disconnects at least m of the sink nodes from the source node. Now in problem 2, choose $F_0 = \mathcal{A}$. Since two graphs are the same, at least m of the demand nodes are disconnected from the supply node s. As a result, final yield is at most $|T| - m$. Since initial yield was $|T|$, $Y(G, F_0) \leq 1 - \frac{m}{|T|}$. Hence, $Y(G, k) \leq 1 - \frac{m}{|T|}$.

($\Leftarrow$) Now the other way, assume the answer to problem 2 is *yes*. It means that there is an initial set of edge failures $F_0 \subseteq$

E with $|F_0| \leq k$ such that $Y(G, F_0) \leq 1 - \frac{m}{|T|}$. First, since all the edges have capacity equal to $|T|$ which is an upper bound for a flow in an edge, after initial set of failures, there is no cascade. Therefore, there is no further edge failures. Second, with the same reason, as long as a demand node is connected to the supply node, its demand can be satisfied. Now since $Y(G, F_0) \leq 1 - \frac{m}{|T|}$, with initial set of failure F_0, at least m of the demand nodes are disconnected from supply node s. In problem 1 choose $\mathcal{A} = F_0$, since the graphs in two problems are the same, by removing set of edges $\mathcal{A}$ from G, at least m of the sink nodes are disconnected from source node s. Since $|\mathcal{A}| = |F_0| \leq k$, the answer to problem 1 is also *yes*.

It can be concluded from this claim that problems 1 and 2 are equivalent. Therefore, problem 2 is also NP-complete. Now since problem 2 is an special case of the minimum yield problem, the minimum yield problem is NP-hard, and hence its decision version is NP-complete. □

SoftUPS: Eliminating the Need and Cost of Battery Backups in the Developing World

Zohaib Sharani, Khushboo Qayyum, Noman Bashir, Affan Syed
SysNet, National University of Computer and Emerging Sciences
Islamabad, Pakistan.
first.last@sysnet.org.pk

ABSTRACT

We propose to demonstrate a smart-home solution coupled with a smart-grid that can eliminate the cost of battery backups used in the developing world. We are developing a smart-home application, SoftUPS, that instruments a home and enforces lower levels of power consumption, providing a way for a grid to reduce demand and prevent whole-scale blackouts. We have built hardware to enable such control and will demonstrate this control using a Lab-of-Things application.

Categories and Subject Descriptors

C.3 [**Special-Purpose and Application-Based Systems**]: Real-time and Embedded Systems; B.m [**Hardware**]: Miscellaneous

Keywords

Demand Response, Demand Side Management, ICTD

1. INTRODUCTION

Many developing countries suffer from an electrical power deficit because of a mismatch between electricity generation potential and its demand. The power regulatory authorities in these countries then have to resort to whole-scale cutoff in the power supply to segments of their consumers. To maintain a semblance of normality during these blackouts, consumers now resort to running a few important devices from a limited amount of energy stored in batteries that are charged through UPS/inverters during normal power supply.

This solution, we argue, is inefficient, costly, and inflexible, and fails to provide any backup under blackouts of long duration. Seetharam et al. identify that these battery backups are not only **inefficient** (with $\approx 50\%$ efficiency), but also have a positive feedback that increases the supply-demand gap [5]. They are **costly** both in terms of installation (around $250) as well as recurring expense in battery replacement every 8-12 months (another $100). The current

e-Energy'14, June 11–13, 2014, Cambridge, UK.
ACM 978-1-4503-2819-7/14/06.
http://dx.doi.org/10.1145/2602044.2602045 .

backups require hard-wiring user-selected essential devices at installation time, and thus are **inflexible** in terms of a user's ability to dynamically reassign power to a different set of appliances. Finally, under long and regular blackouts (like 18hrs/day [3]), the limited backup capacity fails to keep even a small subset of low power and essential devices running.

We propose SoftUPS, an ICT based solution, that provides for consumers the same service as the current UPS + battery backup, i.e. powering a few important devices during enforced load-shedding intervals. SoftUPS essentially provides a way to automatically migrate homes in the developing world to a low-energy state whenever a utility cannot match the current demand. We expect that utilities, with such a capability, can transmit a request for "load-shedding" to our application that enforces such demand reduction, instead of an enforced blackout. As a software-based solution, we will allow the consumer to identify (and dynamically modify) devices they need available during the load-shedding event. Our system will ensure that the power budget of the identified devices is below a particular threshold, and if so, allow *only* these selected appliances to work directly *from the grid* whenever the grid demands a load-shedding event. Thus, by not requiring a battery backup our solution has no losses, no recurring cost, and unlimited flexibility in device operation (within a power-budget), while still providing utilities with the intended effect of load reduction.

We believe our solution's novelty lies in its clear incentive for usage in the developing world where consumers are already *paying* for installation of battery backups that enforce a very low-power consumption profile during blackouts. We see that existing automatic demand response solutions, with their focus on the developed world, do not realize this niche.

2. CHALLENGES IN BUILDING SoftUPS

Our solution requires a mechanism to instrument a home such that the power consumption of individual appliances can be controlled and overall consumption monitored. This objective raises several challenges (beyond the ability to control and monitor), of cost, architecture, misuse, and usability.

Our prototype here addresses the issues of misuse and usability; we demonstrate a controllable switching element, deployable at room level, that allows selecting individual sockets and appliances for low-power operation. We have developed a HomeOS/LoT [4] driver for our device, along with an application that is available (using LoT redirection service) as an HTML5 application on any connected device. We

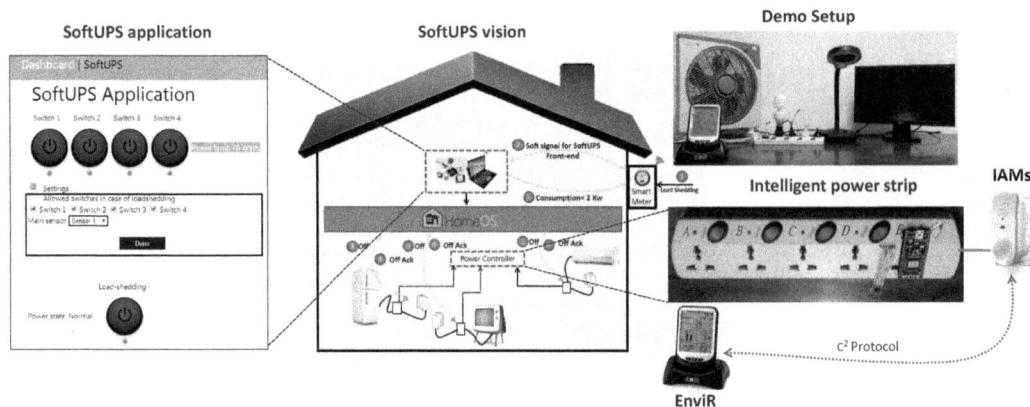

Figure 1: The SoftUPS vision and its prototype implementation as a HomeOS application.

address any potential misuse of our system through a power measurement device that helps enforce our power budget.

We are currently investigating the correct deployment architecture that provides the right tradeoff of cost and observation granularity. Instrumenting every device is a naive and costly option, but the granularity control impacts our the usability and flexibility of our solution.

3. DEMONSTRATING THE SoftUPS IDEA

Overview: Our system comprises the following two components: a) An intelligent Power Strip (iPS) with power monitoring capabilities, and b) A SoftUPS Application over HomeOS (demo video here [2]).

The iPS can demonstrates our ability to control appliances in a single room. Our research shows that room-level switch boards control all power sockets and additional appliances (fans/lighting) from a single location. We use the basic wiring scheme of conventional switch boards, and build our iPS to demonstrate socket level control of plugged in appliances. We augment our iPS with a power monitoring sensor to help enforce limits.

Our SoftUPS application provides a UI to setup policies to view the consumption of the iPS and selection of sockets to shut-off when utilities require load-shedding. This application allows setting a power-budget in theory, informed by power utilities. If this budget is exceeded (by mistake or otherwise) by plugging a higher power device, we enforce the power disconnection to all sockets; essentially the current model of a full blackout.

Implementation Details: Our iPS retrofits a four slot power supply with a RF transceiver (CC2500) controlled by a mbed microcontroller (Figure 1). Furthermore, the on/off state of each socket on the iPS is controlled by mbed using relays. This setup thus provides us with a wireless communication channel to control individual sockets. For power monitoring we use two devices developed by Current Cost [1]; an IAM device for monitoring power consumption of the iPS, and a base station EnivR energy monitor to which the IAM reports its measurements.

Our SoftUPS application is built using custom-developed HomeOS driver for the iPS, and utilizing drivers for their EnviR bases station. Thus our application has both the control (through iPS) and measurement data (through IAM) available to implement our prototype. The SoftUPS application display the available sockets on its UI, with settings option to select which sockets to shut down when utilities want to demand reduction (load-shedding). The UI also shows that the total consumption of the power strip with selected devices turned off, thus allowing the selection to remain below the utility specified threshold, which is also tunable. We emulate the load-shedding event through a button on the UI, which when pressed signals the iPS to block power supply to the selected socket. During this phase, our application continuously monitors the power consumption of the iPS. Thus, when we (for demo purposes) replace the device in a socket with a higher consumption one, such that the allotted consumption threshold is crossed, our application will communicate with the iPS to disconnect all devices. This state is only reset once utilities indicate the end of their load-shedding period.

Conclusion: We thus demonstrate our ability to automatically reduce power consumption of a home, while providing a level of flexibility for the user to select devices that remain available within a threshold. Several aspect of this idea need work, from socket level device disaggregation and security — we aim to target them as part of future work.

4. ACKNOWLEDGMENTS

This work is funded by generous grant from Microsoft Research. We would like to thank and acknowledge Zainab Abaid, Naveed Bhatti, Zaafar Ahmed, and Osama Haq, all of whom helped and provided important feedback in developing the demo as well as proof-reading our paper.

5. REFERENCES

[1] Current Cost. http://www.currentcost.com.
[2] SoftUPS Demo Video.
    http://www.sysnet.org.pk/w/SoftUPS.
[3] DAWN. 14 to 18-hour loadshedding. web site
    http://dawn.com/2013/04/17/
    14-to-18-hour-loadshedding/, April 2013.
[4] Colin Dixon, Ratul Mahajan, Sharad Agarwal, A. J. Brush, Bongshin Lee, Stefan Saroiu, and Paramvir Bahl. An operating system for the home. NSDI'12. USENIX Association, 2012.
[5] Deva P. Seetharam, Ankit Agrawal, Tanuja Ganu, Jagabondhu Hazra, Venkat Rajaraman, and Rajesh Kunnath. Hidden costs of power cuts and battery backups. e-Energy '13. ACM, 2013.

POSTER: Reducing the Electricity Consumption of Large Outdoor LED Advertising Screens

Frank Englert, Ahmad El'Hindi, Daniel Burgstahler, Alaa Alhamoud, Ralf Steinmetz
Multimedia Communications Lab, Technische Universität Darmstadt, Germany
{firstname.lastname}@kom.tu-darmstadt.de

ABSTRACT

Outdoor LED advertising screens have a high power consumption. Those installations can easily reach a power density of 1kW per square meter. This causes not only high electricity costs for the operator but also pollutes the environment with stray light. As the high power consumption is mainly caused by incorrect brightness settings, better control loops could improve the situation. In this paper we propose first steps towards improved brightness control loops which could lead to significant reductions of power consumption as well as stray light. A first evaluation shows that our proposed solution reduces the power consumption of large LED advertising screens by up to 25%.

1. INTRODUCTION

Outdoor LED advertising screens have become ubiquitous inhabitants of modern metropolis. While the exact number of such displays is unknown, according to a Panasonic study, the annual business volume of this market is as high as $1 billion with a growing rate of 20%. With a peak power density exceeding $1kW$ per square meter display area, each of these wall displays consumes huge amounts of electricity and pollutes the environment with stray light [1]. This raises the question, whether there are opportunities to save a significant amount of energy. In this paper we analyzed the power consumption of such screens to determine the saving potential. As result, we identified incorrect brightness settings as main factor for electricity wastage. Building upon that, we developed a better brightness control schema based on the outdoor luminance. First evaluations of this schema show a 25% decrease in the power consumption.

2. STATE OF THE ART

State of the art outdoor LED wall systems as shown in Figure 1, consist of the LED wall itself and a Control Unit. Typically, a computer running a special playback and control software is used as Control Unit. This system sends the video signal to display and also control commands to the

e-Energy'14, June 11–13, 2014, Cambridge, UK.
ACM 978-1-4503-2819-7/14/06.
http://dx.doi.org/10.1145/2602044.2602071.

wall screen. The most commonly used Control Units could adjust the brightness setting in 100 discrete steps. There exist two strategies to adjust the brightness of the LED wall:

1. Time Table based: The brightness of the display is set to a specific value depending on the current date and time. Such time table based algorithms allows reducing the luminance during night times. Although easy to implement, such control algorithms could not achieve optimal control, because they do not consider the actual outdoor luminance.

2. Outdoor luminance based: Newer LED wall screens are equipped with sensors to measure the actual outdoor luminance. As those sensors are mainly developed to reduce the intensity of stray light, their Control Units could switch the brightness in only eight discrete steps. Therefore, a detailed investigation analyzing the energy efficiency of those solutions is required. As shown by [3] such an approach could lead to significant energy savings.

Both brightness control strategies yield suboptimal results from an energy consumption point of view. Thus, in the following sections, we will illustrate solutions to reduce the power consumption of such outdoor LED advertising displays.

3. ADAPTIVE BRIGHTNESS

The goal of this work is to minimize the power consumption of LED walls without negatively affecting the perception of human spectators. Technically spoken, our optimization aims are:

1. Optimal contrast for human spectators.
2. Minimal power consumption.
3. Minimal stray light pollution.

Similar to Moshnyaga et al. [2], we sense the luminance and use a characteristic curve to calculate the brightness setting. Then our solution automatically adjusts the brightness according to the previously calculated setting. This process is shown in Figure 1.

To achieve our optimization goals, the sensor for measuring the outdoor luminance should have a luminance resolution as high as the humans eye together with a high dynamic range. As stated in the Weber-Fechners Law, the human eye responds logarithmically to visual stimuli. Therefore, we decided to use the image data of a video camera for calculating the outdoor luminance. State of the art video equipment is heavily optimized to match the perception characteristics of the human eye and thus yield good luminance readings.

For optimal control, the characteristic curve of the brightness controller should match the logarithmic luminance perception of the human eye. Otherwise, the controller adjusts

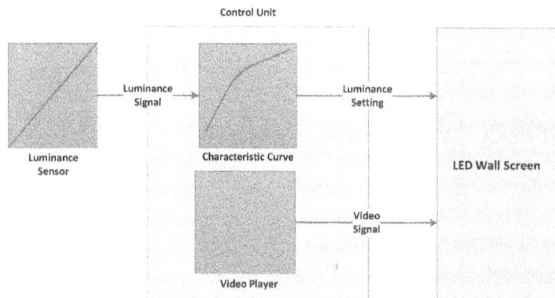

Figure 1: Overview over system setup.

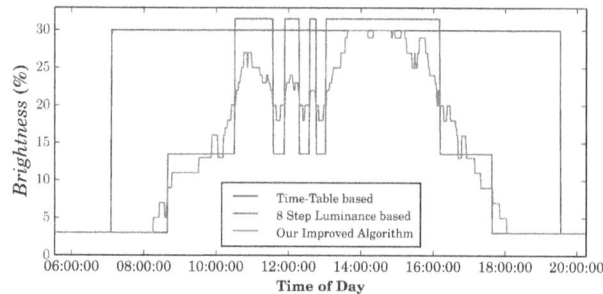

Figure 2: Brightness for different control algorithms

the brightness level too high in dark environments and too low in case of full sunlight. We implemented different approximations for the brightness control curve and adjusted the exact coefficients by manual fine tuning. To do so, we visually inspected and adjusted the brightness setting of the outdoor LED wall under different luminance conditions within one week. A detailed explanation of these algorithms will be omitted due to the space limitations.

4. EVALUATION

The goal of this work is twofold. First, we determine the electric wastage caused by incorrectly controlled LED wall screens. Second, we evaluate our methods for optimal brightness control. Thus, we compare our improved brightness control algorithm with state of the art solutions. To do so, we simulated the power consumption caused by different control algorithms. Building upon that, we conduced measurements in a real world deployment to validate our simulative results.

4.1 Simulation Results

To simulate the power consumption of LED walls, we measured the electricity of a 17 square meter LED wall screen showing a white picture in relation to its brightness setting. As expected, the power consumption rises linear with an increasing brightness setting x: $P_{LED}(x) = ax + b$. In case of our LED wall, the coefficients are $a = 188.3 \frac{W}{step}$ and $b = 2,761W$ for x in $[0...1]$. Using this power consumption model of the wall screen, we simulated the energy demand of different brightness control algorithms under varying light conditions. The response of state of the art algorithms is shown in Figure 2. Obviously, those algorithms neither produce optimal brightness contrast for human spectators nor are they energy efficient. Our improved algorithm consumes round about 36% less energy than the time table based algorithm. Currently, our simulation model has certain limitations. It uses the actual brightness setting as input parameter but ignores the currently shown image completely. This setup might work well for LCD-based systems whose energy consumption is nearly independent from the currently shown image. For LED-based displays, it causes a certain error, because each pixel has multiple LEDs and depending on the actual color of the pixel, these LEDs are controlled individually. We addressed this issue by using the same image for all simulations. However, a future energy model might include additional parameters derived from the image to display. Those parameters could be the image brightness, a sub-sampled version of the image or the image itself.

4.2 Measurement Results

Our simulation does not consider the fact, that different images shown on the display cause differences in the power consumption. Thus, the saving potential calculated by the simulations is too optimistic.

To get meaningful results, we measured the influence of different brightness control algorithms on the power consumption of a real LED wall screen over the period of one month. During this period, the weather conditions ranged from bright sunlight shining directly on the LED wall screen to dark and rainy days. Compared to the time table based brightness control algorithm our solution reduced the power consumption of the LED wall screen in average by 25%. However, this saving potential should be taken as approximation value - the actual saving potential depends on the season as well as on the content shown on the display and our measurement period is too short for well founded statements. A comparison to the luminance based control was impossible to conduct, because our LED wall screen was not equipped with the required hardware.

5. CONCLUSION AND OUTLOOK

The first results show a great electricity saving potential of 25% percent by using appropriate outdoor luminance sensors for controlling the brightness of LED wall screens. This energy saving could be achieved while maintaining optimal contrast for human spectators even under different luminance conditions. To extend this work, we plan an exhaustive long term evaluation of the hereby proposed solution deployed on multiple LED wall screens of different sizes and manufacturers. Furthermore, we will conduct a user study to determine the optimal contrast setting for human spectators.

6. ACKNOWLEDGEMENTS

This work was funded by the German Federal Ministry of Education and Research. The support code of the underlying project is 01IS12054. The authors are fully responsible for the content of this paper.

7. REFERENCES

[1] Ho et al. A Study on Energy Saving and Light Pollution of LED Advertising Signs. 2011.

[2] Moshnyaga et al. A Camera-Driven Power Management of Computer Display. 2012.

[3] Venkatasubramanian. Dynamic Backlight Adaptation for Low-Power Handheld Devices. 2004.

METIS: a Two-Tier Intrusion Detection System for Advanced Metering Infrastructures

Vincenzo Gulisano   Magnus Almgren   Marina Papatriantafilou

Chalmers University of Technology
{vinmas,almgren,ptrianta}@chalmers.se

ABSTRACT

Specification-based intrusion detection systems, the main defense mechanism proposed so far for Advanced Metering Infrastructures, do not provide a comprehensive protection against the wide spectrum of possible attack scenarios. Challenging aspects in this context include the need for timely detection and for novel attack scenario modeling techniques.

This paper introduces *METIS*, a novel two-tier anomaly-based intrusion detection framework that targets such challenges. The framework provides a continuous and fully distributed processing of network traffic by relying on the data streaming processing paradigm. Attack scenarios can be specified by means of the traffic features they affect and their resulting patterns of malicious activities. We overview the framework, presenting the novel detection technique, and provide results from a case study.

Categories and Subject Descriptors

C.3 [**Computer Systems Organization**]: Special-Purpose and Application-Based Systems; C.2.4 [**Computer Systems Organization**]: Computer-Communication Networks— *Distributed Systems*

Keywords

Advanced Metering Infrastructure; Intrusion Detection; Data Streaming

1. INTRODUCTION

Advanced Metering Infrastructures (AMIs) are composed of communication-enabled metering devices that share data and are remotely controlled by energy utilities. Despite the limited number of real attacks documented so far, a considerable amount of possible attack vectors has been uncovered (e.g., by means of penetration testing). Even though specification-based Intrusion Detection Systems[1] (IDSs), the main defense mechanism proposed so far, may detect

e-Energy'14, June 11–13, 2014, Cambridge, UK.
ACM 978-1-4503-2819-7/14/06.
http://dx.doi.org/10.1145/2602044.2602072.

some attacks, they are not suited to provide a comprehensive protection against all possible attack scenarios, especially considering the manual labor required by a security expert to tune such systems to specific installations. More concretely, they might fail in detecting malicious activity residing in between the boundaries of a device's normal behavior (e.g., they might detect a malicious firmware that suppresses consumption readings but probably miss a firmware that lowers bills by slightly reducing reported consumption readings).

Challenges and contributions. We identify two main challenges for an IDS used in the context of AMIs. As discussed in [1], the AMI network consists of several independent networks and a centralized IDS would not have access to the overall traffic. Moreover, its processing capacity could easily be exhausted by the big, fluctuating volume of data generated by AMIs' devices. For these reasons, the IDS should (1) process data in a fully distributed and parallel manner in order to detect malicious activity timely and (2) avoid expensive per-site customization, by providing an efficient way to specify how malicious activities should be detected.

We present *METIS*[1], an anomaly-based IDS that provides continuous and fully distributed analysis of AMIs traffic. It relies on a novel two-tier detection method in which general attack scenarios are specified by means of (i) the traffic features they involve (and their inter-dependencies) and (ii) how the resulting patterns of suspicious events should be interpreted. We overview the framework, presenting its processing model and its detection technique, showing its use and also providing results from a case study.

2. METIS - OVERVIEW

Continuous and distributed traffic analysis. We aim at the design of an IDS that processes data in an online fashion in order to detect malicious activities timely. The need for continuous processing is also motivated by the evolving nature of AMIs, where new devices are deployed on a daily basis. We identify *data streaming*[4] as a suitable processing paradigm for the analysis of AMIs' data flows. With data streaming, on-line analysis is performed by means of directed acyclic graphs of operators referred to as *Continuous Queries*. Operators provide functionality such as data filtering, aggregation and joining. Data streaming allows for

---

[1]Named after the mythology figure standing for good counsel, advice, planning, cunning, craftiness, and wisdom.

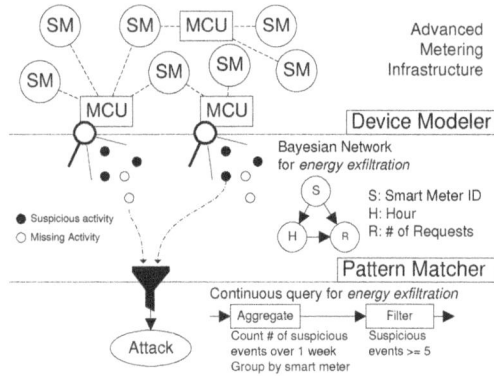

Figure 1: AMI architecture and *METIS* processing overview.

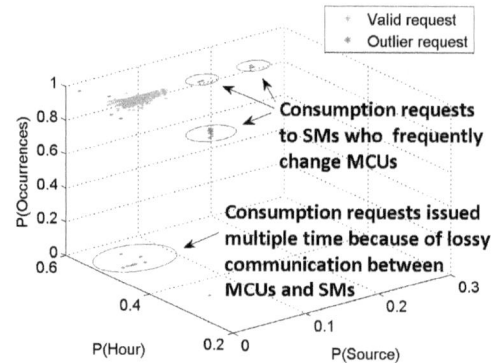

Figure 2: Local Outlier Factor applied to the Bayesian network probabilities.

distributed and parallel processing that can scale accordingly to (i) the increasing number of devices deployed in the network and (ii) the increasing number of attack scenarios being monitored.

Two-tier detection. One of the critical aspects of a defense framework is the way the possible adversary goals need to be specified. To this end, we introduce a novel two-tier detection method in which attack scenarios are specified by the device's traffic features they affect and by the pattern of suspicious events they produce.

Figure 1 presents how the traffic analysis is carried out for a sample AMI composed by Smart Meters (SMs) and Meter Concentrator Units (MCUs) in charge of collecting energy consumption readings. Briefly speaking, *METIS* is composed of two main modules. The *Device Modeler* analyzes each device's traffic and spots suspicious or missing events applying an outlier detection method. The *Device Modeler* relies on a lightweight, yet efficient analysis technique, in which the traffic features that characterize the attack are expressed by means of a Bayesian Network. The secondary analysis is performed by the *Pattern Matcher*, which processes such alerts and requires the user to specify which patterns should be classified as an attack. Such analysis could be performed at dedicated servers, thus relying on more expensive analysis and correlation of the observed alerts.

3. CASE STUDY

Fine grained consumption readings reveal detailed information about household activities [3]. In an energy exfiltration attack scenario, an attacker that gains admin access to an MCU, requests a given SM to report its consumption readings. Notice that a specification-based IDS might fail in detecting such malicious activity if the MCU is actually allowed to retrieve such data from the target SM.

We monitor the traffic of approximately 1,000 SMs connected to 40 MCUs during the months of September to December 2012. We inject 40 simulated energy exfiltration attacks (introducing unauthorized consumption readings) during the month of December. The *Device Modeler*'s Bayesian network and the *Pattern Matcher*'s continuous query are shown in Figure 1. The traffic features we take into account are the smart meter ID (S), the hour (H) and the number of requests (R) observed for each MCU. The *Pattern matcher*

looks for MCUs reporting at least five suspicious requests during a period of one week.

From our evaluation, the framework is able to detect most of the injected attacks. Figure 2 presents the result of the outlier detection method (Local Outlier Factor [2]) and shows which consumption readings are marked as suspicious. Approximately 8% of the events observed at the MCUs are classified as suspicious by the *Device Modeler* (4,000 out of 50,000), while the *Pattern Matcher* provides a True Positive Rate of approximately 91% (36 attacks are detected).

4. CONCLUSION

We propose a two-tier, anomaly-based intrusion detection framework that deals with the security and induced computational challenges of AMIs. We also present a case study that shows it can be flexible for the user to use and can achieve high detection rates. We plan to extend our research considering the detection of a variety of scenarios, including those whose detection is only possible through distributed evidence.

5. REFERENCES

[1] R. Berthier and W. H. Sanders. Specification-based intrusion detection for advanced metering infrastructures. In *IEEE 17th Pacific Rim International Symposium on Dependable Computing (PRDC), 2011*, 2011.

[2] M. M. Breunig, H.-P. Kriegel, R. T. Ng, and J. Sander. Lof: identifying density-based local outliers. In *ACM Sigmod Record*, 2000.

[3] A. Molina-Markham, P. Shenoy, K. Fu, E. Cecchet, and D. Irwin. Private memoirs of a smart meter. In *Proceedings of the 2nd ACM workshop on embedded sensing systems for energy-efficiency in building*, 2010.

[4] M. Stonebraker, U. Çetintemel, and S. Zdonik. The 8 requirements of real-time stream processing. *SIGMOD Rec.*, 2005.

Acknowledgments

This work has been partially supported by the European Comission Seventh Framework Programme (FP7/2007-2013) through the SysSec Project, under grant agreement 257007, through the FP7-SEC-285477-CRISALIS project and through the collaboration framework of Chalmers Energy Area of Advance.

SmartD: Smart Meter Data Analytics Dashboard[*]

Aylin Jarrah Nezhad, Tri Kurniawan Wijaya, Matteo Vasirani, and Karl Aberer
School of Computer and Communication Sciences
École Polytechnique Fédérale de Lausanne (EPFL)
CH-1015 Lausanne, Switzerland
{aylin.jarrahnezhad, tri-kurniawan.wijaya, matteo.vasirani, karl.aberer}@epfl.ch

ABSTRACT

The ability of smart meters to communicate energy consumption data in (near) real-time enables data analytics for novel applications, such as pervasive demand response, personalized energy feedback, outage management, and theft detection. Smart meter data are characterized by big volume and big velocity, which make processing and analysis very challenging from a computational point of view. In this paper we presented SmartD, a dashboard that enables the data analyst to visualize smart meter data and estimate the typical load profile of new consumers according to different contexts, temporal aggregations and consumer segments.

Categories and Subject Descriptors

H.2.8 [**Database Applications**]: Data mining; G.3 [**Probability and Statistics**]: Time series analysis

Keywords

smart meters; visualization; energy consumption analysis

1. INTRODUCTION

Future ICT-based energy systems will rely on an Advanced Metering Infrastructure (AMI), a system that measures and collects data about energy usage and power quality using smart meters installed at the consumer premises [5]. Smart meter data has an important role in several Smart Grid applications and enables novel data analytics tasks, such as energy consumption behavior analysis, theft detection, outage management, pervasive demand response at residential level, and personalized energy feedback. However, processing and analyzing smart meters data is very challenging, because it is characterized by big volume and big velocity, and how to *extract* useful information from it is still an open question.[1]

---

[*]Supported by European Union's Seventh Framework Programme (FP7/2007-2013) 288322, WATTALYST. The authors would like to thank Julien Eberle and Sofiane Sarni for the assistance with GSN.
[1]See Bryan Truex, "Two Opposing Views on Smart Meter Data Analytics", http://bit.ly/LYADfH

---

e-Energy'14, June 11–13, 2014, Cambridge, United Kingdom
ACM 978-1-4503-2819-7/14/06.
http://dx.doi.org/10.1145/2602044.2602046.

In this paper we present SmartD, a dashboard for smart meter data visualization and analysis. SmartD has been built to be (i) seamlessly integrated with existing data collection infrastructures, (ii) intuitive to use, and (iii) easy to extend. To visualize and analyze smart meter data, SmartD supports context selection (e.g., summer, winter, weekend, or weekdays), different temporal aggregations (e.g., hourly, daily, or weekly), and consumer selection (either individual or clusters of consumers). Although this functionality is commonly found in other energy dashboard or time series visualization, SmartD's additional and novel contributions are: (i) estimating the typical hourly load profiles based on demographic information, and (ii) determining the attributes of the demographic profile that are relevant to consumer's energy consumption behavior for a given context. This functionality can be used to predict the typical load profile of new consumers, or to understand the energy consumption behavior of different consumers (e.g., employed vs retired, family vs single).[2]

2. SMARTD

We developed SmartD on top of GSN [2], a widely used middleware for sensor networks deployment. Given that smart meters are essentially sensors, GSN can be seamlessly integrated with an existing smart metering infrastructure, enabling applications running on GSN to receive real-time smart meter readings (push mode) as well as obtaining them from a DB or text files (pull mode). Figure 1 shows the architecture diagram of SmartD.

SmartD needs to be able to (i) retrieve and process smart meter data with big volume and velocity, and (ii) visualize and extract valuable information from that data. While the first capability is provided by GSN, we briefly explain the second in the following sections. We remark that although for demonstration purposes we use the Irish CER dataset [1][3], SmartD can be used with any time series of smart meter data and consumer demographic profiles in the form of <*attribute, value*> tuples.

2.1 Energy Consumption Analysis

For the visualization of energy consumption data (see Figure 2), SmartD has several key features, detailed below.

Temporal aggregations. SmartD supports different time granularities, from half-hourly to monthly. In addition, a set of basic statistical aggregation functions is also provided, such as sum, average, min, and max.[4]

---

[2]We use the terms *energy consumption* and *load* interchangeably.
[3]This dataset contains measurements of approximately 5,000 consumers for 1.5 years (Jul 2009 - Dec 2010)
[4]More sophisticated aggregation functions can be easily added.

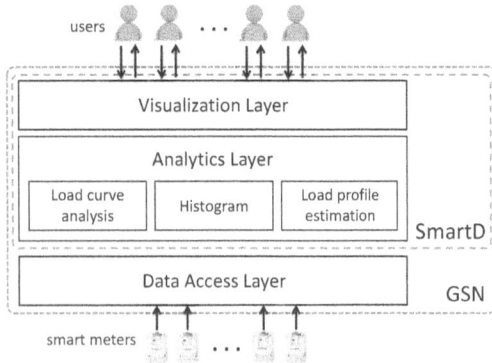

Figure 1: SmartD architecture diagram

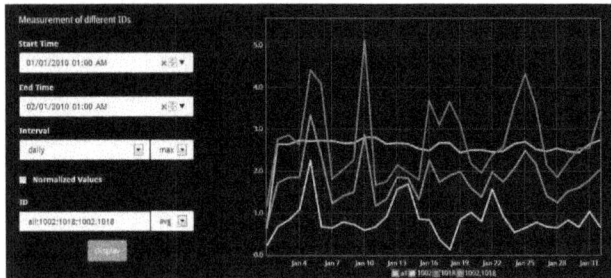

Figure 2: Energy consumption analysis

Consumer aggregations. SmartD supports visualization of energy consumption of a set of individual consumers, clusters of consumers, or a mix of both. We use a simple but flexible grammar $id\big((, id) \mid (; id)\big)^*$ to specify the desired visualization, where id is a consumer identifier, the character ";" separates clusters, and the character "," separates consumers within a cluster. An individual consumer is then expressed as a cluster of one consumer. If a cluster of more than one consumer is specified, the users can choose the functions to aggregate the energy data within the cluster (such as sum, average, min, or max).

Consumer characterization. SmartD provides an option to focus more on consumer demand shape, by plotting z-normalized data. This functionality can be used, e.g., to spot consumers who have morning peak, evening peak, or both.

Histogram. SmartD provides a histogram view with the distribution of energy consumption values, which can be useful to analyze the way people consume energy. For example, we found that the energy consumption of residential consumers follows a log-normal distribution, peaked around their base load, while commercial and industrial consumers follows a normal distribution, peaked around the mean consumption of working hours.

2.2 Energy Consumption Estimation

SmartD supports data analysts by providing insights related to energy consumption behavior. First, it helps to answer questions about consumer load profile given her demographics, such as *what is the difference between load profile of families with and without children?*, or *can we estimate the typical load profile of a new consumer using her socio-demographic information?*. SmartD estimates the load profile of a consumer (see Figure 3), if provided with (a subset of) the consumer demographic information, as well as the context of interest (e.g., weekend, Monday, summer, etc.).

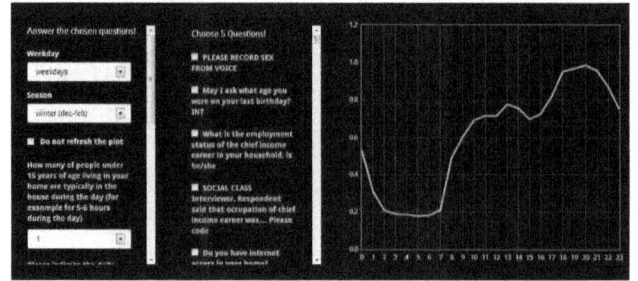

Figure 3: Energy consumption estimation

This is done using *k-nearest neighbor* (*k-NN*), where the best k is determined using *leave-one-out cross-validation*.

Second, SmartD also helps to infer demographic information which significantly influence energy consumption on a specific context, e.g., weekend, Monday, or summer. This is implemented using correlation-based feature selection [4] and *k-NN*, where the features are the demographic information and the target classes are the hourly consumption values. These learning functionalities is developed using the WEKA machine learning library [3].

3. CONCLUSION

In this paper, we presented SmartD, a dashboard for smart meter data analysis and visualization developed on top of GSN. SmartD has been released as an open-source project.[5] SmartD capabilities include visualization of energy consumption data and estimation of the typical load profile of a consumer according to her demographic and contextual information. As future extensions, other functionalities such as customer segmentation [7], interpolation of missing values, and load forecasting [6], could be added.

4. REFERENCES

[1] Smart Metering Trial Data Publication. The Commission for Energy Regulation (CER), 2012.

[2] K. Aberer, M. Hauswirth, and A. Salehi. A Middleware for Fast and Flexible Sensor Network Deployment. In *Proceedings of the 32nd International Conference on Very Large Data Bases*. VLDB Endowment, 2006.

[3] M. Hall, E. Frank, G. Holmes, B. Pfahringer, P. Reutemann, and I. H. Witten. The WEKA Data Mining Software: An Update. *SIGKDD Explor. Newsl.*, 11(1):10–18, Nov. 2009.

[4] M. A. Hall. *Correlation-based Feature Subset Selection for Machine Learning*. PhD thesis, University of Waikato, Hamilton, New Zealand, 1998.

[5] D. Hart. Using AMI to Realize the Smart Grid. In *Power and Energy Society General Meeting - Conversion and Delivery of Electrical Energy in the 21st Century, 2008 IEEE*, pages 1–2, 2008.

[6] S. Humeau, T. K. Wijaya, M. Vasirani, and K. Aberer. Electricity Load Forecasting for Residential Customers: Exploiting Aggregation and Correlation between Households. In *Sustainable Internet and ICT for Sustainability (SustainIT), 2013*, pages 1–6, Oct 2013.

[7] T. K. Wijaya, T. Ganu, D. Chakraborty, K. Aberer, and D. P. Seetharam. Consumer Segmentation and Knowledge Extraction from Smart Meter and Survey Data. In *SIAM International Conference on Data Mining (SDM14)*, 2014.

---

[5]See SmartD's source code, demo video, and supplementary material for this paper at https://github.com/LSIR/smartd

A Social Approach for Predicting Distance-to-Empty in Vehicles

Chien-Ming Tseng, Sohan Dsouza, Chi-Kin Chau

Masdar Institute of Science and Technology, UAE
{ctseng, sdsouza, ckchau}@masdar.ac.ae

ABSTRACT

Distance-to-Empty (DTE) in vehicles depends on several uncertain factors, such as speed, terrain, traffic and driving behavior. Accurate estimation of DTE is vital for not only the scheduling for refueling, but also for the choice of routes for the budget- and/or environmentally-conscious. Traditional approaches often rely on a single driver's personal history. In this paper, we explore a social approach by using other drivers' data to predict the fuel consumption for a given driver along a new route that is not traveled previously. We develop a least-squares regression model and corroborate the performance empirically by an on-road, multi-driver experiment. Our results can enable a new kind of social platform for trip planning based on the shared data among drivers.

1. INTRODUCTION

While in-vehicle information systems are increasingly sophisticated, the information presented from vehicles is not always accurate. One of the major features is Distance-to-Empty (DTE) or alternatively, the fuel consumption for the remaining journey, which are hindered by several uncertain factors, such as speed, terrain, traffic and driving behavior, as well as the intrinsic characteristics of vehicles (e.g., fuel tank capacity, engine load). Accurate prediction of fuel consumption, and thereby DTE, is vital in allowing drivers to know not only when they need to refuel, but also the fuel consumption along different possible routes. In addition, the estimation of DTE is useful for scheduling of refueling, which can optimize the waiting time in the gasoline station.

Previous work relies on using a single driver's personal history for prediction. In contrast, we focus on a social approach by using other drivers' data to predict the DTE for a given driver along a new route. For example, if drivers A, B and C have driven a set of routes X and Y, and only drivers B and C have driven a route Z, we will be able to obtain an estimation for driver A and route Z based on the differences among the routes, and the differences among the drivers' fuel consumption patterns on the same routes.

e-Energy'14, June 11–13, 2014, Cambridge, UK.
ACM 978-1-4503-2819-7/14/06.
http://dx.doi.org/10.1145/2602044.2602073.

To this end, we build on the linear regression approach developed by [4] using a single driver, and extend it to consider multi-driver settings.

2. METHODOLOGY

We adapt the least-squares regression used in [4] to estimate DTE for an electrical vehicle, which also applies to internal combustion vehicles. We first describe the single-driver approach. The drivers' running fuel consumption is computed using a formula provided in [3], with the engine data as inputs, for each slice of sampling time, and added up over a trip to give the total consumption. Training the regression model using the trip data from each driver, we can estimate the DTE for the same drivers in real time. We then extend this single-driver modeling technique to a multi-driver setting. The multivariate regression model in [2] is a blackbox approach, without the detailed knowledge of driving conditions. The regression model estimates the fuel consumption for a route i by

$$F_i(D_j) = \beta_{i0} + \beta_{i1}\chi_{i1} + \beta_{i2}\chi_{i2} + \ldots + \beta_{im}\chi_{im} \quad (1)$$

where (β_{ik}) is a set of (m) unknown coefficients that are determined from the historical data (i.e., the training set). The variables (χ) are the measurable data obtained from the vehicle (e.g., speed, engine parameters), and the response variable, (F_i), is the fuel consumption in a particular route (i) given the data of driver (D_j). Solving (β_i) in Eqn. 1:

$$\beta_i = (\chi^T\chi)^{-1}\chi^T F_i \quad (2)$$

We focus on internal combustion vehicles. The variables χ we employ are listed as follows:

$$\chi = \begin{bmatrix} 1 & \Delta T_a(r_i, D_1) & V_{ave}(r_i, D_1) & I_t(r_i, D_1) & D_c(r_i, D_1) \\ \vdots & \vdots & \vdots & \vdots & \vdots \\ 1 & \Delta T_a(r_i, D_j) & V_{ave}(r_i, D_j) & I_t(r_i, D_j) & D_c(r_i, D_j) \end{bmatrix}$$

where $(T_a(r_i, D_j))$ denotes the ambient temperature of route (i) for the historical data, included to consider that the ambient temperature will affect engine load via the heater or the air conditioner. $(V_{ave}(r_i, D_j))$ denotes the average speed of driving in route (i), since different speeds will cause different fuel consumption in the route. $(I_t(r_i, D_j))$ denotes the total idle time in route (i); we assume that different traffic condition results in different idle time in the route. $(D_c(r_i, D_j))$ denotes the driver and the displacement of the vehicle, since the fuel consumption rate is different for different vehicle types. Here, (j) is the total number of the historical data points.

We next describe the multi-driver extension. Say driver (a) never drove in route (x) before, and we want to estimate the fuel consumption ($F_x(D_a)$) of that driver in that route given the ambient temperature, the average speed, and the idle time. We can establish the relationship between the route (x) and routes ($1 \ldots r$) using the multivariate regression model shown in Eqn. 3. The regression model ($F_r(D_{1\ldots m})$) is the training data set. Since we want to use the data of driver (k) in a different route to determine their fuel consumption in the route they have never driven, the training data set should be ($F_r(D_{1\ldots m}), k \in \{1 \ldots m\}$). However, since ($F_x$) does not include the data of driver (a), the regression model has to be trained without the data of driver (a), resulting in Eqn. 3. Also note that the number of drivers (m) should be greater than the number of routes (r) in order to avoid the ill-condition of the regression model.

$$F_x(D_{1\ldots m}) = \gamma_0 + \gamma_1 F_1(D_{1\ldots m}) + \ldots + \gamma_r F_r(D_{1\ldots m}) \quad (3)$$

where $a \notin \{1 \ldots m\}$ and ($F_i(D_{1\ldots m})$) denotes the fuel consumption of drivers ($1 \ldots m$) in route (i) given ambient temperature, average speed and idle time. Solving for γ_i in Eqn. 1:

$$\gamma_i = (\overline{F}^T \overline{F})^{-1} \overline{F}^T F_n \quad (4)$$

where

$$\overline{F} = \begin{bmatrix} 1 & F_1(D_1) & \ldots & F_r(D_1) \\ \vdots & \vdots & \vdots & \vdots \\ 1 & F_1(D_m) & \ldots & F_r(D_m) \end{bmatrix} F_n = \begin{bmatrix} F_x(D_1) \\ \vdots \\ F_x(D_m) \end{bmatrix}$$

Since we have $F_{1\ldots r}(D_{1\ldots m}), k \in \{1 \ldots m\}$, $F_{1\ldots r}(D_k)$ can be determined and substituted into Eqn. 3 to compute $F_x(D_a)$.[1]

3. EXPERIMENT

We carried out an experiment to corroborate the performance of our approach empirically. The data from three vehicles of different classes were gathered. Our data collection apparatus consisted of Bluetooth ELM327 dongles plugged into the vehicles' onboard diagnostic (OBD) ports and paired with drivers' smartphones and a app is developed for collection and upload of OBD data from the vehicles. [2]

---

[1] If we use only historical data of the driver to predict her fuel consumption, requires dividing the route into many segments based on the characteristic, and is complicated and needs a complete knowledge of fuel consumption of different type of route. On the other hand, social approach allows us to find the fuel consumption between different routes, some of them are very difficult to be separated into segments for analyzing. For the social approach, distance, terrain and traffic data over routes are part of the input of the model, but the model itself is constructed based on how other drivers are affected by these factors at the time they were driving the routes. If something like road blockage or construction affects traffic for a significantly long time, it will also be reflected by the models since the models are periodically updated. Google Maps also provides estimation of traffic and time to destination (TTD), which has already included social approach. Although using a better estimation of TTD may give a better estimation of average speed, it still require a complicated model to take into account of the nuances of a new route with the same average speed, idle time and other conditions.

[2] A) Ford Fusion 2012, 4 cylinder, 2.5 L. B) Hyundai Veloster 2014, 4 cylinder, 1.6 L and C) Lincoln MKX 2007, 6 cylinder, 3.7 L. We chose a 36.3 kilometer-long triangular circuit for the experiment, split up into three segments (routes) of lengths 10km. Each vehicle's driver was assigned a particular driving style: A) cautious, B) moderate, and C) aggressive. The data collection run consisted of two rounds of the circuit, which adds up to about 73 km. Hence, each route was covered twice. The OBD data are mass air-flow, manifold absolute pressure, intake air temperature and engines' RPM, which are then utilized to compute the fuel consumption rate. Furthermore, the geolocation data, accelerometer readings and device identification from the smartphone are also recorded for driving behavior parameters of the model.

4. RESULTS

Using linear regression for the prediction of DTE for each driver along the circuit, we demonstrated that this approach can outperform the vehicles' own DTE estimation models, as seen in Fig. 1. We then applied multi-driver approach to predict fuel consumption for each driver along each run along each route, using the data from them along other routes and other drivers along all routes. The resulting matrix of estimations, and their difference from actual consumption data, is shown in Table 1.

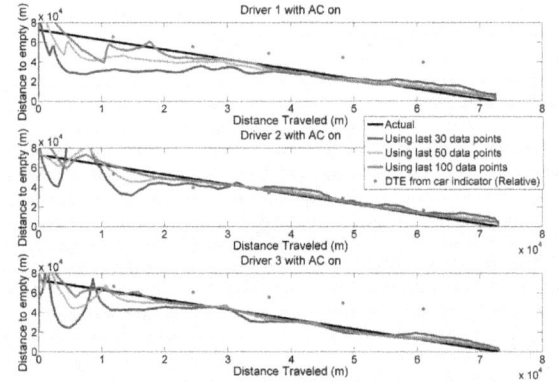

Figure 1: DTE estimated with different-sized terms of fuel intensity (p_{long}). Red dots are estimates given by in-vehicle displays.

Route	Driver A	Driver B	Driver C
1	1.71 (10.0%)	1.23 (17.5%)	1.77 (18.8%)
	1.70 (12.1%)	1.18 (19.4%)	1.84 (18.6%)
2	0.88 (9.6%)	0.61 (10.9%)	0.81 (22.5%)
	0.88 (14.6%)	0.59 (22.1%)	0.75 (30.7%)
3	0.67 (10.2%)	0.57 (7.8%)	0.73 (8.7%)
	0.65 (4.8%)	0.40 (23.2%)	0.73 (20.8%)

Table 1: Estimation of fuel consumption in litres for each run of each route by each driver, with error in parentheses

5. DISCUSSION AND FUTURE WORK

The accuracy of the prediction is limited by the number of training routes, which is in turn limited by the number of drivers. However, the data acquisition system we developed for use in this experiment has been linked to the CloudThink platform [1], which is being expanded to include a network of diverse vehicle data acquisition devices. Apart from the data gathered by running more experiments of our own, we will be acquiring more data from this platform as its user base expands. More data from more drivers over the same routes, and in different climactic and traffic conditions, will help us address the paucity of data and the short, low-consumption trips in the experiments adversely affecting the accuracy of fuel consumption prediction in this particular demonstration. We will also build a social platform for trip planning based on the shared data among drivers.

6. REFERENCES

[1] CloudThink Consortium. Cloudthink homepage. Web page at http://www.cloud-think.com.

[2] R.J. Freund, W.J. Wilson, and P. Sa. *Regression Analysis*. Regression Analysis Series. Elsevier Science, 2006.

[3] Bruce D. Lighter. Map- and maf-based air/fuel flow calculator. Web page at http://www.lightner.net/obd2guru/IMAP_AFcalc.html.

[4] L. Rodgers, E. Wilhelm, and D. Frey. Conventional and novel methods for estimating an electric vehicleâĂŹs âĂŸdistance to emptyâĂŹ. In *Proceedings of the ASME 2013*, Portland, Oregon, USA, 2013.

Self-configurable and Scalable Utility Communications Enabled by Software-Defined Networks

Young-Jin Kim
Bell-Labs, Alcatel-Lucent
young.jin_kim@alcatel-lucent.com

Keqiang He
University of Wisconsin
keqhe@cs.wisc.edu

Marina Thottan
Bell-Labs, Alcatel-Lucent
marina.thottan@alcatel-lucent.com

Jayant G. Deshpande
Bell Labs, Alcatel-Lucent
jayant.deshpande@alcatel-lucent.com

ABSTRACT

Utility communications are increasingly required to support machine-to-machine communications for thousands to millions of end devices ranging from meters and PMUs to tiny sensors and electric vehicles. The Software Defined Network (SDN) concept provides inherent features to support in a scalable and self-configurable manner the deployment and management of existing and envisioned utility end devices and applications. Using the SDN technology, we can create dynamically adaptable virtual network slices to cost-effectively and securely meet the utility communication needs. The programmability of SDN allows the elastic, fast, and scalable deployment of present and future utility applications with varying requirements on security and time criticality. In this work, we design a SDN-enabled utility communication architecture to support scalable deployment of applications that leverage many utility end devices. The feasibility of the architecture over an SDN network is discussed.

Categories and Subject Descriptors

C.2.1 [**Network Architecture and Design**]: Communications

General Terms

Management, Performance, Design, Experimentation

Keywords

Machine-to-Machine (M2M), Self-configurability, Scalability

1. INTRODUCTION

With Smart Grid roll-out, M2M communication networks supporting electric utility applications traffic is undergoing a tremendous change both in the increasing number of new grid applications, and a massive number of communication endpoints that the network must support [1]. Most of this increase in endpoints comes from deployment of sensors, currently limited to a few hundred Remote Terminal Units (RTUs), to thousands to several million sensors including Intelligent Electronic Devices (IEDs), Phasor Measurement Units (PMUs), smart meters, and sensors attached to Distributed Energy Sources (DERs) and Electric vehicles (EVs). In addition the new applications require self-configurable M2M communication networks that can adaptively and scalably meet the needs for performance, reliability, and security.

In this work, we design a new SDN-enabled M2M network architecture. Our M2M network architecture will not only provide

e-Energy'14, June 11–13, 2014, Cambridge, UK.
ACM 978-1-4503-2819-7/14/06.
http://dx.doi.org/10.1145/2602044.2602074

a cost-effective and self-configurable network solution on commoditized SDN switches as network elements, but also has the ability to elastically define virtual network slices with each slice supporting an application (in one utility or across multiple utilities), or a group of similar applications.

Today's M2M Communication Networks

Today we could use the industry standard (i.e., IEEE 802.1Q Virtual LAN [2]) for virtual networking as a M2M communication solution that can accommodate grid applications. However, consider the following deployment scenario of a million scale communication-enabled measurement and monitoring end devices; a relatively-small number (e.g., 100~1000) of network switches; thus, a physical port (called port) in a switch must be logically (not physically) connected to more than one end device (i.e., multiple meters per port via a data concentrator); also, a device must subscribe to more than one VLAN. Unfortunately, the VLAN standard, IEEE 802.1Q, cannot scalably support the scenario due to: the small number of VLANs per-port (Port-based VLANs or Protocol-based VLANs). In the port-based VLAN, an access port between a switch and access devices (not a trunk port between switches) are assigned to a VLAN during a certain time period. In the protocol-based VLAN, one VLAN per protocol is supported. As a result, an access port must be concurrently used by multiple VLANs and only a small number of well-known protocols (i.e., IP, ARP, IPX) are supported. In addition from a security perspective in an IEEE 802.1Q network, all members that are authenticated can directly communicate with each other. As a result, compromising a device (such as computer malwares) can result in the propagation of security threats across the network..

2. BENEFITS OF SDN FOR M2M COMMUNICATIONS

All SDN can provide isolation of different traffic types, applications, and/or endpoint classification. E.g., virtual network slices may be defined for AMI, SCADA, DG/DS/EV, and PMU traffic. Network slices may also be based on geographical or domain considerations (transmission and distribution or security zones). The virtual network slices inherently enhance security with traffic isolation and enabling security, quality of service (QoS), and even network management policies for each network slice. So, a closed group of applications/application type/endpoint group can have its "own virtual network" that is its network slice. Note that the ability to rapidly create required functions with few changes in the physical network makes the network less vulnerable to potential network failures.

Our architecture design offers a programmable open interface to the applications as well as to the network elements for their control, configuration, and management. There is a deliberate shift from fixed network functions serving many applications to per application virtualized functions making introduction of new applications as well as connecting new endpoints in the network more efficient and manageable. The ability to reconfigure a software defined network and rapidly deploy virtualized network functions allows for greater network utilization, global resource optimization, and enhanced scaling. Thus demand driven service and device activation and provisioning will directly lead to dynamic application velocity and scale.

3. SDN-enabled Virtual Utility Network

Our design has been inspired by the SDN concept and the publisher-subscribe (Pub-Sub) paradigm [3]. Fig. 1 represents the overall idea of the SDN-enabled Virtual Utility Network (SVUN) that consists of SDN switches (i.e., OpenFlow switches [4]), M2M clients (publishers or subscribers), and M2M control nodes. The M2M control plane consisting of M2M group manager, authenticator, network manager, and SDN controller provides dynamic and fine-grained membership management and authentication measures for establishing secure and QoS-aware M2M communications (i.e., VLAN per group). Please refer to [5] for details. We emphasize that our unique contribution against other SDN work achieves the complete automation of communication/security configuration by combining M2M group mangers with a SDN controller. Compared to other Pub-Sub work, our approach has the following distinct features: 1) line-speed packet processing and forwarding, 2) per-group VLAN traffic isolation (i.e., VLAN per group), 3) per-group QoS management (i.e., delay-sensitive), and 4) traffic-flow monitoring for load balancing and fail-over.

SVUN' key notions: (1) L4 flow match for access ports, (2) VLAN identifier tagging/stripping for trunk ports, and (3) Pub-Sub communication notion.

Scalability: One important thing is that the SVUN addresses the scalability issue as data from multiple VLANs can concurrently traverse over both access ports and trunk ports. The memory (i.e., TCAM) of SDN switches where flow entries are kept is a major resource since most SDN switches available in today's market have small-size flow tables (i.e., less than 4K flow entries). The scale of flows for M2M data traffic in an SVUN is dependent on the number K of application groups and the number M of group participants. However, the scaling impact of the number of group participants is bounded by the number of SDN switches N due to the effect of VLAN aggregation and multicast in SDN switches. The maximum number of flow entries per SDN switch is $O(K)$ and K is independent of N and also typically smaller than M. This scaling is a unique characteristic of the SVUN.

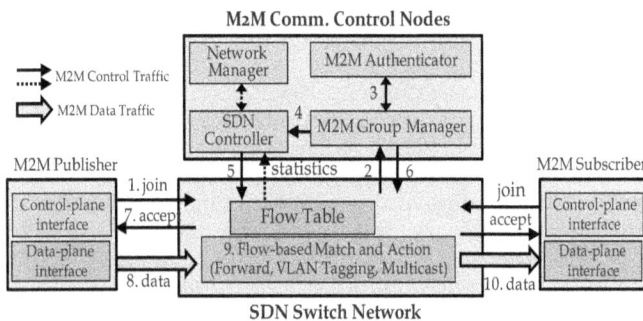

Fig. 1 Schema of an Instance of Our SVUN Architecture

4. FEASIBLITY STUDIES

We discuss a real implementation of SVUN written in Python and C++ and tested in our Lab test bed. In the implementation, an M2M group manager requests a SDN controller of installing

VLAN flow-rules and also let M2M publishers know where publishing data is about to be sent. In the Lab (See Fig 2), we measure three metrics: 1) flow-table occupancy per switch, 2) end-to-end delay of M2M data plane and 3) M2M control plane. The flow-table occupancy shows scalability of our SVUN since the TCAM is critical but has limited resources; the end-to-end delay of M2M data plane is the time difference between when an M2M publisher sends data and when an M2M subscriber receives the data. This metric corresponds to the forwarding performance of SDN switches in M2M data traffic. The end-to-end delay of M2M control plane is the time difference between when a M2M client (as either a M2M publisher or a M2M subscriber) sends a join message to its M2M group manager and when it receive an accept message from its M2M group manager.

Flow Table Occupancy: the maximum number of hard-state flow rules for M2M data traffic is only two irrespective of the number of M2M devices. There exist a small number of soft-state flow rules (deleted after a timer is expired) for connectivity between devices and an M2M group manager.

Delay on aspects of M2M data plane: In principle, once VLAN flow rules for M2M data-plane have been installed, we see line-speed packet lookup and forwarding of TCAM. In the implementation of SVUN, we observed that the end-to-end delay from publishers to subscribers is never more than 150 ns irrespective of the size of data.

Delay on aspects of M2M control plane: M2M control traffic delay is either about 30ms or about 90ms. Compared with M2M data traffic delay, it is fairly high, even though it is tolerable. We observed the following delay sources: 1) flooding-based ARP discovery, 2) TCP connection setup between M2M group manager and M2M clients, 3) A VLAN flow setup for data-plane.

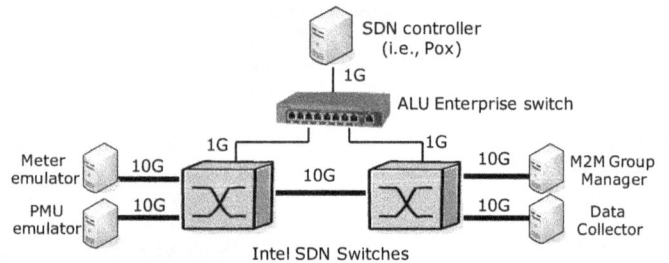

Fig. 2 Our Lab test-bed with two SDN switches

5. REFERENCES

[1] Budka, K., Deshpande J., and Thottan, M, Communication Networks for Smart Grids – Making Smart Grid Real, Springer, 2014.

[2] IEEE Std. 802.1Q-2011, Media Access Control (MAC) Bridges and Virtual Bridged Local Area Networks.

[3] P. Eugster, P. Felber, R. Guerraoui, and A. Kermarrec, The Many Faces of Publish/Subscribe, ACM Computing Surveys, vol. 35, no. 2, June 2003.

[4] OpenFlow Switch Specification Version. 1.0.0, Dec. 2013.

[5] Y-J. Kim, J. Lee, G. Atkinson, H. Kim and M. Thottan, SeDAX: A secure, resilient and scalable platform, IEEE JSAC, vol. 30, no. 6, July 2012.

NITOS Mobile Monitoring Solution:
Realistic Energy Consumption Profiling of Mobile Devices

Stratos Keranidis⊕, Giannis Kazdaridis⊕, Virgilios Passas⊕, Giannis Igoumenos⊕,
Thanasis Korakis⊕, Iordanis Koutsopoulos⊎ and Leandros Tassiulas⊕
○Department of Electrical and Computer Engineering, University of Thessaly, Greece
+Centre for Research and Technology Hellas, CERTH, Greece
⊎Department of Computer Science, Athens University of Economics and Business, Greece
{efkerani, iokazdarid, vipassas, ioigoume, korakis, leandros}@uth.gr, jordan@aueb.gr

ABSTRACT

The unprecedented penetration of "smart" mobile devices in
everyday use case scenarios, along with their energy greedy
profile have motivated researchers in the field of wireless
networking, towards reducing energy consumption wherever
possible. In order to support the design of energy efficient
protocols, in-depth energy consumption profiling of mobile
devices needs to be applied, through long term monitoring and under realistic conditions. To this aim, we have
developed a tiny device able to fit in the battery pack of
smartphones and monitor the resulting power consumption
in an on-line way. In this work, we detail the components
of the developed framework and demonstrate two indicative
scenarios that showcase how the diversity of experimental
conditions and configurations can significantly impact energy consumption.

1. INTRODUCTION

Prompted by the recent emerging technologies, mobile devices have become increasingly sophisticated, providing high
processing capabilities, embedding various hardware components and providing for concurrent execution of multiple
software applications. The limited battery life of modern
mobile devices, along with their increased energy demands,
dictate that design of emerging technologies should be driven
be energy related constraints. In order to support the design
of energy efficient protocols, in-depth energy consumption
profiling of mobile devices needs to be applied, through long
term monitoring and under realistic conditions. Among the
various existing power monitoring platforms, we distinguish
the work in [1] that presents a small-sized device that can be
attached to mobile phones. The obtained measurements are
directly stored to a microSD card and are manually transferred to a dedicated pc for further analysis. Taking a step
further, we introduce the NITOS Mobile Monitoring Solution (MMS) framework that features several more advantages. First, the integration of a bluetooth module that
enables transparent communication with the mobile device,

e-Energy'14, June 11–13, 2014, Cambridge, UK.
ACM 978-1-4503-2819-7/14/06.
http://dx.doi.org/10.1145/2602044.2602047.

allowing for both automatic transferring of obtained measurements and enabling for remote control as well. Second,
the development of an accompanying Android application
that enables logging of mobile device activity to take place
in parallel with the power monitoring procedure, thus allowing for detailed off-line analysis of collected results. In
the next section we present the developed framework as an
extension of our previous work [2].

2. NITOS MMS

Towards the development of a small-sized device, we started
by designing and a Printed Circuit Board (PCB) that integrates all the required components. The core module is the
ATmega32U4 [3], low-power 8-bit micro-controller that runs
at 8MHz. It features 32 KB of flash memory and integrates
a 12 channel Analog to Digital Converter (ADC), with a
resolution of 10-bit. Moreover, the PCB integrates the TI
INA139 [4] high-side current monitoring module that is used
to amplify the voltage drop on current shunt resistors offering high accuracy of analog sampling. In addition, NITOS
MMS is equipped with a microSD slot to enable for external
storage and the RN-42 bluetooth[5] module to enable wireless communication with the mobile phone. The total cost
of the device is less than €35.

In an effort to render the described hardware platform into
a functional framework, we developed appropriate software
to control the programming of the MMS platform, by utilizing open-source Arduino code. Aiming at increasing the
default sampling rate of 4.33 KHz, to enable for increased
sampling accuracy, we properly configured the ATmega32U4
ADC to operate in free-running mode and changed the prescaler
from 62.5 KHz to 500 KHz, resulting in the increased sampling rate of approximately 17 KHz. Through this modification, we enable logging of sampled data to take place
in parallel with ADC conversions, efficiently increasing the
amount of time spent in sample acquisition. By exploiting
the RN-42 module, we transfer the collected measurements
to the smartphone and provide direct access for further processing and depiction of energy consumption data.

The developed platform has been evaluated in comparison
with the high-end NI-6210 data acquisition (DAQ) module
[6] and proved of providing measurements of similar accuracy in the range under consideration. Moreover, as the
proposed measurement procedure is rather generic, it can
be directly applied to most of existing smartphones, since
it only requires a minor modification of the battery. As
Fig. 1(a) shows, our solution is properly powered by the
phone's battery and thus does not require external power

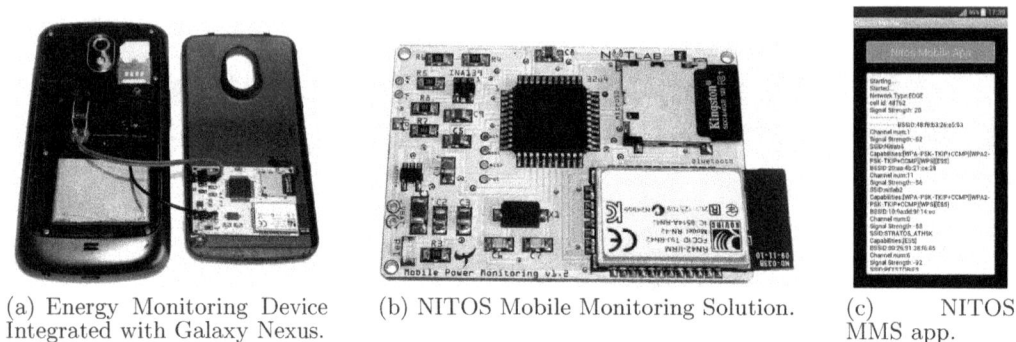

(a) Energy Monitoring Device Integrated with Galaxy Nexus.

(b) NITOS Mobile Monitoring Solution.

(c) NITOS MMS app.

Figure 1: NITOS MMS Hardware and Software Components.

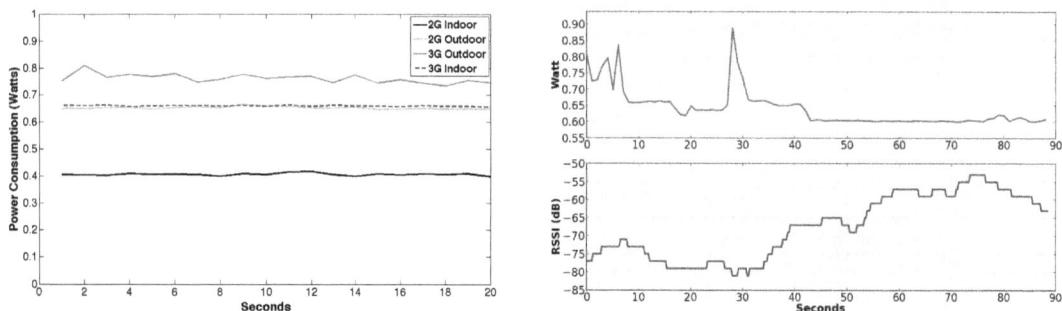

(a) Average Power Consumption during 2G/3G calls in Outdoor/Indoor Locations.

(b) RSSI and Corresponding Power Consumption.

Figure 2: Experimental Results.

supply. Although this design choice does not affect the mobile phone's power consumption, it arises questions related to the impact on the mobile phone's battery lifetime. Due to the low power consumption profile of the various selected components, the proposed device results in a total consumption of 0.043 W and 0.092 W, in idle and monitoring mode accordingly, posing minimal impact on the phone's lifetime.

3. NITOS ANDROID APPLICATION

NITOS MMS application designed and deployed for Android devices, is able to monitor all the information that the Android API exposes, concerning the phone's broadband interface. Each measurement set consists of several variables, such as RSSI, Cell ID, Network Type, Network Operator ID, timestamp and is cached on a local sqlite3 database. To ensure accurate monitoring, the application halts all the unnecessary processes and turns off the non-required interfaces, before triggering the monitoring procedure for both the MMS and mobile phone. Furthermore the application, which is illustrated in Fig. 1(c), exploits any available network connection to off-load the collected data to NITOS [7] server for further processing.

4. EXPERIMENTAL DEMONSTRATION

The prototype device that has been integrated with a Samsung Galaxy Nexus smartphone, as illustrated in Fig. 1(a), will be evaluated under a set of indicative experiments. In the first experiment, we will start by characterising the instantaneous power consumption of the smartphone, during a phone call using the WCDMA 3G interface, while in the second phase we will employ the GSM interface. In Fig. 2(a), we plot the average power consumption, as measured in each different setup and observe higher power consumption for both the 3G and GSM networks in the outdoor environment.

In the second experiment, we will showcase the impact of RSSI fluctuations on the energy consumption of the phone's cellular module. Exploiting the NITOS MMS application, we will collect RSSI measurements alongside with the energy data logging, during a regular phone call. As demonstrated in Fig. 2(b), low RSSI values correspond to higher energy consumption, as it is depicted in the first 40 seconds where the signal ranges from -83 to -68dB.

5. CONCLUSIONS AND FUTURE WORK

In this paper we presented the NITOS MMS that is able to characterise power consumption of mobile devices under real life scenarios. As future work, we seek to integrate the NITOS MMS with mobile phones of volunteers, such as lab members and University students, in order to collect measurements corresponding to the energy that is consumed during long-term execution of everyday life scenarios.

6. ACKNOWLEDGEMENTS

The research leading to these results has received funding from the European Union's Seventh Framework Programme (FP7/2007-2013) under grant agreement n. 258301 (CREW IP project).

7. REFERENCES

[1] A. Schulman, T. Schmid, P. Dutta, and N. Spring. Demo: Phone power monitoring with battor. MobiCom '11, 2011.

[2] S. Keranidis, G. Kazdaridis, V. Passas, T. Korakis, I. Koutsopoulos, and L. Tassiulas. Online Energy Consumption Monitoring of Wireless Testbed Infrastructure Through the NITOS EMF Framework. WiNTECH '13, 2013.

[3] "ATmega32U4", http://goo.gl/MY3qbh.

[4] "Texas Instruments INA139", http://goo.gl/rPQLB.

[5] "RN-42 Bluetooth Module", http://goo.gl/zLyYVv.

[6] "NI-6210 DAQ module", http://goo.gl/oFSJw.

[7] "NITOS Wireless Testbed", http://nitlab.inf.uth.gr/.

Predicting Peak-Demand Days in the Ontario Peak Reduction Program for Large Consumers

Yuheng Helen Jiang, Ryan Levman, Lukasz Golab and Jatin Nathwani
University of Waterloo, Canada
{y29jiang,rslevman,lgolab,nathwani}@uwaterloo.ca

ABSTRACT

In this paper, we propose a heuristic algorithm for day-ahead prediction of the top K days having the highest peak hourly demand for electricity over a given year. This problem, which arises in the context of critical peak pricing in Ontario, Canada, is difficult because we may have to wait till the end of the year to find out which K days ended up being the peak days. Our solution is to leverage short-term load forecasts and call tomorrow a peak day if it has sufficiently high probability of being a peak day in the time window covered by the forecast. Using Ontario demand data from 2007 till 2013, we show that our algorithm may need to call about $2K$ peak days to ensure that most if not all of the actual K peak days are included.

1. INTRODUCTION

Reducing peak electricity consumption is an important problem, which has led to a variety of peak pricing schemes in many jurisdictions. In this paper, we analyze the Five-Coincident-Peaks (5CP) program that affects large industrial and commercial consumers (whose monthly peak exceeds 5 megawatts) in the province of Ontario, Canada. In this program, large consumers pay heavy surcharges for the electricity they consumed during the five days with the highest peak hourly demand [1]. For some customers, these surcharges are higher than their volumetric charges [3].

Ontario's 5CP program is different to, e.g., California's Critical Peak Pricing [2], in which utilities choose which days will be peak-pricing days according to some criteria, and they notify the participating customers one day in advance. In 5CP, Ontario's Electricity System Operator (IESO) waits till the end of the year and applies the surcharge to each large consumer based on its contribution to the load (at the peak hour) on the actual five peak days of this year. Thus, without the benefit of hindsight, it is difficult for consumers to know when to curtail load in order to avoid surcharges.

We propose a practical algorithm that, at the end of every day, predicts whether tomorrow will be one of the five peak days of the current year, given only the publicly-available information such as short-term and long-term load forecasts and historical load statistics. We define the *precision* of such an algorithm as the fraction

e-Energy'14, June 11–13, 2014, Cambridge, UK.
ACM 978-1-4503-2819-7/14/06.
http://dx.doi.org/10.1145/2602044.2602076.

of days identified by it that are in fact peak days, and *recall* as the fraction of actual peak days that were identified as such by the algorithm. For example, suppose that the actual peak days for some year were June 1, July 2, July 3, July 25 and August 8. Suppose that during the course of this year, the algorithm predicts the following *six* days as being peak days: June 1, July 1, July 2, July 3, July 20 and August 8. Its precision is $\frac{4}{6}$ and recall is $\frac{4}{5}$.

Obtaining perfect recall is easy: we predict that each day will be a peak day. Of course, precision will be very low and there will be many false alarms, causing customers to curtail operations unnecessarily and lose business. Ideally, we should achieve high precision (few false alarms) and high recall (few missed alarms).

The IESO publishes 12-month load forecasts, but they are not accurate because Ontario's peak demand is strongly correlated with daily high temperatures, especially in the summer when the daily peak is caused by high air-conditioning use in the afternoon. The 14-day short-term forecasts are quite accurate, and the proposed algorithm uses these as described below.

2. OUR SOLUTION

At the beginning of the year, we are given the actual peak hourly demand for each day in the past year and the IESO 12-month long-term forecast for the current year. At the end of each day in the current year, we will be given the actual peak demand for that day, the 14-day short-term forecast from the IESO and the weather forecast for tomorrow. At the end of each day, the algorithm will compute a probability that tomorrow will be one of the five peak days between the beginning of the year and 14 days from today. If this probability exceeds a threshold τ (which will be defined shortly), the algorithm calls tomorrow as one of the five peak days so that consumers may react accordingly. Since Ontario has been a summer-peaking province since 2005, rather than running the algorithm for an entire year, we only run it from May 1 to September 30.

Throughout the year, we maintain another threshold, τ_D, which is a lower bound for a peak day, i.e., any day whose peak demand forecast is below τ_D will never be called as a peak day. For the initial value of τ_D, we use the maximum peak demand from the IESO long-term forecast, minus a Load-Forecast-Uncertainty (LFU) value of 1600 megawatts. The LFU value is published by the IESO and is related to the uncertainty of the long-term forecast. We also apply two filtering criteria based on domain knowledge: Saturdays and Sundays will never be called as peak days, and nor will days whose weather forecast is not *extreme*, which we define as 30 degrees Celcius or higher. These filtering criteria are meant to avoid false positives.

Let D_i be the actual peak hourly demand on day i and let $\hat{D}_{iL}$ be the estimated peak hourly demand on day $i+L$ as of day i based on the IESO short-term forecast.

Table 1: Computing ranking probabilities. Define $\theta(x,y)$ as follows: $\theta(x,y) = P(Rank_{future} = x) \times P(Rank_{past} = y)$

Final Ranking	Formula
$P(Rank_{overall} = 1)$	$\theta(1,1)$
$P(Rank_{overall} = 2)$	$\theta(1,2) + \theta(2,1)$
$P(Rank_{overall} = 3)$	$\theta(1,3) + \theta(2,2) + \theta(3,1)$
$P(Rank_{overall} = 4)$	$\theta(1,4) + \theta(2,3) + \theta(3,2) + \theta(4,1)$
$P(Rank_{overall} = 5)$	$\theta(1,5) + \theta(2,4) + \theta(3,3) + \theta(4,2) + \theta(5,1)$

Calculating Probabilities

To compute the ranking probabilities over short-term forecasts, we need to identify their distributions. According to the chi square goodness-of-fit test, we verified that the residuals of the short-term forecasts, computed by $\hat{D}_{iL} - D_i$, from 2006 till 2013 are normally distributed with a mean of zero and some standard deviation that depends on L. Thus, every short-term forecast is a random variable with a mean equal to the forecast value and a standard deviation computed from historical data.

We need the following three probabilities. $P(Rank_{future} = j)$ is the probability of $\hat{D}_{i1}$ ranking j^{th} among the 14 days for which we have a short-term forecast, i.e., among $\hat{D}_{i1}$ to $\hat{D}_{i,14}$. $P(Rank_{past} = j)$ is the probability of $\hat{D}_{i1}$ ranking j^{th} compared to the peak demand on the days we have seen so far, i.e., D_1 to D_i. $P(Rank_{overall} = j)$ is the probability of $\hat{D}_{i1}$ ranking j^{th} within the days we have seen plus those for which we have a short-term forecast, i.e., D_1 to D_i and $\hat{D}_{i1}$ to $\hat{D}_{i,14}$.

Assuming that the short-term forecasts for different days are independent, $P(Rank_{future} = j)$ and $P(Rank_{past} = j)$ are easy to compute. For example:

$$P(Rank_{future} = 1) = \prod_{j=1}^{14} P(\hat{D}_{i1} \geq \hat{D}_{ij}) \qquad (1)$$

Since we assumed that the residuals of the short-term forecast are normally distributed, we compute $P(\hat{D}_{i1} \geq \hat{D}_{ij})$ using the probability density function for a normal distribution. $P(Rank_{overall} = j)$ is a bit more complex. Table 1 shows how to compute it for j between one and five. For example, $\hat{D}_{i1}$ can rank second overall under two conditions: either it ranks first in the past and second in the short-term future, or it ranks second in the past and first in the short-term future.

The Algorithm

Figure 1 gives the pseudocode. If the day-ahead peak demand forecast exceeds the lower bound τ_D and tomorrow is a weekday and the weather forecast is extreme (line 2), then we compute the required probabilities (lines 4-6) and we check if tomorrow has a high probability of ranking fifth or higher. If this probability exceeds the threshold τ_p, we predict that tomorrow will be a peak day.

We then check if the lower bound τ_D should be adjusted (lines 9-12). If tomorrow's weather forecast is not extreme, but the demand forecast exceeds the lower bound, then we should raise the lower bound to tomorrow's peak demand forecast (lines 9-10). On the other hand, if tomorrow's weather is expected to be extreme but the lower bound on the peak demand is not going to be exceeded, then we should lower the lower bound (lines 11-12).

To choose a value for τ_p, we use the following data-driven approach. Using the actual and estimated demand data from the pre-

```
1. FOR i=May 1 to Sep 29
2.    IF D̂_{i1} ≥ τ_D and weekday and extreme weather forecast
3.       FOR j=1 to 5
4.          Compute P(Rank_future = j)
5.          Compute P(Rank_past = j)
6.          Compute P(Rank_overall = j) based on Table 1
7.       IF P(Rank_overall ≤ 5) ≥ τ_p
8.          Predict "tomorrow will be a peak day"
9.    ELSE IF D̂_{i1} ≥ τ_D and not extreme weather
10.       τ_D = D̂_{i1}
11.    ELSE IF D̂_{i1} < τ_D and extreme weather
12.       τ_D = D̂_{i1}
```

Figure 1: Proposed algorithm for the 5CP problem.

vious year, we compute $P(Rank_{overall} \leq 5)$ for each day in the past year. We then check this probability for the actual 5CP days and choose τ_p to be the minimum of these. For example, in 2012, each actual 5CP day had $P(Rank_{overall} \leq 5)$ above 0.1, so for 2013 we can set $\tau_p = 0.1$.

Experimental Evaluation

We implemented the proposed algorithm in Matlab and computed its precision and recall on Ontario's demand data from 2007 till 2013. The historical load, short-term and long-term forecast data were downloaded from the IESO Website at `ieso.ca`. Figure 2 shows the results: for each year, we plot the precision, recall and the number of called peak days. The average recall across the seven years is 0.94 and it varied from 0.8 to 1, i.e., the peak days called by the algorithm included four or all five of the actual peak days for that year. The average precision is 0.55 and it varied from 0.4 to 0.7. The number of called peak days varied from 7 to 11. Thus, to identify four or five of the actual five peak days, we may need to call a total of about 10 days as peak days.

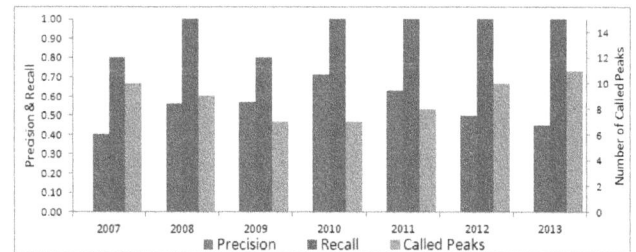

Figure 2: Precision, recall and the number of called peak days from 2007 to 2013.

3. REFERENCES

[1] The 5CP program.
`http://ieso-public.sharepoint.com/Pages/Participate/Settlements/Global-Adjustment-for-Class-A.aspx`

[2] J. Bode, C. Churchwell, S. George, and F. Sullivan. 2012 California statewide non-residential critical peak pricing evaluation. Technical report, Freeman, Sullivan & Co, 2013.

[3] J. Spears. Ontario power fee sets new record. Accessed on 18 October 2013, at `http://www.thestar.com/business/economy/2013/09/03/ontario_power_fee_sets_new_record.html`.

Comparing Apples to Oranges: Energy Benchmarking of Supermarkets with Limited Data

Maathangi Sankar, Venkata Ramakrishna P,
Shiva R. Iyer, Venkatesh Sarangan,
Arunchandar Vasan,
Innovation Labs, Tata Consultancy Services,
IIT Madras Research Park, Chennai, India
venkataramakrishna.p@tcs.com

Anand Sivasubramaniam
Dept. of Comp. Sci. & Eng.
Pennsylvania State University
University Park, PA 16802, USA
anand@cse.psu.edu

ABSTRACT

Current approaches for benchmarking building energy consumption are either too data intensive to be feasible in practice or too data agnostic to be useful. We present a limited data approach where in, instead of using minutiae required for accurate HVAC modeling, we model the heating/cooling loads, the drivers for HVAC. This allows us to see how a building's (i) weather independent consumption compares to the optimal value and (ii) weather dependent consumption compares with its expected heating/cooling loads. Based on this two dimensional metric, we benchmark 94 geographically diverse supermarket stores and present our findings.

Keywords

Building energy management, supermarkets, Benchmarking, Energy modeling

1. ENERGY BENCHMARKING

Given the end user activities, occupancy patterns, age of a building, and the constraints imposed by the building's design and ambient conditions, benchmarking attempts to determine how far is the building's actual energy consumption from the optimal value. Determining this is non-trivial owing to the huge parameter space involved. Nevertheless, benchmarking energy consumption of buildings is required to identify: (i) the outliers in terms of better/worse performance and (ii) possibilities of improvement.

Existing approaches & Limitations. Buildings are typically benchmarked using energy use intensity (EUI). EUI is obtained by normalizing the overall energy usage with respect to parameters such as total floor space, number of occupants, and working hours. However, such benchmarking may not be accurate due to the possible non-linear influence of factors such as occupancy, area, operational schedules, and weather on energy consumption. Two alternatives to EUI based benchmarking exist.

In *data-driven benchmarking*, parameters such as building type, floor area, location, occupancy and energy use are collected from an *ensemble* of buildings. A regression model for energy consumption as a function of these parameters is then derived from this data. Individual buildings are compared with respect to the average performance and appropriately ranked [4]. Standard ranking methods such as EnergyStar, Cal-Arch, and BEE, follow this strategy. However, this approach can only indicate how well a building is doing compared to its peer group. The entire peer group may be inefficient, which could cause an inefficient building to be rated as being efficient.

In *model based benchmarking*, an energy model for each *individual* building is defined. The model parameters are calibrated for an ideal energy behavior adjusted for the building's age. The model's ideal energy consumption is then estimated through simulations. The building's actual energy consumption is benchmarked against this estimated value and opportunities for improvement are identified by a sensitivity study on the model parameters [2]. As the model can be customized for each building, the benchmarking is done against absolute values thereby mitigating the drawbacks of data-driven relative benchmarking.

The efficacy of model-driven benchmarking is limited by its exacting requirements on data availability. For instance, to create an accurate energy model of a building, one would require the age adjusted efficiency and performance curves of each of the HVAC and/or refrigeration system components. Further, researchers have also shown that simulation tools can introduce uncertainty (as much as 22%) in estimating the energy consumed by HVAC systems [3].

2. PROPOSED APPROACH

There is a need for an absolute benchmarking methodology that neither requires data on HVAC systems nor estimates the energy consumed by HVAC systems. We propose such an approach where in, instead of using a model to estimate the *energy* consumed by a building's HVAC system, we use the model to estimate the building's *ideal heating and cooling demands that drive the HVAC operations*. The heating/cooling demands are more innate to a building's structure, lay-out and operations. The ideal heating and cooling demands are independent of the building's HVAC systems. Hence such a modeling does not require any data on the HVAC systems.

We categorize the energy consumed by a building into two components: weather independent and weather dependent. We estimate the ideal energy consumption of weather independent component and compare it with the component's actual consumption in the building; for the weather dependent component, we estimate the building's ideal heating and cooling loads rather than the energy consumed to service these loads. We then compare this ideal load with the building's actual weather dependent energy consumption.

Limitations. While we can identify that the HVAC system in a building as a whole is inefficient, the inefficiencies cannot be drilled down to individual components such as a chiller or blower. The

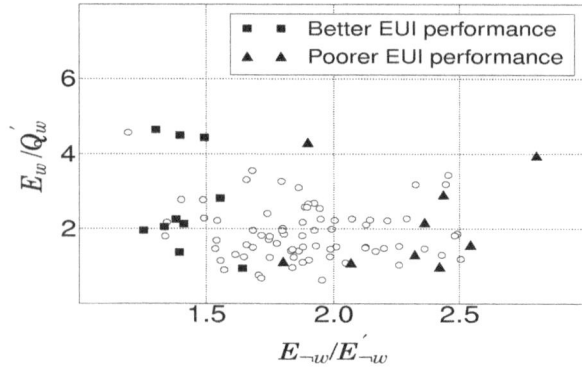

(a) Performance of case study stores under the proposed benchmarking and EUI (kWh/m^2) based standard.

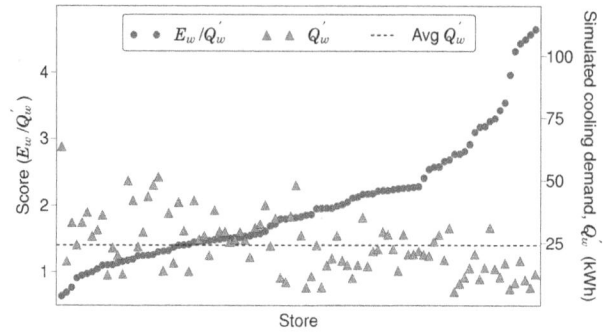

(b) Stores with poor weather dependent performance have possibly over-sized HVAC systems.

Figure 1: Results of our two dimensional benchmarking on a real world supermarket chain of 94 stores.

inefficiencies in individual HVAC components of buildings with poor HVAC performance can be identified through a subsequent deeper study.

Challenges. In conventional EUI based benchmarking and data driven benchmarking, a building can be ranked using just the aggregate energy consumption value. This value is easier to obtain since it could be obtained directly from the utility bills. However, in the proposed two dimensional scheme, a building's energy consumption has to be specified in terms of two orthogonal components – viz. weather independent consumption and weather dependent consumption. As with the EUI based schemes, we assume that only the aggregate consumption of a building is made available (i.e, we do not expect a building to have any sub-metering to monitor the consumption of individual activities/equipment). Given this, a suitable methodology for dis-aggregating the overall energy consumption value into the two orthogonal components is required.

While this may sound challenging, by exploiting the following key observations, it is possible to design a dis-aggregation technique that performs satisfactorily in practice: (i) In certain industry verticals (such as retail outlets, supermarkets, restaurants, and hotels) the individual facilities under a single enterprise are homogeneous in terms of business activities, operations, and even building layout with similar thermal zoning. This uniformity implies that the individual building designs and operations can be reasonably 'templatized' for each enterprise. (ii) During winter, when the facilities have insignificant cooling demand (with the heating being done by gas), their electricity consumption will roughly equal their weather independent consumption.

3. REAL WORLD CASE STUDY

Using the proposed methodology, we benchmark a set of geographically diverse 94 stores from a supermarket using only those data that can be easily gathered. Our model leverages the studies done by organizations such as US National Renewable Energy Laboratory (NREL) to create suitable model templates for the benchmarking exercise [1].

The performance of the various stores along the two orthogonal dimensions is shown in Figure 1(a). The X axis gives the ratio of the actual weather independent energy consumption $E_{\neg w}$ over the expected weather independent energy consumption $E'_{\neg w}$. The Y axis represents the ratio of the actual weather dependent energy consumption $E_{\neg w}$ over the expected weather dependent cooling demand $Q'_{\neg w}$. Lower values along each of these dimensions indicate a better energy performance. The graph shows that the store

population has a significant spread along both the axes. More importantly, *we find that stores that do well in one dimension need not necessarily do well in the other dimension.*

A naive benchmark EUI (kWh/m^2) reference figure for supermarkets has been prescribed by the standard authorities for the case study geography. We ranked the case study stores as per this benchmark value too. The plot in Figure 1(a) also identifies the top 10% of the performers and the worst 10% of the performers as per this EUI metric on our benchmarking axes. The top and worst stores as per the naive benchmarking align towards the left and right respectively in the plot. This suggests that the EUI benchmarking value seems to be heavily influenced by the weather independent consumption.

Our benchmarking, in conjunction with our energy dis-aggregation approach, gives insights on possible causes for poor energy performance of stores. For instance, we notice from Figure 1(b) that stores that have lesser cooling loads seem to perform poorly in weather dependent energy consumption. A possible reason could be that the stores have an oversized HVAC system that has been sized for the average enterprise cooling load.

To conclude, we believe that the proposed two dimensional benchmarking methodology, together with the dis-aggregation approach, is well suited for objectively benchmarking a large set of homogeneous buildings from any vertical especially when data availability is limited.

4. REFERENCES

[1] M. Deru, K. , D. Studer, K. Benne, B. Griffith, P. Torcellini, B. Liu, M. Halverson, D. Winiarski, M. Rosenberg, et al. Us department of energy commercial reference building models of the national building stock. 2011.

[2] B. T. Griffith, N. Long, P. Torcellini, R. Judkoff, D. Crawley, and J. Ryan. *Methodology for modeling building energy performance across the commercial sector.* National Renewable Energy Laboratory, 2008.

[3] S. Shrestha and G. Maxwell. Empirical validation of building energy simulation software: Energyplus. In *Proceedings of Building Simulation 2011: 12th Conference of International Building Performance Simulation Association, Sydney*, pages 2935–2942, 2011.

[4] W. Xuchao, R. Priyadarsini, and L. Siew Eang. Benchmarking energy use and greenhouse gas emissions in singapore's hotel industry. *Energy Policy*, 38(8):4520–4527, 2010.

SURF and SURF-PI: A File Format and API for Non-Intrusive Load Monitoring Public Datasets

Lucas Pereira, Nuno Nunes
Madeira-ITI, University of Madeira
Polo Científico e Tecnológico da Madeira, floor -2
Caminho da Penteada, Funchal, Madeira, Portugal
lucas.pereira@m-iti.org, njn@uma.pt

Mario Bergés
Civil and Environmental Engineering,
Carnegie Mellon University
5000 Forbes Avenue, Pittsburgh, PA, USA
marioberges@cmu.edu

ABSTRACT

In this paper we propose a common file format and API for public Non-Intrusive Load Monitoring (NILM) datasets such that researchers can easily evaluate their approaches across the different datasets and benchmark their results against prior work. The proposed file format enables storing the power demand of the whole house along with individual appliance consumption, and other relevant metadata in a single compact file, whereas the API supports the creation and manipulation of individual files and datasets in the proposed format.

Categories and Subject Descriptors

D.2.13 [**Software Engineering**]: Reusable Software – *reusable libraries.*

Keywords

Energy Disaggregation, Datasets, File Format, API.

1. INTRODUCTION

NILM, first introduced by George Hart in his seminal work [1], is the process of estimating the energy consumption of individual appliances given only current and voltage measurements taken at a limited number of locations in the electric distribution of a building. Yet, despite decades of research and recent efforts towards creating public datasets (e.g. [2] and [3]) to validate and improve the existing approaches, very few formal evaluations (e.g. [4]) of the technology have been carried out so far, thus raising questions about the large scale applicability of this technology. We argue that one of the reasons for this is the difficulty of objectively comparing the performance of different algorithms given the lack of public datasets and the wide differences between the ones currently available. In fact, only recently there has been a serious effort to homogenize the existing datasets and provide a single interface to run evaluations [5] to which we wish to contribute by proposing SURF and SURF-PI, a common file format and programming interface to support the creation and manipulation of public NILM datasets, to help

homogenize the whole process of systematically evaluating NILM algorithms across different datasets.

2. SURF FILE FORMAT

The proposed format is an extension of the Waveform Audio File Format (WAVE) that supports the storage of digital audio data and metadata annotations according to the underlying chunk structure that is defined by the Resource Interchange File Format (RIFF) standard. There are four main reasons behind expanding this format and not another: i) data and metadata are all stored in a single compact file, thus limiting the number of artifacts that need to be managed; ii) the possibility of adding custom chunks without breaking the file consistency; iii) the resulting files are optimized to have little overhead; and iv) the mature programming interfaces that exist for a diversity of programming languages, hence facilitating the expansion and portability of the proposed format and API.

The SURF file format is currently composed of 13 chunks each one containing its own header and data bytes. Eight chunks are inherited from the WAVE format, one from the RIFF standard, and the remaining four are custom chunks created to supplement the files with relevant metadata. Next we describe the underlying structure of the SURF format.

2.1 Power Demand Data

The power demand data is defined in the Format chunk (*sampling rate, sample size* and *channels*) and stored in the Data chunk. The data values are stored uncompressed (to preserve the original signal) in little-endian byte order and scaled to the interval]-1,1[.

2.2 Individual Appliance and User Activities

Individual appliance activities correspond to the changes in the power demand that are triggered when individual loads change their operating mode (e.g. going from *on* to *off* and vice-versa), whereas user activities are groups of related individual appliances activities (e.g. combine the clothes-washer, dryer and iron activities to form the *"laundry"* user activity). All these activities have a corresponding timestamp (user activities also have an end timestamp) that are mapped to the corresponding sample number in the power demand data.

These activities are embedded in the SURF files using the Cue, Associated Data List, Label and Labeled Text chunks. Each activity is represented by their respective positions in the power demand data and a JSON formatted string with its details (see figure 1). For example, the following two JSON strings correspond to a refrigerator activity that was mapped to sample (position) 19394633, and a working activity that involves using the desktop computer, monitor and printer:

```
{"ID": 1101, "Type": 1, "Position": 19394633,
"Timestamp": "2011-10-24 05:45:57.040",
"Appliance_ID": 111, "Appliance_Label":
"Refrigerator"}
```

```
{"ID": 10021, "Activity_ID": 111,
"Activity_Label": "Working" "Start_Position":
14300225, "End_Position": 15000377,
"Start_Timestamp": "2011-10-21 21:05:14.940",
"End_Timestamp": "2011-10-22 00:23:18.056",
"Appliance_Activity_IDs": [1201, 1209, 1303, 1304,
1305, 1401, 1402, 1403], "Total Power": 1290}
```

2.3 Metadata

By default the RIFF standard enables metadata fields in the Info chunk, some of which we have repurposed according to our requirements: *artist* (renamed *dataset creator*), *title*, *date created*, *comment* and *copyright*. Likewise, we have also used the Note chunk to add localized metadata directly in the power demand data (e.g. when some appliance is added or removed from the buildings' electric circuit).

Furthermore, to enable a richer set of metadata we also complemented the SURF files with custom chunks, specifically created for this effect: i) Config: for configuration specific metadata (e.g. initial timestamp and calibration values); ii) External: metadata that refers to variables external to the dataset (e.g. the sensing hardware that was used); iii) Appliances: a list of the existing appliances; and iv) Activities: a list of the existing user activities.

3. SURF PROGRAMMING INTERFACE

The SURF-PI was implemented combining and extending several open source Java libraries for audio edition. The current version enables three main types of operations: i) **Create / Update**: functions to write, edit and delete the available chunks, e.g. *WritePower(powerData)*, and *SetApplianceActivity(position, jsonString)*; ii) **Read**: functions to read the chunks data, e.g. *GetFormat(), GetUserActivity(id); GetAppliances()*; and iii) **Query**: functions for NILM specific queries, e.g. *GetIntervalConsumption(startPosition, endPosition)*, and *GetActivityConsumption(activityID)*.

Additionally, since most of the annotation data are done using JSON we have implemented validation schemas using the JSON Schema Draft 4 to remove ambiguity and errors that may occur when creating the dataset files. We believe that having such a specification is especially important if we consider the possibility of extending or porting this API to other programming languages.

4. CONCLUSION AND FUTURE WORK

In this paper we have presented SURF and SURF-PI, a file format and programming interface for NILM datasets.

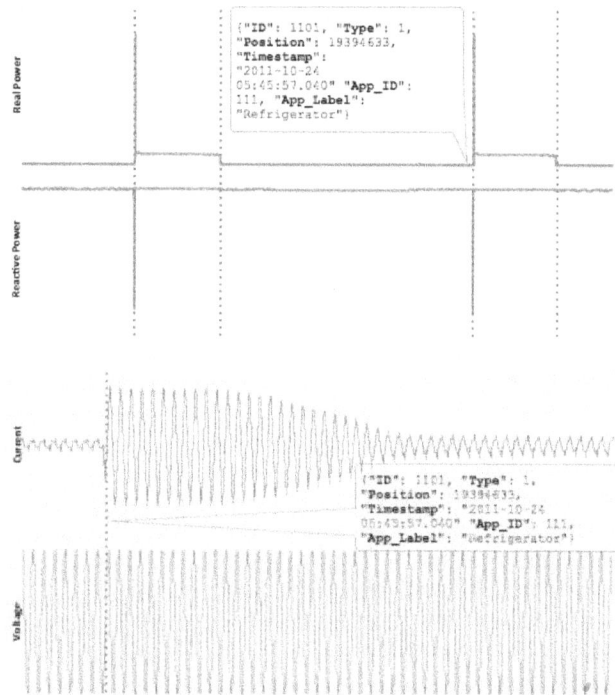

Figure 1. Refrigerator activity: real and reactive power at 60 Hz (top), current and voltage at 12 kHz (bottom).

We are now working towards proving the general applicability of this work and to this end we are converting some of the existing datasets to our format. Furthermore, since our work aims at generalizing NILM research, future work will involve evaluating and benchmarking previously proposed algorithms across the different datasets using SURF and SURF-PI. Likewise, it is very likely that different researchers will have different requirements regarding the proposed API, annotations and metadata, therefore we will be, soon, releasing a stable and documented open-source version of this work that will be accessible from: *http://aveiro.m-iti.org/software/surf*.

5. REFERENCES

[1] G. Hart, "Nonintrusive appliance load monitoring," *Proc. IEEE*, vol. 80, no. 12, 1992.

[2] Z. Kolter and M. Johnson, "REDD: A public data set for energy disaggregation research," *SustKDD '11*.

[3] K. Anderson et al., "BLUED: A Fully Labeled Public Dataset for Event-Based Non-Intrusive Load Monitoring Research," *SustKDD '12*.

[4] Electric Power Research Institute, "Non-Intrusive Load Monitoring (NILM) Technologies for End-Use Load Disaggregation: Laboratory Evaluation I." [Online]. Available: http://tinyurl.com/kloo5wq.

[5] N. Batra et al., "NILMTK: An Open Source Toolkit for Non-intrusive Load Monitoring," *e-Energy '14*.

Efficient PMU Data Dissemination in Smart Grid

Kedar Khandeparkar, Pratik Patre,
Swadesh Jain, Krithi Ramamritham
Indian Institute of Technology, Mumbai, India
{kedark,pbpatre11,swadeshjain,krithi}@cse.iitb.ac.in

Rajeev Gupta
IBM Research, India
grajeev@in.ibm.com

ABSTRACT

Next-generation Smart Grid will be a highly data driven system
with sensors deployed across the grid and analytics being performed
on the data collected for intelligent and timely decision making.
This paper proposes novel techniques for filtering as much data as
possible early in the dissemination network so that applications get
the required data without imposing exorbitant bandwidth requirements while ensuring low latency.

1. INTRODUCTION

A power grid is a large complex network of power generation,
transmission, and distribution systems. The demands for increased
reliability, distributed generation, integration of renewable sources,
and requirements of making the grid more stable are pushing the
development of the Smart Power Grid. A large number of monitoring and sensing devices, Phasor Measurement Units (PMUs), are
being deployed throughout the transmission network that provide a
continuous stream of informative data by providing GPS synchronized measurements of various electrical signals such as voltage,
current, phase angles, frequencies, etc. Phasor Data Concentrators
(PDCs) at one or more levels integrate and aggregate the PMU data.
Lower level PDCs (LPDCs) aggregate data from PMUs which are
geographically located at different places, time align the data, and
send the aggregated data to the applications at higher levels or su-
per PDCs (SPDCs). Different monitoring and control applications
perform computations on the sensed data to make intelligent decisions and ensure efficient utilization and reliable operation of the
grid. However given the large volume and velocity of the data generated by the sensors, collecting all the data at the centralized site
continuously for application execution is not scalable. It may result in wastage of bandwidth and increase the latencies, which can
affect the fulfillment of QoS requirements associated with the applications.

In this paper,we primarily focus on the question, *How do we design data dissemination techniques to efficiently share the communication infrastructure between applications with vastly different
QoS requirements such that the QoS requirements of all applications are satisfied?* We address the problem of executing smart grid

e-Energy'14, June 11–13, 2014, Cambridge, UK.
ACM 978-1-4503-2819-7/14/06.
http://dx.doi.org/10.1145/2602044.2602079 .

applications by designing application specific PMU data dissemination techniques without affecting the QoS requirements of the
applications. The proposed techniques not only reduce the processing time at the application site but also reduce the network traffic
by adopting data filtering techniques. We describe how application semantics can be used to design intelligent data dissemination
techniques. We take angular stability monitoring as an example
application and show the effectiveness of semantic aware data dissemination using real PMU data for Northern Indian grid.

2. SEMANTICS-AWARE DATA FILTERING AND COMMUNICATION

We need the semantics-aware distributed query processing approach to achieve the better utilization of communication infrastructure. Semantics are of two kinds: data semantics– involving
physical meaning of data, their characteristics, etc., and application
semantics– whether the application is monitoring and control application or an operator display application, what the application
priorities are, how the application semantics maps to data semantics, etc.

We now summarize the three high level approaches we consider
in this paper. These approaches differ with respect to the distribution of application execution and the nature of data forwarded to
higher level PDCs.

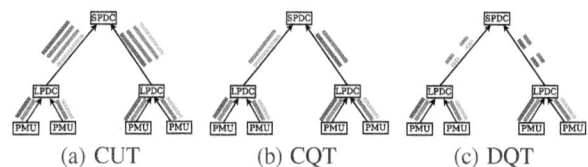

Figure 1: Message transmission in CUT, CQT, and DQT

2.1 CUT

A typical approach for application execution is the Centralized
execution with Unqualified data forwarding Technique (CUT). Here
applications execute at a single site (say, SPDC) and, as shown in
Figure 1(a), LPDCs forward all the data received from downstream
PMUs to SPDC, irrespective of whether the data is relevant to the
application. CUT requires static bandwidth reservation. Clearly
this approach wastes data bandwidth. We need to design application data needs aware communication solutions which would flexi-
bly share the bandwidth between various applications while meeting the data requirements of various applications.

2.2 CQT

Exploiting knowledge of which data is required for which application leads to the Centralized execution with Qualified data forwarding Technique (CQT). In this case, LPDCs transfer only some of the streams to the higher level PDCs. For CQT, we need to identify the data requirements at every application node. These requirements are disseminated to various PDCs and routers. An LPDC receives all the data from PMUs. This data can be seen as a number of streams from each PMU, say, one each for 3 voltage phases, frequency, phasors, etc. As part of CQT, each PDC or router will forward only a sub-set of these streams depending on the application semantics. Thus, each router selects a sub-set of streams, aggregates the data based on their time-stamp, if possible, and these combined packets are forwarded to the higher level PDCs or SPDC.

2.3 DQT

In Distributed execution with Qualified data forwarding Technique (DQT), the application at SPDC is divided into coordinated sub-applications (sub-queries) and executed in a distributed manner at LPDCs. We show that it is sufficient to monitor these sub-queries, over one data stream or data from a limited geographical region, to monitor the application query. These sub-applications forward the relevant filtered and aggregated data from LPDCs to SPDC, as shown in Figure 1(c). This helps in filtering a large amount of data before it is collected at the site. This in-network query processing is application semantics-aware and hence achieves high amount of filtering when *the system is steady* and also ensures detection of any unstable situation when the application is state is changing. In the next section we describe angular stability as the example application and show how the DQT scheme can be implemented for this application.

3. ANGULAR STABILITY

In angular stability application, we need to monitor multiple buses and send alert if the difference in the phase angles is above the specified threshold. It should be noted that, if f is the frequency of the electrical signal, phase angle θ_t at time t can be modeled as:

$$\theta_t = f \times t \times 360° + \theta_0 \ (mod\ 360°)$$

where, f is the phasor frequency in Hz, t is measurement time in seconds, and θ_0 is the phase angle at time $t = 0$. If the frequencies for PMU_i and PMU_j, corresponding to θ^i and θ^j, are equal ($f_i = f = f_j$), individual values of phase angles, with time, will be parallel to each other.

In DQT, rather than sending all the phase values to the application, thresholds to the phase angles are determined, such that LPDC needs to sends the phase angle values to the SPDC only if it crosses the specified thresholds. Since, phase angle values vary with time, rather than a fixed threshold, we need to have time varying thresholds over individual values of phase angles which bounds the angles with an upper bound and a lower bound. These two upper and lower bound constraints should vary linearly with time, should be parallel to each other, and the distance between them should be less than or equal to the value of phase angle difference threshold (say, θ_{Th}).

Let us assume that, for a pair of phase angles at two ends of a bus, initially θ^i is greater than θ^j. If β_i is the distance of the upper bound from linear equation estimating θ_t^i and β_j is the distance of the lower bound from linear equation estimating θ_t^j, we get,

$$\beta_i + \beta_j = \theta_{\mathbf{Th}}^{\mathbf{ij}} - (\theta_0^i - \theta_0^j) \qquad (1)$$

We can then set different values for β_i and β_j. Thus the linear constraints, for both θ^i and θ^j, are:

$$\theta_0^j - \beta_j \leq (\theta^i - f \times t \times 360)\ (mod\ 360°) \leq \theta_0^i + \beta_i$$
$$\theta_0^j - \beta_j \leq (\theta^j - f \times t \times 360)\ (mod\ 360°) \leq \theta_0^i + \beta_i \qquad (2)$$

The values of β_i and β_j can be dynamically obtained using various methods outlined in [1]. If the frequencies of the buses are different, the linear estimation models of phase angles at both the buses are not parallel. In this method, we derive the equation of the linear bounding constraints based on the average frequency ($f_{avg} = (f_i + f_j)/2$), i.e., use f_{avg} in the above equation while dividing the β values in proportion to the corresponding frequency values.

4. PERFORMANCE EVALUATION

For our experiments, we emulated the PMUs and PDCs using a grid simulator [2]. We implemented angular stability monitoring queries at SPDC where the SPDC receives data from 2 local PDCs and determined whether the difference in the phase angles is above the specified threshold. We used PMU data from a Northern-Indian grid line for these experiments. This data included the data when grid was stable as well as during a blackout. The buses (PMUs) were located at: Agra, Bassi, Dadri, Kanpur, Moga, Mumbai, and Hisar; mostly in northern Indian towns which were affected by a blackout during 30th and 31st July 2012. PMU data rate was 50 Hz and data frame size was 74 bytes. which had 16 bytes of header and 58 bytes of payload (3 voltage phasors, 3 current phasors, 1 frequency, 1 angle). We emulated the three methods of data dissemination, CUT, CQT, and DQT.

Average data rates from LPDC to SPDC, in Kb/s were, 586.4, 186.4, 158.4 for the three approaches CUT, CQT, and DQT, respectively. As expected, CUT approach incurs the highest bandwidth consumption compared to CQT and DQT. Average latency to get the application results at SPDC was 2881 μsecs for CUT. Reduction in data requirement also leads to reduction in total latency for CQT and DQT: CQT approach reduces latency by 15% whereas the DQT approach reduces average latency by as much as 80%.

5. CONCLUSION AND FUTURE WORK

We designed various in-network query processing techniques which allow for flexible bandwidth sharing of real time applications. The techniques are application semantics-aware due to which high data filtering is achieved when the grid was stable. This leads to significant message reduction which translated to latency reduction for critical applications. In the future, we will be exploring whether other aggregation processing techniques can be explored depending on the specifics of a given query over smart grid data

Acknowledgments

We would like to acknowledge contributions by Gopal, Prof. Soman, and Prof. Kulkarni from EE department at IIT Bombay in understanding the electric grid.

6. REFERENCES

[1] R. Gupta and K. Ramamritham, "Distributed execution of continuous queries," in *ICDE 2014*, 2014.

[2] K. Khandeparkar and N. Pandit, "Design and implementation of IEEE c37.118 based phaser data concentrator and pmu simulator for wide area measurement system," *Technical Report, Department of Electrical Engineering, IIT, Bombay.*, May, 2012.

Designing Sensor Sets for Capturing Energy Events in Buildings

Tom Lovett[1], Elizabeth Gabe-Thomas[3], Sukumar Natarajan[1],
Matthew Brown[2], Julian Padget[2]
Dept. of Architecture and Civil Engineering[1], Dept. of Computer Science[2], Dept. of Psychology[3]
University of Bath, Bath, UK
{t.r.lovett,e.gabe-thomas,s.natarajan,m.brown,j.a.padget}@bath.ac.uk

ABSTRACT

We study the problem of designing sensor sets for capturing energy events in buildings. In addition to direct energy sensing methods, e.g. electricity and gas, it is often desirable to monitor energy use and occupant activity through other sensors such as temperature and motion. However, practical constraints such as cost and deployment requirements can limit the choice, quantity and quality of sensors that can be distributed within each building, especially for large-scale deployments. In this paper, we present an approach to select a set of sensors for capturing energy events, using a measure of each candidate sensor's ability to predict energy events within a building. We use constrained optimisation – specifically, a bounded knapsack problem (BKP) – to choose the best sensors for the set given each sensor's predictive value and specified cost constraints. We present the results from a field study of 4 UK homes with temperature, light, motion, humidity, sound and CO_2 sensors, showing how valuable yet expensive sensors are often not chosen in the optimal set.

Categories and Subject Descriptors

H.4 [**Information Systems Applications**]: Miscellaneous

Keywords

Energy use; sensing; intelligence; interaction; ENLITEN

1. INTRODUCTION AND PRIOR WORK

To tackle the problem of energy usage reduction in buildings, researchers have used sensing technology to capture and analyse buildings' energy use so that efficiency can be improved and methods of lowering energy demand can be explored, e.g. through changing occupants' energy-related behaviour. The first step in enabling behavioural change is the gathering and sensing of pertinent data. As such, key questions emerge about how best to approach energy sensing: what sensors should we use? How many do we need? How intrusive and costly is the installation? Direct energy sensing with electricity and gas sensors is commonplace [3], but direct sensing alone does not account for total energy use, nor does it allow for non-trivial analyses of the often individualistic causal factors involved in energy consumption. There are two key contributions in this paper:

- A method for assigning a value to a sensor in terms of its utility in capturing human activities that involve energy consumption in a building.

- A method for the selection of maximal value sensor sets subject to practical constraints such as budget and sensor quantities.

The closest work to the study in this paper is Zhang *et al.*'s study of feature selection for occupancy classification in office spaces [6]. Here, the authors explore the relative information gain – or uncertainty coefficients – as a value measure for a small range of sensors using intermittent ground truth gathered in an office environment. We use a different measure of sensor value in a domestic environment, but our results broadly support Zhang *et al.*'s, which show that sound and CO_2 sensors appear to be the most effective at detection; albeit for energy events in ours, and occupancy events in theirs. By incorporating sensor costs, however, we show that these sensors are not always the best ones to choose for maximising sensor value given a set of constraints.

2. APPROACH

2.1 Constrained Optimisation

The knapsack problem is a simple integer linear program that seeks to find the optimal combination of n distinct items that maximises the total value of a weight-constrained knapsack, given that each item has a value and a weight. More formally, given n distinct items, where each item i has a corresponding value v_i, number of copies x_i and weight w_i, and an overall weight constraint W, the knapsack problem seeks to:

$$\text{maximise:} \quad \sum_{i=1}^{n} v_i x_i$$
$$\text{subject to:} \quad \sum_{i=1}^{n} w_i x_i \leq W \quad x_i \in \{0, \ldots, c_i\} \tag{1}$$

Where c_i is an upper bound on the number of copies of each item. c_i could be viewed as a sensor quantity limit, e.g. a stock limit. The above problem is a bounded knapsack problem (BKP), which does not restrict the items in the knapsack to one copy each.

e-Energy'14, June 11–13, 2014, Cambridge, UK.
ACM 978-1-4503-2819-7/14/06.
http://dx.doi.org/10.1145/2602044.2602080.

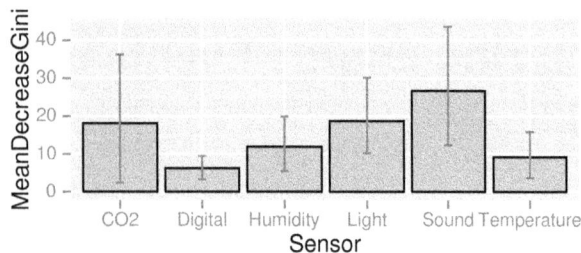

Figure 1: Mean Gini impurity decrease over all features for each sensor.

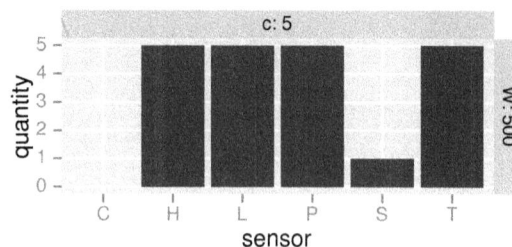

Figure 2: Example sensor set as output by the BKP algorithm for W=500 and c=5.

2.2 Defining Sensor Values and Costs

To perform feature selection, we use a random forest process on a set of extracted features. A random forest is an ensemble learning method that combines a set of decision tree classifiers, each of which is comprised of a random sample of input variables (in our case, extracted features). For brevity, we refer the reader to Breiman's description of the random forest method for a detailed overview [1]. We use random forests to measure the value of each extracted sensor feature using the average decrease in node impurities (Gini measure) from splitting the decision trees on that feature.

As with the choice of value measure, the choice of cost measure is likely to be context-dependent. An obvious choice is the financial cost of each sensor, but more complex cost functions could be designed that incorporate, for example, sensor energy costs, installation effort or sensor reliabilities. In addition to budgetary constraints, logical constraints can be introduced that restrict the chosen sensor set to particular subsets of the overall power set (all 2^n possible choices of sensor set from n sensors).

2.3 Field Study

In order to demonstrate how a sensor set for capturing energy events can be chosen, we present the results of a field study in a set of domestic buildings in the UK. We recruited 4 homes to be studied for 7 consecutive days. Within certain rooms in each home – each room common to each home – we installed the following sensors: temperature in °C, light in lux, CO_2 in ppm, motion in $\{0, 1\}$ and sound level in dB, each sampled once per minute.

To capture a record of ground truth events in each home, we asked the primary occupant to record energy-related events around the home throughout the week in a diary study. To define the energy events, we used Oxford University's Multinational Time Use Study (MTUS) data [2], selecting domestic event codes that classify energy-consuming events around the home. We dismissed data during which the occupants did not log anything, i.e. the ground truth was unknown.

For each of the sensors, we calculated the following features: raw value at timestep k, y_k; first order difference: $\Delta(y_k) = y_{k+1} - y_k$; second order difference, $\Delta^2(y_k) = \Delta(y_{k+1}) - \Delta(y_k)$; and simple moving average over a m minute window.

3. RESULTS

For the random forest process, data is split .7 training, .15 validation and .15 test. Each forest consists of 500 trees, with 4 variables randomly sampled per split; no replacement. We used the *R* package "randomForest" [4] to run the random forest process with the aforementioned parameters. This package uses Breiman's approach [1].

For the BKP, we use Pferschy's $\mathcal{O}(nW)$ BKP algorithm described in [5]. For the moving average feature, we set m – the moving average window – to 20 minutes for each sensor. The sensor values for the BKP are set to the mean Gini decrease measures for each sensor. For the sensor costs, we use the approximate financial cost of the sensors in our study setup: 215 for CO_2, 20 for humidity, 16 for light, 115 for sound and 17 for temperature. The study participants logged 392 events in total over the 7 days (A = 119, B = 59, C = 77, D = 137).

Figure 1 shows the mean Gini impurity decrease for each sensor, averaged over the sensor's features. Figure 2 shows a set of example sensor sets output by the BKP algorithm for given weight constraints W and upper bounds on the sensor quantities c_i.

4. DISCUSSION AND CONCLUSION

The key implication of this work relates to the utilisation of environmental sensors as predictors of energy events in buildings. The sensors in our study are designed to measure a particular environmental property, e.g. temperature, rather than direct energy use – something that devices such as current clamps attached to electricity meters and plug power monitors do. The sensor values show that temperature, humidity, light, CO_2, sound and motion sensors are useful predictors of energy use, though their predictive values do vary both across sensors and between homes. The main limitations of our work relate to the context of sensing, the range of sensors and the study size.

In this paper, we presented a process for designing sensor sets to capture energy events in buildings. The key contributions lie in the use of random forests to produce a measure of sensor value *a priori*, and the implementation of a bounded knapsack problem (BKP) solver that chooses an optimum sensor set given a set of costs and values.

5. REFERENCES

[1] L. Breiman. Random Forests. *Machine Learning*, 45(1):5–32, 2001.
[2] K. Fisher and J. Gershuny. Multinational Time Use Study. Chapter 3: Activity Codes, July 2013. Retrieved from http://www.timeuse.org/sites/ctur/files/858/mtus-user-guide-chapter-3.pdf. Dec 2013.
[3] J. Froehlich, E. Larson, S. Gupta, G. Cohn, M. Reynolds, and S. Patel. Disaggregated end-use energy sensing for the smart grid. *Pervasive Computing, IEEE*, 10(1):28–39, 2011.
[4] A. Liaw and M. Wiener. Classification and Regression by randomForest. *R News*, 2(3):18–22, 2002.
[5] U. Pferschy. Dynamic programming revisited: improving knapsack algorithms. *Computing*, 63(4):419–430, 1999.
[6] R. Zhang, K. P. Lam, Y.-S. Chiou, and B. Dong. Information-theoretic environment features selection for occupancy detection in open office spaces. *Building Simulation*, 5(2):179–188, 2012.

A Novel Heuristics-based Energy Management System for a Multi-Carrier Hub enriched with Solid Hydrogen Storage

Rosario Proietto
Onyx Technology s.r.l.
via Adolfo Ravà
n. 124, 00142, Roma, Italy
+390687675337
proietto.rosario@gmail.com

Diego Arnone
Engineering I.I. S.p.A.
viale della Regione Siciliana N.O.
n.7275, 90146, Palermo, Italy
+390917511734
diego.arnone@eng.it

Massimo Bertoncini
Engineering I.I. S.p.A.
via Riccardo Morandi n.32,
00148, Roma, Italy
+390683074240
massimo.bertoncini@eng.it

Alessandro Rossi
Engineering I.I. S.p.A.
viale della Regione Siciliana N.O.
n.7275, 90146, Palermo, Italy
+390917511735
alessandro.rossi@eng.it

Diego La Cascia
Università degli Studi di Palermo
viale delle Scienze s.n.c.,
90128, Palermo, Italy
+3909123860298
diego.lacascia@dieet.unipa.it

Rosario Miceli
Università degli Studi di Palermo
viale delle Scienze s.n.c.,
90128, Palermo, Italy
+3909123860285
rosario.miceli@unipa.it

Eleonora Riva Sanseverino
Università degli Studi di Palermo
viale delle Scienze s.n.c.,
90128, Palermo, Italy
+3909123860262
eleonora.rivasanseverino@unipa.it

ABSTRACT

In this paper, an efficient optimization algorithm for the energy management of a grid-connected energy hub plant is proposed. The Simulated Annealing algorithm is adopted for the solution of the energy management problem aiming at the profit maximization for the owner of the energy hub plant. The use of a heuristic algorithm was required by the non-linearity of the efficiencies of each component in the energy transformation stages. The proposed heuristics is applied to a large energy hub, corresponding to the simulation of the test-bed that is being designed and developed inside the ongoing INGRID European research project.

Categories and Subject Descriptors

H.4 [**Information Systems Applications**]: Decision Support.

General Terms

Algorithms, Management, Measurement, Design.

Keywords

Energy Management Systems, Energy Storage, Electric Grid balancing, Renewable Sources integration, Simulated Annealing, Energy supply and demand matching.

e-Energy'14, Jun 11-13 2014, Cambridge, United Kingdom
ACM 978-1-4503-2819-7/14/06.
http://dx.doi.org/10.1145/2602044.2602081

1. INTRODUCTION

The distributed energetic production from Renewable Energy Sources (RES) is rapidly expanding so that, sometimes, in particularly sunny or windy places, the "green" energy produced is comparable to, or greater than, the energy adsorbed by the loads connected to the distribution grid. Because of their inherent non-controllable variability as well as partial unpredictability the power produced by RES can cause stability issues and can degrade the quality of the power in the grid. In order to address these issues, the INGRID FP7 European co-funded project [1] is studying several solutions to balance power supply and demand by shifting the electricity adsorption or modulating the energy injected into the grid in cooperation with the Distribution System Operator (DSO). The main objective of this work consists of designing, implementing and testing an innovative Energy Management System (EMS) [2][3] by means of a heuristic based methodology.

2. SYSTEM DESCRIPTION

The system currently under development will be instantiated in a concrete 39 MWh energy storage facility that will be deployed and will operate in Troia (Puglia region, Italy). The system reported in Fig. 1 is composed by the following subsystems: an internal RES based plant, a Water Electrolyser (WE) for hydrogen production, a Hydrogen Solid-state Storage (HSS) system, a Fuel Cell (FC) and an Electrical Vehicle Recharge System (EVRS).

The system takes into account the electric grid connection, the possibility to receive information from both the electricity and the hydrogen markets, and also the possibility to inject the produced hydrogen into the methane pipeline. The system communicates with the DSO, which provides the desired power consumption or generation profiles which are taken into consideration for the optimisation of the profit. The system may also provide ancillary services at the grid connection point by activating the FC when a specific function is requested by the DSO.

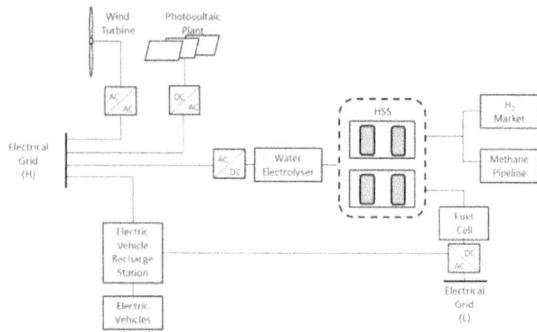

Fig. 1 Managed system block diagram

The HSS is based on a metal hydride technology and consists of two storage subsystems: one tailored to the hydrogen market and the methane pipeline (*open loop*), the other to the FC for the production of electricity (*closed loop*).

3. THE ENERGY MANAGEMENT SYSTEM

In the energy management problem, the objective function is the economic benefit for the plant owner. The function to be optimized has many additive terms. Some of them have non-linear coefficients considering the Water Electrolyser or the Fuel Cell efficiencies, basically derived from the converters used as systems to interface the grid. In order to correctly manage the INGRID system, the Simulated Annealing (SA) algorithm was implemented and appropriately fitted. The EMS sets the plant configuration on the basis of the input data coming from each subsystem in order to modulate the electricity adsorption/supply. The EMS operates considering a reference time horizon, which is subdivided in elementary time slots. The architecture consists of the overlapping of two operational time stages: scheduling time and real time. The scheduling and real time are superimposed in the same time slot and the EMS re-schedules for the entire time horizon [4]. The EMS is connected to the Distribution Management System (DMS), the Electricity Market, the RES forecasting system, the Hydrogen Production and Distribution System (H2P&DS), the Fuel Cell management system, and the Intelligence Dispenser (ID) that manages the EVRS. In particular, the H2P&DS is the system that manages the WE, the HSS, and receives information about the hydrogen sale. The DMS represents the DSO interface which communicates with the EMS by means of the IEC 61850 protocol.

4. SIMULATIONS RESULTS

A MATLAB script has been designed, written and successfully tested to implement the SA based EMS. The following data refer to the MATLAB implementation and to the plant depicted in Fig. 1. The WE rated power is equal to 1152 kW and its minimum value has been set to 460 kW. The FC nominal power is 1000 kW, the hydrogen storage capacity of the *closed loop* tanks is equal to 556.16 Nm^3 of hydrogen, while the *open loop* tanks has a capability of 4449.28 Nm^3.

In our simulation, the system has to satisfy a hydrogen request equal to 1012 Nm^3 for the *open loop* at the end of the day. The round trip efficiency is set to 0.4, the parameter to convert

electricity into hydrogen is equal to 5 kWh/Nm^3 (WE parameter), and a parameter equal to 0.56 Nm^3/kWh is considered to convert hydrogen into electricity. In the following figure, how the EMS operates is reported.

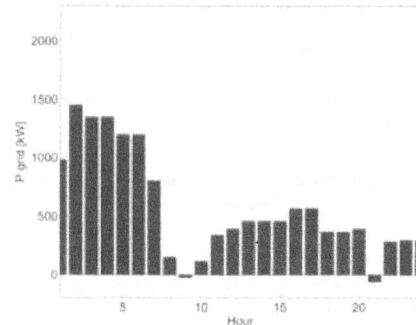

Fig. 2 Electricity adsorbing from electric grid (H)

The blue histogram in Fig. 2 shows the optimal plant configuration during 24 hours, whereas the dashed trend represents the DSO request. The economically optimal solution carried out by the EMS is far from the DSO request because the demonstrator does not follow a master-slave approach. The simulation shows that the integration of a metal hydride based storage as a buffer system in *closed loop* requires that a considerable incentive has to be given to obtain an economically sustainable solution. Despite the poor *closed loop* efficiency, the demonstrator allows to adsorb and convert the excess of electricity coming from the grid, e.g., in presence of power reverse flow, exploiting the *open loop* features.

5. ACKNOWLEDGMENTS

This work is part of the INGRID project, co-funded by the European Commission within the FP7 Framework Programme. Authors thank the members of the INGRID Consortium as well as the European Commission for supporting any project dissemination activities. This work reflects only the authors' views. The Commission is not liable for any use that may be made of the information contained therein.

6. REFERENCES

[1] INGRID (High-capacity hydrogen-based green-energy storage solutions for grid balancing) European FP7 co-funded project: http://www.ingridproject.eu.

[2] D. Arnone, M. Bertoncini, A. Rossi, F. D'Errico, C. García-Santiago, D. Moneta, C. D'Orinzi "An ICT-based Energy Management System to Integrate Renewable Energy and Storage for Grid Balancing", in *Proceedings of the fourth international conference on Future energy systems* (e-Energy '13). ACM, New York, NY, USA, 259-260.

[3] A. Rossi, D. Arnone, M. Bertoncini, D. Moneta, "Sistema di gestione energetico innovativo con stoccaggio a idrogeno per l'integrazione di fonti rinnovabili a supporto del bilanciamento della rete", accepted to AEIT 2013, October 2013, Palermo, Italy.

[4] Eleonora Riva Sanseverino, Maria Luisa Di Silvestre, Mariano Giuseppe Ippolito, Alessandra De Paola, Giuseppe Lo Re, "An execution, monitoring and replanning approach for optimal energy management in microgrids", Energy, vol. 36, n. 5, pp. 3429-3436, May 2011.

Household Electricity Demand Forecasting - Benchmarking State-of-the-Art Methods

Andreas Veit, Christoph Goebel, Rohit Tidke,
Christoph Doblander and Hans-Arno Jacobsen
Department of Computer Science, Technische Universität München
andreas.veit@tum.de, christoph.goebel@tum.de,
rohittidke@gmail.com, doblande@in.tum.de

ABSTRACT

We benchmark state-of-the-art methods for forecasting electricity demand on the household level. Our evaluation is based on two data sets containing the power usage on the individual appliance level. Our results indicate that without further refinement the considered advanced state-of-the-art forecasting methods rarely beat corresponding persistence forecasts. Therefore, we also provide an exploration of promising directions for future research.

Categories and Subject Descriptors

I.2.6 [**Artificial Intelligence**]: Learning

Keywords

Smart Grid; Smart Home; Load Forecasting

1. INTRODUCTION

In this study, we evaluate state-of-the-art forecasting methods for their applicability for household load forecasting. Accurate load forecasts can greatly enhance the micro-balancing capabilities of smart grids, if they are utilized for control operations and decisions like dispatch, unit commitment, fuel allocation and off-line network analysis [1]. Further, accurate load forecasts can help utilities to select customers that are suitable for demand response programs like proposed by [6]. First studies have analyzed the potential of consumption forecasts for individual households [7, 8]. However, most work focuses on disaggregation of electricity consumption (e.g., [2, 3, 4]). Our results show the forecasting methods provide little value, if not embedded into a framework that adapts to individual household attributes, motivating an exploration of promising directions for future research.

2. EXPERIMENT

The technical details of the data pre-processing and experimental setup are explained in the technical report [5].

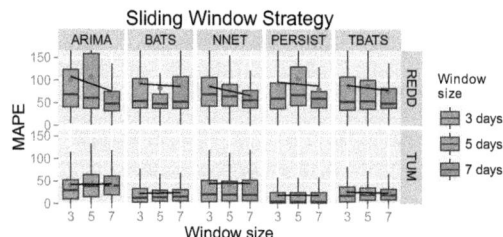

Figure 1: MAPE for varying window sizes.

We use two data sets measuring the power consumption of individual appliances of a household at intervals of 1 to 3 seconds. The TUM data set covers nine month and has a very stable consumption pattern. The Reference Energy Disaggregation Data Set (REDD) [4] covers 18 days and has more frequent and higher fluctuations in consumption. We use different forecasting methods that are all provided by the R forecast package: As benchmark, we use the persistence method, where forecasts equal the last observation. Further, we use Autoregressive Integrated Moving Average (ARIMA), i.e., `auto.arima()`, exponential smoothing state space models, i.e., `bats()` and `tbats()` and feed-forward neural networks with a single hidden layer, i.e., `nnetar()`. We used three sampling strategies: The *sliding window strategy* divides the data set into windows, moving forward on the data, after a model has been trained and tested. The *day type strategy* joins each day of the week of consecutive weeks into separate data sets. The *hierarchical day type strategy* first forecasts individual appliances to then compute the aggregated forecast. We use data granularities from 15 to 60 minutes intervals, forecasting horizons from 15 minutes to 24 hours and window sizes from 3 to 7 days. We measure the model quality by the Mean Absolute Percentage Error (MAPE), because it is a relative measure and can be used to compare the performance on different data sets.

3. EXPERIMENTAL RESULTS

Overall we observe that the considered advanced state-of-the-art *forecasting methods rarely beat corresponding persistence forecasts*. This is especially true for the TUM data set. Further, our *results differ largely between the two data sets*, i.e., the accuracy on the TUM data set is almost constantly higher than on the REDD data set. This could be due to the more stable consumption pattern in the TUM data set, which is easier to predict. In addition, Figure 1 shows boxplots and linear trend lines of MAPE for different

Figure 2

Sliding Window Strategy

REDD (MAPE, forecasting horizon in minutes vs. sampling granularity in minutes)

Horizon	ARIMA 15	ARIMA 30	ARIMA 60	BATS 15	BATS 30	BATS 60	NNET 15	NNET 30	NNET 60	PERSIST 15	PERSIST 30	PERSIST 60	TBATS 15	TBATS 30	TBATS 60
1440	146	146	117	127	92	92	150	121	102	113	118	117	106	61	96
720	103	109	84	111	69	69	85	65	55	93	105	103	87	57	74
180	96	95	66	112	89	74	78	80	50	93	103	83	99	83	81
60	90	86	51	116	75	59	90	54	52	91	71	60	105	70	63
30	83	91		129	57		93	49		71	75		116	72	
15	48			76			85			54			72		

TUM

Horizon	ARIMA 15	ARIMA 30	ARIMA 60	BATS 15	BATS 30	BATS 60	NNET 15	NNET 30	NNET 60	PERSIST 15	PERSIST 30	PERSIST 60	TBATS 15	TBATS 30	TBATS 60
1440	56	55	50	32	36	33	47	43	50	35	34	29	28	30	32
720	55	55	55	33	42	42	62	55	68	31	31	29	41	41	45
180	42	44	46	18	23	25	41	39	46	17	15	13	21	23	26
60	27	29	30	13	13	17	38	39	42	10	9	10	15	15	22
30	22	25		9	10		36	35		8	6		11	13	
15	19			7			35			6			10		

Day Type Strategy

REDD

Horizon	ARIMA 15	ARIMA 30	ARIMA 60	BATS 15	BATS 30	BATS 60	NNET 15	NNET 30	NNET 60	PERSIST 15	PERSIST 30	PERSIST 60	TBATS 15	TBATS 30	TBATS 60
1440	95	84	76	69	53	49	119	83	65	61	60	46	65	55	48
720	97	94	84	70	56	52	126	95	79	63	63	46	65	55	57
180	66	62	53	66	60	63	122	77	97	69	74	66	53	55	64
60	82	56	47	60	52	48	181	75	56	58	68	59	67	45	50
30	112	62		63	64		205	95		53	61		77	40	
15	91			36			206			8			66		

TUM

Horizon	ARIMA 15	ARIMA 30	ARIMA 60	BATS 15	BATS 30	BATS 60	NNET 15	NNET 30	NNET 60	PERSIST 15	PERSIST 30	PERSIST 60	TBATS 15	TBATS 30	TBATS 60
1440	67	55	37	30	34	33	41	31	31	24	24	25	21	32	29
720	60	53	34	28	19	19	23	10	12	11	9	10	11	16	15
180	47	39	27	18	13	15	11	4	7	4	4	6	8	12	13
60	37	32	24	11	15	15	8	5	8	3	6		5	10	10
30	31	30		7	15		12	6		3	6		2	11	
15	29			8			20			5					

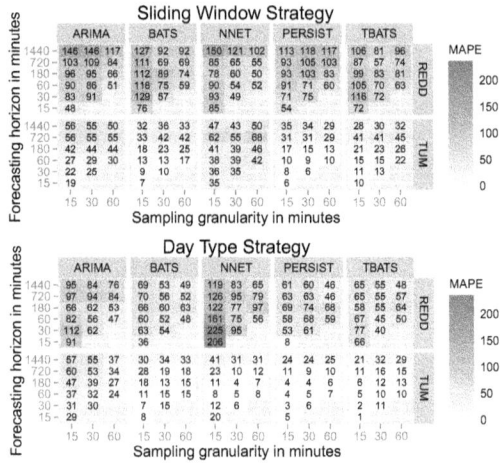

Figure 2: MAPE for varying horizons and granularities.

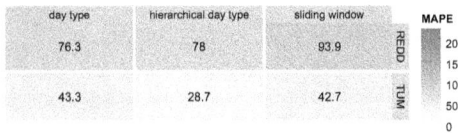

	day type	hierarchical day type	sliding window
REDD	76.3	78	93.9
TUM	43.3	28.7	42.7

Figure 3: Mean MAPE for ARIMA with different strategies.

window sizes in the sliding window strategy. The results indicate that *increasing window sizes improve the results* of the ARIMA, NNET and TBATS methods on the REDD data set, but not on the TUM data set. Because the days in the TUM data are so similar, additional training data might not provide new important information. Further, Figure 2 shows heatmaps of MAPE from the sliding window and day type strategies for different granularities and forecasting horizons. The results indicate that for almost every method, *longer forecasting horizons lead to lower accuracy*. However, the exponential smoothing methods BATS and TBATS seem more robust against increasing horizons than the other methods. Further, especially on the REDD data set, *lower granularities lead to better accuracy*. In particular, the exponential smoothing strategies BATS and TBATS and the neural network outperform the persistence method for granularities of 30 and 60 minutes. Furthermore, Figure 2 shows that for almost every method *a division of the data into day type windows improves the forecast accuracy*. In addition, Figure 3 compares all three strategies for the ARIMA method indicating that the *hierarchical strategy can greatly improve accuracy* on the TUM data set. This is a surprising result, as generally the prediction of aggregated loads tend to result in higher precision.

4. DISCUSSION AND FUTURE WORK

We have evaluated a wide range of state-of-the-art methods and strategies for short-term forecasting of household electricity consumption based on actual data. Although our current data is limited, we were able to gain useful insights. Overall, the considered advanced forecasting methods only rarely beat the accuracy of persistence forecasts. Further, most of the methods benefit from larger training sets, split-

ting the data into sets of particular day types and predicting based on disaggregated data from individual appliances. Furthermore, the achievable accuracy in terms of average MAPE is surprisingly low, ranging between 5 and 150%. Thus, our work motivates more research investigating how accuracy can be increased. First, introducing further features, e.g., from occupancy, temperature or brightness sensors, could improve prediction accuracy, because when a device is switched on/off it takes time until the average wattage accounts for the change. Second, many devices have a very predictable consumption pattern once switched on. Thus, it could be beneficial to detect concrete events (e.g., on/off) and based on these events derive a future consumption pattern. Third, we only considered consistent data sets. However, in real world settings load forecasts need to be performed even in situations with missing data. Thus, future work should investigate how to handle temporary sensor outages, which could distract the prediction algorithms. Last, our results differ largely between the two data sets. It is unclear, how common the characteristics of these data sets are. However, the necessary data for carrying out more representative studies is currently missing. Future work will focus on the design of such frameworks.

5. REFERENCES

[1] D. Bunn and E. Farmer. Review of short-term forecasting methods in the electric power industry. *Comparative models for electrical load forecasting*, 1985.

[2] S. Humeau, T. K. Wijaya, M. Vasirani, and K. Aberer. Electricity load forecasting for residential customers: Exploiting aggregation and correlation between households. In *Sustainable Internet and ICT for Sustainability (SustainIT), 2013*. IEEE, 2013.

[3] W. Kleiminger, C. Beckel, T. Staake, and S. Santini. Occupancy Detection from Electricity Consumption Data. In *Proceedings of the 5th ACM Workshop on Embedded Systems For Energy-Efficient Buildings*. ACM, 2013.

[4] J. Z. Kolter and M. J. Johnson. Redd: A public data set for energy disaggregation research. In *proceedings of the SustKDD workshop on Data Mining Applications in Sustainability*, 2011.

[5] A. Veit, C. Goebel, R. Tidke, C. Doblander, and H.-A. Jacobsen. Household electricity demand forecasting - benchmarking state-of-the-art methods. Technical Report arXiv:1404.0200, arXiv.org, 2014.

[6] A. Veit, Y. Xu, R. Zheng, N. Chakraborty, and K. Sycara. Multiagent coordination for energy consumption scheduling in consumer cooperatives. In *Proceedings of the 27th AAAI Conference on Artificial Intelligence*. AAAI, July 2013.

[7] H. Ziekow, C. Doblander, C. Goebel, and H.-A. Jacobsen. Forecasting household electricity demand with complex event processing: insights from a prototypical solution. In *Proceedings of the Industrial Track of the 13th ACM/IFIP/USENIX International Middleware Conference*. ACM, 2013.

[8] H. Ziekow, C. Goebel, J. Struker, and H.-A. Jacobsen. The potential of smart home sensors in forecasting household electricity demand. In *2013 IEEE International Conference on Smart Grid Communications (SmartGridComm)*. IEEE, 2013.

Appliance Usage Profiling for Energy Management and Healthcare

Simeng Jia[1], Ayomi Bandara[2], Tim Lewis[2], Mahesh Sooriyabandara[2]

[1] Dept of Electrical and Electronic Engineering, University of Bristol,Bristol, BS8 1UB, UK
[2] Toshiba Research Europe Ltd, 32 Queen Square, Bristol, BS1 4ND, UK
simeng.jia.2011@my.bristol.ac.uk, {ayomi.bandara, tim.lewis, maheshs}@toshiba-trel.com

1. INTRODUCTION

Residential energy consumption is steadily increasing year after year and this constitutes a siginificant proportion of the total buildings energy consumption. With this in mind, analyses of electricity consumption in residential households have grown in the recent years. Prediction of energy usage and estimating energy usage behavior in general, is an important aspect of energy management solutions; from the end of the utility providers this will help the estimation of the demand for energy and from the energy consumers end this will help to generate appropriate advice for significant energy/cost savings. There have been a number of recent efforts for analyzing user behaviors, learning user preferences and predicting user activities. The goal of the work presented in this paper is to study the energy consumers' behavior in terms of appliance usage. By using the past energy data for the individual appliances in a household, this work tries to build profiles for appliance use for each household and these profiles may vary for different days of the week, for different months/ seasons and so on depending on the household occupants' routine. The constructed appliance usage profiles will provide a wealth of information relating to the routines and lifestyles of the occupants (e.g. wake up times, meal times, habits such as frequent television viewing, cooking and eating behavior etc.). The profiling method can also be generally applied for analyzing other behaviors such as sleeping profiles. Such profiles once identified, will provide a valuable input towards the development of effective energy management and home automation systems, for providing energy saving tips and for taking appropriate automated control action. This knowledge will not only be useful in an energy management viewpoint, but also from a healthcare management viewpoint. For instance, this can point to unhealthy lifestyles (for example identifying constant television viewing even in good weather) or the change of behavior patterns for elderly occupants that may cause concern. In such cases, relevant health officials can be informed as appropriate and/ or preventive advice and action can be taken.

e-Energy'14, June 11–13, 2014, Cambridge, UK.
ACM 978-1-4503-2819-7/14/06.
http://dx.doi.org/10.1145/2602044.2602083 .

2. APPLIANCE USAGE PROFILILNG

In this work, we are aiming to find for an individual household and for each individual appliance, the usage behavior for the different classes of days (termed as Appliance Usage Profile). This will indicate, for the 24 hour period of the day, the probability of the appliance being used in a given time. The different 'classes' (of days) can vary depending on the appliance concerned and the routines of the individual households. For example, for a household with a single occupant, who is full-time employed in routine work, this can correspond to a week-day and week-end. However, this is likely to vary hugely depending on the lifestyles of the occupants involved and numerous other factors such as weather, season, events etc. In order to extract the appliance usage profiles, we need for each given time, the energy data indicating whether the appliance was on or off, i.e. whether it is being used or not. The granularity of energy data we consider in this work is minutely.

Let $a \in A$ denote an appliance in a given household where A denotes the set of appliances in the household. Daily usage for appliance a will be the usage data over a 24 hour period, and for this study we consider the frequency of available data to be every one minute. Thus, the daily use will be a function $d_a = \{(x,y)|x = \{1, 2, \ldots, 1440\}, y = \{0,1\}\}$, representing used/ not used behavior of the given appliance for each minute of the day. For each appliance a, the clustering approach will identify a set of clusters $C_a = \{c_{a_1}, c_{a_2}, \ldots, c_{a_n}\}$, where c_{a_k} identifies a group of Daily Usages d_a where usage of appliance a is similar and n_a is the number of clusters associated with appliance a. The appliance usage profile for a given appliance a (P_a) will consist of a number of sub-profiles such that $P_a = \left\{p_{a_{c_{a_1}}}, p_{a_{c_{a_2}}}, \ldots, p_{a_{c_{a_n}}}\right\}$ where $p_{a_{c_{a_k}}}$ identifies the profile associated with the kth cluster c_{a_k} for the appliance. Each sub-profile is a function $p = \{(x,y)|x = \{1, 2, \ldots, 1440\}, y = (0,1)\}$, which is obtained by computing the average over the Daily Usages d that were included in the cluster c_{a_k}. That is:

$$p_{a_{c_{a_k}}} = \left\{(x,y)|x = \{1, 2, \ldots, 1440\}, \frac{1}{m}\sum_{k=1}^{m} d_a(x,z)\right\} \text{ where}$$

d represents the daily usages associated with the cluster c_{a_k} and m is the number of days included in the cluster. A given sub-profile $p_{a_{c_{a_k}}}$, will identify the most likely usage behavior for a day that will fall into the cluster c_{a_k}. This effectively will indicate the probability of the use of the appliance a, for each minute of a day in that given cluster.

Table 1: Households used in the experiment and Demographics.

	House1	House2	House3
Appliance monitored	Computer Lounge-lamp Kettle Microwave	TV Dishwasher	TV Cooker Kettle
No. of Adults	1	1	2
No. of Children	0	1	2
Employment status	Retired	Part-time employed	Part-time employed/ Unemployed
Type of house	Semi-detached	Semi-detached	Mid-terraced

2.1 Experiment and Results

The 3eHouses dataset (3eHouses European Union FP7 Project : http:// www. 3ehouses.eu/) was used in this experiment, which covers energy data obtained from over 100 houses and each house's data contains energy data coming from several appliances. For the purpose of this experiment, three households were chosen with each house containing a varying number of appliances. The relevant details of the households used in the experiment are shown in Table 1. For the profiling process, five months of data was used as a training set. The detailed results obtained for the appliances are not included in this paper, however, Figure1 provides a graphical illustration of a sub-profile obtained for one of the appliances. In this graph, the x axis shows the 24 hour time of day, and the y axis shows the probability of the appliance being used, which will range between 0 and 1. As apparent from profiles obtained for the individual appliances, these can disclose a wealth of information regarding the occupants such as: their wake-up times, meal times, television viewing patterns, meal types they usually have (the amount of cooker using time or microwave use may link to home cooked meals/ ready meals / eating out) and other lifestyle facts. Although we intuitively expect to see a weekly pattern in the appliance usage, this wasn't present in some appliances. This is probably due to the lifestyles and work routines of the household occupants concerned in this experiment. Where a weekly pattern is apparent, this can be used to predict the appliance usage for a future date.

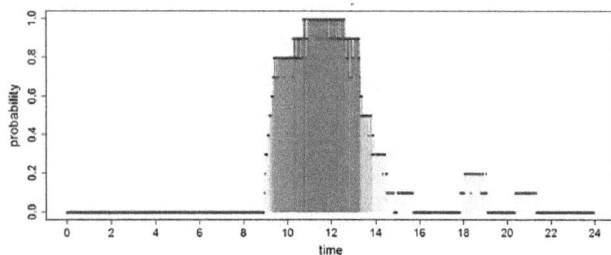

Figure 1: Sub-profile corresponding to the use of Cooker on Sundays for House-3

3. USING APPLIANCE USAGE PROFILES

As mentioned earlier, the usage of certain appliances showed a weekly cycle. Where the appliance use can be linked to weekly cycle, the associated sub-profiles can be used for effectively predicting the appliance usage for a future date. That is, given the appliance usage profiles obtained from historic data, for a given future day and for each hour of the day, a prediction is made as to whether the appliance will be used or not. Please note, that the prediction is done on an hourly basis here, which is more reasonable than trying to predict on a minutely basis. The first step in the prediction process is to construct the hourly sub-profiles for each cluster (which is different to sub-profiles explained in the previous section, which are minutely). Once the hourly sub-profiles are obtained this is used to derive a prediction corresponding to each such hourly sub-profile. This is done using a probability threshold t, and if the probability of use in a given hour is greater than this threshold as indicated in the hourly sub-profile, the prediction is that the appliance will be used, otherwise the prediction will be, that appliance will not be used. We have constructed the usage profiles using 5 months (March 2012 - July 2012) of data as the training data set. For prediction, we use as test data, the days in the month of May 2013. We have applied the prediction approach for 4 of the appliances in Table 1. The detailed results of prediction cannot be discussed here due to limited space, however, the prediction resulted in good rates of accuracy (ranging between 78% and 97% for the four appliances).

In addition to appliance usage prediction, another potential benefit and application of appliance usage profiles, is the use of this knowledge in generating customized energy advice. Also, the energy usage behavior profiles disclose many aspects relating to the lifestyle of the occupants. Therefore, if the behavior profiles indicate an unhealthy lifestyle, it will be in the best interests of the occupants to offer them advice about changing their behavior and to inform them of possible consequences if the unhealthy behaviors are continued.

4. CONCLUSIONS AND FURTHER WORK

In this paper we have proposed an approach for profiling appliance usage of a household's occupants by making use of energy consumption data collected from individual appliances. The approach has been validated on energy data collected from 3 households and the results demonstrate the usefulness of the approach in understanding the user behavior. Also, it has been shown, how the constructed profiles can be used for predicting appliance usage for a future day. The initial results of the prediction approach shows encouraging results with good rates of accuracy.

However, consideration of the other factors (such as the work routines of the individual occupants, weather and external events) other than the profiles obtained from the energy data alone, will be beneficial in improving the prediction results. Also, more research and experimentation needs to be carried out on more varied data sets, with more occupants having different demographics and lifestyles. This will enable the results of findings to be interpreted and validated.

Putting Smart Meters to Work – Beyond the Usual

Kartik Palani, Nabeel Nasir, Vivek Chil Prakash, Amandeep Chugh, Rohit Gupta,
Krithi Ramamritham*
Department of Computer Science, Indian Institute of Technology, Bombay
{kartik, nabeel, vivekcp, amandeepchugh, rohitg, krithi}@cse.iitb.ac.in

ABSTRACT

The paper shows how smart meters can be put to work, beyond their traditional use, towards explaining abnormal and unexpected patterns in the behavior of electrical appliances. We describe two kinds of uses, by visualizing and analyzing smart meter data for an academic building. The first gives us the ability to find anomalous appliance behaviors and the other helps to discover sub-optimal energy consumption patterns. The goal is to stress the fact that the ubiquitous smart meter can act as a sensor not only for monitoring consumption but also for detecting interesting energy usage patterns.

Categories and Subject Descriptors

H.4 [**Information Systems Applications**]: Miscellaneous

Keywords

Smart Meter; Smart Buildings; Anomaly Detection

1. ANOMALY DETECTION

In a large building, quite often malfunctioning devices go unnoticed. Sometimes, these anomalous devices draw large current, thereby adding to the building's consumption, unnecessarily. The ability to analyze the power consumption of a building at various levels of granularity aids in detecting such usage patterns. To observe anomalous behavior we propose a setup that measures data at a macro-level (one smart meter per building) as well as at a micro-level (smart meters in every room of the building).

1.1 Macro Analysis

In this section we describe a fault that we detected by analyzing the building's smart meter data.

---

*The authors would like to thank DeitY, Govt. of India and TCS for their generous support of this work.

When an inductive load turns on, it is characterized with a spike in the current drawn. However, one commonly detected anomaly is a spike of unexpectedly high amplitude that occurs periodically. Figure 1 shows one such occurrence that we noticed in our academic building. Thirty to sixty Ampere spikes occurring every three minutes and lasting two hours were observed on the second phase. Our previous experiments had helped create profiles of appliances typically used in the building. However, none of the appliance signatures contained spikes with these characteristics!

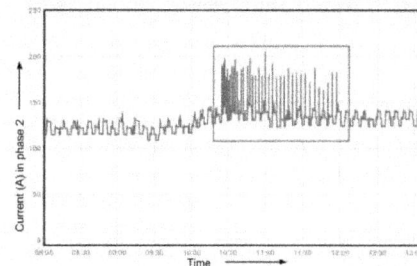

Figure 1: Periodic spikes with unexpectedly high amplitudes

On a non-working day, these spikes were observed again. Taking advantage of the low building occupancy, we were able to isolate the anomalous device: using the room occupancy log for the building, we inferred the list of occupied rooms. Further inspection showed that only one of them had heavy-duty inductive loads (in this case air conditioners), which might have caused the anomaly. We operated the sixteen ACs in the room sequentially until we identified the malfunctioning AC. (It is worth noting that our building is not centrally air-conditioned; each room/hall has one or more AC units, each operating independently.)

We found that the anomalous behavior was due to compressor overload trip, caused by compressor malfunction or non-function. One of the reasons for this is the locked rotor state of compressor. In a single phase compressor a capacitor is required to move the compressor from locked rotor state to running state. If the capacitor is faulty this doesn't happen and a huge current is drawn (about 4-6 times the norm). This causes the overload relay to trip. Following this, we replaced the capacitor in the AC and the spikes stopped occurring.

1.2 Micro Analysis

To reduce peak power consumption, we have deployed the Thermal Comfort Band Maintaining algorithm [1] to control the execution of the several ACs in our lab; this algorithm al-

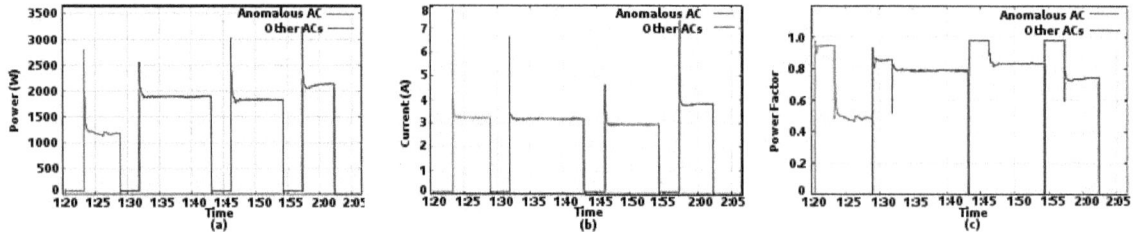

Figure 2: The power (a), current (b) and power factor (c) plots of the anomalous AC

lows only a subset of the ACs to operate at a time while still maintaining the thermal comfort level. Figure 2 (a) presents one instance of this execution where ACs run one after another. But we were surprised by the behavior of AC1, which showed a power consumption profile that is different from the others!

In order to find the cause of the anomaly, we plotted the current profiles for each of the ACs, as shown in Figure 2 (b) and were surprised to see that they were similar. This meant that for the ACs, either the supplied voltage or the power factor was different, inferred from the following relation:

$$Actual Power = V \cdot I \cdot \cos \phi$$

where $V = voltage$, $I = current$, $\cos \phi = power\ factor$

ACs powered by the same power source, receive the same supply voltage. However, a comparison of the power factors, as shown in Figure 2 (c), revealed that the misbehaving AC had a sub-optimal power factor.

We found that the anomalous AC had a coolant leak. The compressor in an AC converts the coolant from low pressure to high pressure, and moves the coolant through its refrigeration cycle. Lower amount of coolant implies lesser work for the compressor. Thus, the current drawn was not being efficiently converted to useful work, leading to a drop in the power factor.

This exercise led us to the following findings:

- To detect anomalies such as the one presented, *knowing parameters like voltage and power factor, in addition to knowing the current, is vital.* These can only be measured by smart meters, in contrast to other metering devices like clamp-on meters, which measure only current. This strengthens our choice of using a smart meter as a sensor to identify anomalies.
- Although macro-analysis can give us significant insights into the electrical consumption patterns and also help detect anomalies, its major drawback is that smaller changes in consumption patterns remain inconspicuous. For such cases, micro-analysis, at the sub-building level becomes essential.

2. SUB-OPTIMAL BEHAVIOR DETECTION

In a building, it is noticed that the base load, i.e., the load at zero occupancy, is not zero. This generally arises due to server rooms, since the servers and the air conditioners that maintain the right operating conditions for them run all the time. However, it is noticed that rooms other than server rooms show such behavior.

An analysis of our lab's electricity consumption data showed that at zero occupancy multiple computers were still running. Since all the computers in the lab are of the same make, we know the average consumption of a single computer (∼45W). For our lab, we had three computers running because they either host applications or act as database servers. Thus the average consumption at zero occupancy should have been around 135W (as shown in Figure 3). However, we were surprised to find that the average consumption at night, when the lab was unoccupied, was around 380W.

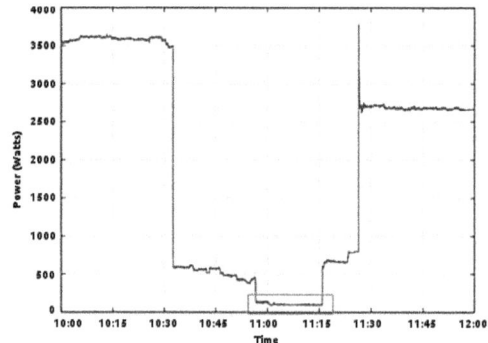

Figure 3: The aggregate usage data when three computers are running has been marked

A survey revealed that many users were leaving their computers on through the night. Further probing showed that the users, occasionally, access their computers remotely. However, given the low frequency of such occurrences, the excess energy usage is worth avoiding.

Having a common computer in the lab with a separate login for each of the users would drastically reduce power consumption while preserving user privacy. This way a user may remotely login to this centralized machine and perform necessary computations. Also, any other computer that is left on at zero occupancy can be queried and turned off.

3. CONCLUSION

We believe that the work described here is just the beginning in terms of exploiting the many facets of smart meter data analytics. We are currently working on algorithms to automatically detect anomalies and optimize usage using the smart meter data. We believe that in the presence of both tangible as well as virtual sensors in smart buildings, this data can be mined for extracting insights that will be useful not only for achieving energy usage optimization but also for fault isolation and identification and services optimization and consolidation among many others.

4. REFERENCES

[1] KARMAKAR, G., KABRA, A., AND RAMAMRITHAM, K. Coordinated scheduling of thermostatically controlled real-time systems under peak power constraint. In *Real-Time and Embedded Technology and Applications Symposium (RTAS), 2013 IEEE 19th* (2013), pp. 33–42.

Unobtrusive Power Proportionality for HPC Frameworks *

Arka Bhattacharya
University of California, Berkeley
arka@eecs.berkeley.edu

David Culler
University of California, Berkeley
culler@cs.berkeley.edu

ABSTRACT

Building power proportional High Performance Computing (HPC) clusters comprising of servers which are not power-proportional is a well-studied problem, and has the potential to provide large energy savings [2]. However, a large emphasis on maintaining cluster uptime disincentivizes system administrators from deploying prior research techniques that introduce changes to existing software configurations, modify the existing cluster job management framework, change user job submission procedures, or fail in unpredictable ways due to frequent server power cycling [3].

We present *Hypnos*, a meta-system that tackles the challenge of implementing power proportionality **unobtrusively** in an HPC cluster with an existing job management framework. Hypnos makes no changes to the existing cluster software or network stack, and uses only the standard interfaces exposed by the existing cluster framework to (a) obtain server state and job information, (b) add/remove servers from the existing framework's purview, (c) infer the cluster's scheduling logic, and (d) handle reliability challenges when servers fail to run jobs, boot up, or race conditions develop between Hypnos and the existing cluster scheduler.

We evaluated Hypnos by deploying it on a production HPC cluster running the framework - Torque [4]. Hypnos was able to achieve a 36% reduction in energy consumption (compared to an optimal of 37.5%) while circumventing over 1500 network and software faults over a 21-day deployment.

Categories and Subject Descriptors

C.4 [**Performance Of Systems**]: Reliability, availability, and serviceability; C.5.5 [**Performance Of Systems**]: Computer System Implementation—*Servers*

---

*For a full version of this work, refer to [1]. This work was funded by NSF Grants CPS-0932209 and CPS- 0931843.

Keywords

Power Proportionality; Unobtrusive; Meta-system; High-Performance Computing; Reliability

1. HYPNOS DESIGN

Hypnos uses the observation that most existing HPC job management frameworks (e.g Torque, Oracle Grid Engine, IBM Load Sharing Facility) expose three interfaces which allow unobtrusive power management - (a) An interface to add / remove servers from the cluster framework's purview (b) An interface exposing server state information, and (c) An interface exposing details of jobs submitted to the cluster and their constraints. Hypnos resides on the existing cluster framework's master node, and comprises of three modules - the Framework Interface Layer, a Server State Machine(SSM) and Failure Handler(FH) for each server, and the Power Management Algorithm(PMA).

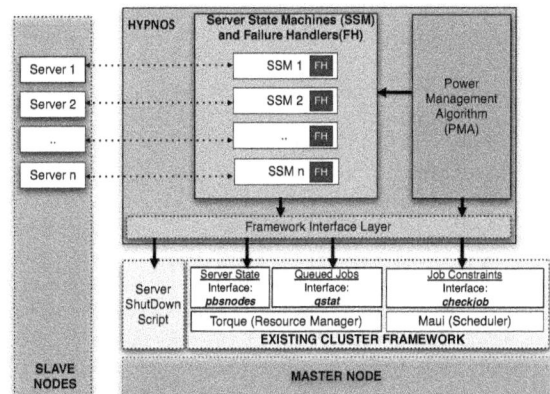

Figure 1: Hypnos System Design. The interfaces Hypnos uses on an HPC cluster running Torque is *pbsnodes*, *qstat* and *checkjob*. Other HPC frameworks have analogous interfaces which Hypnos could use.

Framework Interface Layer: This layer obtains the information required by the other Hypnos modules from the interfaces exposed by the cluster's job management framework, and can be re-written for different cluster frameworks. The Torque-specific interfaces used in our implementation is shown in Figure 1.

Power Management Algorithm(PMA): The PMA implements a wakeup and shutdown control loop using the job information obtained through the Framework Interface Layer and the server state information reported by the Server State Machines. The PMA wakes up servers if existing queued jobs cannot be bin-packed on to the set of already powered-up servers (or the set of servers that are currently waking up). The shutdown control loop shuts down servers in case they have been idling for more than a user-specified threshold, provided powering them down does not affect the cluster's minimum spinning-reserve[1] capacity.

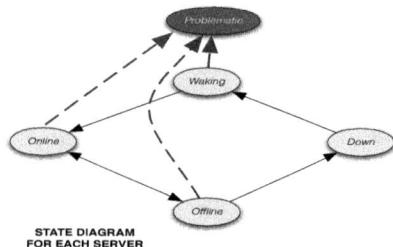

Figure 2: State Machine maintained for each server

Server State Machine(SSM), Failure Handler(FH): Hypnos utilizes the information obtained through the cluster framework's interfaces and the state transitions ordered by the PMA, to implement a Server State Machine (SSM) and a failure handler (FH) for each server. Each server can be in 5 possible states(Figure 2):

(a) `Online`: signifying that the server is powered up and is either executing jobs or is idle;

(b) `Down`: signifying that the server is powered off;

(c) `Offline`: a state a server goes through before it transitions to the `Down` state from the `Online` state. If a job has been scheduled on it due to a race condition between Hypnos and the existing cluster framework, the server is brought back to the `Online` state.

(d) `Waking`: is an intermediate transition state between `Down` and `Online` to account for the time elapsed between servers being commanded to power up and when they become ready to execute jobs.

(e) `Problematic`: signifying that Hypnos has inferred either (a) a failure which renders the server incapable of executing jobs, or (b) some discrepancy between the server's state as maintained by Hypnos and the information obtained from the cluster framework's interfaces. Such inference may happen when a server was presumed by Hypnos to be in the `Online`, `Offline` or `Waking` states. Depending on the state a server transitions to `Problematic` from, Hypnos considers the possible reasons for such a discrepancy, and gracefully handles them through that server's Failure Handler (FH) module. (For details, see [1])

Hypnos thus achieves *unobtrusiveness* by virtue of its meta-system design, where it sits on top the cluster's master node and only uses the interfaces exposed by the existing cluster framework. Hypnos achieves *reliability* by maintaining a state-machine for each server, and periodically corroborating its presumed state of the server with the information obtained from the cluster framework's interfaces. Hypnos is also *extensible*, due to the decoupling of the Framework

Interface Layer, the Power Management Algorithm, and the server-specific SSM and FH modules. The wakeup and shutdown control loops in the PMA can be optimized in isolation (without having to worry about reliability) to take into account cluster-specific workload features such as its diurnal patterns or its burstiness (e.g [5]).

2. EVALUATION

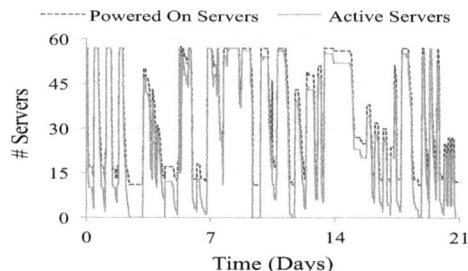

Figure 3: Number of servers kept powered-on closely matched the number of active servers when Hypnos was deployed

Hypnos was evaluated over 21 days on a 57-server cluster consisting of 51 Dell PowerEdge 1850 servers (192W idle / 292W peak), and 6 Dell PowerEdge 1950 servers (253W idle / 387W peak). It achieved a 36% energy savings (37.5% ideal), while serving over 3650 jobs and subverting over 1500 failures, such as a server failing to load essential networked services (e.g the Networked File System) or local filesystem errors which caused the inability of a powered-up server to run jobs. Figure 3 shows that Hypnos was able to power down idle servers, thus, closely matching the number of powered-up servers to the number of *active* servers (servers running jobs).

3. REFERENCES

[1] Arka Bhattacharya and David E. Culler. Hypnos: Unobtrusive power proportionality for hpc frameworks. Technical Report UCB/EECS-2014-29, EECS Department, University of California, Berkeley, Apr 2014.

[2] Luiz André Barroso and Urs Hölzle. The case for energy-proportional computing. *Computer*, 40(12):33–37, December 2007.

[3] Edmund B. Nightingale, John R. Douceur, and Vince Orgovan. Cycles, cells and platters: an empirical analysisof hardware failures on a million consumer pcs. In *Proceedings of the sixth conference on Computer systems*, EuroSys '11, pages 343–356, New York, NY, USA, 2011. ACM.

[4] Torque Resource Manager. http://www.adaptivecomputing.com/products/open-source/torque/.

[5] Kai Wang, Minghong Lin, Florin Ciucu, Adam Wierman, and Chuang Lin. Characterizing the impact of the workload on the value of dynamic resizing in data centers. In *ACM SIGMETRICS Performance Evaluation Review*, volume 40, pages 405–406. ACM, 2012.

---

[1]The spinning reserve is a set of idle servers kept powered up to service smaller/interactive HPC jobs

Is The Grass Greener? Mining Electric Vehicle Opinions

Tommy Carpenter
University of Waterloo
tcarpent@uwaterloo.ca

Lukasz Golab
University of Waterloo
lgolab@uwaterloo.ca

Sohail Javaad Syed
University of Waterloo
sjavaad@uwaterloo.ca

ABSTRACT

Electric Vehicles (EVs) are envisioned to play a large role in the transition from fossil fuel to renewables based transportation. However, their sales thus far are nominal compared to traditional car sales. It has been difficult for manufacturers to measure owners' initial perceptions in order to build improved vehicles more drivers are likely to adopt. Sentiments towards EVs have mostly been determined using either field trials or large surveys of drivers, both of which are problematic. We build a system that mines EV owners' sentiments from online forums. Our system has three main uses. First, it graphs the percentage of positive and negative opinions for each vehicle feature of interest, e.g., *battery capacity*, giving the user a high level product overview. There is currently no easily-consumable review system for EVs. Second, it allows the user to read opinions about the specific features they are most interested in without searching though irrelevant text. In our case study, we find only 3% of the comments on EV ownership forums express opinions on the features. The system therefore reduces the space of text the user must read by 97%, even assuming they wish to read all opinions about all features. Finally, in addition to mining the same perceptions found during expensive field trials, our system finds perceptions that were only realized after the owners possessed their EVs for an extended period of time, i.e., perceptions not available during shorter trials. The system extracts and classifies opinions with a precision and recall of ≈60%, which is on par or better than previous opinion mining systems.

Categories and Subject Descriptors

H.3.1 [**Information Storage And Retrieval**]: Content Analysis and Indexing—*Linguistic processing*

Keywords

Electric vehicles; sentiment analysis; opinion mining

e-Energy'14, June 11–13, 2014, Cambridge, UK.
Copyright is held by the owner/author(s). Publication rights licensed to ACM.
ACM 978-1-4503-2819-7/14/067 ...$15.00.
http://dx.doi.org/10.1145/2602044.2602050.

1. INTRODUCTION

As concerns over climate change and oil availability rise, most utilities and auto manufacturers are preparing for the introduction of electric vehicles (EVs) into the electrical and transportation systems. Major auto manufacturers such as Chevrolet and Nissan have introduced EVs into their product line, and there are now competing manufacturers that specialize in building EVs, e.g., Tesla Motors. However, the sales of these vehicles are currently insignificant compared to traditional car sales[1].

Manufacturers and researchers have traditionally employed two methods to understand drivers' mobility preferences and requirements, hoping to build improved models more drivers are likely to adopt. First, several organizations have held EV field trials where EVs were loaned to participants in exchange for their feedback. However, because vehicles are expensive and must be shared amongst participants, they are usually limited in both size and duration, thus conclusions are drawn from a small number of (still) inexperienced drivers. Second, some have conducted large online surveys to measure drivers' general perceptions towards EVs, but targeting similar surveys specifically to owners is difficult.

Owner perceptions are vital for manufacturers to build improved models more aligned with drivers' mobility preferences and requirements. We build a system that freely and automatically mines EV ownership forums (e.g., [4, 5]) for these opinions, which are buried in mostly irrelevant text. In our case study using a comprehensive list of EV features, adoption barriers, and a large corpus built from online forums, we find ≈97% of the corpus contains no opinions about any product features. Thus, it is laborious[2] to extract these opinions valuable to prospective buyers, marketers (for determining what features should be advertised) and manufacturers (for determining what features should be improved). With our system, users define the set of features they are interested in, and are presented with a list of positive and negative statements about only those features and several visualizations of this data.

Our main contributions are:

---

[1]In 2013 in North America, Tesla sold 22,450 Model S models, Nissan sold 22,610 Leaf models, and Chevrolet sold 23,094 Volt models [1, 2]. While these sales are largely increased from prior years ([3] gives EV sales per month and cumulative sales), they still represents < 2% of car sales.
[2]compared to, for example, the ease of buying a digital camera with hundreds of online numerical or star-based reviews

1. We extend previous review mining systems with several new optimizations and EV domain knowledge to build a powerful EV opinion mining system (Section 4).

2. We evaluate our system using a corpus of 330,000 sentences and a manually labeled corpus of 8,000 sentences containing product features. Using these corpora, we demonstrate the system's text reduction capability and its precision and recall (Section 5).

We have open-sourced our system for use [6] because many prior sentiment mining systems are unavailable.

2. TERMINOLOGY

In this paper we use the following notation:

- $\mathcal{P} = \{P_1, P_2, ...\}$ represents a *product space*.
- $\mathcal{F}^p = \{\vec{\mathbf{F}}_1^{\,p}, \vec{\mathbf{F}}_2^{\,p}, ...\}$ represents the *feature space* of $p \in \mathcal{P}$, where $\vec{\mathbf{F}}_i^{\,p}$ is a vector of synonyms describing feature i. For example, for the feature *fuel economy* this vector may be

  $< fuel\ economy,\ efficiency,\ gas\ mileage,\ fuel\ efficiency,\ mpg.. >$

- $\mathcal{O}$ represents the *opinion phrase space*, the set of all opinion phrases recognized.
- We refer to an opinion o about feature f as a (f, o) pair.
- Where appropriate, we abbreviate "neutral" with N, positive with $+$, and negative with $-$.

3. OVERVIEW AND RELATED WORK

Customers usually desire certain specifications or features when shopping for expensive products, especially vehicles. One buyer may seek performance while another may look for top safety ratings. For these reasons, we build a *feature-based opinion mining* (FBOM) system. In FBOM, the term "feature" refers to a product feature or attribute. Such a system is concerned with extracting and classifying individual opinionative statements about specific product features, rather than classifying text at the document level. There are five main phases in FBOM:

1. Building a text corpus to be mined

2. Defining or mining the product and product features of interest

3. Extracting sentence fragments from the corpus containing opinions about those features; these fragments denoted as (f, o) pairs.

4. Classifying each (f, o) pair as $\{+, N, -\}$

5. Aggregating results and computing various statistics

In this section, we first discuss previous field trials and surveys conducted to elicit EV opinions, and the problems with these approaches (Section 3.1). We then present work on adjective polarity classification (Section 3.2) and existing FBOM systems (Section 3.3).

3.1 Eliciting Electric Vehicle Opinions

Related work in determining drivers' opinions of EVs is split into two categories: field trials and surveys of non-EV owners. We discuss these works and their limitations here.

Various EV field trials that have taken place [7–15]. In these trials, participants were supplied with EVs and monitored. Monitoring consisted of drivers recording their trip information in travel diaries, surveys and interviews throughout the trials. In some cases, vehicles were also fitted with

GPS data loggers that recorded location and charging information. While field trials are useful for drawing conclusions about drivers' experiences with and perceptions towards EVs, they are subject to at least two limitations. First, field trials are expensive because multiple EVs must be purchased or leased for the trial. It is therefore expensive, especially for academic researchers, to conduct field trials with a large number of participants for significant durations. During short trials, drivers may not have time to adjust to driving EVs or have time to derive well-informed conclusions. Conclusions from field trials are consequently drawn from a small number of still-inexperienced drivers. Large (in terms of number of participants) and long (temporally) field trials are needed to resolve such issues. Second, some drivers stated they changed their normal driving habits during the trials to fully explore and "push" the vehicles' capabilities, thus the results may not indicate whether EVs are suitable for their "normal" driving behavior. This behavior is similar to the *Hawthorne effect*, which states subjects in an experiment often alter their behavior for the duration of an experiment [16].

Researchers and manufacturers have also conducted large online surveys [17–25]. In these surveys, drivers were asked about their perceptions towards EVs and their perceived advantages and disadvantages. Because these were not targeted specifically to EV owners, the respondents were mostly drivers with little or no experience with EVs. A benefit of conducting these surveys is that thousands of drivers can be interviewed at little or no cost. However, they only gauge drivers' general interest in adopting EVs and do not measure owners' perceptions.

3.2 Word and Sentence Polarity Classification

There are four main approaches to classifying opinion phrases. Work discussed here is not specific to FBOM but to sentiment classification in general.

1. *Lexicon methods* [26–33] start with a small set of classified *seed words*. These sets are then grown using synonyms derived from WordNet [34] or other glosses—for each word, the word's synonyms are added to the classified set, and this process is repeated as desired.

2. *Semantic methods* [35–38] classify the sentiments of words and sentences based not only on lexicons, but also on the semantic rules of the English language. For example, two adjectives joined by *and* are likely to share the same polarity, e.g., *sunny* and *beautiful*.

3. *Distance methods* [39–43] measure the polarity of a given word based on the *distance* of that word from a set of positive and negative seed words. Distance is normally computed via WordNet or by analyzing the co-occurence of words in a large corpus, with an example function being $d(word, good) - d(word, bad)$ where $d(x, y)$ gives the distance (computed via WordNet) from word x to word y. Another common distance measure is *pointwise mutual information* [44].

4. *Classification methods* [45–49] treat the problem of determining the polarity of opinion phrases as a machine learning problem. Rather than learning the sentiment of individual words, a classifier is trained to classify sentences directly. These authors manually label sentences, train a polarity classifier based on this labeled training data, and then classify sentences in the unlabeled data using the trained classifier.

Some opinion phrases are context-dependent and pose a challenge for opinion mining systems. Ding et al. [26] give an algorithm for querying the sentiment of such phrases. They first attempt to query all opinion phrases in a sentence using a lexicon approach. They then use an algorithm which considers syntactical constructs and the sentiments in neighboring sentences to classify unclassified phrases per these lexicons. We explain how our context-dependent handling differs in Section 4.5. Two other works have also studied classifying context-dependent adjectives [50, 51]. While we use a simpler approach then their methods, they provide avenues for extending our system in future work. Our system combines context-dependent adjective handling with a lexicon approach.

3.3 Feature-Based Review Mining

Hu and Lui define the concept of feature-based opinion mining [30] and introduce the first FBOM system, Opinion Observer [31]. Their system first builds $\mathcal{F}^p$, then finds and summarizes positive and negative opinions corresponding to each feature. The authors use a lexicon to determine the sentiment polarity of adjectives in sentences containing product features, then classify sentences based on the number of positive and negative words in a sentence. While we later show this approach is insufficient, the Opinion Observer system was the precursor to other FBOM systems.

In subsequent work, these authors improve their system. Hu and Lui [29] expand on the product feature identification phase. The authors present an association rule mining process to build $\mathcal{F}^p$. The mining process finds noun phrases (e.g., *digital camera*) that are likely to be product features. Pruning rules are used to trim the set of mined product features. Lui, Hu, and Cheng [31] further update their system to use supervised learning for detecting *implicit features*, e.g., *fast* refers to the feature *performance*. Finally, Ding, Lui, and Yu [26] update their system with a better sentiment classifier. For each feature f in a sentence, the authors compute a scoring function based on all adjectives in the sentence and their distance from f. Hence, if there are two features, the adjectives closest to each will influence their scores the most, but all adjectives have a non-zero contribution to the score of all features. This improvement better classifies (f, o) pairs than simply averaging the classification of all adjectives.

Scaffidi et al. [52] build a system called "Red Opal" which allows users to search for products based on the ratings of specific product features. Products are ranked feature-wise based on numerical review ratings, like those found on Amazon, rather than opinion words in the reviews. While the system achieves good results when numerical reviews are available (which they are typically on online retailers), it is not applicable to our problem as the system cannot mine forums, article comments, or other text.

Popescu and Etzioni [48] present a competing system to Hu's. Their system OPINE uses different algorithms for building $\mathcal{F}^p$ and mining/classifying (f, o) pairs. To mine (f, o) pairs, the authors use *syntactical templates* such as <feature> is <value>—if a sentence matches this pattern, (feature, value) is mined as an (f, o) pair. These syntactical templates motivated our use of *chunking* to parse (f, o) pairs, as further explained in Section 4.3. This resolves problems with Hu's system because not all opinions in a sentence are associated with every feature in the sentence. They use

statistics and classifier-based methods for classifying word sentiments, as opposed to Hu's lexicon based approach.

Jin et al. [49, 53] build a novel system called Opinion Miner. Their system trains a hidden Markov model (HMM) to find (f, o) pairs *and* classify them; the only work we know of to merge these two steps. The HMM is trained using linguistic constructs, syntactical templates, and word sentiments. The HMM learns to mine constructs such as "negative opinion about [feature]", instead of first finding (f, o) pairs and then separately classifying each pair. The authors manually tag certain constructs, then use synonyms, antonyms, linguistic constructs, and other bootstrapping techniques to grow the set of training examples for the HMM. Our system does not combine the mining and classification phases, but we plan to evaluate this merged approach in future work (see Section 7).

Zhang et al [54] use a graph mining approach to rank several products according to various product features. The authors divide opinionative sentences into two sets, those that express opinions on just one product (subjective), and those that compare two or more products (comparative). Products are treated as nodes in a "feature graph". Subjective sentences and their classification are used to weigh nodes, while comparative sentences and their classification are used to weigh edges between the two products being compared. Then a pageRank algorithm is used to rank the set of nodes according to the feature. In the future, when many EV models are sold and EV sales increase, this work may help compare several EV models.

Other researchers have improved upon these systems. Kobayashi et al. [55] suggest a domain-knowledge-driven feature and opinion phrase selection process, instead of the general association mining techniques offered by Hu et al. They introduce an iterative algorithm that generates candidate features and opinion phrases, and manually select those that are valid. In each iteration, more candidates are selected based on the prior iteration, and the process is repeated until an iteration goes by where the human selects no candidates. Zhuang et al. [37] present a case study of Hu's system using movie reviews. The authors incorporate domain knowledge using supervised learning into feature and opinion keyword mining. For example, they have several movie fans manually tag reviews for features, feature opinions, and cast members. Several other systems similar to these [56–58] have also been built, but the systems described above are representative of the various approaches taken in building FBOMs.

4. SYSTEM ARCHITECTURE

We now describe our opinion mining system.

4.1 Mining Overview

Our mining system is depicted in Figure 1. Forums are first crawled using Scrapy [59], a python web crawling framework, then subsequently cleaned (see Section 4.2) and split into individual sentences. Sentences are mined for (f, o) pairs using a process known as *chunking* (see Section 4.3). Sentence fragments containing (f, o) pairs, known as chunks, are then classified for sentiments (see Section 4.4, 4.5). Finally, the results are output. We note our system has several limitations; we propose improvements in Section 7.

This process builds upon previous work. Like Zhuang et al. [37] and Kobayashi et al. [55], we incorporate domain knowledge (DK) into our mining process, specifically in the

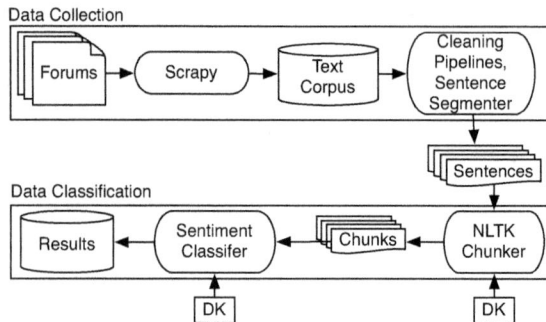

Figure 1: System Architecture

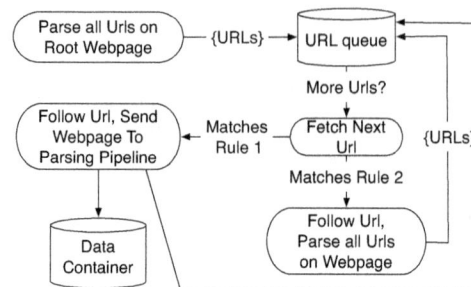

Figure 2: Recursive Scrapy Webcrawling

chunking and querying phases. For feature mining, a part of the chunking phase, we use Hu's association mining technique [29] and then manually prune and collapse the feature set like Kobayashi et al. [55]. We note this is feasible because there are fewer than one hundred common features one may talk about within the context of a car. For parsing sentences, our use of chunking is similar to using syntactical templates like Kobayashi, Popescu, and Zhuang [37, 48, 55], but more powerful (see Section 4.3.3). We use our own methods for the classification stage but partially rely on an open-source sentiment dictionary, the MPQA Opinion Corpus [60, 61]. Like Ding et al. [26], we handle context opinions, but we introduce two new constructs to handle context-dependent opinions (see Section 4.4).

4.2 Data Collection and Preprocessing

We use the Python Scrapy package [59] to collect EV reviews from the Web. Scrapy is a system in which the user writes *spiders* containing two sets of regular expressions (regex). Crawled URLs matching any expression in the first set are *content pages*, and are sent to a *parsing pipeline*. Crawled URLs matching any expression in the second set are *linking* pages which hold links to other (content & linking) pages. The recursive crawling process is depicted in Figure 2.

We preprocess the data before mining it. First, we remove all HTML tags and links. We then convert all characters to lowercase. Next, we iterate through a large list of common typos [62] and fix common misspellings. Finally, we iterate through a list of contractions [63] and expand them. This is done because words such as *not* are *valence shifters* which change the sentiment of opinion phrases as discussed in the following section.

4.3 Parsing Via Chunking

English is not a regular language [64], thus arbitrary English sentences cannot be parsed using regular expressions. Fortunately, most of the sentence constructs people use can be. In the following two sections, we describe our sentence parsing methodology, *chunking*, which works by grouping part of speech (pos) tags with regex. We also describe its advantages over prior work. To the best of our knowledge, we are the first work to use this parsing method.

4.3.1 NLTK Chunking

We use the Python NLTK (*Natural Language Toolkit* [65]) package to parse sentences using *chunking* [66], which makes use of regex to group word sequences with particular parts of speech (pos) together.

A context free grammar (CFG) is a set of production rules of the form $A \to B$, where this denotes A can be replaced with B in any "string" in the language. In the context of parsing natural language, CFGs state "replace instances of B with the higher-level notion of A". For instance, the rule <verb-phrase> $\to$ <subject><verb> replaces the tags <subject><verb> with <verb-phrase>. Chunking is simply an *extended CFG* (E-CFG), a CFG in which the right hand side of production rules can be regex. While E-CFGs provide no functional benefit over traditional CFGs—they describe exactly the same set of languages [67]—an infinite number of CFG production rules may be needed to express the same rule of an E-CFG [67]. The regex operators $\{+, *\}$ provide *compactness*—a way to specify an infinite number of patterns that greatly condense the set of needed rules.

To parse sentences using chunking, we first tag the sentences for pos (we use NLTK, but several tagging tools are available). This produces a list of tuples of the form $[(word_1, pos), (word_2, pos)...]$ for each sentence. We then define a NLTK *chunking grammar*, a series of regex executed on these tagged sentences that combines tuples into *chunks*. The expressions in the chunking grammar are executed in-order and are non-overlapping; that is, words consumed during one chunking will not be part of another chunk. Each expression attempts to match a sequence of tags. The standard regex tokens $\{*, ., +, ?\}$ can be used to capture arbitrarily long groups of tags, and allow for optional parts of speech. For example, the rule X:

$$X: \{\text{<}det\text{>}?\text{<}noun\text{>}\text{<}verb\text{>}+\text{<}adverb\text{>}*\text{<}adjective\text{>}+\}^3$$

chunks both *the (product-name) is really superb* and *my (product-name) has been reliable*.

The chunking grammar can include as many rules as desired. The most specific rules should be defined first in the grammar since rules are executed in order, and rules with the most flexibility (achieved through the use of the $\{?, +, *\}$ regex tags) should come last in the grammar. With a well-crafted grammar only a few rules are needed; all results presented in Section 5 come from a grammar with only six (albeit complex) rules.

4.3.2 Mining Features Using Domain Knowledge

The goal of the chunking phase is to mine (f, o) pairs. To find chunks containing features, during the tagging phase described above, sentences are searched for all synonyms for all features. Matches are tagged with a special <feature> tag which is included somewhere in every chunking rule.

---

[3] <det> refers to a *determiner* such as *this* or *my*

244

To build the feature space $\mathcal{F}^p$, we first manually create a *seed* set of features and define a few synonyms for each. We then use *word frequencies, collocations,* and *concordance,* to build and expand the sets above. We use basic word frequencies to generate candidate features missing from the seed feature set—if a noun has a high frequency, it is likely a feature or a feature synonym. We then manually review these results, because not all common nouns are features; e.g., *road* is quite common in our EV review database. Next, we use NLTK's collocation functionality, which produces bigrams and trigrams with high-scoring mutual information—sets of two and three words that often occur together. Multiple-noun features like *battery capacity* and non-adjective opinion phrases like *warranty issues* are found this way. Finally, we use NLTK's concordance functionality. Concordance shows the words surrounding each usage of the target word, e.g., *concordance("battery", k)* prints each occurrence of *battery* with the $k/2$ surrounding words on both sides. Manually reviewing concordance helps identify multi-word features.

Tagging and chunking also allows us to easily handle *implicit features,* words that are both features and opinion phrases. Before chunking a sentence, we replace the part-of-speech tags of implicit features with a special tag $<IF>$. Upon finding a tuple $(w, <\text{IF}>)$, we look up the the feature using w in an inverted dictionary that maps feature synonyms to features, and also use w as the opinion phrase. For example, we define *noisy* as a synonym for the feature *sound,* and also as a negative opinion for that feature.

4.3.3 Advantages Of Chunking

In this section, we provide intuition as to why chunking works better than methods used in prior work for mining (f, o) pairs. We briefly define the notion of *valence shifters* since it is integral to the following discussion—valence shifters are words that invert the semantic meaning of a sentence, such as *not,* as in *do not buy this.* Parsing and handling valence shifters is essential to any review mining system [35].

Prior work in FBOM uses one of two methods to classify (f, o) pairs. The first method is to compute a scoring function using the sentiment of adjectives in the sentence and their proximity to features or products. These methods are insufficient if used on a sentence-wide basis (as opposed to using the scoring function within one particular chunk, which we have not seen in prior work), because sentence structure plays a vital role in the meaning of sentences. Consider two simple sentences:

s_0 : {it does not have good [feature]}

s_1 : {the [feature1] is not good, but its [feature2] is excellent}

Sentences like s_0 are problematic for these methods because the feature is close to the positive opinion *good,* but the opinion is negative. Including rules such as "invert the sentiment if a valence shifter like *not* is found in the sentence" would incorrectly classify s_1 as negative for product2. The solution is to apply the valence inversion rule to only the first part of s_1. We iterate over tagged sentences and replace the part-of-speech tags of valence shifters, products, and features (as described above) with unique tags. These tags are then included in our chunking grammar rules; for example:

r_0 : {$<verb><valenceshft><$"have/has"$><opinion><feature>$}

r_1 : {$<feature><verb><valenceshft>?<opinion>$}

Using the discussed VS inversion rule, s_0 triggers r_0 which correctly classifies it as negative. Moreover, s_1, chunked as $[the\ (r_1),\ but\ its\ (r_1)]$ fails to trigger r_0 because the sentence structure does not match, triggers r_1 which correctly classifies it as negative for [product1], and triggers r_1 again which correctly classifies it as positive for [product2].

The second method used to mine (f, o) pairs in prior work is to parse sentences according to syntactical templates [37, 48, 55]. Chunking is a more expressive form of these templates. The chunking grammar allows templates to contain optional tags and repeated tags, which allows for a much more concise grammar. Theoretically, an infinite number of fixed syntactical templates may be needed to specify a single chunking rule, due to the power of the regex operators $\{+, *\}$. In practice, one of the most useful features of chunking is the allowance of optional tags. Rules with well-placed optional valence shifters and "filler" words can capture many sentence constructs in a single rule, e.g,

{$<valenceshft>?<opinion><$"with"$><det>?<article>?<feature>$}

matches all of "*no problems with the $<feat>$*", "*problems with my $<feat>$*", "*no issues with my $<feat>$*", etc.

Thus, chunking has advantages over scoring based methods and template based methods. Moreover, a scoring function can be used within each chunk; even though each chunk contains only one feature, it may contain multiple, sometimes conflicting opinion phrases. A scoring function can classify the chunk with respect to the feature by weighing each opinion phrase in the chunk.

Finally, we do not compare chunking to the HMM approach used by Jin et al. [49], as their system parses and classifies simultaneously while we do not merge these two steps.

4.4 Handling Context-Dependent Opinions

Before discussing our sentiment querying algorithm, we introduce two concepts to handle context-dependent opinions phrases (CDOPs)—phrases that change their sentiment given their context.

For some features, more or less is always better, e.g., *performance* and *price.* We refer to such features as *positively and negatively oriented features. Intensity modifiers* like *low* and *high* change their context when referring to such features. For example, note the orientations of the following (f, o) pairs:

$$(\text{Range, low}) \rightarrow -$$
$$(\text{Range, high}) \rightarrow +$$
$$(\text{Maintenance, low}) \rightarrow +$$
$$(\text{Gear, low/high}) \rightarrow N$$

$$\dots$$

For each feature of interest, we specify whether the feature is positively, negatively, or non oriented. We also maintain a list of intensity modifiers (many can be found in Paradis [68]) for querying the oriented features. We empirically find that most CDOPs are of this type, so correctly specifying the orientation of features correctly classifies most CDOPs.

Some opinion phrases which are not intensity modifiers can also change their sentiment given their context, for example *cheap quality* vs. *cheap price*. Given this, we define a *product-feature sentiment dictionary*, $S_{f \in \mathcal{F}^p}^{p \in \mathcal{P}}[o \in \mathcal{O}]$, for each {product, feature} pair (p, f). These dictionaries are small and only contain phrases that have a sentiment when referring to (p, f) that is different than the sentiment it holds when used in other contexts. They produce a label when queried with an opinion phrase o if o is defined to be context-dependent for that feature, or "unknown" otherwise:

$$S[Car, \ Quality](cheap) \rightarrow -$$
$$S[Car, \ Price](cheap) \rightarrow +$$
$$S[Car, \ Performance](awesome) \rightarrow \text{unknown}$$

We perform a laborious but worthwhile domain knowledge (DK) input process to build these dictionaries. In addition to manually adding CDOPs into these dictionaries, we label a portion of the training data and use our system to classify these sentences. We print opinion phrases that are found in both correct and incorrect sentences, because if a phrase is missing from a feature-specific dictionary, it is likely classified correctly for some features and incorrectly for others. We then manually review these results and iterate this process several times, each time adding phrases into the appropriate dictionaries.

4.5 Sentiment Querying

When querying the sentiment of a (f, o) pair, several rules are checked in order. Whenever a rule triggers, a sentiment label is returned and the rest of the rules are not checked.

1. If o is an intensity modifier and f is an oriented feature, we use the following sub-rules, one of which must trigger:

$$(o : +, f : +) \rightarrow \text{return } +$$
$$(o : +, f : -) \rightarrow \text{return } -$$
$$(o : -, f : +) \rightarrow \text{return } -$$
$$(o : -, f : -) \rightarrow \text{return } +$$

2. If querying the product-feature sentiment dictionary S_f^p returns a label, the label is returned.

3. If querying the *default sentiment dictionary* (see below) returns a label, the label is returned.

4. Return neutral (N).

This process always returns a label, because if rules 1-3 fail to trigger, N is returned. If the 4th rule triggers, it is likely that the opinion phrase is seldom used or misspelled—after modifying the freely available MPQA Opinion Corpus [60, 61], our default sentiment dictionary contains over 6,800 opinion phrases.

We now compare our handling of context-dependent opinions with Ding et al.'s. Their algorithm sacrifices classification accuracy for improved recall, because they first query opinion phrases using lexicons, and then treat *all* unknown phrases (per these lexicons) as context-dependent and attempt to classify them as such. However, many adjectives are simply neutral, and using their algorithm to classify all neutral phrases leads to *over-classification*, since some of their rules will trigger even when the phrase was neutral. We take the opposite approach and under-classify, because we would rather mine fewer sentences with high accuracy (there are no shortage of opinions online) than many sentences inaccurately. Since all phrases in the feature-specific dictionaries are manually added context-dependent phrases, if line 2 returns a label, it can only be wrong if there is a

parsing or tagging error. Moreover, if line 2 does not return a label, one of two cases must hold—either the phrase is not context-dependent, or the phrase is missing from the dictionary. In the former case, the phrase is classified as normal in the default dictionary. In the latter, a classification error may occur, but this is uncommon because the space of CDOPs that are *not* of the intensity-modifier type is small.

4.6 Other Optimizations

Here we detail various optimizations designed to improve the accuracy of our opinion mining system.

1. We find many sentences (which we were incorrectly classifying) implicitly ask a question or talk about a hypothetical scenario. Words and phrases such as *wondering*, *curious*, and *as long as* were common in sentences that containing an opinion phrase but do not express an opinion, such as *I am curious as to whether the battery lasts a long time*. We use 16 such phrases we manually found and classify all sentences containing these as neutral.

2. Other words nullify opinions only within a chunk; we classify chunks containing such words as neutral, but process other chunks in the sentence as normal. Words like *can*, *may*, and *will* state something will hold in a particular situation, or offer a suggestion, such as "driving too fast may decrease your battery efficiency"; this sentence is not expressing a sentiment, but rather offers a suggestion.

3. Words such as *costs* make classification difficult because they are used in different contexts. Adding *costs* as a synonym for the feature *price* leads to poor accuracy, because too many sentences refer to the cost of something other than the vehicle, e.g., *electricity is cheap*. However, if it is used near the feature *car*, the sentence is likely referring to the *price* of the vehicle. We implement dictionaries of *feature changers*; words that when used near one feature indicate the sentence is referring to another feature. As another example, the word *handles* near the feature *car* indicates that the sentence is not a general sentiment about the car, but rather referring to the car's *performance*.

4. We use a list of "nullifying-synonyms", words near features that indicate the sentence is not actually referring to any feature of interest (in contrast to those just discussed that indicate the sentence is referring to a different feature). For example, if the phrase *12 volt* occurs near the feature *battery*, the sentence is probably referring to the smaller battery in the vehicle, and not the main EV battery.

5. Our mining system handles non-adjective opinions (NAOs) such as *disgrace* and *problem*, whereas most previous work does not. We maintain a list of NAOs, and define the sentiment of these words/phrases. Before chunking a sentence, we replace the tags of words contained in this list with a special tag, and include this special tag in our chunking grammar in the same places we include the tag for an adjective. As an example, *complaint*, while not an adjective, often expresses a negative opinion.

5. EVALUATION METHODOLOGY

Here we discuss our system evaluation methodology. We first define our evaluation metrics (Section 5.1), then our corpora generation (Section 5.2) and definitions used in our results (Section 5.3).

5.1 Evaluation Metrics

Let

- c_f^+, c_f^- represent the number of sentences about feature f classified as $+,-$.
- $\star\left(c_f^+\right), \star\left(c_f^-\right)$ represent the number of sentences classified as $+,-$ for feature f that we also classify as $+,-$ for feature f. We stress "for feature f" because it is possible, and common among classification errors, that the label is correct but the opinion phrase is referring to a different feature.
- t_f^+, t_f^- represent the number of sentences about feature f in the corpus that we classify as $+,-$.

Our two evaluation metrics, *opinion precision* and *opinion recall*, compute for each feature f are defined as:

$$\text{precision}(f) = \frac{\star\left(c_f^+\right) + \star\left(c_f^-\right)}{c_f^+ + c_f^-}$$

$$\text{recall}(f) = \frac{\star\left(c_f^+\right) + \star\left(c_f^-\right)}{t_f^+ + t_f^-}$$

Precision penalizes for incorrect classifications while recall penalizes for failing to mine (f, o) pairs. Chunks misclassified as $(+/-)$ are reflected in precision, and $(+/-)$ chunks classified as neutral are reflected in recall.

5.2 Experimental and Ground Truth Corpus Generation

For our experimental evaluation, we crawled the owner discussion forums for the two best selling EVs—the Nissan Leaf [5] and Chevrolet Volt [4] ownership forums. We crawled every forum post existing on both sites as of February 1st 2013. This led our *experimental corpus* containing 107,293 Volt sentences and 220,906 Leaf sentences. We then classified this corpus using our system which filtered out all sentences containing no features. This left 10,519 Volt sentences and 19,799 Leaf sentences. Next, we sampled a random ≈25% of these and manually labeled them. This led to a *ground truth corpus* containing 2,566 Volt sentences and 5,514 Leaf sentences that contain at least one feature.

We note that due to our labeling methodology, our measure of recall is not "true recall", because we first filter out all sentences which contain no synonyms in our feature set. However, some sentences may refer to a feature implicitly or using a rare synonym. While we include some implicit features and many feature synonyms, we cannot exhaustively include all. To measure true recall, we would randomly read a portion of the experimental corpus without first filtering. However, due to the large percentage of sentences that contain no features ($> 90\%$ as shown), we hypothesize this may lead to very few classified sentences and hence be a wasteful effort. Given this, we believe first filtering out sentences which do not contain any feature synonyms is reasonable.

5.3 Definitions

Here we define the non-obvious features of electric vehicles used in our graphs:

- *General* refers to any opinion referring to the *car* itself and not a specific feature, such as *this car is amazing*.
- *Range anxiety* is the term given to EV drivers' fear of being stranded en route to their destination due to a lack of range and charging.

- Current EV batteries (Lithium Ion) lose capacity over time as they are repeatedly charged and discharged, and if they are subjected to extreme temperatures [69]. *Degradation* refers to the effect of charging and climate on a batteries capacity and life.
- We denote anything related to heating and cooling, including features such as heated seats and pre-warming (warming the EV while it is still plugged in at home), as *HVAC*.
- *Carwings* [70] and *Onstar* [71] are products included with the Leaf and Volt respectively that provide various feedback, charging, and safety services to drivers.
- *MiscFeats* refers to a mix of other features including regenerative breaking and navigation systems.

6. RESULTS

We now describe our evaluation results. We claim our system has three main benefits:

- The system graphs the percentage of positive and negative opinions for each feature, giving the user a high-level product overview. This is not currently available for prospective EV buyers.
- The system significantly reduces the space of text the user must read if he or she is interested in determining what other drivers thought about various features.
- The system measures EV owners' perceptions towards EVs. These perceptions include those drawn from expensive field trials in addition to perceptions that were only realized after owning the vehicle for an extended prior of time.

In the following three sections, we support these claims. We then discuss our system's accuracy and recall in Section 6.4. We note the results shown are for the ≈25% of the corpus we manually labeled (as discussed in §5.2) as the ground truth corpus—we do not present any unverified results from the unlabeled segment of the corpus.

6.1 High Level Polarity Breakdown

The polarity of sentences in the ground truth corpus is shown in Figures 3 and 4. There are three bars for each feature. The first shows the polarity distribution of sentences we classified (c^+, c^-, c^N), the second shows the distribution of those correctly classified $\left(\star\left(c^+\right), \star\left(c^-\right), \star\left(c^N\right)\right)$, and the last shows the distribution of ground truth sentences (t^+, t^-, t^N). The numbers above the bars show the number of sentences containing that feature. Examining these figures quickly gives the user a high-level view of opinions about the various product features.

6.2 Text Reduction

Figures 3 and 4 also demonstrate the text reduction capability of our system. As discussed in Section 5.2, our experimental corpus contains ≈ 330,000 sentences but only ≈10% contain at least one feature. Moreover, we see in Figures 3 and 4 that ≈ 70% of sentences containing a feature are neutral (based on our random sampling). Extrapolating from these metrics, we hypothesize only $330,000 * .1 * .3 = 9,900$ of the original sentences contain positive or negative opinions about a feature. This results in a ≈97% reduction of text compared to searching through the forums, even if the user wishes to read every opinion about every feature.

Leaf Polarity Breakdown

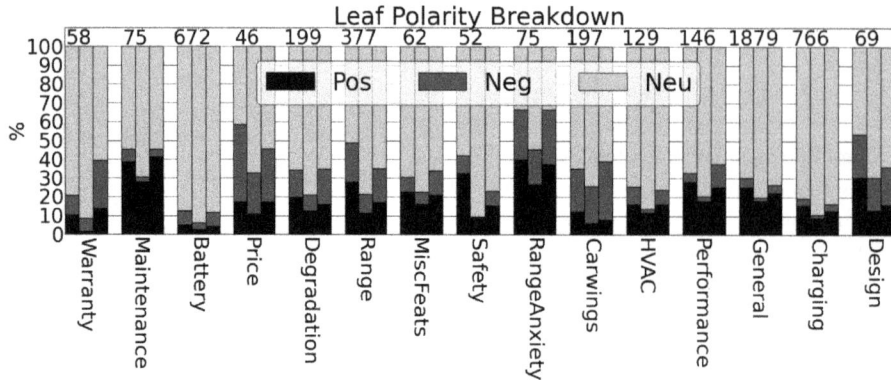

Figure 3: Leaf polarity breakdown

Volt Polarity Breakdown

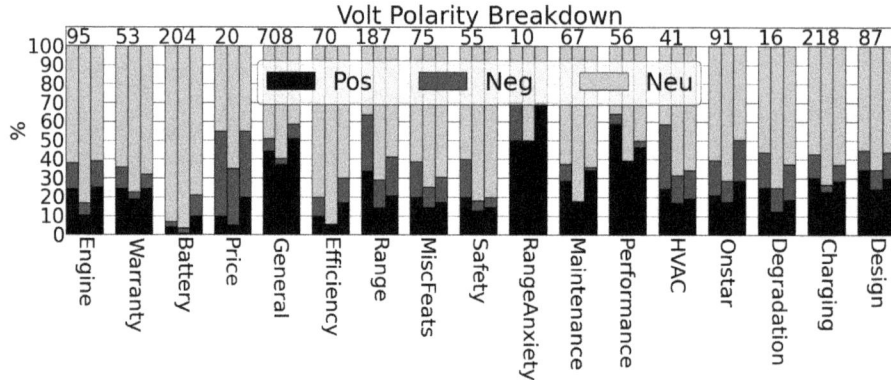

Figure 4: Volt polarity breakdown

Leaf Performance Metrics

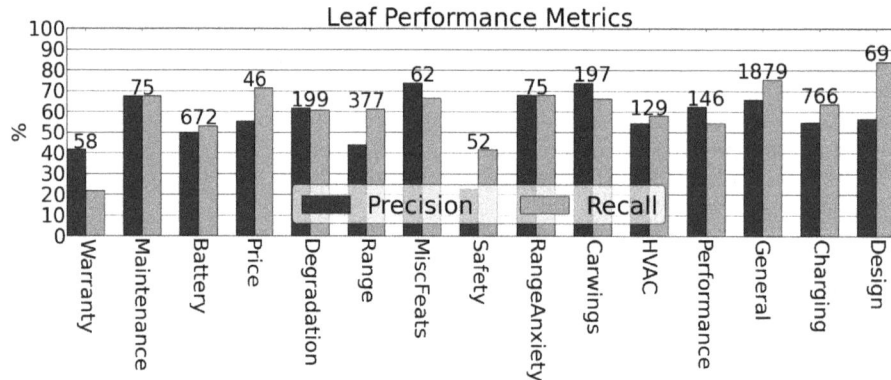

Figure 5: Leaf performance metrics

Volt Performance Metrics

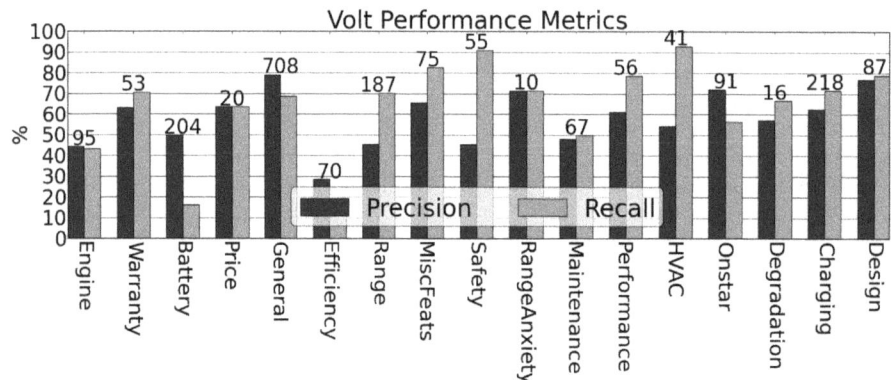

Figure 6: Volt performance metrics

6.3 Insights

We present some insights derived by examining Figures 3 and 4 and reading the classified sentences.

Several mined perceptions support conclusions from field trials and driver surveys. *Price* and *range anxiety* are commonly cited as the two largest EV adoption barriers [69]; Figures 3 and 4 support this hypothesis. For the Leaf, a battery electric vehicle (BEV) that contains no gasoline engine like the Volt, the majority of sentiments about range and range anxiety are negative. Sentiments on range anxiety for the Volt are positive because the Volt is designed to eliminate range anxiety (it has a gasoline engine in addition to the battery). For price, the majority of sentiments for both products are negative (note that there are few sentiments included for price; this problem is discussed in §6.5). *Maintenance* is commonly cited as a major selling point of BEVs—the absence of an engine means fewer moving parts that can fail and less fluids to change. From Figure 3, we see that sentiments towards maintenance for the Leaf are overwhelmingly positive. Field trials often conclude that participants enjoy the EV *charging* process compared to the refueling process—we also find that sentiments towards charging are positive for both vehicles. Reading the classified sentences reveals that many drivers receive free charging at work, have little need for public charging and are thus not concerned about the lack of public charging stations, and live in areas with time-of-day electricity pricing so they are able to charge overnight cheaply. As a final example, the majorly positive sentiments for the *general* category reveals some expected early adopter bias. While many drivers may express concern about the set of features they dislike, most end their discussions with comments like "*... but I love my Leaf*".

We are also able to derive insights that were only perceived after the owners had their vehicles for a significant duration of time. Such insights are not possible to elicit from field trials. The most important such example is owners' experience with *battery degradation*, the effect of repeated charging and climate on battery capacity over time. While it is known that climate and charging cycles affect battery life, it is unknown to what extent this is the case [69]. We find that some owners are experiencing non-trivial battery degradation and about 50% of sentiments towards degradation are negative. Manufacturers can use these sentiments in unison with the owners' location (if available on the forum) to derive conclusions about the effect of climate on battery capacity, e.g., we find that owners in hot regions such as Arizona and southern California post more often about degradation. Closely related are sentiments on *warranty*, which are mostly negative, because some owners have filed for battery replacements through battery warranties against capacity loss. Reading classified statements from warranty and maintenance reveals other vehicle problems of interest to manufacturers, such as the replacement and maintenance rate of various parts. These problems may not appear in shorter duration field trials. We end by noting we are currently implementing the tracking of owners' sentiments over time as further discussed in §7. Field trials have attempted to determine how perceptions change over time, for example, by interviewing participants both before and after the trial. However, because individual participants in trials are often only given a vehicle for a few weeks or months, their opinions may not change as much as they would over a period of years. Thus, tracking owners' opinions over time online can

reveal insights about how perceptions change with vehicle experience on a longer scale.

6.4 Performance Metrics

Figures 5 and 6 show the precision and recall of our system on the ground truth corpus. The sum over both products equals the size of the ground truth corpus ($\approx$8,000 sentences). The performance is on par with or better than prior FBOM systems discussed in Section 3.3. In the next section, we show several examples of both solvable and unsolvable classification errors; the English language is simply too ambiguous and complex to mine without error.

While our results are on par with prior opinion mining systems, we emphasize two of our contributions. First, prior FBOM systems have focused on products for which easily consumable reviews *are* available. For example, Hu and Lui [30] focus on digital camera reviews, Kobayashi et al. [55] focus on movie reviews, and Scaffidi et al. [52] focus on any product with numerical reviews. While these authors contribute to mining opinions on specific features, a useful addition for consumers, an easily-consumable review system of some form exists for these products (e.g., Amazon and IMDB). We present the first work on mining opinions for a new product for which text has thus far been the main review medium. Moreover, if EVs are not improved and customer adoption barriers are not solved, there may never be a comprehensive database of EV reviews. Second our system is open source [6], and the package includes our domain knowledge input and all manually built lists and dictionaries. Future researchers or users that wish to extend the system have a comprehensive starting point. In contrast, the three closest prior systems are either closed source or unavailable—Opinion Miner is proprietary [53], the Opinion Observer system turned into the proprietary OpinionEQ [72,73], and the OPINE system was never released by the authors.

6.5 Insightful Classification Errors

We present here a few problematic sentences because they give insight into the complexities of opinion mining.

Some features are hard to mine or classify opinions for. For example, our system performs poorly on classifying opinions related to *safety*. We find the word *issue* is heavily overloaded but used often—in some instances it is used synonymously with *hazard*, such as *that is a safety issue!*, and in other cases it is used synonymously with *feature*, e.g., *grounded charging is a safety issue*. Our system also performs poorly on classifying *warranty* opinions for similar reasons. For example, it is difficult to tell programmatically when the phrase *not covered* is used as a negative or neutral sentiment. Sometimes posters state facts with this phrase, e.g., *the windshield is not covered in your warranty*, and other times to express frustration, such as *the repair was not covered by my warranty*. Moreover, notice that *price*, even though it is cited as a major adoption barrier, has very few comments. We find too many posts comment on the price of something other than the price of the vehicle, such as the price of charging and electricity. After experiencing a high rate of classification errors regarding this feature, we tuned our system to only classify a chunk as referring to *price* if the chunk contained both a synonym of *price and* a synonym of *General* such as *car, Volt, Leaf*, etc. This led to a tradeoff: from Figures 5 and 6 we see our system performs well with respect to precision and recall for *price*, but

Sentence	Class	Tr	Problem	Solution
The standard warranty is more than enough.	N(Warranty)	+	more than enough not recognized as an opinion	add it to the DSD
My Carwings sometimes hangs.	N(Carwings)	−	hangs not recognized	add it as − to the Carwings FSD
This car is a blast to drive!	−(General)	+	blast is context dependent	add it as + to the General FSD
The dealer showed me how to perform the recommended maintenance	+(Maintenance)	N	recommended is context dependent	add it as N to the Maintenance FSD
Capacity loss is greatest at the beginning of the battery's life.	+(Degradation)	N	greatest is context dependent	add it as N to the Degradation FSD
I love my Audi, it is a great car.	+(General)	N	Subject error	classify chunks w/ other popular car names as N; see Sec. 4.6 number 2
I had a low battery warning.	−(Battery)	N	warning is context dependent	classify chunks w/ this phrase as N
It has a 5 star safety rating.	N(Safety)	+	5 star not recognized	add it as + to the Safety FSD
The hot weather kills my range.	N(Range)	−	kills, a verb, not recognized as an opinion	add it as a non-adjective opinion to the Range FSD.

Table 1: Solvable errors. "FSD" denotes "feature-specific dictionary", and "DSD" refers to the default sentiment dictionary

Sentence	Class	Tr	Problem
"It was charge free."	+(Charging)	N	poster is not referring to charging but rather the price of something. However, sometimes posters talk about free charging.
The Volt is the best car ever and I will never go back to a crude ICE	−(General)	+	ICE most often refers to the Volt's ICE, but sometimes to non hybrid vehicles in general.
My new radio has far less degradation near mountains.	+(Degradation)	N	here the poster is referring to radio signal degradation; static near mountains, power lines, or tunnels.
It felt like the engine was on.	+(Engine)	N	like is a tough word. Even within the context of one feature, it can be used as a comparator or as a positive sentiment (more common).
I love everything about this car, with the exception of the exterior.	N(Exterior)	−	Chunking error. We find most opinions do not "cross over" commas, hence commas are not included in chunking rules. Here the valence shifter "exception" loses the opinion to negate—love, since it is not in the chunk.

Table 2: "Better left unsolved" errors

Sentence	Class	Tr	Problem
The Leaf handles 99% of my annual driving."	N(General)	?	Should this be +? What's the +/− Cutoff?
I get around 80 mpg."	N(Efficiency)	?	Should this be + for Efficiency? Cutoff?
The Leaf is very easy to push.	+(General)	?	This might mean the poster's car died, or something related to performance/handling?
Level 2 charging is very efficient.	+(Charging)	?	Should this be +? The poster may either be happy with their charging experience or just stating a fact.
I never worry about my mileage.	+(Efficiency)	?	Is the poster stating a fact or that they have plenty of range?
I am sad my Volt is in for maintenance.	−(Maintenance)	?	is the poster disappointed the car requires maintenance, or are they stating they miss driving their car?

Table 3: Subjective ambiguity errors

the number of classified sentences to draw conclusions from is small. Conversely, our system classifies *General* opinions well for both products, for which there are many. This is because sentences expressing general sentiments are often clear and brief, e.g., *I love my Leaf!* and *this is an excellent car*.

Table 1 shows examples of errors fixable by updating the feature-specific sentiment dictionaries, updating the default sentiment dictionary, or other adding other domain knowledge (DK) as shown. Others errors are "better left unsolved"—tuning the system to correct these creates larger problems elsewhere. Sometimes a feature synonym is used in two different contexts, e.g, "ice" can refer to an engine (Internal Combustion Engine) or the weather condition. We set the system according to which usage is most common, but errors will occur when the word is used in the less common context. Others represent chunking errors where changing the chunking grammar to fix the error caused more problems in other sentences because the offending sentence structure is uncommon. Finally, some words are context-dependent even

within the context of one feature. We accept such errors, exampled in Table 2, as necessary due to the ambiguity and complex structure of English. Finally, some ambiguous sentences can be classified differently by different human readers. Some correspond to a parameter which sounds positive to some, such as "100 miles per gallon", but for which it is hard to impose a strict cutoff for which all human readers agree, e.g., "all mileages over X are positive". Others are ambiguous sentences that could be classified in either direction. Examples of such errors are shown in Table 3.

7. CONCLUSIONS & FUTURE WORK

Understanding EV owners' experiences with and perceptions towards EVs is helpful for manufacturers to build later-generation models more aligned with drivers' mobility preferences and requirements. Unfortunately, it is expensive to conduct field trials and difficult for researchers to distribute surveys specifically to EV owners. We build an opinion mining system that classifies opinions found in EV ownership forums. Our system helps the user obtain a high-level overview of opinions on various product features, and greatly reduces the space of text the user is required to read to extract opinions. These opinions are useful to prospective buyers, marketers (what features should be advertised?) and manufacturers (what features should be improved?). To build this system, we combine prior opinion mining systems with several new optimizations and our EV domain knowledge. We furthermore open sourced our system for extension by other researchers, as we find most prior opinion mining systems are unavailable. We end with several avenues for extending and improving our work:

1. At the time of system implementation, Tesla's sales were still well nominal compared to Nissan's and Chevrolet's EV sales. However, Tesla's Model S sales are now nearly equivalent (see footnote 1). We thus plan to add Tesla support to our system.

2. We are working to see how sentiments change over time by analyzing sentiments periodically, e.g., monthly. It would be interesting to see how perceptions change with vehicle experience and whether sentiments fluctuate with gas, electricity, and vehicle prices. It is possible to see the temporal change for individual owners if they post using a user name, and for owners that post anonymously, we can examine how collective sentiments change.

3. We do not currently perform pronoun resolution. A poster may explicitly mention a feature in one sentence and then write several more opinionative sentences about the same feature using pronouns easily resolved by a human reader. Our system only categorizes opinionative sentences where an explicit or implicit feature is found. Pronoun resolution, while difficult, may be used to infer the features being discussed.

4. We aggregate data for each individual product in a separate database. When mining for product p, we assume all (f, o) pairs found in the database for p refer to p. This produces erroneous results when a poster discusses another product in their post. Future work should detect the product being discussed from the context.

5. We do not perform spam or malicious text detection. We treat all sentences equally even though some may contain sentences injected by malicious sources, such as drivers who oppose a particular brand, or advertisements posted by spamming bots.

6. Our methods for building the feature-specific dictionaries and lists of oriented adjectives are simple; we use pre-built lists and manually add others. This part of our system can be improved using recent work in the field of classifying context-dependent adjectives [50, 51].

7. We do not distinguish between chunks referring to one product and chunks comparing two products like Zhang et al [54]. Modifying the chunking grammar to include comparative templates may reduce classification errors.

8. In all but one prior FBOM systems, (f, o) mining and classification are distinct phases, hence we adopt this approach. However, Jin et al. [49], merge these two phases. In future work we will evaluate this combined approach.

8. REFERENCES

[1] A. Ohnsman, "Tesla rises after model s sales in 2013 exceed forecast," 2014. Accessed March 29th 2014. http://www.bloomberg.com/news/2014-01-14/tesla-delivered-6-900-cars-in-fourth-quarter-executive-says.html.

[2] J. Voelcker, "Plug-in electric car sales for 2013 near double previous year's," 2014. Accessed March 29th 2014. http://www.greencarreports.com/news/1089443_plug-in-electric-car-sales-for-2013-almost-double-last-years.

[3] Electric Drive Transportation Association, "Electric drive sales dashboard," 2014. Accessed March 29th 2014. http://electricdrive.org/index.php?ht=d/sp/i/20952/pid/20952.

[4] "Forum: Volt ownership forum." http://gm-volt.com/forum/forumdisplay.php?16-Volt-Ownership-Forum.

[5] "My Nissan Leaf Discussion Forums." http://www.mynissanleaf.com/.

[6] T. Carpenter, "A Python Electric Vehicle Sentiment Analysis System." http://www.tommyjcarpenter.com/code/evsentiment.html.

[7] L. Bunce, M. Harris, and M. Burgess, "Charge up then charge out? Drivers' perceptions and experiences of electric vehicles in the UK," *Transportation Research Part A*, vol. 59, Jan. 2014.

[8] A. Everett, M. Burgess, M. Harris, S. Mansbridge, E. Lewis, C. Walsh, and S. Carrol, "Initial Findings from the Ultra Low Carbon Vehicle Demonstrator Programme," *Technology Strategy Board Report*, 2011.

[9] S. Pichelmann, T. Franke, and J. F. Krems, "The Timeframe of Adaptation to Electric Vehicle Range," *Lecture Notes in Computer Science*, vol. 8005, no. Chapter 69, 2013.

[10] T. Franke and J. F. Krems, "What drives range preferences in electric vehicle users?," *Transport Policy*, vol. 30, Nov. 2013.

[11] T. Franke, F. Bühler, P. Cocron, I. Neumann, and J. F. Krems, "Enhancing sustainability of electric vehicles: A field study approach to understanding user acceptance and behavior," *Advances in Traffic Psychology*, 2012.

[12] T. Turrentine, D. Garas, A. Lentz, and J. Woodjack, "The UC Davis MINI E Consumer Study," *University of California Davis Institute of Transportation Studies Report*, vol. UCD-ITS-RR-11-05, 2011.

[13] E. Graham-Rowe, B. Gardner, C. Abraham, S. Skippon, H. Dittmar, R. Hutchins, and J. Stannard, "Mainstream consumers driving plug-in battery-electric and plug-in hybrid electric cars: A qualitative analysis of responses and evaluations," *Transportation Research Part A*, vol. 46, no. 1, 2012.

[14] S. Carroll, "The Smart Move Trial: Description and Initial Results," *Centre of Excellence for Low Carbon and Fuel Cell Technologies Report*, 2010.

[15] K. Kurani, "Plug-In Hybrid Electric Vehicle (PHEV) Demonstration and Consumer Education, Outread, and Market Research Program," *University of California Davis Institute of Transportation Studies Report*, vol. UCD-ITS-RR-09-21, 2009.

[16] R. Macefield, "Usability Studies and the Hawthorne Effect," *Journal Of Usability Studies*, vol. 2, May 2007.

[17] K. Lebeau, J. V. Mierlo, P. Lebeau, O. Mairesse, and C. Macharis, "Consumer attitudes towards battery electric vehicles: a large-scale survey," *International Journal of Electric and Hybrid Vehicles*, vol. 5, no. 1, 2013.

[18] R. M. Krause, S. R. Carley, B. W. Lane, and J. D. Graham, "Perception and reality: Public knowledge of plug-in electric vehicles in 21 U.S. cities," *Energy Policy*, vol. 63, Dec. 2013.

[19] O. Egbue and S. Long, "Barriers to widespread adoption of electric vehicles: An analysis of consumer attitudes and perceptions," *Energy Policy*, vol. 48, Sept. 2012.

[20] Deloitte, "Unplugged: Electric vehicle realities versus consumer expectations," *Deloitte Report*, 2011.

[21] S. Musti and K. M. Kockelman, "Evolution of the household vehicle fleet: Anticipating fleet composition, PHEV adoption and GHG emissions in Austin, Texas," *Transportation Research Part A*, 2011.

[22] A. Peters and E. Dütschke, "How do Consumers Perceive Electric Vehicles? A Comparison of German Consumer Groups," *Journal of Environmental Policy & Planning*, Jan. 2014.

[23] EPRI, "Characterizing Consumers' Interest in and Infrastructure Expectations for Electric Vehicles:Research Design and Survey Results," *EPRI Report*, 2010.

[24] Deloitte, "Gaining traction: A customer view of electric vehicle mass adoption in the U.S. automotive market," *Deloitte Report*, 2010.

[25] Ernst & Young, "Gauging interest for plug-in hybrid and electric vehicles in select markets," *Ernst & Young Report*, 2010.

[26] X. Ding, B. Liu, and P. S. Yu, "A Holistic Lexicon-Based Approach to Opinion Mining," *WSDM*, 2009.

[27] A. Esuli and F. Sebastiani, "Determining Term Subjectivity and Term Orientation for Opinion Mining," *EACL*, 2006.

[28] S.-M. Kim and E. Hovy, "Determining the Sentiment of Opinions," *COLING*, 2004.

[29] M. H. Liu and Bing, "Mining Opinion Features in Customer Reviews," *AAAI*, 2004.

[30] M. Hu and B. Liu, "Mining and Summarizing Customer Reviews," *KDD*, 2004.

[31] B. Liu, M. Hu, and J. Cheng, "Opinion Observer: Analyzing and Comparing Opinions on the Web," *WWW*, May 2005.

[32] A. Esuli and F. Sebastiani, "PageRanking WordNet Synsets: An Application to Opinion Mining," *ACL*, 2007.

[33] A. Esuli and F. Sebastiani, "SENTIWORDNET: A Publicly Available Lexical Resource for Opinion Mining," *LREC*, 2006.

[34] "WordNet: a lexical database for English." http://wordnet.princeton.edu/.

[35] A. KENNEDY and D. INKPEN, "Sentiment Classification of Movie Reviews Using Contextual Valence Shifters ," *Computational Intelligence*, 2006.

[36] V. Hatzivassiloglou and K. R. McKeown, "Predicting the Semantic Orientation of Adjectives," *ACL*, 2012.

[37] L. Zhuang, F. Jing, and X.-Y. Zhu, "Movie Review Mining and Summarization," *CIKM*, 2006.

[38] A. Andreevskaia and S. Bergler, "Mining WordNet for Fuzzy Sentiment: Sentiment Tag Extraction fromWordNet Glosses," *Annual Meeting of The European Chapter of The Association of Computational Linguistics*, 2006.

[39] H. Takamura, T. Inui, and M. Okumura, "Extracting Semantic Orientations of Words using Spin Model," *ACL*, 2005.

[40] M. Taboada, C. Anthony, and K. Voll, "Methods for Creating Semantic Orientation Dictionaries," *LREC*, 2006.

[41] P. D. Turney, "Thumbs Up or Thumbs Down? Semantic Orientation Applied to Unsupervised Classification of Reviews," *ACL*, 2002.

[42] P. D. Turney and M. L. Littman, "Measuring Praise and Criticism: Inference of Semantic Orientation from Association," *ACM Transactions on Information Systems*, 2003.

[43] M. Gamon and A. Aue, "Automatic identification of sentiment vocabulary: exploiting low association with known sentiment terms," *The ACL workshop on feature engineering for machine learning in NLP*, 2005.

[44] E. Terra and C. L. A. Clarke, "Frequency estimates for statistical word similarity measures," in *NAACL*, vol. 1, 2003.

[45] T. Wilson, J. Wiebe, and R. Hwa, "Just how mad are you? Finding strong and weak opinion clauses," *AAAI*, 2004.

[46] M. Gamon, A. Aue, S. Corston-Oliver, and E. Ringger, "Pulse: Mining Customer Opinions from Free Text," *Intelligent Data Analysis*, 2005.

[47] A. Esuli and F. Sebastiani, "Determining the Semantic Orientation of Terms through Gloss Classification," *CIKM*, 2005.

[48] A.-M. Popescu and O. Etzioni, "Extracting Product Features and Opinions from Reviews," *HLT*, 2005.

[49] W. Jin, H. H. Ho, and R. K. Srihari, "OpinionMiner: A Novel Machine Learning System for Web Opinion Mining and Extraction," *KDD*, 2009.

[50] M. Tsytsarau and T. Palpanas, "Disambiguating Dynamic Sentiment Ambiguous Adjectives," *Proceedings of the 23rd International Conference on Computational Linguistics*, 2010.

[51] M. Wen and Y. Wu, "Mining the Sentiment Expectation of Nouns Using Bootstrapping Method," *IJCNLP*, 2011.

[52] C. Scaffidi, K. Bierhoff, E. Chang, M. Felker, H. Ng, and C. Jin, "Red Opal: Product-Feature Scoring from Reviews," *EC*, 2007.

[53] OpenDover, "Opinion Miner." http://www.opendover.nl/opinion-miner-0.

[54] K. Zhang, R. Narayanan, and A. Choudhary, "Voice of the Customers: Mining Online Customer Reviews for Product Feature-based Ranking," *WOSN*, 2010.

[55] N. Kobayashi, K. Inui, Y. Matsumoto, K. Tateishi, and T. Fukushima, "Collecting Evaluative Expressions for Opinion Extraction," *IJCNLP*, 2004.

[56] M. Eirinaki, S. Pisal, and J. Singh, "Feature-based opinion mining and ranking," *Journal of Computer and System Sciences*, vol. 78, no. 4, 2012.

[57] B. A. Ojokoh and O. Kayode, "A feature-opinion extraction approach to opinion mining," *Journal of Web Engineering*, vol. 11, no. 1, 2012.

[58] S. Mukherjee and P. Bhattacharyya, "Feature Specific Sentiment Analysis for Product Reviews," *Lecture Notes in Computer Science*, vol. 7181, 2012.

[59] "Scrapy." http://scrapy.org/.

[60] T. Wilson, "Mpqa opinion corpus." http://www.cs.pitt.edu/mpqa/.

[61] T. A. Wilson, *Fine-grained Subjectivity and Sentiment Analysis: Recognizing the Intensity, Polarity, and Attitudes of Private States*. PhD thesis, University of Pittsburgh, 2008.

[62] "Wikipedia: Lists of common misspellings/for machines." http://en.wikipedia.org/wiki/Wikipedia: Lists_of_common_misspellings/For_machines.

[63] "Wikipedia:list of english contractions." http://en.wikipedia.org/wiki/Wikipedia: List_of_English_contractions.

[64] A. Clark, C. Fox, and S. Lappin, eds., *The Handbook of Computational Linguistics and Natural Language Processing*. Blackwell Handbooks in Linguistics, John Wiley & Sons, 2010.

[65] "NLTK 2.0 documentation." http://nltk.org/.

[66] "Nltk: Extracting information from text." http://nltk.googlecode.com/svn/trunk/doc/book/ch07.html.

[67] J. Albert, D. Giammarresi, and D. Wood, "Normal form algorithms for extended context-free grammars," *Theoretical Computer Science*, vol. 267, 2000.

[68] C. Paradis, *Degree modifiers of adjectives in spoken British English*. Lund studies in English, Lund University Press, 1997.

[69] A. G. Boulanger, A. C. Chu, S. Maxx, and D. L. Waltz, "Vehicle Electrification: Status and Issues," *Proceedings of the IEEE*, vol. 99, June 2011.

[70] Nissan Carwings. http://www.nissanusa.com/innovations/carwings.article.html.

[71] OnStar. https://www.onstar.com/web/portal/home.

[72] OpinionEQ, "Sentiment Analysis with Unmatched Accuracy." http://www.opinioneq.com/.

[73] B. Liu and M. Hu, "Opinion Mining, Sentiment Analysis, and Opinion Spam Detection." http://www.cs.uic.edu/~liub/FBS/sentiment-analysis.html.

Online Welfare Maximization for Electric Vehicle Charging with Electricity Cost

Zizhan Zheng and Ness B. Shroff
Department of Electrical and Computer Engineering
The Ohio State University
{zheng.497, shroff.11}@osu.edu

ABSTRACT

The accelerated adoption of EVs in the last few years has raised concerns that the power grid can get overloaded when a large number of EVs are charged simultaneously. A promising direction is to implement large scale automated scheduling of EV charging at public facilities, by exploiting the time elasticity of charging requests. In this work, we study the problem of online EV charging for maximizing the total value of served vehicles minus the energy cost incurred. In contrast to most previous works that assume a fixed capacity constraint while ignoring the electricity cost, we adopt a convex cost model for the system operator together with a concave valuation model for the vehicle owners. We design an online algorithm for balancing the two and prove a bound on its competitive performance for a general class of valuation and cost functions.

Categories and Subject Descriptors

I.2.8 [**Problem Solving, Control Methods, and Search**]: Scheduling; I.1.2 [**Algorithms**]: Analysis of algorithms

Keywords

Electric vehicle charging; deferrable load control; online algorithms

1. INTRODUCTION

The past few years have witnessed increasing interest in Electrical Vehicles (EVs) including both plug-in hybrid electric vehicles (PHEVs) and fully electric vehicles, driven by the advances in battery technology and the necessity of reducing carbon emissions and dependence on petroleum. It is projected that the adoption of EVs is likely to accelerate in the next decade. For instance, the U.S. government calls for deploying 1 million PHEVs by 2015 [17], and a recent Gartner report estimates that by 2020, 10% of all vehicle sales will be EVs [13].

The accelerated adoption of EVs, however, leads to the concern that when a large number of EVs are charged simultaneously in a local area, which is likely to happen in the near future, the local power grid can easily get overloaded. To address the problem, a promising direction is to investigate large scale automated scheduling of EV charging [1, 8, 10]. The key observation is that vehicle owners often exhibit some flexibility in their charging requests, including the time period of getting charged, and in the case of PHEVs, the total amount as well. By exploiting the statistical multiplexing gain and the time elasticity of charging requests, coordinated charging can greatly improve energy efficiency while meeting the utility of vehicle owners. Such a scheme can be implemented in public areas such as parking garages and working places, as envisioned in [8].

In this work, we study the problem of online EV charging for maximizing the total value of served vehicles minus the energy cost incurred. As in [10, 18, 19], each request is characterized by a time window that models the time elasticity of the vehicle owner, a concave function that models the non-increasing marginal valuation for incremental unit of electricity, and a charging rate limit. Moreover, we model the energy cost at any time as a convex function of the total load at that time. The convex cost model has been widely adopted for modeling energy cost, and reflects the fact that each additional unit of power for meeting the increased load is more expensive to obtain [14, 16].

We have designed an online algorithm to this problem that requires no knowledge of future requests while achieving a comparable efficiency as the optimal offline solution. Our analysis is built upon a recently developed primal-dual framework for competitive analysis of online algorithms [6, 12], while allowing a more general class of utility and cost functions. In addition to EV charging, our study applies to welfare maximization of other types of resources where the demand side has a concave utility and exhibits time elasticity, while the supply side incurs a convex cost, e.g., scheduling of computing tasks in a data center and allocating bandwidth in a communication network.

There are several online algorithms designed for coordinated EV charging [7,8,10,19]. In [10], a greedy algorithm is proposed for maximizing the total valuations of vehicle owners subject to a capacity constraint of the distribution network. To cope with the strategic behavior of selfish agents, the algorithm is extended to an online mechanism by allowing some pre-allocated units to be burned. The approach is further extended in [19] to allow multiple charging rates. In another direction, the problem of EV charging with commitment is considered in [7, 8], where each agent requests a fixed amount of resource, and a request has to be either accepted or rejected at its arrival time. A penalty is incurred if an accepted request is not fulfilled by the deadline.

However, most previous works on EV charging assume a capacity constraint while ignoring the electricity cost. One exception is [8], where a linear cost is considered together with a linear valuation. For a large system with high peak load, however, it is often more expensive to generate the supplementary power for meeting the peak load, and a convex cost model better reflects the real cost of electricity [14, 16]. On the other hand, the problem of minimizing a convex energy cost for serving deferrable electric load has also been considered, under the assumption that all the requests have to be satisfied in full [14]. In practice, however, the charging demand of an EV often exhibits some flexibility in terms of the total amount needed, which is better captured by a concave valuation function. Moreover, the approach in [14] does not provide any worst-case performance guarantee. Our approach generalizes these two extreme cases by modelling flexibilities in both the demand and the supply, a better reflection of the reality, while ensuring a performance bound even in the worst-case. In the o ine setting, welfare maximization for electrical load management with general concave valuations and convex costs has been considered in [16]. However, the problem has not been studied in the *online* setting to the best of our knowledge. In a di erent context, a recent work considered the problem of pricing a set of items with general production cost to a sequence of buyers to maximize social welfare or profit [3]. The approach does not apply to expiring resources like electricity and does not consider the time elasticity of demand.

Our main contribution can be summarized as follows.

- We develop an online algorithm that balances the total value of served vehicles and the total energy cost for charging.

- For continuous charging rate (and under some further assumptions to be defined precisely in Section 4), we establish a performance bound of our online algorithm compared with the optimal o ine algorithm, based on a characterization of the concavity (resp. convexity) of the valuation functions (resp. cost functions). We further study the competitive performance of our algorithm for concrete examples of valuation and cost functions.

- Simulation results show that our algorithm achieves close to optimal performance even when the charging rate is discrete, compared with the optimal o ine solution with continuous charging rate.

The remainder of this paper is organized as follows. We present the system model and the welfare optimization problem in Section 2. Our online algorithm is developed in Section 3, where we also present two heuristics as baselines. The competitive performance of our algorithm is studied in Section 4. We evaluate our algorithm in Section 5, and conclude the paper in Section 6.

2. SYSTEM MODEL AND PROBLEM FORMULATION

In this section, we discuss our system model and major assumptions made, and present the optimization problem to be studied.

Consider a system operator that manages multiple charging points. As in [10, 19, 20], we assume that there are enough charging points so that no agent needs to wait to be charged. A time-slotted system is considered. In any time-slot t, the operator incurs a cost $g_t(z_t)$ for serving a total amount z_t (kWh) of charging request. Note that $g_t(\cdot)$ may vary over t in general. We assume that $g_t(\cdot)$ is non-decreasing and convex, $g_t(0) = 0$, and $g_t(\cdot)$ is known to the operator [1]. Let $\mathcal{N} = \{1, ..., N\}$ denote a set of agents, each operating a single EV on behalf of its owner. Each agent i is described by its *type* $\theta_i = (f_i, a_i, d_i, X_i, Y_i)$, where $f_i(\cdot)$ specifies its valuation function, X_i denotes its maximum charging rate, i.e., the maximum amount of electricity that i can charge in any time-slot, and Y_i is the maximum amount of electricity that i would like to obtain, beyond which, there is no extra value. Agent i arrives at the beginning of time-slot a_i, and departs by the end of time-slot d_i, and obtains a valuation $f_i(y_i)$ if it receives a total amount of electricity y_i on departure. Such a total energy requirement model with continuous service rate has been used in [1, 9] for modeling energy demand of EVs and other deferrable electric loads. As in [19], we assume that $f_i(\cdot)$ is non-decreasing and concave, and $f_i(0) = 0$ for any i. Note that Y_i can be incorporated into the definition of f_i. We choose to separate them for the sake of clarity. We assume that the agents always report their true types on their arrivals. Extension of our online algorithm to a truthful online mechanism will be part of our future study. Let $D = \max_i(d_i - a_i + 1)$ denote the maximum time elasticity of any requests.

Agents are sorted by their arrival times (ties are broken arbitrarily). Let T denote the last departure time, i.e., $T = \max_{i \in \mathcal{N}} d_i$. Let x_{it} denote the amount of electricity that agent i obtains at time t, and let $\mathbf{x} \triangleq \{x_{it} : 1 \leq i \leq N, 1 \leq t \leq T\}$. Our objective is to maximize the social welfare of both the system operator and the customers, that is, the total valuations of customers minus the total electricity cost:

$$\max_{\mathbf{x}} \quad \sum_{i=1}^{N} f_i(\sum_{t=1}^{T} x_{it}) - \sum_{t=1}^{T} g_t(\sum_{i=1}^{N} x_{it})$$
$$\text{s.t.} \quad 0 \leq x_{it} \leq X_i, \qquad \forall i, t,$$
$$x_{it} = 0, \qquad \forall i, t \notin [a_i, d_i],$$
$$\sum_{t=1}^{T} x_{it} \leq Y_i, \qquad \forall i.$$

We note that the o ine problem is a convex optimization problem, which can be solved to any accuracy in polynomial time for a large class of f and g. Our objective, however, is to study the problem in the more challenging online setting, where agents of di erent types arrive on the fly, and at any time t, the system operator only has the information of agents that are currently in the system and that have left the system by t. Our objective is to design online algorithms that are competitive with respect to the optimal o ine algorithm. An online algorithm is q-competitive for some $q \geq 1$ if it achieves at least $1/q$ of the optimal o ine social welfare in the worst case [4].

As we will discuss in Section 4, our analysis focuses on the continuous setting when f_i and g_t are continuously di erentiable, and x_{it} are continuous. However, our algo-

---

[1] At any time t, it is sufficient for our algorithm to know $g_\tau(\cdot)$ for $\tau \in \{t, t+1, ..., t+D-1\}$, where $D = \max_i(d_i - a_i + 1)$.

Table 1: Notation List

$\mathcal{N}$	Set of agents (charging requests)
N	Total number of requests
T	Last departure time
g_t	Cost function at time t
$c_{t,k}$	Marginal cost for serving the k-th unit at time t
z_t	Total amount of electricity consumed at time t
f_i	Valuation function of agent i
$v_{i,k}$	Marginal valuation of the k-th unit for agent i
a_i, d_i	Arrival time, departure time of agent i
θ_i	Type of agent i, where $\theta_i = (f_i, a_i, d_i, X_i, Y_i)$
D	$\max_{i \in \mathcal{N}}(d_i - a_i + 1)$
x_{it}	Amount of electricity given to agent i at time t
y_i	Total amount of electricity given to agent i
X_i	Maximum charging rate of agent i
Y_i	Maximum amount of electricity required by agent i
δ	Charging unit
γ	Revocation coefficient

rithm applies to more general forms of f_i and g_t, and to the discrete case when the values of x_{it} need to be a multiple of some charging unit δ. In the discrete case, we define $v_{i,k} = f_i(k\delta) - f_i((k-1)\delta)$ as the k-th *marginal valuation* to agent i. Then we have $f_i(y_i) = \sum_{k=1}^{\lfloor y_i/\delta \rfloor} v_{i,k}$. The concavity of f_i implies that $v_{i,k} \geq v_{i,k+1}, \forall i, k$. Hence, a discrete valuation function can be equivalently defined as a vector of marginal valuations. Similarly, we define $c_{t,k}$ as the k-th marginal cost for the cost function g_t. The convexity of g_t then implies that $c_{t,k} \leq c_{t,k+1}, \forall t, k$. Note that the continuous case can be viewed as an extreme of the discrete case when $\delta \to 0$. To simplify the notation, we also use marginal valuation (cost) to denote the derivative of a continuous valuation (cost) function. Simulation results show that our algorithm achieves close to optimal performance even when x_{it} are discrete, compared with the continuous offine optimal (note that in general, it is NP-hard to find the optimal (offine) solution in the discrete case).

In our analysis and evaluation, we will consider the following commonly adopted valuation and cost functions as examples (our analysis applies to more general f and g). For cost functions, we will consider $g_t(z_t) = c_t z_t^\alpha$ for some $c_t > 0$ and $\alpha \geq 1$, where c_t varies over time, which has been widely adopted for modeling energy cost [14]. We also consider two extensions to this model that incorporate free renewable energy and base load, respectively (see Section 4.3). For valuation functions, we will consider $f_i^1(y_i) = v_i \log(1 + y_i)$ and $f_i^2(y_i) = v_i y_i^\beta$ for $v_i > 0$ and $\beta \in [0,1]$. Note that when the parameter v_i is identical for all the agents, f_1 and f_2 are closely related to the well-known notions of proportional fairness and α-fairness [15], respectively.

3. ONLINE ALGORITHMS

In this section, we present our online algorithms for the EV charging problem. We first consider the case when f and g are continuously differentiable, and x_{it} are continuous. Extensions to more general f and g and to discrete x_{it} will be discussed at the end of the section. We start with two simple online solutions adapted from existing algorithms proposed in related settings [12, 19] (Section 3.1). A careful study of these algorithms reveals their weakness in our context. They also serve as baselines in our simulations (see Section 5). We then propose a more sophisticated solution in 3.2.

3.1 Two Simple Algorithms

The first algorithm we consider is adapted from an online algorithm for a multi-speed EV charging problem proposed in [19], where instead of the electricity cost, a capacity constraint is considered. The objective is to maximize the total valuations of all the agents subject to a constraint on the total amount that can be served at any time. For any agent i, let y_{it} denote the total amount of electricity that agent i received by time t. An agent i is *active* at time t if $t \in [a_i, d_i]$ and $y_{it} < Y_i$. The online algorithm greedily serves the active requests in each time-slot as follows. At any time t, active agents are served in a non-decreasing order of $f_i'(y_{it})$ subject to the capacity constraint and the charging rate limit of each agent. Let z_t denote the current load at time t. To adapt this algorithm to our problem, we observe that when electricity cost is introduced, it is beneficial to serve agent i at time t only if $f_i'(y_{it}) > g_t'(z_t)$. We therefore modify the algorithm as follows.

Per-Time Allocation (PT): At each time t, active agents are served in a non-decreasing order of their marginal valuations, subject to their charging rate constraint. The process repeats until $\max_i f_i'(y_i) \leq g_t'(z_t)$.

Note that PT does not exploit time elasticity explicitly. As an illustrative example, consider a system of three agents, and assume $g_t(z_t) = 0.5z_t^2$ for all t. Agent 1 and 2 arrive at time 1, where $\theta_1 = (1.5y_1, 1, 2, 1, 1)$ and $\theta_2 = (1.5y_2, 1, 1, 1, 1)$ (see Figure 1 (a)). Since the two agents have the same marginal valuation, they can be served in any order. Assuming they are served with equal chance, each of them receives 0.75 units in the first time-slot, so that the marginal valuation of each agent equals to the marginal cost in the first time-slot, both equal to 1.5. Agent 2 then departs at the end of time-slot 1 and agent 3 arrives at the beginning at time-slot 2 where $\theta_3 = (2y_3, 2, 3, 2, 3)$. Note that at time 2, agent 3 receives 2 units while agent 1 (still in the system) is not served as it has lower marginal valuation than agent 3. Finally, at time 3, agent 3 receives 1 more unit since $Y_3 = 3$ and then departs. The total welfare achieved can be computed as $1.5 \times (0.75 + 0.75) + 2 \times 3 - 0.5 \times (1.5^2 + 2^2 + 1^2) = 4.625$.

The second algorithm that we consider is originally proposed for serving computing tasks using a single machine with speed scaling [21]. In this context, each job requires certain amount of CPU cycles, and the power consumption at any time is a function of the processor speed. The objective is to minimize the total energy consumption for serving all the requests (partial fulfillment is not beneficial) subject to their deadline constraints. We consider the greedy online algorithm recently proposed in [12]. In contrast to PT, a plan is made for each request at its arrival time to exploit the time elasticity of requests. The algorithm can be interpreted in our context as follows. A schedule is found for each request at its arrival time, which remains fixed for its entire lifetime in the system. To serve agent i, the time slots in $[a_i, b_i]$ of minimum load (given the current allocations made) are first considered, subject to the charging rate constraint. The process repeats until i's request is satisfied. The algorithm then moves on to the next agent. A simple approach to adapt this algorithm to our setting is to stop allocation for agent i when $f_i'(y_i) \leq \min_{\tau \in [a_i, b_i]} g_\tau'(z_\tau)$.

On-Arrival Allocation (OA): At each time t, for each agent i that arrives at t, the load of all the time slots $\tau \in [a_i, d_i]$ with minimum $g_\tau'(z_\tau)$ are increased for serving i, sub-

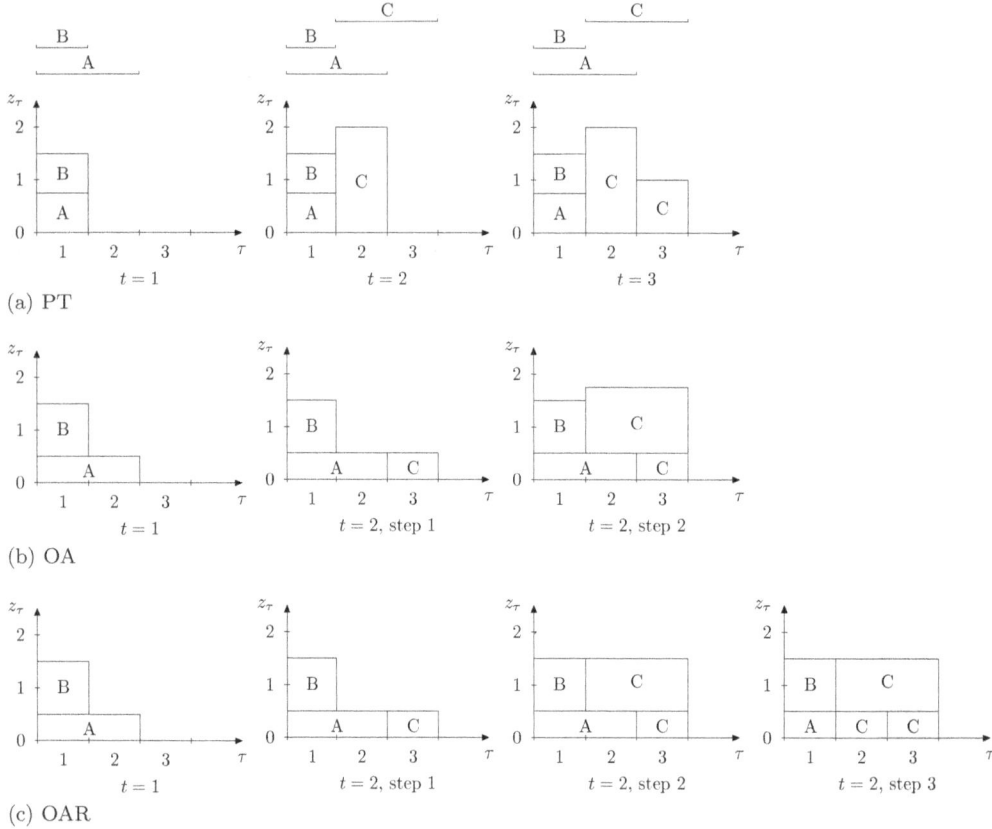

Figure 1: An example of EV charging with three agents.

ject to the charging rate constraint, until $f_i'(y_i) \leq \min_{\tau \in [a_i, b_i]} g_\tau'(z_\tau)$.

Consider the three agent example again. In the beginning of time-slot 1, a plan is made for agent 1 first. Agent 1 receives 0.5 unit in time-slot 1 and 0.5 unit in time-slot 2 (see Figure 1(b)). Agent 2 then receives 1 unit in time-slot 1. When agent 3 arrives at time 2, time-slot 3 is first considered for serving agent 3 as it has the minimum load. Once the load of time 3 increases to 0.5, the load of time-slot 2 increases together with that of time-slot 3 until agent 3 receives its maximum required amount of 3 units, with 1.25 unit served in time 2 and 1.75 unit served in time 3. The total welfare achieved in this case is $1.5 \times (1 + 1) + 2 \times 3 - 0.5 \times (1.5^2 + 1.75^2 + 1.75^2) = 4.8125$.

Discussion: The main problem with the PT algorithm is that the time elasticity of requests is largely ignored. In particular, the algorithm tends to serve requests as fast as possible subject to the charging rate constraint, which can lead to a high cost. Consider a simple example with m agents of the same type $\theta_i = (y_i, 1, m, 1, 1)$, and $g_t(z_t) = 0.25z_t^2$ for all t. Then PT will serve all the agents in the first $m/2$ time-slots, with two agents served together in each of these time-slots, leading to a welfare of $m - m/2 = 0.5m$. On the other hand, in the optimal solution, each agent is served 1 unit in a different time-slot, leading to a welfare of $m - 0.25m = 0.75m$. This result can be made worse when the marginal cost is smaller. In general, we expect that PT performs worse when the average time elasticity is high and traffic load varies over time (so that the time elasticity can potentially be exploited), which is confirmed in

our simulations. The example reveals that instead of making decisions for each time-slot separately, a plan for the future is needed to reduce the cost.

On the other hand, the OA algorithm tends to reduce electricity cost by making a plan for each agent as early as possible. However, since a schedule for each request is fixed at its arrival time and cannot be modified for its entire lifetime, it can prevent future requests with higher marginal valuations from being served. This can happen especially when the system load is relatively high. For instance, consider the three agent example in Figure 1(b) again. The key observation is that the welfare can be improved if part of the allocation to agent 1 can be revoked to serve agent 3. Note that the decision for agent 3 is made at the beginning of time 2, where the allocation for agent 1 at time 2 can still be modified. In making the scheduling decision for agent 3, when the load of both time-slots 2 and 3 increase to 1.5, the marginal cost in both time slots equals to the marginal valuation of agent 1. Starting from that point, instead of further increasing the load, it is more efficient to displace the allocation made for agent 1 at time 2 and reassign the units to agent 3 (see Figure 1(c)). The total welfare is then improved to $1.5 \times (1 + 0.5) + 2 \times 3 - 0.5 \times (1.5^2 \times 3) = 4.875$.

3.2 An Online Algorithm with Revocation

Based on the above discussion, we then design an online algorithm that combines two key ideas: (1) for any request, a tentative schedule that looks into the future is needed for exploiting the time elasticity of requests; (2) tentative allocations made for existing requests should be revocable for serving new requests with higher valuations. Our algorithm is built upon the framework of OA, where for any agent i, a tentative schedule is determined at its arrival time a_i. In making the decision, however, allocations within the interval $[a_i, d_i]$ made for previous agents can be reassigned to agent i if the marginal valuation of the latter is higher than the marginal valuation of the former by a factor $\gamma \geq 1$. The parameter γ is called **revocation coefficient** and is selected by the algorithm according to the shapes of the valuation and cost functions. Approaches for determining a desired γ will be studied in Section 4.

We now discuss our On-Arrival Allocation with Revocation (OAR) algorithm in detail. The algorithm maintains the total amount of electricity consumed in each time-slot t, denoted as z_t, which is initialized to 0. At any time t, for each agent i that arrives at t, a tentative schedule is made for i as follows. For each time-slot $\tau \in [a_i, b_i]$, let $x_{i\tau}$ denote the amount of electricity given to i in time τ, and let $y_i = \sum_\tau x_{i\tau}$ denote the total amount that i receives. These variables are initialized to 0. The tentative schedule for agent i is made in multiple iterations (lines 3-41). In each iteration, certain amount of electricity is allocated to i until y_i equals to Y_i, the maximum amount that agent i requires, or when there is no benefit of serving more for i.

In each iteration, let H denote the set of time-slots in $[a_i, d_i]$ where agent i can receive more electricity subject to its charging rate limit (line 4). Let dc denote the minimum marginal cost in these time-slots, and let H' denote the set of time-slots in H that achieves this minimum (line 9). These are the most cost-effective time-slots for serving i. Moreover, let J denote the set of agents from which the current allocation can potentially be revoked for serving i (lines 10-11). These agents have to satisfy the following necessary conditions:

- They arrived before i;
- They have received some amount in H';
- Their marginal valuation (with respect to their current allocations) is less than $f_i'(y_i)/\gamma$, where $\gamma \geq 1$ is the revocation coefficient, and no larger than dc.

If J is nonempty, let dv denote the minimum marginal valuation for agents in J, and let J' denote the set of agents in J that achieves the minimum. Otherwise, let $dv = dc$ and $J' = \emptyset$ (lines 12-18).

If neither dc nor dv is less than $f_i'(y_i)$, there is no benefit of serving more for agent i. The algorithm moves on to the next agent (lines 19-21). Otherwise, we set $H' = \emptyset$ if $dv < dc$, since in this case, it is more cost-effective to revoke existing allocation instead of allocating more. The algorithm then invokes a procedure Increment to identify a small increment δ_τ for each $\tau \in H'$, and a small amount δ_j to be displaced for each $j \in J'$ (line 25). The procedure Increment identifies the maximum possible amount of increment (revocation) while meeting the following criteria:

- The new value of y_i after increment (revocation) is bounded by Y_i;
- The new marginal cost (valuation) of these time-slots (agents) after increment (revocation) should still equal to each other, and no larger than the derivatives of untouched time-slots in H and agents in J, and that of $f_i'(y_i)$;
- If $\delta_j > 0$ is applied to an agent $j \in J'$, then δ_j should be small enough so that $f_j'(y_j) \leq f_i'(y_i)/\gamma$ after revocation.

On-Arrival Allocation with Revocation (OAR)

$z_t \leftarrow 0, \forall t$
$\gamma \leftarrow \gamma^*$ as determined by Equation (12)
In each time-slot t

```
 1: for each agent i that arrives at t do
 2:     x_{iτ} ← 0, y_i ← 0, ∀i, τ
 3:     while y_i ≤ Y_i do
 4:         H ← {τ : a_i ≤ τ ≤ d_i, x_{iτ} < X_i}
 5:         if H == ∅ then
 6:             break
 7:         end if
 8:         dc ← min_{τ∈H} g'_τ(z_τ)
 9:         H' ← {τ ∈ H : g'_τ(z_τ) == dc}
10:         J ← {j < i : x_{jτ} > 0 for some τ ∈ H',
11:              f'_j(y_j) < f'_i(y_i)/γ, f'_j(y_j) ≤ d_c}
12:         if J == ∅ then
13:             dv ← dc
14:             J' ← ∅
15:         else
16:             dv ← min_{j∈J} f'_j(y_j)
17:             J' ← {j ∈ J : f'_j(y_j) == dv}
18:         end if
19:         if f'_i(y_i) ≤ min(dc, dv) then
20:             break
21:         end if
22:         if dv < dc then
23:             H' ← ∅
24:         end if
25:         ({δ_j}, {δ_τ}) ← Increment(H, J, H'J', y_i)
26:         for τ ∈ H' do
27:             z_τ ← z_τ + δ_τ, x_{iτ} ← x_{iτ} + δ_τ, y_i ← y_i + δ_τ
28:         end for
29:         for j ∈ J' do
30:             δ_0 ← δ_j
31:             for τ ∈ H' and x_{jτ} > 0 do
32:                 δ_1 ← min(δ_0, x_{jτ}, X_i − x_{iτ})
33:                 x_{jτ} ← x_{jτ} − δ_1, y_j ← y_j − δ_1
34:                 x_{iτ} ← x_{iτ} + δ_1, y_i ← y_i + δ_1
35:                 δ_0 ← δ_0 − δ_1
36:                 if δ_0 ≤ 0 then
37:                     break
38:                 end if
39:             end for
40:         end for
41:     end while
42: end for
```

The load in each time-slot $\tau \in H'$ then increases by δ_τ, and the allocation of i is updated accordingly (lines 26-28). Similarly, for each agent $j \in J'$, total amount of δ_j is displaced from the time-slots in H' where j has non-zero allocation, which is reassigned to i subject to the charging rate constraint of i (lines 29-40).

Remark 1: When the functions f and g have constant or linear derivatives, the procedure Increment can be easily implemented to identify the maximum possible increment (revocation) subject to the required conditions. For general f and g, however, it can be difficult to satisfy the criteria above exactly while still making some progress in each step, and some approximation might be needed. We will adopt the following simple solution in our simulations. In each iteration, only consider one time-slot τ in H' or one agent j in J', and increase the load of τ or revoke the allocation of j by a small fixed amount $\delta > 0$, where δ can be adjusted to trade off the accuracy and the time complexity. We call this procedure Simple-Increment.

One advantage of introducing a step size δ is that the algorithm can then be easily extended to non-differentiable f and g, and to the discrete case where x_{it} requires to be a multiple of a charging unit (a given system parameter). In the later case, we can simply set δ to be the charging unit, and replace all the derivatives by marginal valuations or marginal costs. An extra unit of agent i is served at time τ only if the marginal valuation of the next unit of i is higher than the marginal cost for serving one more unit at time τ. Similarly, a unit of agent j is displaced by a unit of agent i only if the marginal valuation of the next unit of i is higher than the marginal valuation of the last unit of j.

Remark 2: With Simple-Increment applied, the time complexity of the OAR algorithm can be determined as follows. Let N denote the number of agents, $Y = \max_i Y_i$ the maximum battery size of an EV, and $D = \max_i(d_i - a_i + 1)$ the maximum time elasticity of any agent. Each agent then requires $O(Y/\delta)$ iterations to schedule, and the time complexity of one iteration is dominated by computing the set J (lines 10-11), which requires $O(ND)$ time. Therefore, the algorithm has a time complexity of $O(\frac{Y}{\delta}N^2D)$.

4. ANALYSIS OF ONLINE ALGORITHMS

We next study the performance of our online algorithm presented in the previous section, by adopting a primal-dual framework [6, 12]. As a classic tool for the design and analysis of approximation algorithms in the offline setting, primal-dual approach has recently been successfully applied to online optimization with linear objectives [5,6]. More recently, this approach has been extended to online non-linear optimization as well. In particular, it has been used in [12] to prove competitive results for the online energy minimization algorithm in the special case when the cost function is a power function, as we mentioned in Section 3.1. Our analysis extends this approach by considering both a general convex cost and a general concave valuation function. To strike a balance between the two, our approach is to properly determine the value of the revocation coefficient γ according to the shapes of the valuation and cost functions. In our proof, we need the following assumption (in addition to the assumptions made in Section 2).

ASSUMPTION 4.1. *f and g are continuously differentiable and strictly increasing; x_{it} are continuous (and can be arbitrarily small); and the Increment procedure (discussed in Section 3.2) can by implemented exactly.*

As we mentioned in Section 3.2, our algorithm applies to the more general setting where a discrete charging unit δ can be introduced. We expect that, when the unit δ can be made small enough[2], similar competitive results as the ones established below can be obtained for more general f and g, e.g., a piecewise linear concave or convex function, with little loss, at the expense of a higher complexity of the algorithm. Extending our results to the setting where δ is a given system parameter is part of our future work. On the

---

[2]This can be made more precisely as follows. Consider a system with a single request i and a single time-slot t, where $a_i \leq t \leq d_i$. Let C_{it} denote the optimal amount of request i scheduled at time t that maximizes the welfare (ignoring other requests and other time slots). Let $C = \min_{i,t} C_{it}$. Effectively, C can be viewed as a notion of the capacity of the system. Then we require that $\delta \ll C$.

other hand, we observe in our simulations (see Section 5) that our algorithm achieves close to optimal performance even under the discrete setting.

4.1 Preliminaries

To illustrate the primal-dual approach, we first rewrite the primal problem as follows:

$$\max_{\mathbf{x},\mathbf{y}} \quad F(\mathbf{x},\mathbf{y}) = \sum_i f_i(y_i) - \sum_t g_t(\sum_i x_{it})$$

$$\text{s.t.} \quad y_i \leq \sum_t x_{it}, \quad \forall i, \tag{1}$$

$$x_{it} \leq X_i, \quad \forall i, t, \tag{2}$$

$$x_{it} = 0, \quad \forall i, t \notin [a_i, d_i], \tag{3}$$

$$x_{it} \geq 0, \quad \forall i, t, \tag{4}$$

$$0 \leq y_i \leq Y_i, \quad \forall i. \tag{5}$$

where $\mathbf{x} \triangleq \{x_{it}\}$ and $\mathbf{y} \triangleq \{y_i\}$.

We introduce a dual variable λ_i for the first constraint for each i, and a dual variable μ_{it} for the second constraint for each i and t. Let $\lambda \triangleq \{\lambda_i\}$ and $\mu \triangleq \{\mu_{it}\}$. Let $\mathcal{X}$ denote the set of $\mathbf{x}$ that satisfies constraints (3) and (4), and let $\mathcal{Y}$ denote the set of $\mathbf{y}$ that satisfies the last constraint. We consider the following dual function

$$
\begin{aligned}
G(\lambda,\mu) &= \max_{\mathbf{x}\in\mathcal{X},\mathbf{y}\in\mathcal{Y}} \sum_i f_i(y_i) - \sum_t g_t(\sum_i x_{it}) \\
&\quad + \sum_i \lambda_i(\sum_t x_{it} - y_i) + \sum_{i,t} \mu_{it}(X_i - x_{it}) \\
&= \max_{\mathbf{x}\in\mathcal{X},\mathbf{y}\in\mathcal{Y}} \sum_i (f_i(y_i) - \lambda_i y_i) + \sum_{i,t} \mu_{it} X_i \\
&\quad + \sum_t \Big[\sum_i (\lambda_i - \mu_{it})x_{it} - g_t(\sum_i x_{it}) \Big]
\end{aligned}
\tag{6}
$$

By the weak duality theorem [2], the dual function yields an upper bound on the optimal solution of the initial problem for any $\lambda_i \geq 0$ and $\mu_{it} \geq 0, \forall i, t$. The main idea of the online primal-dual approach is to set dual variables $(\widehat{\lambda}, \widehat{\mu})$ based on the values of the primal variables $(\overline{\mathbf{x}}, \overline{\mathbf{y}})$ determined by a (deterministic) online algorithm such that $G(\widehat{\lambda}, \widehat{\mu}) \leq qF(\overline{\mathbf{x}}, \overline{\mathbf{y}})$ for some $q \geq 1$, which then implies that the online algorithm is q-competitive.

4.2 Analysis

We now study the performance of OAR. Our analysis is centered at the choice of revocation coefficient γ based on a characterization on the level of concavity (resp. convexity) of f (resp. g). By the concavity of f and the assumption that $f(0) = 0, f(y) \geq 0, \forall y \geq 0$, we have $f'(y)y \leq f(y)$ for any $y \geq 0$ (a formal proof can be found in [2]). Based on this observation, we use $\phi_f(y) = \frac{f'(y)y}{f(y)}$ to characterize the convexity of f at point y (see Figure 2 for an example), and define $\phi_f = \max_{y\geq 0} \phi_f(y)$. For instance, when $f(y) = vy^\beta$ for some $v > 0, \beta \leq 1$, we have $\phi_f = \beta$. Similarly, we consider $\phi_g(z) = \frac{g'(z)z}{g(z)}$ as a characterization of the convexity of g at point z, and define $\phi_g = \min_{z\geq 0} \phi_g(z)$. Moreover, for a given set of agents $\mathcal{N}$ and a time horizon T, we define $\phi_f = \max_{i\in\mathcal{N}} \phi_{f_i}, \phi_g = \min_{t\in T} \phi_{g_t}$.

Consider an agent i scheduled by OAR. Let $\{\widetilde{x}_{it}\}$ denote the initial allocation made for i at its arrival, $\widetilde{y}_i = \sum_t \widetilde{x}_{it}$

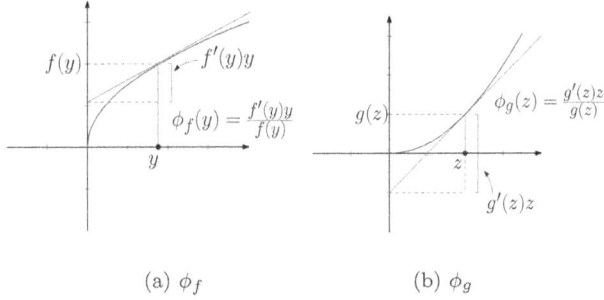

(a) ϕ_f (b) ϕ_g

Figure 2: Characterization of concavity (convexity) by ϕ_f (ϕ_g).

the total amount of electricity given to i initially, and $\tilde{z}_{i,t}$ the load in time-slot t right after the initial decision for i is made. Let $\{\overline{x}_{it}\}$, $\overline{y}_i$, and $\overline{z}_t$ denote the corresponding values in the final allocation. We then set the dual variables as

$$\widehat{\lambda}_i = \begin{cases} \max_{\tau:\widetilde{x}_{i\tau}>0} g'_\tau(\widetilde{z}_{i,\tau}) & \text{if } \widetilde{y}_i = Y_i, \\ f'_i(\widehat{y}_i) & \text{if } \widetilde{y}_i < Y_i. \end{cases}$$

$$\widehat{\mu}_{it} = \begin{cases} \widehat{\lambda}_i - g'_t(\widetilde{z}_{i,t}) & \text{if } \widetilde{x}_{it} > 0, \\ 0 & \text{if } \widetilde{x}_{it} = 0. \end{cases}$$

That is, if $\widetilde{y}_i = Y_i$, $\widehat{\lambda}_i$ is set to the maximum marginal cost for time slots where i has been initially allocated some amount. Otherwise, $\widehat{\lambda}_i$ is set to the derivative of f_i at $\widehat{y}_i$. Moreover, $\widehat{\mu}_{it}$ satisfies the following complementary slackness condition.

LEMMA 4.1. $\widehat{\mu}_{it} = 0$ when $\widetilde{x}_{it} < X_i$.

PROOF. For any agent i and time-slot t, if $\widetilde{x}_{it} = 0$, then $\widehat{\mu}_{it} = 0$ by the definition. Assume $\widetilde{x}_{it} > 0$. We need to show that $\widehat{\lambda}_i = g'_t(\widetilde{z}_{i,t})$. First note that when agent i is initially scheduled in OAR, time-slots with minimum marginal cost are always considered first. Therefore, we must have $g'_t(\widetilde{z}_{i,t}) = \max_{\tau:\widetilde{x}_{i\tau}>0} g'_\tau(\widetilde{z}_{i,\tau})$ by the assumption that $\widetilde{x}_{it} < X_i$. If $\widetilde{y}_i = Y_i$, we then have $\widehat{\lambda}_i = \max_{\tau:\widetilde{x}_{i\tau}>0} g'_\tau(\widetilde{z}_{i,\tau}) = g'_t(\widetilde{z}_{i,t})$. Next consider the case $\widetilde{y} < Y_i$. We must have $f'_i(\widehat{y}_i) \geq g'_t(\widetilde{z}_{i,t})$ since $\widetilde{x}_{it} > 0$. Moreover, since $\widetilde{x}_{it} < X_i$, we must have $f'_i(\widehat{y}_i) = g'_t(\widetilde{z}_{i,t})$; otherwise i can be served a larger amount at time-slot t by the assumption that the derivatives are continuous. Therefore, we again have $\widehat{\lambda}_i = g'_t(\widetilde{z}_{i,t})$. $\square$

Our objective is to establish an upper bound of $G(\widehat{\lambda}, \widehat{\mu})$ in terms of the objective value obtained by the online algorithm, namely, $\sum_i f_i(\overline{y}_i) - \sum_t g_t(\overline{z}_t)$. Our analysis is built upon the framework in [12]. We first consider the last term in (6), $\max_{x\in\mathcal{X}} \sum_t \left[\sum_i (\widehat{\lambda}_i - \widehat{\mu}_{it})x_{it} - g_t(\sum_i x_{it}) \right]$. Let $\{\widehat{x}_{it}\}$ denote the values of $\{x_{it}\}$ that maximize $\sum_i (\widehat{\lambda}_i - \widehat{\mu}_{it})x_{it} - g_t(\sum_i x_{it})$ subject to the constraints (3) and (4). Let $j = \text{argmax}_{i:a_i\leq t\leq b_i} \widehat{\lambda}_i - \widehat{\mu}_{it}$. It is then clear that, without loss of optimality, we can set $\widehat{x}_{it} = 0$ for $i \neq j$, and the problem can be simplified to $\max_{x_{jt}\geq 0}(\widehat{\lambda}_j - \widehat{\mu}_{jt})x_{jt} - g_t(x_{jt})$. Since $\widehat{\lambda}_i - \widehat{\mu}_{it} = g'_t(\widetilde{z}_{i,t})$ for any agent i with $\widetilde{x}_{it} > 0$, and the load of a time-slot never decreases, we can take j as any agent that is served in time-slot t in its final allocation, and the objective is maximized at $\widehat{x}_{jt} = \overline{z}_t$. Therefore, the last term in (6) becomes $\sum_t (g'_t(\overline{z}_t)\overline{z}_t - g_t(\overline{z}_t))$.

We then consider the first term in (6), $\max_{y\in\mathcal{Y}} \sum_i (f_i(y_i) - \widehat{\lambda}_i y_i)$. For each i, let $\widehat{y}_i$ denote the value of $y_i \leq Y_i$ that

maximizes $f_i(y_i) - \widehat{\lambda}_i y_i$. Then we must have $f'_i(\widehat{y}_i) = \widehat{\lambda}_i$ or $\widehat{y}_i = Y_i$. By the definition of $\widehat{\lambda}_i$, we observe that $\widehat{y}_i = \widetilde{y}_i$. Hence, the first term becomes $\sum_i (f_i(\widetilde{y}_i) - \widehat{\lambda}_i \widetilde{y}_i)$. We then have

$$\begin{aligned} G(\widehat{\lambda}, \widehat{\mu}) &= \sum_i (f_i(\widetilde{y}_i) - \widehat{\lambda}_i \widetilde{y}_i) + \sum_{i,t} \widehat{\mu}_{it} X_i \\ &\quad + \sum_t (g'_t(\overline{z}_t)\overline{z}_t - g_t(\overline{z}_t)) \\ &= \sum_i f_i(\widetilde{y}_i) - \sum_i (\widehat{\lambda}_i \widetilde{y}_i - \sum_t \widehat{\mu}_{it} X_i) \\ &\quad + \sum_t (g'_t(\overline{z}_t)\overline{z}_t - g_t(\overline{z}_t)). \end{aligned} \tag{7}$$

Consider the second term in (7), we have

$$\begin{aligned} \sum_i (\widehat{\lambda}_i \widetilde{y}_i - \sum_t \widehat{\mu}_{it} X_i) &= \sum_i (\sum_t \widehat{\lambda}_i \widetilde{x}_{it} - \sum_t \widehat{\mu}_{it} X_i) \\ &\overset{(a)}{=} \sum_i \sum_t (\widehat{\lambda}_i - \widehat{\mu}_{it}) \widetilde{x}_{it} \\ &= \sum_i \sum_t g'_t(\widetilde{z}_{i,t}) \widetilde{x}_{it} \\ &\overset{(b)}{\geq} \sum_t \sum_i g'_t(\sum_{j\leq i} \overline{x}_{jt}) \overline{x}_{it} \\ &\overset{(c)}{\geq} \sum_t g_t(\overline{z}_t). \end{aligned} \tag{8}$$

where (a) follows from Lemma 4.1, (b) follows from the fact that x_{it} never increases after initial allocation in OAR and the convexity of g_t (recall that agents are sorted by their arrival times), and (c) follows from the convexity of g_t (see Figure 3 for an explanation).

From (7) and (8), we now have

$$G(\widehat{\lambda}, \widehat{\mu}) \leq \sum_i f_i(\widetilde{y}_i) + \sum_t g'_t(\overline{z}_t)\overline{z}_t - 2\sum_t g_t(\overline{z}_t). \tag{9}$$

Recall that our objective is to derive an upper bound of $G(\widehat{\lambda}, \widehat{\mu})$ in terms of $\sum_i f_i(\overline{y}_i) - \sum_t g_t(\overline{z}_t)$. To this end, we first make the following key observation, which establishes an upper bound for $\sum_i f_i(\widetilde{y}_i)$ in terms of $\sum_i f_i(\overline{y}_i)$ as shown in the lemma.

LEMMA 4.2. $\sum_i f_i(\widetilde{y}_i) \leq \frac{\gamma}{\gamma-1} \sum_i f_i(\overline{y}_i)$.

PROOF. We will show $\sum_i (\gamma-1)(f_i(\widetilde{y}_i) - f_i(\overline{y}_i)) \leq \sum_i f_i(\overline{y}_i)$, which implies the lemma. To simplify the description, we prove the statement for the discrete version of OAR. To this end, we view the charging opportunity in each time-slot as multiple units of size δ. To abuse the notation a little bit,

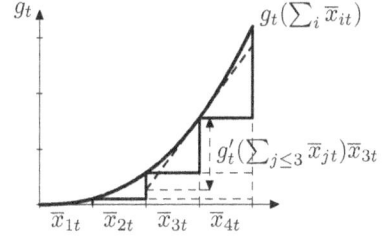

Figure 3: An example that shows $\sum_i g'_t(\sum_{j\leq i} \overline{x}_{jt})\overline{x}_{it} \geq g_t(\sum_i \overline{x}_{it})$ in (8).

259

we redefine f_i in terms of units, and let $\tilde{y}_i$ and $\overline{y}_i$ denote the number of units allocated to agent i in the beginning and in the end, respectively. The k-th unit that agent i obtains has a marginal valuation $v_{i,k} = f_i(k) - f_i(k-1)$. Assume $\overline{y}_i < \tilde{y}_i$. User i went through a sequence of revocations after its initial allocation, where units of higher indices (and hence lower marginal valuations) are displaced first. All the units with index $\overline{y}_i$ and less are not reallocated. We note that by allowing units of different sizes, the following proof applies to the continuous case as well.

For agent i, each unit with index $\overline{y}_i + 1$ or higher went through a sequence of reallocations, represented by (i_1,k_1), $(i_2,k_2),...,(i_n,k_n)$, where in each pair, the first element denotes the agent that holds the unit, and the second element denotes the index of the unit for that agent. Each agent obtains the unit from the previous owner, and i_1 is the first agent that is allocated the unit and i_n the last. Let S denote the set of units over all the time-slots that has even been reallocated. For each unit $s \in S$, let $(i_1^s,k_1^s),(i_2^s,k_2^s),...,(i_{n_s}^s,k_{n_s}^s)$ denote the corresponding sequence of reallocations. Define $V_s = \sum_{m=1}^{n_s-1} v_{i_m^s,k_m^s}$, the sum of marginal valuations over all the agents in the sequence except the last one. We then observe that $\sum_i(f_i(\tilde{y}_i) - f_i(\overline{y}_i)) = \sum_{s\in S} V_s$, since any reallocation is with respect to a unit in S. On the other hand, $\sum_i f_i(\overline{y}_i) \geq \sum_{s\in S} v_{i_{n_s}^s,k_{n_s}^s}$, where the righthand side is the sum of marginal valuations of all the units in S with respect to the final agent that has the unit. The inequality follows from the fact that some units, once allocated to an agent, are never reallocated.

By the above observation, to prove the lemma, it is then sufficient to show that $(\gamma-1)V_s \leq v_{i_{n_s}^s,k_{n_s}^s}$ for any s. Consider one such unit with sequence $(i_1,k_1),(i_2,k_2),...,(i_n,k_n)$, where s is omitted to simplify the notation. According to OAR, (i_{m-1},k_{m-1}) is displaced by (i_m,k_m) only if $v_{i_m,k_m} \geq \gamma v_{i_{m-1},k_{m-1}}$. We prove by induction on $n \geq 2$. For $n = 2$, $(\gamma-1)V = (\gamma-1)v_{i_1,k_1} \leq v_{i_2,k_2}$. Assume the statement holds for $n \leq r$. For $n = r+1$, we have

$$
\begin{aligned}
(\gamma-1)V &= (\gamma-1)\sum_{m=1}^{r} v_{i_m,k_m}\\
&= (\gamma-1)\sum_{m=1}^{r-1} v_{i_m,k_m} + (\gamma-1)v_{i_r,k_r}\\
&\leq v_{i_r,k_r} + (\gamma-1)v_{i_r,k_r}\\
&= \gamma v_{i_r,k_r}\\
&\leq v_{i_{r+1},k_{r+1}}. \qquad \square
\end{aligned}
$$

We then establish connections between the total valuation obtained and the total cost incurred by our algorithm in the following lemma and its corollary, which paves the way toward our main result.

LEMMA 4.3. $\gamma\sum_i f_i'(\overline{y}_i)\overline{y}_i \geq \sum_t g_t'(\overline{z}_t)\overline{z}_t$.

PROOF. Consider any time instance in serving requests using algorithm OAR. Let x_{it} denote the current allocation made for agent i in time-slot t, y_i the total allocation currently made for agent i, and z_t the current load in time-slot t. We claim that $\gamma f_i'(y_i) \geq g_t'(z_t)$ for any t such that $x_{it} > 0$. Otherwise, there must be a piece of demand from another agent j with derivative at least $\gamma f_i'(y_i)$ that is served by increasing the load at t, which, however, should have been served by displacing the allocation of i. It follows that $\gamma f_i'(\overline{y}_i) \geq g_t'(\overline{z}_t)$ for any t where $\overline{x}_{it} > 0$. Therefore,

$$
\begin{aligned}
\gamma\sum_i f_i'(\overline{y}_i)\overline{y}_i &= \sum_i\sum_t \gamma f_i'(\overline{y}_i)\overline{x}_{it}\\
&\geq \sum_i\sum_t g_t'(\overline{z}_t)\overline{x}_{it}\\
&= \sum_t g_t'(\overline{z}_t)\sum_i \overline{x}_{it}\\
&= \sum_t g_t'(\overline{z}_t)\overline{z}_t. \qquad \square
\end{aligned}
$$

We further have the following corollary.

COROLLARY 4.1. $\sum_i f_i(\overline{y}_i) \geq \frac{\rho_g}{\gamma\rho_f}\sum_t g_t(\overline{z}_t)$.

PROOF. By the definition of ρ_f and ρ_g, we have

$$
\begin{aligned}
\sum_i f_i(\overline{y}_i) &\geq \sum_i f_i'(\overline{y}_i)\overline{y}_i/\rho_f\\
&\geq \sum_t g_t'(\overline{z}_t)\overline{z}_t/(\gamma\rho_f) \quad \text{(Lemma 4.3)}\\
&\geq \frac{\rho_g}{\gamma\rho_f}\sum_t g_t(\overline{z}_t). \qquad \square
\end{aligned}
$$

From (9), Lemmas 4.2 and 4.3, and Corollary 4.1, we have

$$
\begin{aligned}
G(\hat{\lambda},\hat{\mu}) &\leq \sum_i f_i(\tilde{y}_i) + \sum_t g_t'(\overline{z}_t)\overline{z}_t - 2\sum_t g_t(\overline{z}_t)\\
&\overset{(a)}{\leq} \frac{\gamma}{\gamma-1}\sum_i f_i(\overline{y}_i) + \sum_t g_t'(\overline{z}_t)\overline{z}_t - 2\sum_t g_t(\overline{z}_t)\\
&\overset{(b)}{\leq} \frac{\gamma}{\gamma-1}\sum_i f_i(\overline{y}_i) + \gamma\sum_i f_i'(\overline{y}_i)\overline{y}_i - 2\sum_t g_t(\overline{z}_t)\\
&\overset{(c)}{\leq} \left(\frac{\gamma}{\gamma-1} + \gamma\rho_f\right)\sum_i f_i(\overline{y}_i) - 2\sum_t g_t(\overline{z}_t) \quad (10)\\
&\overset{(d)}{\leq} \frac{(\frac{1}{\gamma-1}+\rho_f)\rho_g - 2\rho_f}{\frac{1}{\gamma}\rho_g - \rho_f}\left[\sum_i f_i(\overline{y}_i) - \sum_t g_t(\overline{z}_t)\right].
\end{aligned}
$$
(11)

where (a) follows from Lemma 4.2, (b) follows from Lemma 4.3, (c) follows from the definition of ρ_f, and (d) follows from Corollary 4.1 and simple algebra. Given ρ_f and ρ_g, the coefficient in (11) can be minimized by choosing the revocation coefficient to be

$$
\gamma^* = \frac{\rho_g - 2 + \sqrt{\frac{2}{\rho_g} - (1+\frac{1}{\rho_f})\rho_g + 2}}{\rho_g - 1}. \quad (12)
$$

Therefore, we obtain the following main result:

THEOREM 4.1. *OAR is* $\frac{(\frac{1}{\gamma^*-1}+\rho_f)\rho_g - 2\rho_f}{\frac{1}{\gamma^*}\rho_g - \rho_f}$-*competitive, where*
$$
\gamma^* = \frac{\rho_g-2+\sqrt{\frac{2}{\rho_g}-(1+\frac{1}{\rho_f})\rho_g+2}}{\rho_g-1}.
$$

Remark 3: The fact that the total valuation obtained is at least a factor $\rho \triangleq \frac{\rho_g}{\gamma\rho_f}$ of the total cost incurred in algorithm OAR, as proved in Corollary 4.1, is critical for deriving the competitive factor in (11) from the weaker form of (10). It can be seen that for a fixed γ, a larger ρ implies a smaller competitive factor. In particular, for a given problem instance, the factor ρ can be improved by replacing $_f$ and $_g$ with $\max_i \phi_{f_i}(\overline{y}_i)$ and $\min_t \phi_{g_t}(\overline{z}_t)$, respectively. A further improvement is discussed in Example 4 below.

4.3 Examples

We now apply Theorem 4.1 to some concrete examples of valuation and cost functions. In the examples, all the agents are assumed to have the same type of valuation functions and the system operator has the same type of cost functions in all the time-slots. But the parameters of the functions vary over agents and time, respectively.

Example 1: $f_i(y_i) = v_i \log(1 + y_i)$ for some $v_i > 0$, and $g_t(z_t) = c_t z_t^\alpha$ for some $c_t > 0$ and $\alpha \geq 1$. In this case, we have $_f = 1$ since $\phi_{f_i}(y_i) = \frac{[\log'(1+y_i)]y_i}{\log(1+y_i)} \to 1$ as $y_i \to 0$, and $_g = \alpha$ since $(z^\alpha)'z = \alpha z^\alpha$. Therefore, $\gamma^* = \frac{\alpha - 2 + \sqrt{(\alpha-1)^2 + 1}}{\alpha - 1}$. In particular, consider the case when the cost function has a linear derivative, that is, $\alpha = 2$, we have $\gamma^* = \sqrt{2}$, and OAR is $\frac{2}{(\sqrt{2}-1)^2}(< 12)$-competitive. In general, the competitive factor obtained at γ^* increases as α approaches to 1 (see Figure 4(a)). On the other hand, we observe that $\phi_{f_i}(y_i)$ is decreasing on y_i and approaches to 0 as $y_i \to \infty$. Hence, for a given problem instance, when $\overline{y}_i$ is relatively large for most requests, a smaller competitive factor can be expected.

Example 2: $f_i(y_i) = v_i y_i^\beta$ for some $v_i > 0$ and $\beta \in [0, 1]$, and $g_t(z_t) = c_t z_t^\alpha$ for some $c_t > 0$ and $\alpha \geq 1$. In this case, we have $_f = \beta$ and $_g = \alpha$. In particular, when $\alpha = 2, \beta = 1/2$, we have $\gamma^* = 2$, and OAR is 4-competitive. In general, the competitive factor increases as α/β approaches to 1 (see Figure 4(b)). However, we note that in the extreme case when $\alpha = \beta = 1$, that is, when both the valuation and the cost functions are linear, the algorithm OA proposed in Section 3.1 is optimal and revocation is not needed.

In both examples, we observe that the value of γ^* increases as α/β increases in most cases, and is minimized when $\alpha/\beta \to 1$. This can be explained from Corollary 4.1 and Lemma 4.2. When $_g/_f$ is small, a small γ is needed to maintain the multiplicative factor in Corollary 4.1. On the other hand, when $_g/_f$ is large, a large γ is desirable as it minimizes $\frac{\gamma}{\gamma-1}$, the multiplicative factor connecting the valuations of the initial and final allocation proved in Lemma 4.2.

Example 3 (free renewable energy): $g_t(z_t) = c_t[(z_t - z_t^0)^+]^\alpha$ for $c_t > 0, \alpha > 1, z_t^0 > 0$, where $(x)^+ \triangleq \max(x, 0)$. We use z_t^0 to model the amount of free renewable energy available at time t. Note that $g_t(z_t)$ is continuously differentiable for $\alpha > 1$, and $g_t'(z_t) = c_t \alpha[(z_t - z_t^0)^+]^{\alpha-1}$. Hence, $g_t'(z_t)z_t \geq \alpha g_t(z_t)$, and $\phi_{g_t} \geq \alpha$. Therefore, a non-zero renewable energy supply actually helps with the competitive performance (assuming it is predictable).

Example 4 (non-zero base load): $g_t(z_t) = c_t[(z_t + z_t^0)^2 - (z_t^0)^2]$ for some $c_t > 0, z_t^0 > 0$, where z_t^0 models the base load in the system that is out of the control of the operator. We have $\phi_{g_t} = 1$ since $\phi_{g_t}(z_t) = \frac{g_t'(z_t)z_t}{g_t(z_t)} = \frac{2(z_t + z_t^0)}{z_t + 2z_t^0} \to 1$ as $z_t \to 0$. On the other hand, $\phi_{g_t}(z_t)$ is increasing on z_t and approaches 2 as $z_t \to \infty$. Therefore, a single worst-case ϕ_{g_t} is not very expressive. Below we outline an approach for improving Corollary 4.1, which can also be applied to other cost functions with increasing $\phi_{g_t}(z_t)$.

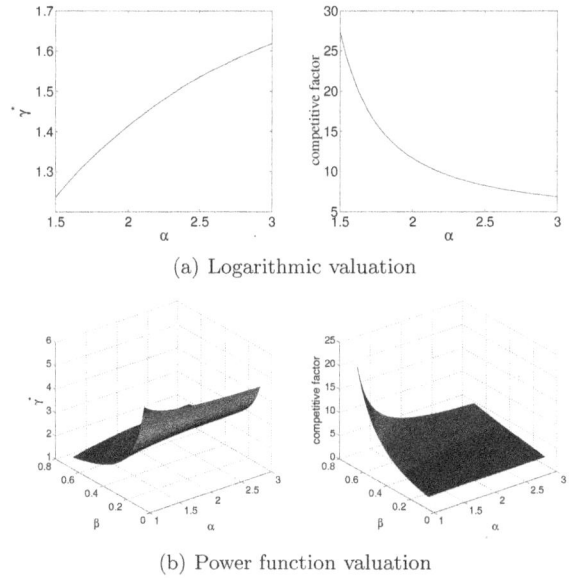

(a) Logarithmic valuation

(b) Power function valuation

Figure 4: Competitive performance for two types of valuation functions. In both (a) and (b), α is the power of the cost function, and in (b), β is the power of the valuation function.

First, we define $\gamma_t = \max_{i:\overline{x}_{it} > 0} \frac{g_t'(\overline{z}_t)}{f_i'(\overline{y}_i)}$. Then by a similar argument as in the proof of Lemma 4.3, we have $\gamma_t \leq \gamma$, and $\sum_i f_i'(\overline{y}_i)\overline{y}_i \geq \sum_t \frac{1}{\gamma_t} g_t'(\overline{z}_t)\overline{z}_t$. Now apply a similar proof of Corollary 4.1, we get $\sum_i f_i(\overline{y}_i) \geq \frac{1}{_f}\sum_t \frac{\phi_{g_t}(\overline{z}_t)}{\gamma_t} g_t(\overline{z}_t)$. For any time-slot with $\overline{x}_{it} > 0$, we must have $f_i'(\overline{y}_i) \geq g_t'(0)$. Therefore, $\gamma_t \leq \frac{g_t'(\overline{z}_t)}{g_t'(0)} = \frac{2(z_t + z_t^0)}{2z_t^0}$; hence, $z_t \geq (\gamma_t - 1)z_0$. It follows that $\phi_{g_t}(\overline{z}_t) \geq \frac{2((\gamma_t - 1)z_0 + z_0)}{(\gamma_t - 1)z_0 + 2z_0} = \frac{2\gamma_t}{\gamma_t + 1}$; hence, $\phi_{g_t}(\overline{z}_t)/\gamma_t \geq \frac{2}{\gamma_t + 1} \geq \frac{2}{\gamma+1}$. Therefore, $\sum_i f_i(\overline{y}_i) \geq \frac{2}{(\gamma+1)_f}\sum_t g_t(\overline{z}_t)$. In contrast, if Corollary 4.1 is applied with $_g = 1$, we get $\sum_i f_i(\overline{y}_i) \geq \frac{1}{\gamma_f}\sum_t g_t(\overline{z}_t)$. Since $\frac{2}{(\gamma+1)} > \frac{1}{\gamma}$ whenever $\gamma > 1$, a smaller competitive factor can be obtained using this approach.

5. EVALUATION

In this section, we evaluate the performance of our online algorithm using simulations. We compare our OAR algorithm with PT and OA. The Simple-Increment approach discussed in Section 3.2 is used to implement all the three algorithms, where a discrete increment δ (i.e., the charging unit) is applied in each iteration. For our algorithm, the revocation coefficient γ is determined by Theorem 4.1. We study the performance of these algorithms under different values of δ, and compare them with the optimal offline solution (with continuous charging rate), obtained using the CVX toolbox [11]. Our results show that the OAR algorithm performs clearly better than PT and OA and achieves close to the offline optimal welfare under various settings. The simulation results also illustrate scenarios when PT or OA does not perform well.

5.1 Setup

In our simulations, we assume that the number of new arrivals of charging requests in each time-slot follows a Poisson distribution with mean λ_{arr}, independent of other time-slots. The active duration of each request follows an ex-

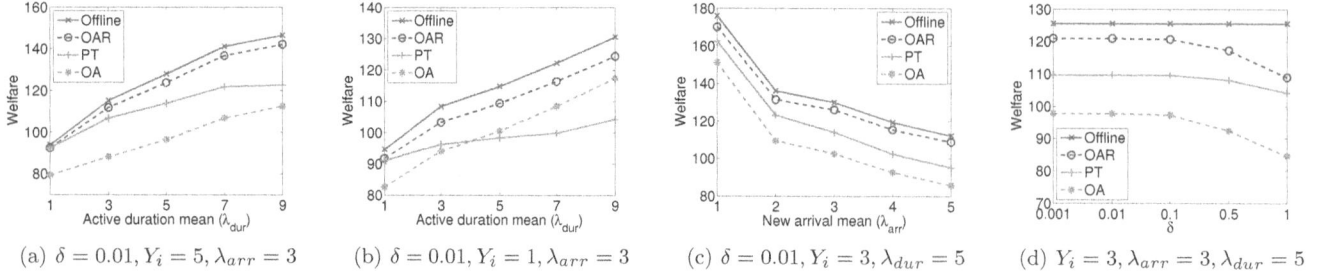

(a) $\delta = 0.01, Y_i = 5, \lambda_{arr} = 3$ (b) $\delta = 0.01, Y_i = 1, \lambda_{arr} = 3$ (c) $\delta = 0.01, Y_i = 3, \lambda_{dur} = 5$ (d) $Y_i = 3, \lambda_{arr} = 3, \lambda_{dur} = 5$

Figure 5: Simulation results for logarithmic valuation function and quadratic cost.

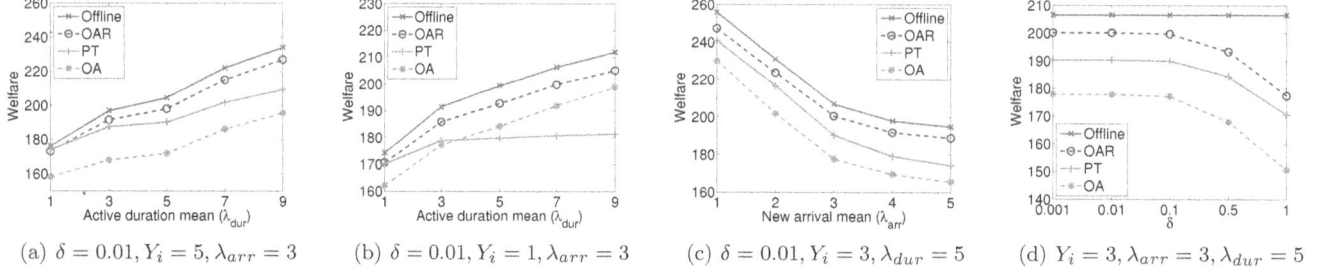

(a) $\delta = 0.01, Y_i = 5, \lambda_{arr} = 3$ (b) $\delta = 0.01, Y_i = 1, \lambda_{arr} = 3$ (c) $\delta = 0.01, Y_i = 3, \lambda_{dur} = 5$ (d) $Y_i = 3, \lambda_{arr} = 3, \lambda_{dur} = 5$

Figure 6: Simulation results for power valuation function and quadratic cost.

ponential distribution of mean λ_{dur}, independent of other requests. All the time-slots have the same cost function $g_t(z_t) = z_t^2$. All the requests have the same type of valuation functions. Two types are considered: $f_i^1(y_i) = v_i \log(1 + y_i)$ and $f_i^2(y_i) = v_i\sqrt{y_i}$. The coefficients v_i are generated from a uniform distribution in $[1,10]$. All the requests have the same charging rate limit $X_i = 1$ and the same maximum charging amount Y_i. The charging unit δ is chosen from $\{0.001, 0.01, 0.1, 0.5, 1\}$. Each figure below illustrates the average results over 50 independent scenarios generated under a given set of parameters, where 50 requests are generated in each scenario.

5.2 Results

The simulation results for logarithmic valuation function together with the quadratic cost are given in Figure 5. We first set $\delta = 0.01$ and plot the results in Figures 5(a)-5(c). Since δ is small enough compared with X_i and Y_i, the results closely reflect what can be expected in the continuous charging rate regime. In Figure 5(a), we fix $Y_i = 5$ and $\lambda_{arr} = 3$, and plot the welfare achieved by different algorithms versus the active duration mean (λ_{dur}). We make the following observations: (1) Our algorithm achieves close to optimal welfare; (2) All the algorithms achieve better welfare for a larger λ_{dur}, which reflects the benefit of introducing demand-side time elasticity; (3) The gap between PT and our algorithm (and the offline optimal) increases for larger λ_{dur}, which is due to the fact that PT does not take the time elasticity of requests into account explicitly when making charging decisions; and (4) Compared with PT, OA can better utilize large λ, but it has the lowest welfare among the four algorithms. The situation changes when we fix $Y_i = 1$ instead as shown in Figure 5(b). In this case, OA performs better than PT except when λ_{dur} is very small. The intuition is that a small Y_i implies that the traffic load is relatively low (compared to the cost). Hence, there is an opportunity to flatten the load to reduce the cost when time elasticity allows, which, however, is not well utilized by PT. From Figures 5(a) and 5(b),

we also observe that our algorithm achieves close to optimal performance even when the average time elasticity is low, while the performance of PT and OA vary under different scenarios.

Figure 5(c) shows the impact of mean arrival rate (λ_{arr}) on the performance of the algorithms. Since we fix the number of requests to be 50, a larger λ_{arr} leads to a lower welfare due to the higher density of the load. Moreover, since the number of new requests in each time-slot follows a Poisson distribution, a larger λ_{arr} also leads to a larger variance in the arrival process. We observe that our algorithm always achieves close to optimal performance. On the other hand, the gap between PT and the optimal increases for a larger λ_{arr}. This is also the case for OA, and can be more easily seen when the valuation functions are power functions (see Figure 6(c)). For PT, the problem is due to the fact that time elasticity has been largely ignored, which, however, is beneficial especially when the variance in workload is high. On the other hand, OA suffers from the weakness that requests of high valuations can be blocked especially when the system load is high.

We then study the impact of different charging unit δ. The results are given in Figure 5(d), where we fix $\lambda_{arr} = 3, \lambda_{dur} = 5$, and vary δ in $\{0.001, 0.01, 0.1, 0.5, 1\}$. The offline optimal is still computed by assuming a continuous charging rate since finding an optimal solution for a discrete charging rate is computationally difficult. We observe that there is little performance loss for the three online algorithms when δ is changed from 0.001 to 0.1. Therefore, a good competitive performance can be achieved at a relatively low complexity (recall that OAR has a time complexity of $O(\frac{Y}{\delta}N^2D)$ as discussed in Section 3.2). On the other hand, the performance of the online algorithms clearly drop when δ is close to 1, the charging rate limit, due to the inherent integrality gap. However, we observe that our algorithm still performs better than the other two even in this regime.

The simulation results for power valuation function and quadratic cost are given in Figure 6, where we observe similar trends as in the logarithmic valuation case discussed above.

6. CONCLUSION

To improve the energy efficiency in supporting large scale EV charging, an e ective approach is to study coordinated charging schemes that can exploit the flexibilities at both the demand side and the supply side. In this work, we propose an online algorithm for scheduling deferrable charging requests to balance the total value of vehicle owners and the total cost for providing charging service. Assuming that the charging rate is continuous, we characterize the competitive performance of our algorithm in terms of the concavity of the valuation function and the convexity of the cost function. Numerical results demonstrate that our algorithm achieves close to optimal performance even for discrete charging rates.

7. ACKNOWLEDGMENTS

This work is supported in part by a grant from the National Science Foundation ECCS-1232118.

8. REFERENCES

[1] A. Subramanian, M. Garcia, A. Dom´nguez-Garc´a, D. Callaway, K. Poolla, and P. Varaiya. Real-time scheduling of deferrable electric loads. In *Proc. of ACC*, 2012.

[2] D. P. Bertsekas. *Nonlinear Programming, 2nd edition*. Athena Scientific, 1999.

[3] A. Blum, A. Gupta, Y. Mansour, and A. Sharma. Welfare and profit maximization with production costs. In *Proc. of FOCS*, 2011.

[4] A. Borodin and R. El-Yaniv. *Online Computation and Competitive Analysis*. Cambridge University Press, 2005.

[5] N. Buchbinder and J. Naor. Online primal-dual algorithms for covering and packing. In *Proc. of the 13th Annual European Symposium on Algorithms*, 2005.

[6] N. Buchbinder and J. Naor. The design of competitive online algorithms via a primal-dual approach. *Foundations and Trends in Theoretical Computer Science*, 3(2-3):93 263, 2007.

[7] S. Chen, T. He, and L. Tong. Optimal deadline scheduling with commitment. In *Allerton Conference on Communication, Control and Computing*, 2011.

[8] S. Chen and L. Tong. iEMS for large scale charging of electric vehicles: Architecture and optimal online scheduling. In *Proc. of SmartGridComm*, 2012.

[9] L. Gan, U. Topcu, and S. H. Low. Optimal decentralized protocol for electric vehicle charging. *IEEE Transactions on Power Systems*, 28(2):940 951, 2013.

[10] E. H. Gerding, V. Robu, S. Stein, D. C. Parkes, A. Rogers, and N. R. Jennings. Online mechanism design for electric vehicle charging. In *Proc. of AAMAS*, 2011.

[11] M. Grant and S. Boyd. CVX: Matlab software for disciplined convex programming, version 2.0 beta. http://cvxr.com/cvx, Sept. 2013.

[12] A. Gupta, R. Krishnaswamy, and K. Pruhs. Online primal-dual for non-linear optimization with applications to speed scaling. In *10th Workshop on Approximation and Online Algorithms (WAOA)*, 2012.

[13] T. Koslowski. The electric vehicle s value chain and technology evolution. Technical report, Gartner Inc., 2009.

[14] I. Koutsopoulos and L. Tassiulas. Optimal control policies for power demand scheduling in the smart grid. *IEEE Journal on Selected Areas in Communications*, 30(6):1049 1060, 2012.

[15] T. Lan, D. Kao, M. Chiang, and A. Sabharwal. An axiomatic theory of fairness in network resource allocation. In *Proc. of IEEE Infocom*, 2010.

[16] N. Li, L. Chen, and S. H. Low. Optimal demand response based on utility maximization in power networks. In *Power and Energy Society General Meeting*, 2011.

[17] B. Obama and J. Biden. New Energy for America. http://energy.gov/sites/prod/files/edg/media/Obama_New_Energy_0804.pdf, 2009.

[18] V. Robu, E. H. Gerding, S. Stein, D. C. Parkes, A. Rogers, and N. R. Jennings. An online mechanism for multi-unit demand and its application to plug-in hybrid electric vehicle charging. *Journal of Artificial Intelligence Research*, 48:175 230, 2013.

[19] V. Robu, S. Stein, E. H. Gerding, D. C. Parkes, A. Rogers, and N. R. Jennings. An online mechanism for multi-speed electric vehicle charging. In *Proc. of AMMA*, 2011.

[20] S. Stein, E. H. Gerding, V. Robu, and N. R. Jennings. A model-based online mechanism with pre-commitment and its application to electric vehicle charging. In *Proc. of AAMAS*, 2012.

[21] F. Yao, A. Demers, and S. Shenker. A scheduling model for reduced cpu energy. In *Proc. of FOCS*, 1995.

NILMTK: An Open Source Toolkit for Non-intrusive Load Monitoring

Nipun Batra[1], Jack Kelly[2], Oliver Parson[3], Haimonti Dutta[4], William Knottenbelt[2],
Alex Rogers[3], Amarjeet Singh[1], Mani Srivastava[5]

[1]Indraprastha Institute of Information Technology Delhi, India {nipunb, amarjeet}@iiitd.ac.in
[2] Imperial College London {jack.kelly, w.knottenbelt}@imperial.ac.uk
[3] University of Southampton {osp, acr}@ecs.soton.ac.uk
[4] CCLS Columbia {haimonti@ccls.columbia.edu}
[5] UCLA {mbs@ucla.edu}

ABSTRACT

Non-intrusive load monitoring, or energy disaggregation, aims to separate household energy consumption data collected from a single point of measurement into appliance-level consumption data. In recent years, the field has rapidly expanded due to increased interest as national deployments of smart meters have begun in many countries. However, empirically comparing disaggregation algorithms is currently virtually impossible. This is due to the different data sets used, the lack of reference implementations of these algorithms and the variety of accuracy metrics employed. To address this challenge, we present the Non-intrusive Load Monitoring Toolkit (NILMTK); an open source toolkit designed specifically to enable the comparison of energy disaggregation algorithms in a reproducible manner. This work is the first research to compare multiple disaggregation approaches across multiple publicly available data sets. Our toolkit includes parsers for a range of existing data sets, a collection of preprocessing algorithms, a set of statistics for describing data sets, two reference benchmark disaggregation algorithms and a suite of accuracy metrics. We demonstrate the range of reproducible analyses which are made possible by our toolkit, including the analysis of six publicly available data sets and the evaluation of both benchmark disaggregation algorithms across such data sets.

Categories and Subject Descriptors

I.5 [**Pattern Recognition**]: Applications
; I.2 [**Artificial Intelligence**]: Learning   *Parameter learning*

Keywords

energy disaggregation; non-intrusive load monitoring; smart meters

e-Energy'14, June 11–13, 2014, Cambridge, UK.
Copyright 2014 ACM 978-1-4503-2819-7/14/06 ...$15.00.
http://dx.doi.org/10.1145/2602044.2602051 .

1. INTRODUCTION

Non-intrusive load monitoring (NILM), or energy disaggregation, aims to break down a household s aggregate electricity consumption into individual appliances [1]. The motivations for such a process are threefold. First, informing a household s occupants of how much energy each appliance consumes empowers them to take steps towards reducing their energy consumption [2]. Second, personalised feedback can be provided which quantifies the savings of certain appliance-specific advice, such as the financial savings when an old inefficient appliance is replaced by a new efficient appliance. Third, if the NILM system is able to determine the time of use of each appliance, a recommender system would be able to inform the household s occupants of the savings of deferring appliance use to a time of day when electricity is either cheaper or has a lower carbon footprint.

Such benefits have drawn significant interest in the field since its inception 25 years ago. In recent years, the combination of smart meter meter deployments [3, 4] and reduced hardware costs of household electricity sensors has led to a rapid expansion of the field. Such rapid growth over the past five years has been evidenced by the wealth of academic papers published, international meetings held (e.g. NILM 2012[1] and EPRI NILM 2013[2]), startup companies founded (e.g. Bidgely and Neurio) and data sets released, (e.g. REDD [5], BLUED [6] and Smart* [7]).

However, three core obstacles currently prevent the direct comparison of state-of-the-art approaches, and as a result may be impeding progress within the field. To the best of our knowledge, each contribution to date has only been evaluated on a single data set and consequently it is hard to assess whether such approaches generalise to new households. Furthermore, many researchers sub-sample data sets to select specific households, appliances and time periods, making experimental results more difficult to reproduce. Second, newly proposed approaches are rarely compared against the same benchmark algorithms, further increasing the difficulty in empirical comparisons of performance between different publications. Moreover, the lack of reference implementations of these state-of-the-art algorithms often leads to the reimplementation of such approaches. Third, many papers target different use cases for NILM and therefore the ac-

---
[1]http://www.ices.cmu.edu/psii/nilm/
[2]http://goo.gl/dr4tpq

curacy of their proposed approaches are evaluated using a different set of performance metrics. As a result the numerical performance calculated by such metrics cannot be compared between any two papers. These three obstacles have led to the proposal of successive extensions to state-of-the-art algorithms, while a direct comparison between new and existing approaches remains impossible.

Similar obstacles have arisen in other research fields and prompted the development of toolkits specifically designed to support research in that area. For example, PhysioToolkit offers access to over 50 databases of physiological data and provides software to support the processing and analysis of such data for the biomedical research community [8]. Similarly, CRAWDAD collects 89 data sets of wireless network data in addition to software to aid the analysis of such data for the wireless network community [9]. However, no such toolkit is available to the NILM community.

Against this background, we propose NILMTK[3]; an open source toolkit designed specifically to enable easy access to and comparative analysis of energy disaggregation algorithms across diverse data sets. NILMTK provides a complete pipeline from data sets to accuracy metrics, thereby lowering the entry barrier for researchers to implement a new algorithm and compare its performance against the current state of the art. NILMTK has been:

released as open source software (with documentation[4]) in an effort to encourage researchers to contribute data sets, benchmark algorithms and accuracy metrics as they are proposed, with the goal of enabling a greater level of collaboration within the community.

designed using a modular structure, therefore allowing researchers to reuse or replace individual components as required. The API design is influenced by `scikit-learn` [10], which is a machine learning library in Python, well known for its consistent API and complete documentation.

written in Python with flat file input and output formats, in addition to high performance binary formats, ensuring compatibility with existing algorithms written in any language and designed for any platform.

The contributions of NILMTK are summarised as follows:

We propose NILMTK-DF (data format), the standard energy disaggregation data structure used by our toolkit. NILMTK-DF is modelled loosely on the REDD data set format [5] to allow easy adoption within the community. Furthermore, we provide parsers from six existing data sets into our proposed NILMTK-DF format.

We provide statistical and diagnostic functions which provide a detailed understanding of each data set. We also provide preprocessing functions for mitigating common challenges with NILM data sets.

We provide implementations of two benchmark disaggregation algorithms: first an approach based on combinatorial optimisation [1], and second an approach

based on the factorial hidden Markov model [5, 11]. We demonstrate the ease by which NILMTK allows the comparison of these algorithms across a range of existing data sets, and present results of their performance.

We present a suite of accuracy metrics which enables the evaluation of any disaggregation algorithm compatible with NILMTK. This allows the performance of a disaggregation algorithm to be evaluated for a range of use cases.

The remainder of this paper is organised as follows. In Section 2 we provide an overview of related work. In Section 3 we present NILMTK and describe its components. In Section 4 we demonstrate the empirical evaluations which are enabled by NILMTK, and provide analyses of existing data sets and disaggregation algorithms. Finally, in Section 5 we conclude the paper and propose directions for future work.

2. BACKGROUND

The field of non-intrusive load monitoring was founded 25 years ago when Hart proposed the first algorithm for the disaggregation of household energy usage [1, 12]. However, the majority of research prior to 2011 had been evaluated using either lab-based or simulated data and hence the performance of disaggregation algorithms in real households had remained unknown. More recently, national deployments of smart meters have prompted a renewed interest in energy disaggregation. We now discuss recent research which has contributed new data sets (Section 2.1), disaggregation algorithms (Section 2.2) and evaluation metrics (Section 2.3) to the field. In Section 2.4 we discuss general purpose toolkits, and finally in Section 2.5 we formalise the NILM problem drawing upon notation used in prior literature.

2.1 Public Data Sets

In 2011, the Reference Energy Disaggregation Dataset (REDD) [5] was introduced as the first publicly available data set collected specifically to aid NILM research. The data set contains both aggregate and sub-metered power data from six households, and has since become the most popular data set for evaluating energy disaggregation algorithms. In 2012, the Building-Level fUlly-labeled dataset for Electricity Disaggregation (BLUED) [6] was released containing data from a single household. However, the data set does not include sub-metered power data, and instead records events triggered by appliance state changes. As a result, it is only possible to evaluate whether changes in appliance states have been detected (e.g. washing machine turns on), rather than the assignment of aggregate power demand to individual appliances (e.g. washing machine draws 2 kW power). More recently, the Smart* [7] data set was released, which contains household aggregate power data from three households, while sub-metered appliance power data was only collected from a single household.

In 2013 the Pecan Street sample data set was released [13], which contains both aggregate and sub-metered power data from 10 households. Later, the Household Electricity Survey data set was released [14], which contains data from 251 households although aggregate data was only collected for 14 households. The Almanac of Minutely Power dataset (AMPds) [15] was also released that year containing both

[3]Code: http://github.com/nilmtk/nilmtk (release v0.1.0 was used for this paper)
[4]Documentation: http://nilmtk.github.io/nilmtk

Data set	Institution	Location	Duration per house	Number of houses	Appliance sample frequency	Aggregate sample frequency
REDD (2011)	MIT	MA, USA	3-19 days	6	3 sec	1 sec & 15 kHz
BLUED (2012)	CMU	PA, USA	8 days	1	N/A*	12 kHz
Smart* (2012)	UMass	MA, USA	3 months	3	1 sec	1 sec
Tracebase (2012)	Darmstadt	Germany	N/A	N/A	1-10 sec	N/A
Sample (2013)	Pecan Street	TX, USA	7 days	10	1 min	1 min
HES (2013)	DECC, DEFRA	UK	1 or 12 months	251	2 or 10 min	2 or 10 min
AMPds (2013)	Simon Fraser U.	BC, Canada	1 year	1	1 min	1 min
iAWE (2013)	IIIT Delhi	Delhi, India	73 days	1	1 or 6 sec	1 sec
UK-DALE (2014)	Imperial College	London, UK	3-17 months	4	6 sec	1-6 sec & 16 kHz

Table 1: Comparison of household energy data sets. *BLUED labels state transitions for each appliance.

aggregate and sub-metered power data from a single household. Subsequently, the Indian data for Ambient Water and Electricity Sensing (iAWE) [16] was released, which contains both aggregate and sub-metered power data from a single house. Most recently, the UK Domestic Appliance-Level Electricity data set [17] (UK-DALE) was released which contains data from four households using both aggregate meters and individual appliance sub-meters. Unfortunately, subtle differences in the aims of each data set have led to completely different data formats being used. As a result, a time-consuming engineering barrier exists when using the data sets, each of which are in different formats. This has resulted in publications using only a single data set to evaluate a given approach, and consequently the generality of results over large numbers of households are rarely investigated. We summarise these data sets in Table 1.

2.2 Disaggregation Algorithms & Benchmarks

The REDD data set was proposed along with a performance result of a benchmark disaggregation algorithm using 10 second data across five of the six households [5]. Kolter and Jaakkola later proposed an extension to the benchmark algorithm [18], however the extension was only evaluated using features extracted from 15 kHz data from a single house from the data set, and therefore the performance results are not directly comparable. Later, Zeifman [19] and Johnson and Willsky [20] evaluated various approaches using the same data set, although both selected a different subset of appliances and calculated an artificial household aggregate from these appliances, therefore simplifying the disaggregation problem and preventing a numerical comparison with other publications. Subsequently, Parson et al. [21] and Rahayu et al. [22] both proposed new approaches, although each were evaluated using a different set of four houses from the REDD data set, again preventing a numerical comparison between publications. Last, Batra et al. [23] evaluated their approach on the REDD data set using a different household to Kolter and Jaakkola. As a result, it has not been possible to deduce whether one approach is preferable to another from the literature.

The BLUED data set was introduced along with a benchmark algorithm [6], but has since only been used by one other publication [24]. Similarly, AMPds has only been used to evaluate disaggregation algorithms proposed by the data set authors [15]. Clearly, the variety of different formats is slowing the uptake of new data sets, and also preventing algorithms from being tested across multiple data sets.

It is essential to compare newly proposed disaggregation algorithms to the state of the art in order to assess the increase in an algorithm s performance. However, the lack of available reference implementations of state-of-the-art disaggregation algorithms has led to authors often comparing against more basic benchmark algorithms. This problem is further compounded since there is no single consensus on which benchmarks to use, and as a result most publications use a different benchmark algorithm. For example, Kolter and Jaakkola compared their approach to a set of decoupled HMMs [18], Parson et al. and Batra et al. both evaluated their approaches against variants of their own approaches [21, 23], Zeifman compared their approach to a Bayesian classifier, while Rahayu et al. and Johnson and Willsky both compared against a factorial hidden Markov model (FHMM) [22, 20]. Clearly, further publications would benefit from openly available benchmark algorithms against which newly proposed algorithms could be easily compared.

2.3 Evaluation Metrics

The range of different application areas of energy disaggregation has prompted a number of evaluation metrics to be proposed. For example, four disaggregation metrics labelled *energy correctly assigned* have recently been used to evaluate the performance of disaggregation algorithms using the REDD data set. First, Kolter and Johnson [5] proposed an accuracy metric which captures the error in assigned energy normalised by the actual energy consumption in each time slice averaged over all appliances, which was also later used by Rahayu et al. [22] and Johnson and Willsky [20]. However, large errors in the assigned energy in some time slices will result in a negative accuracy, making this an ill-posed metric. Second, Kolter and Jaakkola [18] proposed an equivalent metric wherein the error is presented individually for each appliance rather than an average across all appliances. Third, Parson et al. [21] proposed a metric which captures the error in assigned energy consumed over the complete duration of the data set rather than per time slice. This metric allows overestimates and underestimates in the assigned energy in different time slices to cancel out, and therefore does not represent all disaggregation errors. Fourth, Batra et al. [23] proposed a subtly different metric to Kolter and Johnson [5], in which error is reported instead of accuracy, and also energy assigned to an incorrect appliance is double counted as both an overestimate of one appliance s energy consumption and an underestimate of another. The differences between these four metrics prevent numerical compar-

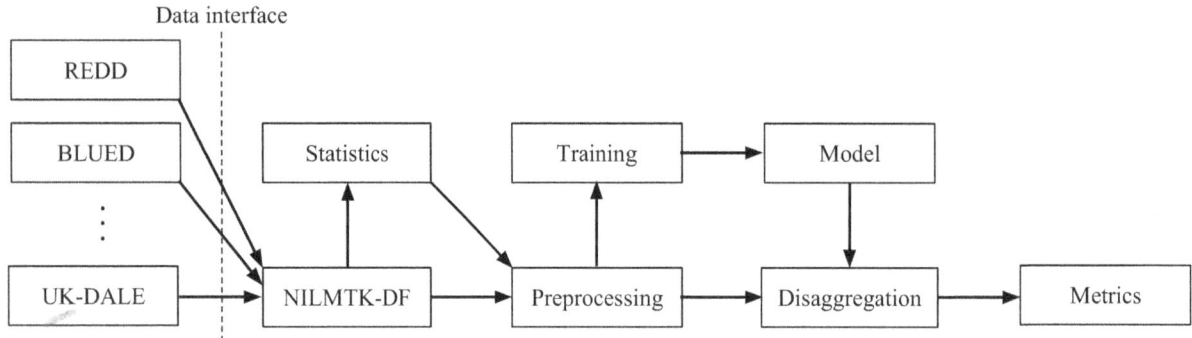

Figure 1: NILMTK pipeline. At each stage of the pipeline, results and data can be stored to or loaded from disk.

isons between publications, and motivate the use of common metrics.

2.4 General Purpose Toolkits

Although no toolkit currently exists specifically for energy disaggregation, various toolkits are available for more general machine learning tasks. For example, `scikit-learn` is a general purpose machine learning toolkit implemented in Python [10] and `GraphLab` is a machine learning and data mining toolkit written in C++ [25]. While such toolkits provide generic implementations of machine learning algorithms, they lack functionality specific to the energy disaggregation domain, such as data set parsers, benchmark disaggregation algorithms, and energy disaggregation metrics. Therefore, an energy disaggregation toolkit should extend such general toolkits rather than replace them, in a similar way that `scikit-learn` adds machine learning functionality to the `numpy` numerical library for Python.

2.5 Energy Disaggregation De nition

The aim of energy disaggregation is to provide estimates, $\hat{y}_t^{(n)}$, of the actual power demand, $y_t^{(n)}$, of each appliance n at time t, from household aggregate power readings, $\bar{y}_t$. Most NILM algorithms model appliances using a set of discrete states such as o , on, intermediate, etc. We use $x_t^{(n)} \in \mathbb{Z}_{>0}$ to represent the ground truth state, and $\hat{x}_t^{(n)}$ to represent the appliance state estimated by a disaggregation algorithm.

3. NILMTK

We designed NILMTK with two core use cases in mind. First, it should enable the analysis of existing data sets and algorithms. Second, it should provide a simple interface for the addition of new data sets and algorithms. To do so, we implemented NILMTK in Python due to the availability of a vast set of libraries supporting both machine learning research (e.g. `Pandas`, `scikit-learn`) and the deployment of such research as web applications (e.g. `Django`). Furthermore, Python allows easy deployment in diverse environments including academic settings and is increasingly being used for data science.

Figure 1 presents the NILMTK pipeline from the import of data sets to the evaluation of various disaggregation algorithms over various metrics. In the remainder of this section we discuss each module of the pipeline: the NILMTK data format, the data set diagnostics and statistics, preprocessing, disaggregation, model import and export and finally we describe accuracy metrics.

3.1 Data Format

Motivated by our discussion in Section 2.1 of the wide differences between multiple data sets released in the public domain, we propose NILMTK-DF; a common data set format inspired by the REDD format [5], into which existing data sets can be converted. NILMTK currently includes importers for the following six data sets: REDD, Smart*, Pecan Street, iAWE, AMPds and UK-DALE. BLUED was excluded due to the lack of sub-metered power data, the Tracebase data set was excluded due to the lack of household aggregate power data and HES was excluded due to time constraints.

After import, the data resides in our NILMTK-DF in-memory data structure, which is used throughout the NILMTK pipeline. Data can be saved or loaded from disk at multiple stages in the NILMTK processing pipeline to allow other tools to interact with NILMTK. We provide two CSV flat file formats: a rich NILMTK-DF CSV format and a strict REDD format which allows researchers to use their existing tools designed to process REDD data. We also provide a more efficient binary format using the Hierarchical Data Format (HDF5). In addition to storing electricity data, NILMTK-DF can also store relevant metadata and other sensor modalities such as gas, water, temperature, etc. It has been shown that such additional sensor and metadata information may help enhance NILM prediction [26].

Another important feature of our format is the standardisation of nomenclature. Di erent data sets use di erent labels for the same class of appliance (e.g. REDD uses refrigerator whilst AMPds uses FGE) and di erent names for the measured parameters. When data is first imported into NILMTK, these diverse labels are converted to a standard vocabulary [27].

In addition, NILMTK allows rich metadata to be associated with a household, appliance or meter. For example, NILMTK can store the parameters measured by each meter (e.g. reactive power, real power), the geographical coordinates of each house (to enable weather data to be retrieved), the mains wiring defining the meter hierarchy (useful if a single appliance is measured at the appliance, circuit and aggregate levels), whether a single meter measures multiple appliances and whether a specific lamp is dimmable. Our full NILM Metadata schema is described in [27].

Through such a combination of metadata and standard nomenclature, NILMTK allows for analysis of appliance data across multiple data sets. For example, users can perform queries such as: what is the energy consumption of refrigerators in the USA compared to the UK? .

We have defined a common interface for data set importers which, combined with the definition of our in-memory data structures, enables developers to easily add new data set importers to NILMTK.

3.2 Data Set Diagnostics

Since no data set is perfect, researchers are required to explore the characteristics of each data set before disaggregation approaches can be evaluated. To help diagnose these issues, NILMTK provides diagnostic functions including:

Detect gaps: Many NILM algorithms assume that each sensor channel is contiguous. However, this assumption is violated when sensors are o or malfunctioning. A gap exists between any pair of consecutive samples if the time elapsed between them is larger than a predefined threshold.

Dropout rate: The dropout rate is the total number of recorded samples, divided by the number of expected samples (which is the length of the time window under consideration multiplied by the sample rate).

Dropout rate (ignoring gaps): To quantify the rate at which a wireless sensor drops samples due to radio issues, we first remove large gaps where the sensor is o and subsequently calculate the dropout rate for the remaining contiguous sections.

Up-time: The up-time is the total time for which a sensor was recording. It is the last timestamp, minus the first timestamp, minus the duration of any gaps.

Diagnose: NILMTK provides a single `diagnose` function which checks for all the issues we have encountered.

3.3 Data Set Statistics

Distinct from *diagnostic* statistics, NILMTK also provides functions for exploring appliance usage, e.g.:

Proportion of energy sub-metered: Data sets rarely sub-meter every appliance or circuit, and as a result it is useful to quantify the proportion of total energy measured by sub-metered channels. Prior to calculating this statistic, all gaps present in the mains recordings are masked out of each sub-metered channel, and therefore any additional missing sub-meter data is assumed to be due to the meter and load being switched o .

Section 3.2 and 3.3 have described a subset of the diagnostic and statistical functions in NILMTK.

Further functions are listed in in the statistics section of the online documentation.[5]

3.4 Preprocessing of Data Sets

To mitigate the problems with di erent data sets, some of which were presented in Section 3.2, NILMTK provides several preprocessing functions, including:

Downsample: As seen in Table 1, the sampling rate of appliance monitors varies from 0.008 Hz to 16 kHz across the data sets. The downsample preprocessor down-samples data sets to a specified frequency using aggregation functions such as mean, mode and median.

Voltage normalisation: The data sets presented in Table 1 have been collected from di erent countries, where voltage fluctuations vary widely. Batra et al. showed voltage fluctuates from 180-250 V in the iAWE data set collected in India [16], while the voltage in the Smart* data set varies

across the range 118-123 V. Hart suggested to account for these voltage fluctuations as they can significantly impact power draw [1]. Therefore, NILMTK provides a voltage normalisation function based on Hart s equation:

$$Power_{normalised} = \left(\frac{Voltage_{nominal}}{Voltage_{observed}} \right)^2 \times Power_{observed} \quad (1)$$

Top-k appliances: It is often advantageous to model the top-k energy consuming appliances instead of all appliances for the following three reasons. First, the disaggregation of such appliances provides the most value. Second, such appliances contribute the most salient features, and therefore the remaining appliances can be considered to contribute only noise. Third, each additional modelled appliance might contribute significantly to the complexity of the disaggregation task. Therefore, NILMTK provides a function to identify the top-k energy consuming appliances.

NILMTK also provides preprocessing functions for fixing other common issues with these data sets, such as: (i) interpolating small periods of missing data when appliance sensors did not report readings, (ii) filtering out implausible values (such as readings where observed voltage is more than twice the rated voltage) and (iii) filtering out appliance data when mains data is missing.

Each data set importer defines a `preprocess` function which runs the necessary preprocessing functions to clean the specific data set.

A detailed account of preprocessing functions supported by NILMTK can be found in the online documentation.[6]

3.5 Training and Disaggregation Algorithms

NILMTK provides implementations of two common benchmark disaggregation algorithms: combinatorial optimisation (CO) and factorial hidden Markov model (FHMM). CO was proposed by Hart in his seminal work [1], while techniques based on extensions of the FHMM have been proposed more recently [5, 11]. The aim of the inclusion of these algorithms is not to present state-of-the-art disaggregation results, but instead to enable new approaches to be compared to well-studied benchmark algorithms without requiring the reimplementation of such algorithms. We now describe these two algorithms.

Combinatorial Optimisation: CO finds the optimal combination of appliance states, which minimises the di erence between the sum of the predicted appliance power and the observed aggregate power, subject to a set of appliance models.

$$\hat{x}_t^{(n)} = \underset{x_t^{(n)}}{\operatorname{argmin}} \left| \bar{y}_t - \sum_{n=1}^{N} \hat{y}_t^{(n)} \right| \quad (2)$$

Since each time slice is considered as a separate optimisation problem, each time slice is assumed to be independent. CO resembles the subset sum problem and thus is NP-complete. The complexity of disaggregation for T time slices is $O(TK^N)$, where N is the number of appliances and K is the number of appliance states. Since the complexity of CO is exponential in the number of appliances, the approach is only computationally tractable for a small number of modelled appliances.

Factorial Hidden Markov Model: The power demand of each appliance can be modelled as the observed value of

---

[5] http://nilmtk.github.io/nilmtk/stats.html

[6] http://nilmtk.github.io/nilmtk/preprocessing.html

a hidden Markov model (HMM). The hidden component of these HMMs are the states of the appliances. Energy disaggregation involves jointly decoding the power draw of n appliances and hence a factorial HMM [28] is well suited. A FHMM can be represented by an equivalent HMM in which each state corresponds to a different combination of states of each appliance. Such a FHMM model has three parameters: (i) prior probability (π) containing K^N entries, (ii) transition matrix (A) containing $K^N \times K^N$ or K^{2N} entries, and (iii) emission matrix (B) containing $2K^N$ entries. The complexity of exact disaggregation for such a model is $O(TK^{2N})$, and as a result FHMMs scale even worse than CO. From an implementation perspective, even storing (or computing) A for 14 appliances with two states each consumes 8 GB of RAM. Hence, we propose to validate FHMMs on preprocessed data where the top-k appliances are modelled, and appliances contributing less than a given threshold are discarded. However, it should be noted that more efficient pseudo-time algorithms could alternatively be used for inference over both CO and FHMM.

For algorithms such as FHMMs, it is necessary to model the relationships amongst consecutive samples. Thus, NILMTK provides facilities for dividing data into continuous sets for training and testing. While we have discussed supervised and non-event based algorithms here, NILMTK also supports event based and unsupervised approaches.

3.6 Appliance Model Import and Export

Many approaches require sub-metered power data to be collected for training purposes from the same household in which disaggregation is to be performed. However, such data is costly and intrusive to collect, and therefore is unlikely to be available in a large-scale deployment of a NILM system. As a result, recent research has proposed training methods which do not require sub-metered power data to be collected from each household [11, 21]. To provide a clear interface between training and disaggregation algorithms, NILMTK provides a *model* module which encapsulates the results of the training module required by the disaggregation module. Each implementation of the module must provide import and export functions to interface with a JSON file for persistent model storage. NILMTK currently includes importers and exporters for both the FHMM and CO approaches described in Section 3.5.

3.7 Accuracy Metrics

As discussed in Section 2.3, a range of accuracy metrics are required due to the diversity of application areas of energy disaggregation research. To satisfy this requirement, NILMTK provides a set of metrics which combines both general detection metrics and those specific to energy disaggregation. We now give a brief description of each metric implemented in NILMTK along with its mathematical definition.

Error in total energy assigned: The difference between the total assigned energy and the actual energy consumed by appliance n over the entire data set.

$$\left| \sum_t y_t^{(n)} - \sum_t \hat{y}_t^{(n)} \right| \tag{3}$$

Fraction of total energy assigned correctly: The overlap between the fraction of energy assigned to each appliance and the actual fraction of energy consumed by each appliance over the data set.

$$\sum_n \min\left(\frac{\sum_n y_t^{(n)}}{\sum_{n,t} y_t^{(n)}}, \frac{\sum_n \hat{y}_t^{(n)}}{\sum_{n,t} \hat{y}_t^{(n)}} \right) \tag{4}$$

Normalised error in assigned power: The sum of the differences between the assigned power and actual power of appliance n in each time slice t, normalised by the appliance's total energy consumption.

$$\frac{\sum_t \left| y_t^{(n)} - \hat{y}_t^{(n)} \right|}{\sum_t y_t^{(n)}} \tag{5}$$

RMS error in assigned power: The root mean square error between the assigned power and actual power of appliance n in each time slice t.

$$\sqrt{\frac{1}{T} \sum_t \left(y_t^{(n)} - \hat{y}_t^{(n)} \right)^2} \tag{6}$$

Confusion matrix: The number of time slices in which each of an appliance's states were either confused with every other state or correctly classified.

True positives, False positives, False negatives, True negatives: The number of time slices in which appliance n was either correctly classified as being on (TP), classified as being on while it was actually off (FP), classified as off while is was actually on (FN) and correctly classified as being off (TN).

$$TP^{(n)} = \sum_t \text{AND}\left(x_t^{(n)} = on, \hat{x}_t^{(n)} = on \right) \tag{7}$$

$$FP^{(n)} = \sum_t \text{AND}\left(x_t^{(n)} = off, \hat{x}_t^{(n)} = on \right) \tag{8}$$

$$FN^{(n)} = \sum_t \text{AND}\left(x_t^{(n)} = on, \hat{x}_t^{(n)} = off \right) \tag{9}$$

$$TN^{(n)} = \sum_t \text{AND}\left(x_t^{(n)} = off, \hat{x}_t^{(n)} = off \right) \tag{10}$$

True/False positive rate: The fraction of time slices in which an appliance was correctly predicted to be on that it was actually on (TPR), and the fraction of time slices in which the appliance was incorrectly predicted to be on that it was actually off (FPR). We omit appliance indices n in the following metrics for clarity.

$$TPR = \frac{TP}{(TP + FN)} \tag{11}$$

$$FPR = \frac{FP}{(FP + TN)} \tag{12}$$

Precision, Recall: The fraction of time slices in which an appliance was correctly predicted to be on that it was actually off (Precision), and the fraction of time slices in which the appliance was correctly predicted to be on that it was actually on (Recall).

$$Precision = \frac{TP}{(TP + FP)} \tag{13}$$

$$Recall = \frac{TP}{(TP + FN)} \tag{14}$$

Data set	Number of appliances	Percentage energy sub-metered	Dropout rate (percent) ignoring gaps	Mains up-time per house (days)	Percentage up-time
REDD	9, 16, 23	58, 71, 89	0, 10, 16	4, 18, 19	8, 40, 79
Smart*	25	86	0	88	96
Pecan Street	13, 14, 22	75, 87, 150	0, 0, 0	7, 7, 7	100, 100, 100
AMPds	20	97	0	364	100
iAWE	10	48	8	47	93
UK-DALE	4, 12, 53	19, 48, 82	0, 7, 22	36, 102, 470	73, 84, 100

Table 2: Summary of data set results calculated by the diagnostic and statistical functions in NILMTK. Each cell represents the range of values across all households per data set. The three numbers per cell are the minimum, median and maximum values. AMPds, Smart* and iAWE each contain just a single house, hence these rows have a single number per cell.

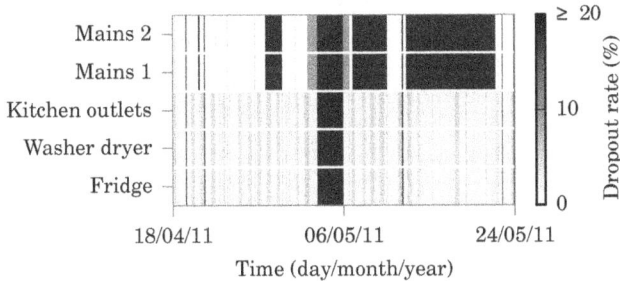

Figure 2: Lost samples per hour from a representative subset of channels in REDD house 1.

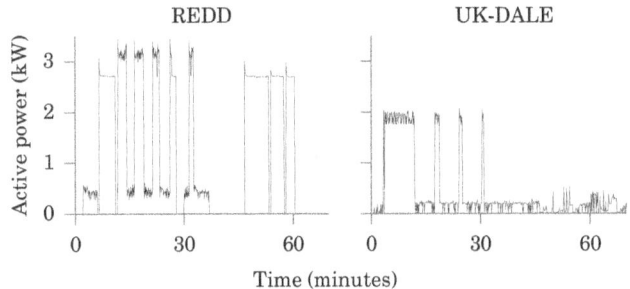

Figure 3: Comparison of power draw of washing machines in one house from REDD (USA) and UK-DALE.

F-score: The harmonic mean of precision and recall.

$$F\text{-}score = \frac{2.Precision.Recall}{Precision + Recall} \qquad (15)$$

Hamming loss: The total information lost when appliances are incorrectly classified over the data set.

$$HammingLoss = \frac{1}{T}\sum_t \frac{1}{N}\sum_n \text{XOR}\left(x_t^{(n)}, \hat{x}_t^{(n)}\right) \qquad (16)$$

4. EVALUATION

We now demonstrate several examples of the rich analyses supported by NILMTK. First, we diagnose some common (and inevitable) issues in a selection of data sets. Second, we show various patterns of appliance usage. Third, we give some examples of the effect of voltage normalisation on the power demand of individual appliances, and discuss how this might affect the performance of a disaggregation algorithm. Fourth, we present summary performance results of the two benchmark algorithms included in NILMTK across six data sets using a number of accuracy metrics. Finally, we present detailed results of these algorithms for a single data set, and discuss their performance for different appliances.

4.1 Data Set Diagnostics

Table 2 shows a selection of diagnostic and statistical functions (defined in Section 3.2 and 3.3) computed by NILMTK across six public data sets. BLUED, Tracebase and HES were not included for the same reasons as in Section 3.1. The table illustrates that AMPds used a robust recording platform because it has a percentage up-time of 100%, a dropout rate of zero and 97% of the energy recorded by the mains channel was captured by the sub-meters. Similarly, Pecan Street has an up-time of 100% and zero dropout rate.

However, two homes in the Pecan Street data registered a proportion of energy sub-metered of over 100%. This indicates that some overlap exists between the metered channels, and as a result some appliances are metered by multiple channels. This illustrates the importance of data set metadata (proposed as part of NILMTK-DF in Section 3.1) describing the basic mains wiring.

Figure 2 shows the distribution of missing samples for REDD house 1. From this we can see that each mains recording channel has four large gaps (the solid black blocks) where the sensors are off. The sub-metered channels have only one large gap. Ignoring this gap and focusing on the time periods where the sensors are recording, we see numerous periods where the dropout rate is around 10%. Such issues are by no means unique to REDD and are crucial to diagnose before data sets can be used for the evaluation of disaggregation algorithms or for data set statistics.

4.2 Data Set Statistics

Energy disaggregation systems must model individual appliances. Hence, as well as diagnosing technical issues with each data set, NILMTK also provides functions to visualise patterns of behaviour recorded in each data set. For example, different appliances draw a different amount of power (e.g. a toaster draws approximately 1.57 kW), are used at different times of day (e.g. the TV is usually on in the evening) and have different correlations with external factors such as weather (e.g. lower outside temperature implies more usage of electric heating). Furthermore, load profiles of different appliances of the same type can vary considerably, especially appliances from different countries (e.g. the two washing machine profiles in Figure 3). Some disaggregation systems benefit by capturing these patterns (for example, the conditional factorial hidden Markov model

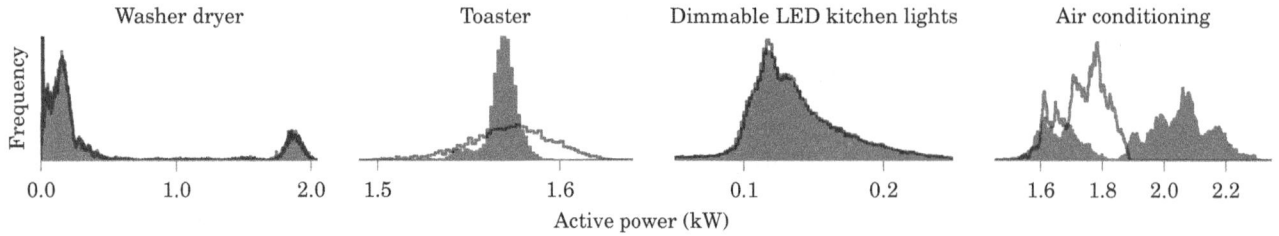

Figure 4: Histograms of power consumption. The filled grey plots show histograms of normalised power. The thin, grey, semi-transparent lines drawn over the filled plots show histograms of un-normalised power.

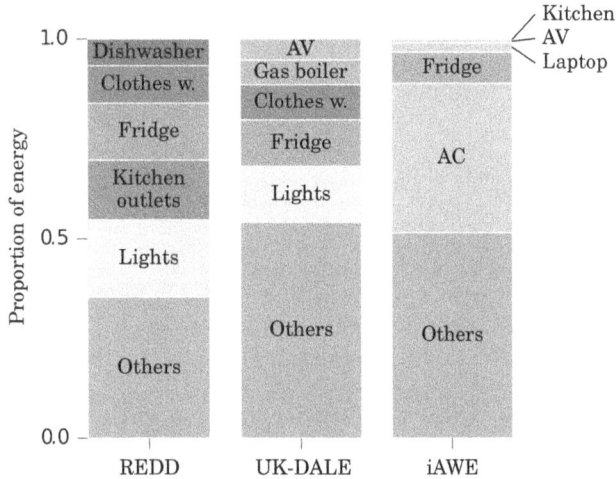

Figure 5: Top five appliances in terms of the proportion of the total energy used in a single house (house 1) in each of REDD (USA), iAWE (India) and UK-DALE.

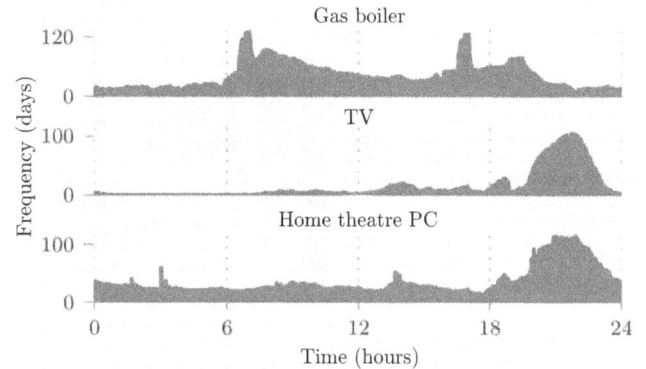

Figure 6: Daily appliance usage histograms of three appliances over 120 days from UK-DALE house 1.

(CFHMM) [11] can model the influence of time of day on appliance usage). In the following sections, we present examples of how such information can be extracted from existing data sets using NILMTK, covering the distribution of appliance power demands (Section 4.2.1), usage patterns (Section 4.2.2) and external dependencies (Section 4.2.3).

4.2.1 Appliance power demands

Figure 4 displays histograms of the distribution of powers used by a selection of appliances (the washer dryer, toaster and dimmable LED kitchen lights are from UK-DALE house 1; the air conditioning unit is from iAWE). Appliances such as toasters and kettles tend to have just two possible power states: on and off. This simplicity makes them amenable to be modelled by, for example, Markov chains with only two states per chain. In contrast, more complex appliances such as washing machines, vacuum cleaners and computers often have many more states.

Figure 5 shows examples of how the proportion of energy use per appliance varies between countries. It can seen that the REDD and UK-DALE households share some similarities in the breakdown of household energy consumption. In contrast, the iAWE house shows a vastly different energy breakdown. For example, the house recorded in India for the iAWE data set has two air conditioning units which account for almost half of the household's energy consumption, whilst the example household from the UK-DALE data set does not even contain an air conditioner.

4.2.2 Appliance usage patterns

Figure 6 shows histograms which represent usage patterns for three appliances over an average day, from which strong similarities between groups of appliances can be seen. For example, the usage patterns of the TV and Home theatre PC are very similar because the Home theatre PC is the only video source for the TV. In contrast, the boiler has a usage pattern which occurs as a result of the household's occupancy pattern and hot water timer in mornings and evenings.

4.2.3 Appliance correlations with weather

Previous studies have shown correlations between temperature and heating/cooling demand in Australia [29] and between temperature and total household demand in the USA [30]. Such correlations could be used by a NILM system to refine its appliance usage estimates [31].

Figure 7 shows correlations between boiler usage and maximum temperature (appliance data from UK-DALE house 1, temperature data from UK Met Office). The correlation between external maximum temperature and boiler usage is strong ($R^2 = 0.73$) and it is noteworthy that the x-axis intercept (19 C) is approximately the set point for the boiler thermostat.

4.3 Voltage Normalisation

Normalisation can be used to minimise the effect of voltage fluctuations in a household's aggregate power. Figure 4 shows histograms for both the normalised and un-normalised appliance power consumption. Normalisation produces a noticeably tighter power distribution for linear resistive appliances such as the toaster, although it has little effect on constant power appliances, such as the washer dryer or LED

Data set	Train time (s)		Disaggregate time (s)		NEP		FTE		F-score	
	CO	FHMM	CO	FHMM	CO	FHMM	CO	FHMM	CO	FHMM
REDD	3.67	22.81	0.14	1.21	1.61	1.35	0.77	0.83	0.31	0.31
Smart*	3.40	46.34	0.39	1.85	3.10	2.71	0.50	0.66	0.53	0.61
Pecan Street	1.72	2.83	0.02	0.12	0.68	0.75	0.99	0.87	0.77	0.77
AMPds	5.92	298.49	3.08	22.58	2.23	0.96	0.44	0.84	0.55	0.71
iAWE	1.68	8.90	0.07	0.38	0.91	0.91	0.89	0.89	0.73	0.73
UK-DALE	1.06	11.42	0.10	0.52	3.66	3.67	0.81	0.80	0.38	0.38

Table 3: Comparison of CO and FHMM across multiple data sets.

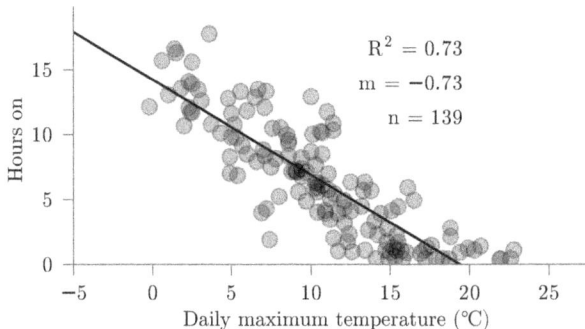

Figure 7: Linear regression showing correlation between gas boiler usage and external temperature. R^2 **denotes the coefficient of determination,** m **is the gradient of the regression line and** n **is the number of data-points (days) used in the regression.**

kitchen ceiling lights. Moreover, for non-linear appliances such as the air conditioner, normalisation increases the variance in power draw. This is in conformance with work by Hart [1] which proposed a modified approach to normalisation:

$$Power_{normalised} = \left(\frac{Voltage_{nominal}}{Voltage_{observed}} \right) \times Power_{observed} \quad (17)$$

For linear appliances such as the toaster, = 2, whereas for appliances such as fridge, Hart found = 0.7. Thus, we believe the benefit of voltage normalisation is dependent on the proportion of resistive loads in a household.

4.4 Disaggregation Across Data Sets

We now compare the disaggregation results across the first house of six publicly available data sets. Again, BLUED, Tracebase and HES were not included for the same reasons as in Section 3.1. Since all the data sets were collected over di erent durations, we used the first half of the samples for training and the remaining half for disaggregation across all data sets. Further, we preprocessed the REDD, UK-DALE, Smart* and iAWE data sets to 1 minute frequency using the down-sampling filter (Section 3.4) to account for different aggregate and mains data sampling frequencies and compensating for intermittent lost data packets. The small gaps in REDD, UK-DALE, SMART* and iAWE were interpolated, while the time periods where either the mains data or appliance data were missing were ignored. AMPds and the Pecan Street data did not require any preprocessing.

Since both CO and FHMM have exponential computational complexity in the number of appliances, we model only those appliances whose total energy contribution was

greater than 5%. Across all the data sets, the appliances which contribute more than 5% of the aggregate include HVAC appliances such as the air conditioner and electric heating, and appliances which are used throughout the day such as the fridge. We model all appliances using two states (on and o) across our analyses, although it should be noted that any number of states could be used. However, our experiments are intended to demonstrate a fair comparison of the benchmark algorithms, rather than a fully optimised version of either approach. We compare the disaggregation performance of CO and FHMM across the following three metrics defined in Section 3.7: (i) fraction of total energy assigned correctly (FTE), (ii) normalised error in assigned power (NEP) and (iii) F-score. These metrics were chosen because they have been used most often in prior NILM work. F-score and FTE vary between 0 and 1, while NEP can take any non-negative value. Preferable performance is indicated by a low NEP and a high FTE and F-score. The evaluation was performed on a laptop with a 2.3 GHz i7 processor and 8 GB RAM running Linux. We fixed the random seed for experiment repeatability, the details of which can be found on the project github page.

Table 3 summarises the results of the two algorithms across the six data sets. It can be observed that FHMM performance is superior to CO performance across the three metrics for REDD, Smart* and AMPds. This confirms the theoretical foundations proposed by Hart [1]; that CO is highly sensitive to small variations in the aggregate load. The FHMM approach overcomes these shortcomings by considering an associated transition probability between the di erent states of an appliance. However, it can be seen that CO performance is similar to FHMM performance in iAWE, Pecan Street and UK-DALE across all metrics. This is likely due to the fact that very few appliances contribute more than 5% of the household aggregate load in the selected households in these data sets. For instance, space heating contributes very significantly (about 60% for a single air conditioner which has a power draw of 2.7 kW in the Pecan Street house and about 35% across two air conditioners having a power draw of 1.8 kW and 1.6 kW respectively in iAWE). As a result, these appliances are easier to disaggregate by both algorithms, owing to their relatively high power demand in comparison to appliances such as electronics and lighting. In the UK-DALE house the washing machine was one of the appliances contributing more than 5% of the household aggregate load, which brought down overall metrics across both approaches.

Another important aspect to consider is the time required for training and disaggregation, again reported in Table 3. These timings confirm the fact that CO is exponentially quicker than FHMM. This raises an interesting insight: in households such as the ones used from Pecan Street and

Appliance	NEP		F-score	
	CO	FHMM	CO	FHMM
Air conditioner 1	0.3	0.3	0.9	0.9
Air conditioner 2	1.0	1.0	0.7	0.7
Entertainment unit	4.2	4.1	0.3	0.3
Fridge	0.5	0.5	0.8	0.8
Laptop computer	1.7	1.8	0.3	0.2
Washing machine	130.1	125.1	0.0	0.0

Table 4: Comparison of CO and FHMM across different appliances in iAWE data set.

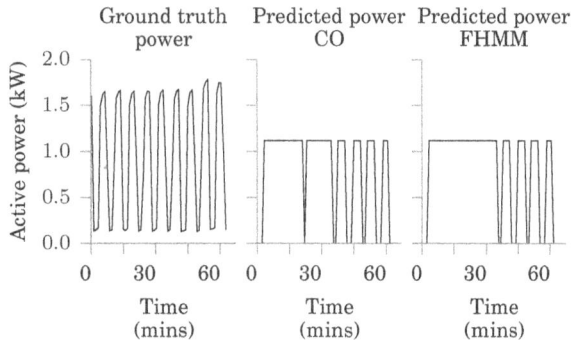

Figure 8: Predicted power (CO and FHMM) with ground truth for air conditioner 2 in the iAWE data set.

iAWE in the above analysis, it may be beneficial to use CO over a FHMM owing to the reduced amount of time required for training and disaggregation, even though FHMMs are in general considered to be more powerful. It should be noted that the greater amount of time required to train and disaggregate the AMPds data is a result of the data set containing one year of data, as opposed to the Pecan Street data set which contains one week of data, as shown by Table 1.

4.5 Detailed Disaggregation Results

Having compared disaggregation results across different data sets, we now give a detailed discussion of disaggregation results across different appliances for a single house in the iAWE data set. The iAWE data set was chosen for this experiment as the authors provided metadata such as set temperature of air conditioners and other occupant patterns. Table 4 shows the disaggregation performance across the top six energy consuming appliances, in which each appliance is modelled using two states as before. It can be seen that CO and FHMM report similar performance across all appliances. We observe that the results for appliances such as the washing machine and switch mode power supply based appliances such as laptop and entertainment unit (television) are much worse when compared to HVAC loads like air conditioners across both metrics. Furthermore, prior literature shows that complex appliances such as washing machines are hard to model [32].

We observe that the performance accuracy of air conditioner 2 is much worse than air conditioner 1. This is due to the fact that during the instrumentation, air conditioner 2 was operated at a set temperature of 26 C. With an external temperature of roughly 30 − 35 C, this air conditioner reached the set temperature quickly and turned off the com-

pressor while still running the fan. However, air conditioner 1 was operated at 16 C and mostly had the compressor on. Thus, air conditioner 2 spent much more time in this intermediate state (compressor off, fan on) in comparison to air conditioner 1. Figure 8 shows how both FHMM and CO are able to detect on and off events of air conditioner 2. Since air conditioner 2 spent a considerable amount of time in the intermediate state, the learnt two state model is less appropriate in comparison to the two state model used for air conditioner 1. This can be further seen in the figure, where we observe that both FHMM and CO learn a much lower power level of around 1.1 kW, in comparison to the rated power of around 1.6 kW. We believe that this could be corrected by learning a three state model for this air conditioner, which comes at a cost of increased training and disaggregation computational and memory requirements.

5. CONCLUSIONS AND FUTURE WORK

In this paper, we proposed NILMTK; the first open source toolkit designed to allow empirical comparisons to be made between energy disaggregation algorithms across multiple data sets. The toolkit defines a common data format, NILMTK-DF, and includes parsers from six publicly available data sets to NILMTK-DF. The toolkit further facilitates the calculation of data set statistics, diagnosing problems and mitigating them via preprocessing functions. In addition, the toolkit includes implementations of two benchmark disaggregation algorithms based on combinatorial optimisation and the factorial hidden Markov model. Finally, NILMTK includes implementations of a set of performance metrics which will enable future research to directly compare disaggregation approaches through a common set of accuracy measures. We demonstrated several analyses facilitated by NILMTK including: use of statistics functions to detect missing data, learning of appliance models from sub-metered data, comparing disaggregation algorithms across multiple data sets and breakdown algorithm performance by individual appliances.

Future work will focus upon the addition of recently proposed training and disaggregation algorithms and data sets. For instance, larger data sets such as HES could also provide additional insight into disaggregation performance. In addition, recently proposed algorithms which do not require sub-metered power data for their unsupervised training could be compared against the current supervised algorithms. An additional direction for future work could be the use of a semantic wiki to maintain a comprehensive, communal database of appliance metadata. Finally, the inclusion of a household simulator (e.g. [33]) would allow disaggregation algorithms to be evaluated in a wider variety of settings than those represented by publicly available data sets.

6. ACKNOWLEDGEMENTS

Nipun Batra would like to thank TCS Research and Development for supporting him through a PhD fellowship and EMC, India for their support, and the Department of Electronic and Information Technology (Government of India) for funding the project (Grant Number DeitY/R-&D/ITEA/4(2)/2012). Jack Kelly thanks the EPSRC for his Doctoral Training Account and Intel for their Ph.D. Fellowship grant. Oliver Parson thanks the EPSRC for his Doctoral Prize Award. The authors thank the anonymous reviewers for their feedback, and also Denzil Correa, PhD student IIIT Delhi for his valuable comments.

7. REFERENCES

[1] G. W. Hart. Nonintrusive appliance load monitoring. *Proceedings of the IEEE*, 80(12):1870 1891, 1992. doi:10.1109/5.192069.

[2] S. Darby. The e ectiveness of feedback on energy consumption. *A Review for DEFRA of the Literature on Metering, Billing and direct Displays*, 2006.

[3] California Public Utilities Commission. Final Opinion Authorizing Pacific Gas and Electric Company to Deploy Advanced Metering Infrastructure. Technical report, 2006.

[4] Department of Energy & Climate Change. Smart Metering Equipment Technical Specifications Version 2. Technical report, UK, 2013.

[5] J. Z. Kolter and M. J. Johnson. REDD: A public data set for energy disaggregation research. In *Proceedings of 1st KDD Workshop on Data Mining Applications in Sustainability*, San Diego, CA, USA, 2011.

[6] K. Anderson, A. Ocneanu, D. Benitez, D. Carlson, A. Rowe, and M. Bergés. BLUED: A fully labeled public dataset for Event-Based Non-Intrusive load monitoring research. In *Proceedings of 2nd KDD Workshop on Data Mining Applications in Sustainability*, pages 12 16, Beijing, China, 2012.

[7] S. Barker, A. Mishra, D. Irwin, E. Cecchet, P. Shenoy, and J. Albrecht. Smart*: An open data set and tools for enabling research in sustainable homes. In *Proceedings of 2nd KDD Workshop on Data Mining Applications in Sustainability*, Beijing, China, 2012.

[8] A. L. Goldberger, L. A. Amaral, L. Glass, J. M. Hausdor , P. C. Ivanov, R. G. Mark, J. E. Mietus, G. B. Moody, C.-K. Peng, and H. E. Stanley. PhysioBank, PhysioToolkit, and PhysioNet: components of a new research resource for complex physiologic signals. *Circulation*, 101(23):e215 e220, 2000. doi:10.1161/01.cir.101.23.e215.

[9] D. Kotz and T. Henderson. Crawdad: A community resource for archiving wireless data at dartmouth. *Pervasive Computing, IEEE*, 4(4):12 14, 2005. doi:10.1109/MPRV.2005.75.

[10] F. Pedregosa, G. Varoquaux, A. Gramfort, V. Michel, B. Thirion, O. Grisel, M. Blondel, P. Prettenhofer, R. Weiss, V. Dubourg, J. Vanderplas, A. Passos, D. Cournapeau, M. Brucher, M. Perrot, and E. Duchesnay. Scikit-learn: Machine learning in Python. *Journal of Machine Learning Research*, 12:2825 2830, 2011. arXiv:1201.0490.

[11] H. Kim, M. Marwah, M. F. Arlitt, G. Lyon, and J. Han. Unsupervised Disaggregation of Low Frequency Power Measurements. In *Proceedings of 11th SIAM International Conference on Data Mining*, pages 747 758, Mesa, AZ, USA, 2011. doi:10.1137/1.9781611972818.64.

[12] K. C. Armel, A. Gupta, G. Shrimali, and A. Albert. Is disaggregation the holy grail of energy efficiency? The case of electricity. *Energy Policy*, 52:213 234, 2013. doi:10.1016/j.enpol.2012.08.062.

[13] C. Holcomb. Pecan Street Inc.: A Test-bed for NILM. In *International Workshop on Non-Intrusive Load Monitoring*, Pittsburgh, PA, USA, 2012.

[14] J.-P. Zimmermann, M. Evans, J. Griggs, N. King, L. Harding, P. Roberts, and C. Evans. Household Electricity Survey. A study of domestic electrical product usage. Technical Report R66141, DEFRA, May 2012.

[15] S. Makonin, F. Popowich, L. Bartram, B. Gill, and I. V. Bajic. AMPds: A Public Dataset for Load Disaggregation and Eco-Feedback Research. In *IEEE Electrical Power and Energy Conference*, Halifax, NS, Canada, 2013.

[16] N. Batra, M. Gulati, A. Singh, and M. B. Srivastava. It s Di erent: Insights into home energy consumption in India. In *Proceedings of the Fifth ACM Workshop on Embedded Sensing Systems for Energy-E ciency in Buildings*, 2013. doi:10.1145/2528282.2528293.

[17] J. Kelly and W. Knottenbelt. UK-DALE: A dataset recording UK Domestic Appliance-Level Electricity demand and whole-house demand. *ArXiv e-prints*, 2014. arXiv:1404.0284.

[18] J. Z. Kolter and T. Jaakkola. Approximate Inference in Additive Factorial HMMs with Application to Energy Disaggregation. In *Proceedings of the International Conference on Artificial Intelligence and Statistics*, pages 1472 1482, La Palma, Canary Islands, 2012.

[19] M. Zeifman. Disaggregation of home energy display data using probabilistic approach. *IEEE Transactions on Consumer Electronics*, 58(1):23 31, 2012. doi:10.1109/TCE.2012.6170051.

[20] M. J. Johnson and A. S. Willsky. Bayesian Nonparametric Hidden Semi-Markov Models. *Journal of Machine Learning Research*, 14:673 701, 2013. arXiv:1203.1365.

[21] O. Parson, S. Ghosh, M. Weal, and A. Rogers. Non-intrusive load monitoring using prior models of general appliance types. In *Proceedings of the 26th AAAI Conference on Artificial Intelligence*, pages 356 362, Toronto, ON, Canada, 2012.

[22] D. Rahayu, B. Narayanaswamy, S. Krishnaswamy, C. Labbe, and D. P. Seetharam. Learning to be energy-wise: Discriminative methods for load disaggregation. In *3rd International Conference on Future Energy Systems*, pages 1 4, 2012. doi:10.1145/2208828.2208838.

[23] N. Batra, H. Dutta, and A. Singh. INDiC: Improved Non-Intrusive load monitoring using load Division and Calibration. In *International Conference of Machine Learning and Applications*, Miami, FL, USA, 2013.

[24] K. Anderson, M. Berges, A. Ocneanu, D. Benitez, and J. Moura. Event detection for non intrusive load monitoring. In *Proceedings of 38th Annual Conference on IEEE Industrial Electronics Society*, pages 3312 3317, 2012. doi:10.1109/IECON.2012.6389367.

[25] Y. Low, J. Gonzalez, A. Kyrola, D. Bickson, C. Guestrin, and J. M. Hellerstein. Graphlab: A new parallel framework for machine learning. In *Conference on Uncertainty in Artificial Intelligence*, Catalina Island, CA, USA, 2010. arXiv:1006.4990.

[26] A. Schoofs, A. Guerrieri, D. T. Delaney, G. O Hare, and A. G. Ruzzelli. ANNOT: Automated Electricity Data Annotation Using Wireless Sensor Networks. In *Proceedings of the 7th Annual IEEE Communications Society Conference on Sensor Mesh and Ad Hoc Communications and Networks*, Boston, MA, USA, 2010. doi:10.1109/SECON.2010.5508248.

[27] J. Kelly and W. Knottenbelt. Metadata for Energy Disaggregation. *ArXiv e-prints*, Mar. 2014. arXiv:1403.5946.

[28] Z. Ghahramani and M. I. Jordan. Factorial hidden markov models. *Machine learning*, 29(2-3):245 273, 1997. doi:10.1023/A:1007425814087.

[29] Richard de Dear and Melissa Hart. Appliance Electricity End-Use: Weather and Climate Sensitivity. Technical report, Sustainable Energy Group, Australian Greenhouse Office, 2002.

[30] A. Kavousian, R. Rajagopal, and M. Fischer. Determinants of residential electricity consumption: Using smart meter data to examine the e ect of climate, building characteristics, appliance stock, and occupants behavior. *Energy*, 55(0):184 194, 2013. doi:10.1016/j.energy.2013.03.086.

[31] M. Wytock and J. Zico Kolter. Contextually Supervised Source Separation with Application to Energy Disaggregation. *ArXiv e-prints*, 2013. arXiv:1312.5023.

[32] S. Barker, S. Kalra, D. Irwin, and P. Shenoy. Empirical characterization and modeling of electrical loads in smart homes. In *IEEE International Green Computing Conference*, pages 1 10, Arlington, VA, USA, 2013. doi:10.1109/IGCC.2013.6604512.

[33] J. Liang, S. K. K. Ng, G. Kendall, and J. W. M. Cheng. Load Signature Study - Part II: Disaggregation Framework, Simulation, and Applications. *IEEE Transactions on Power Delivery*, 25(2):561 569, 2010. doi:10.1109/TPWRD.2009.2033800.

Algorithms for Upgrading the Resolution of Aggregate Energy Meter Data

Harshad Khadilkar[I], Tanuja Ganu[I], Zainul Charbiwala[I], Lim Chee Ming[U],
Sathyajith Mathew[U], Deva P Seetharam[I]
[I]IBM India Research Lab   [U]University of Brunei Darussalam

ABSTRACT

Metering of the energy supplied to consumers is an important component of operations for utility providers. Several schemes have been employed for this purpose, including traditional postpaid and prepaid metering, and more advanced smart metering technology. Analysis of the data generated by these meters has the potential to provide insights into consumer characteristics and power consumption patterns, including consumer segmentation and anomaly detection. We describe the di erent types of power purchase and consumption data, as well as the analytics algorithms that can be applied to them. Most applications developed for energy meter data require high resolution information of the type provided by smart meters, thus leaving aggregate prepaid or postpaid meter schemes at a disadvantage. In this paper, we present analytics-based methodologies to upgrade aggregate prepaid and postpaid meter data resolution, which will allow smart meter analytics to be applied without expensive infrastructure upgrades.

Categories and Subject Descriptors

H.4 [**Information Systems Applications**]: Miscellaneous

General Terms

Energy Metering, Prepaid, Postpaid, Smart Meters

Keywords

Analytics Algorithms, Data Resolution Upgrade

1. INTRODUCTION

Energy metering technology has been in development since the 1880s [1]. Energy meters can be broadly classified into two types: postpaid and prepaid meters. The traditional business model for electricity retail involves the installation of postpaid meters at customer premises and subsequent billing for the amount of energy consumed during the previous billing period (typically a month or a quarter). Since

these meters rarely have access to communication facilities, they must be read and billed manually. Prepaid meters are gaining popularity because they simplify billing operations, especially in areas where utility providers face severe non-payment issues. This metering scheme requires the customers to make advance payment for their energy. Prepaid meters are being used in many countries including Brunei, India, Ireland, South Africa and Sudan [2, 3, 4].

Conventional metering schemes (both prepaid and postpaid) are limited by the aggregate nature of measurement, which does not allow tracking of the rate of energy consumption as a function of time. This information is important for utility providers, since it can be leveraged for applications such as time-of-use pricing, demand response programs and fine-grained spatio-temporal load forecasts [5]. This shortcoming is addressed by the use of smart meters, which can record the amount of energy consumed as a function of time [6]. These meters can directly communicate time-stamped consumption data to meter data management systems. Residual concerns with regard to cost and data privacy have restricted their popularity at present [7]. Consequently, there is a need for low-cost solutions to the problem of obtaining high-resolution data from energy meters. As far as the authors can determine, the algorithm presented in Sec. 4 is the first e ort to address the issue with a purely analytical approach. The principal advantage of this methodology is that no hardware changes or retrofitting is required to the aggregate energy meters.

In Sec. 3, we discuss the applicability of various analysis algorithms to di erent types of energy consumption data. Sec. 4 presents algorithms for extracting fine-grained temporal consumption details from the aggregate consumption data reported by conventional postpaid and prepaid meters. We present a convergence analysis for the proposed algorithms, as well as a derivation of the corresponding error bounds. In Sec. 5, we validate our assumptions using actual empirical data and also evaluate the estimation algorithms using real-world and synthetic datasets.

2. RELATED WORK

Analysis of energy meter data has received wide attention in past literature. The emphasis has been on applications such as segmentation of consumers into groups based on similarity of usage [8, 9], predicting consumer behaviour [10] and setting of power tari s [11, 12]. Most prior studies focus on smart meter data because of the high resolution that it provides. Such data is important for applications such as fraud detection [13, 14] and real-time consumer feedback [15]. We review some of these applications in Sec. 3.

The problem of recovering high-resolution data from low-resolution aggregate data has been addressed in multiple fields of research. Data fusion in wireless networks presents challenges when the sensors are separated spatio-temporally [16]. Upgrade algorithms for sensor data are also developed in the field of compressed sensing [17, 18]. It is necessary to interpolate data being received from low-resolution sensors, in order to combine it effectively with high-resolution sensors. The problem considered in this paper has a similar objective, with aggregate energy meter data being used to estimate dynamic energy consumption.

The concept of combining data from multiple proximal sensors into a single high-resolution data stream is frequently used in climate modelling [19, 20, 21] and image processing [22]. Analogously, in this paper we combine the meter readings of consumers with similar consumption patterns to estimate dynamic energy consumption for each consumer.

3. ALGORITHMS FOR DATA ANALYSIS

As discussed in the previous section, the three major types of metering mechanisms are (i) prepaid meters, (ii) postpaid meters, and (iii) smart meters. The corresponding data formats can be broadly classified as *purchase data* for prepaid meters, *aggregate consumption* for postpaid meters, and *dynamic consumption* for smart meters. In this section, we describe the analysis algorithms that can be applied to each type of data without any interconversion. Algorithms for upgrading the resolution of purchase and aggregate consumption data are described in Sec. 4.

3.1 Analysis of purchase data

Prepaid meter data consists of logs of the number of units purchased by each consumer, with the corresponding time (and possibly location) stamps. In the absence of ground truth about rate of energy consumption, analysis algorithms for this type of data are limited to characterization of the trends in energy purchased. In this paper, we use data from Brunei Darussalam for studying these patterns empirically. The time range for this data covers three years, from January 2010 to December 2012.

It is possible to use the prepaid data to identify segments of nominal purchase patterns, using standard cluster analysis techniques such as k-means [23]. A sample plot with 7 consumer segments is shown in Fig. 1. The X axis in the figure depicts the progression of time from Jan 2010 to Dec

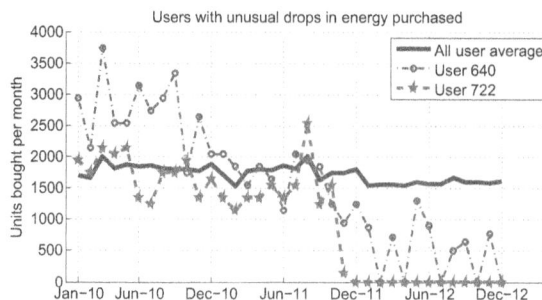

Figure 2: Purchase-based outlier detection.

2012, and the Y axis shows the average monthly purchased energy for each consumer segment. Each consumer in the data is mapped to one of the seven segments. This type of consumer segmentation facilitates the automated detection of *outliers*, or consumers whose purchase patterns are not similar to any of the common patterns seen in the data. Such information may be used for further analysis, with fraud detection being an example. Fig. 2 shows a sample plot for two outliers detected in the prepaid data. The two highlighted users can be seen to have stopped purchasing energy midway through the period of analysis. This behaviour could be indicative of illegal activities such as energy purchases from unauthorized dealers. Note that aggregate data only enables us to detect gross changes in consumption patterns. A more effective anomaly detection mechanism - one that is sensitive and that can pinpoint the cause of the anomaly - requires high resolution data. This further motivates the necessity of developing algorithms such as those presented in Sec. 4.

3.2 Analysis of aggregate consumption data

Utilities collect aggregate consumption data from meters primarily for billing. The meter reading interval typically coincides with the billing period, which may range from a few weeks to a few months. Although aggregate meter readings are temporally sparse, they can nevertheless be used for some analytical applications. One example is that of inferring connectivity models of electricity grids. The connectivity model of a distribution network provides the underlying interconnection between various assets (such as transformers) and customers in the grid. Prior literature has shown that meter readings from a subset of the distribution points are sufficient to estimate grid connectivity [24]. The accuracy of this information deteriorates over time due to repairs, maintenance, and balancing efforts. Partial or incorrect connectivity information leads to delays and higher costs in identifying the true location of a malfunction.

Analysis of aggregate consumption data can reveal insights about consumer segments, patterns in their behavior, and potential theft [25]. It can also be used at a macro scale to determine economic development metrics. For example, the World Bank uses national energy and electricity production in their World Development Reports [26]. Additionally, Lorenz curves (commonly used by economists to estimate income inequality) are sometimes used to combine energy access and consumption into a single equity metric [27, 28]. Using data from Norway, the US, El Salvador, Thailand, and Kenya, prior studies show that the distribution of energy across consumers in industrialized nations is far more

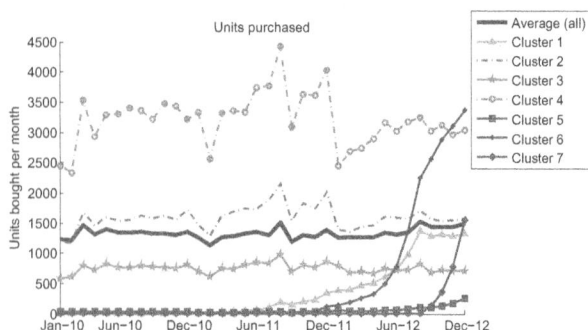

Figure 1: Segments of residential consumers separated into 7 clusters based on unit purchases. Large users can be seen to have reduced energy purchases in 2012.

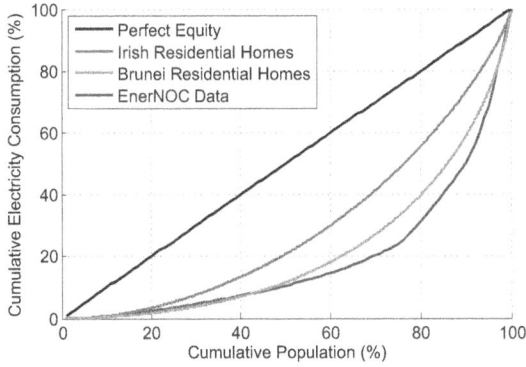

Figure 3: Lorenz curve comparison between commercial (EnerNOC) and residential (Brunei Darussalam and Ireland) aggregate consumption data.

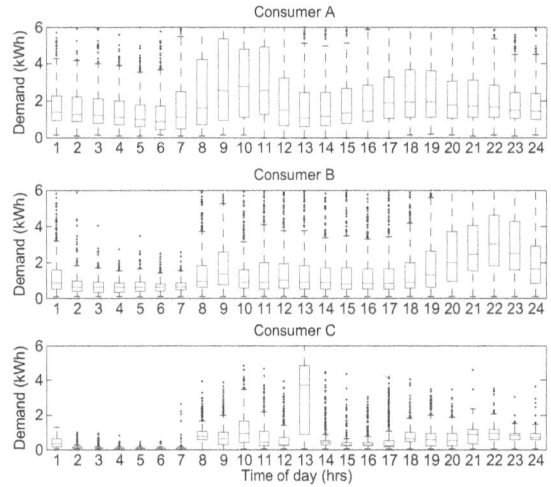

Figure 4: Selecting consumers for specific DR events based on their hourly dynamic consumption data

uniform than in developing nations. Fig. 3 shows a comparison of the Lorenz curves for 100 commercial consumers in the US and 57156 and 782 residential consumers from Brunei Darussalam and Ireland respectively. The curves illustrate the higher disparity in commercial enterprises than in residential consumers, owing to the wider spectrum of companies served by the utility.

3.3 Analysis of dynamic consumption data

The proliferation of real-time sensing and feedback in electricity grids has enabled their evolution into *smart grids*. Smart meters perform sensing functions at the individual household level in smart grids [29]. These meters record energy consumption with fine granularity (5 minute to 30 minute intervals). The use of two-way communication between smart meters and utilities has allowed the implementation of applications such as outage detection, identification of demand response (DR) potential and the detection of consumption anomalies and energy theft [30, 31].

Demand response programs aim to provide higher system reliability by altering consumer demand in response to available supply and economic conditions [32, 33, 34]. These programs identify the target set of consumers based on criteria such as the day of week, time of day, peak loads and demand variability. For example, Fig. 4 shows representative smart meter data for three residential consumers in Ireland, measured over a period of six months. The variability of demand on collated on an hourly basis is shown in the form of box plots. The higher the variability of demand, the greater is the potential flexibility of the consumer. From Fig. 4, it is seen that consumer A is the most suitable for demand response in the morning, while both consumers A and B can be targeted in the evening. Note that such insights are only available through high resolution consumption data. They cannot be directly derived from traditional power purchase data or aggregate postpaid consumption data.

Anomalous consumption patterns could indicate energy theft, and are a major concern for utility providers. A common vector for energy theft is to bypass the energy meters at certain times of the day (such as late nights) or on certain days of the week (such as weekends) [35]. It is observed that only a fraction of non-technical losses due to fraud are ever detected using historical aggregated consumption data. However, dynamic consumption data can be used for theft detection through advanced data analysis techniques [36, 37]. Similarly, smart meter data combined with context data (weather, public events) and demographic attributes can also used for consumer segmentation [38]. For the endusers, real-time feedback about energy usage [13, 14] can help reduce energy costs by taking advantage of time of use pricing [15]. In summary, insights from dynamic smart meter data enable utility providers to maintain efficient and reliable grid operations, while also allowing consumers to use energy more e ectively.

4. UPGRADING DATA RESOLUTION

The analytics algorithms that are applicable to di erent types of meter data were described in Sec. 3. It was shown that the data produced by smart meters is the most useful for deep analytics and for real-time applications. The underlying property of smart meter data that makes it more useful than postpaid or prepaid meter data, is its high resolution. However, this richness of information is accompanied by higher cost, because of the accompanying communication and sensing infrastructure that needs to be installed.

In this section, we present algorithms that can upgrade the resolution of prepaid and postpaid meter data without any additional hardware installation. These algorithms are based on the similarity of consumption patterns across consumers within a single segment. As such, the temporal resolution that they can achieve is a function of the minimum time interval between data samples across di erent consumers. The traditional postpaid regime receives meter readings for di erent consumers tagged with the day of reading. Thus, the best temporal distinction between data samples is one day. As a result, this section focuses on converting aggregate meter readings to an estimate of daily consumption. We emphasize that the algorithms themselves are applicable to any two time scales, as long as the stated assumptions regarding the underlying consumption patterns are satisfied. For example, the same algorithms presented in Sec. 4.1 and Sec. 4.2 can be used to upgrade daily consumption data to an estimate of 15-minute consumption.

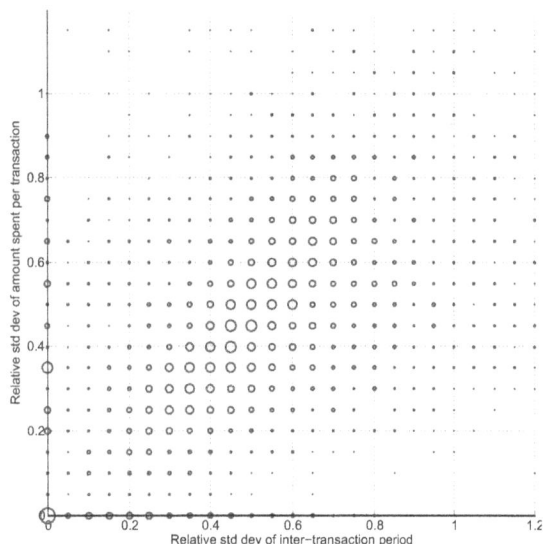

Figure 5: Transaction amount and inter-transaction period characteristics in prepaid data. Both axes are normalized by the corresponding averages for each customer.

4.1 Estimation of aggregate consumption from purchase data

Energy utilities using the prepaid meter model typically only have access to transaction data. Any conversion from monetary transactions to high-resolution consumption estimates necessarily involves an intermediate step where aggregate consumption is estimated. Therefore, in the following development, we only describe an algorithm to form a noisy estimate of aggregate consumption from prepaid transaction information. Sec. 4.2 develops the subsequent method for converting noisy aggregate consumption data to estimates of daily consumption.

Fig. 5 shows the transaction behaviour of consumers in Brunei Darussalam for the years 2010 and 2011. The Y axis shows the standard deviation in the amount per transaction for residential consumers, normalized by the average amount per transaction. The X axis shows the analogous statistic for the inter-transaction period. The size of each circle is proportional to the frequency with which the corresponding (x, y) coordinate is seen in the data. It can be seen that the behaviour across all consumers varies considerably, with the most common cases falling in the region where both sets of standard deviation are 50% of the mean. It is, however, possible to determine some estimate of the aggregate consumption based on the following assumption.

A-1 Consumers recharge their prepaid meters when the residual units in the meter drop below a certain threshold. The threshold itself may vary from consumer to consumer.

It is reasonable to expect that most consumers will have a threshold below which they judge themselves to be in danger of running out of electricity, and will therefore have an urge to recharge their meters. This assumption is clearly not valid in all cases, as seen from Fig. 5. However, in absence of accompanying consumption data with the prepaid transaction data set, we will proceed to estimate aggregate energy consumption based on **A-1**. In steady state, the threshold

number of units will always be present in the meter. Each fresh transaction will simply add to this number and the meter will subsequently count down back to the threshold value. The value will act like a displaced zero with the following consequence:

P-1 All units purchased during one transaction are consumed by the time when the next transaction takes place. If u_1 units are purchased at time t_1 and u_2 units are subsequently purchased at time t_2, then it follows that u_1 units are consumed over the period from t_1 to t_2.

The estimate of aggregate consumption obtained using **P-1** can be fed into the algorithm described in Sec. 4.2 to estimate dynamic energy consumption. In effect, this two-step procedure converts prepaid transaction data into estimates of dynamic energy consumption.

4.2 Estimation of dynamic consumption from aggregate consumption data

In the following development, we focus on estimating daily consumption from an aggregate consumption measurement period of M days. As noted earlier, the same algorithm is applicable to any other pair of time scales. We use data from EnerNOC, a US-based utility provider, to test the validity of the assumptions made in the following treatment. Commercial energy consumption data from this provider is freely available online for a set of 100 consumers and a duration of one year [39]. The raw data is available from the utility in the form of 5-minute energy consumption information for each consumer. This is artificially aggregated in order to emulate postpaid meter readings, thus allowing us to compare the results of the estimation algorithm with ground truth.

4.2.1 Background assumptions

We will make the following assumptions before we begin the discussion of using aggregate consumption data for forming an estimate of dynamic consumption.

A-2 Monthly meter readings are taken for different consumers on different days, each aggregated over M days.

We will denote the aggregate consumption by $F_c(i)$, where $c \in \{1, 2, \ldots, N\}$ is the index of the consumer and i is the day when the reading is taken.

A-3 The consumption for each user c can be mapped to a single consumption pattern through some one to one mapping function. In this paper, we will use a simple scaling factor a_c.

This factor may be calculated based on context information such as area of premises and occupancy, or by base-lining average consumption over a previous time period. Fig. 6 depicts empirical daily energy consumption for consumers subscribing to EnerNOC. The upper plot in the figure shows the actual spread of consumption for each of the 100 users over a 60 day period. The value of the scaling constant a_c is assumed to be equal to the median daily consumption for each consumer, and the lower plot shows the resulting normalized values. The variability of the daily consumption values can be seen to be substantially smaller in the lower plot, compared to the upper plot. Fig. 7 quantifies this improvement by comparing the spread in the original data

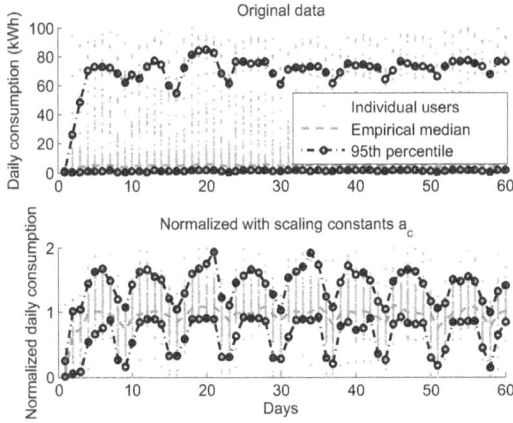

Figure 6: Comparison of the spread in daily energy consumption in the original data (top plot) and the spread in data normalized using the scaling constants a_c.

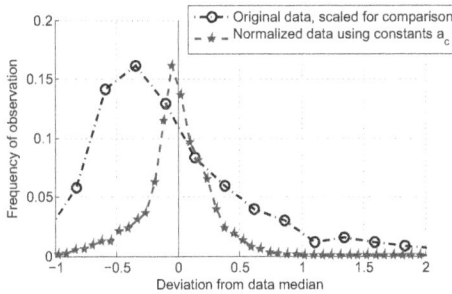

Figure 7: The distribution of normalized data around the median of the normalized data. The original data has been scaled by the original median for comparison.

with that in the normalized data. The original data has been scaled by a single value (median daily consumption) across all consumers, while the normalized data has been scaled using the estimated constants a_c. It can be seen that the scaling factors substantially reduce the differences across consumers, allowing the estimation of a common consumption pattern for the entire data set.

The normalized daily consumption will be denoted by $f(i)$ with i being any integer (negative values for past days), and the aggregate reading for each consumer can be calculated by the following relation.

$$F_c(i) = \sum_{j=i-M+1}^{i} a_c \, f(j).$$

The normalized *aggregate* consumption is the same across all users (according to **A-3**) and is denoted by $y(i) = \frac{F_c(i)}{a_c}$. We will now proceed to make an assumption that will allow us to build an algorithm for estimating daily consumption.

A-4 The underlying consumption function $f(i)$ is periodic with a (possibly unknown) period T. We will denote the daily consumption values by $\{z_1, z_2, \ldots, z_T\}$, and note that $z_1 = f(1) = f(T+1)$ and so on. As a con-

sequence, the normalized aggregate consumption also becomes periodic with $y(1) = y(T+1)$ and so on.

The periodicity assumption allows us to define linear relations between the daily consumption and aggregate consumption values. Periodicity is a property seen in real-world empirical energy consumption data, as shown in Sec. 5. These relations can be solved either by directly inverting the coefficient matrix (denoted by $\mathcal{B}$ in Sec. 4.2.4) or through the iterative procedure described in Sec. 4.2.2, subject to the following three properties.

P-2 If the period T is exactly equal to the measurement period M, it is not possible to construct an algorithm for estimating daily consumption from aggregate data.

This follows from the observation that $T = M$ gives us linear equations with the same set of variables (the T unknowns $\{z_1, z_2, \ldots, z_T\}$) and the same coefficients for each equation. The equations are linearly dependent, the coefficient matrix is singular, and no estimation of the individual variables is possible [40]. A minor extension of this linear dependency argument gives us two additional properties.

P-3 Estimation of daily consumption is also not possible if T and M have one or more common prime factors.

P-4 Exact estimation of daily consumption is possible if the period T is known and the measurement period M has no common prime factors with T. The number of aggregate readings required for this estimation is T.

If there are no common prime factors between T and M, we can write T linearly independent equations with T readings $\{y(1), \ldots, y(T)\}$, and simply invert the coefficient matrix to calculate the exact values of each of the unknowns $\{z_1, z_2, \ldots, z_T\}$ [40]. We will make one final assumption before proceeding to develop an iterative estimation algorithm for daily consumption.

A-5 The period T can be independently calculated from prior empirical data.

This is a reasonable assumption to make, with one possible approach for calculating T involving matching the aggregate supply and demand characteristics for the utility provider.

4.2.2 Iterative estimation algorithm

If the period T is known exactly, and there is no noise in the system and in the measurements, then inverting the linear relation between daily and aggregate consumption is the simplest way of estimating daily consumption. However, these conditions are unlikely to be satisfied in a realistic setting. When there is noise in the data and/or trends in consumption, it is desirable to implement the estimation procedure over a rolling window of size T. For large T, it is expected that an iterative algorithm initialized with the estimates from the previous window will be computationally faster than solving the full set of linear equations each time. The functional period T can be very large when real-time estimation of consumption is required. For example, 15-minute resolution estimates with a consumption periodicity of one day (1440 minutes) will imply $T = \frac{1440}{15} = 96$. The computational time for the algorithm is even more important if real-time demand response signals are to be generated based on the consumption estimates.

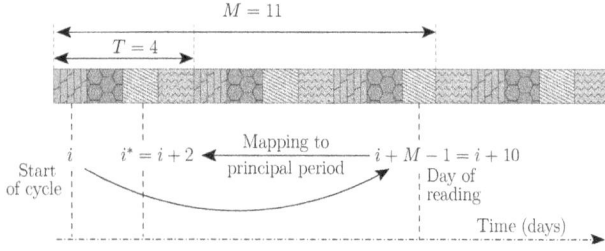

Figure 8: Relation between the start of the measurement cycle i, and the reading date mapped to the principal period i^*. For illustration, it is assumed that $T = 4$ and $M = 11$.

The uniqueness of the solution to a non-singular linear system of equations [40] ensures that the problem formulation satisfies one of the necessary conditions for convergence of iterative update algorithms [41]:

P-5 If conditions **A-4** and **A-5** are met and T and M have no common prime factors, then there is only one unique solution $\{z_1, z_2, \ldots, z_T\}$ to an observed aggregate consumption pattern $\{y(1), \ldots, y(T)\}$.

We now proceed to define the structure of the estimation algorithm. Let us assume that the period T is known, and denote the estimated daily consumption variables by $\hat{z}_i$ and the predicted normalized aggregate consumption by $\hat{y}(j)$. We further assume that the measurement period is M and that $n = \frac{M}{T}$ is the number of full functional cycles in each measurement period. Consider a measurement cycle that begins on day i. The normalized reading for this cycle will be $y(i + M - 1)$, taken on day $(i + M - 1)$. By the periodicity assumption, this reading will be equal to $y\left((i + M - 1) - T \left\lfloor \frac{i+M-1}{T} \right\rfloor\right)$, which falls within the principal period $\{1, \ldots, T\}$. For simplicity, we will use the symbol i^* to denote the mapping of $(i + M - 1)$ to the principal period. Fig. 8 clarifies the relation between i and i^*. We now define the iterative update algorithm for each variable $\hat{z}_i$ to be,

$$\hat{z}_i^+ = \hat{z}_i^- + k \left[y(i^*) - \hat{y}(i^*)\right], \tag{1}$$

where $\hat{z}_i^-$ is the estimate of z_i before the update step and $\hat{z}_i^+$ is the estimate after the update step. Only one $\hat{z}_i$ is updated at a time. The predicted measurement $\hat{y}(i^*)$ is calculated using the relation,

$$\hat{y}(i^*) = n \sum_{j=1}^{T} \hat{z}_j + \sum_{m=i}^{i^*} \hat{z}_m. \tag{2}$$

Note that the second summation may involve a roll-over if $i^* < i$. In that case, the summation will be evaluated over $\hat{z}_m$ with $m \in \{i, i+1, \ldots, T, 1, 2, \ldots, i^*\}$. The estimation mechanism in Eq. (1) is to compensate for the prediction error by increasing the estimate of the first day in the measurement cycle, with a gain equal to k. **P-5** guarantees that termination can occur only with the unique solution.

4.2.3 Selection of the update gain k

There are two types of error associated with the iterative algorithm given by Eq. (1). The first kind is introduced by noise in the aggregate measurements, and fundamentally limits the accuracy of the estimated daily consumption (independently of the estimation algorithm). A treatment of this kind of error is given in Sec. 4.2.4. The second type

of error relates to successive iterations of Eq. (1) for the same set of T aggregate readings, and is a property of the applied estimation algorithm. We can show that this can be driven to zero through a judicious selection of the update gain k. The post-update estimation error can be computed by subtracting Eq. (1) from the true value z_i:

$$z_i - \hat{z}_i^+ = z_i - \hat{z}_i^- - k \left[y(i^*) - \hat{y}(i^*)\right]$$

$$= z_i - \hat{z}_i^- - k \left[\left(n \sum_{j=1}^{T} z_j + \sum_{m=i}^{i^*} z_m\right) - \left(n \sum_{j=1}^{T} \hat{z}_j + \sum_{m=i}^{i^*} \hat{z}_m\right)\right]$$

$$= z_i - \hat{z}_i^- - k \left[n \sum_{j=1}^{T} (z_j - \hat{z}_j) + \sum_{m=i}^{i^*} (z_m - \hat{z}_m)\right]$$

$$z_i - \hat{z}_i^+ = [1 - (n+1)k](z_i - \hat{z}_i^-)$$

$$- (n+1)k \sum_{m=i+1}^{i^*} (z_m - \hat{z}_m)$$

$$- nk \left[\sum_{j=1}^{i-1} (z_j - \hat{z}_j) + \sum_{p=i^*+1}^{T} (z_p - \hat{z}_p)\right]. \tag{3}$$

The last step follows from the fact that there are $(n+1)$ copies of individual error terms $(z_j - \hat{z}_j) \; \forall j \in \{i, \ldots, i^*\}$, and n copies for all other j. Consider evaluating Eq. (3) for $i = 1$, and let 1^* be the equivalent of i^*. If we denote the error terms $(z_j - \hat{z}_j)$ by e_{rj} where $j \in \{1, \ldots, T\}$ and r is the iteration number, then the error for $j = 1$ after the first iteration is given by,

$$e_{11} = \begin{bmatrix} (1 - (n+1)k) & -(n+1)k & \ldots & -nk \end{bmatrix} \begin{bmatrix} e_{01} \\ e_{02} \\ \vdots \\ e_{0T} \end{bmatrix}. \tag{4}$$

For ease of representation, consider the simple case where $T = 3$ and $M = 2$, which means that the consumption pattern repeats every third day and measurements are taken on every second day. The number of complete cycles involved in each reading is $n = 0$ and $1^* = 2$ (last day of the measurement period which started on day 1). Instantiating Eq. (4) for this example, the error after the first update is,

$$e_{11} = \begin{bmatrix} (1 - k) & -k & 0 \end{bmatrix} \begin{bmatrix} e_{01} \\ e_{02} \\ e_{03} \end{bmatrix}$$

$$\begin{bmatrix} e_{11} \\ e_{02} \\ e_{03} \end{bmatrix} = \begin{bmatrix} (1-k) & -k & 0 \\ 0 & 1 & 0 \\ 0 & 0 & 1 \end{bmatrix} \begin{bmatrix} e_{01} \\ e_{02} \\ e_{03} \end{bmatrix} = \mathcal{A}_1 \begin{bmatrix} e_{01} \\ e_{02} \\ e_{03} \end{bmatrix}. \tag{5}$$

The next update corresponds to the aggregate reading $z_3 + z_1$, and is equivalent to substituting $i = 3$ in Eq. (1). This update will use the updated version of $\hat{z}_1$ with the corresponding error e_{11}. Therefore, the post-update error vector in Eq. (5) is now modified to,

$$\begin{bmatrix} e_{11} \\ e_{02} \\ e_{13} \end{bmatrix} = \begin{bmatrix} 1 & 0 & 0 \\ 0 & 1 & 0 \\ -k & 0 & (1-k) \end{bmatrix} \begin{bmatrix} e_{11} \\ e_{02} \\ e_{03} \end{bmatrix}$$

$$\begin{bmatrix} e_{11} \\ e_{02} \\ e_{13} \end{bmatrix} = \begin{bmatrix} 1 & 0 & 0 \\ 0 & 1 & 0 \\ -k & 0 & (1-k) \end{bmatrix} \mathcal{A}_1 \begin{bmatrix} e_{01} \\ e_{02} \\ e_{03} \end{bmatrix} = \mathcal{A}_3 \mathcal{A}_1 \begin{bmatrix} e_{01} \\ e_{02} \\ e_{03} \end{bmatrix}.$$

The final update in the first stage of iteration will be for $\hat{z}_2$, and the error terms after this step will be given by,

$$\begin{bmatrix} e_{11} \\ e_{12} \\ e_{13} \end{bmatrix} = \begin{bmatrix} 1 & 0 & 0 \\ 0 & (1-k) & -k \\ 0 & 0 & 1 \end{bmatrix} \begin{bmatrix} e_{11} \\ e_{02} \\ e_{13} \end{bmatrix} = \mathcal{A}_2 \begin{bmatrix} e_{11} \\ e_{02} \\ e_{13} \end{bmatrix}$$

$$\begin{bmatrix} e_{11} \\ e_{12} \\ e_{13} \end{bmatrix} = \mathcal{A}_2 \mathcal{A}_3 \mathcal{A}_1 \begin{bmatrix} e_{01} \\ e_{02} \\ e_{03} \end{bmatrix} = \mathcal{A} \begin{bmatrix} e_{01} \\ e_{02} \\ e_{03} \end{bmatrix}. \tag{6}$$

In the last step, we have denoted the product of the three error update matrices by the matrix $\mathcal{A}$. The entries of this matrix are only a function of k and are well known. All further iterations involve the same three update steps, and are equivalent to pre-multiplying Eq. (6) by $\mathcal{A}$ each time.

P-6 The convergence of the estimation algorithm is determined by the eigenvalues of $\mathcal{A}$. As the system is discrete, errors e_{rj} are guaranteed to decay to 0 i the dominant eigenvalue is smaller than 1 in magnitude [42].

The $\mathcal{A}$ matrix can be calculated for any period T once the order of updates is known ($\hat{z}_1$ $\hat{z}_3$ $\hat{z}_2$ in Eq. (6)). The update gain can be selected by calculating the eigenvalues of the corresponding $\mathcal{A}$ matrix as a function of k, and choosing any value that guarantees stability, as shown in Sec. 5.

4.2.4 Confidence bounds for estimation errors

In the following development, we consider the e ect of error in the aggregate measurements on the estimates of daily consumption. We assume a structure for the introduction of noise into the system, and then proceed to analyse the problem for various properties of the noise function.

A-6 There is an underlying periodic function z_i with period T ($i \in \{1, 2, \ldots, T\}$), and the actual daily consumption is the sum of z_i and some form of additive noise.

The assumption of periodicity is not restrictive, because (i) periodicity is seen in most real-world data sets for energy consumption, and (ii) the noise terms can account for small variations in the estimation of T.

The simplest case to analyse is that for a single consumer, where the estimation algorithm uses T successive aggregate readings to compute $\hat{z}_i$. Since each reading period is M days long, the total time period before these estimates can be computed is equal to MT. We make the following assumption for analysing the statistical properties of the estimated daily consumption for a single consumer:

A-7 Additive noise in consumption on day i is equal to w_i, zero-mean, independent and identically distributed (i.i.d). The consumption on day i is thus ($z_i + w_i$).

We have not specified the distribution of w_i beyond the i.i.d assumption, because:

P-7 As long as the noise is zero-mean i.i.d, the central limit theorem ensures that the sum of the noise variables approaches a zero-mean normal distribution with variance equal to the variance of $\sum w_i$ [43].

The jth normalized aggregate measurement for a single consumer will be given by the relation,

$$y(jM) = \sum_{i=(j-1)M+1}^{jM} (z_i + w_i),$$

and will be composed of M days. The periodicity assumption implies that $z_{j+T} = z_j$, but this relation need not hold true for the noise terms w_j. The set of values $\{\hat{z}_1, \ldots, \hat{z}_T\}$ will be estimated from the measurements $\{y(M), \ldots, y(MT)\}$. There are MT i.i.d noise terms involved with no overlap between readings, thus implying the following property:

$$\text{var}(y(jM)) = \text{var}\left(\sum_{i=(j-1)M+1}^{jM} (z_i + w_i) \right)$$

$$= \underbrace{\text{var}\left(\sum_{i=(j-1)M+1}^{jM} z_i \right)}_{\text{constants}} + \underbrace{\text{var}\left(\sum_{i=(j-1)M+1}^{jM} w_i \right)}_{M \text{ i.i.d variables}}$$

$$= 0 + M \, \text{var}(w_i).$$

P-8 The variance of each aggregate reading $y(jM)$ is M times the variance of each day s consumption.

Let us denote the nominal daily consumption $[z_1, \ldots, z_T]'$ by Z, where $'$ is the matrix transpose operator. Similarly, let the estimated daily consumption be $\hat{Z} = [\hat{z}_1, \ldots, \hat{z}_T]'$, and the vector of aggregate readings be $Y = [y(M), \ldots, y(MT)]'$. Regardless of the method of estimation (matrix inversion or the iterative algorithm), the estimated daily consumption is the unique solution of the relation $\mathcal{B} \hat{Z} = Y$, where $\mathcal{B}$ is composed of the coefficients of $\hat{z}_i$ in Eq. (2). The entries of this matrix are equal to the number of copies of each z_i in the aggregate readings, and are equal to n or $(n+1)$. **P-4** tells us that $\mathcal{B}$ is non-singular and hence invertible. The estimated daily consumption is thus given by,

$$\hat{Z} = \mathcal{B}^{-1} Y.$$

The error bounds for the estimation algorithm are related to the statistical properties of $\hat{Z}$:

P-9 The estimation procedure is unbiased since the expectation of the estimate of daily consumption is given by,

$$\mathbb{E}[\hat{Z}] = \mathbb{E}[\mathcal{B}^{-1} Y] = \mathcal{B}^{-1} \mathbb{E}[Y] = Z.$$

The last equality follows from **A-7** (the noise in each aggregate reading is zero-mean). To calculate the variance of $\hat{Z}$, we first calculate the expectation of the outer product $\hat{Z}\hat{Z}'$:

$$\mathbb{E}[\hat{Z}\hat{Z}'] = \mathbb{E}[(\mathcal{B}^{-1} Y)(\mathcal{B}^{-1} Y)']$$
$$= \mathcal{B}^{-1} \mathbb{E}[YY'](\mathcal{B}^{-1})'. \tag{7}$$

The right hand side of Eq. (7) is easy to compute numerically, because the matrix $\mathcal{B}$ is well known and $\mathbb{E}[YY']$ can be approximated using observed aggregate readings. Equivalently, the left hand side can be directly calculated from the empirical mean of $\hat{Z}\hat{Z}'$. In either case, we note the following property for single-customer consumption estimation.

P-10 While the estimate $\hat{Z}$ can be computed from T aggregate readings, several more sets of aggregate readings are required to compute the error bounds on $\hat{Z}$.

The variance of each z_i can be calculated from the diagonal elements of $\mathbb{E}[\hat{Z}\hat{Z}']$ using the following relation.

$$\text{var}(\hat{z}_i) = \mathbb{E}[\hat{z}_i^2] - (\mathbb{E}[\hat{z}_i])^2.$$

A combination of **P-9** and the central limit theorem allows us to equate the variance of the estimates $\hat{z}_i$ to the variance of the errors $(z_i - \hat{z}_i)$.

P-11 For a sufficiently large number of aggregate readings, the error $(z_i - \hat{z}_i)$ is Gaussian with zero mean and standard deviation $\sigma_i = \sqrt{\text{var}(\hat{z}_i)}$.

When there are multiple consumers in the data, the analysis is different from that of the single-consumer case. We show that the variability across consumers tends to increase the estimation error, but if the consumer segmentation has been correctly carried out, increasing the number of consumers in the data set helps drive the error down. We will assume that **A-3** nominally holds true, but that there may be a temporary increase/decrease in each customer s consumption relative to the normalized mean (from **A-3**, the normalization constant for each consumer c is a_c). Therefore, the noise in the aggregate readings across consumers and over the measurement time period M will have two sources.

A-8 Individual trends in consumption (not accounted for by the normalization by a_c) for each consumer c are represented by the i.i.d random variable v_c. In addition, the random variation around the nominal pattern for consumer c on day i is represented by w_{ci}, also i.i.d with $i \in \{1, 2, \ldots, M\}$. The total energy consumption for consumer c on day i is given by $z_{ci} = z_i + v_c + w_{ci}$, where z_i is the mean nominal consumption for that particular consumer segment.

As a consequence of this assumption, the normalized aggregate reading for consumer c for a measurement period starting on day i is given by,

$$y_c(i + M - 1) = \sum_{j=i}^{i+M-1} z_{cj}$$

$$= \underbrace{\sum_{j=i}^{i+M-1} z_j}_{\text{Mean trend}} + \underbrace{M\,v_c}_{\text{Cust. specific}} + \underbrace{\sum_{j=i}^{i+M-1} w_{cj}}_{\text{Random variation}} \ .$$

In order to be able to estimate the mean trend of consumption, we compute the average across consumers of all readings taken on day $(i + M - 1)$. Let $\mathcal{C}_i$ denote the set of consumers whose meter readings are taken on this day, and let $|\mathcal{C}_i|$ be the number of such consumers. Then the average normalized reading $y(i + M - 1)$ is given by,

$$y(i + M - 1) = \frac{1}{|\mathcal{C}_i|} \sum_{c\,\mathcal{C}_i} y_c(i + M - 1)$$

$$= \frac{1}{|\mathcal{C}_i|} \sum_{c\,\mathcal{C}_i} \sum_{j=i}^{i+M-1} z_j + \frac{M}{|\mathcal{C}_i|} \sum_{c\,\mathcal{C}_i} v_c$$

$$+ \frac{1}{|\mathcal{C}_i|} \sum_{c\,\mathcal{C}_i} \sum_{j=i}^{i+M-1} w_{cj}.$$

Since the mean trend z_j is the same across consumers, the first summation opens out and we get,

$$y(i + M - 1) = \sum_{j=i}^{i+M-1} z_j + \frac{M}{|\mathcal{C}_i|} \sum_{c\,\mathcal{C}_i} v_c$$

$$+ \frac{1}{|\mathcal{C}_i|} \sum_{c\,\mathcal{C}_i} \sum_{j=i}^{i+M-1} w_{cj}. \qquad (8)$$

Each batch of T variables for the mean trend $\{\hat{z}_i, \ldots, \hat{z}_{i+T-1}\}$ is computed using the set of T consumer-averaged readings $\{y(i+M-1), \ldots, y(i+M+T-2)\}$. Computing the variance of (8) provides useful insights into the estimation accuracy:

$$\text{var}(y(i + M - 1)) = \text{var}\left(\sum_{j=i}^{i+M-1} z_j\right) + \text{var}\left(\frac{M}{|\mathcal{C}_i|} \sum_{c\,\mathcal{C}_i} v_c\right)$$

$$+ \text{var}\left(\frac{1}{|\mathcal{C}_i|} \sum_{c\,\mathcal{C}_i} \sum_{j=i}^{i+M-1} w_{cj}\right)$$

$$= 0 + \frac{M^2}{|\mathcal{C}_i|^2} \text{var}\left(\sum_{c\,\mathcal{C}_i} v_c\right)$$

$$+ \frac{1}{|\mathcal{C}_i|^2} \text{var}\left(\sum_{c\,\mathcal{C}_i} \sum_{j=i}^{i+M-1} w_{cj}\right)$$

$$= \frac{M^2 |\mathcal{C}_i|}{|\mathcal{C}_i|^2} \text{var}(v_c) + \frac{M |\mathcal{C}_i|}{|\mathcal{C}_i|^2} \text{var}(w_{cj}).$$

P-12 The variance of each consumer-averaged aggregate reading is thus given by,

$$\text{var}(y(i + M - 1)) = \frac{M^2}{|\mathcal{C}_i|} \text{var}(v_c) + \frac{M}{|\mathcal{C}_i|} \text{var}(w_{cj}). \quad (9)$$

Note the difference between **P-8** and **P-12**. While the variance in the former case scaled linearly with M, the variance in the latter case scales quadratically with M. However, it is possible to drive this variance down by increasing the number of readings $|\mathcal{C}_i|$ taken on any given day. The measurement period M at which the first term in Eq. (9) starts dominating the second term depends on the relative ratio between $\text{var}(v_c)$ and $\text{var}(w_{cj})$. This fact emphasizes the necessity of accurate consumer segmentation: $|\mathcal{C}_i|$ should not be increased at the cost of an increase in $\text{var}(v_c)$.

The same procedure as demonstrated in Eq. (7) can be used for estimating the confidence bounds on $\hat{z}_i$. The only modification required is that the empirical values of Y used for calculating the expectation will be the consumer-averaged aggregate readings, instead of the time-averaged readings for a single consumer.

5. EXPERIMENTAL EVALUATION

We now validate the data resolution upgrade algorithm described in Sec. 4.2. Simulated data is used for evaluating the iterative estimation algorithm and the confidence bounds for the single consumer case. Empirical data from EnerNOC, a utility based in the United States, is used for evaluating the confidence bounds for estimation of daily consumption for multiple consumers. We reiterate that the raw data has a resolution of 5 minutes, and is artificially aggregated in order to simulate postpaid meter readings. Fig. 9 shows that data from consumers subscribing to this utility has strong periodicity with a principal period of one week

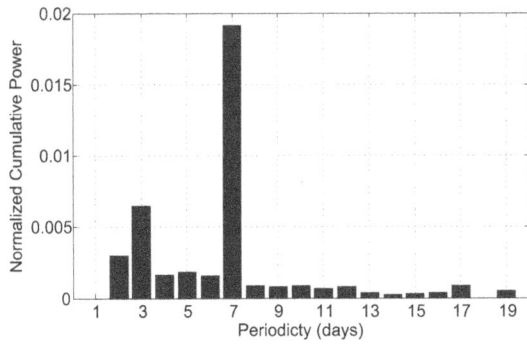

Figure 9: Validation of the assumption of periodicity in energy consumption, for the EnerNOC data set.

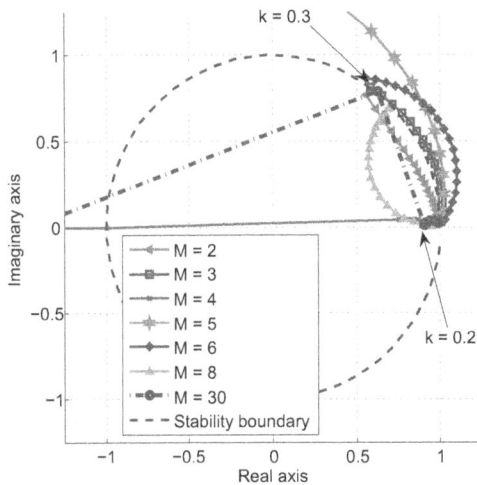

Figure 10: The evolution of the dominant eigenvalue of $\mathcal{A}$ for a weekly consumption cycle, and various values of M. Locations of $k = 0.2$ and $k = 0.3$ for $M = 30$ are marked.

Figure 11: Simulated estimation runs for $T = 7$ and $M = 30$. The case with $k = 0.2$ converges to the correct estimates, while that with $k = 0.3$ does not. The magnitudes of the corresponding dominant eigenvalues of $\mathcal{A}$ are 0.914 and 1.008.

($T = 7$). It depicts the cumulative normalized power spectral distribution for daily energy consumption for all the users in the data set, and indicates that the consumption patterns across users are not only periodic, but have the same periodicity.

Fig. 10 illustrates the implications of **P-6** for the case of a weekly consumption cycle and for various potential values of the aggregate measurement period M. Each curve traces the locus of the dominant eigenvalue of $\mathcal{A}$, parametrized by the gain k. A monthly measurement cycle can be approximated by the curve for $M = 30$. The unit circle in Fig. 10 marks the boundary of the stable region for the iterative algorithm. All the curves originate at $(1, 0)$ for $k = 0$. This value represents the open-loop case, when the coefficient matrix $\mathcal{A}$ is the identity matrix. Choosing a value of k such that the dominant eigenvalue falls within the unit circle ensures convergence of the algorithm (1), and vice versa. Conformance to this property is demonstrated for simulated data in Fig. 11, where the iterative algorithm is seen to converge for $k = 0.2$ (within the unit circle in Fig. 10) but not for $k = 0.3$ (outside the unit circle).

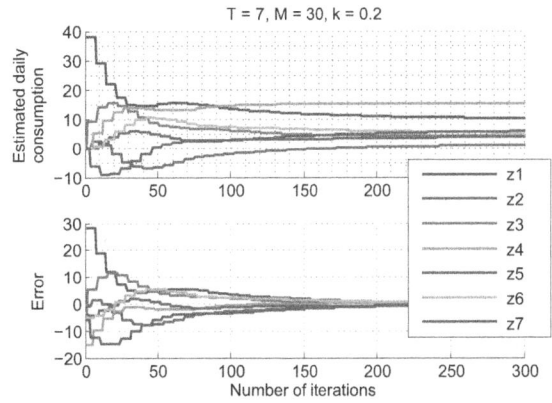

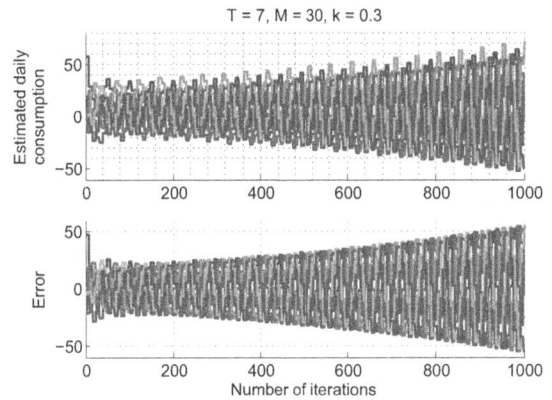

An illustration of the confidence bounds derived in **P-11** for the single-consumer case is shown in Fig. 12. The nominal daily consumption was assumed to be $\{z_1, \ldots, z_7\} = \{50, 20, 80, 40, 110, 90, 140\}$, with a measurement cycle of 30 days. Uncorrelated random noise $w_j \quad \mathcal{N}(0, 0.5)$ was added to the nominal values, and the algorithm (1) was used to estimate the daily consumption. $\mathbb{E}[YY']$ was calculated empirically by taking aggregate consumption readings over several cycles. The 99.7% error bounds in Fig. 12 are equivalent to ± 3 standard deviations of the estimated noise in $\hat{Z}$. Since the confidence intervals for individual $\hat{z}_i$ are nearly equal to each other, only one set is shown.

Analogous bounds for consumption estimates based on data from multiple consumers are shown in Fig. 13. The estimates are based on a real-world data set consisting of 100 consumers subscribing to the utility EnerNOC. The data was available for a period of one year. The normalization constant a_c for each consumer was calculated by computing the average daily consumption for that consumer over the first four months in the data. The remaining eight months were used for testing the estimation algorithm.

Aggregate meter readings were simulated based on the measured daily consumption for each consumer. The date of reading i_c for each consumer c was generated from a uniform distribution on the range $[1, M]$, where M was the length of the measurement period. The normalized aggregate read-

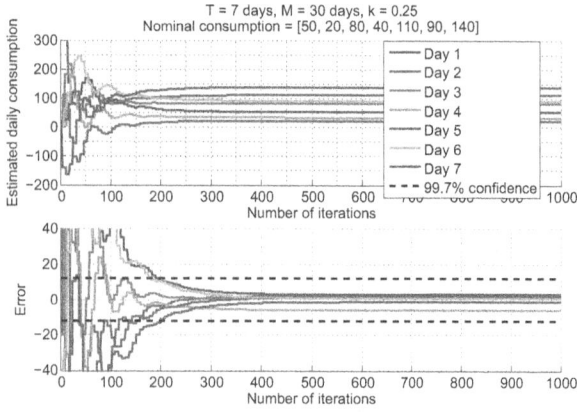

Figure 12: Dynamics of the estimation algorithm and error bounds for a single consumer.

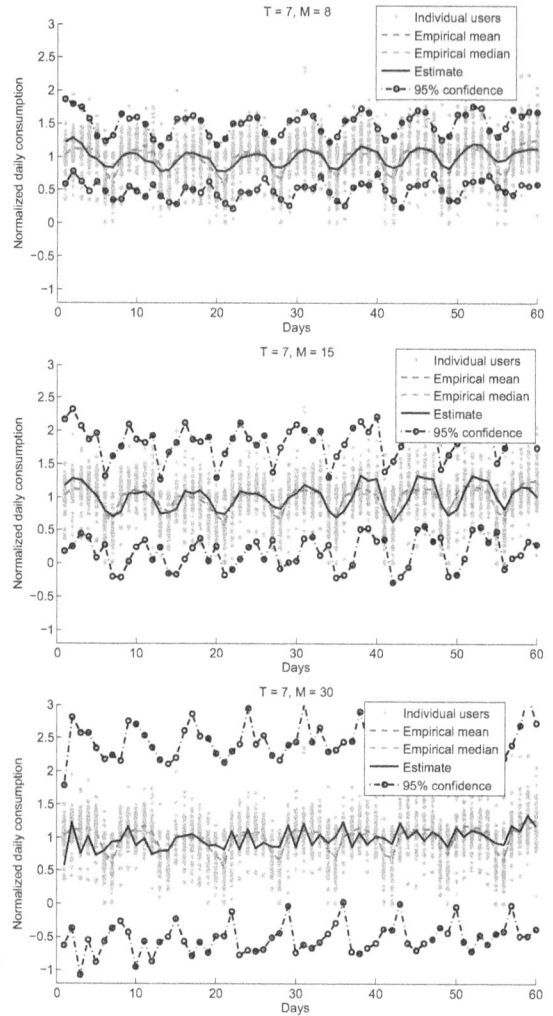

Figure 13: Estimation of the mean trend and error bounds for measurement periods $M = 8$, 15 and 30 days. The same number of aggregate readings are taken per day, in all three cases. It can be seen that the confidence intervals grow larger with increasing M.

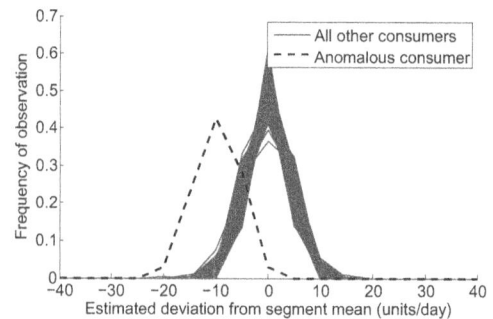

Figure 14: Distribution of estimated consumer-specific deviation v_c.

ings for that consumer were calculated by summing the daily consumption over the time periods $[i_c - M + 1, i_c]$, $[i_c + 1, i_c + M]$ and so on, and then dividing each sum by the constant a_c. Since the data set was limited both in terms of number of consumers and the available time period, the number of readings $|\mathcal{C}_i|$ generated for any particular day i was inversely proportional to the measurement time period M. As a consequence, Eq. (9) suggests that the estimation quality for the mean as well as the tightness of the confidence bounds will deteriorate rapidly with increasing M.

Fig. 13 illustrates this property by using three sample values for M. The ground truth for daily consumption for all 100 consumers is depicted by the light pink dots, while the actual mean consumption across all consumers is shown by a dashed red line. The estimated consumption, based on readings aggregated over M days, is shown with a solid black line and the corresponding 95% confidence intervals (± 2 standard deviations) by hollow black circles. Eq. (9) indicates that the confidence intervals are related to the variation v_c *across consumers* rather than the random noise w_{ci} around the *mean trend*. The estimates as well as the bounds are based on the empirical value of $\mathbb{E}[YY']$, and can therefore be improved by increasing the number of readings (either by increasing the number of consumers or by taking more readings over the course of time). The case with $M = 8$ is seen to produce the tightest confidence intervals, with 95% of all consumers falling within the corresponding confidence bounds on each day.

The dominance of the noise term v_c over w_{cj} in Eq. (9) can be seen when recovering the consumption estimates for each consumer, scaled back to the original values. Since the trend v_c is expected to dominate the random variation w_{cj}, the estimate for each consumer is computed by shifting the estimated segment means $\hat{z}_i$ by an amount proportional to the difference in the individual readings $y_c(i)$ and the mean reading $y(i)$. Empirical results show that this adjustment reduces the RMS error in daily consumption for 94% of consumers in the data set. If the trend v_c were not dominating w_{cj}, this procedure would increase/decrease the RMS error in a purely random fashion: a 50% performance. The significantly better results seen in empirical data show that the $M^2 \operatorname{var}(v_c) \quad M \operatorname{var}(w_{cj})$ assumption in **P-12** is valid.

Finally, we demonstrate the application of the estimation algorithm for identifying and analysing anomalous consump-

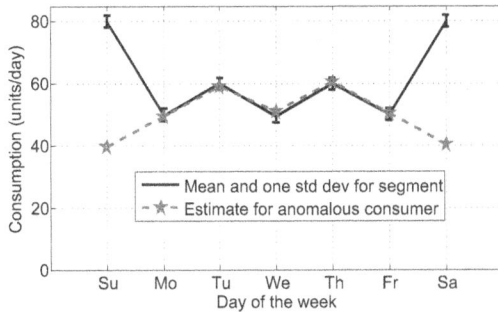

Figure 15: Estimated daily consumption across all consumers, as well as for the anomalous consumer.

tion patterns. We simulate daily consumption for a set of 1400 consumers with a periodicity of $T = 7$, and a nominal daily consumption pattern of $[80, 50, 60, 50, 60, 50, 80]$ units. Meter readings are taken in a staggered fashion, with a measurement time period of $M = 30$ days for each consumer. The consumer-specific deviation v_c in each measurement cycle is drawn from the normal distribution $\mathcal{N}(0, 1)$ while the daily random variation w_{cj} is drawn from the distribution $\mathcal{N}(0, 10)$. Only one of the 1400 consumers is assumed to have a consumption of 40 units on the first and last day of each weekly consumption cycle, as opposed to 80 units. The estimation algorithm is run on simulated data for several measurement cycles, and the estimated consumer-specific variation v_c is noted. It can be seen from Fig. 14 that the anomalous consumer shows a clear difference from the rest of the consumers, even though the standard deviation of w_{cj} is an order of magnitude larger than that of v_c. Estimation of daily consumption based only on aggregate readings from the anomalous consumer is shown in Fig. 15. It clearly emphasizes the differentiation capabilities of the algorithm presented in Sec. 4.2.

6. CONCLUSION

Our objective in writing this paper was to present a comparative study of the technical limits for analysing each type of meter data (prepaid, postpaid and smart meters). We characterized the usefulness of several algorithms for analysing aggregate as well as dynamic consumption data. These functions include consumer segmentation as well as automated detection of anomalous consumption patterns. The depth of insight available from the data was shown to improve with data resolution. Consequently, we also described analytical approaches to extract fine-grained temporal consumption details from coarse-grained aggregate consumption data. The proposed algorithms were analysed from the point of view of stability and the statistical properties of estimation error. Empirical data was used to show the efficacy of the estimation algorithms for several applications, including the detection and characterization of anomalous consumption patterns. We believe that the methodology presented in this paper can be applied effectively by utility providers for acquiring high quality consumption data from existing infrastructure, at relatively low cost.

Acknowledgements

The authors would like to thank Abdul Salam Bin Hj Abdul Wahab and Norihramniza Hj Ramlee from the Energy Department at the Prime Minister s Office, Brunei Darussalam and Siti Kadzijjah Binti Abd Lati and Pg Jamra Weira Bin Pg Hj Petra from the Department of Electrical Services, and Abdul Aziz bin Haji Mohamad Ali from the University of Brunei Darussalam for providing prepaid purchase data.

7. REFERENCES

[1] D. Dahle, A brief history of meter companies and meter evolution, http://www.watthourmeters.com/history.html.

[2] Electric Ireland, Pay as you go meters, https://www.electricireland.ie/ei/residential/manage-your-account/pay-as-you-go.jsp.

[3] A. Raj, Prepaid meters to plug power theft and loss of revenue, http://www.telegraphindia.com/1130319/jsp/bihar/story_16687604.jsp#.UtuqL3nT62w.

[4] Standard Transfer Specification (STS) Committee, STS membership growth, http://www.sts.org.za.

[5] F. E. R. Commission, Assessment of demand response and advanced metering, http://www.ferc.gov/legal/sta -reports/2013/oct-demand-response.pdf.

[6] Smart Grid Deployment Tracker 3Q13, http://www.navigantresearch.com/research/smart-grid-deployment-tracker-3q13.

[7] D. Cornish, The case against smart meters, http://www.wired.co.uk/news/archive/2012-12/21/smart-meters.

[8] S. J. Moss, M. Cubed, and K. Fleisher, Market segmentation and energy efficiency program design, *California Institute for Energy and Environment Berkeley*, 2008.

[9] S. Ramos, Z. Vale, J. Santana, and J. Duarte, Data mining contributions to characterize MV consumers and to improve the suppliers-consumers settlements, in *IEEE Power Engineering Society General Meeting*, 2007, pp. 1 8.

[10] A. Albert and R. Rajagopal, Smart meter driven segmentation: What your consumption says about you, *IEEE Transactions on Power Systems*, vol. PP, no. 99, pp. 1 12, 2013.

[11] C. Flath, D. Nicolay, T. Conte, C. Dinther, and L. Filipova-Neumann, Cluster analysis of smart metering data, *Business & Information Systems Engineering*, vol. 4, no. 1, pp. 31 39, 2012.

[12] T. Räsänen and M. Kolehmainen, Feature-based clustering for electricity use time series data, in *Proceedings of the 9th International Conference on Adaptive and Natural Computing Algorithms*, ser. ICANNGA 09. Berlin, Heidelberg: Springer-Verlag, 2009, pp. 401 412.

[13] OPOWER, Opower: Energy reporting, http://opower.com/products/energy-reporting.

[14] Bidgely, Itemize your energy bill, http://www.bidgely.com/.

[15] T. Bapat, N. Sengupta, S. K. Ghai, V. Arya, Y. B. Shrinivasan, and D. Seetharam, User-sensitive scheduling of home appliances, in *Proceedings of the*

2nd ACM SIGCOMM workshop on Green networking.
ACM, 2011, pp. 43 48.

[16] D. Ganesan, S. Ratnasamy, H. Wang, and D. Estrin, Coping with irregular spatio-temporal sampling in sensor networks, *SIGCOMM Comput. Commun. Rev.*, vol. 34, no. 1, pp. 125 130, January 2004.

[17] D. Donoho, Compressed sensing, *IEEE Transactions on Information Theory*, vol. 52, no. 4, pp. 1289 1306, 2006.

[18] Y. Tsaig and D. Donoho, Extensions of compressed sensing, *Signal Processing*, vol. 86, no. 3, pp. 549 571, 2006.

[19] A. Moberg, D. Sonechkin, K. Holmgren, N. Datsenko, and W. Karlen, Highly variable northern hemisphere temperatures reconstructed from low- and high-resolution proxy data, *Letters to Nature*, vol. 433, pp. 613 617, December 2004.

[20] T. Mitchell and P. Jones, An improved method of constructing a database of monthly climate observations and associated high-resolution grids, *International Journal of Climatology*, vol. 25, no. 6, pp. 693 712, May 2005.

[21] P. Jones, T. Osborn, K. Bri a, C. Folland, E. Horton, L. Alexander, D. Parker, and N. Rayner, Adjusting for sampling density in grid box land and ocean surface temperature time series, *Journal of Geophysical Research: Atmospheres*, vol. 106, no. D4, pp. 3371 3380, February 2001.

[22] D. Long, P. Hardin, and P. Whiting, Resolution enhancement of spaceborne scatterometer data, *IEEE Transactions on Geoscience and Remote Sensing*, vol. 31, no. 3, pp. 700 715, 1993.

[23] J. MacQueen, Some methods for classification and analysis of multivariate observations, in *Symposium on mathematical statistics and probability*, Berkeley, CA, 1967.

[24] V. Arya, T. Jayram, S. Pal, and S. Kalyanaraman, Inferring connectivity model from meter measurements in distribution networks, in *Proceedings of the fourth international conference on Future energy systems.* ACM, 2013, pp. 173 182.

[25] C. Bandim, J. Alves Jr, A. Pinto Jr, F. Souza, M. Loureiro, C. Magalhaes, and F. Galvez-Durand, Identification of energy theft and tampered meters using a central observer meter: a mathematical approach, in *Transmission and Distribution Conference and Exposition, 2003 IEEE PES*, vol. 1. IEEE, 2003, pp. 163 168.

[26] World Bank, World development reports, http://www.worldbank.org.

[27] A. Jacobson, A. D. Milman, and D. M. Kammen, Letting the (energy) gini out of the bottle: Lorenz curves of cumulative electricity consumption and gini coefficients as metrics of energy distribution and equity, *Energy Policy*, vol. 33, no. 14, pp. 1825 1832, 2005.

[28] J. L. Gastwirth, The estimation of the lorenz curve and gini index, *The Review of Economics and Statistics*, vol. 54, no. 3, pp. 306 316, 1972.

[29] S. Harrison, Smart Metering Projects Map, http://bit.ly/GSs1o5, 2013.

[30] Z. Pollock, The True ROI of Smart Meter Deployments, http://bit.ly/1dK33jW, July 2013.

[31] S. Depuru, L. Wang, and V. Devabhaktuni, Smart meters for power grid: challenges, issues, advantages and status, *Renewable and Sustainable Energy Reviews*, vol. 15, no. 6, pp. 2736 2742, 2011.

[32] N. Armaroli and V. Balzani, The future of energy supply: challenges and opportunities, *Angewandte Chemie International Edition*, vol. 46, no. 1-2, pp. 52 66, 2007.

[33] U.S. Department of Energy, Benefits of demand response in electricity markets and recommendations for achieving them, 2006, http://eetd.lbl.gov/ea/emp/reports/congress-1252d.pdf.

[34] K. Spees and L. Lave, Impacts of responsive load in PJM: load shifting and real time pricing, *The Energy Journal*, vol. 29, no. 2, pp. 101 122, 2008.

[35] K Rowland, Detecting theft and enhancing billing processes only two of many potential applications, http://www.intelligentutility.com/article/12/03/meter-data-applied, March 2012.

[36] S. McLaughlin, D. Podkuiko, and P. McDaniel, Energy theft in the advanced metering infrastructure, *Critical Information Infrastructures Security*, vol. 6027, pp. 176 187, 2010.

[37] S. Depuru, L. Wang, and V. Devabhaktuni, Electricity theft: overview, issues, prevention and a smart meter based approach to control theft, *Energy Policy*, vol. 39, no. 2, pp. 1007 1015, 2011.

[38] T. Wijaya, T. Ganu, D. Chakraborty, K. Aberery, and D. P. Seetharam, Consumer Segmentation and Knowledge Extraction from Smart Meter and Survey Data, in *SIAM International Conference on Data Mining*, 2014.

[39] EnerNOC, 2012 Commercial Energy Consumption Data, http://open.enernoc.com/data/.

[40] E. Kreyszig, *Advanced Engineering Mathematics.* John Wiley & Sons, 2010.

[41] D. Bertsimas and J. Tsitsiklis, *Introduction to Linear Optimization.* Athena Scientific, 1997.

[42] R. Williams and D. Lawrence, *Linear State-Space Control Systems.* John Wiley & Sons, 2007.

[43] D. Bertsekas and J. Tsitsiklis, *Introduction to Probability.* Athena Scientific, 2008.

EnergyLens: Combining Smartphones with Electricity Meter for Accurate Activity Detection and User Annotation

Manaswi Saha , Shailja Thakur , Amarjeet Singh , Yuvraj Agarwal

Indraprastha Institute of Information Technology, Delhi   Carnegie Mellon University
{manaswis, shailja1275, amarjeet}@iiitd.ac.in,   yuvraj.agarwal@cs.cmu.edu

ABSTRACT

Inferring human activity is of interest for various ubiquitous computing applications, particularly if it can be done using ambient information that can be collected non intrusively. In this paper, we explore human activity inference, in the context of energy consumption within a home, where we define an activity as the usage of an electrical appliance, its usage duration and its location. We also explore the dimension of identifying the occupant who performed the activity. Our goal is to answer questions such as Who is watching TV in the Dining Room and during what times? . This information is particularly important for scenarios such as the apportionment of energy use to individuals in shared settings for better understanding of occupant s energy consumption behavioral patterns. Unfortunately, accurate activity inference in realistic settings is challenging, especially when considering ease of deployment. One of the key di er-ences between our work and prior research in this space is that we seek to combine readily available sensor data (i.e. home level electricity meters and sensors on smartphones carried by the occupants) and metadata information (e.g. appliance power ratings and their location) for activity inference.

Our proposed EnergyLens system intelligently fuses electricity meter data with sensors on commodity smartphones the Wifi radio and the microphone to infer, with high accuracy, which appliance is being used, when its being used, where its being used in the home, and who is using it. EnergyLens exploits easily available metadata to further improve the detection accuracy. Real world experiments show that EnergyLens significantly improves the inference of energy usage activities (average precision= 75.2%, average recall= 77.8%) as compared to traditional approaches that use the meter data only (average precision = 28.4%, average recall = 22.3%).

Categories and Subject Descriptors

C.3 [**Special-Purpose and Application-Based Systems**]: Real-time and embedded systems

Keywords

Smart Meters; Smartphones; Energy Disaggregation; Activity Detection; User Association

1. INTRODUCTION

Smartphones, over the past few years, have seen unprecedented growth across the world. In many markets, such as the US, they have long since surpassed sales of traditional feature phones. While many factors have contributed to their popularity, the most important perhaps is the increase in device capabilities as supported by higher end components such as multi-core processors, ample memory and storage, and a plethora of embedded sensors. These sensors in turn are used in novel ways by smartphone apps as well as by researchers to build context aware systems [15, 20, 30].

Our work explores the use of these pervasive smartphone platforms for detailed activity inference of individuals within a home setting, which can help occupants make better decisions around their routine daily activities. In particular, we consider the context of activities that lead to energy usage by occupants in a residential setting. This is particularly important since buildings are known to consume significant proportion of energy consumption in both developed and developing countries (45% to 47% of the total energy consumption in the US [5] and India [35] respectively). Smart electricity meters have also been widely deployed with the intention of having complete coverage over the next decade even in the developing countries such as India. Wide scale adoption of smart meters is motivated by several reasons including remote and easy data collection for billing purposes and implementation of new billing practices such as time of day based pricing.

To provide users with finer grained breakdown of their energy usage, there has been much research within the context of direct energy metering [34] or indirect inference using Non-Intrusive Load Monitoring (NILM) techniques [13, 22]. NILM techniques in particular are attractive since they often require a single smart meter and then employ complex machine learning algorithms [14] to disaggregate energy usage at the appliance level. To further improve the accuracy of NILM algorithms, researchers have proposed additional sensors such as EMI detectors[8, 26] and room-level motion and light sensors [27], which are often impractical from an ease of deployment perspective. To our knowledge, the combination of smartphones and smart electricity meters have not been used before for activity inference in the context of understanding energy usage.

In this paper, we present EnergyLens, a system that leverages two easily available data sources within homes — energy usage data from smart meters and sensor data from smartphones — for accurate activity inference and its annotation to individual home occupants. We define an activity as the usage *(when)* of an electrical appliance *(what)* within a home, as attributed to a specific occupant *(who)*, along with the room *(where)* the appliance is located. In other words, our goal with EnergyLens is to answer questions such as "Who is watching the TV in the dining room and during what times?". Energy consumption information at this granularity is particularly useful to apportion energy usage among occupants in a shared setting as well as understand behavioral patterns for energy usage. Prior work [6] shows, for example, that providing feedback to users about their energy use can help bring about a change in their usage.

Our primary goals in the design of EnergyLens were ease of deployment, widespread applicability and low cost data collection. As a result, while there are numerous sensors available on a modern smartphone we chose to use only WiFi and audio from the microphone since they are available even on low cost devices. Similarly, we only assume the availability of total real power data from a smart meter. While meters that provide additional information such as power factor are available, they are typically more expensive and are not widely deployed in our experience. This information is augmented with metadata information that tags appliances with their power consumption and room location for use by EnergyLens. This metadata was chosen since it is primarily static and requires a one time effort to collect it per home.

EnergyLens therefore combines WiFi based localization and audio-based appliance detection with NILM for appliance classification using meter data. Importantly, we show that even simple algorithms for each of the components — localization, audio classification, and NILM — when used in combination yield good overall accuracy for user activity detection. To show the effectiveness of EnergyLens for accurate activity inference (appliance, location and the identity of the occupant), we validated it in three different residential scenarios: (a) a controlled residential setting with a single occupant; (b) a controlled shared residence with multiple occupants; and (c) a real residential setting with a single occupant over multiple days. Note, we discuss the challenges of evaluating EnergyLens in a real home setting with multiple occupants in Section 6.

In summary, we make the following contributions:

We present the design and implementation of **EnergyLens**, a novel algorithm that fuses sensor data from smartphones and energy meter data for activity inference in a residential setting;

We deployed EnergyLens in both controlled and real world settings, to evaluate different use scenarios. Extensive data collection from these deployments show that EnergyLens is significantly accurate than using the energy meter data alone, particularly in real settings;

Using empirical data, we extensively discuss the impact of different factors such as simultaneous usage of appliances with similar power consumption and phone's orientation, on detection accuracy of EnergyLens and challenges thereof for real world activity classification for energy consumption in buildings.

2. USAGE SCENARIO

We now describe the underlying assumptions and the usage mode of the EnergyLens system. We assume that users have an installed smart meter to measure power usage (real power) for their home. While additional information such as power factor can be further useful to improve EnergyLens accuracy, we do not assume that it is readily available. We further assume that this power data is accessible by the server running EnergyLens over the web.

Training using Smartphones: EnergyLens users are assumed to have a basic Android smartphone with the ability to sample microphone audio and WiFi signal strength. During an initial *training phase*, users run the EnergyLens application and visit each room in their house for a few minutes to provide room-level location annotations. Within each room, the users are required to switch on the appliances they want EnergyLens to identify, wait for some time for its power consumption to reach a steady state and then turn it off. Each of these appliance on-off durations are then annotated, with a recognizable name such as "Fan" or "Kettle" or "Microwave", in the EnergyLens smartphone application. These appliance annotations are then used to train both the audio based classifier (Section 3.1.3) and the meter based NILM algorithm (Section 5). In a home with multiple occupants, where the smartphone models are not identical, this training process has to be repeated for each device *type*. This is due to our observation that microphone audio and WiFi fingerprints vary significantly across different phone models. After the training phase, EnergyLens server learns the necessary models that can then be applied to infer activity during actual usage.

Actual Usage Scenario: As the users start to use EnergyLens in their daily lives, we assume that they mostly carry their phones with them as they move around the house. In other words, EnergyLens assumes that the energy usage events — such as turning an appliance ON or OFF — takes place in the same location as the smartphone's location. During the activity, microphone audio is sampled and necessary features are extracted from it on the phone itself. Extracted features from the audio stream, along with the data from WiFi scans are sent to the server. Our EnergyLens algorithm executes on the server and identifies *who* performed *what* activity *where* in the home, and *when* they performed it. This annotated energy usage activity can then be presented to the user through the EnergyLens app, or by logging on to a website, or sent to them using a different modality.

3. ENERGYLENS OVERVIEW

At a high level, the goal of EnergyLens is to infer appliance activity and associate it with an occupant by fusing sensory data from smartphones, energy data from smart electricity meters, and metadata information about the appliances in a home. The two main aspects of EnergyLens are therefore the different sensor data sources, and the EnergyLens algorithm that we have developed to perform the activity inferences. We describe these components in detail below.

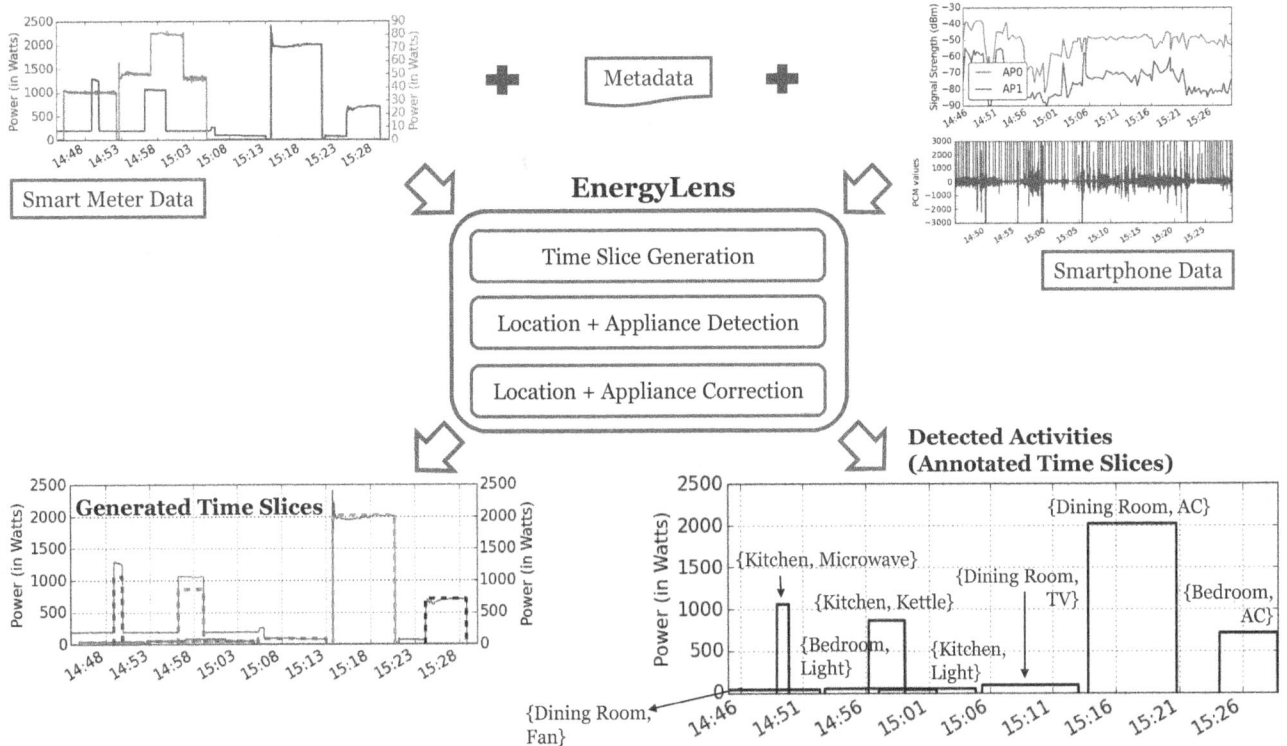

Figure 1: EnergyLens Overview. Smart meter data, appliance metadata and phone data (WiFi scans and audio signals) are taken as inputs. Time Slice Generation (Stage I) generates time slices (shown in dotted lines) from meter data. These time slices are used by Location and Appliance Detection Stages (II and III shown together here). This generates a set of annotated time slices. If location or appliance were misclassified, then Location and Appliance Correction Stages (IV and V) rectify the errors and generate the final set of annotated time slices.

3.1 System Components and Data Sources

3.1.1 Meter data for NILM

We use the total power measurements, sampled at 1Hz, from the whole house electricity meter to create time slices which define a period of activity for each appliance. EnergyLens uses a simple edge detection and edge matching algorithm to retrieve these time slices which are then labeled during the localization and appliance detection stages (see Section 3.2 for details).

3.1.2 WiFi-based localization

WiFi fingerprinting has been a popular technique for indoor localization for many years. EnergyLens uses a simple WiFi fingerprinting technique that has been adapted from RADAR [2]. Our EnergyLens app captures the received signal strengths (RSS) of the nearby access points by doing periodic WiFi scans. For every scan, the phone logs a timestamp and the MAC address, SSID and RSSI values of all the visible APs. These logs are then periodically uploaded to the server for further processing. At the server side, kNN algorithm is used to match and classify the received fingerprints with the stored fingerprints (collected during the training phase) to infer the room-level location for a given time slice.

3.1.3 Audio-based appliance detection

EnergyLens uses the smartphone microphone to capture audio samples when appliances are in use. Collected audio data is then processed by an audio processing pipeline implemented in our EnergyLens mobile app. This audio processing pipeline has primarily two stages: (1) pre-processing; and (2) feature extraction. The first stage involves *sampling audio at 8kHz for a period of 10 seconds at every 20 seconds interval* (i.e. duty-cycle = 10/20 = 50%). These samples are then combined together into *frames* with a frame size of 500ms. Next, we apply a Hamming window function to each of the frames before passing it on to the next stage. For each of the resulting frames, *13 Mel-Frequency Cepstral Coefficient (MFCC) features* are computed on the phone. Prior work on acoustic background recognition [19, 28] have shown that MFCC is effective in non-speech audio recognition. These features are then periodically sent to the server for audio classification using the model learned from the training data, while the raw audio data is discarded. Performing the feature computation on the phone helps preserve user privacy, while also significantly reducing the amount of data uploaded to the server.

3.1.4 Metadata

EnergyLens further uses additional information, that is static and can be easily collected. This additional data consists of two different meta information about appliances present in the home:

Appliance Location Mapping: Room-level location tagged for each appliance.

Appliance Power Mapping: Measured power for each appliance, extracted from the meter data collected during the training phase (Section 2), is used to tag each

Appliance	Location	Power(W)
AC	Dining Room	1950
Microwave	Kitchen	1150
Kettle	Kitchen	950
AC	Bedroom	670
TV	Dining Room	80
Fan	Dining Room	45
Fan	Bedroom	45
Light	Bedroom	45

Table 1: *Metadata*: Appliance Location Power Mapping

appliance with its power consumption. This information is critical for standard NILM algorithm as well.

Using these two pieces of metadata, we create a table with this information   Appliance Location Power Mapping (hereafter labeled as *Metadata*). A snapshot of the *Metadata* for an example home is shown in Table 1.

3.2 EnergyLens Algorithm

Our proposed EnergyLens algorithm itself comprises of five key stages, as illustrated in Figure 1, with each stage described in detail below.

Stage I: Time Slice Generation

In this stage, the electricity meter data is used to generate time slices i.e. when di erent activities are performed. Each time slice is annotated with its observed power consumption, using meter data, for further stages. The sensor stream for the total real power from the electricity meter is taken as the input. This stage primarily involves two steps - *Edge Detection* and *Edge Matching*.

Edge Detection: In this step, we generate all the rising and falling edges from the meter data stream S_i. Each edge $e_i = (m_i, t_i) \in E_i$ consists of a tuple containing magnitude m_i and time t_i at which the event occurred. m_i is a signed value that captures the power change of an electrical event above a minimum threshold m_t. From the detected edges, we discard edges where:

A falling edge occurs before a rising edge of similar magnitude.

Rising and falling edges of similar magnitude occur within a very small time duration. This results in filtering out immediate ON and OFF events.

Multiple rising (or falling) edges (of similar magnitude) are generated within a time duration. Only the last rising or falling edge is retained amongst such a set while the rest are discarded.

Edge Matching: The filtered edges from the previous step are converted into time slices using a threshold based matching algorithm. We use edge magnitude m_i to match rising and falling edges. Due to an initial surge of power when an appliance is turned on, the magnitude of rising edges are typically higher than the corresponding falling edges. However, in some cases e.g. when there is a heating element that increasingly consumes higher power, the magnitude of falling edges turns out to be higher. Therefore, for each falling edge, the matching algorithm looks for rising edges with magnitude within $\pm p\%$ of the falling edge. Amongst such candidate rising edges for a falling edge, we select the rising edge with the least di erence in magnitude with the falling edge. Selected rising and falling edges are

paired to create a time slice $t_s = (t_r, t_f, mag_t)$ where t_r is the start time (time for the rising edge), t_f is the end time (time for the falling edge) and mag_t is the power consumption of the time slice. The final set of time slices T_s, thus created, is passed onto the next stage.

Stage II: Location Detection

In this stage, every time slice in T_s is annotated with a location. For each of the time slices inferred, the WiFi scan data from the phone is used to infer where an activity is performed. From the WiFi scan data stream, we first summarize a minute s worth of data by taking the mean of signal strength samples received from each of the access points (APs) separately. Using these individual summarized values from the di erent access points, we form a feature vector $< rssi_1, rssi_2, \ldots, rssi_k >$ where k is the number of visible access points. We ignore APs with less than -85dBm signal strength since they are close to the noise floor. This feature vector is fed into the kNN algorithm to classify every time period (here, a minute) with one of the room locations. Thereafter, a location label which is in majority for the duration of a given time slice is selected as the location for the corresponding time slice. If the duration of the time slice is smaller than the sampling rate of WiFi scan, they are discarded at this stage.

Stage III: Appliance Detection

For all the location annotated time slices, audio recognition is performed to determine the appliance in use. We use an SVM classifier on the 13 MFCC features (extracted from the audio data) received from the phone. Prior work has shown SVM to perform the best for appliance recognition [36, 32]. From the predicted labels for a time slice, the label which is in majority is selected as the appliance being used during that period.

At the end of Stage III, EnergyLens obtains what appliance is used, when it is used and where it is used, which are collectively referred to as an *activity* . The identity is implicit for a single occupant setting. For a multiple occupant scenario, User Association is done after the Location and Appliance Detection stages (explained in the next subsection). Hereafter, we compare the classified detection for both appliance and location and verify if the combination of classified appliance and location match with the metadata. For all the unmatched entries, we perform the Location and Appliance Correction stages as described below.

Stage IV: Location Correction

In this stage, we use the *Metadata* to extract all the appliances listed to be at the same location as the classified location for a given time slice. For each of these appliances, we compare their power consumption from the *Metadata* with the observed power from the meter. For all time slices where the comparison results do not match (indicator of incorrect location classification), the classified location of the time slice is corrected to the location of the appliance (from amongst all the appliances in the *Metadata*) with the closest match in terms of power consumption. For a non-unique match, if all the matched entries have the same appliance and location (indicating multiple same appliances in the same location), then we use this location for correction. Otherwise, the misclassified location of the time slice is left unchanged.

Stage V: Appliance Correction

We detect an incorrect appliance classification by comparing the power consumption (from *Metadata*) of the classified ap-

Setting	Experiment Type	Appliances Used	Duration
Controlled	Single Occupant	Fans, Lights, AC, TV, Microwave, Kettle	6 hours
Controlled	Multi-Occupant	Fans, Lights, AC, TV, Microwave, Kettle	3 hours
Real	Single Occupant	Lights, TV, Microwave, Kettle	4 days

Table 2: Empirical Dataset Description

Exp#	Description	Appliances Used	Objective
1	Ideal scenario - use of dissimilar appliances with phone kept outside the pocket	Fans, Lights, AC, TV, Microwave, Kettle	Assess algorithm performance
2	Use of dissimilar appliances with phone kept inside the pocket		
3	Use of both similar and dissimilar appliances simultaneously		
4	Realistic scenario - multiple events with combination of similar and dissimilar appliances used simultaneously		
5	Use of similar appliances simultaneously across different rooms	Lights, Fans, TV	Assess impact on time slice accuracy
6	Use of dissimilar appliances used simultaneously across different rooms	Fans, AC, TV, Microwave, Kettle	

Table 3: Controlled experiments for single occupant setting. Here, similar appliances refers to those that lie within the same power consumption range. E.g. Microwave and Kettle lie within 800 – 1200W range; Fans and Lights fall within 30 – 45W range.

pliance with the power consumption observed in the location corrected time slices from the previous stage. For correcting these misclassified appliances, we find all the appliances in the predicted location (using *Metadata*) and select the one with the closest match in terms of power consumption. Again, for a non-unique match, if all the matched entries have the same appliance label then we use this label for correction. Else, we leave the entry with misclassified appliance unchanged.

Multi-Occupant Setting

User Association Stage: For a multi-occupant setting, each time slice further needs to be associated with a user to specify who is performing the activity. For each of the generated time slices after Stage I, location and appliance detection (Stages II and III) are performed on data from each of the occupant s smartphones. Note that each smartphone acts as a proxy for an occupant. At the end of Stage III, each time slice gets multiple sets of <location, appliance> tuples associated with it. The number of occupants determines the number of sets generated for each time slice.

We take the generated set of annotations (each set corresponding to an occupant) for every time slice and match the classified location and inferred power consumption with the *Metadata*. If only one of the sets match with the metadata, then the corresponding occupant is associated with this time slice. If, however, the matching process results in a non-unique match, then we select the set with the least difference from the metadata in terms of power consumption. A non-unique match at the end of this process indicates that the corresponding occupants were all present at the same location where the activity was being done during that period and hence the time slice is associated with all of these occupants.

4. EXPERIMENTAL SETUP

We now describe the experimental setup that we used to evaluate EnergyLens. We conducted experiments in two phases: (1) student volunteers from IIIT-Delhi conducting the experiments in controlled settings; (2) involved experiments in a real world setting.

Controlled Experiments

We used a well furnished 3 room apartment with common appliances such as a refrigerator, television, microwave, kettle, room level air conditioning units, multiple lights and fans. All the appliances were used during the experiments. Multiple experiments were performed to emulate the single occupant and the multi-occupant settings. The participants were closely monitored to observe their behavior while performing the activity. They were given a script to follow which mentioned the appliances they had to use and the duration of use. Their actions were not influenced in any way by the authors monitoring these experiments. We collected ground truth manually by annotating each event by the authors as it was being done.

Real World Experiments

The second phase experiments were done in the one of faculty residences at IIIT-Delhi. An apartment with a single occupant, consisting of 6 rooms and 8 different types of appliances, was selected. The appliances in the apartment include TV, lights, fans, microwave, room level Air Conditioner (AC), refrigerator, washing machine and kettle. No fans or AC were used during the data collection phase as the experiments were conducted during early winter. The refrigerator was not considered in our approach but it was running in the background for the entire experiment duration of a week. Appliances used during the week were TV, lights, microwave and kettle. The smartphone used by the

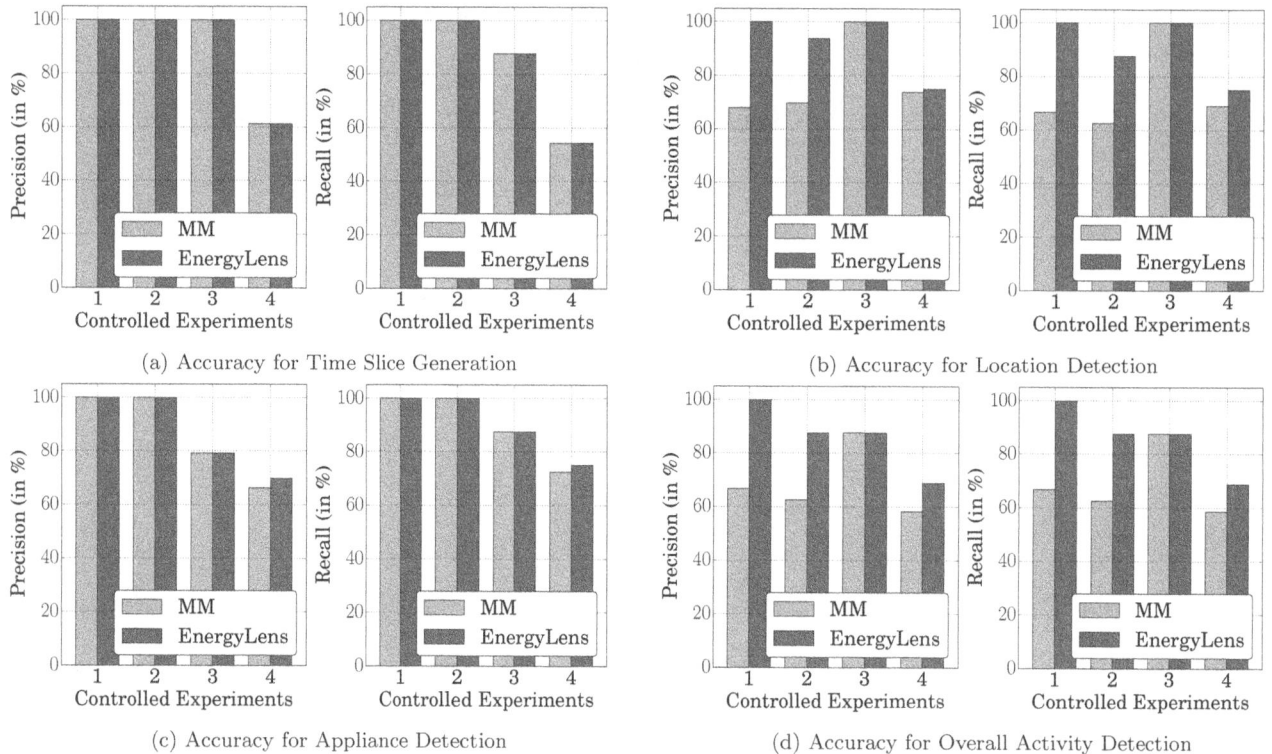

(a) Accuracy for Time Slice Generation

(b) Accuracy for Location Detection

(c) Accuracy for Appliance Detection

(d) Accuracy for Overall Activity Detection

Figure 2: Component wise Precision and Recall for all the controlled experiments (single occupant). Refer Table 3 for experiment details. Here, MM stands for Meter + Metadata (as explained in Section 5).

occupant was a Samsung Galaxy S4 with our EnergyLens application installed. Data description is presented in Table 2. Out of a total 7 experimental days, we obtained 4 days of useful data.

For collecting ground truth, we used the paper-pen method wherein we stuck a paper next to each appliance of interest. The occupant of the home was requested to enter the ON and OFF time as she used appliances during the experiment week. Labeled ground truth was collected every evening from the apartment and was compared with smart meter data for the previous day. Any discrepancies observed in the labels, through manual comparison with smart meter data, were duly discussed with the home occupant and rectified to ensure true validity of the ground truth.

For both phases, the smart meter data was collected at 1Hz. The phone sensors namely, WiFi scan and audio, were sampled every 20 seconds. Audio sampling was performed for 10 seconds every 20 seconds. The phone uploaded data every 5 minutes to the central server. Appliance metadata (appliances, their location and observed power) for both apartments was collected before the experiments and was done by measuring the real power consumption of the appliances as described in Section 2.

5. EVALUATION

We evaluate our EnergyLens system (combining phone sensors with meter data), as described in Section 3.2, by comparing its performance (in terms of activity detection accuracy) with a NILM only approach. For the NILM only approach, which we refer to as **Meter + Metadata (MM)**, *Metadata* information is used in combination with smart

meter power data to determine the appliance and its location. For the MM approach, the time slices are generated (as described in Section 3.2 Stage I), and are labeled with the appropriate appliance and location by matching the observed power from the meter with the *Metadata*. Activity detection accuracy is measured in terms of:

Precision: calculated as the ratio of the number of activities correctly identified and the total number of identified activities.

Recall: calculated as the ratio of the number of activities correctly identified and the total number of activities done during the experiment duration.

5.1 Performance Analysis

We conducted several experiments, as listed in Table 3, to emulate different realistic scenarios for evaluating the detection accuracy of EnergyLens.

5.1.1 EnergyLens inference evaluation

In this section, we show the activity detection accuracy of EnergyLens together with the accuracy of its individual components, namely, time slice generation (*when*), location detection (*where*) and appliance detection (*what*). We present the results for both controlled and real world experiments in a single occupant setting. To present the component wise accuracy, we use the ground truth after Stage I. In other words, to report the location and appliance detection accuracy, we use ground truth time slices over which we run the detection algorithm and report the accuracy for the individual components.

Day	Approach	Time Slice Generation	Location Detection	Appliance Detection	Activity Detection
1	MM	33.3 / 27.3	66.4 / 62.9	55.3 / 57.9	49.6 / 29.3
	EnergyLens	37.5 / 27.3	90.6 / 87.5	100 / 100	91.7 / 87.5
2	MM	30.7 / 50.0	51.9 / 61.2	62.5 / 50.0	14.3 / 11.2
	EnergyLens	33.3 / 50.0	76.2 / 85.7	100 / 100	76.2 / 85.7
3	MM	70.0 / 77.8	85.0 / 80.0	35.5 / 46.7	22.4 / 26.7
	EnergyLens	70.0 / 77.8	88.1 / 85.7	88.6 / 85.7	68.6 / 71.4
4	MM	70.0 / 63.6	63.7 / 72.0	28.3 / 50.0	27.4 / 22.0
	EnergyLens	77.8 / 63.6	91.1 / 88.9	61.1 / 77.8	64.5 / 66.7

Table 4: Precision/Recall (P/R) of activity detection accuracy for a single occupant real setting. MM stands for Meter + Metadata (as explained in Section 5).

Exp#	Approach	User Association		Activity Detection	
		User 1	User 2	User 1	User 2
1	MM	NA		44.7 / 46.4	75.0 / 75.0
	EnergyLens	80.0 / 80.0	80.0 / 80.0	60.0 / 100	100 / 100
2	MM	NA		100 / 100	25.0 / 25.0
	EnergyLens	66.7 / 50.0	75.0 / 60.0	100 / 100	75.0 / 75.0
3	MM	NA		30.0 / 40.0	66.7 / 66.7
	EnergyLens	83.3 / 83.3	20.0 / 20.0	70.0 / 80.0	80.0 / 80.0

Table 5: Precision/Recall (P/R) of activity detection and user association accuracy for a multi occupant controlled setting. To report activity detection accuracy per occupant for MM approach, the occupant labels are taken from the ground truth.

Figure 2 shows the precision and recall achieved across experiments 1 – 4 (See Table 3). For Experiment 1, wherein the participant complied with all the assumptions made by the algorithm and kept the phone out of their pocket most of the times, EnergyLens achieved 100% precision and recall for activity detection. With phone being kept inside the pocket for Experiment 2, the overall inference accuracy for EnergyLens reduces, primarily due to the poor location detection accuracy caused due to the varying orientation of the phone (as explained in Section 5.1.3). Similarly, in Experiment 3, the accuracy of EnergyLens was lower due to reduced appliance detection accuracy, caused due to mis-classifications by the audio recognition algorithm. Appliance correction stage was unable to rectify these misclassifications as *Metadata* had multiple appliances with similar power consumption at the classified location.

During complex appliance usage events, as emulated in Experiment 4 wherein multiple appliances (combination of similar and dissimilar appliances in terms of power consumption) were used simultaneously across different rooms, EnergyLens is able to achieve 68.93% precision and 68.75% recall which is higher than MM approach which achieves 58.19% precision and 58.23% recall.

Real world experiments for the single occupant setting, as shown in Table 4, further corroborate that EnergyLens always performs at least as good and in most cases much better than the meter only approach (MM). The average precision and recall for EnergyLens was 75.2% and 77.8% while for MM approach, it was 28.4% and 22.3%. MM approach compares the observed power consumption obtained from meter data with the metadata to determine location and appliance. For similar appliances (e.g. lights and fans), which were used extensively by the occupant, MM was not able to distinguish them. This resulted in low appliance detection accuracy which brought down the activity detection accuracy. In contrast, EnergyLens used phone data for determining the location and appliance which if misclassified was corrected with the help of metadata. This combination of phone with meter improved the activity detection accuracy significantly as seen in Table 4.

5.1.2 User Association Accuracy

In this section, we report the accuracy of the user association component of EnergyLens wherein *Precision* and *Recall* are calculated separately for each user. We only present the results of controlled experiments for the multi-occupant setting. Real world scenarios present a lot of challenges (as discussed in Section 6) which makes the problem of user association non-trivial. Further, obtaining ground truth for such settings is a significant challenge. Detailed instrumentation is required to monitor the occupants activities to identify their actual location and appliance activity which we plan to undertake in the future.

In order to test the performance of our user attribution algorithm, we conducted several controlled experiments where we emulated realistic scenarios. Each experiment involved doing a set of activities by two participants based on a script given to them. The results of these experiments are shown in Table 5. The table lists user association accuracy along with the activity detection accuracy for each occupant. For the MM approach, it is evident that meter data cannot be used in isolation to determine the identity of the occupant who did an activity. Therefore, to determine the activity detection accuracy per occupant, we feed pre-annotated user time slices to the MM algorithm. This reduced the multi-occupant case to the single occupant case for this approach.

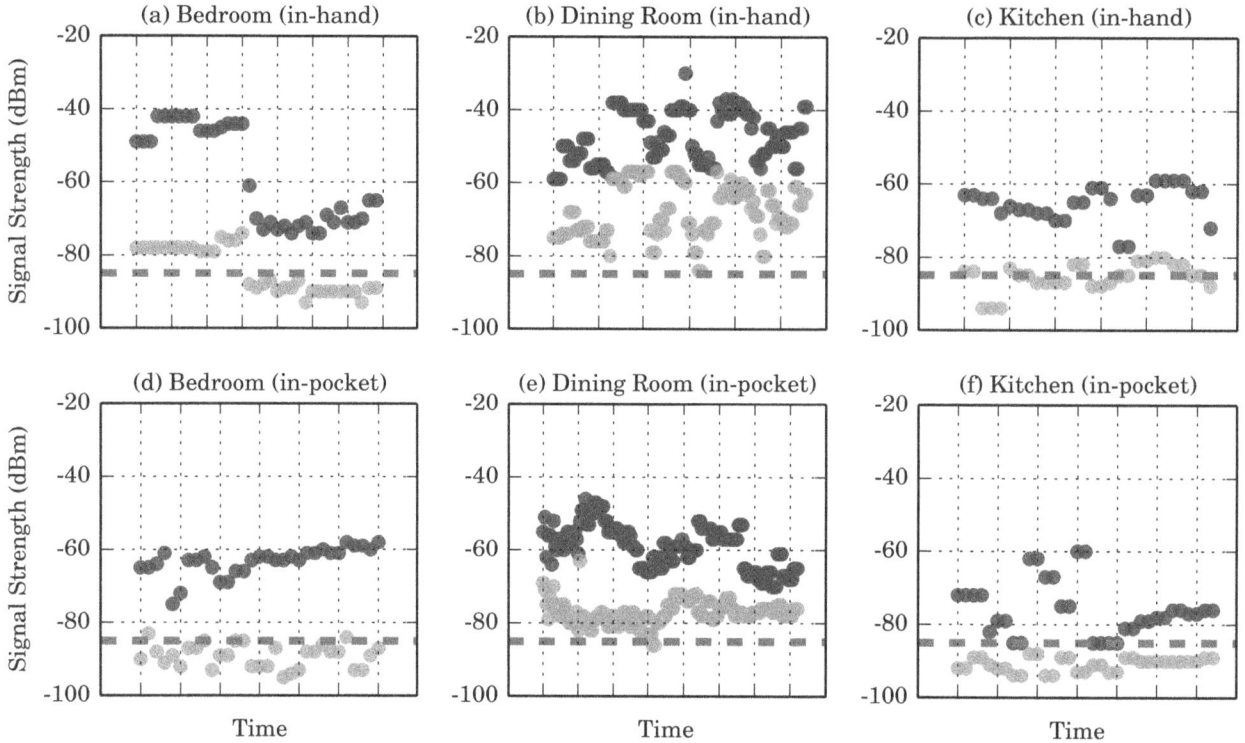

Figure 3: Illustration of signal attenuation caused due to phone orientation. Each color represents the signal strength from a di erent access point (maroon representing the AP inside the apartment where experiment was conducted). The line drawn at -85dBm denotes that all signal strength values below -85dBm are discarded by EnergyLens.

The results listed in Table 5 look promising and they demonstrate the importance of smartphones in attributing energy to individuals. As pointed out earlier, the accuracy of individual components a ect the overall activity detection and user association accuracy. We see the e ect of poor location detection accuracy on user association in Experiment 3 for the second occupant. The misclassifications caused by the detection algorithm was due to the poor quality of location data obtained from the phone when it was kept in the pocket during the experiment. The next section (Section 5.1.3) explains the impact of phone s orientation in detail.

5.1.3 Impact of Phone Orientation on Location Detection Accuracy

In this section, we analyze how the orientation of phone, i.e. phone s position while performing activities, a ects location detection accuracy.

We performed two experiments, referred as Exp 1 and 2 in Table 3. In the first experiment, the phone was carried in hand or placed on the table while doing the activities. In experiment 2, the phone was kept inside the pocket all the time. Four access points (APs) were seen in the vicinity of the apartment; one of them being the AP of the apartment in which experiments were conducted. Out of the four, two APs had less than -85dBm signal strength and were therefore not used by EnergyLens. Two APs were visible across all three rooms. The AP in the apartment was kept in the dining room.

Figure 3 shows the signal strength received from the two visible APs for each room. Observations obtains from experiment 1 and 2 are shown in Figure 3a Figure 3c and Figure 3d Figure 3f respectively. Since the apartment AP was in the dining room, the signal attenuation is negligible and thus doesn t a ect the detection accuracy for this room. However, signals from the second AP which were comparatively weaker in the Bedroom and Kitchen, gets further attenuated due to phone s orientation and a ects the localization accuracy for these rooms.

The experiments were conducted in an apartment building inside IIIT-Delhi campus in India where very few access points were seen in the vicinity. The accuracy is expected to be much more when the number of access points increase in number (which is relatively common in the US).

5.1.4 Impact of Sampling Intervals on Appliance Detection Accuracy

To assess the impact of the sampling interval on the accuracy of appliance detection, we conducted an experiment where multiple appliances were used (experiment 4 in Table 3) with audio sampling done every 20 seconds for a period of 10 seconds. We sub-sampled this data to obtain data with sampling intervals from 40 seconds to 180 seconds. Table 6 shows the appliance detection accuracy of the algorithm for di erent sampling intervals. Since the usage of appliances during this experiment was well separated in terms of power consumption and usage times, and 10 second audio data was observed to be sufficient for classification

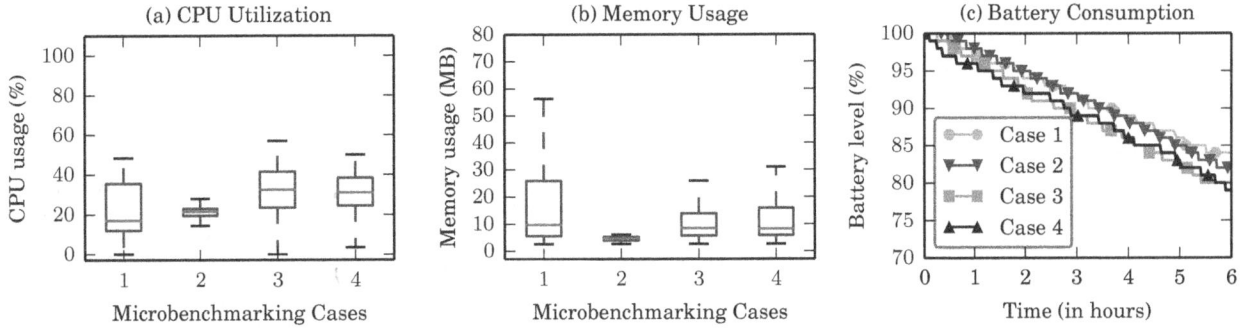

Figure 4: Microbenchmarking of EnergyLens in terms of CPU, memory and battery usage. The four cases are: (1) Wifi sampling only (2) Audio Sampling only (3) Wifi and Audio sampling together (4) EnergyLens with sampling and data upload

Sampling Interval(s)	EnergyLens	
	Precision(%)	Recall(%)
20	69.8	75.0
40	66.0	68.8
60	67.3	71.9
80	67.2	71.9
100	68.9	75.0
120	64.1	65.6
140	59.3	62.5
160	62.8	62.5
180	64.1	65.6

Table 6: Impact of Sampling Intervals on Precision/Recall of Appliance Detection Accuracy

purposes, the appliance detection accuracy remains approximately constant across different sampling intervals. This shows that for such infrequent appliance usages (which are common in real world settings as well), we can reduce the sampling interval for audio sampling without significantly affecting the inference accuracy.

5.1.5 Impact of Simultaneous Activity on Time Slice Generation Accuracy

Simple edge detection and edge matching algorithm for inferring usage durations, as used in the current implementation of EnergyLens, are accurate when the used appliances differ in terms of their power consumption. However, when appliances with similar power consumption (such as fans and lights; microwave and electric kettle) are used simultaneously then it becomes difficult for the edge matching algorithm to correctly associate an ON event with a corresponding OFF event.

We conducted three controlled experiments (refer Table 3): first with dissimilar appliances (fan, microwave, TV, AC, kettle) working at the same time (experiment 6), second with multiple similar appliances (mostly lights and fans) used simultaneously across rooms (experiment 5), and the third with a combination of similar and dissimilar appliances used concurrently (experiment 3). These experiments yielded 100/80, 62.5/45.5 and 100/87.5 of precision/recall respectively, illustrating that the current time slice generation algorithm finds it difficult to differentiate between appliances

with similar power consumption. We believe that additional use of power factor will help differentiate between appliances of similar power consumption and will significantly improve the accuracy for such usage scenarios.

5.2 EnergyLens Application Profiling

In order to characterize the system and energy impact of EnergyLens mobile application, we conducted tests to benchmark the impact of different components of EnergyLens. We used a Sony Xperia SP smartphone with 1.7 GHz dual core processor and 1 GB RAM for the evaluation. The audio sampling rate was set to 8kHz and was sampled for 10 seconds at an interval of 20 seconds. The phone also scanned for WiFi APs every 20 seconds. The collected and processed data was uploaded every 5 minutes to the central server.

5.2.1 Application Overhead

We collected system's total CPU and memory usage for a duration of 3 hours each, for the cases: (a) System with Wifi turned ON and without EnergyLens installed (baseline case) (b) System with EnergyLens installed and background data collection process enabled. Background running processes were constant for both cases. Mean memory usage of the system for the baseline case was found to be 240MB and 256MB for EnergyLens. The memory overhead of EnergyLens was observed to be 16MB, only a 6% increase in usage. The mean CPU usage was 13% and 22% for cases (a) and (b) respectively. Therefore, the difference in usage (CPU overhead of EnergyLens) was found to be 9%. This increase in CPU utilization of EnergyLens can be reduced with adaptive sampling techniques which we leave as a future work.

5.2.2 Microbenchmarking

The microbenchmarking tests were conducted to quantify the effect of the individual components of EnergyLens, namely Wifi sampling, audio sampling and data upload. We measured the CPU, memory and battery usage for four cases: (1) App with Wifi sampling only (2) App with audio sampling only (3) App with Wifi and audio sampling together (4) EnergyLens App with audio and Wifi sampling with periodic data uploads. CPU and memory measurements were taken every second using Android's *adb* utility over a period of 3 hours each. Battery runs were done over a period of 6 hours each where the residual battery level was logged once every 20 seconds by the mobile application during data sampling.

CPU and Memory Footprint: Figure 4a and Figure 4b show the CPU and memory usage of the smartphone for each of the four cases. The mean memory usage is 17MB, 4MB, 10MB and 11MB for cases 1 4 respectively and the mean CPU usage of the four cases is 23%, 21%, 32% and 30% respectively. From Figure 4a and Figure 4b, we see that the audio sampling (case 2) component s impact is less than Wifi sampling component (case 1) in terms of CPU and memory usage both. The upload component (case 4) doesn t add much memory overhead (only 1MB) when compared to case 3. Similarly, the mean CPU usage of case 3 and case 4 also remains the same. Thus, we can conclude that the additional periodic uploads (case 4) doesn t add any significant overhead on the system s performance when compared to case 3.

Energy footprint: The battery drain was observed to be 2.67%, 3%, 3.33% and 3.5% per hour for cases 1 4 respectively. They correspond to 37.4 hours, 33.3 hours, 30.0 hours and 28.5 hours of battery life. From Figure 4c, we observe that the di erence in battery usage for case 3 and case 4 is not remarkable (just 5% increase from case 3) which reaffirms that the upload component doesn t add any significant overhead on the system s performance. On the contrary, the audio sampling (case 2) component s battery usage is 12% more than Wifi sampling component (case 1), making it the most power hungry component of EnergyLens (case 4). With the battery lifetime of approximately 28.5 hours for the smartphone with EnergyLens application running in the background, we can conclude that EnergyLens is comparable to the normal usage scenarios and it does not reduce battery life of a device perceptibly.

6. DISCUSSION AND LIMITATIONS

EnergyLens seeks to address a very complex problem of identifying and disaggregating energy usage per appliance and associating each usage with a particular user. The current implementation of EnergyLens tries to achieve this objective with a basic set of sensors from mobile phones and home level electricity meters, chosen to keep the overall cost of deployment and maintenance low. We now discuss several challenges that arise while using such a restricted set of sensing modalities for this complex problem.

We note that energy attribution in a multi-occupant setting can not be done by using meter data alone and therefore adding phone information becomes critical. We further show that, by combining even the most simplistic algorithms for localization, appliance detection and NILM, EnergyLens can provide better accuracy for activity inference as compared to NILM only techniques. A natural extension of our work is to investigate more complex algorithms, such as Factorial HMM for NILM [24], sound separation techniques such as Computational Auditory Scene Analysis (CASA) [3] for audio-based appliance detection and localization techniques such as UnLoc [31] and Ariel [12], to further improve accuracy, particularly for more complex scenarios such as in multi-occupant homes. Use of additional sensors for both smartphones and energy meters can provide additional contextual information that can be used to further improve the accuracy. Examples of these additional context information include detection of ambient light using the phone light sensor, improved location classification using camera [1], radio

ranging such as the one provided by Bluetooth Low Energy and power factor to help distinguish loads. Finally, a simple extension of EnergyLens can be to use events on the meter data to trigger sensing for mobile phone audio and WiFi, thereby reducing the overall energy burden due to EnergyLens.

In terms of deployment and use of our system, there are a number of practical considerations that a ect the overall inference accuracy. Examples of these considerations include phone orientation a ecting WiFi-based localization accuracy, scenarios when the user is not carrying the phone with them while performing any appliance usage and scenarios wherein the user initiates an appliance activity (e.g. start a microwave) and then leaves the room to return back after a time when the activity is still underway. Such considerations are further complicated for the multi-occupant scenario. Examples of complex multi-occupant scenarios include simultaneous switching of appliances by di erent users across di erent rooms, movement of users across di erent rooms while the appliance usage (e.g. television being ON) in each of the rooms is ongoing and one user s phone is in a room where the second user is present, though without her phone, while initiating an appliance usage activity. These complex scenarios, for both single and multi-occupant case, potentially require both additional sensing information and more sophisticated inference algorithms that also decide when to use or ignore di erent context information.

Since EnergyLens uses smartphone sensors such as audio from the microphone, privacy is a natural concern. Preprocessing the audio on the phone itself while sending only the inferred values to the EnergyLens server for analysis, mitigates such privacy concerns in EnergyLens. Furthermore, the data analysis for activity inference is simple enough to be easily run on a local computer in the occupants home, further alleviating any privacy concerns.

7. RELATED WORK

Location based services using WiFi on phones as a sensor (e.g. LifeMap [4] and ParkSense [20]) as well as acoustic sensing applications using phones (e.g. SpeakerSense [16] and SocioPhone [15]) have been proposed. Smartphones in a way provide an ideal platform to host many of these applications. Motivated by the ubiquity of smartphones and their increasing sensing capabilities, EnergyLens looks at a previously unexplored dimension of residential energy monitoring by leveraging smartphone sensors together with smart meter data for improved electrical appliance activity detection accuracy. We now present related work across the three dimensions of EnergyLens: location inference, audio classification and appliance detection. To the best of our knowledge, there does not exist any other work that addresses the complex combination of inference including who , what , when and where for activities in residential setting.

Several techniques, other than the WiFi fingerprinting methods, have been proposed over the years for indoor localization. These techniques use additional sensors e.g. microphone sound, camera [1] and light [25] to improve the overall localization accuracy. EnergyLens can potentially improve its localization accuracy by utilizing such additional smartphone sensors and incorporating some of these sophisticated techniques rather than simple nearest neighbor approach based on WiFi fingerprinting, currently used in this work.

Several frameworks have been proposed for building context aware applications using audio as a sensing modality. These include SoundSense [17] for distinguishing voice and music from ambient noise, Jigsaw [18] for human activity inferences and iSleep [9] for detecting sleep quality. Recently, Auditeur [21], a general purpose acoustic event detection platform for smartphones was proposed that enable applications to register for receiving notifications for the desired audio events as classified within their framework. Several of the techniques used in these frameworks for audio processing on the phone can also be incorporated into EnergyLens for improving the overall detection accuracy.

Energy monitoring in a residential setting involves multiple facets e.g. NILM work using smart meters for energy monitoring and disaggregation [10, 7, 14]; use of additional sensing modalities that indirectly monitors the environment for e ects caused due to energy usage [8]; combining meters with other ambient sensors such as light, temperature, motion and acoustic signals [13, 23]; and very recently using smartphones only [30, 29]. EnergyLens does not require deploying and managing additional sensors but endeavors to better solve the problem of energy monitoring by leveraging smartphone sensors for improved appliance detection and recognition.

Of the recent work, AppliSense [33] has some aspects that are related to our work. AppliSense, propose a NILM algorithm to disaggregate appliance energy use. They also propose using a smartphone UI to help users label appliances as part of their training phase. The crucial di erentiator is that they don t actually propose, or use, any of the smartphone sensors for the actual disaggregation algorithm. In contrast, the key contribution of EnergyLens is the idea of combining sensor readings from smart meters and user s smartphones for improved energy use inference in order to answer the *who, what, where* and *when* questions of energy apportionment. Kay et al. [11] presented the case for apportionment in a building. They studied di erent apportionment policies and how sensor systems could be used to further enable this. EnergyLens takes a step further and proposes an actual system to provide the key pieces of information required for apportioning energy in homes.

8. CONCLUSIONS

This paper presents the design and implementation of EnergyLens , a system for accurate activity inference in homes specifically to disaggregate energy and apportion usage to the occupants. The key contribution of EnergyLens is a novel sensor fusion algorithm that utilizes sensor data from occupants smartphones and that from a smart meter to improve inference accuracy as compared to traditional NILM approaches. In contrast to prior approaches that propose to address this problem using additional sensors and complex algorithms, we show that even simple NILM, audio-based classification and WiFi-based localization methods provide sufficient accuracy in realistic settings.

We highlight several challenges that impact the inference accuracy for the complex problem at hand. These include the impact of phone orientation, diverse usage scenarios especially for the multi-occupant case, collection of ground truth data for establishing the accuracy and simultaneous switching of appliances with similar power consumption profiles. While the current implementation of EnergyLens seeks reasonable accuracy in many such complex scenarios, we

plan to enrich our system with additional sensing modalities both from the smartphone (e.g. light sensor, camera) and the smart meter (e.g. power factor) together with more sophisticated inference algorithms. The flip side, however, of using sophisticated inference algorithms will be the increased computation demand; EnergyLens is currently lightweight enough to run on a laptop class machine.

9. ACKNOWLEDGEMENTS

Authors would like to acknowledge the support provided by ITRA project, funded by DEITy, Goverment of India, under grant with Ref. No. ITRA/15(57)/Mobile/HumanSense/ 01. This work was also supported in part by NSF grant SHF-1018632. We wish to thank our anonymous reviewers for their feedback to help improve the paper.

10. REFERENCES

[1] M. Azizyan, I. Constandache, and R. Roy Choudhury. SurroundSense: Mobile phone localization via ambience fingerprinting. In *Proc. of the 15th Annual International Conference on Mobile computing and networking*, pages 261 272. ACM, 2009.

[2] P. Bahl and V. N. Padmanabhan. RADAR: An in-building RF-based user location and tracking system. In *Proc. of the 19th Annual Joint Conference of the IEEE Computer and Communications Societies*, volume 2, pages 775 784. IEEE, 2000.

[3] G. J. Brown and M. Cooke. Computational auditory scene analysis. *Computer Speech & Language*, 8(4):297 336, 1994.

[4] J. Chon and H. Cha. Lifemap: A smartphone-based context provider for location-based services. *IEEE Pervasive Computing*, 10(2):58 67, 2011.

[5] DOE. Buildings Energy Data Book. *Department of Energy*, March 2009.

[6] J. Froehlich, L. Findlater, and J. Landay. The design of eco-feedback technology. In *Proc. of the CHI Conference on Human Factors in Computing Systems*, pages 1999 2008. ACM, 2010.

[7] H. Gonçalves, A. Ocneanu, M. Bergés, and R. Fan. Unsupervised disaggregation of appliances using aggregated consumption data. In *The 1st KDD Workshop on Data Mining Applications in Sustainability*, 2011.

[8] S. Gupta, M. S. Reynolds, and S. N. Patel. ElectriSense: Single-point Sensing using EMI for Electrical Event Detection and Classification in the Home. In *Proceedings of the 12th ACM international conference on Ubiquitous Computing (Ubicomp)*, pages 139 148. ACM, 2010.

[9] T. Hao, G. Xing, and G. Zhou. iSleep: unobtrusive sleep quality monitoring using smartphones. In *Proc. of the 11th ACM Conference on Embedded Networked Sensor Systems*, page 4. ACM, 2013.

[10] G. W. Hart. Nonintrusive appliance load monitoring. *Proceedings of the IEEE*, 80(12):1870 1891, 1992.

[11] S. Hay and A. Rice. The case for apportionment. In *Proc. of the 1st ACM Workshop on Embedded Sensing Systems for Energy-E ciency in Buildingss*, pages 13 18. ACM, 2009.

[12] Y. Jiang, X. Pan, K. Li, Q. Lv, R. P. Dick, M. Hannigan, and L. Shang. Ariel: Automatic wi-fi

based room fingerprinting for indoor localization. In *Proc. of the 14th ACM Conference on Ubiquitous Computing*, pages 441 450. ACM, 2012.

[13] Y. Kim, T. Schmid, Z. Charbiwala, and M. Srivastava. ViridiScope: design and implementation of a fine grained power monitoring system for homes. In *Proc. of the 11th International Conference on Ubiquitous computing*, pages 245 254. ACM, 2009.

[14] J. Z. Kolter, S. Batra, and A. Ng. Energy Disaggregation via Discriminative Sparse Coding. In *Advances in Neural Information Processing Systems*, pages 1153 1161, 2010.

[15] Y. Lee, C. Min, C. Hwang, J. Lee, I. Hwang, Y. Ju, C. Yoo, M. Moon, U. Lee, and J. Song. SocioPhone: Everyday Face-to-Face Interaction Monitoring Platform Using Multi-Phone Sensor Fusion. In *Proc. of the 11th International Conference on Mobile Systems, Applications, and Services*. ACM, 2013.

[16] H. Lu, A. B. Brush, B. Priyantha, A. K. Karlson, and J. Liu. SpeakerSense: energy efficient unobtrusive speaker identification on mobile phones. In *Pervasive Computing*, pages 188 205. Springer, 2011.

[17] H. Lu, W. Pan, N. D. Lane, T. Choudhury, and A. T. Campbell. SoundSense: scalable sound sensing for people-centric applications on mobile phones. In *Proc. of the 7th International Conference on Mobile systems, applications, and services*, pages 165 178. ACM, 2009.

[18] H. Lu, J. Yang, Z. Liu, N. D. Lane, T. Choudhury, and A. T. Campbell. The Jigsaw continuous sensing engine for mobile phone applications. In *Proc. of the 8th ACM Conference on Embedded Networked Sensor Systems*, pages 71 84. ACM, 2010.

[19] L. Ma, B. Milner, and D. Smith. Acoustic environment classification. *ACM Transactions on Speech and Language Processing*, 3(2):1 22, 2006.

[20] S. Nawaz, C. Efstratiou, and C. Mascolo. ParkSense: a smartphone based sensing system for on-street parking. In *Proc. of the 19th Annual International Conference on Mobile Computing & Networking*.

[21] S. Nirjon, R. F. Dickerson, P. Asare, Q. Li, D. Hong, J. A. Stankovic, P. Hu, G. Shen, and X. Jiang. Auditeur: A mobile-cloud service platform for acoustic event detection on smartphones. In *Proc. of the 11th International Conference on Mobile systems, applications, and services*. ACM, 2013.

[22] S. N. Patel, T. Robertson, J. A. Kientz, M. S. Reynolds, and G. D. Abowd. At the flick of a switch: Detecting and classifying unique electrical events on the residential power line. In *Proc. of the 9th International Conference on Ubiquitous computing*, pages 271 288. Springer, 2007.

[23] D. E. Phillips, R. Tan, M.-M. Moazzami, G. Xing, J. Chen, and D. K. Yau. Supero: A sensor system for unsupervised residential power usage monitoring. In *IEEE International Conference on Pervasive Computing and Communications*, volume 18, pages 66 75, 2013.

[24] D. Rahayu, B. Narayanaswamy, S. Krishnaswamy, C. Labbe, and D. P. Seetharam. Learning to be energy-wise: Discriminative methods for load disaggregation. In *3rd International Conference on Future Energy Systems*, pages 1 4, 2012.

[25] N. Ravi and L. Iftode. Fiatlux: Fingerprinting rooms using light intensity. In *Adjunct Proc. of the Fifth International Conference on Pervasive Computing*. Citeseer, 2007.

[26] A. Rowe, M. Berges, and R. Rajkumar. Contactless Sensing of Appliance State Transitions Through Variations in Electromagnetic Fields. In *Proc. of the 2nd ACM Workshop on Embedded Systems For Energy-E cient Buildings*, 2010.

[27] V. Srinivasan, J. Stankovic, and K. Whitehouse. FixtureFinder: discovering the existence of electrical and water fixtures. In *Proceedings of the 12th International Conference on Information Processing in Sensor Networks*, pages 115 128. ACM, 2013.

[28] Z. C. Taysi, M. A. Guvensan, and T. Melodia. TinyEars: spying on house appliances with audio sensor nodes. In *Proc. of the 2nd ACM Workshop on Embedded Sensing Systems for Energy-E ciency in Buildings*, pages 31 36. ACM, 2010.

[29] M. Uddin and T. Nadeem. EnergySni er: Home energy monitoring system using smart phones. In *Proc. of 8th International Wireless Communications and Mobile Computing Conference*, pages 159 164. IEEE, 2012.

[30] M. Uddin and T. Nadeem. MachineSense: detecting and monitoring active machines using smart phone. *Mobile Computing and Communications Review*, 16(4):16 17, 2012.

[31] H. Wang, S. Sen, A. Elgohary, M. Farid, M. Youssef, and R. R. Choudhury. No need to war-drive: Unsupervised indoor localization. In *Proc. of the 10th International Conference on Mobile systems, applications, and services*, pages 197 210. ACM, 2012.

[32] J.-C. Wang, H.-P. Lee, J.-F. Wang, and C.-B. Lin. Robust environmental sound recognition for home automation. *IEEE Transactions on Automation Science and Engineering*, 5(1):25 31, 2008.

[33] M. Weiss, A. Helfenstein, F. Mattern, and T. Staake. Leveraging smart meter data to recognize home appliances. In *IEEE International Conference on Pervasive Computing and Communications*, pages 190 197. IEEE, 2012.

[34] T. Weng, B. Balaji, S. Dutta, R. Gupta, and Y. Agarwal. Managing Plug-Loads for Demand Response within Buildings. In *Proc. of the 3rd ACM Workshop on Embedded Sensing Systems For Energy-E ciency In Buildings*, 2011.

[35] J.-P. Zimmermann, M. Evans, J. Griggs, N. King, L. Harding, P. Roberts, and C. Evans. Household Electricity Survey. A study of domestic electrical product usage. Technical Report R66141, DEFRA, May 2012.

[36] A. Zoha, A. Gluhak, M. Nati, M. A. Imran, and S. Rajasegarar. Acoustic and device feature fusion for load recognition. In *Proc. of the 6th IEEE International Conference Intelligent Systems*, pages 386 392. IEEE, 2012.

Deltaflow: Submetering by Synthesizing Uncalibrated Pulse Sensor Streams

Meghan Clark, Bradford Campbell, and Prabal Dutta
Electrical Engineering and Computer Science Department
University of Michigan
Ann Arbor, MI 48109
{mclarkk,bradjc,prabal}@umich.edu

ABSTRACT

Current submetering systems suffer from prohibitive device costs, invasive installations, and burdensome maintenance. In this paper we present Deltaflow, a submetering system that can estimate the power draw of individual loads by augmenting aggregate measurements with very simple sensors. The key insight is that we can drastically reduce sensor complexity by encoding information in the mere existence of a radio transmission, rather than the contents of that transmission. A sensor consisting simply of a radio and an energy-harvesting power supply tuned to harvest a side-channel emission of energy consumption (e.g. light, heat, magnetic field, vibration) will exhibit an activation frequency that is correlated with the power draw of the load to which it is affixed. These sensors report their activations to the data-processing backend, which can determine the actual power draw by incorporating ground truth aggregate measurements such as those provided by utility meters. The server maps sensor activations to energy consumption by observing when the aggregate measurement and the sensor activation frequency change simultaneously. The server iteratively partitions the system history into discrete states which are used to construct and solve instances of a linear optimization problem. Solutions to the problem reveal the mapping from pulse frequencies to individual load power draw. This systems approach to submetering results in deployments that are easy to install and maintain, while contributing zero additional load, enabling building owners and occupants to simply affix tags to energy consumers and automatically begin receiving real-time power draw readings.

Categories and Subject Descriptors

B.m [**HARDWARE**]: Miscellaneous—*Miscellaneous*

General Terms

Design, Experimentation, Measurement, Performance

Keywords

Energy harvesting, Power metering, Data aggregation, Intermittent power, Submetering, Non-intrusive load monitoring

e-Energy'14, June 11–13, 2014, Cambridge, UK.
ACM 978-1-4503-2819-7/14/06.
http://dx.doi.org/10.1145/2602044.2602070.

1. INTRODUCTION

Buildings account for a significant share of resource use in the U.S.: they consume 39% of the energy, 73% of the electricity, 55% of the natural gas, and 12% of the water. Powering them results in $400 billion in annual expenditures. If current trends continue, by 2025 buildings worldwide will consume more energy than the transportation and industry sectors combined. Moreover, "between 60 and 80 percent of the energy used in commercial office buildings is consumed by tenants within their spaces," yet, "no widely available tools exist to help tenants understand their energy consumption or to compare it against their peer groups," claims a recent U.S. National Science and Technology Council (NSTC) study [17]

The same NSTC study states that the "refined measurement of electricity and water use represent a key enabler for the improved performance of new and existing buildings," and adds that, "For building operators, a detailed record of system performance provides a critical means of... focusing future design and retrofit activities on the most cost-effective energy and water system improvements," and, "For building occupants, detailed information on consumption promotes resource conservation through behavioral changes." [17] A recent U.S. National Science Board (NSB) study adds, "One critical focus area is developing measurement science to enable the development of zero-energy buildings." [16]

Unfortunately, today's metering technologies are ill-suited to the measurement task at hand. Existing whole-building metering systems provide little visibility into the contributions of individual loads. Non-intrusive load monitoring (NILM) techniques provide some additional insights, but they do not scale beyond a few loads, they often require training or association of loads to their signatures, and they can typically identify only the largest loads. Plug-load meters provide much greater visibility but they are costly and limited in their coverage to easily accessible electrical loads. Hybrid approaches also exist that augment NILM with additional sensors that aid disaggregation, but the devices are often costly, the sensors require periodic battery maintenance, and the algorithms often assume appliance states are known *a priori*.

To address the challenges with prior approaches, this paper proposes not to replace, but rather to augment, existing whole-building or panel-level metering techniques with a new class of simple and easily-deployed energy-harvesting sensors and a novel algorithm that combines data from both new and existing meters to infer the contributions from individual loads. We envision a future in which building owners or occupants can simply and directly tag end loads like a ceiling light, shower head, or range top with small and inexpensive sensors. The sensors *indirectly* monitor the load by harvesting the energy that a load emits when operating (e.g. the light emitted from a bulb). The sensor activations are received by a base station, time-stamped, and forwarded to the cloud for processing.

Our prior work has shown the viability of energy harvesting energy meters [4]. In particular, we have shown that the energy emitted from many electrical loads is roughly proportional to the energy consumed by that load, and that by harvesting this side-channel energy, it is possible to intermittently power sensors whose activation interval (and in turn packet transmission period) approximately encodes the underlying energy use. We call this the "Monjolo" principle and envision many different kinds of "pulse" sensors that could be constructed using this principle.

Such sensors represent a modern reinterpretation of the decades-old pulsed-output meters that measure electricity, gas, and water, but with one crucial difference. Whereas traditional meters are calibrated to output one pulse per useful billing quanta (e.g. 1 W-hr, 1 CCF, or 1 gal), our proposed meters would usually not be, and often could not be, calibrated *a priori*. We hypothesize that by using statistical methods to correlate the timing of the packet pulse train from instrumented loads with readings from existing aggregate electricity, gas, or water meters, we can obtain individual estimates without intrusive metering.

In an ideal measurement setting, all loads would be instrumented and energy-harvesting sensors would respond instantly to changes in load power draws. However, satisfying these conditions is usually undesirable for reasons of cost and coverage, and potentially impossible for energy-harvesting sensors that must accrue energy for some time before becoming active. To mitigate the effects of delayed sensor response, we employ algorithmic techniques to partition the power draw history into periods of rapid change and relative stability. Then, by analyzing the sensor pulse trains, we identify those adjacent periods in which it is likely that only the monitored loads changed, discarding those changes attributable to uninstrumented loads. Representative data points for the remaining stable periods are then used to construct a regression problem that determines the sensor calibration. This allows us to deploy uncalibrated sensors, which reduces cost, and then employ parameter estimation to calibrate the sensors *in situ*.

While today's centimeter-scale prototype sensors are built from off-the-shelf parts, we imagine that in the future the sensors will be built from integrated circuit technology laminated into smart labels with energy-harvesting front-ends, eventually making them small, inexpensive, and easy-to-deploy. Indeed, contemporaneous research has already demonstrated the viability of fully-functional sensor systems at the millimeter-scale [13]. Our approach imposes minimal sensor requirements, allowing the future sensors to be drop-in replacements. We believe that one of Deltaflow's greatest strengths is sensor agnosticism. Since the disaggregation algorithm simply analyzes uncalibrated pulse trains, pulse counting serves as a layer of abstraction over the physical details of how the pulse measurement is generated. This means the system naturally supports a heterogeneous collection of pulse-counting devices. It makes no difference whether the devices measure electricity, water, or gas–or even whether the measurements are aggregated at the level of plug loads, individual circuits, panel boxes, whole buildings, or entire campuses–the same techniques apply. Collectively, these Deltaflow properties address cost and coverage challenges, and enable scalable deployment and widespread adoption.

To evaluate the viability and drawbacks of this approach, we employ several types of sensors in various configurations with real loads. We find that our pulse-counter calibration methods are able to disaggregate power draw in cases with complete sensor coverage, with unmonitored loads, and with heterogeneous sensor types. Further, we show that our approach is able to provide breakdowns of total energy usage suitable for solving the submetering problem. Finally, we identify limitations and opportunities for future work.

2. RELATED WORK

Numerous methods exist to measure and disaggregate electrical loads in residential and commercial buildings including non-intrusive load monitoring, plug-load monitoring, and hybrid approaches. In this section, we discuss these approaches, identify their drawbacks, and contrast them with Deltaflow.

2.1 Non-Intrusive Load Monitoring

Whole-building meters [5, 25] provide an overall view of electricity or water use, but they do not disaggregate the data in a way that allows either precise or approximate attribution to the various individual loads comprising the whole. Analytics can take meter data and disaggregate the readings using appliance signatures with a technique called non-intrusive load monitoring or NILM [8]. This approach works well when the loads are sufficiently few (e.g. typically no more than 6-7), mostly large (e.g., air conditioners and stoves), and have distinctive signatures (e.g. refrigerators and ovens). NILM has difficulty with smaller loads (e.g. electronics) or multiple instances of a particular load (e.g. several 60 W light bulbs), or a large collection of loads (e.g. in an office building).

Extensions of the general NILM approach use higher frequency sampling (e.g. MHz) of the current and voltage waveforms, higher dimensional data (e.g. real and reactive power), and complex signatures (e.g. wideband spectra arising from the flick of a switch or a toggle of a faucet) to identity individual loads [2,6,7,19], but these approaches still require training to associate the loads to their signatures, are susceptible to small changes in the environment (e.g. moving a load from one outlet to another), and are costly due to the use of high-rate sampling and processing. In contrast with NILM techniques, our approach can scale to a much larger number of loads of any type, even if they have similar or identical signatures. By instrumenting individual loads with inexpensive, indirect, and inaccurate sensors, Deltaflow can distinguish identical loads and disaggregate the contributions of individual loads.

2.2 Plug-Load Metering

At the other extreme, plug load meters allow individual loads to be measured [9, 14, 18, 20, 22, 24, 26]. Standalone meters display usage data locally, which supports casual use but not automated aggregation and analysis. Networked energy meters send their data to servers for analysis and visualization. However, plug load metering faces some coverage and cost disadvantages. Some loads are built-in or hard-to-access, including ceiling lights, HVAC equipment, and major appliances, making them ill-suited to such meters (although NILM techniques can sometimes identify these loads). Furthermore, at a price point of $25-$50 for standalone meters and $75-$250 for networked meters, covering a home or office can cost thousands or tens of thousands of dollars, making widespread monitoring prohibitively expensive.

In contrast with intrusive plug load meters, our approach supports indirect measurements of a load—like a ceiling light's radiant output or an air conditioner's vibrations—rather than their electrical inputs, which makes instrumenting built-in or difficult-to-access loads easier. In addition, the kinds of indirect sensors we envision—that harvest energy from light, heat, magnetic fields, and vibrations—could be constructed at the chip-scale and built into "peel-and-stick" sensor tags, much like RFID chips today. Although our mesoscale sensors deployed in modest numbers today are centimeter-scale systems, prototypes of some of the basic sensors, complete with an energy-harvesting front end, energy storage, and a processor and a radio, have been demonstrated at the millimeter-scale [13], providing some evidence that peel-and-stick sensors may soon be viable and inexpensive.

2.3 Hybrid Approaches

Due to the drawbacks of both the NILM and direct metering approaches, some recent efforts have explored hybrid models in which additional sensors augment NILM and aid with disaggregation [11, 12, 15, 23]. The extra sensors help NILM scale beyond a half-dozen loads by providing it an additional signal that reflects the state of an individual load. Sensors that detect the on-off states [10] or more finely quantized energy emissions of appliances including light, sound, and magnetism [21], have been shown to aid greatly in disaggregation. However, the former approach requires foreknowledge of the states of the instrumented loads, and the latter approach requires modeling the physical transfer functions for each type of energy emission sensor. Additionally, a major scalability impediment of earlier hybrid approaches is the cost of the sensors and the overhead of periodic battery replacement. Low-cost, mains-powered sensors that detect appliance state can address these problems, but they are currently limited to electrical plug loads [27].

In contrast with prior work that attempts to directly measure side-channel emissions (including ones that harvest the side-channel energy and use it to power active sensors [1, 3, 15]), or inexpensively measure plug loads, we propose to leverage emerging "Monjolo" sensors that simply harvest the side-channel energy and transmit a radio packet when enough energy has been accumulated to do so [4, 28], making the activation rate a proxy for power. Harvesting just enough to send a packet requires less energy than revenue-grade sensing and is easier to install, thus enabling smaller and less expensive—but also cruder—sensors. Such simple sensors, while easier to deploy and operate, are not easily calibrated.

However, much of what the sensors lose in individual quality, they gain through sheer numbers in conjunction with data fusion and optimization algorithms. Like the NILM and hybrid disaggregation techniques, Deltaflow uses a whole-building meter (or, in the case of large buildings, unit-, zone-, or floor-level meters). In our model, data from the whole-building meter is combined with the activation frequency data from a multitude of inexpensive energy-harvesting sensors to infer the contributions of individual loads. We model the relationship between a sensor's activation rate and the underlying energy flow using a combination of time series partitioning heuristics and linear optimization techniques.

3. OVERVIEW

The goal of the Deltaflow system is to provide a breakdown of the total electrical energy consumption of a building at the individual load level. Deltaflow accomplishes this using a calibrated, accurate aggregate meter and an array of simple, pulse-based sensors attached to each load. Each pulse sensor operates according to a simple principle: the higher the power draw of the load, the greater the frequency of the pulses. The Deltaflow system uses these pulse streams as hints about each load to disaggregate the aggregate measurement into each individual load's contribution.

The Deltaflow system architecture is shown in Figure 1. A power meter that is monitoring aggregate energy flow upstream from the target loads (e.g., a utility meter) reports aggregate measurements to the Deltaflow server. Additionally, the individual loads to be metered are instrumented with a suitable pulse sensor that transmits a representative pulse stream to the Deltaflow server. By augmenting the aggregate measurements with pulse frequencies that change as the individual load's power draw changes, the Deltaflow server characterizes the sensor's response to changes in the power state of the load it is attached to. The server uses these models of the sensors to perform calibrated disaggregation and provide power draw estimates for the individual loads being monitored.

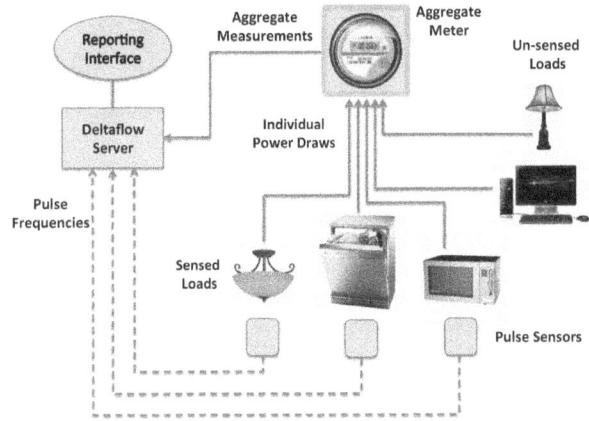

Figure 1: System architecture. The Deltaflow server takes in aggregate power draw measurements and the activation frequencies of energy-harvesting sensors attached to individual loads. By augmenting aggregate power measurements with sensor activation (or pulse) frequencies that are correlated with power draw, Deltaflow determines the individual energy consumption of the sensed loads. The system is able to function even if some loads remain unsensed.

4. DESIGN

In this section we describe common types of aggregate meters, the pulse sensors we use to monitor loads, and the algorithm used by the Deltaflow server to disaggregate loads.

4.1 Aggregate Meters

Aggregate meters provide a calibrated stream of ground truth measurements that represent the sum of all of the individual loads or consumers in the system or subsystem. Common household aggregate meters exist for electricity, water, and natural gas. In some cases unit-, zone-, or floor-level aggregates may be more appropriate than whole-building meters. Currently, while many utility meter readings are difficult to access and provide a temporal resolution that is quite coarse, being revenue-grade devices, they are quite accurate. Trends suggest that in the future detailed readings may become more readily accessible. In the meantime, commercial whole-house meters that provide higher temporal resolution, like The Energy Detective [5], are available on the market.

4.2 Energy-Harvesting Sensors

The pulse sensors the Deltaflow system uses are based around a simple observation: the act of energy consumption often emits side channels of energy that can be harvested to intermittently power a sensor node. For example, powering an AC load creates a changing magnetic field around the wires running to the load, lighting a room generates a harvestable light source, and drawing a hot bath causes pipes to be warmer than the surrounding air. Capturing these side-channel energy sources to power a sensor node creates a suitable pulse sensor that follows the principle in Section 3. As the power draw of the energy-consuming load increases, so does the magnitude of the side-channel emission, and this in turn causes the sensor node to activate more frequently. These activations are the "pulses" from the pulse sensors. Even though we employ energy-harvesting sensors to generate these pulses, any meter that operates on this principle (including most utility meters in existence today) will satisfy our requirements.

(a) Coilcube   (b) Split-core   (c) Gecko

Figure 2: Pulse sensors. Examples of the energy-harvesting pulse sensors we use attached to the loads they meter. Monitored loads include a plug-load, a circuit in a panel box, and a recessed can light. The latter two loads are easily monitored using our approach.

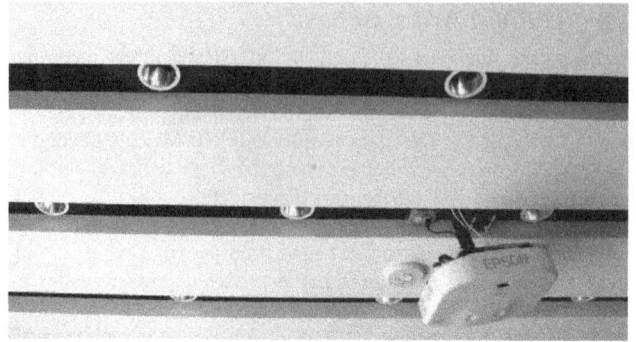

Figure 3: Recessed ceiling lights. Lights such as these are traditionally difficult to meter due to limited access to their wiring and uncertainty about the topology of the lighting circuit. Our Gecko sensors are easily and unobtrusively installed in fixtures such as these. See Figure 2(c) for a closeup view of the sensor mounting.

The Deltaflow pulse sensors are based on the Monjolo principle [4], a simple energy-harvesting design that entails three basic components: a harvester, a processor with non-volatile storage, and a radio. The energy-harvesting power supply accumulates charge over time and activates the computational core of the node when enough energy has accrued. Upon activation, the node transmits a wireless packet, discharges any remaining energy, and resumes charging once again. The node also stores the activation count to stable storage and transmits this information in each packet. The Deltaflow server receives these packets and interprets each packet as one (or more) pulse(s) for disaggregation purposes.

While simple, this design offers two major advantages: it requires no batteries and can be used to measure any energy source that can be harvested. Removing batteries simplifies deployment and eliminates the maintenance cost of replacing them. Harvesting side-channel emissions of power draw, such as magnetic inductance, heat, light, or vibration enables sensing of otherwise difficult-to-measure energy sources, such as ceiling lights, shower heads, or built-in appliances. Additionally, these sensors abstract the heterogeneity of their power sources and sensor types by eschewing direct measurements in exchange for a single homogeneous interface— pulse rate as proxied by activations or radio packet transmissions.

We adjust our specific implementation to address two common network problems: packet loss and flooding. First, because radio packets can be dropped, each sensor keeps a local counter of its own activations in nonvolatile memory and transmits this count every time it sends a packet. This way, the receiver can still calculate the rate of activations even if a packet is lost. Second, if one or more of the sensors has a very high activation rate it could easily flood the wireless channel by sending packets at every activation. To prevent this, we use a "timing" capacitor with a large resistor in parallel. At every activation, the sensor checks the voltage on the capacitor. If it is below a threshold, the node transmits and then recharges the timing capacitor. If it is above a threshold, the node simply increments the counter and waits for its next activation. The following sections describe the specific devices we employ as pulse sensors for three representative load classes.

4.2.1   AC Power Meter

In order to harvest from an AC power source, we use a current transformer. The magnetic field of the AC line induces a current in the transformer and the output of the transformer is then rectified and harvested. We call the AC power pulse sensor Coilcube, which comes in two forms. The plug-load (Figure 2(a)) version sits between the wall outlet and the load, and contains the phase line leading to the AC load wrapped around a current transformer. The coil, the harvesting power supply, and the sensor node core fit in a small enclosure into which the load is plugged. Although

it might seem odd to design a plug-load pulse sensor, it allows us to both illustrate the viability of the approach and deploy a near-zero power sensor [4]. The second version uses a split-core current transformer that can be clipped easily around a wire running to a breaker in a circuit panel (Figure 2(b)). The other electronics are small and can be installed with the transformer in the panel box. This design is ideal for unobtrusively monitoring an entire circuit.

4.2.2   Light Meter

The light meter, called Gecko, enables Deltaflow to measure the energy contribution of ceiling lights, such as those in Figure 3 that are otherwise challenging to measure. Harvesting is based on a small amorphous solar cell. All of the other required electronics fit in a space approximately the same size as the solar cell. This results in a small sensor that can easily be deployed near a light bulb to unobtrusively meter the light as shown in Figure 2(c).

4.3   Disaggregation Methodology

As Figure 1 shows, the Deltaflow server receives two input streams: aggregate ground truth measurements (e.g. Watt or Whr) and pulse frequencies from each sensor attached to the instrumented loads. The server uses each of the pulse streams to decompose the aggregate measurements into the contributions from each load.

4.3.1   Sensor Calibration

The server starts by trying to estimate a *calibration function* for each sensor. This calibration function must be determined at run-time, and not *a priori*, for two main reasons: manufacturing differences, as shown in Figures 4(a) and 4(b), and sensor placement, which is unknown until after installation yet affects the response of the light-based pulse meters, as shown in Figures 4(c) and 4(d). We determine the sensor specific calibration function by first noting that the sensor pulse frequency, s_i, of load i is a function of the power draw of load i

$$s_i = f_i(p_i) \qquad (1)$$

Examples of this relationship are shown for Coilcube sensors in Figures 5(a) and 5(b) and for Gecko sensors in Figures 5(c) and 5(d). Given that we know s_i and want to determine p_i, we can express the relationship as:

$$p_i = f_i^{-1}(s_i) = g_i(s_i) \qquad (2)$$

Then, given a pulse rate, we can determine a power estimate for each sensed load using the calibration function g_i.

|(a) Coilcube Variation | (b) Gecko Variation | (c) Gecko Distance Dependence | (d) Gecko Angle Dependence |

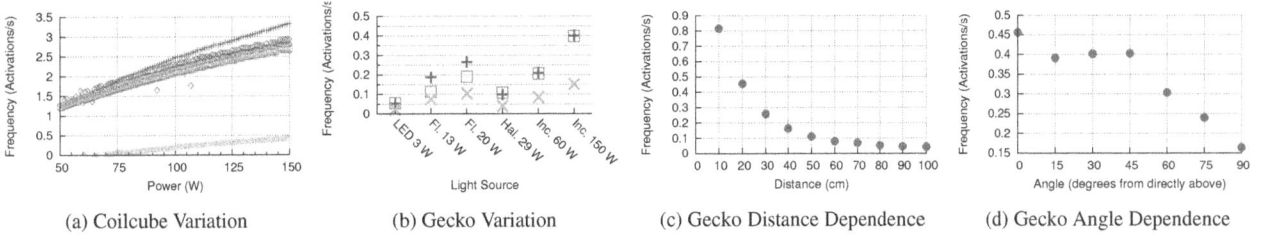

Figure 4: Motivation for runtime calibration. Figures 4(a) and 4(b) show that the pulse rate of different instances of the same sensor type varies over the same range of loads. This suggests that a single calibration function cannot be used for all instances of a particular sensor type. Figures 4(c) and 4(d) show the effect of placement on the pulse rate of Gecko sensors. As the distance and angle from the light source varies, so does the pulse rate. Therefore, factory calibration is inadequate; calibration must be performed after installation.

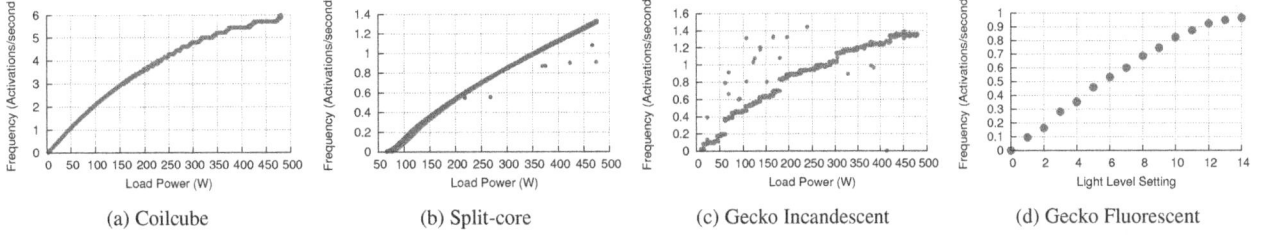

|(a) Coilcube | (b) Split-core | (c) Gecko Incandescent | (d) Gecko Fluorescent |

Figure 5: Pulse sensor activation rate vs load power. The activation rate of Coilcube, Split-core, and Gecko sensors is shown as the primary load is swept across a range of values. All sensors demonstrate a roughly monotonically increasing relationship with primary load power, but some noisy outliers are clearly visible as well.

To determine each g_i we use information about how the pulse streams change when the aggregate measurements change. However, to avoid searching through the infinite space of possible functions, we choose a general form of g_i with which to work. We additionally assume that the general form will be the same for every instance of a particular type of sensor. Requiring foreknowledge of the function for each class of sensor is reasonable because it can be determined once, at design time. This shifts the burden of configuration from sensor users to manufacturers.

We use datasets like those in Figure 5 to estimate the sensor calibration function. We find that the best-fit functions are second-order polynomials, and therefore make the assumption that the calibration function can be approximated by a monotonically increasing polynomial of degree two or less. Thus Equation 2 becomes:

$$p_i = {}_i s_i^2 + {}_i s_i + {}_i \qquad (3)$$

Now, to determine the calibration function, Deltaflow need only choose the coefficient parameters $_i$, $_i$, and $_i$ for each sensor that best fit with historical data.

4.3.2 Full Coverage

To determine the polynomial coefficients, we start with the simplest case: assume all n loads comprising the aggregate are metered. If we let M_t be the ground truth aggregate meter reading at time t and let $s_{i,t}$ be the pulse frequency for sensor i attached to load i at time t, then we have the relationship:

$$M_t = \sum_{i=1}^{n} p_i(s_{i,t}) \qquad (4)$$

Using the least squares method, let $\mathbf{M}$ be a vector of aggregate measurements M_t taken at different times t. Let $\mathbf{A}$ be a matrix of calibration function terms derived from pulse frequencies, where each row $\mathbf{A}_i$ is a vector of all the terms in each sensor's calibration

function at time t, stripped of their coefficients.

$$\mathbf{A}_i = \begin{bmatrix} s_{1,t}^2 & s_{1,t} & 1 & s_{2,t}^2 & s_{2,t} & 1 & \dots & s_{n,t}^2 & s_{n,t} & 1 \end{bmatrix} \qquad (5)$$

Let $\overline{x}$ be the vector of coefficients where $x_{i,j}$ is the coefficient of the jth term in the calibration function for sensor i.

$$\overline{x} = \begin{bmatrix} 1 & 1 & 1 & \cdots & n & n & n \end{bmatrix} \qquad (6)$$

Given data points for aggregate power draw and sensor pulse frequencies from some m different points in time, Equation 4 can be written in matrix form as:

$$\mathbf{M} = \mathbf{A}\,\overline{x} \qquad (7)$$

$$\mathbf{M} = \begin{bmatrix} s_{1,t_1}^2 & s_{1,t_1} & 1 & \dots & s_{n,t_1}^2 & s_{n,t_1} & 1 \\ s_{1,t_2}^2 & s_{1,t_2} & 1 & \dots & s_{n,t_2}^2 & s_{n,t_2} & 1 \\ \vdots & \vdots & \vdots & \ddots & \vdots & \vdots & \vdots \\ s_{1,t_m}^2 & s_{1,t_m} & 1 & \dots & s_{n,t_m}^2 & s_{n,t_m} & 1 \end{bmatrix} \begin{bmatrix} 1 \\ 1 \\ 1 \\ \vdots \\ n \\ n \\ n \end{bmatrix} \qquad (8)$$

With these definitions, we can formulate our optimization problem as:

$$\min_{\overline{x}} \quad \|\mathbf{M} - \mathbf{A}\,\overline{x}\|_2^2 \qquad (9)$$

The solution to this problem is the value of $\overline{x}$—i.e. the set of coefficients for our calibration functions—that gives load estimates that best match our aggregate readings.

Note that while our calibration functions may be non-linear, by providing the values of each non-linear term we have reduced calibration to a linear least squares problem. Use of the l_2 norm makes the regression more susceptible to noisy outliers than the l_1 norm, but it is much easier to compute. Outlier identification techniques can be used if the system converges to an unsatisfactory result.

305

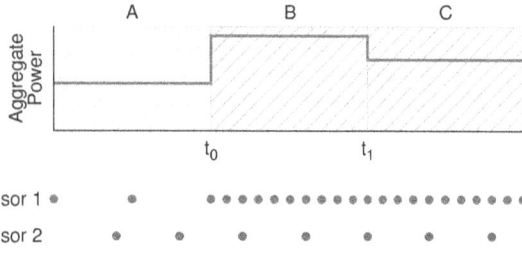

Figure 6: Effect of hidden loads. The change in aggregate power at time t_0 is attributed to the load metered by Sensor 1 whose frequency changes at that time. The aggregate also changes at t_1, but since neither sensor changes, we attribute the change at t_1 to a hidden load and ignore state C. This allows us to discard the effects of non-aliasing uninstrumented hidden loads.

4.3.3 Partial Coverage

The above approach describes finding the calibration coefficients in the ideal case when all loads are instrumented. Unfortunately, that approach does not work if even a single load is left uninstrumented, as Equation 4 no longer holds. The aggregate M_t now becomes the sum of both sensed loads and *hidden loads*.

$$M_t = \sum_{i=1}^{n} p_i(s_{i,t}) + \sum_{i=1}^{k} h_{i,t} \tag{10}$$

Let us assume that there are no aliasing hidden loads—that is, no hidden load changes at the same time as a sensed load. In that case, we can choose to select just those data points that represent states where sensed loads changed. Figure 6 illustrates such a situation. At time t_0 the pulse frequency of Sensor 1 changes along with the aggregate. However, at time t_1, the aggregate changes but both Sensor 1 and Sensor 2's frequencies stay the same. We attribute the change in aggregate power to a hidden load and ignore state C. We examine aliasing loads further in the discussion section.

For a data set in which between any two times $t = 0$ and $t = 1$ only sensed loads change, the following holds true:

$$M_1 - M_0 = \left(\sum_{i=1}^{n} p_i(s_{i,1}) + \sum_{i=1}^{k} h_{i,0} \right) - \left(\sum_{i=1}^{n} p_i(s_{i,0}) + \sum_{i=1}^{k} h_{i,0} \right)$$

$$\Delta M_t = \sum_{i=1}^{n} p_i(s_{i,1}) - p_i(s_{i,0})$$

$$\Delta M_t = \sum_{i=1}^{n} (\ _i s_{i,1}^2 + \ _i s_{i,1} + \ _i) - (\ _i s_{i,0}^2 + \ _i s_{i,0} + \ _i)$$

$$\Delta M_t = \sum_{i=1}^{n} \ _i(s_{i,1}^2 - s_{i,0}^2) + \ _i(s_{i,1} - s_{i,0}) \tag{11}$$

When calculating the change in estimated load power draw, the constant term $\ _i$ drops out of the model. However, due to the energy-harvesting nature of our pulse sensors, we know that when the load power draw p_i is zero, the pulse rate s_i is also zero. This means that $\ _i$ must be zero as well for all i. Our calibration function is now of the form:

$$p_i = \ _i s_i^2 + \ _i s_i \tag{12}$$

If we define a new matrix $\Delta \mathbf{A}$ such that

$$\Delta \mathbf{A}_i = \left[(s_{1,t_1}^2 - s_{1,t_0}^2) \quad (s_{1,t_1} - s_{1,t_0}) \quad \ldots \right] \tag{13}$$

then

$$\Delta \mathbf{A} \, \overline{x} = \Delta \mathbf{M} \tag{14}$$

Solving the optimization problem

$$\min_{\overrightarrow{x}} \quad ||\Delta \mathbf{M} - \Delta \mathbf{A} \, \overline{x}||_2^2 \tag{15}$$

will give us the coefficients for all of the calibration functions. Many existing libraries provide optimizers that can easily solve optimization problems of this formulation. In our implementation we used the non-negative linear least squares function provided by Python's SciPy library.

4.3.4 State Identification

The data points used to construct the optimization problem critically determine the performance of the regression. For example, when a load changes power states, the aggregate may reflect the change sooner than the pulse sensor which only activates once enough energy has accrued to power the sensor, thus causing a synchronization error. We find that identifying steady states in the data (using heuristic thresholds) and selecting a median or mean data point to represent the state compensates for this error. These data points are then used to determine the deltas between distinct adjacent stable states when constructing the calibration Equation 14.

5. EVALUATION

In this section, we evaluate Deltaflow's ability to identify the individual contributions of multiple loads comprising an aggregate under several conditions: when all loads are instrumented, in the presence of uninstrumented (hidden) loads, when monitoring loads with non-unity power factors, and when monitoring a load tree as one might find in a home.

5.1 Methodology

To evaluate Deltaflow we conduct several experiments consisting of a set of loads designed to test Deltaflow in different conditions. In each test, each load is monitored by a pulse sensor and a calibrated meter to collect ground truth. All loads are additionally plugged into a common calibrated meter to obtain aggregate measurements. Each load is operated to expose its power states and to simulate normal usage. The resulting ground truth and pulse data streams are collected during the experiment and then saved to be processed offline. The processing step removes the power overhead of the ground truth meters, runs the disaggregation algorithms, and computes statistics about the estimations including absolute and percentage error.

5.2 Full Instrumentation of Loads

We evaluate Deltaflow's baseline performance with an experiment in which all loads in the system are metered with pulse sensors. Figure 7(a) shows the setup of the three loads, all light bulbs with four states each. The loads are switched between states at random intervals in such a way that all state combinations are visited. Figures 7(b) to 7(d) show Deltaflow's disaggregation. Deltaflow is able to identify transitions and steady states of the loads to determine the calibration function for each pulse sensor. It then applies that calibration function to the subsequently observed pulses. In the steady state for each load, the absolute error in Deltaflow's estimates is no greater than 15 W, with average error of 5.9 W, 6.3 W, and 7.5 W, and average percent error of 12.3%, 12.3%, and 11.5%, for Loads A, B, and C, respectively. When a load transitions, Deltaflow identifies the transition and then updates its estimate, while momentarily exhibiting a higher estimation error.

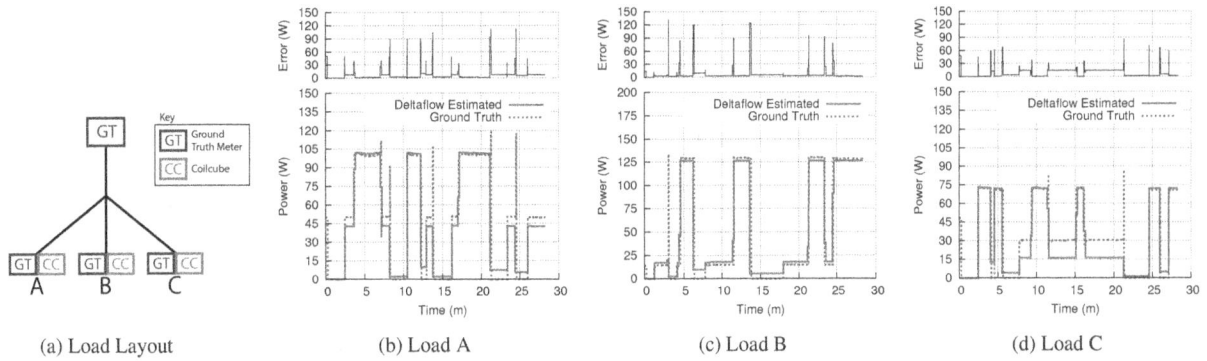

(a) Load Layout   (b) Load A   (c) Load B   (d) Load C

Figure 7: Deltaflow operating on stateful loads with instrumentation of all loads. Three loads are metered as shown in Figure 7(a). Figures 7(b) to 7(d) show the ground truth for each load and the resulting Deltaflow estimates, with graphs of the absolute error above. In steady state the error is 15 W with the only significant errors occurring during load state transitions.

The error spikes are due to the fact that Deltaflow's accuracy is constrained by the update latency of the pulse sensors. These sensors may not report a change in pulse frequency instantly, which in turn results in a race condition: aggregate measurements arrive before the pulse sensors react, causing Deltaflow to exhibit an estimation lag, which results in short periods of high error until the pulse sensors "catch up."

This experiment demonstrates Deltaflow's ability to disaggregate within reasonable error bounds. While not sufficient for scientific or revenue-grade metering, Deltaflow supports the goal of submetering loads and providing information about the energy consumption contribution of loads in a building. The delay surrounding transitions could be addressed with minor modifications to the pulse sensors themselves. Reconfiguring the pulse meters to transmit a pulse immediately after a sudden change in load power would enable Deltaflow to respond to changes quicker.

5.3 Selective Instrumentation of One Load

To explore selective instrumentation—for example, when one might want to instrument only one or just a few loads—we evaluate the case when not all loads are metered. We run the same experiment as in Section 5.2 but ignore the pulse data from the sensors attached to loads A and C. Figure 8 shows the ground truth for the single metered load and the power estimate curve from Deltaflow overlaid on the aggregate power trace for the three loads.

Even in the presence of transitions in the aggregate with no matching change in any pulse stream, Deltaflow is able to provide a power estimate for the sensed load comparable with the estimate provided in the case of full coverage. With one metered load, the average error of the power estimates is 12.5%, marginally worse than the case with full coverage, which exhibits a 12.3% estimation error.

The calibration function that Deltaflow estimates compensates for the sensed load and hidden loads changing at the same time. At $t = 7.5$ in Figure 8, the aggregate increases by 45 W while the sensed load increases only 14 W. Deltaflow correctly does not attribute the entire increase to the sensed load.

5.4 Power Factor Effects

As observed in prior work [4], Coilcube sensors have a different relationship between load power and pulse frequency depending on a load's power factor. To investigate how well Deltaflow handles loads with non-unity power factors, we construct the following setup: two loads with very similar power draws but with different power factors are run independently with the same Coilcube sensor. The first load, an AC fan, draws approximately 11.1 W with a

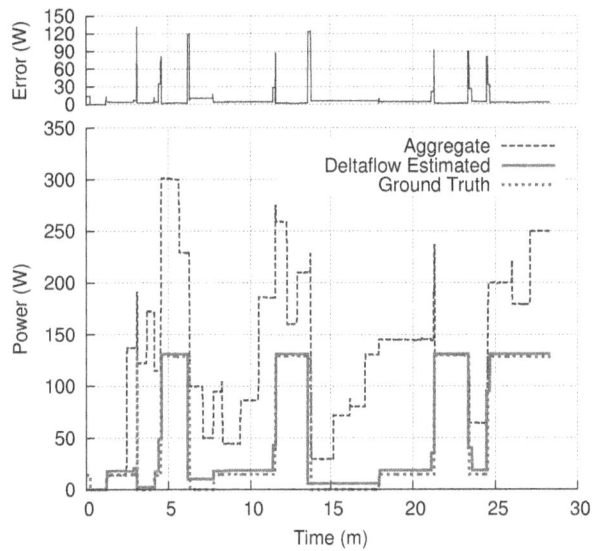

Figure 8: Deltaflow monitoring one sensed load and multiple hidden loads. This figure shows the ground truth and Deltaflow estimated power for the single sensed load, as well as the ground truth aggregate for a tree containing the sensed load and two unmonitored (hidden) loads. In steady state, Deltaflow tracks ground truth reliably, with a slight overestimate. Significant error occurs in the transitions until the sensor frequency stabilizes and Deltaflow is able to correct. Deltaflow successfully ignores state transitions that belong to hidden loads.

power factor of 0.6. The second load, an incandescent light bulb, draws 10.8 W with a power factor of 1.0. The power factor of the two loads and the activation rate of the sensor are shown in Figure 9(a). While the power draws are very similar, the different power factors cause the same sensor to activate at different rates.

Deltaflow adapts to the different activation rates and generates different calibration functions for the AC fan and light bulb as shown in Figure 9(b). This demonstrates that Deltaflow can adapt to the difference in power factor. Figure 9(c) shows the resulting power estimates for each load. The estimates for the AC fan and light bulb differ from ground truth by 6.0% and 6.9%, respectively. From two different activation rates from the same sensor, Deltaflow accurately maps the rates to the correct power magnitudes by adapting to the load.

307

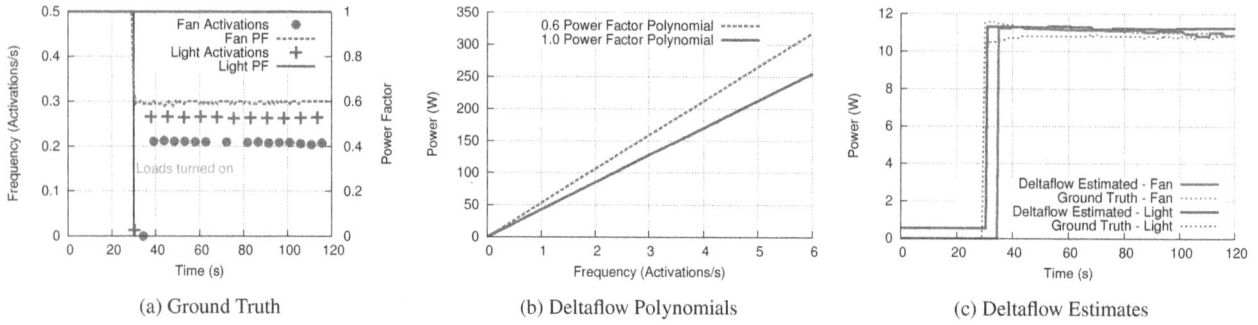

| (a) Ground Truth | (b) Deltaflow Polynomials | (c) Deltaflow Estimates |

Figure 9: Effect of different power factors on the Deltaflow system. Two loads, an AC fan and an incandescent light bulb, with very similar power draws but different power factors are measured. Figure 9(a) shows the power factor of each load over time and the corresponding activation frequency when the same Coilcube sensor is attached to each load. Although the power draw is the same for both loads, the different power factors cause the sensor to report different activation frequencies. Figure 9(b) shows the polynomials that Deltaflow generates for each of the loads. These polynomials differ due to the activation rate differences. Figure 9(c) shows the estimated power draw matches ground truth for each load even though the same Coilcube generates different activation frequencies when measuring the same power draw.

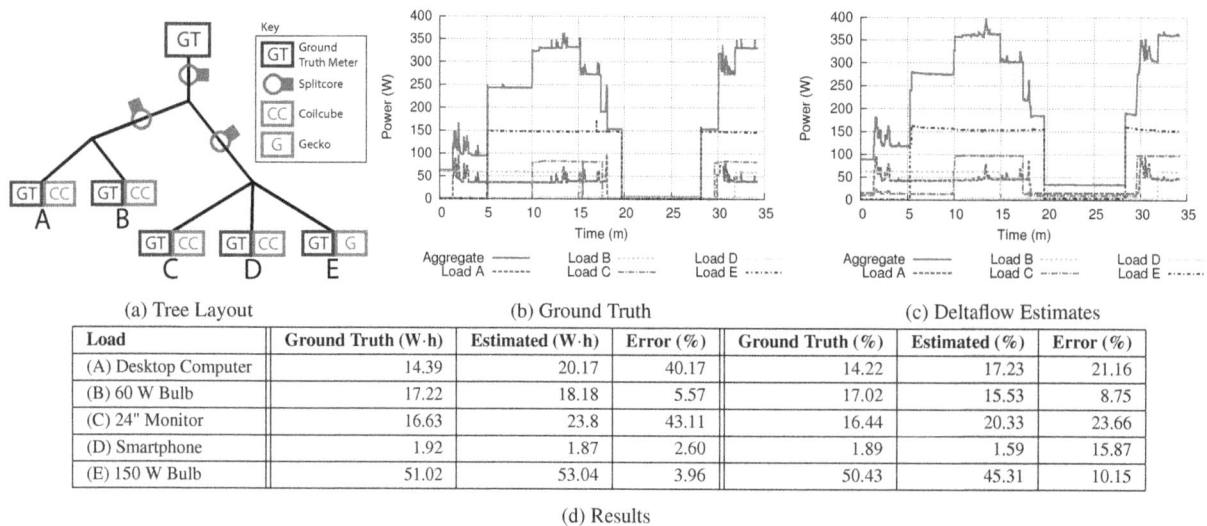

| (a) Tree Layout | (b) Ground Truth | (c) Deltaflow Estimates |

Load	Ground Truth (W·h)	Estimated (W·h)	Error (%)	Ground Truth (%)	Estimated (%)	Error (%)
(A) Desktop Computer	14.39	20.17	40.17	14.22	17.23	21.16
(B) 60 W Bulb	17.22	18.18	5.57	17.02	15.53	8.75
(C) 24" Monitor	16.63	23.8	43.11	16.44	20.33	23.66
(D) Smartphone	1.92	1.87	2.60	1.89	1.59	15.87
(E) 150 W Bulb	51.02	53.04	3.96	50.43	45.31	10.15

(d) Results

Figure 10: Deltaflow performance on a realistic tree of loads. Figure 10(a) shows the hierarchy of loads and the corresponding sensors. Figure 10(b) shows the ground truth power traces for the aggregate and each load. Figure 10(c) shows the Deltaflow estimates for all five loads and an estimated aggregate for comparison purposes. Figure 10(d) shows the breakdown of overall energy usage by each load and the estimate provided by Deltaflow, as well as the percent of the total energy usage each load represents. While the error for loads (C) and (E), which change power states at similar times, is high (> 40%), Deltaflow handles loads that transition independently successfully. Also, Deltaflow is able to successfully integrate streams from multiple types of pulse counting sensors.

5.5 Load Tree

To mimic a realistic load tree as one might find in a residential or commercial building, we construct a load hierarchy and instrument it with pulse sensors as shown in Figure 10(a). The five loads at the leaves of the tree are (A) desktop computer, (B) 60 W incandescent light bulb, (C) 24" monitor, (D) smartphone charger, and (E) 150 W incandescent light bulb. The 150 W light bulb is monitored with a Gecko sensor and the other four loads are attached to Coilcube sensors. Three split-core current transformer sensors monitor the aggregate and each main branch of the tree. Each load and the aggregate is also metered with a ground truth meter, so we have full knowledge of the power draws.

Figure 10(b) shows ground truth power for each load as well as the aggregate, and Figure 10(c) shows the resulting estimates of power draw from the Deltaflow system and the sum of the estimates to form an estimate of the aggregate. The primary error in

Deltaflow's results is overestimation. Notably, between $t = 20$ min and $t = 28$ min, all loads except for (D) are off, causing the ground truth aggregate to be very low. However, Deltaflow estimates the off loads at a higher power state, causing the estimated aggregate to be significantly higher. This error primarily stems from the design of the pulse meters. When no current is flowing to each load, the energy-harvesting pulse meters are unable to report any pulses. Without data from the pulse streams, Deltaflow does not update its estimate for the load power until it receives a new pulse, which it then uses to backfill the missing data. This causes it to overestimate during periods in which most loads are turned off and there are no transitions. To compensate for this error, heuristics could be added that predict the likelihood the load is off given no incoming pulses and update the estimates accordingly. Alternately, the pulse sensors could be modified to report their state if they detect a sudden loss in harvestable energy income.

To quantify how Deltaflow performs in a use-case likely to be relevant to consumers, we explore how well Deltaflow estimates kilowatt-hours (kWh), the unit of energy by which consumers typically buy their electricity. Further, we evaluate how well Deltaflow is able to disaggregate the total kWh consumed into the percent contribution of each load. This information would be particularly useful for a consumer to determine where to direct effort when seeking energy efficiencies. Figure 10(d) shows this breakdown. The percent error of the estimated kWh values for loads (B), (D), (E) is under 6%. These loads tended to change independently of other loads, allowing Deltaflow to better determine their calibration functions and disaggregate the total to these loads. Loads (A) and (C), however, are likely used together and transitioned power states at similar times. This adversely affects Deltaflow's ability to successfully disambiguate two loads leading to the relatively high (> 40%) errors in the kWh estimation. These errors would likely be reduced with a longer running experiment that exhibits a greater number of transitions that Deltaflow could use for calibration.

Also included in Figure 10(d) is a breakdown of each load based on the fraction of the total kWh each load consumes. While the errors in absolute kWh are still present in the breakdown, general trends about load consumption are still clear in the Deltaflow estimates: load (E) dominates the contributions of the other loads, loads (A), (B), and (C) have approximately the same contribution, and load (D) is an insignificant fraction of the total. These results show that Deltaflow supports critical comparative analyses of this nature that are essential for determining how best to invest constrained resources toward increasing efficiencies.

Figure 10 also demonstrates the effectiveness of integrating pulse meters that are based on different types of sensors and energy-harvesting front ends. Monitoring load (E) with only a Gecko node does not hinder Deltaflow's ability to disaggregate the load. Although we use only three different kind of pulse sensors in these experiments, we envision many other kinds might be used in the future to monitor not only electricity, but water and gas as well.

6. DISCUSSION

Designing a system with few constraints on input data and few assumptions about sensor calibration results in some limitations, but it also offers many opportunities for improvement.

6.1 Limitations

The Deltaflow system has some obvious limitations, which we now discuss, as well as possible ways to address them.

6.1.1 State Identification

A major challenge in achieving high accuracy is correctly identifying when a load is in a power state that would be useful for the regression engine, particularly if Deltaflow is processing in real-time. Poor state identification leads to inaccurate curves being fit to model the pulse-counter frequencies. We believe that techniques such as stepwise approximation algorithms and histogramming can be added to Deltaflow to improve state identification and make Deltaflow more robust to highly variable loads.

6.1.2 Environmental Bias

Pulse sensors may be triggered by more than simply the targeted load, causing pulses that are not correlated to the power draw of the load being metered. One example of this is the solar cell-based sensors that can be activated by ambient light, as shown in Figure 11. This type of error could be compensated for by using additional sensors that are designed to only capture environmental bias conditions and subtracting their pulses from the affected sensors.

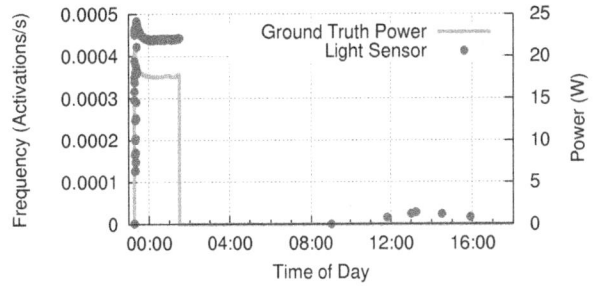

Figure 11: Effect of ambient light on Gecko sensors. A Gecko node is placed in a lamp shade near a window. When the light turns on shortly before midnight, the sensor correctly activates in response. Long after the light is turned off, however, the sensor activates several times between 9:00 AM and 4:00 PM in response to ambient sunlight. These activations are false positive and they must be accounted for to ensure robustness disaggregation.

However, differentiating between the load and environmental sensors may require supplying the system with additional metadata, which may complicate deployments.

6.1.3 Aliased Loads

It is possible for an unmonitored (hidden) load to change power states simultaneously with a monitored load such that the change in the aggregate that corresponds to the metered load is masked. Similarly, two monitored loads that change power states simultaneously will cause a single change in the aggregate, making disaggregation between those two loads difficult. In the first scenario, we assume that this case will not occur too frequently, and while it will be a source of error when it happens, over time the error will be mitigated. In the second case, it may be acceptable to group the power draw of items that transition simultaneously, as that likely represents a composite load that can be thought of as a single load, like a TV and surround sound speaker system.

6.1.4 Privacy

Conveying information via the characteristics of the transmission channel instead of the content obviously raises security and privacy issues, due to potential leakage of the occupant activities as they are performed within a private space.

While content can be encrypted, it is much more difficult to hide from a malicious observer the transmission frequency. In order to obscure the timing characteristics of sensor wakeups so that they are not detectable by a third party but are still available to the intended recipient, we must convey timing information over a regular encryptable data channel, not a side-channel.

To report wakeups over a regular data channel, the sensors need to transmit periodically and provide a recent history of wakeup times within each transmission. However, storing and reporting time-series data is a challenge as the intermittently-powered energy-harvesting sensors that we use are unable to support real-time clocks (RTCs). To provide these highly-constrained sensors with a notion of temporal history, we propose an unconventional method for representing the passage of time.

The main resources that our sensors have for carrying the effects of past states into the present is their timing capacitor and flash memory. If the sensors record the voltage level of their timing capacitor upon wakeup, then Deltaflow need only convert a report of these voltage levels into the corresponding wallclock times to obtain the time-series and subsequent sensor wakeup frequency.

To map voltages to time, we propose a two phase approach consisting of *model acquisition* and *secure sensing*. During model acquisition, when a sensor powers itself it immediately transmits an encrypted packet containing the current timing capacitor voltage level. These transmissions allow Deltaflow to build a model of the load power-timing capacitor relationship. During secure sensing, the sensor records voltage levels upon wakeup. The sensor periodically transmits that history to the server which reconstructs it using the initial model, thus preserving some level of privacy.

6.2 Future Work

We envision four key areas for future work. These areas focus on improving the deployability and automation of the system by providing real-time processing capabilities, supporting redundant sensors, removing the need to specify the parameterized form of the calibration function, and miniaturizing the sensors.

6.2.1 Real-time Processing

In a practical deployment, the disaggregation system will likely need to update in real time. This presents unique challenges over static data processing because a sensor's activation frequency at a given time is unknown until the next pulse is received. If a pulse stream suddenly stops, Deltaflow loses its information source.

One possible solution is to assume that a load will stay constant. This means that the activation rate will also stay constant, and Deltaflow can predict the latest time by which the next pulse should arrive. If the pulse does not arrive by the expected time, there are four possible explanations: the load has reduced its power draw, the load has turned off completely, a packet has been lost, or the sensor has been lost (i.e. is broken or has been removed).

If Deltaflow estimates the expected arrival time of the next sensor pulse for each sensor, it can identify missing pulses and accommodate them by incrementally reducing the power estimate for the load until the server receives the next pulse or the estimate reaches zero. If the load reduces its power draw, then this process will draw a line that slopes down to the new estimate. If the load turns off, then this method will converge to a power estimate of zero.

If a packet is lost, then using this method will cause Deltaflow's estimate to dip during real-time operations. However, packets from the pulse sensors contain sequence numbers that allow the system to retroactively correct the estimate when the next pulse is received. How *post facto* corrections are used is a different matter.

If the sensor is lost, then Deltaflow will generate an incorrect estimate for that load. The aggregate will not drop, however, so the error of the estimated aggregate will increase. When the error is greater than a certain threshold, Deltaflow is alerted to the fact that its system model is no longer accurate. Problematic sensors can be identified using techniques like the largest normalized residual test, which is used for detecting faulty sensors during the bad data processing phase of power system state estimation. Once the bad sensor is identified, Deltaflow can alert the user and re-run the regression problem without that sensor to determine an updated system model. This method of monitoring the error and re-running when the error exceeds a threshold can be used to compensate for other error sources, such as changing power factors, new sensors, and changes in load characteristics.

6.2.2 Multiple Sensors

One potential method for reducing error in the system is to add multiple sensors per load, e.g. using both a Gecko and Coilcube sensor on the same lamp. This would both provide additional hints for the Deltaflow system and remove the current constraint that allows at most one sensor per load.

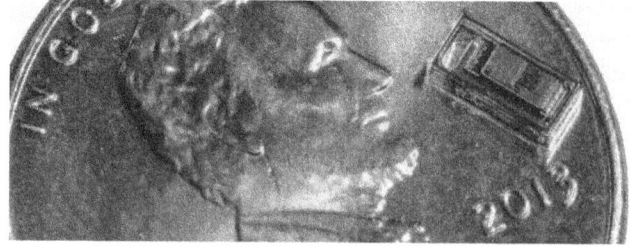

Figure 12: A mm-scale sensor node that integrates a solar cell, processor, radio, and battery that provides much of the pulse sensor functionality. This illustrates that the "peel-and-stick" sensor tags we envision will soon be viable.

Extending Deltaflow to support multiple sensors would involve adding a method for determining which sensors represent the same load. This could be done by observing that a set of sensors are synchronized in their pulse frequency deviations, perhaps by observing the sensor covariance matrix. However, due to differences in sensor response times, determining their synchronized behavior may be difficult, requiring that sensor traces be partitioned into stable and volatile segments. Manually augmenting the system with metadata would be an effective but labor-intensive and perhaps error-prone fallback should efforts at automation prove too complex.

6.2.3 Adaptive Models

Currently, Deltaflow requires that the monotonically increasing calibration function for the sensors be provided in a general form *a priori*. Our implementation uses non-negative least squares regression to enforce the monotonicity constraint, but this may rule out monotonically increasing functions with negative coefficients. A more general approach may be to use semi-definite programming to establish the monotonicity constraint. It may also be possible to eliminate all foreknowledge of the calibration function. Calculus of variations is an analytical tool that can discover arbitrary functions that minimize some other function. If these techniques could be used to discover the functions at runtime that minimize the error of the estimated aggregate, then we could eliminate assumptions about the form of the calibration function.

6.2.4 "Peel-and-stick" Sensors

While the current generation of sensors are functional, we envision a future generation of pulse sensors that are truly peel-and-stick, like RFID tags are today. Figure 12 shows an example of such a sensor. At this scale, the sensor could be integrated into laminated tags and easily affixed to loads.

7. CONCLUSIONS

A recent U.S. National Science and Technology Council report states that the ability to submeter electricity and water in modern buildings is critical to meeting Federal sustainability targets, but the same report also notes the difficulty of submetering at scale. This paper explores a new approach to submetering that does not suffer from many of the drawbacks of current systems. We leverage recent advances in inexpensive—but low-quality—energy-harvesting sensors that can be deployed broadly and propose new algorithms to processing their intermittent, inaccurate, and noisy data streams. Our results show that it is possible to deploy small, unobtrusive, inaccurate, and uncalibrated sensors, and yet still be able to estimate individual contributions to an aggregate load. Miniaturizing the sensors and supporting other modalities will soon pave the way to pervasive, fine-grained, "peel-and-stick" submetering solutions.

8. ACKNOWLEDGMENTS

Special thanks to Jake Abernethy for introducing the initial regression formulation, Quentin Stout for sanity checks on partial coverage and state detection, Jeremy Hoskins for suggesting calculus of variations as a way to discover calibration functions, and the students of Lab 11 for all the reviews, food, and support. This work was also supported in part by the TerraSwarm Research Center, one of six centers supported by the STARnet phase of the Focus Center Research Program (FCRP), a Semiconductor Research Corporation program sponsored by MARCO and DARPA. This material is based upon work partially supported by the US Agency for International Development, the National Science Foundation under grants CNS-0964120, CNS-1111541, and CNS-1350967, and generous gifts from Intel, Qualcomm, and Texas Instruments.

9. REFERENCES

[1] T. Campbell, E. Larson, G. Cohn, J. Froehlich, R. Alcaide, and S. N. Patel. WATTR: A method for self-powered wireless sensing of water activity in the home. Ubicomp '10, 2010.

[2] G. Cohn, S. Gupta, J. Froehlich, E. Larson, and S. N. Patel. GasSense: Appliance-level, single-point sensing of gas activity in the home. Pervasive '10, 2010.

[3] Cooper Power Systems. Energy Harvesting (EH) Power Supply and Repeater. http://www.cooperindustries.com/content/public/en/power_systems/products/automation_and_control/amr_ami/energy_harvesting.html, 2014.

[4] S. DeBruin, B. Campbell, and P. Dutta. Monjolo: An energy-harvesting energy meter architecture. In *Proceedings of the 11th ACM Conference on Embedded Networked Sensor Systems*, SenSys '13, 2013.

[5] Energy, Inc. TED The Energy Detective. http://www.theenergydetective.com/, 2013.

[6] J. Froehlich, E. C. Larson, T. Campbell, C. Haggerty, J. Fogarty, and S. N. Patel. Hydrosense: infrastructure-mediated single-point sensing of whole-home water activity. In *UbiComp'10*, pages 235–244, 2009.

[7] S. Gupta, M. S. Reynolds, and S. N. Patel. Electrisense: Single-point sensing using emi for electrical event detection and classification in the home. In *UbiComp'10*, 2010.

[8] G. Hart. Nonintrusive appliance load monitoring. *Proceedings of the IEEE*, 80(12):1870–1891, 1992.

[9] X. Jiang, S. Dawson-Haggerty, P. Dutta, and D. Culler. Design and implementation of a high-fidelity ac metering network. In *Proceedings of the 2009 International Conference on Information Processing in Sensor Networks*, IPSN '09, pages 253–264, 2009.

[10] D. Jung and A. Savvides. Estimating building consumption breakdowns using on/off state sensing and incremental sub-meter deployment. In *Proceedings of the 8th ACM Conference on Embedded Networked Sensor Systems*, SenSys '10, pages 225–238, 2010.

[11] Y. Kim, T. Schmid, Z. M. Charbiwala, J. Friedman, and M. B. Srivastava. NAWMS: nonintrusive autonomous water monitoring system. In *Proceedings of the 6th ACM conference on Embedded network sensor systems*, SenSys '08, pages 309–322, 2008.

[12] Y. Kim, T. Schmid, Z. M. Charbiwala, and M. B. Srivastava. Viridiscope: design and implementation of a fine grained power monitoring system for homes. Ubicomp '09, pages 245–254, New York, NY, USA, 2009.

[13] Y. Lee, S. Bang, I. Lee, Y. Kim, G. Kim, M. H. Ghaed, P. Pannuto, P. Dutta, D. Sylvester, and D. Blaauw. A modular 1 mm^3 die-stacked sensing platform with low power I^{2}C inter-die communication and multi-modal energy harvesting. In *IEEE Journal of Solid-State Circuits*, volume 48, 2013.

[14] J. Lifton, M. Feldmeier, Y. Ono, C. Lewis, and J. Paradiso. A platform for ubiquitous sensor deployment in occupational and domestic environments. In *Information Processing in Sensor Networks, 2007. IPSN 2007. 6th International Symposium on*, pages 119–127, 2007.

[15] P. Martin, Z. Charbiwala, and M. Srivastava. DoubleDip: Leveraging thermoelectric harvesting for low power monitoring of sporadic water use. In *Proceedings of the 10th ACM Conference on Embedded Network Sensor Systems*, SenSys '12, pages 225–238, 2012.

[16] National Science Board. Building a sustainable energy future: U.S. actions for an effective energy economy transformation, Aug. 2009.

[17] NSTC–Committee on Technology. Submetering of building energy and water usage: Analysis and recommendations of the subcommitte on buildings technology research and development, Oct. 2011.

[18] P3 International. Kill-A-Watt wireless. http://www.p3international.com/products/consumer/p4220.

[19] S. Patel, T. Robertson, J. Kientz, M. Reynolds, and G. Abowd. At the flick of a switch: Detecting and classifying unique electrical events on the residential power line. Ubicomp '07. 2007.

[20] N. B. Priyantha, A. Kansal, M. Goraczko, and F. Zhao. Tiny web services: Design and implementation of interoperable and evolvable sensor networks. In *Proceedings of the 6th ACM Conference on Embedded Network Sensor Systems*, SenSys '08, pages 253–266, 2008.

[21] A. Rowe, M. Berges, and R. Rajkumar. Contactless sensing of appliance state transitions through variations in electromagnetic fields. In *Proceedings of the 2nd ACM Workshop on Embedded Sensing Systems for Energy-Efficiency in Building*, BuildSys '10, 2010.

[22] Smarthome. iMeter Solo. http://www.smarthome.com/2423A1/iMeter-Solo-INSTEON-Power-Meter-Plug-In/p.aspx.

[23] V. Srinivasan, J. Stankovic, and K. Whitehouse. Fixturefinder: Discovering the existence of electrical and water fixtures. In *Proceedings of the 12th International Conference on Information Processing in Sensor Networks*, IPSN '13, pages 115–128, 2013.

[24] Watts up? Watts up? .net. https://www.wattsupmeters.com/secure/products.php?pn=0&wai=0&spec=1.

[25] Wattvision. Wattvision: The Smart Energy Sensor. http://www.wattvision.com/, 2013.

[26] T. Weng, B. Balaji, S. Dutta, R. Gupta, and Y. Agarwal. Managing plug-loads for demand response within buildings. In *Proceedings of the Third ACM Workshop on Embedded Sensing Systems for Energy-Efficiency in Buildings*, BuildSys '11, pages 13–18, 2011.

[27] T. Wu and M. Srivastava. Low-cost appliance state sensing for energy disaggregation. In *Proceedings of the Fourth ACM Workshop on Embedded Sensing Systems for Energy-Efficiency in Buildings*, BuildSys '12, 2012.

[28] L. Yerva, B. Campbell, A. Bansal, T. Schmid, and P. Dutta. Grafting energy-harvesting leaves onto the sensornet tree. In *Proceedings of the 11th International Conference on Information Processing in Sensor Networks*, IPSN '12, pages 197–208, 2012.

Author Index

www.ingramcontent.com/pod-product-compliance
Lightning Source LLC
Chambersburg PA
CBHW080927220326
41598CB00034B/5706